A BYZANTINE
MONASTIC OFFICE,
1105 A.D.

A BYZANTINE MONASTIC OFFICE, 1105 A.D.

Houghton Library, MS gr. 3

JEFFREY C. ANDERSON &
STEFANO PARENTI

THE CATHOLIC UNIVERSITY
OF AMERICA PRESS

Washington, D.C.

Design and typesetting by Kachergis Book Design

Cataloging-in-Publication Data available
from the Library of Congress
ISBN 978-0-8132-3637-7

CONTENTS

ILLUSTRATIONS

PREFACE

I wish to thank Leslie A. Morris, curator of manuscripts at the Houghton Library for allowing me to study the Psalter, which is here published by permission of the Houghton Library, Harvard University. The value of the manuscript was recognized by Prof. Robert F. Taft, SJ, who encouraged its publication. Stefano Parenti carefully reviewed the text and an early draft of the English translation was read and commented upon by Stamatina McGrath. Much of the final draft of both the text and the translation was carefully reviewed and commented upon by my colleague Prof. Robert H. Jordan. The Department of Fine Arts and Art History and the Columbian College of Arts and Sciences at George Washington University offered funding for the translation of part 2 of the publication. I offer my warmest thanks to all for their generous help and support.

JEFFREY C. ANDERSON
Professor Emeritus
George Washington University
Washington, D.C.

For the completion of this work, begun too long ago to still have to await its conclusion, I must thank many people: my friend and colleague Prof. Robert F. Taft, SJ, who asked me to work on the Cambridge codex, and Prof. Dirk Krausmüller, who allowed me to use his unpublished transcription of the *Hypotyposis* of Nicetas of Stoudios prior to the edition by Parpulov. At the Library of the Academy of Sciences in Sofia, I consulted the microfilms of the Sinai manuscripts when they were made available to scholars through the great generosity of Dr. Gabriela Georgieva, in an atmosphere of courteous collaboration. I am grateful to Prof. Agamemnon Tselikas, through the good offices of Prof. Maria Luisa Agati, for the microfilm of the Lesbos, Leimonos 295. I am also grateful to Dr. Alda Spotti and the staff of the Italian Center for Manuscript Studies of the "Vittorio Emanuele" Central National Library in Rome: their kindness is well known to those who have had the opportunity to conduct research at the Center, which deserves wider recognition. Finally, I would like to thank the Institute for Patristic Studies of Thessaloniki, which I consulted during Professor Euthymios Litsas's tenure as supervisor of the microfilms.

STEFANO PARENTI

Facoltà di Liturgia

Pontificio Ateneo S. Anselmo

Rome

June 30, 2010

ABBREVIATIONS

AB	*Analecta Bollandiana*
BA	Biblioteca Ambrosiana, Milan
BAV	Biblioteca Apostolica Vaticana, Rome (Vatican City)
BB	Biblioteca della Badia, Grottaferrata
BBTT	Belfast Byzantine Texts and Translations
BC	Biblioteca Casanatense, Rome
BCA	Bibliothèque des Cahiers archéologiques
BELS	Bibliotheca Ephemerides Liturgicae "Subsidia"
BHG	Bibliotheca Hagiographica Graeca
BiblBasil	*Bibliotheca Basiliana Universalis*, ed. Fedwick
BL	British Library, London
BollGrott	*Bollettino della Badia Greca di Grottaferrata*
BM	Biblioteca Marciana, Venice
BMFD	*Byzantine Monastic Foundation Documents*, ed. Thomas and Hero
BML	Biblioteca Medicea Laurenziana, Florence
BNE	Biblioteca Nacional de España, Madrid
BNF	Bibliothèque Nationale de France, Paris
BNU	Biblioteca Nazionale Universitaria, Turin
BodL	Bodleian Library, Oxford
BSl	*Byzantinoslavica*
BZ	*Byzantinische Zeitschrift*
C	Cambridge, Harvard University, Houghton Library, gr. 3
CC	Corpus Christianorum
CFHB	Corpus Fontium Historiae Byzantinae

CPG	*Clavis Patrum Graecorum*, ed. Geerard
DChAE	Δελτίον τῆς Χριστιανικῆς ἀρχαιολογικῆς ἑταιρείας
DOP	*Dumbarton Oaks Papers*
EBE	Ἐθνικὴ Βιβλιοθήκη τῆς Ἑλλάδος, Athens
GIM	Государственный Исторический Музей, Moscow
HA	Ὡρολόγιον τὸ μέγα περιέχον ἅπασαν τὴν ἀνήκουσαν αὐτῷ ἀκολουθίαν, 5th ed.
HR	Ὡρολόγιον περιέχον τὴν ἡμερονύκτιον ἀκολουθίαν μετὰ τῶν συνήθων προσθήκων, 2nd ed.
LB	Liturgy of St. Basil: ed. Trempelas, *Αἱ τρεῖς λειτουργίαι*
LCh	Liturgy of St. John Chrysostom: ed. Trempelas, *Αἱ τρεῖς λειτουργίαι*
LXX	*Septuaginta. Id est Vetus Testamentum graece iuxta LXX interpretes*, ed. Rahlfs
MDion	Μονὴ Διονυσίου, Mount Athos
MDoch	Μονὴ Δοχειαρίου, Mount Athos
MHS	*Μέγας ἱερὸς συνέκδημος* (Athens, n.d.)
MI	Μονὴ Ἰβήρων, Mount Athos
MK	Μονὴ Κουτλουμουσίου, Mount Athos
ML	Μονὴ Λειμῶνος, Lesbos
MML	Μονὴ Μεγίστης Λαύρας, Mount Athos
MP	Μονὴ Παντοκράτορος, Mount Athos
MR	*Μηναῖα τοῦ ὅλου ἐνιαυτοῦ*, 4 vols. (Rome, 1885–1901)
MSC	Μονὴ Ἁγίας Αἰκατερίνης, Mount Sinai
MV	Μονὴ Βατοπεδίου, Mount Athos
NT	*Novum Testamentum Graece*, ed. Nestle and Aland
OCA	Orientalia Christiana Analecta
OCP	*Orientalia Christiana Periodica*
ODB	*The Oxford Dictionary of Byzantium*, ed. Kazhdan et al.
ÖNb	Österreichische Nationalbibliothek, Vienna
P	Paris, BNF, gr. 331
PaR	*Παρακλητικὴ ἤτοι ὀκτώηχος ἡ μεγάλη* (Rome, 1885)

PB	Πατριαρχικὴ Βιβλιοθήκη, Jerusalem
PG	*Patrologiae cursus completus. Series graeca*, ed. Migne
PL	*Patrologiae cursus completus. Series latina*, ed. Migne
REB	*Revue des études byzantines*
RGB	Российская Государственная Библиотека, Moscow
RNB	Российская Национальная Библиотека, St. Petersburg
RSBN	*Rivista di studi bizantini e neoellenici*
SC	Sources Chrétiennes
SH	Subsidia Hagiographica
ST	Studi e Testi
SVThQ	*St. Vladimir's Theological Quarterly*
TR	*Τριῴδιον κατανυκτικὸν περιέχον ἅπασαν τὴν ἀνήκουσαν αὐτῷ ἀκολουθίαν τῆς ἁγίας καὶ μεγάλης τεσσαρακοστῆς* (Rome, 1879)
TSMO	Typologie des sources du moyen âge occidental
Ubibl	Universitätsbibliothek, Erlangen
VizVrem	*Византийский Временник*
WAM	Walters Art Museum, Baltimore

PART 1

TEXT AND TRANSLATION

Jeffrey C. Anderson

INTRODUCTION

The liturgical psalter, Cambridge, Houghton Library, MS gr. 3, was donated to Harvard University by Edward Everett.[1] Over his lifetime (1794–1865), Everett was a graduate of Harvard College, Eliot Professor of Greek Literature, and president of the University. While studying for his doctorate at Göttingen, Everett took the opportunity to travel in search of Greek manuscripts, which were rare in America at the time. On a visit to Istanbul, in 1818, he was given the opportunity to buy five Greek manuscripts and some leaves with Greek text. The offer was made by the British Consul General, acting on behalf of the "family of a Greek prince in decay."[2] As Georges Papazoglou has shown, the "Greek prince" was Nikolaos Karatzas, a Phanariot who had amassed a substantial library.[3] With the exception of a copy of the *Chronicle* composed by the twelfth-century author Michael Glykas, the manuscripts purchased by Everett were liturgical in nature (Gospel lection-

1. S. De Ricci and W. Wilson, *Census of Medieval and Renaissance Manuscripts in the United States and Canada*, 3 vols. (New York: H. W. Wilson, 1935–40), 1:971; N. Kavrus-Hoffmann, "Catalogue of Greek Medieval and Renaissance Manuscripts in the Collections of the United States of America. Part V.1: Harvard University, The Houghton Library," *Manuscripta* 54 (2010): 85–102, with bibliography; L. Nees, "An Illuminated Byzantine Psalter at Harvard University," *Dumbarton Oaks Papers* [hereafter "*DOP*"] 29 (1975): 205–24; A. Cutler, *The Aristocratic Psalters in Byzantium*, Bibliothèque des Cahiers archéologiques [hereafter "BCA"] 13, 35–36 (Paris: Picard, 1984); I. Spatharakis, *The Portrait in Byzantine Illuminated Manuscripts*, Byzantina Neerlandica VI (Leiden: E. J. Brill, 1976), 44–48; G. R. Parpulov, *Toward a History of Byzantine Psalters*, 2 vols. (PhD diss., University of Chicago, 2004), 1:118–24.

2. E. Everett, "An Account of Some Greek Manuscripts Procured at Constantinople in 1819, and now Belonging to the Library of the University at Cambridge," *Memoirs of the American Academy of Arts and Sciences* 4 (1820): 409–15.

3. G. Papazoglou, "Un manuscrit inconnu provenant de la bibliothèque de l'archonte phanariote Nikolaos Karatzas," *Revue des études byzantines* [hereafter "*REB*"] 49 (1991): 255–61, discusses the other notes pertaining to provenance.

ary, praxapostolos, liturgical sermons of Gregory of Nazianzen). Upon his return to America, Everett promptly donated the books to the university, and all are now in the Houghton Library (Gk. MSS 3–8).[4]

The psalter that Everett acquired from Karatzas had been in Istanbul for over two centuries. A note dated 1589, written on fol. A, states that the book belonged to Michael Kantakouzenos, father of Andronikos who used it to learn the psalms.[5] This Michael was the notorious book collector Michael ("Son of Satan") Kantakouzenos of Constantinople, whose vast library was sold at his death, in 1578, eleven years before the date given in the note.[6] Papazoglou has argued that Michael had apparently given the psalter to his son, who was thirty-six years old in 1589, when the note was written. Owing to the transaction the manuscript escaped the liquidation of the Kantakouzenos library to remain within the family until it passed to Nikolaos Karatzas, who may have given it to his son, from whom it came to Edward Everett.[7]

Although the Harvard Psalter contains no explicit testimony as to where and for whose use it was made, the manuscript does have evidence of when it was finished. The scribe included a set of Paschal tables (fols. 285–86). They begin with the entry: "The year 6613 [1105 A.D.]; indiction 13; solar cycle 5; lunar cycle 1; apokreos: February 12; Pascha by [Mosaic] Law: Monday of the first week of April [April 3]; Pascha of the Christians [Easter]: April 9," and continue for nineteen more years to A.M. 6632 [1124 A.D.].[8] The table gives the reader two of the most important points for the changing liturgical

4. De Ricci and Wilson, *Census*, 1:971–72.

5. + τῶ ψαλτηρι(ον) ὑπάρχει Μηχαήλ Καντακουζενοὺ, τοῦ κυρ[ήτζ]η ἀνδρονῖκου, κ(αὶ) ἐπῖασε να τὸ μανθάνει ἐν μηνῖ ἰουλιου, ιζ, ἡμέρ(α) δⁿ τῆς ἁγίας Αἰκατερηνας, ετους ζϙζ ἀπὸ Χ(ριστο)ῦ καταβασεως ετους αφπθ [The psalter belongs to Michael Kantakouzenos, the father of Andronikos, and he got it to learn in the month of July, the 17th, Wednesday of St. Catherine's day, in the year 7097, years from Christ's incarnation: 1589].

6. D. Nicol, *The Byzantine Family of Kantakouzenos (Cantacuzenus), ca. 1100–1460. A Genealogical and Prosopographical Study*, Dumbarton Oaks Studies XI (Washington, D.C.: Dumbarton Oaks Center for Byzantine Studies, 1968), v–vi; and on the library: G. Papazoglou, *Βιβλιοθήκες στὴν Κωνσταντινούπολη τοῦ ιϛ′ αἰῶνα (κώδ. Vind. hist. gr. 98)* (Thessaloniki, 1983), 327–67.

7. G. Papazoglou, "Le Michel Cantacuzène du codex Mavrocordatianus et le possesseur homonyme du Psautier de Harvard," *REB* 46 (1988): 163–65; Papazoglou, "Un manuscrit de la collection des Cantacuzènes à la Pierpont Morgan Library de New York," *Byzantion* 67 (1997): 522–23.

8. ἔτ(ους), ͵ϛχιγ′, ἰνδ(ικτῶνος) ιγ′, κύ(κλος) (ἡλίου) ε′, κύ(κλος) (σελήνης) α′· ἡ ἀποκρέ(α) φε(βρουαρίου) ιβ′, νομι(κὸν) πάσχ(α) ἀπριλλί(ου) εἰς τ(ὰς) β′, ἡμέ(ρα) α′, χρ(ιστιανῶν) π(άσ)χ(α) ἀπριλλ(ίου) θ′. νομι(κὸν) πάσχ(α). Passover is known in some manuscripts as ἰουδαϊκὸν πάσχα; see A. Mentz, *Beiträge zur Osterfestberechnung bei den Byzantinern* (PhD diss., Albertus-Universität of Königsberg, 1906), 43.

seasons: apokreos (the first week of partial abstinence leading up to Lent) and Easter (the first Sunday after the first full moon following the spring equinox). Although one might connect the tables to the use of the manuscript in a monastery (see below), their inclusion is actually a function of the content of the book; many copies of the psalter have such tables, including ones with no apparent liturgical use as well as others made for lay reading.[9] If one believes that the scribe was a practical man, then the first entry is that of the year in which the manuscript was finished, 1105. Nothing in the handwriting or illustration casts doubt on this conclusion. The illustration, in fact, supports the early twelfth-century date, and points to Constantinople as the place where the manuscript was made.

The Harvard Psalter is illustrated, mainly in the psalms. Its miniatures were the subject of an important article published by Lawrence Nees in 1975.[10] In his study of the manuscript, Nees brought together a number of other works illustrated in a similar style. On the strength of Nees's findings, other scholars have contributed attributions to the group, which is now both extensive and varied.[11] Appearing as early as the last decade of the eleventh century and lasting as late as the middle of the twelfth, the manner of illustration exemplified by the Psalter represents a significant movement. Although no work has yet come to light with the name of a patron who can be placed in the capital—as is so often the case with luxury manuscripts—it is difficult to imagine the phenomenon the group represents as one occurring outside Constantinople and its unique base of patronage. The only full-page illustration appears on fol. 8v.[12] It shows the Deesis with David, who is placed outside the frame but next to the Theotokos (fig. 1).

9. See, for example, Rome, BAV, gr. 752 of 1059 (E. De Wald, *The Illustrations of the Manuscripts of the Septuagint*, vol. 3, *Psalms and Odes*, part 2, *Vaticanus Graecus 752* [Princeton, N.J.: Princeton University Press, 1942]) and Washington, Dumbarton Oaks Collection, cod. 3, made, in 1084, for use by a layman (S. Der Nersessian, "A Psalter and New Testament Manuscript at Dumbarton Oaks," *DOP* 19 [1965]: 155–83).

10. Nees, "Psalter." See also his contribution to *Illuminated Greek Manuscripts from American Collections*, ed. G. Vikan (Princeton, N.J.: Art Museum, Princeton University, 1973), 128–29.

11. The contributions are recounted in J. Anderson, "The Walters Praxapostolos and Liturgical Illustration," Δελτίον τῆς Χριστιανικῆς ἀρχαιολογικῆς ἑταιρείας [hereafter "DChAE"] 19 (1996–97): 10–13.

12. Nees, "Psalter," fig. 1. Also known in another psalter from roughly the same time: Berlin, Universität, Abteilung für Christliche Archäologie und kirchliche Kunst, cod. 3807: G. Stuhlfauth, "A Greek Psalter with Byzantine Miniatures," *Art Bulletin* 15 (1933): 311–26, fig. 8.

Fig. 1: Cambridge, Houghton Library, Harvard University, MS Gr. 3, fol. 8v: Deesis
with David and prostrate monk

At her feet is a small figure who may represent the manuscript's patron and donor, its user, or possibly its scribe; he is, unfortunately, too small and the surface too abraded to offer much information. He is depicted in proskynesis; with his left hand he reaches out to cup Christ's foot and the fingers of his right hand touch its toes. Portrayed with an oval face and possibly no beard, he either wears a grey cap or has grey hair. His long undergarment is ochre, but the overgarment has entirely flaked away; from stains on the sheet, the overgarment appears to have been painted a dark color, possibly black or deep olive. The color scheme of ochre tunic and medium to very dark brown overgarment is that of the monks' habits in the Princeton *Heavenly Ladder*, made about a generation before the Harvard Psalter, as well as in other works around the same time.[13] A figure shown at a smaller scale and prostrate appears in a number of frontispiece and dedication miniatures; sometimes the figure is identified as the donor, as in Mt. Athos, MML, A.103, whereas in others he may be the scribe, as seems to be the case with Paris, BNF, Coisl. gr. 79, fol. 2v.[14] In the Psalter, the man may be the owner and user of the book, who has had himself depicted touching Christ's body, albeit the Lord's foot and in gesture of supplication in keeping with the tenor of the monk's prayers in the book itself. In fact, the entire composition, a Deesis that includes David and the prostrate monk, can be considered an emblem of the text, which for several of the offices was used privately by the owner in his cell.

The Harvard Psalter represents a recent phenomenon of the time—the richly produced liturgical text—though admittedly ones this rich are rare. Among the other contemporary or nearly contemporary examples are the charter of the monastery of the Theotokos Kecharitomene (Paris, BNF, gr. 384), founded by Eirene Doukaina,[15] the Evergetis Synaxarion in Athens (Athens, EBE, 788),[16] and Paris, BNF, gr. 331, discussed below.

---

13. Princeton University Library, MS Garrett 16, in S. Kotzabassi and N. P. Ševčenko, *Greek Manuscripts at Princeton, Sixth to Nineteenth Century. A Descriptive Catalogue* (Princeton, N.J.: Princeton University Press, 2010), 115–23, figs. 129–68, with some exceptions.

14. MML = Μονὴ Μεγίστης Λαύρας, Mount Athos; BNF = Bibliothèque Nationale de France, Paris. The Lavra manuscript is a lectionary donated by the anonymous man at the feet of the Theotokos (see Spatharakis, *Portrait*, 78–79, fig. 45); the Paris Chrysostom shows a tiny figure near the emperor's feet and the inscription suggests that he is the scribe (ibid., 112, fig. 72).

15. P. Gautier, "Le typikon de la Théotokos Kécharitôménè," *REB* 43 (1985): 10.

16. EBE = Ἐθνικὴ Βιβλιοθήκη τῆς Ἑλλάδος, Athens. *The Synaxarion of the Monastery of the Theotokos Evergetis*, 2 vols., ed. and trans. R. H. Jordan (Belfast: Belfast Byzantine Enterprises, 2000–2007).

Description and Contents

The Harvard Psalter is a quarto measuring 23 ¼ x 17 ¾ cm. It is composed of heavy parchment of average preparation, and originally consisted of 282 folios; the leaf between fols. 187 and 188 was omitted from the foliation and the one between fols. 184 and 185 is lost. For the text of the psalms and odes (fols. 9r–232v) the scribe ruled the leaves throughout for a single column of text in pattern[17] 31C1a with 21 lines per leaf in a block measuring 16.7 x 10.9 cm (fig. 1). For the horologion and calendar (fols. 233r–281v) he changed to the simpler pattern 12C1 and increased the number of lines to 22, inscribed in a block measuring 16.8 x 12.2 cm (fig. 2).

The scribe copied the text in minuscule using a dull brown ink common in Middle Byzantine manuscripts, and the rubrics he wrote in semi-uncial using a thin carmine ink (cool red). Many of the additions he added in the margins are also in red. The unnumbered quires are regular quaternions except for the illustrated block in gathering fols. 214–16 and the gathering at the end of the horologion, fols. 273–81. Two other manuscripts have been attributed to or associated with the work of the scribe of the Harvard Psalter; one is the psalter Mt. Athos, MI, cod. 22, and the other a Gospel book in Baltimore, WAM, W 522.[18] Although possible, such attributions tend to be difficult and inconclusive owing to the formalized nature of the scripts, which, to borrow a characterization from Nigel Wilson, are "copper plate."

The manuscript opens with one complete gathering of prefatory material: an introduction written by Michael Psellos in political verse (fols. 1r–7v),[19] and the full-page image of the Deesis (fol. 8v); following the introductory ma-

---

17. J.-H. Sautel, *Répertoire de réglures dans les manuscrits grecs sur parchemin* (Turnhout: Brepols, 1995).

18. WAM = Walters Art Museum, Baltimore; MI = Μονὴ Ἰβήρων, Mount Athos. The former by Parpulov, *Byzantine Psalters*, 1:120, and the latter by Parpulov in "A Catalogue of the Greek Manuscripts at the Walters Art Museum," *Journal of the Walters Art Museum* 62 (2004): 89. Kavrus-Hoffmann, "Catalogue," 98, suggests a similar hand is found in another Psalter: Philadelphia, Free Library, MS E 189.

19. *Michaelis Pselli poemata*, ed. L. Westerink (Stuttgart: Teubner, 1992), 1–13; copying the text, the scribe omitted lines 71, 123, 263, 298, which were later added in the margins. In the space left at the foot of fol. 7v a hand other than the scribe's added a brief quotation from John Chrysostom's Sixteenth Homily on Ephesians: "παιδευόμεθα τοίνυν ὅτι ... πῦρ" (J.-P. Migne, ed., *Patrologiae cursus completus. Series graeca.* 161 vols. [Paris, 1857–66], 62:112) [hereafter "PG"].

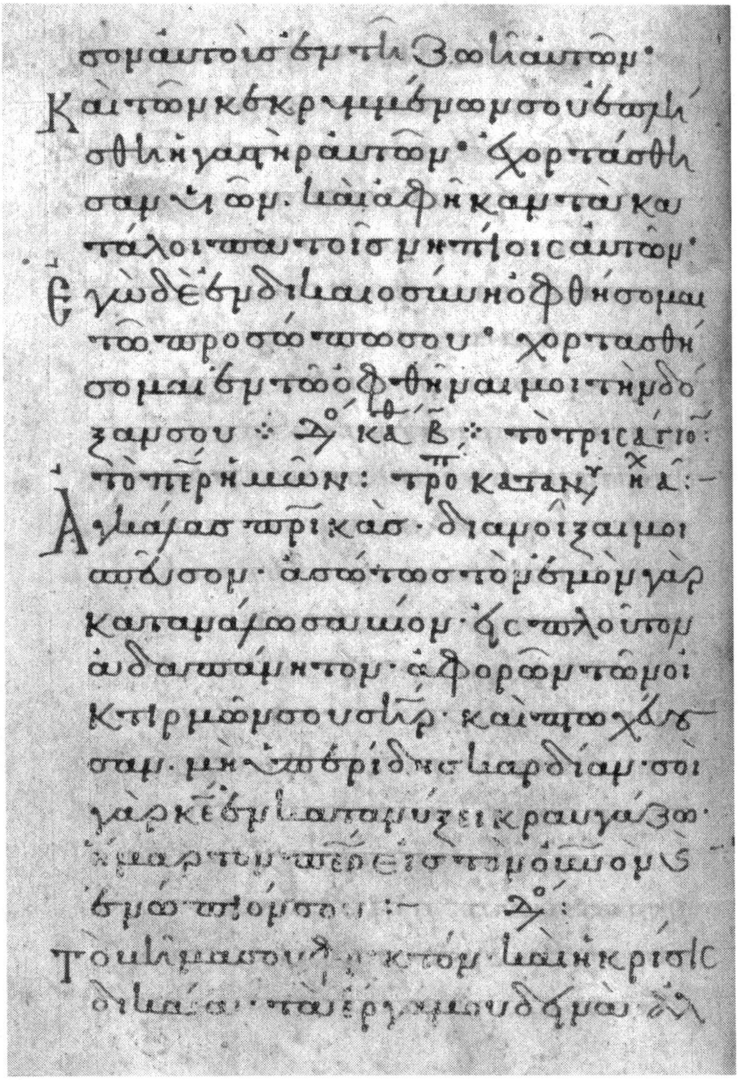

Fig. 2: Cambridge, Houghton Library, Harvard University, MS Gr. 3, fol. 24v: Ps 16:14b–15 and beginning of liturgical supplements of Kathisma 2

terials are the psalms and odes with supplements (fols. 8r–232v), a horologion (fols. 233r–261v), synaxarion-menologion (fols. 262r–281v), guides to setting the dates of feasts governed by the lunar cycle, and a brief excerpt from the *Exposition fidei* of John of Damascus (fols. 282r–289v, not transcribed here).[20]

The scribe employed graphic conventions to call attention to the major divisions of the text, which is written more or less continuously so as not to waste valuable parchment. A cross of four dots sets off the titles to the canonical hours (fols. 242v, 244r, 245v, 252v, 253v), the interhours (fols. 251v, 252r), as well as the liturgical office called "the Typika" (fols. 245v, 247v), the ritual before communion (fol. 248v), the office of Holy Thursday (fol. 248v), the prayers before communion (fol. 249v), and the prayers after communion (fol. 251r). A line sets off the Trinitarian Hymns of matins (fol. 263v) as well as the prokeimena to "Everything that has breath" (fol. 238v), and another is drawn at the end of the typika (fol. 248v). Lines also call attention to the start of the calendar and before each of the months. Finally, a cross of four dots sets off the word "then" following the second prayer for the dead in compline (fol. 260r). In the synaxarion-menologion, the scribe used red ink to highlight a number of feasts: the conception of John the Baptist (Sep. 23), the Theotokos's ascent to the Holy of Holies (Nov. 21), Christmas (Dec. 25), the Feast of Lights (Jan. 6), Feast of the Annunciation (Mar. 25), Feast of the Metamorphosis (Aug. 6), and Easter Sunday.

The Greek Text

The scribe wrote in a neat, legible hand. He copied the psalter supplements (part I) in full, neither truncating passages nor abbreviating words. As a result, the non-biblical additions match the psalms in appearance; figure 2 shows fol. 24v, which contains Psalm 16:14b–15 and, beginning at line 9, the start of the supplements to kathisma 2. When copying the horologion (part II) and synaxarion-menologion (part III), the scribe often abbreviated words, following a tradition of medieval Greek texts that was based on the need to conserve material. Letters the scribe omitted in the copying of troparia and prayers he indicated by conventional signs, whereas the liturgi-

20. B. Kotter, *Die Schriften des Johannes von Damaskos* (Berlin: De Gruyter, 1973), 2:61.

cal instructions must be read without the benefit of compendia, often from only two or three letters serving to designate an entire word; owing to their formulaic nature and familiarity from other liturgical books, the instructions are rarely in doubt (see fig. 3, fol. 240v with the end of matins and start of the first hour in line 13). When a question arises over what the scribe intended, the letters supplied appear in angle brackets. These and other additions in angle brackets must be treated as conjectures.

In transcribing the text, I have added the iota subscripts and ignored the occasional double dotting of iota and upsilon, though the scribe's use of the diaeresis is followed in the transcription. The rare cases of itacism have been corrected, unless they create a possible reading or occur in a proper name. The scribe is careful with accents, including enclitics. The exception is when the word preceding the enclitic has a circumflex on the penult (for example, ῥῦσαι); in these instances the scribe almost invariably fails to shift the accent. I transcribe the numbers as written unless the context seems better served otherwise; thus, I leave ὁ N' as "the fiftieth psalm."

Possibly the greatest difference between the manuscript and the transcription arises in punctuation (and the attendant accent changes). For the most part, both the troparia and prayers are heavily punctuated. The frequent breaks, and in particular the number of semicolons (·), can hinder the ability of modern readers to follow the meaning. The horologion was intended to be used in performance, both corporate and individual, so the phrases are broken more often than is required by modern, silent reading.

Prose passages copied in the Harvard Psalter, it should be noted, are just as heavily punctuated as the hymns. The scribe sometimes used the margins for the mode designations, psalm numbers, points at which "Glory to the Father ..." or "Both now and forever ..." should be said, to signal that a passage is a prayer, and for his corrections. All marginalia have been integrated at points where I think they belong in a strictly linear text (and notes call attention to their original locations). I also group passages into paragraphs of related material and give a paragraph to each complete troparion and prayer, whereas the scribe wrote in continuous blocks.

This is the publication of a single manuscript, and not a critical edition of several manuscripts of identical content. Reference is occasionally made to contemporary or earlier works: the ninth-century Horologion Cod. Si-

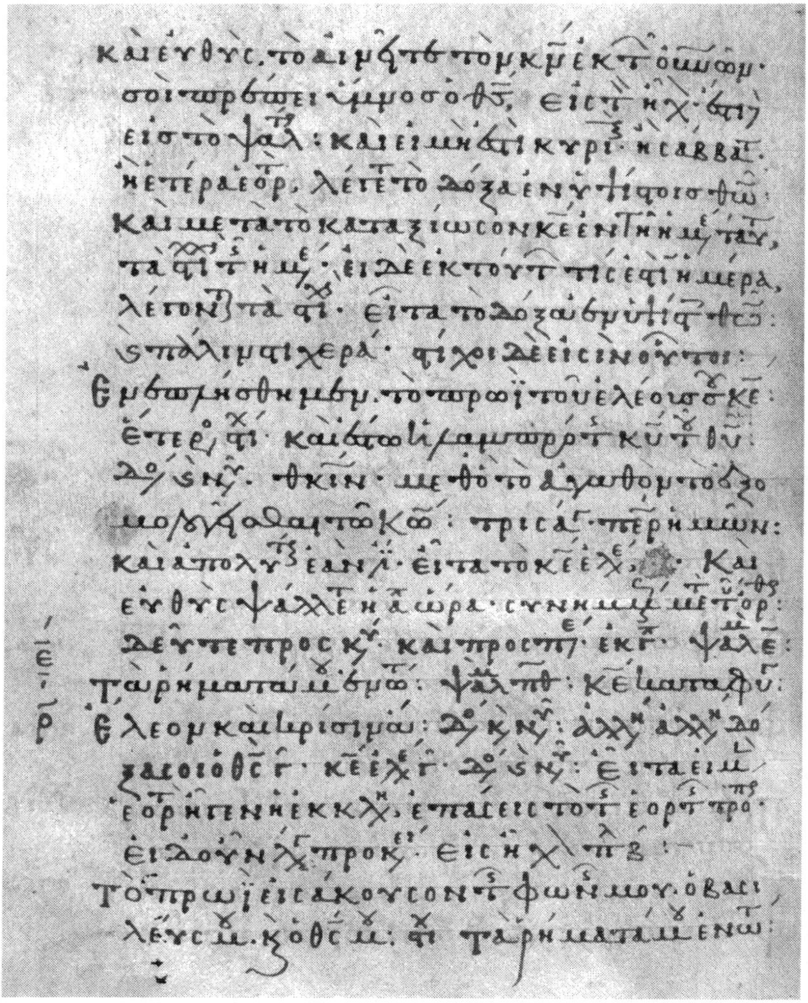

Fig. 3: Cambridge, Houghton Library, Harvard University, MS Gr. 3, fol. 240v:
end of matins and beginning of the first hour

nai. 863, published by J. Mateos,[21] the Evergetis Synaxarion, edited by R. Jordan,[22] and the Messina Typikon, edited by M. Arranz.[23] I have given a greater place to the twelfth-century prayer book Paris, BNF, gr. 331, referred to as "P" in the notes to the text; it is one of three medieval manuscripts used by I. Phountoulis in his edition of the *cursus* of the Sleepless Monks (Akoimetoi).[24] Like the Harvard Psalter, the prayer book is illustrated, though modestly so. Its scribe wrote in a bold minuscule of the type associated with liturgical manuscripts made for performance, whereas the manner of the Harvard Psalter is less expansive and, as noted, relies heavily on abbreviation. The Paris prayer book was made for private use; it contains a brief office for each of the twenty-four hours of the day; these generally consist of a psalm, three troparia, and a prayer. Placed at proper intervals are the offices of matins, the third, sixth, and eighth hours, the typika, and vespers; at the end are communion prayers and the long prayer to the Theotokos that is also found in the Harvard Psalter (fols. 191r–195r).

Other differences noted in the translation are difficult to evaluate along simple lines, but one can say that many of the different wordings found for troparia in the modern editions were already in circulation by the start of the twelfth century. This leads to the question of just how the scribe of the Harvard Psalter composed the text. A clue may lie in several of the pieces the scribe copied more than once: the prayer associated with Psalm 50 (Κύριε ὁ Θεὸς ἡμῶν, ὁ τὴν διὰ μετανοίας) and the two troparia Ὁ χρόνος τῆς ζωῆς μου and Τοῦ σταυροῦ σου τὸ ξύλον. In each case, the scribe gives a slightly different rendering, although the differences are insignificant. Generally speaking, the text (or the manuscript from which it was copied) appears to stand somewhere between oral and written traditions; the scribe or compiler seems occasionally to rely on memory as he arranges familiar material.

---

21. J. Mateos, "Un Horologion inédit de Saint-Sabas. Le codex sinaïtique grec 863 (IXe siècle)," in *Mélanges Eugène Tisserant*, 3:47–76 (Vatican City: Biblioteca Apostolica Vaticana, 1964).

22. *Synaxarion of Evergetis*, ed. Jordan.

23. M. Arranz, *Le Typicon du monastère du Saint-Sauveur à Messine. Codex Messinensis gr. 115*, *A.D. 1131* (Rome: Pontificium Institutum Orientalium Studiorum, 1969).

24. I. Phountoulis, *Εἰκοσιτετράωρον ὡρολόγιον*, Κείμενα Λειτουργικῆς 16 (Thessaloniki, 1977); and, on the monastery and its offices, Phountoulis, *Ἡ εἰκοσιτετράωρος ἀκοίμητος δοξολογία* (Athens: Aster, 1963). See also A. Kazhdan et al., eds., *The Oxford Dictionary of Byzantium* [hereafter "*ODB*"] (Oxford: Oxford University Press, 1991), 1:46, on the Akoimetoi; for the Paris. gr. 331, see Parenti, § III.7–8, V.

Translation

The translation with its notes has been made—above all else—for those who are not students of the monastic offices, but who wish to follow their observance by one monk in one Byzantine house. Meeting this goal requires a structured format with annotations and additions, all bracketed in some way or another. The liturgical instructions appear in plain text and everything spoken in italics. This convention can be said to mirror the scribe's selective use of red and brown inks, minuscule and semi-uncial forms of writing to signal changes from instruction to the voiced passages. But where the scribe tends to write in continuous blocks, I have often separated each element of an office, giving it a separate line.

Some of the troparia, prokeimena, and formulas the scribe wrote out in full, but most he merely signaled using an incipit; and often he did not bother to write formulaic endings that he assumed the user already knew. If only a few words or a sentence remain to complete a prayer or formula, I add them in angle brackets. In most cases, reference is given to a source, but all must be treated as conjecture. When the scribe has given only an incipit, the reader is referred to a printed edition where the full text can be found; these references are given within parentheses following the incipit. Owing to the nature of Greek and how troparia were composed, the opening words often cannot be rendered in acceptable English. I have therefore used the editions cited in parentheses to give an adequate opening phrase, with the occasional result that words in the translation may not appear in the Greek text. Some of the technical terms describing parts of the Byzantine office are merely transliterated; for a few others, English terms have come into use and I employ them. The complex terminology used in denoting the parts of offices is placed within the historical context by Stefano Parenti, to whose accompanying essay I refer using the designation "Parenti §" followed by his section number.

Byzantine liturgical hymns exist in a number of translations made for devotional use.[25] The translators employ language and phrasing that, in the

---

25. For example, in English, Mother Mary and K. Ware, *The Festal Menaion* (London: Faber, 1969), and by the same authors, *The Lenten Triodion* (London: Faber and Faber, 1978); and for

case of English, often recall the King James Bible (1611). The translation here was made for the purpose of studying a historical document. In making it, I have aimed for a literal rendering of the Greek into English and have avoided archaisms while attempting to preserve some of the character of the original. Whenever possible I keep to the order of clauses, deviating when necessary to meet the requirements of English syntax, which relies far more heavily on word order than does Greek. Occasionally, participles are rendered as active verbs and other changes are made to suit English usage. It is sometimes necessary to add words, often pronouns carried over from previous clauses; they appear within parentheses. Finally, I treat the phrase Χριστὸς ὁ Θεός as if it were the common Χριστὸς ὁ Θεὸς ἡμῶν, translating it "Christ our God."

Quotations from the Bible are rendered according to *The Septuagint Version of the Old Testament with an English Translation* for the Septuagint and the Revised Standard Version for the New Testament.[26] Direct quotations from scripture and passages recalling ones from the liturgy appear in boldface; although intrusive, the typographic shift helps clarify changes in verb tense or points at which the syntax seems to slacken. Many direct quotations, it should be stressed, are modified to fit the grammar of the sentence in which they are embedded, so careful study of them as an aspect of medieval composition would require returning to the Septuagint and Greek New Testament. The language of the Byzantine horologion is steeped in the Septuagint, and I have tried to note only deliberate quotation (in boldface), obvious paraphrase (signaled by the abbreviation for *confer*), and words that derive particular significance from their use in a biblical passage. Though seemingly objective, the application of these criteria involves considerable subjectivity. I have not called attention to common epithets for the Deity that are derived from scripture: "full of pity" (Ex 34:6, etc.), "merciful" (ibid.), "patient" (ibid.), "much merciful" (ibid.), "who knows the hearts of mankind" (Acts 1:24), "comforter" (Jn 14:26) and so on.

French, *La Prière des Heures (Horologion)* (Chevetogne: Éditions de Chevetogne, 1975). Others are listed in R. Taft, "The Byzantine Office in the *Prayerbook* of the New Skete: Evaluation of a Proposed Reform," *Orientalia Christiana Periodica* [hereafter "*OCP*"] 48 (1982): 369–70.

26. The English translation of the LXX by Lee C. L. Brenton published by Samuel Bagster in London, 1879, and in New York by Harper and Brothers, under the title *The Septuagint Version of the Old Testament, with an English Translation; and with Various Readings and Critical Notes.*

Scope and Purpose of the Manuscript

The Harvard manuscript is a liturgical psalter intended for use in private and group devotion. Effectively, two components comprise the bulk of the manuscript: the psalter with liturgical supplements and a horologion that gives the rituals of the monastic hours; to them is appended a calendar of fixed and movable celebrations and the hymns appropriate to them.

Psalms and Kathismata

The psalms can be said to lie at the heart of monastic devotion, and they were used in various ways in the monk's daily regime of prayer, confession, and supplication. Single verses, called prokeimena, introduce troparia (short non-biblical hymns), readings,[27] or other ritual units;[28] sometimes they serve as brief, apparently independent chants.[29] Entire psalms appear at points in the offices, often but not invariably early,[30] and they may be grouped in triplets of fixed psalms.[31] David's penitential psalm, Psalm 50, was chanted on a number of occasions throughout the day, when it was often paired with a prayer using language based upon it.[32]

With the exception of Psalm 151, the psalms are also divided into twenty numbered units, known as kathismata, each subdivided into three sections. The number of psalms in each kathisma varies between one and ten, but the number of verses each contains is less variable.[33] At the completion of each kathisma, the scribe added a set of ritual elements that follow a consistent pattern (fig. 2); the monk says the Trisagion ("Holy God, holy and

27. See, for example, the weekday prokeimena of vespers, 154–56; in other sources the prokeimenon precedes a biblical reading (see 157n123).

28. See the Sunday matins prokeimena said before the "Let everything that has breath …," 100–102.

29. See the prokeimenon following the set of three psalms at the opening of the first hour when there is no festal hymn, 110. See Parenti § III.9.2 on prokeimena.

30. See Ps 26 at the start of mesonyktikon, the office here absorbed into the beginning of matins, 84, or Ps 118 at compline, 172.

31. See the tripsalmos at the start of the first hour, 110, and the paired triplets, the hexapsalmos, of matins and compline, 88, 160.

32. For example, 82.

33. 1: Pss 1–8. 2: Pss 9–16. 3: Pss 17–23. 4: Pss 24–31. 5: Pss 32–37. 6: Pss 38–45. 7: Pss 46–54. 8: Pss 55–63. 9: Pss 64–69. 10: Pss 70–76. 11: Pss 77–84. 12: Pss 89–90. 13: Pss 91–100. 14: Pss 101–4. 15: Pss 105–8. 16: Pss 109–17. 17: Ps 118. 18: Pss 119–33. 19: Pss 134–42. 20: Pss 143–50.

mighty ...."),[34] the Lord's Prayer ("Our father ...."), two troparia, a theotokion (a troparion in honor of the Virgin Mary, the Theotokos), the Kyrie eleison ("Lord, have mercy") repeated forty times, and finally a prayer.[35] With the exception of the Trisagion and Lord's Prayer, the liturgical supplements are copied out in full. Recitation of the kathismata may have two places in the monk's daily devotions, one corporate and the other private. Group recitation of the kathismata, termed stichologia and translated here as "continuous psalmody," is ordered as a regular part of the Sunday office of matins.[36] The manuscript specifies two kathismata, but from other sources we know that kathismata were chanted daily at matins and their number could change with the liturgical seasons. At the Constantinopolitan monastery of St. John Stoudios, where an influential reform of monastic ritual was undertaken in the century following the end of Iconoclasm, anywhere from one to four kathismata were said at matins, depending on the season or celebration.[37] At Stoudios and other monasteries of the time kathismata were also performed at vespers (although omitted with some regularity), and at the first, third, sixth, and ninth hours.[38] In addition to their use in corporate worship, the kathismata may have been chanted privately. In his commentary on the Harvard Psalter, Stefano Parenti advances the proposition that the monk recited kathismata at moments throughout the entire day, ending with the tenth and the office for trespasses at the close of the day,[39] followed by kathismata eleven through twenty said during the night.[40]

34. One of a number of common, generally short formulas that are never written out in full; they are given on 27–28.

35. See the example following the first kathisma, 30–32.

36. 96.

37. "Rule of the monastery of St. John Stoudites," in *Byzantine Monastic Foundation Documents*, ed. J. Thomas and A. Constantinides Hero (Washington, D.C.: Dumbarton Oaks Research Library and Collection, 2000) [hereafter "*BMFD*"] 1:102, 105, 106; see also Messina: Arranz, *Typicon de Messine*, xxxvi.

38. Where they come before Ps 140, 152: Arranz, *Typicon de Messine*, xliv. One or two kathismata open vespers at the Evergetis monastery: see the synaxarion (*Synaxarion of Evergetis*, ed. Jordan) and J. Klentos, "The *Synaxarion* of Evergetis: algebra, geology and Byzantine monasticism," in *Work and Worship at the Theotokos Evergetis 1050–1200*, ed. M. Mullett and A. Kirby (Belfast: Belfast Byzantine Enterprises, 1997), 350–52. In the Harvard Psalter, Ps 118 ("The blameless"), which happens to be the seventeenth kathisma, is said at compline, 172, but I do not think this would be considered a kathisma. Performance of kathismata at the first, third, sixth, and ninth hour is suggested by a note in the Evergetis Synaxarion: *Synaxarion of Evergetis*, ed. Jordan, 1:496.

39. See 52.   40. Parenti, § V.

Odes and Canons

Following Psalm 151, the scribe copied nine biblical odes.[41] As the "canon" this particular choice plays an important role in matins and compline. The nine are grouped in triplets,[42] and are chanted with non-biblical liturgical poetry, for example, compositions specific to the saint or feast of the day. Two important service manuals that are roughly contemporary with the Harvard manuscript show how rich and variable the canons could be. One is the ritual typikon of the monastery of San Salvatore at Messina, published by Miguel Arranz and thought to generally reflect Stoudite practice.[43] The other is the synaxarion of the Constantinopolitan monastery of the Theotokos Evergetis, edited by R. Jordan. (Unlike the liturgical psalter, these two works give detailed, day-by-day instructions.) That the nine odes were considered to be a kind of three-part ritual unit is underscored by the appearance of biblical poetry in other parts of the manuscript. Two of what we now call odes are referred to as "prayers" in the manuscript, and the scribe copied them as part of the supplements to the kathismata, not among the nine odes comprising the canon. The first is the Prayer of Manasses,[44] used as the concluding prayer for kathisma 16, where it appears in the manuscript, and additionally chanted at both mesonyktikon and compline. The second is the Prayer of Hezekiah,[45] which serves as the prayer to close kathisma 17, where the scribe copied it. The Ode of Symeon is recited toward the end of vespers, although the scribe did not write out this brief canticle.[46]

---

41. As numbered by the scribe—Ode 1: Ex 15:1–9. 2: Dt 32:1–43. 3: 1 Kgs (= 1 Sm) 2:1–10. 4: Hab 3:2–19. 5: Is 26:9–20. 6: Jon 2:3–10. 7: Dn 3:26–45, 8:52–56. 8: Dn 3:52–88. 9: Lk 1:46–55, 68–79 (Magnificat and Benedictus).

42. See Parenti § III.7.2.2.

43. Arranz, *Typicon de Messine*, 408–9. See also H. Schneider, "Die Biblischen Oden in Jerusalem und Konstantinopel," *Biblica* 30 (1949): 253–55, 262–66; and R. Taft, "Mount Athos: A Late Chapter in the History of the Byzantine Rite," *DOP* 42 (1988): 189–90.

44. Ode 12 in *Septuaginta: Id est Vetus Testamentum graece iuxta LXX interpretes*, ed. A. Ralphs, 3rd ed. (Stuttgart: Privilegierte württembergische Bibelanstalt, 1949).

45. Ode 11 in *Septuaginta*, ed. Rahlfs.

46. Ode 13 (Lk 2:29–32) in *Septuaginta*, ed. Rahlfs: 181.

Horologion and the Monastic Hours

The second part of the manuscript contains the horologion, the order of service for the monastic hours—traditionally matins; the first, third, sixth and ninth hour; vespers; compline; and the night office of mesonyktikon.[47] The horologion of the Psalter combines corporate with private devotions and treats the traditional offices in a manner that reflects contemporary Constantinopolitan practice. The horologion opens on two prayers said upon rising from sleep; they are likely done individually and in private.[48] Following them is a grand office celebrated communally and combining several rituals; it begins with those for the forgiveness of sins and the remembrance of the dead, followed by mesonyktikon, matins (orthros), and the first hour, all of which flow together without intervening titles or obviously marked breaks in the manuscript (fig. 3, showing, on fol. 240v, line 13, the end of matins and beginning of the first hour). Following matins—as I will call it in short—are the third, sixth, and ninth "great" hour, which, like all subsequent hours and rituals, the scribe clearly titled. The third hour evokes the descent of the Holy Spirit at Pentecost (Acts 2:1–4, 15), whereas the sixth and ninth hours recall Christ's last hours on the cross (see Mt 27:45–46; Mk 15:33–34; Lk 23:44–46). The next hour is vespers (lychnikon, lamp-lighting), followed by compline (apodeipnon, after supper), which completes the daily cursus of formal observances.

Typika and Mesoria

To the canonical hours, the compiler added a somewhat loosely organized set of rituals and supplements, which he inserted between the ninth hour and vespers. The first is the office of the typika, said after the sixth hour on days when the eucharistic liturgy is celebrated, but when it is not, after the ninth hour, where it is copied; at the end of the typika is a brief ritual performed before the liturgy. The scribe then gives the additional psalms and troparia for the first, third, sixth, and ninth hour on Maundy Thursday. These are special interhours, or mesoria, that were added after the

47. In general see R. Taft, *The Liturgy of the Hours in East and West: The Origins of the Divine Office and Its Meaning for Today*, 2nd ed. (Collegeville, Minn.: Liturgical Press, 1993).
48. 80–82.

canonical hours. Then come the communion prayers, one set said before receiving communion and the other after, and all four written in the first person singular, signifying that they were said privately.[49] Finally there are the interhours for the first, third, sixth, and ninth great hour for Good Friday as well as those added on the Saturday before Easter Sunday; outside of the three days of Holy Week, no mention is made of interhours, as these were performed, privately or corporately, in other houses of the time.[50]

The third, sixth, and ninth hour were celebrated privately in the monk's room.[51] These hours are relatively short, and their only variable element is the troparion of a feast or saint, when one is celebrated in "the church." To find the additional troparia the monk turned to the calendar following the horologion; in it he found the celebrations and associated troparia for both movable days, determined on the basis of Easter, and the fixed celebrations of the calendar year, which began on September 1. Many of the troparia fixed for the first, sixth, and ninth hours are not contained in the manuscript, but presumably their daily use meant that the monk learned them early on.

Communal Offices: Matins, Vespers, Compline

The other three offices—matins, vespers, and compline—were communal celebrations for which the monks all gathered to participate. The three communal hours, and particularly matins and compline, are lengthy and complex in nature on account of the many variable elements that needed to be taken into account. The Harvard manuscript covers the main factors governing the choices that needed to be made. The first is the day of the week, whether Sunday, the weekdays Monday through Friday, Saturday, or one of the individual weekdays. At the start of matins, for example, the "Alleluia" is specified daily except Saturday and Sunday, when "God is the Lord" is ordered. There are also elements that change daily; the matins Hymns of

---

49. 140–42.

50. D. Krausmüller, "Private vs communal: Niketas Stethatos's Hypotyposis for Stoudios, and patterns of worship in eleventh-century Byzantine monasteries," in *Work and Worship at the Theotokos Evergetis*, ed. Mullett and Kirby, 310–11; see also the mid-eleventh-century rules of Nikon of the Black Mountain in *BMFD* 1:385 [7], and a note to Nov. 15 in the Evergetis Synaxarion (*Synaxarion of Evergetis*, ed. Jordan, 1:200).

51. As at Stoudios, when performed corporately only during Lent: Krausmüller, "Private vs communal," 319.

Light in the first mode, for instance, are different on each day of the week.[52] In compiling the order of service for matins, the scribe faced the problem of specifying the weekday changes within the sequential, linear confines of a continuously written text; after giving the instruction for chanting the "God is the Lord" on Saturday,[53] he turns to the Sunday ritual, specifying it as far as the prokeimena to "Everything that has breath ..." and then returning, with some repetition, to where he left off.[54]

The second structural element is the mode of the week. Chanting is done in one of eight modes: modes one through four, plagal modes one and two, barys, and plagal mode four. The modes are said to be "groups of melodies of a certain type built upon a number of basic formulae."[55] Each week has its own mode; the church begins with the first mode in the week following Easter, then moves week-by-week through the remaining seven before beginning again at the first and repeating the cycle. For a small number of hymns—such as the matins Hymns of Light and Trinitarian Hymns[56]—the scribe copied the complete selections arranged by mode, and the user chose the one or ones that were appropriate. The modes of the troparia are generally fixed. Any given hour, therefore, would contain elements in different modes.

The third factor that needed to be taken into account is the feast day, or celebration honoring a saint, when appropriate troparia and other non-biblical poetry would be chanted. Other aspects of performance could also be affected. At Sunday matins "God is the Lord" is chanted in the mode of the week, unless it is a feast or saint's day, then it is chanted in the mode of the troparion for that day's feast.[57] The horologion contains little about the great liturgical periods, particularly Lent.[58] It specifies that on Monday through Wednesday of Holy Week a troparion said in conjunction with the "Alleluia" replaced the Trinitarian Hymns, and there are the added troparia

52. 104–6.   53. 96–100.

54. 96.

55. Egon Wellesz, *A History of Byzantine Music and Hymnography,* 2nd ed. (Oxford: Oxford University Press, 1961), 303.

56. Respectively, 104–8, and 90–96.

57. 88.

58. See, for example, the rules governing the use and number of kathismata during the liturgical seasons and on feast days at the monastery of San Salvatore, Messina (Arranz, *Typicon de Messine,* 3–5).

for the interhours of Holy Week, but little else is specified as changing with the liturgical seasons, other than the additions and substitutions cited for certain days in the calendar of movable feasts.

Personnel

Despite what may at first seem to be offices described in considerable detail, the horologion actually gives only a basic order of service—the skeletal structure—and it may be useful to note what the compiler leaves out. In a large monastery of Middle Byzantine times, the communal offices might be organized and supervised by a substantial number of monks charged with separate duties. They could include the doorman, who admonished late-comers and kept watch for those trying to leave before the dismissal, a brother who awakened monks nodding off in fatigue, and the superior who might participate in minor ways along with the ekklesiarch. The ekklesiarch (in a nunnery the ekklesiarchissa) was charged with the arrangements for each communal office, including the requirements of the cantor (psaltes), who supervised one or two choirs. When the eucharistic liturgy was performed the priest officiated with the assistance of the deacon.

The horologion tells us little to nothing about the roles of the priest, deacon, and cantor. It incorporates ritual elements and prayers associated with the eucharistic liturgy, but makes no mention of the priest and, with one exception, the deacon who would have conducted the service. From Abbot Timothy's typikon for the Theotokos Evergetis we know that the priest was present at matins and compline, as was also likely to have been the case in the monastery where the Psalter was used.[59] The beginning of matins is signaled in the Harvard manuscript by "Glory to the holy, consubstantial and indivisible Trinity, always, now and forever and ever. Amen."[60] From the typika of Stoudios, Evergetis, and St. Sabas, we learn that the first line is said by the priest, and Evergetis adds that the "Amen" is said by the ekklesiarch.[61] At the Stoudios monastery the prayer following Psalm 50 was said by the

---

59. Evergetis typikon of Abbot Timothy (*BMFD* 2:473–75, 475–76).

60. 86.

61. Stoudios (*BMFD* 1:98); Evergetis (*BMFD* 2:476); St. Sabas (A. Dmitrievskij, *Описание литургических рукописей храня в библиотеках православнаго Востока*, 3 vols. [St. Petersburg, 1895–1917, reprinted in Hildesheim: G. Olms, 1965], 321).

priest at matins, but in the Harvard Psalter, where the prayer is twice written out in full, the rubric seems to indicate that it is said by the congregation.[62] The participation of the deacon is cited once in the horologion—in the chanting of the prokeimena to the "Let everything that has breath ..."—and the only mention of the cantor comes in the same sequence of responsory prokeimena.[63]

Books

Arranging and leading the communal hours and the liturgy required a small library of specialized books, none mentioned in the horologion. The priest read from a book of prayers (euchologion) and the biblical lessons were chanted from the Gospel lectionary, the Prophetologion (Old Testament readings), and Apostolos (readings from Acts and Epistles). In preparing for the performance of the hours, the ekklesiarch arranged for the cantor the specialized volumes containing the propers of the day, including the troparia only given here in their opening phrases; among the many service books needed are the Oktoechos (hymns in the eight modes), Pentekostarion (offices for Eastertide), and Triodion (for Lent), in which the hymns and other devotional units are organized by mode and liturgical season.[64] When the Harvard manuscript orders the monks to do poetic kathismata and canons, or hypakoe, it does not provide the actual hymns needed to do so. Judging by the twelfth-century liturgical typika of the monasteries of San Salvatore at Messina and the Theotokos Evergetis (its synaxarion), prose readings were also a regular part of matins.[65] The horologion here makes no reference to biblical, patristic, or hagiographic readings at any point other than the Sunday reading from the Gospel lectionary.[66] In the vespers ritual, the prokeimenon that is associated with a reading from the Old Testament is given, but no reference to a reading follows;[67] instead, the scribe writes "After the prokeimenon say, 'Deign, O Lord ...'" At Messina, the "Deign, O

62. See 52, 82–84. For Stoudios, see M. Arranz, "Les prières presbytérales des matins byzantines," OCP 37 (1971): 426–28.

63. Respectively, 100, 102.

64. Wellez, Byzantine Music, 139–45, describes these and others.

65. Synaxarion of Evergetis, ed. Jordan, 3:163–205, lists the many.

66. 98.

67. Synaxarion of Evergetis, ed. Jordan, 1:6 [V.4–5]; Arranz, Typicon de Messine, 12.15–17.

Lord . . ." is chanted directly after the reading.[68] But at the Evergetis the same prokeimenon could, it appears, occasionally be a free-standing element, so it is difficult to determine with confidence whether there was or was not a reading at this point in the monastery for which the Psalter was made. In light of the number of copies of the liturgical homilies of Gregory of Nazianzen or the edition of saints' lives by Symeon Metaphrastes produced in the eleventh century for monastic use—not to mention biblical and patristic works—the omission from the horologion of any mention of readings seems to be a decision based on the assumption that the book's owner was an auditor not a reader or monk with specific responsibility for the services.

Most of the components of the hours are chanted, and although the mode is often given there is no musical notation to offer further guidance. The instruction in the menologion for the birth of the Theotokos, celebrated on September 7, gives the troparion and orders that it be chanted in the first mode to the melody of the troparion "When the stone had been sealed," reminding us that the hymns were sung. A number of troparia are repeated often through the week, so presumably they were committed to memory. But the monks go through a vast amount of hymnographic material of various kinds at the three communal services. We cannot assume anything like a hymnal at the back of every pew, but then neither can we take it for granted that the monastic congregation chanted or said everything cited in the orders of service. Some elements may have been performed by the choir(s) or by the soloist.[69] The cantor may have started a chant before it was taken up by the congregation following his lead.[70] We also know that cantors used hand signals when leading the choir(s), and it is possible that the congregation of monks, called the "people" in the manuscript, were positioned in such a way as to be able to follow the cantor's lead; this seems to be explicit at the Evergetis.[71] Finally, it should be noted that in our attempt to understand aspects of performance, the scribe or compiler offers us little help. In the manuscript he uses three verbs for performance, chant (ψάλλω), sing (ἐπᾴδω), and what

---

68. Arranz, *Typicon de Messine*, xliv–xlv.

69. As the December 25 vespers and matins at the Evergetis monastery (*Synaxarion of Evergetis*, ed. Jordan, 1:328–32, 334–38).

70. Ibid., 1:356.

71. Ibid., 1:330, 337. N. Moran, *Singers in Late Byzantine and Slavonic Painting* (Leiden: E. J. Brill, 1986), 38–47.

I have rendered as "say" (λέγω), instead of the more restrictive "recite." I suspect his use of these words is at times imprecise.

Places and Times for Offices

Finally, the horologion omits mention of where things happen and when they happen. The scribe gave only the sequence of observations and, in the case of the office of the typika, the circumstance under which the sequence would change; the scribe does not tell the user at what times he should gather with the others in church or rise in his room to chant an hour. Such instruction would have been unnecessary because a brother was designated to keep time and sound the semantron, a length of wood or metal struck rhythmically with a mallet, to signal the start of the office. The one indication in the manuscript that the times of the observances were not consistently fixed throughout the year comes indirectly in the form of the brief notes at the start of each month of the fixed cycle; they give the number of daylight and night time hours.[72] Other sources also indicate that the times of when the hours were celebrated were not invariable. Combing the Messina typikon, Arranz has established the times throughout the year when the San Salvatore monks performed their offices, and John Klentos has done the same for the Evergetis monastery.[73] Their results cannot be applied to the monk who used the Harvard manuscript; nevertheless, they reveal the possible degree of variation in timing the observances, which themselves differed in length over the course of the year. Where the monks gathered is also unspecified, and we cannot assume that everything took place in either the monk's room or the church. At Messina, where the midnight office immediately preceded matins, the monks did not enter the church until the "Glory to God in the highest ..." and so presumably they were gathered in the narthex, as at Stoudios.[74] We also know of processions around monastic precincts, or gatherings to pray and sing at graves, in special chapels, or at the monastic fountain in the courtyard. The Harvard Psalter gives no indication of such things. Although there can be no doubt that the Harvard Psalter reflects

---

72. A note in the Evergetis Synaxarion says that with the lengthening nights Pss 134–35 could be added to nighttime vigils (*Synaxarion of Evergetis*, ed. Jordan, 2:708).

73. Arranz, *Typicon de Messine*, xxxv–xlix; see also Klentos, "*Synaxarion*," 344.

74. Arranz, *Typicon de Messine*, xxxvi; Stoudios (*BMFD* 1:98 [2]).

contemporary monastic practices, some of the things left unspecified, along with ones added, raise the possibility, even if remote, that the book was used outside a monastery for private devotion.[75]

Naming of Elements

A final word on nomenclature. It can seem dauntingly opaque and foreign, but it is only the technical language of the church. The compiler identified the ritual units, the building blocks of the hours, essentially in one of three ways. One was by giving the opening phrase: the "Come, let us worship," "Everything that has breath," or "God is the Lord." Troparia are similarly identified. For the psalms both the opening phrase and the psalm number are given, making it easy to find them in the first part of the manuscript. Other units bear something like a name: the Trisagion, The Trinitarian Hymns; Psalms 148–50 are called the Ainoi (the psalms of praise, or lauds in the Western church). Finally, there are the generic designations for variable elements—Hymns of Light, canons, hypakoe—that may derive from content, place in the service, or some other aspect of the hymn. The roots of these terms do not always lead to a correct understanding of their meaning or implication. The prokeimena, from *prokeimai*, ought to be the things that invariably come before, requiring a close connection with something immediately following, as is generally the case, but as noted above a prokeimenon can at times also be a free-standing unit. The kathismata, from *kathidzo*, ought to be things done sitting down, but the psalms recitations, to which the word often pertains, were performed standing. This last and other problems of naming are taken up by Stefano Parenti in his commentary on the horologion.[76]

---

75. See Parenti § III.9.4.

76. See also the index of liturgical terms in Arranz, *Typicon de Messine*, 376–449, and the glossary in *Synaxarion of Evergetis*, ed. Jordan, 1:571–83.

COMMON, REPEATED
FORMULAS

Alleluia:
> Ἀλληλούϊα, ἀλληλούϊα, δόξα σοι ὁ Θεός.
>
> *Alleluia, alleluia, glory to you, O God.*

Come let us worship (the three-line invitatory formula said before the recitation of psalms; the formula is given slightly differently in the third hour and compline instructions):
> Δεῦτε προσκυνήσωμεν καὶ προσπέσωμεν τῷ βασιλεῖ ἡμῶν Θεῷ.
> Δεῦτε προσκυνήσωμεν καὶ προσπέσωμεν Χριστῷ τῷ βασιλεῖ ἡμῶν Θεῷ.
> Δεῦτε προσκυνήσωμεν καὶ προσπέσωμεν αὐτῷ Χριστῷ τῷ βασιλεῖ καὶ Θεῷ ἡμῶν.
>
> **Come let us worship and fall down before** (Ps 94:6) *the king our God.*
> *Come let us worship and fall down before Christ the king our God. Come let us worship and fall down before him, Christ our king and God.*

Glory ... both now (sometimes said as a continuous unit, sometimes separately at the start and finish of other passages):
> Δόξα Πατρὶ καὶ Υἱῷ καὶ Ἁγίῳ Πνεύματι. Καὶ νῦν καὶ ἀεὶ καὶ εἰς τοὺς αἰῶνας τῶν αἰώνων.
>
> *Glory to the Father and the Son and the Holy Spirit. Both now and always and for ever and ever.*

God is the Lord:

Θεὸς Κύριος, καὶ ἐπέφανεν ἡμῖν, εὐλογημένος ὁ ἐρχόμενος ἐν ὀνόματι Κυρίου (HR 77).[77]

God is the Lord, and he has shined upon us (Ps 117:27); **blessed is he who comes in the name of the Lord** (Ps 117:26).

Heavenly king, comforter:

Βασιλεῦ οὐράνιε, παράκλητε, τὸ πνεῦμα τῆς ἀληθείας, ὁ πανταχοῦ παρὼν καὶ τὰ πάντα πληρῶν, ὁ θησαυρὸς τῶν ἀγαθῶν καὶ ζωῆς χορηγός, ἐλθὲ καὶ σκήνωσον ἐν ἡμῖν καὶ καθάρισον ἡμᾶς ἀπὸ πάσης κηλῖδος καὶ σῶσον, ἀγαθέ, τὰς ψυχὰς ἡμῶν (HR 11).

Heavenly king, comforter, spirit of truth, he who is everywhere and supplies everything, the store of good and giver of life, O you who are good, come dwell among us, cleanse us of all stain and save our souls.

Let everything that has breath:

Πᾶσα πνοὴ αἰνεσάτω τὸν Κύριον. Αἰνεῖτε τὸν Κύριον ἐκ τῶν οὐρανῶν· αἰνεῖτε αὐτὸν ἐν τοῖς ὑψίστοις. Σοὶ πρέπει ὕμνος, τῷ Θεῷ. Αἰνεῖτε αὐτὸν, πάντες οἱ ἄγγελοι αὐτου· αἰνεῖτε αὐτόν, πᾶσαι αἱ δυνάμεις αὐτοῦ. Σοὶ πρέπει ὕμνος, τῷ Θεῷ (HR 122).

Let everything that has breath praise the Lord (Ps 150:6). **Praise the Lord from the heavens; praise him in the highest** (Ps 148:1). **To you is due praise, to God** (Ps 64:2). **Praise him all his angels; praise him all his hosts** (Ps 148:2). **To you is due praise, to God.**

Trisagion:

Ἅγιος ὁ Θεός, ἅγιος ἰσχυρός, ἅγιος ἀθάνατος, ἐλέησον ἡμᾶς (HR 7).

Holy God, holy and mighty, holy and immortal, have mercy on us.

---

77. HR = Ὡρολόγιον περιέχον τὴν ἡμερονύκτιον ἀκολουθίαν μετὰ τῶν συνήθων προσθήκων, 2nd ed. (Rome, 1937).

I

KATHISMATA
AND OFFICE FOR
TRESPASSES

※

Key to Signs and Abbreviations

In the Greek, square brackets [ ] enclose letters or words supplied where a gap occurs in the text. Angle brackets < > enclose words or letters omitted by the scribe without abbreviation signs; braces { } indicate letters written by the scribe but omitted as erroneous. "C" denotes Cambridge, Harvard University, Houghton Library, MS gr. 3, dated 1105. "P" denotes the roughly contemporary Paris, Bibliothèque Nationale de France, gr. 331 (from a microfilm).

In the English translation, anything bracketed is absent from the Greek. Parentheses ( ) enclose four types of additions: words added to meet the requirements of English usage, words added to clarify liturgical directions, references to printed editions when only an incipit is given, and citations of sources and significant parallel passages. Angle brackets enclose words and phrases supplied in cases where the scribe has assumed a conventional ending familiar to the reader, or where he has omitted a word or phrase.

κάθισμα α΄[1]

Τὸ τρισάγιον, τὸ *Πάτερ ἡμῶν*, τροπάριον, ἦχος α΄,
'Εν ἀνομίαις συλληφθεὶς ἐγὼ ὁ ἄσωτος, οὐ τολμῶ ἀτενίσαι εἰς τὸ ὕψος τοῦ οὐρανοῦ, ἀλλὰ θαρρῶν εἰς τὴν φιλανθρωπίαν σου κράζω· 'Ο Θεὸς ἱλάσθητί μοι τῷ ἁμαρτωλῷ καὶ σῶσόν με. |[15v] *Δόξα* .[2]

Εἰ ὁ δίκαιος μόλις σῴζεται, ἐγὼ ποῦ φανοῦμαι ὁ ἁμαρτωλός; Τὸ βάρος καὶ τὸν καύσωνα τῆς ἡμέρας οὐκ ἐβάστασα· τοῖς περὶ τὴν ἑνδεκάτην ὥραν συναρίθμησόν με, ὁ Θεός, καὶ σῶσόν με. Καὶ νῦν.

Θεοτοκίον,[3] *Ἄχραντε Θεοτόκε, ἡ ἐν οὐρανοῖς εὐλογουμένη καὶ ἐπὶ γῆς δοξολογουμένη· Χαῖρε νύμφη ἀνύμφευτε.*

Τὸ *Κύριε, ἐλέησον*, μ΄, εἶτα τὴν εὐχὴν τοῦ Μεγάλου Βασιλείου,[4]
Εὐλογῶ σε, Κύριε, τὸν μόνον μακρόθυμον καὶ ἀνεξίκακον, τὸν καθ' ἑκάστην ἡμέραν καὶ ὥραν μακροθυμοῦντά μοι πλημμελοῦντι, καὶ δόντα ἐξουσίαν πᾶσιν ἡμῖν μετανοίας· διὰ γὰρ τοῦτο σιωπᾷς καὶ ἀνέχη ἡμῶν, Κύριε, ἵνα σε δοξολογῶμεν τὸν οἰκονομοῦντα τοῦ γένους ἡμῶν τὴν σωτηρίαν. Ποτὲ μὲν διὰ φόβων, ἄλλοτε δὲ διὰ παραινέσεων, |[16] *ποτὲ μὲν διὰ προφητῶν, ὕστερον δὲ διὰ παρουσίας τοῦ Υἱοῦ σου ἐπισκεψάμενος ἡμᾶς. Σὺ γὰρ ἔπλασας ἡμᾶς καὶ οὐκ ἡμεῖς· σὺ εἶ ὁ Θεὸς ἡμῶν. 'Εγὼ μέν, Κύριε, οὐκ εἰμὶ ἄξιος ἐπὶ σοῦ φθέγξασθαι, διότι σφόδρα ἁμαρτωλὸς τυγχάνω. Εὐχαριστῶ σοι, Κύριε, ὅτι μου ἐμακροθύμησας τοῖς παραπτώμασι καὶ ἕως τοῦ νῦν ἀτιμώρητόν με εἴασας. 'Εγὼ μὲν γὰρ ἄξιός εἰμι[5] πολλὰ παθεῖν καὶ ἀπορριφῆναι ἀπὸ τοῦ προσώπου σου· ἡ δὲ ἀνεξίκακός σου φιλανθρωπία ἐμακροθύμησεν ἐπ' ἐμοί. Εὐχαριστῶ σοι, Κύριε, εἰ καὶ μὴ τυγχάνω αὐτάρκης πρὸς δοξολογίαν τῆς σῆς ἀνεξικακίας, ἐλέησόν με, Κύριε· κράτησόν μου τὴν ψυχὴν τὸ λοῖπον[6] τῆς*

---

1. Fols. 9–15.
2. δόξα indicated in the margin.
3. θεοτοκίον indicated in the margin here and in other instances.
4. εὐχή indicated a second time in the margin.
5. ἄξιος εἰμὶ: C.
6. λεῖπον: C.

Kathismata 1–10[1])
Kathisma 1[2]

The Trisagion,[3] the *Our Father* (*HR* 8), troparion, mode I:

*I, the prodigal who was **conceived in sins** (Ps 50:7), dare not look to heaven's heights (cf. Ps 102:11; Lk 18:13), but having confidence in your love of mankind, I cry out, "**God, be merciful to me, a sinner** (Lk 18:13), and save me."*

Glory.

If the righteous man be barely saved, where shall I, the sinner, appear *(Prv 11:31, 1 Pt 4:18)? I did not bear the burden of the day and (its) scorching heat (cf. Mt 20:12). Count me among them **near the eleventh hour** (Mt 20:9), God, and save me.*

Both now.

theotokion: *O undefiled Theotokos, you who are blessed in heaven and glorified on earth: hail, bride unwed.*

Lord, have mercy forty times, then the

Prayer of Basil the Great: *I praise you, O Lord, the only one patient and forbearing, who through every day and hour are patient with me as I make mistakes, and who grant the power of repentance to all of us; O Lord, you are silent and hold fast to us for this purpose: that we might glorify you who direct the salvation of our race. At one time through fears, but at another time through counsels, at one time through the prophets, but later through the coming of your son, you watch over us. For you created us, and we did not (create ourselves). You are our God.*

I am not worthy, O Lord, to speak of you because I am deeply sinful. I thank you, O Lord, for you are slow to anger in the face of my transgressions and since up to now you left me unpunished. Truly I am worthy to suffer greatly and to be cast out of your presence,[4] but your forbearing love of mankind was

---

1. The kathismata are arranged in order of the modes: kath. 1-3: mode I; kath. 4-5: mode II; kath. 6-7: mode III; kath. 8-10: mode IV; kath. 11-13: plagal mode I; kath. 14-15: plagal mode II; kath. 16-18: barys mode; kath. 19-20: plagal mode IV. For the use of the kathismata and their supplements in the monk's private devotions, see Parenti, § V.

2. Psalms 1–8. Divided into three sessions (staseis), each marked by *Glory* at its end: first, Pss 1–3; second, 4–6; third, 7–8.

3. Formulas for which no reference is given appear in Common, Repeated Formulas, 27–28.

4. Familiar reminiscence from the LXX, e.g., Ps 50:11.

ζωῆς μου εἰς τὸ |¹⁶ᵛ θέλημά σου, καὶ κυβέρνησον ὡς γινώσκει ἡ εὐσπλαγχνία σου τὴν ταπείνωσίν μου· καὶ μὴ καταπιστεύσῃς μοι τὸ ἔλεός σου, ἀλλ᾽ ὡς γινώσκει ἡ εὐσπλαγχνία σου καὶ ἡ φιλανθρωπία σου. Μόνον παράσχου μοι σταγόνα τοῦ ἐλέους τῆς εὐσπλαγχνίας σου τῷ πλήθει τῶν οἰκτιρμῶν σου, καὶ οὕτως με ἀπόλυσον ἐκ τοῦ σώματος τούτου, πρεσβείαις καὶ ἱκεσίαις τῆς πανενδόξου δεσποίνης ἡμῶν, Θεοτόκου καὶ ἀειπαρθένου Μαρίας, τῶν ἁγίων σου λειτουργῶν καὶ ἀχράντων δυνάμεων, τοῦ ἁγίου καὶ ἐνδόξου προφήτου, προδρόμου καὶ βαπτιστοῦ Ἰωάννου, τοῦ τιμίου καὶ ζωοποιοῦ σταυροῦ καὶ πάντων τῶν ἁγίων τῶν ἀπ᾽ αἰῶνός σοι εὐαρεστησάντων, ὅτι εὐλογητὸς εἶ εἰς τὸν αἰῶνα· ἀμήν.

κάθισμα β᾽⁷

Τὸ τρισάγιον, τὸ Πάτερ ἡμῶν, τροπάριον κατανυκτικόν, ἦχος α᾽,

Ἀγκάλας πατρικὰς διανοῖξαι μοι σπεῦσον, ἀσώτως τὸν ἐμὸν γὰρ κατανάλωσα βίον, εἰς πλοῦτον ἀδαπάνητον ἀφορῶν τῶν οἰκτιρμῶν σου, Σωτήρ, καὶ πτωχεύουσαν μὴ ὑπερίδῃς καρδίαν. Σοὶ γὰρ, Κύριε, ἐν κατανύξει κραυγάζω· Ἥμαρτον, Πάτερ, εἰς τὸν οὐρανὸν καὶ ἐνώπιόν σου. Δόξα.

Τὸ βῆμά σου φρικτὸν καὶ ἡ κρίσις δικαία· τὰ ἔργα μου δεινά, ἀλ|²⁵-λ᾽ αὐτός, ἐλεήμων προφθάσας με, διάσωσον καὶ καὶ κολάσεως λύτρωσαι· ῥῦσαι, Δέσποτα, τῆς τῶν ἐρίφων μερίδος· συναρίθμησον τοῖς δεξιοῖς με προβάτοις καὶ σῶσόν με δέομαι. Καὶ νῦν.

θεοτοκίον, Οἱ τὴν σὴν προστασίαν κεκτημένοι, ἄχραντε, καὶ ταῖς σαῖς ἱκεσίαις τῶν δεινῶν λυτρούμενοι, τῷ σταυρῷ τοῦ υἱοῦ σου ἐν παντὶ φρουρούμενοι, κατὰ χρέως σε πάντες εὐσεβῶς μεγαλύνομεν.

Τὸ Κύριε, ἐλέησον, μ᾽, εἶτα τὴν εὐχήν,

Κύριε Ἰησοῦ Χριστέ, Υἱὲ τοῦ Θεοῦ, Λόγε ἀθάνατε, ὁ μὴ καταισχύνων τοὺς πεποιθότας ἐπὶ σέ, ὁ φιλανθρωπίας Πατήρ, ὁ πάσης παρακλήσεως καὶ οἰκτιρμῶν Θεός, ὁ προαιώνιος καὶ νῦν ὢν ἐν τῇ ἀγαθότητι καὶ διαμένων εἰς

---

7. Fols. 17–24v.

slow to anger at me. I thank you, O Lord; and if I am not capable of glorifying your forbearance, have mercy on me, O Lord. Subject my soul to your will for the rest of my life and direct my course, since your compassion recognizes my lowliness. Do not entrust your mercy to me, except as your compassion and your love of mankind determine. Only grant me a drop of the mercy of your compassion through the fullness of your pity, and in this way release me from this body through the intercessions and supplications of our all-glorious sovereign lady, mother of God and ever-virgin Mary, your holy ministers and immaculate powers, the holy and glorious prophet, forerunner, and baptist John, the precious and life-giving cross, and all the saints who have pleased you throughout the ages, for blessed are you <forever. Amen.>

Kathisma 2[5]

The Trisagion, the *Our Father,* penitential troparion, mode I:

*Hurry, savior, to open up your fatherly arms to me, for I prodigally spent my life, turning my back on the inexhaustible riches of your acts of mercy. Do not ignore my destitute heart. To you, O Lord, I cry out in remorse, "**I have sinned, Father, against heaven and before you**"* (Lk 15:18, 21).

Glory.

Your tribunal strikes fear, but your judgment is just. My deeds are terrible; but, as the merciful one who goes before me (cf. Ps 58:11), keep me safe and deliver me from punishment. Rescue me, O Master, from the fate of the goats; count me among the sheep on your right and save me, I beg.

Both now.

theotokion, *O undefiled one,* We *who possess your protection, O undefiled one, and are delivered from terror by your supplications, being guarded throughout everything by the cross of your son, we all reverently extoll you in our indebtedness.*

Lord, have mercy forty times, then the

prayer, *Lord Jesus Christ, son of God, immortal Word, you do not put to shame those who have placed their trust in you: the father of benevolence, **God of all comfort and mercies*** (2 Cor 1:3). *In (your) goodness (you were) before*

---

5. Psalms 9–16. The three sessions (staseis) are: first, Pss 9, 10; second, 11–13; third, 14–16.

τοὺς αἰῶνας, ἀποδίωξον ἀπ᾽ ἐμοῦ τοῦ δούλου σου |²⁵ᵛ τοὺς παρενοχλοῦντάς μοι πονηροὺς λογισμούς. Σὺ γὰρ ἐπίστασαι, καρδιογνῶστα, ὁ θεωρῶν τὰ κρυπτὰ τῆς καρδίας μου ὅτι ἀκούσιοί εἰσι· συγχώρησόν μοι, Δέσποτα, καὶ μὴ γενέσθω μοι τοῦτο εἰς σύνταγμα ἁμαρτίας, ἀλλ᾽ ἵλεώς μοι γενοῦ· ἐξαπόστειλον τὴν χάριν σου ἐξ ἁγίου θρόνου δόξης σου ἐπὶ τὴν ψυχήν μου τοῦ τάλανος· ἐπισκίασον ἐπ᾽ ἐμὲ ⁸ τὸν δοῦλόν σου· συνέτισόν με, Δέσποτα, καὶ μαθήσομαι τὰς ἐντολάς σου, καὶ ζήσομαι, ἰατρὲ ψυχῶν καὶ σωμάτων, μόνε ἀναμάρτητε δεδοξασμένε Κύριε, ὅτι εὐλογητὸν καὶ αἰνετὸν καὶ δεδοξασμένον τὸ ὄνομά σου ἐν πᾶσι τοῖς ἁγίοις σου· ἀμήν.

κάθισμα γ᾽⁹

Τὸ τρισάγιον, τὸ Πάτερ ἡμῶν, τροπάριον, ἦχος α᾽,

Τὸν πλοῦτον θεωρήσας τῶν ἀρετῶν τοῦ Ἰώβ, συλῆσαι ἐμηχανᾶτο ὁ τῶν δικαίων ἐχθρός, καὶ διαρρήξας τὸν πύργον τοῦ σώματος· τὸν θησαυρὸν οὐκ ἐσύλησε τοῦ πνεύματος· εὗρε γὰρ ὡπλισμένην τὴν τοῦ δικαίου ψυχήν. Ἐμὲ δὲ καὶ γυμνώσας, ἠχμαλώτευσε· |³⁶ προφθάσας οὖν πρὸ τοῦ τέλους, Χριστὲ ὁ Θεός, ῥῦσαί με τοῦ δολίου, Σωτήρ, καὶ σῶσόν με. Δόξα.

Τὸν ἄσωτον ἐζήλωσα ταῖς πράξεσι· τὴν τούτου δὲ μετάνοιαν οὐ κέκτημαι· ἀλλ᾽ ὡς ὑπάρχων ἀκατάληπτος, Κύριε, ἐπίστρεψόν με τὸν γνώμῃ πλανώμενον καὶ κάθαρόν με τοῦ ῥύπου τῶν πταισμάτων μου διὰ τῆς Θεοτόκου κράζοντα· Ἥμαρτον, Πάτερ, εἰς τὸν οὐρανὸν καὶ ἐνώπιόν σου. Καὶ νῦν.¹⁰

θεοτοκίον, Μητέρα σε Θεοῦ ἐπιστάμεθα πάντες· παρθένον ἀληθῶς καὶ μετὰ τόκον εἰδότες, ἐν πόθῳ καταφεύγομεν πρὸς τὴν σὴν ἀγαθότητα· σὲ γὰρ ἔχομεν ἁμαρτωλοὶ προστασίαν· σὲ κεκτήμεθα ἐν πειρασμοῖς σωτηρίαν τὴν μόνην πανάμωμον.

Τὸ Κύριε, ἐλέησον, μ᾽, εἶτα τὴν εὐχὴν |³⁶ᵛ τοῦ ὁσίου Νίκωνος,

Ὁ Θεὸς ὁ δίκαιος καὶ αἰνετός, ὁ Θεὸς ὁ μέγας καὶ ἰσχυρός, ὁ Θεὸς ὁ προαιώνιος, εἰσάκουσον ἁμαρτωλοῦ ἀνδρὸς τῇ ὥρᾳ ταύτῃ. Ἐπάκουσόν

---

8. ἐμε: C.
9. Fols. 25v–35v.
10. καὶ νῦν indicated in the margin.

the ages, and are now, and forever (shall) endure. Rid me, your servant, of the wicked thoughts that disturb me. For you, who know the heart and observe the secrets of my heart, understand that they are beyond my control. Forgive me, O Master, and let this not be on my record of sin, but be merciful to me. From your holy throne of glory send forth your grace on my, a sufferer's, soul; overshadow[6] *me, your servant.* **Instruct me, O Lord, that I will learn your commandments** *(Ps 118:73), and* **that I will live** *(Ps 118:77), O physician of souls and bodies, O glorified Lord, alone without sin, for blessed and praised and glorified is your name among all your saints. Amen.*

Kathisma 3[7]

The Trisagion, the *Our Father*, troparion, mode I:

The enemy of the righteous saw Job's wealth of virtues, and although he devised a plot to rob him, destroying the defenses of his body, he did not rob the treasure of the spirit, because he discovered that the soul of the righteous man was armed for battle. But stripping me bare, he took me prisoner. Overtaking (me) before the end, O Christ my God, rescue me from the treacherous one, and save me, O savior.

Glory.

I emulated the prodigal in deeds, yet I do not have his repentance. But as the incomprehensible one, O Lord, turn me around, I who in (my) mind am going astray. Cleanse me of the filth of my errors, I who cry out through the Theotokos, **"I have sinned, Father, against heaven and before you"** *(Lk 15:18, 21).*

Both now.

theotokion, *We all understand you to be mother of God. Knowing (you) truly to be a virgin even after childbirth, we ardently take refuge in your goodness, for we sinners have you as patron. O you who alone are without flaw, we have gained you as a deliverance in (our) trials.*

Lord, **have mercy** *forty* times, then the

Prayer of the blessed Nikon, *God, you who are the just and the praiseworthy; God, the great and the powerful; God, the eternal: hear a* **sinful man** *(Lk 5:8)*

---

6. For "overshadow" see Lk 1:34.

7. Psalms 17–23. The three sessions (staseis) are: first, Pss 17, 18; second, 19, 20; third, 21–23.

μου ἐν ἰσχύϊ, μὴ μνημονεύων ἐν ταύτῃ μου τῇ προσευχῇ τῶν ἀεὶ καὶ εἰσαεὶ παρακοῶν τῆς ἐμῆς ἐξουδενώσεως. Ἐπάκουσόν μου ἐν πυρὶ προσευχῆς, ὡς ποτὲ τοῦ σοῦ προφήτου Ἠλιοῦ, καὶ διὰ τῶν αὐτοῦ πρεσβειῶν κατάφλεξόν μου τὰς ἀνομίας καὶ τὰς ἁμαρτίας καθάρισον. Ναί,[11] ὁ Θεὸς τῶν ἁγίων δυνάμεων· ναί, ὁ τῶν ἀσωμάτων ποιητής· ναί, ὁ εἰπών, Αἰτεῖτε καὶ λήψεσθε· μὴ βδελύξῃ με τὸν ἀκάθαρτα χείλη κεκτημένον καὶ ἐν ἁμαρτίαις συνεχόμενον. Ἐπάκουσόν μου, ὁ ἐπαγγειλάμε |[37]-νος ὑπακούειν τῶν ἐν ἀληθείᾳ ἐπικαλουμένων σε· κατεύθυνον τὰ διαβήματά μου καὶ τοὺς πόδας μου εἰς ὁδὸν εἰρήνης. Συμπάθησόν μοι πᾶν πλημμέλημα ἑκούσιόν τε καὶ ἀκούσιον, ὁ εἰπών, Γίνεσθε φρόνιμοι ὡς οἱ ὄφεις καὶ ἀκέραιοι ὡς αἱ περιστεραί. Ἐκέκραξα ἐν ὅλῃ καρδίᾳ μου· ἐπάκουσόν μου, Κύριε, ἡ ἐλπὶς πάντων τῶν περάτων τῆς γῆς καὶ τῶν ἐπὶ ξένης μακράν· ἐπιτίμησον πᾶσι τοῖς ἀκαθάρτοις πνεύμασιν ἀπὸ προσώπου τῆς ἀσθενείας μου. Ἐπιλαβοῦ ὅπλου καὶ θυρεοῦ, καὶ ἀνάστηθι εἰς τὴν βοήθειάν μου· ἔκχεον ῥομφαίαν καὶ σύγκλεισον ἐξεναντίας τῶν καταδιωκόντων με· εἶπον, ὦ Κύριε, Κύριε, τῇ ψυχῇ μου· Σωτηρία σοῦ εἰμι ἐγώ. Ὑπαναχωρη|[37v]-σάτω ἀπὸ τῆς ἐμῆς διανοίας πνεῦμα μίσους, καὶ μνησικακίας καὶ φθόνου, πνεῦμα δειλίας, ἀκηδίας, ὑπερηφανίας καὶ πάσης ἄλλης κακίας· καὶ κατασβεσθήτω μου πᾶσα πύρωσις καὶ κίνησις ἐκ διαβολικῆς ἐνεργείας συνισταμένη. Φωτισθήτω μου ἡ ψυχὴ καὶ τὸ σῶμα καὶ τὸ πνεῦμα τῷ φωτὶ τῆς γνώσεώς σου, ἵνα τῷ πλήθει τῶν οἰκτιρμῶν σου καταντήσας εἰς τὴν ἑνότητα τῆς πίστεως καὶ τῆς ἐπιγνώσεως τῆς ἁγίας Τριάδος, εἰς ἄνδρα τέλειον, εἰς μέτρον ἡλικίας, δοξάσω εἰς αἰῶνα αἰῶνος, σὺν ἀγγέλοις καὶ πᾶσι τοῖς ἁγίοις τοῖς ἀπ᾽ αἰῶνος εὐαρεστήσασι σοὶ τῷ Θεῷ,[12] τὸ πάντιμον καὶ φυλακτήριον καὶ σωτήριον καὶ πολυπόθητον ὄνομα τοῦ Πατρὸς |[38] καὶ τοῦ Υἱοῦ καὶ τοῦ ἁγίου Πνεύματος νῦν καὶ ἀεὶ καὶ εἰς τοὺς αἰῶνας τῶν αἰώνων· ἀμήν.

κάθισμα δ᾽[13]

Τὸ τρισάγιον, τὸ Πάτερ ἡμῶν, τροπάριον, ἦχος β᾽,
Ὡς κύματα θαλάσσης ἐπ᾽ ἐμὲ[14] ἐπανέστησαν αἱ ἀνομίαι μου· ὡς σκάφος

---

11. ναί here and in the following clauses has a double accent.
12. An interrogative mark ends phrase.
13. Fols. 38–46v.   14. ἐμέ: C.

at this hour. Hear me in (your) strength, not, at this my prayer, calling to mind the constant and future disobedience of my disregard. Hear me in the fire of prayer as once you did your prophet Elijah,[8] *and through his pleas consume my transgressions and wash away my sins. Truly, you are the God of the holy powers, truly the maker of the incorporeal beings, truly he who said,* **"Ask and you will receive"** *(Jn 16:24). Do not be disgusted with me, the one who has unclean lips and is afflicted by sin. Hear me, you who promised to answer those who truthfully call upon you;* **guide my steps** *(Ps 118:133) and my* **feet along the path of peace** *(Lk 1:79). Show sympathy to me for all my mistakes, both voluntary and involuntary, you who say,* **"Be wise as serpents and innocent as doves"** *(Mt 10:16).* **I have cried with all my heart** *(Ps 118:145). Hear me, O Lord, you who are* **the hope of all the ends of the earth** *(Ps 64:6) and of them far away in a foreign land. Punish all the unclean spirits (, driving them) away from a person of my weakness.* **Take hold of shield and buckler, and arise for my help. Bring forth a sword, and stop the way against them that persecute me; say, Lord, O Lord, to my soul, I am your salvation** *(Ps 34:2–3). Let the spirit of hatred depart from my mind, as well as those of malice and envy, the spirit of cowardice, of torpor, arrogance, and of every other evil. Let all my burning be quenched, as well as the turmoil from devilish influence. Let my soul and body and spirit be illuminated by the light of your knowledge, so that—through the fullness of your mercy,* **arriving at the unity of the faith and of the knowledge of the** *holy* Trinity,[9] **at mature manhood, at the measure of stature** *(Eph 4:13)—I might glorify for ever, with the angels and all the saints that through the ages have been pleasing to you, God, the all-honorable, protecting, saving, and deeply desired name of the Father and of the Son and of the Holy Spirit, now and always and forever and ever. Amen.*

Kathisma 4[10]

The Trisagion, the *Our Father,* troparion, mode II:

My sins rise up against me like an ocean's waves. Alone, like a boat on the

---

8. See 1 Kgs (= LXX 3 Kgs) 18:22–40.

9. *Novum Testamentum Graece,* eds. Nestle and Aland, http://www.nestle-aland.com/en/home/ [hereafter "NT"]: τοῦ υἱοῦ τοῦ Θεοῦ, the Son of God, for τῆς ἁγίας Τριάδος.

10. Psalms 24–31. The three sessions (staseis), are: first, Pss 24–26; second, 27–29; third, 30, 31.

ἐν πελάγει ἐγὼ μόνος χειμάζομαι ὑπὸ πταισμάτων πολλῶν, ἀλλ' εἰς εὔδιον λιμένα ὁδήγησόν με, Κύριε, τῇ |⁴⁷ μετανοίᾳ καὶ σῶσόν με. Δόξα.

Ἐγὼ ὑπάρχω τὸ δένδρον τὸ ἄκαρπον, Κύριε, κατανύξεως καρπὸν μὴ φέρον τὸ σύνολον· καὶ τὴν ἐκκοπὴν πτοοῦμαι καὶ τὸ πῦρ ἐκεῖνο δειλιῶ τὸ ἀκοίμητον· διό σε ἱκετεύω, πρὸ ἐκείνης τῆς ἀνάγκης ἐπίστρεψον καὶ σῶσόν με. Καὶ νῦν.

θεοτοκίον, Θεοτόκε, μὴ παρίδῃς μὲ δεόμενον ἀντιλήψεως τῆς ἀπὸ σοῦ, ἐπὶ σοὶ γὰρ πέποιθεν ἡ ψυχή μου· ἐλέησόν με.

Τὸ Κύριε, ἐλέησον, μ', καὶ εἶθ' οὕτως τὴν εὐχήν,
Ὁ Θεὸς ὁ παντοκράτωρ, ὁ Πατὴρ τοῦ Χριστοῦ σου τοῦ μονογενοῦς σου Υἱοῦ, δός μοι σῶμα ἄσπιλον, καρδίαν καθαράν, νοῦν γρήγορον, γνῶσιν ἀπλανῆ, Πνεύματος ἁγίου ἐπιφοίτησιν πρὸς κτῆσιν καὶ πληροφορίαν τῆς ἀληθείας, διὰ τοῦ |⁴⁷ᵛ Χριστοῦ σου, μεθ' οὗ σοι δόξα σὺν ἁγίῳ Πνεύματι εἰς τοὺς αἰῶνας· ἀμήν.

κάθισμα ε'¹⁵

Τὸ τρισάγιον, τὸ Πάτηρ ἡμῶν, τροπάριον, ἦχος β',
Ἐλέησόν με, ὁ Θεός, ἐλέησόν με, ἐπὶ δυσὶν ὁ Δαυῒδ ἁμαρτήμασιν ἐθρήνει· ἐπὶ μυρίοις ἐγὼ πλημμελήμασι βοῶ σοι. Ἐκεῖνος τὴν |⁵⁶ᵛ στρωμνὴν τοῖς δάκρυσιν ἔβρεχεν· ἐγὼ δὲ ῥανίδα μίαν οὐ κέκτημαι. Ἀπέγνωσμαι καὶ δέομαι· Ἐλέησόν με ὁ Θεός, κατὰ τὸ μέγα σου ἔλεος. Δόξα.¹⁶

Ἐλέησόν με, εἶπεν ὁ Δαυῒδ, κἀγώ σοι κράζω· Ἥμαρτον, Σωτήρ· τὰς ἐμὰς ἁμαρτίας διὰ τῆς μετανοίας ἐξαλείψας, ἐλέησόν με. Καὶ νῦν.¹⁷
θεοτοκίον, Σὲ μεγαλύνομεν, Θεοτόκε, βοῶντες· Χαῖρε, ἀδύτου φωτὸς νεφέλη, αὐτὸν βαστάσασα κόλποις τῆς δόξης τὸν Κύριον.

---

15. Fols. 47v–56.
17. καὶ νῦν indicated in the margin.

16. δόξα indicated in the margin.

open sea, I am storm-tossed by (my) many faults. But you, O Lord, lead me to a calm harbor through repentance and save me.

Glory.

I am the **tree that is without fruit** (Jude 12), O Lord, (the tree) that altogether fails to bear the fruit of contrition. I am terrified at being cut down and fear that fire (cf. Mt 3:10) which never dies out. Therefore I implore you: before this distress,[11] turn me around and save me.

Both now.

theotokion, O *Theotokos, do not ignore me—I who ask you for support—for my soul has put its trust in you. Have mercy on me.*

Lord, have mercy forty times, then thus: the

prayer, *God the almighty, father of your anointed, your only-begotten son, give me an unstained body, a pure heart (cf. Mt 5:8), an alert mind, unerring knowledge, (and) visitation of the Holy Spirit for the possession and assurance of the truth through your Christ, with whom you (are due) the glory along with the Holy Spirit forever. Amen.*

Kathisma 5[12]

The Trisagion, the *Our Father*, troparion, mode II:

"**Have mercy on me, God** (Ps 50:3), **have mercy on me,**" lamented David after two sins; I cry to you after thousands of offenses. He drenched his bed with tears (cf. Ps 6:7); I have not a single drop. I am in despair, and beseech (you): "**Have mercy on me, God, according to your great mercy**" (Ps 50:3).

Glory.

"**Have mercy on me**" (Ps 50:1) said David, and I, too, call out to you, "I have sinned, O savior; blot out my sins through repentance (cf. Acts 3:19) and have mercy on me."

Both now.

theotokion, *We extol you, O Theotokos, crying out, "Hail, cloud of never-*

---

11. In characterizing the end, Christ says (Lk 21:23) that "great distress (ἀνάγκη μεγάλη) shall be upon the earth."

12. Psalms 32–37. The three sessions (staseis) are: first, Pss 32, 33; second, 34, 35 third, 36, 37.

Τὸ Κύριε, ἐλέησον, μ', εἶτα ἡ εὐχή,[18]

Κύριε Σωτήρ μου, ἱνατί με ἐγκατέλιπες; Οἰκτείρησόν με, ὅτι σὺ εἶ μόνος
φιλάνθρωπος· καὶ σῶσόν με τὸν ἁμαρτωλόν, ὅτι σὺ εἶ μόνος ἀναμάρτητος,
χαρακτὴρ καὶ ἀπαύγασμα τοῦ εὐλογημένου Πατρός. Ἔκσπασόν με τοῦ
βορβόρου τῶν ἀνομιῶν μου, ἵνα μὴ ἐμπαγῶ εἰς αἰῶνα αἰῶνος. Λυτρωτὰ |[57]
καὶ ὑπερασπιστὰ τῶν πεποιθότων ἐπὶ σέ, ῥῦσαί με ἐκ τοῦ στόματος τοῦ ἐχθροῦ
μου· ἰδοὺ γὰρ ὡς λέων ὠρυόμενος τοῦ καταπιεῖν με ἐπέρχεται. Ἄστραψον
οὖν τὴν ἀστραπήν σου καὶ διασκόρπισον αὐτοῦ τὴν κορυφουμένην κατὰ
τοῦ δούλου σου δύναμιν· πτοηθήτω καὶ σκορπισθήτω ἀπὸ τοῦ προσώπου
σου, ἀσθενὴς γὰρ αὐτοῦ ἡ ἰσχύς, μὴ φέρουσα στῆναι ἐνώπιόν σου ἢ πρὸ
προσώπου τῶν ἀγαπώντων σε. Ὁρᾷ γὰρ τὸ σημεῖον τῆς χάριτός σου καὶ
πτοεῖται καὶ κατῃσχυμμένος ἀναχωρεῖ ἀπ' αὐτοῦ. Ἱκετεύω οὖν σε, Σωτὴρ τοῦ
κόσμου, Χριστέ· ἐπίβλεψον ἐπ' ἐμὲ καὶ ῥῦσαί με ἐκ τῶν αὐτοῦ σκανδάλων καὶ
μηχανῶν· συγχώρησόν μοι τὸ πλῆθος τῶν ἀνομιῶν μου. Εἰ γὰρ καὶ ἠθέτησα
|[57v] πάντα τὰ ἀγαθὰ ἃ ἐποίησας μετ' ἐμοῦ, Κύριε, Κύριε, καὶ ἔτι νῦν ἀθετῶ,
ἀλλὰ προσπίπτω δεόμενός σου· Κύριε, σῶσόν με, ὅτι πρὸς σὲ κατέφυγον.

Κάθισμα ϛ΄[19]

Τὸ τρισάγιον, τὸ Πάτερ ἡμῶν, τροπάριον ἦχος γ΄,

Παροικοῦσα ἐν τῇ γῇ, ψυχή μου,[20] μετανόησον· χοῦς ἐν τάφῳ οὐχ ὑμνεῖ,
πταισμάτων οὐ λυτροῦται· βόησον Χριστῷ τῷ Θεῷ. Καρδιογνῶστα ἥμαρτον·
πρὶν καταδικάσεις με, ἐλέησον. Δόξα.[21]

Ἐπὶ τῆς δίκης τῆς φοβερᾶς ἄνευ κατηγόρων ἐλεγχθήσομαι,[22] |[69] ἄνευ
μαρτύρων κατακριθήσομαι· αἱ γὰρ βίβλοι τοῦ συνειδότος ἀναπτύσσονται
καὶ τὰ ἔργα τὰ κεκρυμμένα ἀνακαλύπτονται· πρὶν οὖν ἐν ἐκείνῳ τῷ πανδήμῳ
θεάτρῳ μέλλει ἐρευνᾶσθαι τὰ ἐμοὶ πεπραγμένα, ὁ Θεὸς ἱλάσθητί μοι καὶ
σῶσόν με. Καὶ νῦν.[23]

---

18 εὐχή indicated again in the margin.
19. Fols. 57v–68v.
20. ψυχή μου added in the margin without insertion sign.
21. δόξα indicated in the margin.   22. ἐλλεχθήσομαι: C.
23. καὶ νῦν indicated in the margin.

failing light,[13] *you who carried him in the womb: the Lord of Glory"* (Acts 2:8).

Lord, have mercy forty times, then the

prayer, *O Lord my savior, why have you forsaken me* (Ps 21:1 [Mt 27:46])? *Take pity on me, for you are the only one who loves mankind; and save me, the sinner, for you alone are without sin: the image* (cf. Heb 1:3) *and radiance of the blessed Father. Pull me from the mire of my sins, lest I be stuck for eternity. O redeemer and protector of them who trust you* (2 Kg 22:31), *deliver me from the jaws of my enemy, for behold, like a roaring lion* (cf. Ps 21:14; 1 Pt 5:7) *he comes to devour me. Send lightning* (Ps 143:6) *and scatter his power, which soars against your servant* (cf. Ps 58:12). *Let him be frightened and driven out of your presence, for his strength is weak; it cannot bear to stand before you or in the presence of those who love you. He sees the evidence of your grace and is terrified; shamed, he retreats from it. I thus entreat you, O Christ, savior of the world* (Jn 4:42): *look upon me and deliver me from his snares and contrivances. Pardon my multitude of offenses; and if I disregarded all the good things you did with me, Lord, O Lord, and still disregard (them) now, then I fall down, begging: "Save me, O Lord, because I fled to you for refuge"* (Ps 142:9).

Kathisma 6[14]

The Trisagion, the *Our Father,* troparion, mode III:

Repent, my soul, while you sojourn on earth. Dust in a grave sings no praise; mistakes are not excused. Cry to Christ our God, "You who know men's hearts (know) I have sinned. Show mercy before condemning me."

Glory.

At the fearful trial I will be examined without accusers, will be condemned without witnesses. The books of conscience are spread open and the deeds that have been hidden are revealed. Before the things that I have done come to be examined at that gathering of all humanity, God be merciful to me and save me.

Both now.

---

13. See Mt 17:5 ("bright cloud" of Christ's glory at the transfiguration); for ἀδύτος in this context see G. Lampe, *A Patristic Greek Lexicon* (Oxford: Oxford University Press, 1968), s.v.

14. Psalms 38–45. The three sessions (staseis) are: first, Pss 38, 39; second, 40–42; third, 43–45.

θεοτοκίον, Ἕκαστος ὅπου σῴζεται, ἐκεῖ δικαίως καὶ προστρέχει· καὶ ποία ἄλλη τοιαύτη καταφυγή, ὡς ἡ σή,[24] Θεοτόκε, σκέπουσα τὰς ψυχὰς ἡμῶν;

Τὸ Κύριε, ἐλέησον, μ', εἶτα τὴν εὐχήν,

Κύριε, ὁ τὰ ὕψη τῶν οὐρανῶν σπιθαμῇ καὶ τὴν γῆν δρακὶ μετρήσας, ὁ τὰ ἑξαπτέρυγα χερουβὶμ κτίσας, τὴν ἀκατάπαυστον φωνὴν βοᾶν σοι· Ἅγιος, ἅγιος, ἅγιος. Δὸς δόξαν τῷ ὀνόματί σου τῷ ἁγίῳ· ῥῦσαί με ἐκ τῆς χειρὸς τοῦ διαβόλου. Δέσποτα, λήθην |[69v] ποίησον τῶν πολλῶν μου κακῶν, καὶ τῷ πλήθει τῶν οἰκτιρμῶν σου τὴν καθημερινὴν ἄφεσιν παράσχου μοι· ὅτι εὐλογητὸς εἶ εἰς τοὺς αἰῶνας· ἀμήν.

κάθισμα ζ'[25]

Τὸ τρισάγιον, τὸ Πάτερ ἡμῶν, τροπάριον, ἦχος γ',

Ἕως πότε, ψυχή μου, ἐπιμένεις τοῖς πταίσμασιν; Ἕως τίνος λαμβάνεις μετανοίας ὑπέρθεσιν; Λάβε κατὰ νοῦν τὴν κρίσιν τὴν μέλλουσαν· βόησον Κυρίῳ· Ἥμαρτον, ἀναμάρτητε Κύριε, ἐλέησόν με. |[79v] Δόξα.[26]

Βυθιζόμενος ἐν τῷ πελάγει τῶν δεινῶν, κατερρύπωσα[27] ἐν ἁμαρτίαις τὴν ψυχὴν καὶ μὴ ποιήσας ἀγαθόν, ἐν τῇ γεέννῃ ἀπέρχομαι. Φιλάνθρωπε, Σωτήρ μου, οἰκτείρησον δέομαι· ἔκτεινόν μοι ὡς τῷ Πέτρῳ τὴν ἄχραντον χεῖρά σου, καὶ γὰρ ὡς ὁ τελώνης βοῶ σοι· Ὁ Θεὸς ἱλάσθητί μοι καὶ σῶσόν με. Καὶ νῦν.

θεοτοκίον, Καταφυγὴ καὶ δύναμις ἡμῶν, Θεοτόκε· ἡ κραταιὰ βοήθεια τοῦ κόσμου· τῇ πρεσβείᾳ σου σῷζε τοὺς δούλους σου ἀπὸ πάσης ἀνάγκης, μόνη εὐλογημένη.

Τὸ Κύριε, ἐλέησον, μ', εἶτα τὴν εὐχήν,

Κύριε, ὑπὲρ πάντων καὶ διὰ πάντων καὶ ἐν πᾶσιν ὑμνῶ, εὐλογῶ, προσκυνῶ, δοξολογῶ καὶ εὐχαριστῶ σου τῇ ἀγαθότητι, ὅτι ἐρρύσω τὴν ψυχήν μου |[80] ἐκ θανάτου, τοὺς ὀφθαλμούς μου ἀπὸ δακρύων καὶ τοὺς πόδας μου ἀπὸ ὀλισθήματος. Ἥμαρτον εἰς τὸν οὐρανὸν καὶ ἐνώπιόν σου· ἐλέησόν με, Κύριε, καὶ μὴ συναπολέσῃς με ταῖς ἀνομίαις μου, ἀλλὰ δοκίμασόν με ὁ Θεός, καὶ

---

24. The scribe corrected εἶ σύ in the text to ἡ σή.
25. Fols. 69v–79.
26. δόξα indicated in the margin.
27. κατερύπωσα corrected by the scribe, adding a ρ above the line.

theotokion, *Each man rightfully runs to the place where he is saved. O Theotokos, you who shelter our souls, what other refuge is comparable to yours?*

Lord, have mercy forty times, then the

prayer, *O Lord, **you measured heaven's reach in the span of fingers and the earth in a handful** (Is 40:12); you created the six-winged cherubim to cry to you in a never-ceasing voice, "**Holy, holy, holy**" (Is 6:3). **Give glory to your holy name** (Ps 113:9). Deliver me from the hand of the devil. O Master, forget my many evils and in the fullness of your mercy grant me daily forgiveness, for blessed are you forever. Amen.*

Kathisma 7[15]

The Trisagion, the *Our Father,* troparion, mode III:

My soul, how long will you continue in (your) lapses? How long will you accept a delay in repentance? Take thought of the judgment that awaits; cry to the Lord, "I have sinned, O Lord without sin; have mercy on me."

Glory.

*Sinking into a sea of terrors, I defiled my soul with sin; and since I did nothing good, I am going to hell. O lover of mankind, my savior, take pity, I beg, (and) as (you did) to Peter, stretch out to me your immaculate hand, for like the tax collector I cry out to you, "**'God, be merciful to me'** (Lk 18:13) and save me."*

Both now.

theotokion, *O Theotokos, you who are our refuge and strength, the mighty helper of the world, save your servants from all violence by your intercession, O you alone who are blessed.*

Lord, have mercy forty times, then the

Prayer,[16] *O Lord, because of everything, with everything, and in everything, I praise, worship, glorify, and give thanks for your goodness, **for you delivered my soul from death, my eyes from tears, my feet from slipping** (Ps 55:14). I **have sinned against heaven and before you** (Lk 15:18, 21). Have mercy on me, O Lord, and **do not destroy me together with my sins** (Ode 12:13), but*

---

15. Psalms 46–54. The three sessions (staseis) are: first, Pss 46–48; second, 49, 50; third, 51–54.

16. P adds τοῦ ὁσίου Μακαρίου, of the blessed Makarios.

γνῶθι τὴν καρδίαν μου. Ἔτασόν με καὶ γνῶθι τὰς τρίβους μου καὶ ἴδε εἰ ὁδὸς ἀνομίας ἐν ἐμοί, καὶ ἀπόστρεψόν με ἀπ᾽ αὐτῆς καὶ ὁδήγησόν με ἐν ὁδῷ αἰωνίᾳ, ὁ Θεὸς ὁ εἰπών, Ἐγώ εἰμι ἡ ὁδὸς καὶ ἡ ἀλήθεια καὶ ἡ ζωή, ὅτι εὐλογητὸς εἶ εἰς τοὺς αἰῶνας· ἀμήν.

κάθισμα η᾽[28]

Τὸ τρισάγιον, τὸ Πάτερ ἡμῶν, τροπάριον, ἦχος δ᾽,

Τὴν ταπεινήν μου ψυχὴν ἐπίσκεψαι, Κύριε, τὴν ἐν ἁμαρτίαις τὸν βίον ὅλον δαπανήσασαν· ὃν τρόπον τὴν πόρνην δέξαι κἀμὲ Σωτήρ, καὶ σῶσόν με. Δόξα.[29]

Διαπλέων τὸ πέλαγος τῆς πα|[89]-ρούσης ζωῆς, ἐνθυμοῦμαι τὴν ἄβυσσον τῶν πολλῶν μου κακῶν· καὶ μὴ ἔχων τὸν κυβερνήτην λογισμόν, τὴν τοῦ Πέτρου σοι προσφθέγγομαι φωνήν· Σῶσόν με, Χριστέ, σῶσόν με ὁ Θεὸς ὡς φιλάνθρωπος. Καὶ νῦν.

θεοτοκίον, Τὸν Λόγον τοῦ Πατρός, Χριστὸν τὸν Θεὸν ἡμῶν, ἐκ σοῦ σαρκωθέντα ἔγνωμεν, Θεοτόκε παρθένε, μόνη ἁγνή, μόνη εὐλογημένη· διὸ ἀπαύστως σὲ ἀνυμνοῦντες μεγαλύνομεν.

Τὸ Κύριε, ἐλέησον, μ᾽, εἶτα τὴν εὐχήν,

Κύριε, ὡς ἀγαθὸς καὶ φιλάνθρωπος Θεὸς πολλὰ ἐλέη ἐποίησας μετ᾽ ἐμοῦ, ὧν οὐκ ἤμην ἄξιος, ἃ οὐ προσεδόκων ἰδεῖν. Καὶ τί ἀνταποδώσω τῇ σῇ ἀγαθότητι, Κύριε; Εὐχαριστῶ σου τῷ πολυϋμνήτῳ ὀνόματι, εὐχαριστῶ τῇ ἀνεκδιηγήτῳ σου δυνάμει, εὐχαριστῶ |[89v] τῇ ἀνεικάστῳ σου μακροθυμίᾳ· καὶ ἀπὸ τοῦ νῦν με ἐλέησον καὶ βοήθησον καὶ ἀντιλαβοῦ μου καὶ σκέπασόν με, Δέσποτα. Δέσποτα τῶν ἁπάντων, Κύριε, Κύριε οὐρανοῦ καὶ γῆς καὶ πάσης κτίσεως ποιητά, σὺ γινώσκεις τὴν ἀφροσύνην μου· σὺ γὰρ ἐπίστασαι τὰ ἐν νυκτί, τὰ ἐν ἡμέρᾳ, τὰ ἑκούσια, τὰ ἀκούσια, τὰ ἐν γνώσει, τὰ ἐν ἀγνοίᾳ· ὡς ἀγαθὸς καὶ φιλάνθρωπος Θεός, ἐξάλειψον αὐτὰ τῇ δρόσῳ τοῦ ἐλέους σου καὶ ἐλέησον καὶ βοήθησόν μοι, Υἱὲ τοῦ Θεοῦ. Βοήθησόν μοι,[30] ἀγαθὲ Κύριε,

---

28. Fols. 80–88v.
29. δόξα indicated in the margin.
30. Υἱὲ τοῦ Θεοῦ βοήθησόν μοι added in the margin with an insertion sign.

*test me, God, and know my heart. Examine me and know my ways and see
if there is any way of iniquity in me. Turn me from it, and lead me in an
everlasting way* (Ps 138:23, 24), *O God who said, "I am the way and the truth
and the life"* (Jn 14:6), *for blessed are you forever. Amen.*

Kathisma 8[17]

The Trisagion, the *Our Father,* troparion, mode IV:

*Have regard, O Lord, for my humble soul, which squandered an entire
lifetime in sin. Savior, receive me, too, the way that you received the harlot,
and save me.*

Glory.

Sailing[18] *through the sea of this life, I am pondering the pit of my many
evils. Lacking reason as a guide, I address you in the voice of Peter, "Save me*
(Mt 14:30), *O Christ; save me, O God, as the one who loves mankind."*

Both now.

theotokion, *O virgin mother of God, you who alone are pure, alone are
blessed, we know that the Word of the Father, Christ our God, assumed flesh
from you. Singing unceasingly, we extol you for this.*

Lord, have mercy forty times, then the

prayer, *O Lord, as a good and benevolent God, you performed on my behalf
many merciful acts of which I was unworthy, which I did not expect to see. How,
O Lord, might I repay your goodness? I give thanks for your much-praised name,
I give thanks for your indescribable power, I give thanks for your incomparable
patience. From now on, O Master, have mercy on me, help and assist me, and
shelter me. O Master of all, Lord, Lord of heaven and earth and maker of all
creation, you know my foolishness; you understand my (sins) during the night
(and) the day, the voluntary (and) the involuntary ones, (those committed) with
full knowledge, and the ones (done) in ignorance. As a good and benevolent
God, blot them out with the dew of your mercy* (cf. Hos 6:5), *and have mercy*

---

17. Psalms 55–63. The three sessions (staseis) are: first, Pss 55–57; second, 58–60; third, 61–63.

18. I.e., διαπλῶν; see K. Mitsakis, *The Language of Romanos the Melodist,* Byzantinisches
Archiv 11 (Munich: C. H. Beck, 1967), 17 (32).

σὺ εἶ τὸ φῶς καὶ ἡ ἀλήθεια καὶ ἡ ζωή· σὺ γινώσκεις τὴν ἀφροσύνην μου· σὺ γινώσκεις τὸ ἀσθενὲς τῆς φύσεώς μου, οἷς ἐπίστασαι κρίμασι· Κύριε, σῶσόν με.

κάθισμα θ᾿[31]

Τὸ τρισάγιον, τὸ Πάτερ ἡμῶν, τροπάριον, ἦχος δ᾿,
Ταχὺ συνεισέλθωμεν τῷ νυμφίῳ, |⁹⁹ Χριστῷ, ἵνα πάντες ἀκούσωμεν τῆς μακαρίας φωνῆς Χριστοῦ τοῦ Θεοῦ ἡμῶν· δεῦτε οἱ ἀγαπῶντες τὴν οὐράνιον δόξαν, λάβετε ταύτην ἅμα ταῖς φρονίμοις παρθένοις, φαιδρύνοντες τὰς λαμπάδας ὑμῶν διὰ τῆς πίστεως. Δόξα.

Τῇ ἀχλύϊ τῶν παθῶν καὶ τῶν τοῦ βίου ἡδονῶν ἐπισκότηται ὁ νοῦς τῆς ταλαιπώρου μου ψυχῆς· καὶ λογισμὸς κατανύξεως οὐχ ὑπάρχει μοι, ἀλλ᾿ οἴκτειρον Σωτὴρ τὴν ταπείνωσίν μου· καὶ δός μοι λογισμὸν κατανύξεως, ἵνα κἀγὼ πρὸ τέλους βοήσω τῇ εὐσπλαγχνίᾳ σου, Κύριε· Χριστὲ Σωτήρ μου ἀπεγνωσμένον σῶσόν με τὸν ἀνάξιον. Καὶ νῦν.

θεοτοκίον, Ὅτι πάντων ὑπάρχεις τῶν ποιημάτων ὑπερτέρα, ἀνυ |⁹⁹ᵛ‑μνεῖν σε ἀξίως οὐκ εὐποροῦμεν, Θεοτόκε· δωρεὰν αἰτούμέν σε· ἐλέησον ἡμᾶς.

Τὸ Κύριε, ἐλέησον, μ᾿, εἶτα τὴν εὐχήν,
Ὁ Θεὸς ὁ ἐπὶ τῶν χερουβὶμ καθεζόμενος καὶ ὑπὸ τῶν σεραφὶμ δοξαζόμενος, ἐπίβλεψον ἐφ᾿ ἡμᾶς τοὺς ταπεινοὺς καὶ ἀναξίους δούλους σου, καὶ διέγειρον ἡμῶν τὸν νοῦν πρὸς δοξολογίαν τῆς σῆς ἀγαθότητος. Ἐξάρπασον ἡμᾶς ἀπὸ πάσης ἐπιβουλῆς τοῦ ἐχθροῦ, ἵνα τῷ φωτί σου καταλαμπόμενοι καὶ τῇ βουλῇ σου ὁδηγούμενοι πρὸς πᾶν ἔργον ἀγαθόν, ἀξιωθῶμεν καὶ τῆς ἐπουρανίου σου βασιλείας συναριθμούμενοι πᾶσι τοῖς ἐκλεκτοῖς σου· ὅτι σὺ εἶ ὁ Θεὸς ἡμῶν τοῦ ἐλεῆσαι ἡμᾶς χάριτι καὶ φιλανθρωπίᾳ τοῦ Κυρίου ἡμῶν Ἰησοῦ Χριστοῦ, μεθ᾿ οὗ εὐλογητὸς εἶ σὺν τῷ πα|¹⁰⁰‑ναγίῳ Πνεύματι νῦν καὶ ἀεὶ καὶ εἰς τοὺς αἰῶνας τῶν αἰώνων· ἀμήν.

31. Fols. 90–98v.

and help me, O son of God. O good Lord, you who are the light, the truth, and the life (cf. Jn 8:12, 14:6), *help me. You know my foolishness, you know the weakness of my nature, you understand the sentences for them. Lord save me.*

Kathisma 9[19]

The Trisagion, the *Our Father,* troparion, mode IV:

Let us quickly enter along with the bridegroom Christ, so that we might all hear the blessed voice of Christ our God. You who love heavenly praise (cf. Jn 12:43), *come receive it together with the wise virgins, illuminating your lamps through faith.*

Glory.

The mind of my miserable soul is cast into the darkness of passions and life's pleasures. I have no thought of penitence. Take pity on my degradation, savior, and give me thoughts of penitence so that before the end even I, O Lord, will cry for your mercy, "O Christ, my savior, save me, the unworthy one who has fallen into despair."

Both now.

theotokion, *Because you are the pinnacle of all creation, we are not capable of worthily praising you, O Theotokos. Undeservedly, we ask you for our sake, "Have mercy on us."*

Lord, have mercy forty times, then the

prayer, *O God, you **who take your place on the cherubim** (Ps 79:2)[20] and are glorified by the seraphim, look upon us, your humble and unworthy servants, and direct our minds to the glorification of your goodness. Snatch us from the enemy's every scheme, so that we, whom your light shines upon and who are led by your council toward every good work, might be deemed worthy to be numbered among all the elect of your heavenly kingdom; for you are our God, the one to show us mercy through the grace and benevolence of our Lord Jesus Christ, with whom you are blessed along with the all-holy Spirit, now and always and for ever and ever. Amen.*

---

19. Psalms 64–69. The three sessions (staseis) are: first, Pss 64–66; second, 67; third, 68, 69.

20. And elsewhere: 2 Kgs (LXX = 4 Kgs) 19:15, 2 Chr 13:6, Is 37:16, and Dn 3:55.

κάθισμα ι΄[32]

Τὸ τρισάγιον, τὸ *Πάτερ ἡμῶν*, τροπάριον, ἦχος δ΄,

Βεβαρημένος τῷ ὕπνῳ τῆς ῥᾳθυμίας, φαντασιοῦμαι ἀπάτῃ τῆς ἁμαρτίας· ἀλλὰ παράσχου μοι τὸν ὄρθρον τῆς μετανοίας, καταυγάζων μου τὸ ὄμμα τῆς διανοίας, Χριστὲ ὁ Θεός, ὁ φωτισμὸς τῶν ψυχῶν ἡμῶν. Δόξα.[33]

Ὅλον μου τὸν βίον ἐρρύπωσα[34] *τῇ ἁμαρτίᾳ, ὅλον σου τὸν νόμον ἠθέτησα τῇ ῥᾳθυμίᾳ, διὸ προσπίπτων βοῶ· Καρδίαν καθαρὰν κτίσον ἐν ἐμοὶ ὁ Θεός· καὶ πρὸ τοῦ τέλους ἐπιστρέψας, ἐλέησόν με. Καὶ νῦν.*[35]

θεοτοκίον, *Τεῖχος ἀκαταμάχητον ἡμῶν τῶν χριστιανῶν ὑπάρχεις, Θεοτόκε παρθένε· πρὸς σὲ γὰρ καταφεύγοντες ἄτρωτοι διαμένομεν.* |[110v] *καὶ πάλιν ἁμαρτάνοντες, ἔχομέν σε πρεσβεύουσαν· διὸ εὐχαριστοῦντες βοῶμέν σοι· Χαῖρε κεχαριτωμένη, ὁ Κύριος μετὰ σοῦ.*

Τὸ *Κύριε, ἐλέησον*, μ΄, εἶτα τὴν εὐχὴν τοῦ ὁσίου Αὐξεντίου,

Πτωχὸς καὶ πένης αἰνέσουσί σε, Κύριε· Δόξα τῷ Πατρί, δόξα τῷ Υἱῷ, δόξα τῷ ἁγίῳ Πνεύματι τῷ λαλήσαντι διὰ τῶν προφητῶν· ἡ ἐλπίς μου ὁ Θεός, ἡ καταφυγή μου ὁ Χριστός, ἡ σκέπη μου τὸ Πνεῦμα τὸ ἅγιον. Στρατιαὶ ἐν οὐρανοῖς ὕμνον ἀναπέμπουσι καὶ ἡμεῖς οἱ ἐπὶ γῆς τὴν δοξολογίαν· Δημιουργὲ τῶν ἁπάντων, εἶπας καὶ ἐγενήθημεν, ἐνετείλω καὶ ἐκτίσθημεν· πρόσταγμα ἔθου καὶ οὐ παρελεύσεται· Σῶτερ, εὐχαριστοῦμέν σοι. Κύριε τῶν δυνάμεων, ἔπαθες, ἀνέστης, |[111] *ὤφθης, ἀνελήφθης, ἔρχῃ κρῖναι τὸν κόσμον, Σῶτερ τοῦ κόσμου· σὺ γὰρ εἶ Θεὸς τῶν μετανοούντων· ὁ καθήμενος ἐπὶ τῶν χερουβὶμ καὶ τοὺς οὐρανοὺς ἀνοίξας, οἰκτείρησον καὶ σῶσον ἡμᾶς.* κάθισμα ι΄.

Τοῦ μακαριωτάτου μοναχοῦ κυροῦ Γρηγορίου, στίχοι κατανυκτικοί

Ὢ τῆς δριμείας πικρίας τοῦ θανάτου·
ὢ τῶν σκοτεινῶν δαιμόνων τιμωρίας·

---

32. Fols. 100–110.
33. δόξα indicated in the margin.
34. ἐρύπωσα (as Mateos, *Typicon*, 2.34) corrected by scribe, adding ρ above the line.
35. καὶ νῦν indicated in the margin.

Kathisma 10[21]

The Trisagion, the *Our Father,* troparion, mode IV:

*While weighted down by the sleep of apathy, I am deluded by the **tricks of sin*** (Heb 3:13). *Grant me a dawning of repentance, you who illuminate my mind's eye, O Christ our God, you who are the light of our souls.*

Glory.

*I sullied my whole life with sin. In (my) apathy, I disregarded your entire law. Therefore, I fall down and cry, "**Create in me a clean heart, O God** (Ps 50:12); turn me around before the end, and have mercy on me."*

Both now.

theotokion, *O virgin mother of God, you are an unconquerable fortress for us Christians, for when we flee to you for refuge we survive unharmed. Falling into sin again, we have you who take up our cause. For this we who give you thanks cry, "**Hail, full of grace, the Lord is with you**"* (Lk 1:28).

Lord, have mercy forty times, then the

Prayer of the blessed Auxentios, O Lord, **the poor and needy shall praise you** (Ps 73:21): *Glory to the Father, glory to the Son, glory to the Holy Spirit who spoke through the prophets. My hope is God, my refuge is Christ, my shelter is the Holy Spirit. The holy companies in heaven offer up a hymn and we on earth sing the praise: maker of all things, you spoke and we were made* (cf. Pss 32:9, 148:5), *you commanded and we were created* (cf. ibid.), **you made an ordinance and it shall not pass away** (Ps 148:6). *O savior, we thank you. Lord of Hosts, you suffered, you arose, you appeared again* (cf. Lk 24:34), *you were taken up (to heaven), you are returning to judge the world.*[22] *Savior of the world, you are the God of those who repent.* **You who sit on the cherubim** (for example, Ps 79:2), *open the heavens, take pity on us, and save us.* Kathisma 10.[23]

Penitential verses of the most blessed monk Kyr Gregory
What stinging bitterness of death!
What torture by dark demons!

---

21. Psalms 70–76. The three sessions (staseis) are: first, Pss 70, 71; second, 72, 73; third, 74–76.
22. The sentence paraphrases the Creed (*HR* 30–31).
23. The reiteration of the kathisma number acts to separate the troparia and prayer from the additions intervening before the start of the eleventh kathisma.

ὦ οἷον ὄψει, φεῦ, ψυχὴ φόβον, κλόνον
ὥρᾳ θανάτου, πικρίας πεπλησμένου·
οἱ δαίμονες πάρεισιν ἠγριωμένοι,
ἐμὰς φέροντες μυρίας ἀσωτίας·
διατρέχουσιν ἀγγέλων φρυκτωρίαι,
ζητοῦσιν ἰδεῖν πρᾶξιν ἠγλαϊσμένην,
ἀλλ᾽ οὐδὲν εὑρίσκουσιν ἀγαθουργίας·
κατηγοροῦσι δαιμόνων ὁμηγύρεις,
ἕλκουσιν εἰς γέενναν, εἰς ᾅδου χάος· |¹¹¹ᵛ
δίκης τρόπῳ σύρουσιν εἰς τιμωρίας,
τύπτουσι, συντρίβουσιν, αἰκίζουσί σε.
Λοιπὸν στέναξον· δάκρυσον πρὸ τοῦ τέλους·
ματαιότητος κατάγνωθι τοῦ βίου·
μνήσθητι θρήνου τῶν κατακεκριμμένων·
μνήσθητι κλαυθμοῦ τῶν τεταρταρωμένων,
ᾅδου σιωπῆς, πικρίας, ἀηδίας,
πολλῆς ὀδύνης, δακρύων ἀϊδίων·
δεσμῶν ἀλύτων, μαστίγων αἰωνίων·
κρίσιν λογίζου τὴν φρίκης πεπλησμένην,
κλαυθμούς, ὀδυρμοὺς τῶν παρηνομηκότων,
βρυγμούς, στεναγμοὺς τῶν κατεσπιλωμένων,
ὅπως δυνηθῇς ἐκφυγεῖν σαρκὸς πάθη
καὶ παραδείσου τῆς κατοικίας τύχῃς.
Καταξίωσον, ὦ Τριὰς παναγία,
φρίττειν ἀεί με τῆς γεέννης τὴν φλόγα
καὶ τὴν θάλασσαν τοῦ πυρὸς τοῦ παμφάγου,
καὶ τὴν ἄβυσσον, τάρταρον καὶ τὸ σκότος,
ᾅδου τὸ χάος, τὸν θάνατον, τὴν κρίσιν,
πικροὺς λογιστὰς καρδίας ἐνθυμίων,
πράξεις φέροντας εἰς μέσον, καὶ τοὺς λόγους. |¹¹²
Ἐντεῦθεν ὡς ἔλθοιμι θεῖον εἰς φόβον,
καὶ τῆς χαρᾶς τύχοιμι τῆς αἰωνίου.

Oh alas, my soul, you will see such terror (and) tumult
At the hour of death filled with bitterness.
The savage demons approach
Bearing our thousands of profligate acts.
The signal torches of angels are streaming through (my life)
As they search to see action that might give delight,
But they will not discover a single good deed.
Gangs of demons are bringing up charges,
Pulling you down to Gehenna, down into the chasm of hell;
As at a trial they will drag you to torture,
Where they will beat, crush, torment you.
From now on, moan. Weep before the end comes.
Despise life's folly.
Remember the lament of those who have been condemned.
Remember the wailing of those cast into Tartarus,
The silence of Hades, the bitterness, the repugnance,
The great pain, the everlasting tears,
The unbreakable chains, the eternal whippings.
Consider the judgment filled with horror,
The wailing, the lamenting of those who have transgressed,
The gnashing of teeth, the moaning of the utterly filthy,
So that you might gather strength to escape the passions of the flesh
And gain a dwelling place in paradise.
O all-holy Trinity, make me worthy
Always to dread the flame of Gehenna
And the sea of all-consuming fire,
The abyss, Tartarus and the gloom,
Hades's vast emptiness, death, judgment,
The stern auditors of the thoughts of the heart,
Bringing actions into the open and words.
Oh that I might return henceforth to the fear of God
And receive (his) eternal joy!

Ἀκολουθία ὑπὲρ τῶν συμβαινόντων δι' ὅλης
τῆς ἡμέρας σφαλμάτων

Τὸ τρισάγιον· τὸ *Πάτερ ἡμῶν*· τὸ *Κύριε, ἐλέησον, γ'*· τὸ *Δεῦτε
προσκυνήσωμεν*· <ὁ> Ν',[36] *Ἐλέησόν με ὁ Θεὸς κατὰ τὸ μέγα ἔλεός σου,
καὶ κατὰ τὸ πλῆθος τῶν οἰκτιρμῶν σου ἐξάλειψον τὸ ἀνόμημά μου*· καὶ
μετὰ τὸ τελειῶσαι τὸν ψαλμὸν πάλιν λέγε τὸ τρισάγιον, τὸ *Πάτερ ἡμῶν*,
μεθὸ τὰ τροπάρια ταῦτα, *Ἐλέησον ἡμᾶς, Κύριε, ἐλέησον ἡμᾶς, πάσης γὰρ
ἀπολογίας. Δόξα.*[37] *Κύριε ἐλέησον ἡμᾶς· ἐπὶ σοὶ γὰρ πεποίθαμεν. Καὶ νῦν.*[38] *Τῆς
εὐσπλαγχνίας τὴν πύλην ἄνοιξον.* Τὸ *Κύριε, ἐλέησον, κ'*· εἶτα τὴν εὐχὴν ταύτην,

*Κύριε ὁ Θεὸς ἡμῶν, ὁ τὴν διὰ μετανοίας ἄφεσιν τοῖς ἀνθρώποις δωρησάμενος,
καὶ τύπον ἡμῖν ἐπιγνώσεως ἁμαρτημάτων καὶ ἐξομολογήσεως τὴν τοῦ Δαυῒδ
μετάνοιαν πρὸς συγ|*[112v]*-χώρησιν ὑποδείξας· αὐτός, Δέσποτα, πολλοῖς ἡμᾶς καὶ
μεγάλοις περιπεπτωκότας πλημμελήμασιν, ἐλέησον κατὰ τὸ μέγα σου ἔλεος,
καὶ κατὰ τὸ πλῆθος τῶν οἰκτιρμῶν σου ἐξάλειψον τὰ ἀνομήματα ἡμῶν, ὅτι σοὶ
ἡμάρτομεν. Κύριε, τῷ τὰ ἄδηλα καὶ τὰ κρύφια τῆς καρδίας τῶν ἀνθρώπων
γινώσκοντι καὶ μόνῳ ἔχοντι ἐξουσίαν ἀφιέναι ἁμαρτίας. Καρδίαν δὲ καθαρὰν
κτίσας ἐν ἡμῖν καὶ πνεύματι ἡγεμονικῷ στηρίξας ἡμᾶς, καὶ τὴν ἀγαλλίασιν
τοῦ σωτηρίου σου γνωρίσας ἡμῖν, μὴ ἀπορρίψῃς ἡμᾶς ἀπὸ τοῦ προσώπου σου·
ἀλλ' εὐδόκησον, ὡς ἀγαθὸς καὶ φιλάνθρωπος Θεός, μέχρι τῆς ἐσχάτης ἡμῶν
ἀναπνοῆς προσφέρειν σοι θυσίαν δικαιοσύνης καὶ ἀναφορὰν καὶ δέησιν ἐν τοῖς
ἁγίοις σου καὶ οὐρανίοις θυσιαστηρίοις, ἐλέει καὶ φιλανθρωπίᾳ τοῦ μονογενοῦς
σου Υἱοῦ, μεθ' οὗ εὐλογητὸς εἶ σὺν τῷ παναγίῳ καὶ ἀγαθῷ καὶ ζωοποιῷ σου
Πνεύματι νῦν καὶ ἀεὶ καὶ εἰς τοὺς αἰῶνας τῶν αἰώνων· ἀμήν.*

---

36. N' written in the margin.   37. δόξα indicated in the margin.
38. καὶ νῦν indicated in the margin.

(I.2)
Office for trespasses that together we have committed throughout the entire day[24]

The Trisagion, the

Our Father (HR 8),

Lord, have mercy three times,

Come, let us worship and fall down.

Psalm 50: *Have mercy upon me, O God, according to your great mercy, and according to the fullness of your mercies blot out my transgressions.*

And again, after finishing the psalm, say the Trisagion, the

Our Father, after which these troparia,

Have mercy on us, O Lord, have mercy on us (Ps 122:3, Mt 20:30). *We who are sinners lacking any defense* (82).

Glory.

O Lord, have mercy on us, for we have put our trust in you (82).

Both now.

Open to us the gate of compassion (82).

Lord, have mercy twenty times, then this

prayer, *O Lord our God, you have given mankind the gift of remission from sin through repentance, and for our forgiveness have shown us David's repentance as a model of the recognition of sins and confession. Master,* **have mercy on us, who have committed many grievous sins.** *According to your great mercy, and* **according to the fullness of your compassion blot out our transgressions** (Ps 50:3), *for* **we have sinned against you** (Ps 50:6), *O Lord, you who know* **the secrets and the things hidden** (Ps 50:8) *in the hearts of men, and who alone hold the power to forgive sin* (cf. Mt 9:6). **Create in us a clean heart** (Ps 50:12), *and* **establish with us your guiding spirit** (Ps 50:14). *You who made known to us* **the joy of your salvation** (Ps 50:14), **do not cast us out of your presence** (Ps 50:13), *but as a good and benevolent God* **consent** *to our offering you, until our last breath, a* **sacrifice of righteousness and offering** (Ps 50:21) *and supplication at your holy and heavenly altars* (cf. Ps 50:21), *through the mercy and benevolence of your only-begotten Son, with whom you are blessed along with the all-holy, good, and life-giving Spirit, now and always and for ever and ever. Amen.*

---

24. In P the office of the twelfth minor hour of the day concludes with the direction: ποιεῖ δὲ μετὰ τὰς ιβ' ὥρας τρισάγιον ὑπὲρ τῶν συμβαινόντων σφαλμάτων δι' ὅλης τῆς ἡμέρας. For the office see Parenti § II.5.

κάθισμα ια᾽[39]

Τὸ τρισάγιον, τὸ Πάτερ ἡμῶν, τροπάριον, ἦχος πλάγιος α᾽,
Κριτοῦ καθεζομένου καὶ ἀγγέλων ἑστώτων, σάλπιγγος ἠχούσης καὶ φλογὸς καιομένης, τί ποιήσεις ψυχή μου, ἀπαγομένη εἰς κρίσιν; Τότε γὰρ τὰ δεινά σου παρίστανται, τὰ κρυπτά σου ἐλέγχονται ἐγκλήματα· διὸ |[126] πρὸ τέλους βόησον τῷ κριτῇ· ὁ Θεὸς ἱλάσθητί μοι καὶ σῶσόν με. Δόξα.[40]

Ψυχὴ τὰ ὧδε[41] *πρόσκαιρα, τὰ δὲ ἐκεῖθεν αἰώνια· ὁρῶ τὸ δικαστήριον καὶ ἐπὶ θρόνου τὸν κριτὴν καὶ τρέμω τὴν ἀπόφασιν· λοιπὸν σπουδῇ ἐπίστρεψον· ἡ κρίσις ἀσυγχώρητος. Καὶ νῦν.*

θεοτοκίον, *Τὴν ταχεῖάν σου σκέπην καὶ τὴν βοήθειαν καὶ τὸ ἔλεος δεῖξον ἐπὶ τοὺς δούλους σου· καὶ τὰ κύματα, ἁγνή, καταπράϋνον τῶν ματαίων λογισμῶν, καὶ τὴν νοσοῦσάν μου ψυχὴν ἀνάστησον, Θεοτόκε· οἶδα γὰρ οἶδα, πάρθενε, ὅτι ἰσχύεις ὅσα καὶ βούλει.*

Τὸ *Κύριε, ἐλέησον,* μ᾽, εἶτα τὴν εὐχήν,
Κύριε, ὁ Θεὸς ἡμῶν ὁ θέλων πάντας ἀνθρώπους σωθῆναι καὶ εἰς ἐπίγνωσιν ἀληθείας ἐλθεῖν, ὁ μὴ βουλόμενος τὸν θάνατον τοῦ ἁμαρ|[126v]-τωλοῦ, ὡς τὸ ἐπιστρέψαι καὶ ζῆν αὐτόν, ἐλέησόν με τὸν ἁμαρτωλὸν καὶ δώρησαί μοι λογισμὸν πάντοτε ταῖς ἰδίαις ἁμαρτίαις προσέχειν μετὰ αἰσθήσεως καὶ πόνου καρδίας, ἵνα, ἐν αὐταῖς ἀσχολούμενος καὶ τὰς ἀλλοτρίας μὴ γινώσκων, κτήσωμαι τὸν φόβον σου τὸν ἅγιον, δι᾽ οὗ δυνήσομαι ἀπὸ παντὸς κακοῦ ἐκλῖναι καὶ λατρεύειν σοι ἐν καρδίᾳ συντετριμμένῃ καὶ τεταπεινωμένῃ, ὅτι σοὶ πρέπει πᾶσα δόξα, τιμὴ καὶ προσκύνησις νῦν καὶ ἀεὶ καὶ εἰς τοὺς αἰῶνας τῶν.

---

39. Fols. 113–25v.
41. ὧδε: C.

40. δόξα indicated in the margin.

Kathismata 11–20)
Kathisma 11[25]

The Trisagion, the *Our Father*, troparion, plagal mode I:

Once the judge is enthroned and the angels are at attention, a trumpet sounds and flames burn; what, my soul, will you do when you are led away to judgment? At that instant, your terrors will be upon you, the secret charges against you revealed. Therefore, call to the judge before the end, "O God, be merciful to me and save me."

Glory.

Soul, the things here are transitory, those on the other side eternal. I see the courtroom and the judge on the throne, and I quake at the verdict. In the time remaining, reform in earnest; the sentence is not (yet) final.

Both now.

theotokion, *Show your swift shelter, help and mercy to your servants. O you who are pure, calm the waves of profane thoughts; lift up my soul, which has fallen ill, O Theotokos. I know, O virgin, I know that you are capable of whatever you choose.*

Lord, have mercy forty times, then the

prayer, *O Lord, our God* **who desires all men to be saved and to come to the knowledge of the truth** *(1 Tm 2:4), who wants not the sinner's death, so that he (has time to) reform and live, have mercy on me, the sinner, and always give me the understanding to attend to my own sins with discernment and a suffering heart. Thus absorbed in them, and not knowing any other's, I might gain the fear of you that is holy, through which I will be able to turn from all evil and worship you with a heart that is contrite and humbled: for you are due all glory, honor and worship, now and always and for ever <and ever. Amen>.*

---

25. Psalms 77–84. The three sessions (staseis) are: first, Ps 77; second, 78–80; third, 81–84.

κάθισμα ιβ[42]

Τὸ τρισάγιον, τὸ *Πάτερ ἡμῶν*, τροπάριον, ἦχος πλάγιος α·,

Ἐν κλίνῃ κατακείμενος ἁμαρτημάτων πολλῶν, συλοῦμαι τὴν ἐλπίδα τῆς σωτηρίας μου· ὁ γὰρ ὕπνος τῆς ἐμῆς ῥαθυμίας προξενεῖ μου τῇ ψυχῇ τιμωρίαν, ἀλλὰ σύ, ὁ θεὸς ὁ τεχθεὶς ἐκ παρθένου, διέγειρόν με πρὸς τὴν σὴν ὑμνῳδίαν ἵνα δοξάζω σε. Δόξα.[43]

Πάντες ἀγρυπνήσωμεν καὶ Χριστῷ ὑπαντήσωμεν μετὰ πλήθους ἐλαίου[44] *καὶ λαμπάδων φαεινῶν, ὅπως τοῦ νυμφῶνος ἔνδον γενέσθαι ἀξιωθῶμεν· ὁ γὰρ τῆς θύρας ἔξω φθανόμενος ἄπρα*|[136]-*κτα τῷ Θεῷ κέκραγεν· Ἐλέησόν με. Καὶ νῦν.*[45]

θεοτοκίον, Μήτηρ Θεοῦ παναγία, τὸ τεῖχος τῶν χριστιανῶν, ῥῦσαι λαόν σου συνήθως κραυγάζοντά σοι ἐκτενῶς· Ἀντιτάχθητι αἰσχροῖς καὶ ἀλαζόσι λογισμοῖς, ἵνα βοῶμέν σοι· Χαῖρε ἀειπάρθενε.

Τὸ *Κύριε, ἐλέησον*, μ·, εἶτα τὴν εὐχήν,

Κύριε οἰκτίρμον καὶ ἐλεῆμον, μακρόθυμε καὶ πολυέλεε, ἐνώτισαι τὴν προσευχήν μου καὶ πρόσχες τῇ φωνῇ τῆς δεήσεώς μου. Ποίησον μετ᾽ ἐμοῦ σημεῖον εἰς ἀγαθόν, ὁδήγησόν με ἐν τῇ ὁδῷ σου τοῦ πορεύεσθαι ἐν τῇ ἀληθείᾳ σου· εὔφρανον τὴν καρδίαν μου εἰς τὸ φοβεῖσθαι τὸ ὄνομά σου τὸ ἅγιον, διότι μέγας εἶ καὶ ποιῶν θαυμάσια. Σὺ εἶ ὁ Θεὸς μόνος καὶ οὐκ ἔστιν ὅμοιός σοι ἐν θεοῖς, Κύριε, δυνατὸς ἐν ἐλέει |[136v] *καὶ ἀγαθὸς ἐν ἰσχύϊ εἰς τὸ βοηθεῖν καὶ παρακαλεῖν καὶ σῴζειν πάντας τοὺς ἐλπίζοντας εἰς τὸ ὄνομά σου τὸ ἅγιον, τοῦ Πατρὸς καὶ τοῦ Υἱοῦ καὶ τοῦ ἁγίου Πνεύματος νῦν καὶ ἀεὶ καὶ εἰς τοὺς αἰῶνας τῶν αἰώνων.*

κάθισμα ιγ᾽[46]

Τὸ τρισάγιον, τὸ *Πάτερ ἡμῶν*, τροπάριον, ἦχος πλάγιος α·,

Ἐξ ἀμέτρων πταισμάτων ἐγὼ ὁ τάλας τὸν νοῦν ἐν τῷ πελάγει τοῦ βίου κλυδωνιζόμενος, ὡς κυβερνήτην τοῦ παντὸς καθικετεύων βοῶ τὴν σὴν

---

42. Fols. 126v–135v.
44. ἐλέους: C.
46. Fols. 136v–144v.

43. δόξα indicated in the margin.
45. καὶ νῦν indicated in the margin.

Kathisma 12[26]

The Trisagion, the *Our Father*, troparion, plagal mode I:

While lying in a bed of many sins, I am robbed of my hope for salvation. The sleep of my apathy will secure punishment for my soul, but you, God born of a virgin, awaken me to singing hymns that I might glorify you.
Glory.

Let us all keep vigil and go to meet Christ with a supply of oil and lamps burning bright, so that we might be considered worthy to be within the bridal chamber. The one who arrives outside the door cries out to God to no avail, "Have mercy on me."
Both now.

theotokion, *All-holy Mother of God, fortress of Christians, rescue your people who habitually call to you with fervor; range yourself against shameful and false thoughts, so that we might call to you, "Hail, you who are forever virgin."*

Lord, have mercy forty times, then the

prayer, **O Lord, the compassionate and merciful, the patient and rich in mercy** (Ps 85:15), **give ear to my prayer and attend to the voice of my supplication** (Ps 85:6). **Establish with me a sign for good** (Ps 85:17), **guide me in your way to walk in your truth; gladden my heart to fear your holy name** (Ps 85:11), **since you are great and work wonders** (Ps 85:10). **You are the only God** (Ps 85:10), and **there is none equal to you among gods** (Ps 85:8), O Lord strong in mercy and good in strength for helping, encouraging and saving all who put hope in your holy name (cf. Ps 16:7): (that) of the Father and the Son and the Holy Spirit, now and always and for ever and ever. <Amen.>

Kathisma 13[27]

The Trisagion, the *Our Father*, troparion, plagal mode I:

Because of my innumerable mistakes, I, the wretched, am buffeted in my mind on the waves of life's sea. Earnestly entreating you as every man's helms-

---

26. Psalms 85–90. The three sessions (staseis) are: first, Pss 85–87; second, 88; third, 89, 90.
27. Psalms 91–100. The three sessions (staseis) are: first, Pss 91–93; second, 94–96; third, 97–100.

βοήθειαν, Χριστέ· μὴ ἀντανέλῃς ἀπ᾽ ἐμοῦ, ἀλλ᾽ οἴκτειρόν με καὶ σῶσον καὶ ῥῦ|¹⁴⁵-σαι ἐκ τῶν κινδύνων τῆς ἁμαρτίας τὴν ταπεινήν μου ψυχήν. Δόξα.⁴⁷

Θρήνησον, ψυχή μου, τὴν ἑαυτῆς ῥᾳθυμίαν· θέλησον λοιπὸν πρὸ τελευτῆς ἐπιστρέψαι· θορύβων ἀπόστηθι βιωτικῶν· Θεῷ προσκολλήθητι τῷ ἀγαθῷ, καὶ σώσει σε ὡς φιλάνθρωπος. Καὶ νῦν.

θεοτοκίον, Ὁ ἐκ παρθένου ἀνατείλας τῷ κόσμῳ, Χριστὲ ὁ Θεός, υἱοὺς φωτὸς δι᾽ αὐτῆς ἀναδείξας, ἐλέησον ἡμᾶς.

Τὸ Κύριε, ἐλέησον, μʹ, εἶτα τὴν εὐχήν,

Κύριε Ἰησοῦ Χριστέ, Υἱὲ τοῦ Θεοῦ τοῦ ζῶντος, ἄφελε τὴν ὑψηλοφροσύνην καὶ τὴν κενοδοξίαν καὶ τὴν ὑπερηφανίαν καὶ τὴν βλασφημίαν ἀπ᾽ ἐμοῦ τοῦ τάλανος. Ἐξάλειψον τὸ χειρόγραφον τῶν πολλῶν καὶ αἰσχρῶν μου πράξεων, καὶ τοιοῦτόν με ποίησον διανοεῖσθαι καὶ ἔχειν ἑαυτόν, οἷος τῇ ἀληθείᾳ εἰμί. |¹⁴⁵ᵛ Δέσποτα Χριστὲ ὁ Θεὸς ἡμῶν, ὁ μόνος ἀκριβῶς τῆς ἀθλίας μου ψυχῆς τὴν νόσον καὶ τὴν ταύτης θεραπείαν ἐπιστάμενος, ἰάτρευσον αὐτὴν ἕνεκεν τοῦ πλήθους τοῦ ἐλέους σου καὶ τῶν οἰκτιρμῶν σου, ὅσον γὰρ ἐκ τῶν ἔργων μου οὐκ ἔστι μάλαγμα ἐπιθεῖναι, οὔτε ἔλαιον οὔτε καταδέσμους· ἀλλὰ σὺ ὁ μὴ ἐλθὼν καλέσαι δικαίους ἀλλὰ ἁμαρτωλοὺς εἰς μετάνοιαν, ἐλέησον, οἴκτειρον, συμπάθησον καὶ ὁδήγησον εἰς τὴν εὐθεῖαν ὁδόν σου, ἵνα πορευόμενος ἐν τῇ ἀληθείᾳ σου, δυνήσομαι ἐκφυγεῖν τὰ βέλη τοῦ πονηροῦ καὶ οὕτως σταθῆναι ἀκατακρίτως ἐνώπιον τοῦ φοβεροῦ βήματός σου, δοξάζων καὶ ἀνυμνῶν σου τὸ πανάγιον ὄνομα εἰς τοὺς αἰῶνας· ἀμήν.

κάθισμα ιδʹ⁴⁸

Τὸ τρισάγιον, τὸ Πάτερ ἡμῶν, τροπάριον, ἦχος πλάγιος βʹ,

Ἐννοῶ τὴν ἡμέραν τὴν φοβερὰν καὶ θρηνῶ μου τὰς πράξεις τὰς πονηράς. Πῶς ἀπολογήσομαι τῷ ἀθανάτῳ βασιλεῖ; Ποίᾳ δὲ παρρησίᾳ ἀτενίσω τῷ κριτῇ, ὁ ἄσωτος ἐγώ; Εὔσπλαγχνε Πάτερ, Υἱὲ μονογενές, τὸ Πνεῦμα τὸ ἅγιον ἐλέησόν με. Δόξα.

---

47. δόξα indicated in the margin.
48. Fols. 146–54ᵛ.

man, I call for your help; O Christ, do not withdraw it from me, but take pity on me and save and rescue my wretched soul from the dangers of sin.

Glory.

Lament, my soul, your laziness. Be willing to reform in what time remains before the end. Stay away from worldly clamor. Cling to God who is good, and as (the one who is) benevolent he will save you.

Both now.

theotokion, O Christ, you who are God, who came forth into the world from a virgin, revealing through her the **sons of light** (Jn 12:36), have mercy on us.

Lord, have mercy forty times, then the

prayer, Lord Jesus Christ, **son of the living God** (Mt 16:16), take from me, a wretch, haughtiness, vanity, arrogance, and slanderous speech. Blot out the record of my many shameful deeds; and make such a one as me to be mindful and keep myself as I truly am. O Master, Christ, our God (and) the only one who understands perfectly my miserable soul's illness as well as its treatment, cure it **through the fullness of your mercy** (Ps 68:14) and **your compassion** (Ps 68:17), since from my works there is no salve to apply, nor oil or bandages. You who came **to call to repentance not the just but the sinners** (Lk 5:32), have mercy, take pity, sympathize, and lead me along your straight path (cf. Ps 106:7), so that walking in your truth (cf. Ps 85:11) I will have the strength to flee **the arrows of the evil one** (Eph 6:16) and thus to stand uncondemned before your fearful tribunal, glorifying and praising your all-holy name forever. Amen.

Kathisma 14[28]

The Trisagion, the *Our Father,* troparion, plagal mode II:

I am reflecting on the fearful day and bewailing my wicked deeds. How will I defend myself before the immortal King? With what confidence will I—I who am profligate—gaze upon the judge? O compassionate Father, only-begotten Son, Holy Spirit: have mercy on me.

Glory.

---

28. Psalms 101–4. The three sessions (staseis) are: first, Pss 101, 102; second, 103; third, 104.

Εἰς τὴν κοιλάδα τοῦ κλαυθμῶνος, εἰς τὸν τόπον ὅν διέθου, ὅταν καθίσῃς, ἐλεῆμον, ποιῆσαι δικαίαν κρίσιν, μὴ δημοσιεύσῃς μου τὰ κεκρυμμένα· μὴ δὲ καταισχύνῃς με ἐνώπιον τῶν ἀγγέλων, ἀλλὰ φεῖσαί μου ὁ Θεός, καὶ ἐλέησόν με. Καὶ νῦν.

θεοτοκίον, Πολλὰ τὰ πλήθη τῶν ἐμῶν, Θεοτόκε, πταισμάτων· πρὸς σὲ κατέφυγ[ον], ἀγνή, σωτηρίας [δεόμ]ενος. Ἐ|¹⁵⁵–πίσκεψαι τὴν ἀσθενοῦσάν μου ψυχὴν καὶ πρέσβευε τῷ υἱῷ σου καὶ Θεῷ δοθῆναί μοι τὴν ἄφεσιν ὧν ἔπραξα δεινῶν, μόνη εὐλογημένη.

Τὸ Κύριε, ἐλέησον, μ΄, εἶτα τὴν εὐχήν,
Δεόμεθά σου, Κύριε ὁ Θεὸς ἡμῶν, μακροθύμησον ἐφ᾽ ἡμᾶς τοὺς ἁμαρτωλοὺς καὶ φεῖσαι τῶν ἔργων τῶν χειρῶν σου· ὁ εἰδὼς ἡμῶν τὴν ἀσθένειαν, καὶ λύτρωσαι ἡμᾶς ἀπὸ παντὸς πειρασμοῦ καὶ πάντων τῶν ἐνεστώτων καὶ ἐπερχομένων κακῶν, καὶ τοῦ ἄρχοντος τῆς ἐξουσίας τοῦ σκότους· καὶ μετάστησον εἰς τὴν βασιλείαν τοῦ μονογενοῦς σου Υἱοῦ καὶ Θεοῦ ἡμῶν, ὅτι σοῦ ἐστιν ἡ δόξα εἰς τοὺς αἰῶνας· ἀμήν.

κάθισμα ιε΄⁴⁹

Τὸ τρισάγιον, τὸ Πάτερ ἡμῶν, τροπάριον, ἦχος πλάγιος β΄,
Τῶν φρονίμων παρθένων τὸ ἄγρυπνον δώρησαί μοι, Κύριε, καὶ τῆς ψυχῆς μου τὴν λαμπάδα φαίδρυνον ἐλαίῳ τῶν σῶν οἰκτιρμῶν, ἵνα τῶν ἀγγέλων ψάλλω σοι τὸν ὕμνον· Ἀλληλούϊα. Δόξα.⁵⁰

Ψυχή μου, ἱνατί ῥαθυμοῦσα τῇ ἁμαρτίᾳ δουλεύεις; Καὶ ἱνατί ἀσθενοῦσα τῷ ἰατρῷ οὐ προσέρχῃ; Ἀνάνηψον λοιπὸν ἐκ τῶν κακῶν ὧν ἔπραξας, καὶ βόησον πρὸς τὸν σωτῆρα λέγουσα· Ἐλπὶς ἀπελπισμένων, ζωὴ ἀπεγνωσμένων, ἰατρὲ καὶ σωτήρ μου, Κύριε, σῶσόν με. Καὶ νῦν.

θεοτοκίον, Τῆς εὐσπλαγχνίας τὴν πύλην ἄνοιξον ἡμῖν, εὐλογημένη Θεοτόκε· ἐλπίζοντες εἰς σὲ μὴ ἀστοχήσωμεν· ῥυσθείημεν διὰ σοῦ τῶν |¹⁶⁵ περιστάσεων· σὺ γὰρ εἶ σωτηρία τοῦ γένους τῶν ἀνθρώπων.

Τὸ Κύριε, ἐλέησον, μ΄, εἶτα τὴν εὐχὴν τῆς ὑπεραγίας Θεοτόκου,

---

49. Fols. 155–64v.
50. δόξα indicated in the margin.

*When you, the merciful, take the throne to pass righteous judgment **in the valley of weeping, at the place which you appointed*** (Ps 83:7), *do not reveal openly the things I have kept hidden, nor disgrace me in **the presence of the angels*** (Lk 12:9). *Spare me instead, God, and have mercy on me.*

Both now.

theotokion, *Many are the multitudes of my mistakes; I flee to you, O Theotokos, for refuge, asking, immaculate one, for salvation. O you alone who are blessed, look upon my sick soul and intercede with your son and God to grant me forgiveness for the terrible things I did.*

Lord, have mercy forty times, then the

prayer, *We ask you, O Lord our God: have patience with us sinners and spare us, who are the work of your hands. Knowing our weakness, also deliver us from every temptation, all present and future evils, as well as from the ruler of **the power of darkness*** (Lk 22:53). *Remove us to the kingdom of your only-begotten son and our God, for yours is the glory forever. Amen.*

Kathisma 15[29]

The Trisagion, the *Our Father,* troparion, plagal mode II:

Grant me, O Lord, the vigilance of the wise virgins and illuminate the lamp of my soul with the oil of your compassion, so that I may sing to you the hymn of the angels, "Alleluia."

Glory.

Why, my soul, do you serve sin by being sluggish? And why, being weakened, do you not go to the physician? Recover from the evil things that you did. Call to the savior, saying, "Hope of those driven to despair, life to those who have given up, O Lord, my physician and savior, save me."

Both now.

theotokion, *Open to us the gate of compassion, O blessed Theotokos. We put our hope in you; do not let us fail. Through you may we be rescued from misfortune, for you are the race of mankind's deliverance.*

Lord, have mercy forty times, then the

29. Psalms 105–8. The three sessions (staseis) are: first, Ps 105; second, 106; third, 107, 108.

*Παναγία δέσποινα Θεοτόκε, ἀποδίωξον τοὺς πονηροὺς καὶ ἀκαθάρτους
λογισμοὺς ἐκ τῆς ἀθλίας καὶ ταλαιπώρου μου καρδίας, καὶ ἐλέησόν με
τὸν ἁμαρτωλόν, ὅτι ἀσθενὴς καὶ ταλαίπωρος εἰμί, καὶ λύτρωσαί με ἐκ τῶν
πονηρῶν ἐνθυμήσεων καὶ προλήψεων. Κύριε, ἐκ τῶν κρυφίων μου καθάρισόν
με. Κύριε, σὺ οἶδας τὰς ἁμαρτίας μου· σὺ ὡς θέλεις ἐξάλειψον αὐτάς. Ἥμαρτον,
Κύριε· συγχώρησόν μοι διὰ τὸ ὄνομά σου τὸ ἅγιον. Κύριε, δὸς ἡμῖν ἀγαθοὺς
ἀγγέλους ὁδηγοῦντας καὶ κυβερνοῦντας τὴν ἡμῶν ζωήν, πολλὴ γάρ ἐστιν ἡ
καθ' ἡμῶν μανία τῶν δαιμόνων. Ὁ Θεός μου, μὴ ἐγκα|*[165v]*-ταλίπῃς με· οὐδὲν
ἐποίησα ἐνώπιόν σου ἀγαθόν, ἀλλὰ δὸς ἡμῖν κατὰ τὴν σὴν ἀγαθότητα βαλεῖν
ἀρχήν. Κύριε, ὁδήγησόν με πῶς σωθῶ, καὶ μὴ συναπολέσῃς με ταῖς ἀνομίαις
μου, φιλάνθρωπε, ὅτι εὐλογήμενον ὕπαρχει τὸ ὄνομά σου, τοῦ Πατρὸς καὶ τοῦ
Υἱοῦ καὶ τοῦ ἁγίου Πνεύματος νῦν καὶ ἀεὶ καὶ εἰς τοὺς αἰῶνας τῶν αἰώνων.*

κάθισμα ις΄[51]

Τὸ τρισάγιον, τὸ *Πάτερ ἡμῶν,* τροπάριον, ἦχος βαρύς,

*Ἔχουσα, ψυχή μου, τὸ ἰατρεῖον τῆς μετανοίας, πρόσελθε δακρύουσα, ἐν
στεναγμοῖς κραυγάζουσα τῷ ἰατρῷ ψυχῶν τε καὶ σω|*[172v]*-μάτων· Ἐλευθέρωσόν
με, φιλάνθρωπε, ἐκ τῶν ἐμῶν πλημμελημάτων· συναρίθμησόν με τῇ πόρνῃ,
τῷ λῃστῇ καὶ τῷ τελώνῃ, καὶ δώρησαί μοι, ὁ Θεός, τῶν ἀνομιῶν μου τὴν
συγχώρησιν καὶ σῶσόν με. Δόξα.*

*Τοῦ τελώνου τὴν μετάνοιαν οὐκ ἐζήλωσα καὶ τῆς πόρνης τὰ δάκρυα οὐ
κέκτημαι· ἀπορῶ γάρ ἐκ πωρώσεως τῆς τοιαύτης διορθώσεως, ἀλλὰ τῇ σῇ
εὐσπλαγχνίᾳ, ὁ Θεός, σῶσόν με ὡς φιλάνθρωπος. Καὶ νῦν.*

θεοτοκίον, *Ὑπερέβης τὰς δυνάμεις τῶν οὐρανῶν, ὅτι ναὸς ἐδείχθης θεϊκός,
εὐλογημένη Θεοτόκε, ὡς τεκοῦσα Χριστὸν τὸν σωτῆρα τῶν ψυχῶν ἡμῶν.*

Τὸ *Κύριε, ἐλέησον,* μ΄, εἶτα τὴν προσευχὴν τοῦ Μανασσῆ βασιλέως τῶν
Ἰουδαίων,

Κύριε παντοκράτορ, ὁ Θεὸς τῶν πατέρων ἡμῶν ...[52]

---

51. Fols. 165v–172.
52. Ode 12: fols. 172v–174v.

prayer of the most holy Theotokos, *All-holy sovereign lady, mother of God, chase the wicked and unclean thoughts from my wretched and afflicted heart* (cf. Mt 9:4) *and* **have mercy on me, the sinner, for I am weak** (Ps 6:3) *and afflicted; redeem me from wicked ideas and preoccupations.*

O Lord, cleanse me of my secret thoughts. O Lord, you know my sins; blot them out, as is your wish. I have sinned, O Lord; forgive me for your holy name's sake. Give us, O Lord, good angels who guide and direct our life, since the madness of the demons arrayed against us is powerful. My God, **do not forsake me** (Ps 26:9); *I did not a single good thing in your presence, but grant us, according to your goodness, a fresh start. O Lord, you who love mankind, guide me in how I might be saved,* **and do not destroy me with my sins** (Ode 12:13), *for blessed is your name: (that) of the Father and the Son and the Holy Spirit, now and always and for ever and ever.* <*Amen.*>

Kathisma 16[30]

The Trisagion, the *Our Father*, troparion, barys mode:

Having at hand, my soul, the remedy of repentance, go weeping and groaning aloud to the physician of both souls and bodies, "O you who love mankind, free me from my sins. Count me with the harlot, the thief, and the tax collector, and grant me, God, forgiveness for my transgressions and save me."

Glory.

I have not gained the repentance of the tax collector and have not shed the harlot's tears, for I am at a loss because of callous insensitivity to correction such as theirs. But in your compassion, God, save me as the one who loves mankind.

Both now.

theotokion, *You surpassed the powers of the heavens, for you, blessed Theotokos, as she who bore Christ the savior of our souls, were revealed to be a divine temple.*

Lord, have mercy forty times, then the

Prayer of Manasses, king of the Jews, *O Lord Almighty, the God of our fathers …* [Copied in full; cf. LXX, Ode 12][31]

---

30. Psalms 109–17. The three sessions (staseis) are: first, Pss 109–11; second, 112–14; third, 115–17.
31. LXX = *Septuaginta*, ed. Ralphs.

κάθισμα ιζ΄[53]

Τὸ τρισάγιον, τὸ Πάτερ ἡμῶν, τροπάριον, ἦχος βαρύς,
Ὁ τοῦ Πέτρου τὴν ἄρνησιν τοῖς δάκρυσι καθαρίσας καὶ τελώνου τὰ πταίσματα τῷ στεναγμῷ συγχωρήσας· φιλάνθρωπε Κύριε, ἐλέησόν με. Δόξα.[54]

Μετανοεῖν ἐπαγγέλλομαι ἐν τῇ ὥρᾳ τῆς προσευχῆς· καὶ τῶν δεινῶν οὐκ ἀφίσταμαι, συνωθοῦντος τοῦ πονηροῦ, ἀλλ᾽ αἰτῶ σε· ἐξάρπασόν με τούτου, Χριστὲ ὁ Θεός, καὶ σῶσόν με. Καὶ νῦν.

θεοτοκίον, Ὁ καρπὸς τῆς κοιλίας σου, ἄχραντε, τῶν προφητῶν ὑπάρχει καὶ τοῦ νόμου τὸ πλήρωμα· |[184v] διό σε Θεοτόκον ἐν ἐπιγνώσει δοξάζοντες εὐσεβῶς μεγαλύνομεν.

Τὸ Κύριε ἐλέησον, μ᾽, εἶτα τὴν προσευχὴν Ἐζεκίου βασιλέως τῆς Ἰουδαίας, Ἐγὼ εἶπα[55] ἐν τῷ ὕψει τῶν ἡμερῶν μου, πορεύσομαι ἐν πύλαις ᾅδου...[56]

κάθισμα ιη΄[57]

Τὸ τρισάγιον, τὸ Πάτερ ἡμῶν, τροπάριον, ἦχος πλάγιος δ᾽,
Ὄμματι εὐσπλάγχνῳ, Κύριε, ἴδε τὴν ἐμὴν ταπείνωσιν, ὅτι κατὰ μικρὸν ἡ ζωή μου δαπανᾶται, καὶ ἐξ ἔργων ἐν ἐμοὶ οὐχ ὑπάρχει σωτηρία· διατοῦτο[58] δέομαι· Ὄμματι εὐσπλάγχνῳ, Κύριε, ἴδε τὴν ἐμὴν ταπείνωσιν καὶ σῶσόν με. Δόξα.[59]

Ὡς τοῦ κριτοῦ παρόντος μερίμνησον, ψυχή, καὶ τῆς φρικτῆς ἡμέρας τὴν ὥραν ἐννοοῦ· ἡ γὰρ κρίσις ἀνίλεώς ἐστι τοῖς μὴ πράξασιν ἔλεος· διὸ φεῖσαί μου, Σωτήρ, μόνος γὰρ ὑπάρχεις ἀναμάρτητος. Καὶ νῦν.

---

53. Fols. 174v–184.   54. δόξα indicated in the margin.
55. εἶπα: C.
56. Ode 11: fol. 184v; the leaf with Ode 11:13b–Ps 119:5a is missing between fols. 184 and 185.
57. Fols. 185–190v.
58. διατοῦτο: C.
59. δόξα indicated in the margin.

Kathisma 17[32]

The Trisagion, the *Our Father*, troparion, barys mode:

You who cleansed Peter's denial with (his) tears and forgave the tax collector's mistakes with (his) moan, benevolent Lord, have mercy on me.

Glory.

I promise to repent at the hour of prayer! I do not give up terrible things since the evil one urges me on, but I beg you: Snatch me away from him, Christ our God, and save me.

Both now.

theotokion, *The fruit of your womb* (Lk 1:42), *O undefiled one, is the fulfillment of the prophets and the Law* (cf. Mt 5:17); *glorifying you in acknowledgment of this, we piously extol you who are the mother of God.*

Lord, have mercy forty times, then the

Prayer of Hezekiah, king of Judea, *I said at the end of my days, I shall go to the gates of the grave...*[33] [Copied in full; cf. LXX, Ode 11 = Is 38:10–20]

Kathisma 18[34]

The Trisagion, the *Our Father*, troparion, plagal mode IV:

Look on my humanity, O Lord, with a compassionate eye, for my life is being spent little by little, and I have no salvation from (my) works. Because of this, I implore (you), "Look, O Lord, on my humanity with a compassionate eye and save me."

Glory.

Take care, O soul, as if the judge were present, and ponder the hour of the terrible day, for the judgment of those who did not practice mercy is merciless (Jas 2:13). *On this account spare me, O savior, for you alone are without sin.*

Both now.

---

32. Psalm 118. The three sessions (staseis) are: first, vv 1–73; second, 74–131; third, 132–76.
33. Literally Hades.
34. Psalms 119–33. The three sessions (staseis) are: first, Pss 119–23; second, 124–28; third, 129–33.

θεοτοκίον, Προστασία φοβερὰ καὶ ἀκατάληπτε, μὴ παρίδῃς ἀγαθὴ τὰς
ἱκεσίας ἡμῶν, πανύμνητε Θεοτόκε· στήριξον ὀρθοδόξων πολιτείαν· σῷζε οὓς
ἐκέλευσας βασιλεύειν |¹⁹¹ καὶ χορήγησον αὐτοῖς τὴν ἐπουράνιον νίκην· διότι
ἔτεκες Θεόν, μόνη εὐλογημένη.

Τὸ Κύριε ἐλέησον, μʹ, εἶτα εὐχὴ ἱκετήριος εἰς τὴν ὑπεραγίαν Θεοτόκον,
Πολλῶν καὶ μεγάλων ἀπολαύσας τῶν δωρημάτων τοῦ πλαστουργήσαντός
με Θεοῦ, ἀμνήμων τε πάντων φανείς, ὁ ἄθλιος καὶ ἀχάριστος ἐγώ· εἰκότως
παρασυνεβλήθην τοῖς κτήνεσι τοῖς ἀνοήτοις καὶ ὡμοιώθην αὐτοῖς. Πτωχεύων
ταῖς ἀρεταῖς, πλουτῶν τοῖς πάθεσιν, αἰσχύνης πεπληρωμένος, παρρησίας θείας
ἐστερημένος, κατακρινόμενος ὑπὸ Θεοῦ, θρηνούμενος ὑπὸ ἀγγέλων, γελώμενος
ὑπὸ δαιμόνων, ἐλεγχόμενος ὑπὸ τοῦ συνειδότος, ὑπὸ τῶν πονηρῶν μου πράξεων
καταισχυνόμενος, καὶ πρὸ θανάτου νεκρὸς ὑπάρχω· καὶ πρὸ κρί|¹⁹¹ᵛ–σεως
αὐτοκατάκριτος, καὶ πρὸ τῆς ἀτελευτήτου κολάσεως αὐτοτιμώρητος ὑπὸ τῆς
ἀπογνώσεως τυγχάνω. Διὸ δὴ εἰς τὴν σὴν καὶ μόνην καταφεύγω θερμοτάτην
ἀντίληψιν, δέσποινα Θεοτόκε, ὁ τῶν μυρίων ὀφειλέτης ταλάντων, ὁ ἀσώτως
μετὰ πορνῶν τὴν πατερικὴν δαπανήσας οὐσίαν, ὁ πορνεύσας ὑπὲρ τὴν πόρνην,
ὁ παρανομήσας ὑπὲρ τὸν Μανασσῆν, ὁ ὑπὲρ τὸν πλούσιον ἄσπλαγχνος ὤν, ὁ
λαιμαργιῶν δοῦλος, τὸ τῶν πονηρῶν λογισμῶν δοχεῖον, ὁ τῶν αἰσχρῶν καὶ
ῥυπαρῶν λόγων θησαυροφύλαξ, ὁ πάσης ἀκαθαρσίας ἔμπλεως <ὤν>,⁶⁰ καὶ
πάσης ἀγαθοεργίας ἀλλότριος. Ἐλέησόν μου τὴν ταπείνωσιν, ἄχραντε· οἰκτεί
|¹⁹²–ρησόν μου τὴν ἀσθένειαν, πάναγνε. Μεγάλην ἔχεις παρρησίαν πρὸς τὸν
ἐκ σοῦ τεχθέντα ὡς οὐδεὶς ἕτερος· πάντα δύνασαι ὡς Θεοῦ μήτηρ, πάντα
ἰσχύεις ὡς πάντων ὑπερέχουσα κτισμάτων, <καὶ>⁶¹ οὐδέν σοι ἀδύνατον ἐὰν
θελήσῃς. Μόνον μὴ παρίδῃς μου τὰ δάκρυα, δέσποινα· μὴ βδελύξῃ μου τὸν
στεναγμόν· μὴ ἀπώσῃ μου τὸν ἐγκάρδιον πόνον· μὴ καταισχύνῃς μου τὴν εἰς
σὲ προσδοκίαν· ἀλλὰ ταῖς μητρικαῖς σου δεήσεσι τὴν τοῦ ἀγαθοῦ υἱοῦ καὶ
Θεοῦ σου ἀβίαστον βιασαμένη εὐσπλαγχνίαν, ἀξίωσόν με τὸν ἁμαρτωλὸν
καὶ ἀνάξιον καὶ ἀχρεῖον οἰκέτην σου, τὸ πρῶτον καὶ ἀρχαῖον ἐπαναλαβεῖν
τῆς ψυχῆς κάλλος, τὴν τῶν παθῶν ἀποθέσθαι ἀμορφίαν, |¹⁹²ᵛ ἐλευθερωθῆναι
τῆς ἁμαρτίας, δουλωθῆναι τῇ δικαιοσύνῃ, ἐκδύσασθαι τὸν μιασμὸν τῆς
σαρκός, ἐνδύσασθαι τὸν ἁγιασμὸν τῆς ψυχικῆς καθαρότητος, νεκρωθῆναι

---

60. Supplied from P, fol. 191v.
61. Supplied from P, fol. 192.

theotokion, *O you who are a formidable protection beyond comprehension, O Theotokos worthy of all praise, do not, good one, ignore our supplications. Strengthen the commonwealth of orthodox believers; save them whom you commanded to rule and give them the heavenly victory, for you bore God, you who alone are blessed.*

Lord, have mercy forty times, then the

prayer of supplication to the most holy Theotokos,[35] *Though having the benefit of the many, great gifts of the God who fashioned me, and appearing to forget all of them, I am a wretched and ungrateful man; fairly, **I was compared to the senseless cattle, and was something like them** (Ps 48:13). Poor in virtue and rich in misfortune, filled with shame and deprived of divine trust, condemned by God, lamented by angels and mocked by demons, censured by my conscience and shamed by my wicked deeds, I am dead before death, condemned by myself before the judgment, and before the endless punishment (I take) vengeance on myself through despair. Wherefore O sovereign lady, mother of God, I flee for refuge to your unique and warmest succor.*

*I who am **in debt for a thousand talents** (Mt 18:24), the one who spent the paternal inheritance in profligacy with harlots, I am he whose fornication exceeded the harlot's, whose transgression exceeded Manasses's,[36] whose heartlessness exceeds the rich man's, a servant of greed, the vessel of evil thoughts, the treasurer of shameful and filthy speech, he who is overflowing with every impurity and is estranged from every good work. Have mercy on my humility, O you who are undefiled. O all-holy one, take pity on my weakness.*

Like no other you have great confidence in speaking with him to whom you gave birth. As the mother of God, you are capable of everything; you who transcend all created things are strong in everything; nothing is impossible for you, if you wish (it). Only do not ignore my tears, sovereign lady; do not be disgusted at my groaning. Do not ignore the suffering that is in my heart; do not shame the expectations I place in you.

You who by your maternal entreaties compel the uncompellable compassion of your good son and God, consider me, the sinner (who is) your unworthy and

---

35. In both C and P this long prayer is divided by means of decorative initials into paragraphs; the divisions differ in the two manuscripts and do not clarify the structure of the prayer, which has been attributed to Ephrem the Syrian. K. Phrantzola, Ὁσίου Ἐφραίμ τοῦ Σύρου ἔργα, vol. 6 (Thessaloniki: Ekdoseis to Perivoli tes Panagias, 1998), 354–413.

36. Cf. 2 Kgs (LXX = 4 Kgs) 21:1–17.

τῷ κόσμῳ, ζῆσαι τῇ ἀρετῇ. Ὁδοιποροῦντί μοι συνοδεύουσα, ἐν θαλάσσῃ
πλέοντι συμπλέουσα, ἀεὶ πολεμοῦσα τοὺς χαλεπῶς ἀφ' ὕψους πολεμοῦντάς
με δαίμονας, ἀγρυπνοῦντά με ἐνισχύουσα, ὑπνοῦντα διαφυλάττουσα,
παραμυθουμένη θλιβόμενον, ὀλιγοψυχοῦντα παρακαλοῦσα, ἀσθενοῦντα
ῥωννύουσα, ἀδικούμενον ῥυομένη, συκοφαντούμενον ἀθῳοῦσα, καὶ εἰς
θάνατον κινδυνεύοντα συντόμως προφθάνουσα |¹⁹³ φοβερόν με, ὁρατοῖς
καὶ ἀοράτοις ἐχθροῖς δεικνύουσα καθεκάστην, ἵνα γνῶσι πάντες οἱ ἀδίκως
με τυραννοῦντες δαίμονες τίνος δοῦλος ὑπάρχω. Ναί, ὑπεράγαθε δέσποινα
Θεοτόκε, ἐπάκουσόν μου τῆς οἰκτροτάτης δεήσεως, καὶ μὴ καταισχύνῃς με
ἀπὸ τῆς προσδοκίας μου, ἡ ἐλπὶς πάντων τῶν περάτων τῆς γῆς· τὸν βρασμὸν
τῆς σαρκός μου κατάσβεσον· τὸν ἐν τῇ ψυχῇ μου ἐγειρόμενον ἀγριώτατον
κλύδωνα τοῦ ἀκαίρου θυμοῦ καταπράϋνον· τὸν τῦφον καὶ τὴν ἀλαζονείαν
τῆς ματαίας οἰήσεως ἐκ τοῦ νοός μου ἀφάνισον· τὰς νυκτερινὰς φαντασίας
τῶν πονηρῶν πνευμάτων καὶ τὰς καθημερινὰς |¹⁹³ᵛ τῶν ἀκαθάρτων ἐννοιῶν
προσβολὰς ἐκ τῆς καρδίας μου μείωσον. Παίδευσόν μου τὴν γλῶσσαν λαλεῖν
τὰ συμφέροντα· δίδαξόν μου τοὺς ὀφθαλμοὺς τοῦ βλέπειν ὀρθῶς τῆς ἀρετῆς
τὴν εὐθύτητα, τοὺς πόδας μου τρέχειν ἀσκέλιστα ποίησον, τὴν μακαρίαν
ὁδὸν τῶν ἐντολῶν τοῦ Θεοῦ, τὰς χεῖράς μου ἁγιασθῆναι παρασκεύασον,
ἵνα ἀξίως αἴρωνται πρὸς τὸν ὕψιστον. Κάθαρόν μου τὸ στόμα, ἵνα μετὰ
παρρησίας ἐπικαλέσηται Πατέρα τὸν φοβερὸν καὶ ἅγιον. Ἄνοιξόν μου τὰ
ὦτα, ἵνα ἀκούων αἰσθητῶς τε καὶ νοερῶς τὰ γλυκύτερα κηρίου καὶ μέλιτος
τῶν ἁγίων γραφῶν λόγια, ποιῶ αὐτὰ διὰ σοῦ κραταιούμενος.⁶² Δός μοι
καιρὸν |¹⁹⁴ μετανοίας καὶ λογισμὸν ἐπιστροφῆς· αἰφνιδίου με ἐλευθέρωσον
θανάτου· κατακεκρυμμένου με συνειδότος ἀπάλλαξον· τέλος παράστηθί μοι
ἐν τῷ χωρισμῷ τῆς ψυχῆς ἀπὸ τοῦ ἀθλίου τούτου σώματος. Τὴν ἀφόρητον
ἐκείνην ἐλαφρύνουσα βίαν, τὸν ἀνέκφραστον ἐκεῖνον κουφίζουσα πόνον,
τὴν ἀπαραμύθητον παραμυθουμένη στενοχωρίαν, τῆς σκοτεινῆς με τῶν
δαιμόνων λυτρουμένη μορφῆς, τῶν πικροτάτων λογοθεσίων τῶν τελωνῶν
τοῦ ἀέρος καὶ τῶν ἀρχόντων τοῦ σκότους ἐξαιροῦσα,⁶³ τὰ χειρόγραφα τῶν
πολλῶν μου ἁμαρτιῶν διαρρήσσουσα, τῷ Θεῷ με οἰκειοῦσα, τῆς ἐκ δεξιῶν
αὐτοῦ μακα|¹⁹⁴ᵛ-ρίας στάσεως ἐν τῷ φοβερῷ αὐτοῦ κριτηρίῳ καταξιοῦσα,
τῶν αἰωνίων αὐτοῦ καὶ ἀκηράτων ἀγαθῶν ποιοῦσα κληρονόμον, ταύτην σοι

---

62. κρατουούμενος: C.
63. ἐξαίρουσα: C, P, fol. 196.

useless slave, worthy to get back the soul's first and original beauty and to cast off the deformity of the passions, to be freed from sin and to devote myself to righteousness, to strip away the defilement of the flesh and to clothe myself in the sanctity of the purest soul, to become dead to the world and to live by virtue.

As I travel the earth, go with me; as I sail the sea, sail with me, always battling the demons that cruelly assault me from on high, always giving me strength when I am awake, keeping me safe when I sleep, encouraging me when I am distressed, exhorting me when I am discouraged, fortifying me when I grow weak, protecting me when I am wronged, showing my innocence when I am falsely accused, anticipating my fear at suddenly dying, and showing <your strength>[37] to (my) visible and invisible enemies each day, so that all the demons that unjustly tyrannize me may know whose servant I am.

Indeed, most beneficent sovereign lady, mother of God, hope of all the ends of the earth, hear my most pitiful supplication **and make me not ashamed of my expectation** (Ps 118:116). Quell the roiling of my flesh; pacify the very savage wave of untimely anger that rises in my soul. Uproot from my mind the vanity and arrogance of empty conceit. Dispel the nocturnal visions of evil spirits and check the daily assault of impure thoughts from my heart. Instruct my tongue to speak what is profitable, teach my eyes to see clearly the righteousness of virtue, make my feet to walk without tripping on the blessed road of God's command-ments. Prepare my hands for sanctification, so that they might worthily be lifted up to the most high. Cleanse my mouth, so that it might freely call upon the fearful and holy Father. Open my ears so that hearing, with both the senses and the mind, the **teachings** of holy scripture **that are sweeter than honeycomb and honey** (Ps 118:103), I might carry them out strengthened by you.

Give me the opportunity for repentance and the thought of reform; free me from sudden death; deliver me from a conscience that is hidden away; stand by me at the separation of my soul from this miserable body. You who lighten that unendurable violence, who relieve that indescribable suffering, who console the inconsolable distress, who save me from the dark shape of the demons, from the most bitter calculations of the tax collectors of the air and the rulers of darkness, (you) who seize (and) tear apart the ledgers with my many sins, reconciling me to God, you who consider me worthy of a blessed

37. A possible reminiscence of Ps 58:10.

προσάγω τὴν ἐξομολόγησιν, δέσποινα Θεοτόκε, τὸ φῶς τῶν ἐσκοτισμένων μου ὀφθαλμῶν, ἡ παραμυθία τῆς ἐμῆς ψυχῆς, ἡ μετὰ Θεὸν ἐλπίς μου καὶ προστασία, ἣν εὐμενῶς πρόσδεξαι, καὶ καθάρισόν με ἀπὸ παντὸς μολυσμοῦ σαρκὸς καὶ πνεύματος· ἀξιοῦσά με ἐν τῷ παρόντι μὲν αἰῶνι ἀκατακρίτως μετέχειν τοῦ παναγίου καὶ ἀχράντου σώματος καὶ αἵματος τοῦ υἱοῦ καὶ Θεοῦ σου, ἐν τῷ μέλλοντι δὲ τῆς γλυκύτητος τοῦ οὐρανίου δείπνου, τῆς τρυφῆς τοῦ παραδείσου καὶ τῆς βασιλείας τῶν οὐρανῶν, |¹⁹⁵ ἔνθα πάντων ἐστὶν εὐφραινομένων ἡ κατοικία· ἀμήν.

<h1 style="text-align:center">κάθισμα ιθ´⁶⁴</h1>

Τὸ τρισάγιον, τὸ Πάτερ ἡμῶν, τροπάριον, ἦχος πλάγιος δ´,

Ὁ χρόνος τῆς ζωῆς μου συντελεῖται, Δέσποτα, ὁ δὲ φρικτός σου θρόνος λοιπὸν εὐτρεπίζεται, ὁ βίος παρέρχεται, ἡ δὲ κρίσις ἐκδέχεται· ἀπειλοῦσά μοι τοῦ πυρὸς τὴν τιμωρίαν καὶ τὴν φλόγα τὴν ἄσβεστον· δακρύων ὄμβρους πέμψον μοι Σωτήρ, καὶ σβέσον ταύτης τὴν ἰσχὺν ὁ θέλων πάντας ἀνθρώπους σωθῆναι. Δόξα.

Ὡς ἡ πόρνη προσπίπτω σοι, ἵνα λάβω τὴν ἄφεσιν· καὶ ἀντὶ μύρου τὰ δάκρυα ἐκ καρδίας προσ|²⁰⁴ᵛ-φέρω σοι, ἵνα ὡς ἐκείνην οἰκτειρήσῃς με Σωτήρ, καὶ παράσχῃς ἱλασμὸν ἁμαρτιῶν· ὡς αὐτὴ γὰρ κραυγάζω σοι· Λύτρωσαί με τοῦ βορβόρου τῶν ἔργων μου. Καὶ νῦν.⁶⁵

θεοτοκίον, Ἡ νοητὴ πύλη τῆς ζωῆς, ἄχραντε Θεοτόκε, τοὺς προστρέχοντάς σοι πιστῶς λύτρωσαι τῶν κινδύνων, ἵνα δοξάζωμεν τὸν πανάγιον τόκον σου εἰς σωτηρίαν τῶν ψυχῶν ἡμῶν.

Τὸ Κύριε ἐλέησον, μ´, εἶτα τὴν εὐχὴν ταύτην,

Πάλιν ὑπεσκελίσθην ὁ τάλας τὸν νοῦν τῇ πονηρᾷ συνηθείᾳ τῆς ἁμαρτίας δουλεύων· πάλιν ὁ τοῦ σκότους ἄρχων καὶ τῆς ἐμπαθοῦς ἡδονῆς, ὁ γεννήτωρ αἰχμάλωτον εἷλέ με· καὶ ὥσπερ δοῦλον τεταπεινωμένον τῷ ἑαυτοῦ θελήματι καὶ ταῖς ἐπιθυμίαις τῆς σαρκός, δουλεύειν καταναγκάζει με. Καὶ τί ποιήσω,

---

64. Fols. 195–204.
65. καὶ νῦν indicated in the margin.

place at his right hand in his fearful place of judgment, who make (me) an
heir to his eternal and unalloyed good things, to you I offer this confession, O
sovereign lady, mother of God—the light of my eyes, which have been dimmed,
the encouragement of my soul, after God, my hope and patron—kindly accept
it and cleanse me of all defilement of flesh and spirit; make me worthy to par-
take, free of condemnation in this present age, of the all-holy and immaculate
body and blood of your son and God, and in the age to come (to partake) of
the sweetness of the heavenly banquet, the delight of paradise and the kingdom
of heaven, which is **the dwelling of all who rejoice** *(Ps 86:7). Amen.*

Kathisma 19[38]

The Trisagion, the *Our Father,* troparion, plagal mode IV:

The span of my life is drawing to a close, O Master, your terrible throne
is now being prepared, life passes away, the judgment awaits, threatening me
with punishment by fire and the unquenchable flames (cf. Mt 3:12). Send me
showers of tears, savior, and quench its strength, O you **who wish all mankind**
to be saved *(1 Tm 2:4).*[39]

Glory.

Like the harlot I fall down before you so that I might obtain remission; but
instead of myrrh I offer you tears from the heart, so that you, savior, might
take pity on me as you did on her, and might grant atonement for my sins; for,
like her, I cry to you, "Deliver me from the mire of my works."

Both now.

theotokion, *You who are seen by the mind's eye as the gate of life, O unde-*
filed Theotokos, deliver us from danger—we who in faith run to you—so that
for the salvation of our souls we might glorify your all-holy child.

Lord, have mercy forty times, then this

prayer, *Again I stumbled, worthless in mind, a slave to the evil habit of sin*
(cf. Rom 6:6), (and) once again, the ruler of darkness and of passionate plea-
sure, the begetter,[40] *took me prisoner and forces me, like a humiliated slave,*
into servitude to his wishes and the desires of the flesh. **What will I do** *(Mk*

---

38. Psalms 134–42. The three sessions (staseis) are: first, Pss 134–36; second, 137–39; third, 140–42.

39. See above, 86.

40. For ὁ γεννήτωρ as Satan, see Lampe, *Lexicon,* s.v.

|²⁰⁵ Κύριε μου, Κύριε, λυτρωτὰ καὶ ὑπερασπιστὰ τῶν πεποιθότων ἐπὶ σέ; Πρὸς σὲ πάλιν ἐπιστραφήσομαι καὶ στενάξω καὶ συγγνώμην αἰτήσομαι τῶν πεπραγμένων μοι.⁶⁶ ἀλλὰ δέδοικα καὶ τρέμω· μήπως καθεκάστην ἐξομολογούμενος καὶ ἀποχὴν τῶν κακῶν ἐπαγγελλόμενος καὶ καθ' ὥραν ἁμαρτάνων καὶ μὴ ἀποδιδοὺς τὰς εὐχάς μου σοί, τῷ Θεῷ μου, τὴν μακροθυμίαν σου διεγείρω πρὸς ἀγανάκτησιν. Καὶ τίς ὑποίσει, Κύριε, τὸν θυμόν σου; Γινώσκων οὖν τὸ πλῆθος τῶν οἰκτιρμῶν σου καὶ τὴν ἄβυσσον τῆς φιλανθρωπίας σου, πάλιν ἐπιρρίπτω ἐμαυτὸν εἰς τὰ ἐλέη σου καὶ κράζω σοι τὸ Ἥμαρτον, ὁ Θεός, ἐλέησόν με τὸν παραπεσόντα· δὸς χεῖρα βοηθείας τῷ ἐν βορβόρῳ |²⁰⁵ᵛ τῶν ἡδονῶν βεβυθισμένῳ, καὶ μὴ καταλίπῃς, Κύριε, τὸ πλάσμα σου φθαρῆναι ταῖς ἀνομίαις καὶ ταῖς ἁμαρτίαις μου,⁶⁷ ἀλλὰ τῇ συνήθει σου χρηστότητι χρησάμενος, ῥῦσαί με τοῦ μιασμοῦ καὶ τοῦ ῥύπου τῆς σαρκός μου καὶ τῶν ἐμπαθῶν λογισμῶν τῶν καθ' ἑκάστην καταχραινόντων τὴν ἐμὴν ἀθλίαν ψυχήν. Ἰδοὺ γάρ, Κύριε ὁ Θεός μου, οὐκ ἔστι τόπος ἐν ταύτῃ καθαρός, ἀλλ' ὅλη λελέπρωται τὴν ὁλοσώματον ἔχουσα πληγήν. Αὐτὸς οὖν, ὡς ἰατρὸς τῶν ψυχῶν καὶ τοῦ ἐλέους πηγή, καθάρισον ταύτην τῇ τῶν δακρύων μου καθάρσει· ταῦτα προχέων ἐν ἐμοὶ δαψιλῶς, καὶ ἐπίχεε ἐπ' ἐμὲ τὴν φιλανθρωπίαν σου καὶ ἴασαι τὰ συντρίμματα ταύτης. Καὶ δός μοι τὴν ἴασιν |²⁰⁶ καὶ τὴν κάθαρσιν, καὶ μὴ ἀποστρέψῃς τὸ πρόσωπόν σου ἀπ' ἐμοῦ, καὶ ὡς πῦρ καταφάγεταί με τὸ τῆς ἀπογνώσεως πῦρ· ἀλλ' ὅπερ εἶπας ὁ ἀψευδὴς Θεὸς ὅτι μεγάλη χαρὰ γίνεται ἐν οὐρανῷ ἐπὶ τῇ τοῦ ἁμαρτωλοῦ μετανοίᾳ· τοῦτο πραχθείη καὶ ἐπ' ἐμοὶ τῷ ἁμαρτωλῷ, καὶ μὴ κλείσθῃς τὰ ὦτα τῆς εὐσπλαγχνίας σου εἰς τὴν προσευχὴν τῆς μετανοίας μου, ἀλλ' ἄνοιξόν μοι αὐτά, καὶ ὡς θυμίαμα κατεύθυνον αὐτὴν ἐνώπιόν σου. Οἶδας γὰρ τὴν ἀσθένειαν τῆς φύσεως, ὁ πλάστης, καὶ τὸ εὐόλισθον τῆς νεότητος, καὶ παρορᾷς ἁμαρτίας καὶ τὴν μετάνοιαν ἐκδέχῃ τῶν ἐν ἀληθείᾳ ἐπικαλουμένων σέ, ὅτι εὐλογητὸς εἶ εἰς τοὺς αἰῶνας· ἀμήν. |²¹³

κάθισμα κ'⁶⁸

Τὸ τρισάγιον, τὸ Πάτερ ἡμῶν, τροπάριον, ἦχος πλάγιος δ',
Τὴν ἡμέραν ἐκείνην τὴν φοβερὰν ἐννοοῦσα, ψυχή μου γρηγόρησον, ἀνάπτουσα λαμπάδα σου, ἐν ἐλαίῳ φαιδρύνουσα· οὐ γὰρ οἶδας πότε πρὸς σὲ

---

66. μοι written in the margin with an insertion sign.
67. μου added by the scribe above the line.
68. Fols. 206v–213.

10:17), *O Lord, my Lord, redeemer and protector of them who have put trust in you? I will again turn to you. I will groan and will beg forgiveness for what I have done. Yet I fear and I quake, lest in any way—confessing every day and promising to renounce evil, but sinning every hour and not offering my prayers to you my God—I turn your patience into angry exasperation. And who, O Lord, will endure your wrath? Knowing, then, the fullness of your mercy* (Ps 50:3) *and the unfathomable depth of your love for mankind, I again throw myself on your mercy and call out to you, I have sinned* (Ps 50:6); *God, have mercy on me* (Ps 50:3) *who has fallen into error. Give a helping hand to one who is sinking himself into the mire of pleasures, and do not, O Lord, abandon the creation of your hands to destruction on account of my iniquities and sins. Rather, practicing your inherent goodness, save me from defilement, from the uncleanness of my flesh* (cf. 1 Pt 3:21), *and the passionate thoughts that daily cover my wretched soul with spots. Look, O Lord my God: there is no clean place on it. It turned all leprous, having sores over the entire body. You, then, as physician of souls and as a wellspring of mercy, cleanse it through the purification of my tears; as you pour them abundantly over me, also pour your benevolence on me and heal its afflictions. Give me the cure and cleansing, and do not turn your face away from me* (Ps 26:9). *Like fire, the flames of despair are destroying me, but you are the truthful God who said that there will be great joy in heaven over the repentance of the sinner* (cf. Lk 15:7). *Oh, that this be done even for me, the sinner, and that you not shut the ears of your compassion to my prayer of repentance! Open them to me and guide it like incense into your presence. You who formed (us) know the weakness of (our) nature and the instability of youth, you overlook sin and accept the repentance of those who call on you in truth, for blessed are you forever. Amen.*

Kathisma 20[41]

The Trisagion, the *Our Father,* troparion, plagal mode IV:

As you ponder that fearful day, my soul, stay alert. Light your lamp with oil (and) shine forth, for you know not when the voice will come to you saying,

---

41. Psalms 143–50. The three sessions (staseis) are: first, Pss 143, 144; second, 145–47; third, 148–50.

ἐπελεύσεται ἡ φωνὴ ἡ λέγουσα· Ἰδού, ὁ νυμφίος σου· βλέπε οὖν ψυχή μου· μὴ
νυστάξῃς καὶ μείνῃς ἔξωθεν κρούουσα ὡς αἱ πέντε παρθένοι· ἀλλὰ ἀγρύπνως
καρτέρησον, ἵνα ὑπαντήσῃς Χριστῷ ἐν ἐλαίῳ πίονι, καὶ δῴη σοι τὸν νυμφῶνα
τὸν θεῖον τῆς δόξης αὐτοῦ. Δόξα.

Ὁ εἰδώς μου τὸ ἀνέτοιμον τοῦ βίου, μὴ ἐπάξῃς μοι τὸν θάνατον |²¹³ᵛ
αἰφνιδίως. Οἶδας τῆς φύσεώς μου τὸ ῥάθυμον· δός μοι νῦν κατάνυξιν πρὸ
τοῦ τέλους, πρεσβείαις τῆς Θεοτόκου καὶ σῶσόν με. Καὶ νῦν.⁶⁹

θεοτοκίον, Χαριστήριον αἶνον χρεωστικῶς, ὡς ἡ χήρα ἐκείνη δύο λεπτά,
προσφέρω σοι, Δέσποινα, ὑπὲρ πασῶν χαρίτων σου·⁷⁰ σὺ γὰρ ὤφθης σκέπη
μου, ὁμοῦ καὶ βοήθεια πειρασμῶν καὶ θλίψεων ἀεί με ἐξαίρουσα, ὅθεν ὡς ἐκ
μέσης φλογιζούσης καμίνου ῥυσθεὶς τῶν θλιβόντων με. Ἐκ καρδίας κραυγάζω
σοι· Θεοτόκε, βοήθει μοι πρεσβεύουσα Χριστῷ τῷ Θεῷ τῶν πταισμάτων
ἄφεσιν δοθῆναί μοι· σὲ γὰρ ἔχω ἐλπίδα ὁ δοῦλός σου.

Τὸ Κύριε ἐλέησον, μ΄, εἶτα τὴν εὐχὴν τοῦ ἁγίου Γρηγορίου τοῦ θεολόγου,

Σὲ καὶ νῦν εὐλογοῦμεν, Χριστέ μου, Λόγε |²¹⁴ Θεοῦ,
φῶς ἐκ φωτὸς ἀνάρχου καὶ Πνεύματος ταμία,
τριττοῦ φωτὸς εἰς μίαν δόξαν ἀθροιζομένου·
ὃς ἔλυσας τὸ σκότος, ὃς ὑπέστησας τὸ φῶς,
ἵν' ἐν φωτὶ κτίσῃς τὰ πάντα καὶ τὴν ἄστατον ὕλην
στήσῃς⁷¹ μορφῶν εἰς κόσμον καὶ τὴν νῦν εὐκοσμίαν·
ὃς νοῦν ἐφώτισας ἀνθρώπου λόγῳ τε καὶ σοφίᾳ,
λαμπρότητος τῆς ἄνω καὶ κάτω θεὶς εἰκόνα,
ἵνα φωτὶ βλέπῃ τὸ φῶς καὶ γένηται φῶς ὅλον,
σὺ φωστῆρσιν οὐρανὸν κατηύγασας ποικίλοις·
σὺ νύκτα⁷² καὶ ἡμέραν ἀλλήλαις εἴκειν ἠπίως
ἔταξας,⁷³ νόμον τιμῶν ἀδελφότητος καὶ φιλίας·

69. καὶ νῦν indicated in the margin.
71. Scribe breaks after στήσῃς.
73. Scribe breaks after ἔταξας.

70. σου added above the line.
72. νύκτα: C.

*"Behold: your **bridegroom**"* (Mt 25:6). *Watch, then, my soul, lest you nod off in sleep and remain outside, knocking like the five virgins. Instead, keep steadfast without sleeping, so that you may go to meet Christ who is rich with oil, and he grant you the divine bridal chamber of his glory.*

Glory.

You who know my unpreparedness in life, do not strike me suddenly with death. You know the sluggishness of my nature; now, before the end, grant me remorse, through the entreaties of the Theotokos and save me.

Both now.

theotokion, *Like that widow (who gave) two coins,*[42] *I offer you in repayment, O sovereign lady, praise of thanksgiving for all your favors, since you appeared as my shelter and also my help, you who always deliver me from temptations and afflictions, who pulled me away from those who afflict me as if from the midst of a burning oven. I cry to you from the heart, O Theotokos, help me (by) interceding with Christ our God to give me remission for my sins, for I, your servant, put my hope in you.*

Lord, have mercy forty times, then the

prayer of St. Gregory (of Nazianzen) the Theologian,

Even now we bless you, O my Christ, Word of God,
You who are light from uncreated light and the keeper of the Spirit,
Light of the threefold light that is gathered into one glory,
You who dispelled the darkness, the one who set up the light
so that in light you might create all things, and that you might make chaotic matter stable,
Shaping it into the world that is now well ordered.
You (are he) who enlightened the mind of man with both reason and wisdom,
Who made an image below of the splendor that is above,
So that by light he might look upon the light and become wholly light.
You who illuminated the heavens with many-colored lights,
You ordered the night and day to make way gently to one another,
Honoring the law of brotherhood and friendship;
In the one you brought an end to the weariness of our toiling flesh,

42. Cf. Mk 12:42.

καὶ τῇ μὲν⁷⁴ ἔπαυσας κόπους τῆς πολυμόχθου σαρκὸς
τῇ δὲ⁷⁵ ἤγειρας εἰς ἔργα καὶ πράξεις τὰς σοὶ φίλας,
ἵνα τὸ σκότος |²¹⁴ᵛ φυγόντες φθάσωμεν εἰς ἡμέραν,
ἡμέραν τὴν μὴ νυκτὶ τῇ στυγνῇ διαλυομένην.
Σὺ μὲν βάλλοις ἐλαφρὸν ὕπνον ἐμοῖς βλεφάροις,
ὡς μὴ γλῶσσαν ὑμνῳδὸν ἐπὶ πολὺ νεκροῦσθαι·
μηδ'⁷⁶ ἀντίφωνον ἀγγέλων πλάσμα σὸν ἡσυχάζοι·
σὺν σοὶ δὲ κοίτῃ εὐσεβεῖς ἐννοίας ἐταζέτω,
μηδέ τι τῶν ῥυπαρῶν ἡμέρας νὺξ ἐλέγξῃ,
μὴ δὲ παίγνια νυκτὸς ἐνύπνια θροείτω·
νοῦς δὲ καὶ σώματος δίχα σοί, Θεέ, προσλαλείτω,
τῷ Πατρὶ καὶ τῷ Υἱῷ καὶ τῷ ἁγίῳ Πνεύματι,
ᾧ τιμή, δόξα, κράτος, νῦν καὶ ἀεὶ καὶ εἰς τοὺς αἰῶνας τῶν αἰώνων· ἀμήν.

Τοῦ μακαριωτάτου μοναχοῦ κυροῦ Γρηγορίου στίχοι⁷⁷

Ὦ Πάτερ, Υἱέ, Πνεῦμα, Τριὰς ἁγία,
ὅταν καθίσῃς εἰς ἐπηρμένον θρόνον,
ὅτε κρίνῃς με τὸν κατακεκριμμένον
πάντων ὁρώντων καὶ τρόμῳ πεφρικότων·
μὴ διανοίξῃς βιβλίον συνειδότος,
μὴ στηλιτεύσῃς τὰς ἐμὰς ἀσωτίας,
μὴ τοῖς ἐρίφοις τοῖς κεκατηραμένοις
ἐμὲ συνάψῃς τὸν κεκατηρευμένον,
ἀλλὰ προβάτοις τοῖς μεμακαρισμένοις
αἰῶνι τῷ μέλλοντι τῷ σωτηρίῳ.

74. μὲν accented twice.   75. δὲ accented twice.
76. μὴ δ': C.
77. Fol. 232v, written by the scribe at the end of the psalter, following Ps 151, Odes 1–7, Hymn of the Three Youths (Ode 8:52–56), Ode 8 (Ode 8:57–88 and apostles, prophets, etc.), Ode 9 (Ode 9:46–55). Prayer of Zachariah (Ode 9:68–79); in all, fols. 214v–232v.

And in the other you awakened us to our labors and to works pleasing to you,
So that escaping the darkness we might arrive at the day,
Day that is not dispelled by the gloomy night.
Oh, may you cast a light sleep over my eyelids,
So as not to long deaden my tongue that sings (your) praise;
May the antiphonal singing between the angels, the work of your hands,
not be silenced;
Let (my) going to bed test, with your help, my pious intentions;
And let the night not convict any of the foul things of the day;
May the fantasies of the night not upset (my) dreams;
Let the mind, separated from the body, speak with you, O God,
With the Father and the Son and the Holy Spirit,
To whom (is due) honor, glory, power, now and always and for ever and
ever. Amen.

Verses of the most blessed monk Kyr Gregory

Oh Father, Son, Spirit: holy Trinity,
Whenever you take your place on the exalted throne,
When you judge me—one who has (already) been condemned
While all are looking on and shuddering with fear—
May you not open the scroll of my conscience,
May you not announce my prodigality,
May you not join me, the accursed,
With the goats that have been cursed,
But rather with the sheep that have been blessed
With the salvation in the age to come.

II

HOROLOGION

Εὐχὴ ὀφείλουσα λέγεσθαι ἅμα τῷ τοῦ ὕπνου ἐξεγερθῆναι

Εὐχαριστῶ σοι, ἁγία Τριάς, Θεὲ τῶν θεῶν καὶ Κύριε πάσης ἐξουσίας καὶ πνοῆς, ὁ ποιήσας εἰς ἐμὲ τὸν ἁμαρτωλὸν καὶ ἀνάξιον τὸ μέγα σου ἔλεος, καὶ θαυμαστώσας ἐν τῇ ταπεινώσει μου τὴν σὴν ἀγαθότητα· καὶ τὰ νῦν ἐξεγειρόμενος ἀπὸ τῆς ἐφαμάρτου μου στρωμνῆς καὶ τοῦ ὕπνου, δοξολογῶ σου τὴν δύναμιν, μεγαλύνω τὴν εὐσπλαγχνίαν σου καὶ ἀνυμνῶ σου τὸ κράτος. Ἔπιδε πρὸς τὴν ταπείνωσιν τοῦ δούλου σου, καὶ δός μοι βοήθειαν καὶ δύναμιν πρὸς τὸ διὰ τῆς χάριτός σου ἀντιταχθῆναι ὁρατοῖς καὶ ἀοράτοις ἐχθροῖς. Οἶδας γάρ, Κύριε, τὰς καρδίας ἡμῶν, καὶ γινώσκεις ὅτι πρὸς σὲ τὴν ἐλπίδα ἔχομεν καὶ τοὺς τῆς διανοίας ὀφθαλμοὺς ἀνατείνομεν· κἂν διὰ τὰ πονηρὰ ἡμῶν ἔργα καὶ τὰς ἁμαρτίας καταισχυνώμεθα ἐνώπιόν σου μετὰ παρρησίας στῆναι, ἀλλὰ παρὰ σοῦ, διὰ τὸ πλῆθος τῶν οἰκτιρμῶν σου, προσδεχόμεθα καὶ ἐξομολογούμεθά σοι· ὁ Θεός, |²³³ᵛ *Θεὸς ἡμῶν, τὴν βοήθειαν καὶ σωτηρίαν καὶ συντήρησιν παράσχου ἡμῖν, ἵνα εὐλογῶμεν σὺν τῷ Πατρὶ καὶ τὸν Υἱὸν καὶ τὸ ἅγιον Πνεῦμα εἰς τοὺς αἰῶνας τῶν αἰώνων· ἀμήν.*

Εὐχὴ ἑτέρα[78]

Κύριε ὁ Θεὸς ἡμῶν, ὁ διαναπαύσας ἡμᾶς ἐν τῷ ὕπνῳ καὶ παρασχὼν ἡμῖν ἐκ τῆς κοίτης ἐξεγερθῆναι, αὐτός, φιλάνθρωπε βασιλεῦ, πᾶσαν ῥαθυμίαν, πᾶσαν κάκωσιν ψυχῆς καὶ σώματος ἀπόστησον ἀφ' ἡμῶν τῇ ἐνεργείᾳ τοῦ ἁγίου σου Πνεύματος. Πᾶσαν ταραχὴν ἀπέλασον λογισμῶν, πᾶσαν φαντασίαν καὶ ἔννοιαν ἀπρεπῆ, καὶ καταξίωσον ἡμᾶς ἐν καθαρᾷ καρδίᾳ, ἐν νοΐ ἀμετεωρίστῳ πρὸς σὲ μόνον ἀτενίζειν· καὶ τῇ σῇ ἀκορέστῳ ἐπιθυμίᾳ κατεχομένους δοξάζειν καὶ εὐχαριστεῖν σοι κατὰ τὸ μέτρον τῆς ἀσθενείας ἡμῶν, καὶ ἀκαταγνώστως προσφέρειν σοι, ὥσπερ ἀπαρχάς, τὰς πρώτας κινήσεις τῆς καρδίας ἡμῶν τὰς μετὰ τὴν ἐξ ὕπνου ἐξέγερσιν. Ἀσφάλισαι ἡμᾶς ἐν τῇ σῇ χάριτι ἐκ πάσης δαιμονικῆς προσβολῆς, καὶ ἱκάνωσον καὶ κοιταζομένους εὐχαριστεῖν σοι, καὶ ἀνισταμένους δοξολογεῖν σε καὶ πάντοτε ὑμνεῖν σε καθαρῷ συνειδότι, πρεσβείαις τῆς |²³⁴ *ἀχράντου δεσποίνης ἡμῶν Θεοτόκου καὶ ἀειπαρθένου Μαρίας, τῶν θείων καὶ ἱεραρχῶν λειτουργῶν σου σεραφὶμ τῆς πρώτης*

---

78. εὐχὴ ἑτέρα written in the margin.

(II.1
Prayers on Rising, Mesonyktikon [Midnight Hour],
Matins, and First Hour)

Prayer due to be said upon awakening from sleep: *I thank you, O holy Trinity,* **God of gods** (Ps 49:1) *and Lord of all power and spirit, you who showed me, the unworthy sinner, your great mercy and who magnified your goodness in the face of my affliction. Now, upon arising from my bed of sin and from sleep, I glorify your power, I extol your compassion, I praise your strength. Look upon the affliction of your servant, and by means of your grace give me the help and strength to mount a resistance against visible and invisible enemies. You, O Lord, know our hearts, and you understand that we have hope in you and that we lift up the eyes of our minds to you. And if, because of our wicked deeds and sins, we are ashamed to stand in your presence with confidence, nevertheless through the* **fullness of your compassion** (Ps 50:3) *we are received with favor by you and confess to you: O God, our God, give us help, deliverance and protection, so that we might praise, along with the Father, the Son, and the Holy Spirit, for ever and ever. Amen.*

Another prayer: *O Lord our God, you who gave us rest through sleep and allowed us to rise from bed, O benevolent king, by the workings of your Holy Spirit keep us from all torpor, from every affliction of body and soul. Drive away all unsettling thoughts, every fantasy and unseemly idea, and consider us worthy to gaze on you alone with a pure heart (and) mind free of distraction; also (consider us), who are possessed by an insatiable desire for you, worthy to glorify and thank you according to the measure of our weakness, and blamelessly to offer you, as the first fruits of the day, the initial stirring of our hearts upon awakening from sleep. Fortify us with your grace against every demonic assault, and enable us to offer you thanks even in sleep, and to glorify you when we have risen, and constantly to praise you with a clean conscience—through the intercessions of our undefiled sovereign lady, mother of God and ever-pure Mary, your sacred and ministerial seraphim, the first hierarchical order—and to glorify you with the Father and your all-holy, good, and life-giving Spirit, now and always and forever. Amen.*

ἱεραρχίας καὶ διακοσμήσεως καὶ δοξάζειν σε σὺν τῷ Πατρὶ καὶ τῷ παναγίῳ καὶ ἀγαθῷ καὶ ζωοποιῷ σου Πνεύματι νῦν καὶ ἀεὶ καὶ εἰς τοὺς αἰῶνας· ἀμήν.

Καὶ εὐθὺς τὸ *Δεῦτε, προσκυνήσωμεν,* καὶ τὸν Ν'· εἶτα τρισάγιον καὶ τροπάρια,

Ἐλέησον ἡμᾶς, Κύριε, ἐλέησον ἡμᾶς, πάσης γὰρ ἀπολογίας ἀποροῦντες ταύτην σοι τὴν ἱκεσίαν ὡς Δεσπότῃ ἁμαρτωλοὶ προσφέρομεν· Ἐλέησον ἡμᾶς, Κύριε, ἐλέησον ἡμᾶς. Δόξα.[79]

Κύριε, ἐλέησον ἡμᾶς, ἐπὶ σοὶ γὰρ πεποίθαμεν· μὴ ὀργισθῇς ἡμῖν σφόδρα, μηδὲ μνησθῇς τῶν ἀνομιῶν ἡμῶν, ἀλλ' ἐπίβλεψον καὶ νῦν ὡς εὔσπλαγχνος καὶ λύτρωσαι ἡμᾶς ἐκ τῶν ἐχθρῶν ἡμῶν· σὺ γὰρ εἶ Θεὸς ἡμῶν καὶ ἡμεῖς λαός σου, πάντες ἔργα χειρῶν σου, καὶ τῷ ὀνόματί σου ἐπικεκλήμεθα. Καὶ νῦν.

θεοτοκίον, *Τῆς εὐσπλαγχνίας τὴν πύλην ἄνοιξον ἡμῖν, εὐλογημένη Θεοτόκε· ἐλπίζοντες εἰς σέ, μὴ ἀστοχήσωμεν· ῥυσθῶμεν διὰ σοῦ τῶν περιστάσεων, σὺ γὰρ εἶ σωτηρία τοῦ γένους τῶν ἀνθρώπων.*

Κύριε, ἐλέησον, κ'· εὐχὴ[80] *συνάδουσα τῷ πεντηκοστῷ,* |[234v]
Κύριε ὁ Θεὸς ἡμῶν, ὁ τὴν διὰ μετανοίας ἄφεσιν τοῖς ἀνθρώποις δωρησάμενος, καὶ τύπον ἡμῖν ἐπιγνώσεως ἁμαρτημάτων καὶ ἐξομολογήσεως τὴν τοῦ προφήτου Δαυΐδ μετάνοιαν πρὸς συγχώρησιν ὑποδείξας, αὐτός, Δέσποτα, πολλοῖς ἡμᾶς καὶ μεγάλοις περιπεπτωκότας πλημμελήμασι, ἐλέησον κατὰ τὸ μέγα σου ἔλεος, καὶ κατὰ τὸ πλῆθος τῶν οἰκτιρμῶν σου ἐξάλειψον τὰ ἀνομήματα ἡμῶν· ὅτι σοὶ

---

79. δόξα indicated in the margin.
80. εὐχή written again in the margin of fol. 234v, at the start of the prayer.

(Office for forgiveness of sins[43])

And immediately the *Come, let us worship,*[44] and

Psalm 50, then (the)

Trisagion and

troparia:

Have mercy on us, O Lord, have mercy on us (Ps 122:3, Mt 20:30). *We who are sinners lacking any defense make this supplication to you who are our master: Have mercy on us, O Lord, have mercy on us.*

Glory.

O Lord, have mercy on us, for we have put our trust in you; be not irate with us (Is 64:8), *nor remember our iniquities* (Ps 78:8), *but look upon us even now* (Is 64:8) *as one who is compassionate. Save us from our enemies, for you are our God* (cf. Ps 24:5) *and we are your people* (Ps 78:13; cf. Is 64:8); *all men are the work of your hands* (Is 64:7) *and we are called by your name* (cf. Ps 79:19).

Both now.

theotokion: *Open to us the gate of compassion, O blessed Theotokos. We put our hope in you; do not let us fail. Through you let us be rescued from misfortune, for you are the race of mankind's deliverance.*

Lord, have mercy twenty times.

Prayer said together with the fiftieth psalm:[45] *O Lord our God, you have given mankind the gift of remission from sin through repentance, and for our forgiveness have shown us the prophet David's repentance as a model of the recognition of sins and confession. Master, according to your great mercy have mercy on us who have committed many grievous sins, and according to the fullness of your compassion blot out our transgressions* (Ps 50:3). *We*

43. See Parenti § III.4. A communal office.

44. Those formulas for which no reference is given appear in Common, Repeated Formulas, 27–28.

45. The rubric appears elsewhere (see P. P. Trempelas, *Μικρὸν Εὐχολόγιον* [Athens, 1955], 2:216–17) and may travel with the prayer, which is also said at the end of the Office for Trespasses (52) but, perhaps significantly, without the rubric. In some circumstances the prayer is said by the priest (see M. Arranz, "Les prières presbytérales des matins byzantines," *OCP* 37 [1971]: 426–28), but that would not be the case in the Office for Trespasses and may not be here either.

ἡμάρτομεν, Κύριε, τῷ τὰ ἄδηλα καὶ τὰ κρύφια τῆς καρδίας τῶν ἀνθρώπων γινώσκοντι, καὶ μόνῳ ἔχοντι ἐξουσίαν ἀφιέναι ἁμαρτίας. Καρδίαν δὲ καθαρὰν κτίσας ἐν ἡμῖν καὶ πνεύματι ἡγεμονικῷ στηρίξας ἡμᾶς· καὶ τὴν ἀγαλλίασιν τοῦ σωτηρίου σου γνωρίσας ἡμῖν, μὴ ἀπορρίψῃς ἡμᾶς ἀπὸ τοῦ προσώπου σου· ἀλλ' εὐδόκησον, ὡς ἀγαθὸς καὶ φιλάνθρωπος Θεός, μέχρι τῆς ἐσχάτης ἡμῶν ἀναπνοῆς, προσφέρειν σοι θυσίαν δικαιοσύνης καὶ ἀναφορὰν καὶ δέησιν ἐν τοῖς ἁγίοις σου καὶ οὐρανίοις θυσιαστηρίοις, ἐλέει καὶ φιλανθρωπίᾳ τοῦ μονογενοῦς σου Υἱοῦ, μεθ' οὗ εὐλογητὸς εἶ σὺν τῷ παναγίῳ καὶ ἀγαθῷ καὶ ζωοποιῷ σου Πνεύματι νῦν. |²³⁵

Εἶτα τρισάγιον καὶ τροπάρια νεκρώσιμα, Μνήσθητι, Κύριε, ὡς ἀγαθός, τῶν δούλων σου. Δόξα. Μετὰ τῶν ἁγίων ἀνάπαυσον. Καὶ νῦν. Σὲ καὶ τεῖχος καὶ λιμένα. Κύριε, ἐλέησον, ιε'· καὶ τὸ Δεῦτε, προσκυνήσωμεν· ψαλμὸς κς', Κύριος φωτισμός μου καὶ σωτήρ μου· τίνα φοβηθήσομαι; Εἶτα τὸ Κύριε παντοκράτωρ, καὶ τὸ Δόξα ἐν ὑψίστοις Θεῷ καὶ ἐπὶ γῆς εἰρήνη· εἶτα τρισάγιον, μεθ' ὃ τὸ τῆς κυριακῆς ἀναστάσιμον κάθισμα ἢ ἑτέρας ἑορτῆς ἢ ἁγίου τὸ ἀπολυτίκιον καὶ θεοτόκιν.

have sinned against you (Ps 50:6) *O Lord, you who know **the secrets and the
things hidden** (Ps 50:8) in the hearts of men, and who alone hold the power
to forgive sin* (cf. Mt 9:6). ***Create in us a clean heart*** (Ps 50:12), *and **establish
with us your guiding spirit*** (Ps 50:14). *You who taught us **the joy of your
salvation*** (Ps 50:14), ***do not cast us out of your presence*** (Ps 50:13), *but as
a good and benevolent God **consent** to our offering you, until our last breath,
a **sacrifice of righteousness and offering*** (Ps 50:21), *and supplication at your
holy and heavenly altars* (cf. Ps 50:21), *through the mercy and benevolence of
your only-begotten Son, with whom you are blessed along with your all-holy,
good, and life-giving Spirit, now <and always and for ever and ever. Amen>.*

(Remembrance of the Dead[46])

Then (the) Trisagion, and
troparia in remembrance of the dead:
Remember, O Lord, as the one who is good, your servants (HR 38).
Glory.
Give rest with the saints (HR 38).
Both now.
We have you as both fortress and haven (TR 21).[47]
Lord, have mercy fifteen times, and the

(Office of Mesonyktikon[48])

Come, let us worship.
Psalm 26: *The Lord is my light and my savior; whom shall I fear?* then
Lord almighty (Ode 12: Manasses),[49] and the
Glory to God in the highest and peace on earth (Lk 2:14), then (the)
Trisagion, after which the

---

46. See Parenti § III.5.

47. TR = Τριῴδιον κατανυκτικὸν περιέχον ἅπασαν τὴν ἀνήκουσαν αὐτῷ ἀκολουθίαν τῆς ἁγίας
καὶ μεγάλης τεσσαρακοστῆς (Rome, 1879).

48. Midnight office; See Parenti § III.6.

49. The ode numbers correspond to those in *Septuaginta*, ed. Rahlfs; this ode is without
number in the manuscript (fol. 172v).

Λιτῆς δὲ οὔσης ἡμέρας καὶ τοῦ Ἀλληλούϊα μέλλοντος ψάλλεσθαι, λέγει εἰς τὸ παρὸν τρισάγιον τροπάρια καθίσματα κατανυκτικά, ἦχος πλάγιος δ᾽,

Ὡς τοῦ κριτοῦ παρόντος μερίμνησον, ψυχή, καὶ τῆς φρικτῆς ἡμέρας τὴν ὥραν ἐννοοῦ· ἡ γὰρ κρίσις ἀνίλεως ἐστὶ τοῖς μὴ πράξασιν ἔλεος· διὸ φεῖσαί μου Σωτήρ, μόνος γὰρ ὑπάρχεις ἀναμάρτητος. Δόξα.

Ὁ χρόνος τῆς ζωῆς μου συντελεῖται, Δέσποτα, ὁ δὲ φρικτός σου θρόνος λοιπὸν εὐτρεπίζεται, ὁ βίος παρέρχεται, ἡ δὲ κρίσις ἐκδέχεται, ἀπειλοῦσά μοι τοῦ πυρὸς τὴν τιμωρίαν καὶ τὴν φλόγα τὴν ἄσβεστον. Δακρύων ὄμβρους πέμψον μοι καὶ σβέσον αὐτῆς τὴν ἰσχὺν ὁ θέλων πάντας ἀνθρώπους σωθῆναι. |²³⁵ᵛ *Καὶ νῦν.*[81]

Ἰδού, ὁ νυμφίος ἔρχεται ἐν τῷ μέσῳ τῆς νυκτὸς καὶ μακάριος ὁ δοῦλος ὃν εὑρήσει γρηγοροῦντα· ἀνάξιος δὲ πάλιν ὃν εὑρήσει ῥαθυμοῦντα. Βλέπε οὖν, ψυχή μου, μὴ τῷ ὕπνῳ κατενεχθῇς καὶ τῆς βασιλείας ἀποκλεισθῇς, ἀλλὰ ἀνάνηψον κράζουσα· Ἅγιος, ἅγιος, ἅγιος εἶ ὁ Θεός· διὰ τῆς Θεοτόκου ἐλέησον ἡμᾶς.

Τὸ *Κύριε, ἐλέησον,* κ᾽· καὶ εὐθὺς τὸ *Δόξα τῇ ἁγίᾳ καὶ ὁμοουσίῳ καὶ ἀδιαιρέτῳ Τριάδι, πάντοτε καὶ νῦν καὶ ἀεὶ καὶ εἰς τοὺς αἰῶνας τῶν αἰώνων·*

---

81. καὶ νῦν indicated in the margin.

Sunday resurrection hymn,[50] or the apolytikion[51] of another feast or saint, and theotokion.

When it is a weekday[52] and the Alleluia[53] is about to be chanted, say at this Trisagion the penitential troparia kathismata plagal mode IV:

Take care, O soul, as if the judge were present, and ponder the hour of the terrible day, **for the judgment on those who did not practice mercy is merciless** *(Jas 2:13). On this account, spare me, O savior, for you alone are without sin.*

Glory.

The span of my life is drawing to a close, O master, your terrible throne is now being prepared, life passes away, the judgment awaits, threatening me with punishment by fire and the unquenchable flames (cf. Mt 3:12). Send me showers of tears and quench its strength, O you **who wish all mankind to be saved** *(1 Tm 2:4).*

Both now.

Behold, the bridegroom comes *(Mt 25:6) in the middle of the night, and blessed is the servant whom he discovers alert, but the one he finds sluggish is instead (found) unworthy. Take care, my soul, that you are not weighed down by sleep and shut out of the kingdom. Regain your senses, crying, "Holy, holy, holy (Is 6:3) are you, O God; through the (intercession) of the Theotokos, have mercy on us."*

Lord, have mercy twenty times, and immediately

(Matins)

Glory to the holy, consubstantial, and indivisible Trinity, always, now and for ever and ever. Amen.[54]

---

50. The eight anastasima kathismata, one for each of the modes (and now referred to as "apolytikia": *HR* 771–80), consist of a troparion and theotokion; the pair chanted in mode I begins Τοῦ λίθου σφραγισθέντος and Τοῦ Γαβριὴλ φθεγξαμένου.

51. The troparion specific to the feast or saint of the day; the apolytikia are given in the synaxarion-menologion at the end of the offices (part III).

52. A rogation day, meaning, in effect, a weekday to distinguish the structure from those of Saturday, Sunday, and feast days.

53. See below 88.

54. The first line of this three-line formula is said by the priest to signal the beginning of matins (Studios Typikon, *BMFD*, 1:98 [2], when the monks then enter from the narthex to begin; see also St. Sabas Typikon: Dmitrievskij, *Opisanie*, 3:21). Following the invocation is the two-line response, *Glory to God ...*, of the people said before the hexapsalmos (Arranz, *Typicon de Messine*, 197.15–16).

ἀμήν. Δόξα ἐν ὑψίστοις Θεῷ καὶ ἐπὶ γῆς εἰρήνη, ἐν ἀνθρώποις εὐδοκία, λέγε ἐκ τρίτου· Κύριε, τὰ χείλη μου ἀνοίξεις, καὶ τὸ στόμα μου ἀναγγελεῖ τὴν αἴνεσίν σου, δίς· ψαλμὸς γ',[82] Κύριε, τί ἐπληθύνθησαν οἱ θλίβοντές με; λζ', Κύριε, μὴ τῷ θυμῷ σου ἐλέγξῃς με μὴ δὲ τῇ ὀργῇ σου· ξβ', Ὁ Θεὸς ὁ Θεός μου, πρὸς σὲ ὀρθρίζω· ἐδίψησεν. Δόξα καὶ νῦν. Ἀλληλούϊα, ἀλληλούϊα, δόξα σοι, ὁ Θεός, ἐκ γ'· εἶτα πζ', Κύριε ὁ Θεὸς τῆς σωτηρίας μου, ἡμέρας ἐκέκραξα· ρβ', Εὐλόγει, ἡ ψυχή μου, τὸν Κύριον καί, πάντα τὰ ἐντός· ρμβ', Κύριε, εἰσάκουσον τῆς προσευχῆς μου, ἐνώτισαι. |²³⁶ Δόξα καὶ νῦν. Ἀλληλούϊα, ἀλληλούϊα, δόξα σοι, ὁ Θεός, λέγε ἐκ γ'.

Εἶτα κυριακῆς μὲν οὔσης ἢ ἑορτῆς δεσποτικῆς ἢ ἁγίου τῶν ἐπισήμων, ψάλλεται τὸ Θεὸς Κύριος κατὰ τὸν ἦχον τοῦ ἀναστασίμου καθίσματος ἢ[83] τοῦ τῆς ἑορτῆς ἀπολυτικίου ἢ τοῦ ἁγίου. Στίχος α', Ἐξομολογεῖσθε τῷ Κυρίῳ, ὅτι ἀγαθός, ὅτι εἰς τὸν αἰῶνα τὸ ἔλεος αὐτοῦ· στίχος β', Πάντα τὰ ἔθνη ἐκύκλωσάν με, καὶ τῷ ὀνόματι Κυρίου ἠμυνάμην αὐτούς· στίχος γ', Οὐκ ἀποθανοῦμαι, ἀλλὰ ζήσομαι καὶ διηγήσομαι τὰ ἔργα Κυρίου· στίχος δ', Παρὰ Κυρίου ἐγένετο αὕτη καὶ ἔστι θαυμαστὴ ἐν ὀφθαλμοῖς ἡμῶν. Θεὸς Κύριος, καὶ ἐπέφανεν ἡμῖν· καὶ εὐθὺς τὸ τοῦ ἤχου ἀναστάσιμον τροπάριον ἢ τὸ τῆς ἑορτῆς ἢ τὸ τοῦ ἁγίου ἀπολυτίκιον καὶ θεοτοκίον πρὸς τὸν ἦχον.

Εἰ δὲ λιτή ἐστιν ἡμέρα, τὸ Ἀλληλούϊα εἰς τὸν ἦχον, οὗ ὁ πρῶτος στίχος· Διότι φῶς τὰ προστάγματά σου ἐπὶ τῆς γῆς· στίχος β', Καὶ νῦν πῦρ τοὺς ὑπεναντίους ἔδεται· στίχος γ', Πρόσθες κακὰ τοῖς ἐνδόξοις τῆς γῆς· στίχος δ', Οὕτως ἐγενήθημεν τῷ ἀγαπητῷ σου.

---

82. ψαλμός and the numbers γ' through ρμβ' are written in the margin.
83. καί: C.

Glory to God in the highest and on earth peace, among men goodwill (Lk 2:14), say three times.

O Lord, you will open my lips and my mouth will declare your praise (Ps 50:17) two times.

Psalm 3: *O Lord, why are they who afflict me multiplied?*
Psalm 37: *O Lord, rebuke me not in your anger, neither in your wrath.*
Psalm 62: *O God, my God, I cry to you early, my soul has thirsted.*
Glory, both now.
Alleluia, alleluia, glory to you, O God three times, then
Psalm 87: *O Lord God of my salvation, I have cried by day.*
Psalm 102: *Bless the Lord, O my Soul, and all that is within.*
Psalm 142: *O Lord, attend to my prayer; hearken.*
Glory, both now.
Alleluia, alleluia, glory to you, O God, say three times.

Then, when it is Sunday or a feast of the Lord or of a saint of distinction, God is the Lord is chanted according to the mode of the resurrection hymn or (that) of the apolytikion of the feast or saint.[55] First verse: *Give thanks to the Lord for he is good; for his mercy endures forever* (Ps 117:1); second verse: *All the nations compassed me about, but in the name of the Lord I repulsed them* (Ps 117:10); third verse: *I shall not die, but live and recount the works of the Lord* (Ps 117:17); fourth verse: *This has been done of the Lord; and it is wonderful in our eyes* (Ps 117:23); *God is the Lord, and he has shined upon us.*

And immediately (chant) the resurrection troparion[56] of the mode (of the week)—or the troparion of the feast or the apolytikion of the saint—and theotokion according to the mode.

But if it is a weekday (chant) the Alleluia in the mode (of the week), for which the first verse is *For your commandments are a light upon the earth* (Ode 5:9 [Is 26:9]); second verse: *And now fire shall devour the adversaries*

55. On Sunday, God is the Lord would normally be chanted in the mode of the week, that is, the mode of the resurrection hymn, unless a feast or saint were to be celebrated, in which case God is the Lord would be chanted in the mode of the apolytikion.

56. The troparion cited above, 87n50, as the anastasimon kathisma with accompanying theotokion.

Καὶ εὐθὺς τὰ τοῦ ἤχου τριαδικά, εἶτα ἡ στιχολογία καὶ μετὰ τὴν στιχολογίαν ὁ Ν' καὶ οἱ κανόνες καὶ ἡ λοιπὴ⁸⁴ ἀκολουθία τοῦ ὄρθρου. |²³⁶ᵛ

Τὰ τριαδικὰ τῶν ὀκτὼ ἤχων
ἦχος α'⁸⁵

Σωματικαῖς μορφώσεσι τῶν ἀσωμάτων δυνάμεων πρὸς νοερὰν καὶ ἄϋλον ἀναγόμενοι ἔννοιαν, καὶ τρισαγίῳ μελῳδήματι τρισυποστάτου θεότητος δεχόμενοι ἔλλαμψιν, χερουβικῶς βοήσωμεν· Ἅγιος, ἅγιος, ἅγιος εἶ ὁ Θεός, διὰ τῆς Θεοτόκου ἐλέησον ἡμᾶς.

Μετὰ πασῶν τῶν οὐρανίων δυνάμεων χερουβικῶς τῷ ἐν ὑψίστοις βοήσωμεν, τὸν τρισάγιον ἀναπέμποντες αἶνον· Ἅγιος, ἅγιος, ἅγιος εἶ ὁ Θεός, διὰ τῆς.

Ἐξεγερθέντες τοῦ ὕπνου προσπίπτωμέν σοι, ἀγαθέ, καὶ τῶν ἀγγέλων τὸν ὕμνον βοῶμέν σοι, δυνατέ· Ἅγιος, ἅγιος, ἅγιος εἶ ὁ Θεός, διὰ τῆς.

ἦχος β'

Τὰς ἄνω δυνάμεις μιμούμενοι ἐπὶ γῆς, ἐπινίκιον ὕμνον προσφέρομέν σοι, ἀγαθέ· Ἅγιος, ἅγιος, ἅγιος εἶ ὁ Θεός, ὁ ἐν τρισὶν ὑποστάσεσιν καὶ μιᾷ θεότητι προσκυνούμενος.

Ἄκτιστε φύσις, ἡ τῶν ὅλων δημιουργός, τὰ χείλη ἡμῶν ἄνοιξον, ὅπως

---

84. οἱ λοιπ<οὶ>: C.
85. ἦχος α' and the other mode designations are indicated in the margins.

(Ode 5:11 [Is 26:11]); third verse: *Bring more evils on the glorious ones of the earth* (Ode 5:15 [Is 26:15]); fourth verse: *So we have been to your beloved* (Ode 5:17 [Is 26:17]).

And immediately the Trinitarian Hymns of the mode (of the week), then continuous psalmody,[57] and after the continuous psalmody, Psalm 50, the canons, and the remaining office of matins.

The Trinitarian Hymns of the eight modes[58]

Mode I

In corporeal likeness of the incorporeal powers, we are raised up to a spiritual and immaterial understanding, and receive through the thrice-holy chant the illumination of the triune Deity. Let us cry out in the manner of the cherubim , "Holy, holy, holy[59] are you, O God." Through (the intercession of) the Theotokos, have mercy on us.

With all the powers of the heavens let us cry out to him in the highest, as we offer up the thrice-holy praise in the manner of the cherubim, "Holy, holy, holy are you, O God." Through <the intercession of the Theotokos have mercy on us>.

Arising from sleep, let us fall down in supplication before you, O one who is good. Let us cry out to you the hymn of the angels, O mighty one, "Holy, holy, holy are you, O God." Through the <intercession of the Theotokos have mercy on us>.

Mode II

We on earth who emulate the powers above offer a triumphal hymn to you, O one who is good, "Holy, holy, holy are you, O God," who are worshiped as one Deity in three persons.

Uncreated being, the maker of everything, open our lips so that we might

---

57. Stichologia: the recitation of the psalms verse by verse; the number of kathismata is unspecified for weekdays but given below as two for Sundays.

58. The triplet chanted is that in the mode of the week. The final clauses are variable in *HR* 79–85; *TR* 761–65; Παρακλητικὴ ἤτοι ὀκτώηχος ἡ μεγάλη (Rome, 1885), 713–15 [hereafter "*PaR*"]. Here they are completed following the formula used in the first hymn and occasionally thereafter.

59. Cf. Is 6:3.

ἀναγγέλλωμεν τὴν αἴνεσίν σου βοῶντες· Ἅγιος, ἅγιος, ἅγιος εἶ ὁ Θεός, διὰ τῆς Θεοτόκου.

Τῆς κλίνης καὶ τοῦ ὕπνου ἐξεγείρας με, Κύριε· τὸν νοῦν μου φώτισον καὶ τὴν καρδίαν, καὶ τὰ χείλη μου |²³⁷ ἄνοιξον εἰς τὸ ὑμνεῖν σε, ἁγία Τριάς· Ἅγιος, ἅγιος, ἅγιος εἶ.

ἦχος γ᾽

Τριὰς ὁμοούσιε καὶ ἀδιαίρετε, μονὰς τρισυπόστατε καὶ συναΐδιε, σοὶ ὡς Θεῷ τῶν ἀγγέλων τὸν ὕμνον βοῶμεν· Ἅγιος ἅγιος, ἅγιος εἶ ὁ Θεός.

Πατέρα ἄναρχον, Υἱὸν συνάναρχον, Πνεῦμα συναΐδιον, θεότητα μίαν χερουβικῶς δοξάσωμεν· Ἅγιος, ἅγιος, ἅγιος εἶ ὁ Θεός, διὰ τῆς Θεοτόκου ἐλέησον.

Ἀθρόον ὁ κριτὴς ἐπελεύσεται, καὶ ἑκάστου αἱ πράξεις γυμνωθήσονται· ἀλλὰ φόβῳ κράξωμεν ἐν τῷ μέσῳ τῆς νυκτός· Ἅγιος, ἅγιος, ἅγιος εἶ ὁ.

ἦχος δ᾽

Τὸν ἄναρχόν σου Πατέρα, καὶ σέ, Χριστὲ ὁ Θεός, καὶ τὸ πανάγιόν σου Πνεῦμα χερουβικῶς δοξολογεῖν τολμῶντες, λέγομεν· Ἅγιος, ἅγιος, ἅγιος εἶ ὁ Θεός.

Ὡς αἱ τάξεις νῦν τῶν ἀγγέλων ἐν οὐρανῷ, καὶ στάσ<ε>ις φόβῳ ἀνθρώπων ἐπὶ τῆς γῆς, ἐπινίκιον ὕμνον προσφέρομέν σοι, ἀγαθέ· Ἅγιος, ἅγιος, ἅγιος.

Τῶν νοερῶν σου λειτουργῶν προσφέρειν οἱ θνητοὶ τὸν ὕμνον τολμῶντες, λέγομεν· Ἅγιος, ἅγιος, ἅγιος εἶ ὁ.

ἦχος πλάγιος α᾽

Εἰκονίζειν τολμῶντες τὰ νοερά σου στρατεύματα, Τριὰς ἄναρχε, στόμασιν ἀναξίοις βοῶμέν σοι· Ἅγιος, ἅγιος, ἅγιος εἶ ὁ Θεός, διὰ τῆς.

proclaim your praise (cf. Ps 50:17), *crying out, "Holy, holy, holy are you, O God." Through (the intercession of) the Theotokos <have mercy on us>.*

Having awakened me from bed and sleep, O Lord, enlighten my mind and heart; open my lips so as to sing praise to you (cf. Ps 50:17), holy Trinity, "Holy, holy, holy are you <O God." Through the intercession of the Theotokos have mercy on us>.

Mode III

Consubstantial and indivisible Trinity, unity of three Persons coeternal, to you who are God we cry out the hymn of the angels, "Holy, holy, holy are you, O God." <Through the intercession of the Theotokos have mercy on us.>

In the manner of the cherubim let us glorify the Father without beginning, the equally without beginning Son, the coeternal Spirit, one Deity, "Holy, holy, holy are you, O God." Through (the intercession of) the Theotokos have mercy <on us>.

All at once the judge will arrive and each man's deeds will be laid bare; in the middle of the night let us call out in fear, "Holy, holy, holy are you <O God." Through the intercession of the Theotokos have mercy on us>.

Mode IV

Daring to glorify in the manner of the cherubim your Father without beginning and you, Christ our God, and your all-holy Spirit, we say, "Holy, holy, holy are you, O God." <Through the intercession of the Theotokos have mercy on us.>

Now, like the orders of the angels in heaven, we, the companies of men (gathered) in fear on earth, offer to you, O good one, the triumphal hymn, "Holy, holy, holy <are you, O God." Through the intercession of the Theotokos have mercy on us>.

Daring to offer the hymn of the spiritual ones who minister to you, we mortals recite, "Holy, holy, holy are you <O God." Through the intercession of the Theotokos have mercy on us>.

Plagal mode I

Daring to represent your spiritual ranks, O Trinity without beginning, we cry out to you with our unworthy mouths, "Holy, holy, holy are you, O God." Through the <intercession of the Theotokos have mercy on us>.

Ὑμνῳδίας ὁ καιρὸς καὶ δεήσεως ὥρα· ἐκτενῶς |²³⁷ᵛ βοήσωμεν τῷ μόνῳ Θεῷ· Ἅγιος, ἅγιος, ἅγιος εἶ ὁ Θεός.

Ὁ ἐν μήτρᾳ παρθενικῇ χωρηθείς, καὶ τῶν κόλπων τοῦ Πατρὸς μὴ χωρισθείς, σὺν ἀγγέλοις καὶ ἡμᾶς πρόσδεξαι, Χριστὲ ὁ Θεός, βοῶντάς σοι· Ἅγιος, ἅγιος, ἅγιος εἶ ὁ Θεός, διὰ τῆς Θεοτόκου ἐλέησον.

ἦχος πλάγιος β'

Ἀσωμάτοις στόμασιν, ἀσιγήτοις δοξολογίαις τὰ ἐξαπτέρυγα ᾄδουσί σοι τὸν τρισάγιον ὕμνον, ὁ Θεὸς ἡμῶν· καὶ ἡμεῖς οἱ ἐπὶ γῆς ἀναξίοις χείλεσιν αἰνόν σοι ἀναπέμπομεν· Ἅγιος, ἅγιος, ἅγιος εἶ ⁸⁶ ὁ Θεός.

Παριστάμενα φόβῳ τὰ χερουβίμ, ἐξιστάμενα τρόμῳ τὰ σεραφὶμ τὸν τρισάγιον ὕμνον προσφέρει ἀσιγήτῳ φωνῇ, μεθ' ὧν καὶ ἡμεῖς βοῶμεν οἱ ἁμαρτωλοί· Ἅγιος, ἅγιος, ἅγιος εἶ ὁ Θεός, διὰ τῆς Θεοτόκου.

Τριαδικῆς μονάδος θεότητα ἀσυγχύτῳ ἑνώσει δοξάζοντες τῶν ἀγγέλων τὸν ὕμνον βοήσωμεν· Ἅγιος, ἅγιος, ἅγιος εἶ.

ἦχος βαρύς

Τῇ ἀπροσίτῳ θεότητι, τῇ ἐν μονάδι Τριάδι, τῶν σεραφὶμ τὸν τρισάγιον ἀναπέμποντες αἶνον, μετὰ φόβου βοήσωμεν· Ἅγιος, ἅγιος, ἅγιος εἶ ὁ Θεός, διὰ τῆς Θεοτόκου. |²³⁸

Ὁ ὑψίστῳ δυνάμει χερουβικῶς ἀνυμνούμενος, καὶ θεϊκῇ τῇ δόξῃ ἀγγελικῶς προσκυνούμενος, πρόσδεξαι καὶ ἡμᾶς τοὺς ἁμαρτωλοὺς ἀναξίως τολμῶντας κράζειν σοι· Ἅγιος, ἅγιος, ἅγιος εἶ ὁ Θεός.

Ὡς ὕπνον τὸν ὄκνον ἀποθεμένη, ψυχή, διόρθωσιν πρὸς ἔγερσιν δεῖξον τῷ κριτῇ καὶ ἐν φόβῳ βόησον· Ἅγιος, ἅγιος, ἅγιος εἶ ὁ Θεός.

---

86. εἶ added above the line.

It is the time for singing hymns and the hour of supplication; let us fervently cry out to the one God, "Holy, holy, holy are you, O God." <Through the intercession of the Theotokos have mercy on us.>

You who were contained in a virgin womb but were not separated from the bosom of the Father, O Christ our God, accept us who cry out to you with the angels, "Holy, holy, holy are you, O God." Through (the intercession of) the Theotokos have mercy on <us>.

Plagal mode II

With incorporeal mouths (and) unceasing praise, the six-winged beings sing to you, O our God, the thrice-holy hymn, and we who are upon the earth offer up to you praise with unworthy lips, "Holy, holy, holy are you, O God." <Through the intercession of the Theotokos have mercy on us.>

The cherubim frozen in fear, the seraphim struck in amazement, trembling, offer the thrice-holy hymn in a voice that never ceases; we sinners, too, cry out with them, "Holy, holy, holy are you O God." Through (the intercession of) the Theotokos <have mercy on us>.

Glorifying the Deity of a triune monad in a union that is without confusion, let us cry out the hymn of the angels, "Holy, holy, holy are you <O God." Through the intercession of the Theotokos have mercy on us>.

Barys mode

Offering up the thrice-holy praise of the seraphim to the unapproachable Deity, the Trinity in one being, let us cry out in fear, "Holy, holy, holy are you, O God." Through (the intercession of) the Theotokos <have mercy on us>.

You who are praised in song by the cherubim in the highest power and who are worshiped by angels in divine glory, receive us sinners who undeservedly dare to call out to you, "Holy, holy, holy are you, O God." <Through the intercession of the Theotokos have mercy on us>.

Having put off indolence like sleep, O soul, show the judge your reformation to an awakening and cry in fear, "Holy, holy, holy are you, O God." <Through the intercession of the Theotokos have mercy on us.>

ἦχος πλάγιος δ᾽

Εἰς οὐρανὸν τὰς καρδίας ἔχοντες, ἀγγελικὴν μιμησώμεθα τάξιν καὶ ἐν φόβῳ τῷ ἀδεκάστῳ προσπέσωμεν, ἐπινίκιον ἀνακράζοντες αἶνον· Ἅγιος, ἅγιος, ἅγιος εἶ ὁ Θεός.

Ὁρᾶν σε μὴ τολμῶντα τὰ χερουβίμ, ἱπτάμενα κραυγάζει ἀλαλαγμῷ τὸ ἔνθεον μέλος τῆς τρισαγίας φωνῆς· σὺν αὐτοῖς καὶ ἡμεῖς βοῶμέν σοι· Ἅγιος, ἅγιος, ἅγιος εἶ ὁ Θεός.

Κατακαμπτόμενοι τῷ πλήθει τῶν πταισμάτων ἡμῶν καὶ μὴ τολμῶντες ἀτενίσαι τῷ ὕψει σου, τὴν ψυχὴν σὺν τῷ σώματι κλίναντες, μετὰ ἀγγέλων τὸν ὕμνον βοῶμέν σοι· Ἅγιος, ἅγιος, ἅγιος εἶ.

Ταῦτα μὲν ψάλλονται εἰς τὸ Ἀλληλούϊα

Ἐν δὲ τοῖς σάββασι ψάλλεται Θεὸς Κύριος εἰς ἦχον β᾽, εἶτα τὰ τροπάρια ταῦτα, β᾽,[87] Ἀπόστολοι, μάρτυρες καὶ προφῆται. |[238v] Δόξα.[88] Μνήσθητι, Κύριε, ὡς ἀγαθός,[89] τῶν δούλων. Καὶ νῦν. Μήτηρ ἁγία τοῦ ἀφράστου.

Ταῖς δὲ κυριακαῖς ψάλλεται τὸ Θεὸς Κύριος πρὸς τὸν ἐνεστῶτα ἦχον· εἶτα λέγεται τὸ ἀναστάσιμον τροπάριον ἐκ β᾽ καὶ τὸ θεοτοκίον αὐτοῦ, καὶ εὐθὺς ἄρχονται στιχολογεῖν καθίσματα β᾽· εἶτα ἡ ὑπακοὴ τοῦ ἤχου καὶ οἱ

---

87. β᾽ indicated in the margin.
88. δόξα indicated in the margin.
89. τῶν ψυχῶν: C, corrected from fol. 258v.

Plagal mode IV

Having our hearts to heaven, let us emulate the angelic order and fall down in fear before the impartial (one) as we raise our voices in the triumphal hymn, "Holy, holy, holy are you, O God." <Through the intercession of the Theotokos have mercy on us.>

Not daring to look upon you, the cherubim as they fly call out with a shout the divinely inspired song of the thrice-holy expression; with them we, too, cry out to you, "Holy, holy, holy are you, O God." <Through the intercession of the Theotokos have mercy on us.>

Bent down by the multitude of our errors and not daring to gaze up to your height, we bow our soul with the body and along with the angels cry out to you the hymn, "Holy, holy, holy are you <O God." Through the intercession of the Theotokos have mercy on us.> These are chanted at the Alleluia.

On Saturdays God is the Lord is chanted in the second mode, then these troparia, two times:

> *Apostles, martyrs, and prophets* (TR 289).
> *Glory.*
> *Remember, O Lord, as the one who is good, your servants* (TR 289).
> *Both now.*
> *Holy mother of the ineffable light* (TR 289).

On Sundays God is the Lord is chanted in the appointed mode;[60] then the resurrection troparion is said two times with its theotokion,[61] and immediately

> begin continuous psalmody, two kathismata, then the hypakoe[62] of the mode (of the week) and the ([63])

---

60. See above 88, 89n55.

61. For these see above 87n50.

62. Hypakoe: a class of troparion chanted in the mode of the week. They are found in a separate volume: Μέγας ἱερὸς συνέκδημος (Athens, n.d.), 161–68 [hereafter "*MHS*"]: first mode hypakoe begins Ἡ τοῦ λῃστοῦ.

63. Contemporary sources specify a prose reading—whether sermon, commentary or saint's life—following the hypakoe and before the gradual hymns: e.g., *Synaxarion of Evergetis*, ed. Jordan, 1:10 [O.5.h.i]; Arranz, *Typicon de Messine*, 13.15; and possibly the Studios Typikon: *BMFD*, 1:102 [4].

ἀναβαθμοί, ἔπειτα ἀντὶ τοῦ *Ἀνάστηθι* τὸ *Πᾶσα πνοή·* εἶτα τὸ εὐαγγέλιον, καὶ ἀπὸ τοῦ εὐαγγελίου λέγετε *Ἀνάστασιν Χριστοῦ θεασάμενοι* καὶ ὁ Ν'· εἶτα οἱ κανόνες καὶ τὸ ἐξαποστειλάριον τοῦ ἤχου ἀναστασίμον ἢ ἀντὶ τούτου τὸ *Ἅγιος Κύριος ἡμῶν·* εἶτα οἱ Αἶνοι καὶ εἶθ' οὕτως τὰ ἀναστάσιμα στιχηρὰ εἰς τοὺς Αἴνους· εἶτα τὸ *Δόξα ἐν ὑψίστοις Θεῷ καὶ ἐπί·* τὸ *Ἅγιος ὁ Θεός,* γ'· εἶτα ψάλλετε ἡ α' ὥρα καὶ ἀπολύει.

gradual hymns;[64] thereupon, instead of the Arise[65] the
Let everything that has breath (Ps 150:6), then the
Gospel reading;[66] then after the Gospel say
Having seen Christ's resurrection (PaR 549), and
Psalm 50, then
the canons[67] and the
Sunday Hymn of Light[68] of the mode (of the week), or instead of this the
Holy is the Lord our <God>,[69] then the
lauds (Pss 148–50); then in this way:
the resurrection stichera to lauds,[70] then the

64. Anabathmoi: a class of troparion chanted in the mode of the week. They are found in a separate volume. *MHS* 161–68; *PaR* 10: the first mode begins Ἐν τῷ θλίβεσθαι.

65. According to a euchologion of 1153, Cod. Sinai. gr. 973 (Dmitrievskij, *Opisanie*, 2:89.10), the cantor says the prokeimenon Ἀνάστηθι, Κύριε, *Arise, O Lord* (Ps 9:33), immediately before the reading from the Gospel. The order of service here may specify that on Sunday *Let everything that has breath* was said in the place of *Arise, O Lord*, as seems to have been the practice followed at the Evergetis; its synaxarion mentions *Let everything that has breath* only on Sundays (e.g., *Synaxarion of Evergetis*, ed. Jordan, 1:68 [O.7.b]) and a few important feasts (e.g., ibid., 1:30 [O.7.b]). It is also possible that ἀντί should be taken as "before" rather than "instead of"; the rule of San Salvatore cites *Let everything that has breath* not only on Sunday (e.g., Arranz, *Typicon de Messine*, 72.8), but also in conjunction with *Arise, O Lord* (ibid., 73.18–19) and on other days that might not be considered major feasts (e.g., Oct. 7: ibid., 37.29), as well as occasionally at the lauds (e.g., ibid., 83.31). The prokeimena (100–102) read on Sundays in conjunction with the *Let everything that has breath* make extensive use of the verb "to arise." See Parenti § III.7.2.1. A few lines later the scribe gives the prokeimena according to the modes.

66. Eleven morning readings are designated in the medieval Gospel lectionary; see C. Gregory, *Textkritik des Neuen Testamentes*, 3 vols. (Leipzig: J. C. Hinrichs, 1900–1909), 1:364). The readings are also designated in the Cathedral Typikon; see J. Mateos, *Le Typicon de la Grande Église. Ms. Sainte-Croix no 40*, 2 vols., Orientalia Christiana Analecta 165–66 [hereafter "OCA"] (Rome: Pont. Institutum Studiorum Orientalium, 1962–63), 2:170–75. The priest read from the Gospel lectionary in the mode of the week, and a table in the Messina Typikon (Arranz, *Typicon de Messine*, 306–7) clarifies the distribution of the eleven readings among eight modes. Certain feast days occasioned the use of other morning readings (cf. ibid., 134.8: εὐαγγέλιον ἑωθινόν, unspecified further) found in the Gospel lectionary; cf. Gregory, *Textkritik*, 1:365–86, given individually on designated days, but in a separate list in the Cathedral Typikon (Mateos, *Typicon*, 2:181–85).

67. Canons: the biblical Odes with other liturgical material added (Schneider, "Oden," 253–55, 262–66; Arranz, *Typicon de Messine*, 408–9; *Synaxarion of Evergetis*, ed. Jordan, 572–73).

68. Resurrection exaposteilaria: troparia said before the lauds; they are found in another volume. As is true of the Gospel readings, there are eleven Hymns of Light and accompanying theotokia (*PaR* 706–12: the first begins Τοῖς μαθηταῖς συνέλθωμεν). The weekday Hymns of Light are given below at 104–6.

69. Ps 98:9: see below, 104.

70. Stichera: poetic stanzas, which are verses said in conjunction with psalms and composed in each of the eight modes. They are found in a separate volume (*PaR* 20–21, that of the first mode begins Ὑμνοῦμέν σου, Χριστέ). Reference here is to the Sunday stichera. See again below 108.

Προκείμενα ψαλλόμενα ἐν ταῖς κυριακαῖς πρὸ τοῦ εἰπεῖν τὸ Πᾶσα πνοή

Ἦχος α̅,[90] στίχος α̅, *Νῦν ἀναστήσομαι, λέγει Κύριος, θήσομαι ἐν σωτηρίῳ, παρρησιάσομαι ἐν αὐτῷ.* Ὁ λαός, *Νῦν ἀναστήσομαι·* ὁ ψάλτης, *Τὰ λόγια Κυρίου λόγια ἁγνά·* ὁ λαός, *Νῦν ἀναστήσομαι·* ὁ ψάλτης, *Νῦν ἀναστήσομαι, λέγει Κύριος·* καὶ ὁ λαός, *Θήσομαι ἐν σωτηρίῳ.*

Καὶ εὐθὺς τὸ *Πᾶσα πνοὴ αἰνεσάτω τὸν Κύριον* κατὰ τὸν ἦχον, κἂν μὴ |[239] εἰς τὴν καταλογήν, οὗ οἱ στίχοι, *Αἰνεῖτε τὸν Θεὸν ἐν τοῖς ἁγίοις αὐτοῦ, αἰνεῖτε αὐτὸν ἐν στερεώματι δυνάμεως αὐτοῦ· αἰνεῖτε αὐτὸν ἐπὶ ταῖς δυναστείαις αὐτοῦ, αἰνεῖτε αὐτὸν κατὰ τὸ πλῆθος τῆς μεγαλωσύνης· πᾶσα πνοὴ αἰνεσάτω τὸν Κύριον.* Καὶ πάλιν ἀντὶ τοῦ *Ἀνάστηθι,*

εἰς ἦχον β̅, τὸ *Ἐξεγέρθητι, Κύριε ὁ Θεός μου, ἐν προστάγματι, ᾧ ἐνετείλω, καὶ συναγωγὴ λαῶν κυκλώσει σε·* στίχος, *Κύριε ὁ Θεός μου, ἐπὶ σοὶ ἤλπισα· σῶσόν με.*

---

90. ἦχος α̅ indicated in the margin.

Glory to God in the highest, and peace on (doxology: Ode 14).[71]
Holy God (Trisagion) three times, then
chant the first hour and dismiss.[72]

Prokeimena chanted on Sundays before saying the *Let everything that has breath.*[73]

Mode I

First verse: *Now will I arise, says the Lord, I will set them in safety; I will speak to them of it openly* (Ps 11:6).

the people: *Now will I arise.*

the cantor: *The oracles of the Lord are pure oracles* (Ps 11:7).

the people: *Now will I arise.*

the cantor: *Now will I arise, says the Lord.*

and the people: *I will set them in safety.*

Then immediately the *Let everything that has breath praise the Lord* (HR 122) according to the mode (of the week), if it is not in the list,[74] for which the verses are: *Praise God in his holy places; praise him in the firmament of his power. Praise him on account of his mighty acts; praise him according to <his> abundant greatness* (Ps 150:1–2). *Let everything that has breath praise the Lord* (Ps 150:6). Then immediately, instead of the Arise (the *Let everything that has breath*).

In mode II

The *Arise, O Lord my God, according to the decree which you did command, the congregation of nations shall surround you* (Ps 7:7–8).

verse: *O Lord my God, in you have I trusted; save me* (Ps 7:2).

---

71. *HR* 126; the Great Doxology of Sunday. See Parenti § III.7.2.3.

72. The dismissal can involve a brief ritual.

73. The same prokeimena were used in the cathedral (Mateos, *Typicon*, 2:170–75), but without responses specified in its typikon. See Parenti § III.7.2.1.

74. "Kataloge" suggests a memorandum.

εἰς ἦχον γ᾽, Εἴπατε ἐν τοῖς ἔθνεσιν ὅτι Κύριος ἐβασίλευσε, καὶ γὰρ κατώρθωσε τὴν οἰκουμένην, ἥτις οὐ σαλευθήσεται· στίχος α᾽, <Ἄι>σατε τῷ Κυρίῳ ᾆσμα καινόν. Ὁ λαός, Εἴπατε ἐν τοῖς ἔθνεσιν· ὁ διάκονος, τὸ γ᾽, Εἴπατε ἐν τοῖς ἔθνεσιν· ὁ λαός, Καὶ γὰρ κατώρθωσεν.

ἦχος δ᾽, Ἀνάστα, Κύριε, βοήθησον ἡμῖν καὶ λύτρωσαι ἡμᾶς ἕνεκεν τοῦ ὀνόματός σου· στίχος, Ὁ Θεός, ἐν τοῖς ὠσὶν ἡμῶν.

ἦχος πλάγιος α᾽, Ἀνάστηθι, Κύριε ὁ Θεός μου, ὑψωθήτω ἡ χείρ σου, ὅτι σὺ βασιλεύεις εἰς τὸν αἰῶνα καὶ εἰς τὸν αἰῶνα τοῦ αἰῶνος· στίχος, Ἐξομολογήσομαί σοι. |²³⁹ᵛ

ἦχος πλάγιος β᾽,⁹¹ Κύριε, ἐξέγειρον τὴν δυναστείαν σου καὶ ἐλθὲ εἰς τὸ σῶσαι ἡμᾶς· στίχος, Ὁ ποιμαίνων τὸν Ἰσραήλ, πρόσχες.

ἦχος βαρύς, Ἀνάστηθι, Κύριε ὁ Θεός μου, ὑψωθήτω ἡ χείρ σου· στίχος, Ἐξομολογήσομαί σοι, Κύριε.

ἦχος πλάγιος δ᾽, Βασιλεύσει Κύριος εἰς τὸν αἰῶνα, ὁ Θεός σου, Σιών, εἰς γενεὰν καὶ γενεάν· στίχος, Αἴνει, ἡ ψυχή μου, τὸν Κύριον, αἰνέσω Κύριον.

Καὶ μετὰ ταῦτα ὡς καὶ ἐν τῇ ἀρχῇ τούτων, ἤγουν ἐν τῷ πρώτῳ ἤχῳ δεδήλωται, τὸ Πᾶσα πνοὴ εἰς τὸν ἦχον· εἶτα ἑωθινὸν εὐαγγέλιον· εἶτα τὸ Ἀνάστασιν Χριστοῦ θεασάμενοι, προσκυνήσωμεν ἅγιον Κύριον, τὸ Ἐλέησόν

---

91. ἦχος πλάγιος β᾽ indicated in the margin, as are the following two mode designations.

In mode III

*Say among the heathen, the Lord reigns, for he has established the world
so that it shall not be moved* (Ps 95:10).

first verse: *Sing to the Lord a new song* (Ps 95:1).

the people: *Say among the heathen <the Lord reigns>.*

the deacon, three (times), *Say among the heathen <the Lord reigns>.*

the people: *For he has established <the world so that it shall not be moved>.*

Mode IV

Arise, O Lord, help us, and redeem us for your name's sake (Ps 43:27).

Verse: *O God, with our ears <we have heard>* (Ps 43:2).

Plagal mode I

Arise, O Lord my God, let your hand be lifted up (Ps 9:33), *for you reign
forever and ever* (Ps 9:37).

Verse: *I will give thanks to you <O Lord, with my whole heart>* (Ps 9:2).

Plagal mode II

O Lord, stir up your power and come to deliver us (Ps 79:3).

Verse: *Attend, O shepherd of Israel* (Ps 79:2).

Barys mode

Arise, O Lord my God, let your hand be lifted up (Ps 9:33).

Verse: *I will give thanks to you, O Lord <with my whole heart>* (Ps 9:2).

Plagal mode IV

The Lord shall reign forever, even your God, O Sion, to all generations (Ps
145:10).

Verse: *My soul praise the Lord; I will praise the Lord* (Ps 145:1-2).

And after these (prokeimena)—as has been set out at their beginning,
that is, (at the prokeimenon) in the first mode[75]—the *Let everything that has
breath* in the mode (of the week), then the

75. Resumes the order from 98, with a slight change.

με, ὁ Θεός, τοὺς κανόνας, τὰ τῆς ἡμέρας καθίσματα καὶ τὰ ἐξαποστειλάρια, ἤγουν τὸ Ἅγιος Κύριος ὁ Θεὸς ἡμῶν, ἦχος α'· στίχος, Ὅτι ἅγιος ἐστὶν ὁ Θεὸς ἡμῶν· στίχος,[92] *Ἐπὶ πάντας τοὺς λαοὺς ὁ Θεὸς ἡμῶν· τὸ αὐτὸ δὲ καὶ εἰς τὸν λοιπὸν ἦχον, μεθ' ὃ τὸ ἑωθινὸν ἐξαποστειλάριον καὶ τὸ τῆς δεσποτικῆς ἑορτῆς εἰ τύχοιεν.*

Χρὴ δὲ γινώσκειν ὅτι καὶ ἐν ταῖς τῆς ὑπεραγίας Θεοτόκου ἑορταῖς τὸ *Ἅγιος Κύριος ὁ Θεὸς ἡμῶν* ὡς ἐπὶ τὸ πλεῖστον λέγεται· ἐπὶ δὲ τῶν ἁγίων τῶν ἐχόντων τὸ Θεὸς Κύριος, ψάλλετε τὸ *Ὁ οὐρανὸν τοῖς ἄστροις* καὶ εὐθὺς τὸ *Αἰνεῖτε τὸν Κύριον.* Εἰ δὲ λιτὴ ἡμέρα |[240] ἐστίν, καὶ τοῦ Ἀλληλούϊα.

Ἐξαποστειλάρια ψάλλονται κατὰ ἦχον ταῦτα

εἰς ἦχον α'

τῇ β',[93] *Ὁ τὸ φῶς ἀνατέλλων, Κύριε, τὴν ψυχήν μου καθάρισον ἀπὸ πάσης ἁμαρτίας, προστασίαις τῶν ἀσωμάτων, καὶ σῶσον ἡμᾶς. τῇ πρεσβείᾳ τῶν ἁγίων. ταῖς πρεσβείαις τῆς Θεοτόκου, καὶ σῶσον ἡμᾶς.*

92. στίχος indicated in the margin.
93. τῇ β written in the margin.

morning Gospel reading, then

Having seen Christ's resurrection, let us worship the holy Lord (PaR 549).
Have mercy on me, O God (Ps 50).

canons,

poetic kathismata of the day,[76] and

Hymns of Light, that is: *Holy is the Lord our God* (Ps 98:9) in the first mode; verse: *For the Lord our God is holy* (Ps 98:9); verse: *Over all the people is our God* (Ps 98:2); the same (again) in the remaining mode,[77] after which the

Morning Hymn of Light[78] and that of the feast of the Lord,[79] if it happens to be one.

It is necessary to know that on the feasts of the all-holy Theotokos the (Hymn of Light) *Holy is the Lord our God* is also generally said; for the saints that have God is the Lord,[80] chant the (troparion) *You who as God adorned the heavens with stars*[81] and then immediately the *Praise the Lord* (lauds: Pss 148–50). If it is a weekday also (chant) the Alleluia.

(Hymns of Light[82])

These Hymns of Light are chanted according to the mode (of the week):

In mode I

On Monday

Lord, you who brought forth the light, purify my soul of all sin through the patronage of the incorporeal beings and save us.

---

76. Poetic kathismata: compositions dedicated to the feast, saint or saints of the day said in conjunction with the canon of biblical odes. On a feast day or when there is one saint, the chant generally follows the third ode (*Synaxarion Evergetis*, ed. Jordan, 1:8 [O.9.a], 18 [O.9.a]), and after the third and sixth when there are two chants (ibid., 14 [O.4]). Interrupting the recitation of the odes for liturgical poetry is specified for compline below, 166.

77. I am uncertain as to the meaning of "remaining"; it may mean that after *Holy is the Lord our God* is said in mode one it is repeated in the mode of the week.

78. Heothinon exaposteilarion: eleven compositions. They are found in a separate volume (PaR 706–12; first heothinon, mode I begins Εἰς τὸ ὄρος τοῖς μαθηταῖς).

79. The manuscript does not contain exaposteilaria for feasts of the Lord.

80. Specified in the synaxarion-menologion (part III).

81. The troparion is a variant of *HR* 120; see Parenti § III.7.2.2.

82. Now commonly referred to as the "photagogika." The Sunday Hymn of Light, absent from this list, is cited above 98. Bracketed additions are from *HR* 78–79.

τῇ γ', τῇ πρεσβείᾳ τοῦ Προδρόμου.

τῇ δ', τῇ δυνάμει τοῦ σταυροῦ.

τῇ ε', τῇ πρεσβείᾳ τῶν ἀποστόλων.

τῇ παρασκευῇ, πάλιν τῇ δυνάμει τοῦ σταυροῦ.

τὸ δὲ σάβατον, Ὁ οὐρανὸν τοῖς ἄστροις. Ὁ καὶ νεκρῶν καί. Ὁ γλυκασμός.

ἦχος β'[94]
Τὸ φῶς σου τὸ ἀΐδιον ἐξαπόστειλον, Κύριε, καὶ φώτισον τὴν καρδίαν μου, προστασίαις τῶν ἀσωμάτων, καὶ σῶσον.

ἦχος γ'
Ἐξαπόστειλον τὸ φῶς σου, Χριστὲ ὁ Θεός, καὶ φώτισον τὴν καρδίαν μου, προστασίαις τῶν ἀσωμάτων, καὶ σῶσόν με.

ἦχος δ'
Ὁ τὸ φῶς ἀνατέλλων τῷ κόσμῳ σου, τὴν ἐν σκότῳ ψυχήν μου ὑπάρχουσαν.

94. ἦχος β' and the following six mode designations are indicated in the margin.

<Lord, you who brought forth the light, purify my soul of all sin> through the intercession of the saints <and save us>.

<Lord, you who brought forth the light, purify my soul of all sin> through the intercessions of the Theotokos and save us.

On Tuesday

through the intercession of the Forerunner <and save us>.

On Wednesday

by the power of the cross <and save us>.

On Thursday

through the intercession of the apostles <and save us>.

On Friday

again *by the power of the cross <and save us>.*

Saturday

<You who as God adorned> the heavens with stars.
<You who have authority over the living> and the dead (HR 122).
The sweetness <of the angels> (HR 120).

Mode II

Send forth your everlasting light (cf. Ps 42:3), O Lord, and illuminate my heart through the patronage of the incorporeal beings and save <me>.

Mode III

Send forth your light (Ps 42:3), *O Christ, you who are God, illuminate my heart through the patronage of the incorporeal beings and save me.*

Mode IV

You who make the light to rise for your world <purify of all sin>[83] *my soul, which lives in darkness.*

83. ἀπὸ πάσης ἁμαρτίας καθάρισον supplied from P, and see *HR* 119.

ἦχος πλάγιος α'
Φωτοδότα Κύριε, ἐξαπόστειλον τὸ φῶς σου καὶ φώτισον τὴν καρδίαν μου.

ἦχος πλάγιος β'
Πρεσβείαις, Κύριε, τῶν ἀσωμάτων σου, καταύγασον τὰς ψυχὰς ἡμῶν φωτὶ τῷ ἀϊδίῳ σου.

εἰς ἦχον πλάγιον δ' καὶ εἰς τὸν βαρὺν ὁμοίως
Φῶς ὑπάρχων, Χριστέ, φώτισόν με σύ, τῇ δυνάμει. |²⁴⁰ᵛ

Καὶ εὐθὺς τὸ Αἰνεῖτε τὸν Κύριον ἐκ τῶν οὐρανῶν· Σοὶ πρέπει ὕμνος, ὁ Θεὸς εἰς τὸν ἦχον, ἔστι δὲ εἰς τὸ ψαλτ<ή>ρ<ιον>· καὶ εἰ μὴ ἐστὶ κυριακὴ ἢ σάββατον ἢ ἑτέρα ἑορτὴ λέγετε τὸ Δόξα ἐν ὑψίστοις Θεῷ, καὶ μετὰ τὸ Καταξίωσον, Κύριε, ἐν τῇ ἡμέρᾳ ταύτῃ τὰ στιχηρὰ τῆς ἡμέρας. Εἰ δὲ ἐκ τούτων τίς ἐστὶν ἡμέρα λέγονται τὰ στιχερά, εἶτα τὸ Δόξα ἐν ὑψίστοις Θεῷ καὶ πάλιν στιχερά. Στίχοι δέ εἰσιν οὗτοι· Ἐνεπλήσθημεν τὸ πρωῒ τοῦ ἐλέους σου, Κύριε· ἕτερος στίχος, Καὶ ἔστω ἡ λαμπρότης Κυρίου τοῦ Θεοῦ. Δόξα καὶ νῦν. θεοτόκιν, μεθ' ὃ τὸ Ἀγαθὸν τὸ ἐξομολογεῖσθαι τῷ Κυρίῳ· τρισάγιον· Πάτερ ἡμῶν, καὶ ἀπολυτίκιον ἐάν ἐστιν, εἶτα τὸ Κύριε, ἐλέησον [ ]⁹⁵ καὶ εὐθὺς ψάλλεται ἡ α' ὥρα συνημμένως μετὰ τοῦ ὄρθρου.

95. Short gap in the text.

Plagal mode I

Light-giving Lord, **send forth your light** *and illuminate my heart.*

Plagal mode II

Through the intercessions, O Lord, of your incorporeal beings flood our souls with your everlasting light.

Plagal mode IV, as well as barys mode

Being light, O Christ, illuminate me by the power <of the cross and save me>.

Immediately the

Praise the Lord from the heavens (lauds: Pss 148–50).

Praise becomes you, O God (Ps 64) in the mode (of the week); it (the psalm) is in the psalter; and, unless it is Sunday or Saturday or another feast, say the *Glory to God in the highest* (doxology[84]) and after the (line) *Deem worthy, O Lord, on this day*[85] the day's stichera.[86] But if any day is (one) of these,[87] the stichera are said (and) then the *Glory to God in the highest* and (the) stichera again. The verses are these: *We have been satisfied in the morning with your mercy, O Lord* (Ps 89:14); the other verse: *And let the brightness of the Lord our God be upon us* (Ps 89:17).

Glory, both now.

Theotokion,[88] after which

It is good to give thanks to the Lord (Ps 91),[89]

Trisagion,

Our Father (HR 8) and the

apolytikion,[90] if there is one, then

---

84. See Parenti § III.7.2.3.

85. Phrase toward the end (14:30) of the Great Doxology: *HR* 127.

86. Presumably the verses cited above at the lauds; cf. 99n70.

87. I.e., Saturday or Sunday or a feast day.

88. The theotokion said toward the end of matins in the mode of the week; it is found in a separate volume (*HR* 787–815, *PaR* 719–31: the first mode theotokion begins Ἄχραντε Θεοτόκε, ἡ ἐν οὐρανοῖς).

89. P specifies Ps 91:2–3.

90. The troparion of the feast or saint of the day from the synaxarion-menologion (part III).

Δεῦτε, προσκυνήσωμεν καὶ προσπέσωμεν, ἐκ γ΄· ψαλμὸς ε΄,[96] Τὰ ῥήματά μου ἐνώτισαι· ψαλμὸς πθ΄, Κύριε, καταφυγή· ρ΄,[97] Ἔλεον καὶ κρίσιν ᾄσομαι. Δόξα καὶ νῦν. Ἀλληλούϊα, ἀλληλούϊα, δόξα σοι, ὁ Θεός, γ΄. Κύριε, ἐλέησον, γ΄· Δόξα καὶ νῦν. Εἶτα εἰ μὲν ἑορτὴν ἦγεν ἡ ἐκκλη<σία>, ἐπάσεις τὸ τῆς ἑορτῆς τροπάριον· εἰ δ᾽ οὖν, λέγε προκείμενον εἰς ἦχον πλάγιον β΄, Τὸ πρωῒ εἰσάκουσον τῆς φωνῆς μου, ὁ βασιλεύς μου καὶ ὁ Θεός μου· στίχος, Τὰ ῥήματά μου ἐνώτισαι· |[241] ἕτερος στίχος, Ὅτι πρὸς σὲ προσεύξομαι, Κύριε. Δόξα καὶ νῦν. Τί σε καλέσωμεν τὴν κεχαριτωμένην; Τὰ διαβήματά μου κατεύθυνον. Εἶτα τὸ τρισάγιον, τὸ Πάτερ ἡμῶν, τροπάριον,

Χριστέ, τὸ φῶς τὸ ἀληθινὸν τὸ φωτίζον πάντα ἄνθρωπον εἰς τὸν κόσμον ἐρχόμενον, σημειωθήτω ἐφ᾽ ἡμᾶς τὸ φῶς τοῦ προσώπου σου, ἵνα ἐν αὐτῷ ὀψώμεθα φῶς ἀπρόσιτον· καὶ κατεύθυνον τὰ διαβήματα ἡμῶν πρὸς ἐργασίαν τῶν θείων ἐντολῶν σου, πρεσβείαις τῆς Θεοτόκου, καὶ σῶσον ἡμᾶς. Δόξα καὶ νῦν.

Τὴν ὑπερένδοξον τοῦ Χριστοῦ μητέρα καὶ τῶν ἀγγέλων ἁγιωτέραν

---

96. ε΄ written again in the margin.
97. ρ΄ written in the margin.

Lord, have mercy [...][91] times

and without interruption the first hour is immediately chanted with matins.[92]

(First Hour)

Come, let us worship and fall down three times.

Psalm 5, *Hearken to my words*

Psalm 89, *Lord, you have been our refuge*

Psalm 100, *I will sing to you, O Lord, of mercy and judgment*

Glory, both now.

Alleluia, alleluia, glory to you, O God three times.

Lord, have mercy three times.

Glory, both now.

Then if the church is to celebrate a feast, you will sing the troparion of the feast; otherwise, say the prokeimenon in plagal mode II: *In the morning hear my voice* (Ps 5:4), *my king and my God* (Ps 5:3); verse: *Hearken to my words <O Lord>* (Ps 5:2); the other verse: *For to you, O Lord, will I pray* (Ps 5:3).[93] *Glory, both now.*

(theotokion:) *What are we to call you who are **full of grace*** (Lk 1:28)?

Guide my steps (Ps 118:133–35, 70:8; HR 139), then the

Trisagion,

Our Father,

troparion: *O Christ, you who are **the true light that comes into the world illuminating every man** (Jn 1:9), **let the light of your countenance be marked upon us** (Ps 4:7), so that in it we might see (cf. Ps 35:10) **the unapproachable light** (1 Tm 6:16). **Guide our steps** (Ps 118:133) toward the work of your sacred commandments, through the intercessions of the Theotokos and save us.*

Glory, both now.

Let us unceasingly sing with heart and mouth of the most glorious mother

91. The number is lost; in P it is three times.

92. The twelfth-century typikon of the monastery of the Theotokos Evergetis refers to the melding of matins and the first hour as "customary"; *BMFD*, 2:473. The scribe does not break the text or give a title (fig. 3).

93. For a description of how this prokeimenon was chanted see Arranz, *Typicon de Messine*, 200.4–8. For the performative implications of the difference between this instruction and the structurally similar ones for the third, sixth, and ninth hours see Parenti § III.9.2.

ἀσιγήτως ὑμνήσωμεν, καρδίᾳ καὶ στόματι, Θεοτόκον αὐτὴν ὁμολογοῦντες, ὡς κυρίως γεννήσασαν Θεὸν σεσαρκωμένον, καὶ πρεσβεύουσαν ἀπαύστως ὑπὲρ τῶν ψυχῶν ἡμῶν.

Κύριε, ἐλέησον, μʹ· εἶτα τὴν εὐχήν, Ὁ ἐν παντὶ καιρῷ καὶ πάσῃ ὥρᾳ· καὶ μετὰ τὸ πληρῶσαι τὴν εὐχὴν ταύτην μετάνοιαι ιεʹ· καὶ εὐχὴ τῆς αʹ ὥρας,

Ὁ Θεὸς ὁ αἰώνιος, τὸ ἄναρχον καὶ ἀΐδιον φῶς, ὁ πάσης φύσεως δημιουργός, ἡ τοῦ ἐλέους πηγή, τὸ τῆς ἀγαθότητος πέλαγος, |²⁴¹ᵛ ἡ τῆς φιλανθρωπίας ἀνεξιχνίαστος ἄβυσσος, ἐπίφανον ἡμῖν τὸ φῶς τοῦ προσώπου σου. Λάμψον ἐν ταῖς καρδίαις ἡμῶν, νοητὲ ἥλιε τῆς δικαιοσύνης, καὶ τῆς σῆς εὐφροσύνης τὰς ψυχὰς ἡμῶν πλήρωσον. Δίδαξον ἡμᾶς τὰ σὰ μελετᾶν ἀεὶ καὶ φθέγγεσθαι κρίματα καὶ ἐξομολογεῖσθαί σοι διηνεκῶς τῷ ἡμετέρῳ Δεσπότῃ καὶ εὐεργέτῃ. Τὰ τῶν χειρῶν ἡμῶν ἔργα πρὸς τὸ σὸν κατεύθυνον θέλημα, καὶ πράττειν ἡμᾶς τὰ σοὶ εὐάρεστα καὶ φίλα εὐόδωσον, ἵνα καὶ διὰ τῶν ἀναξίων ἡμῶν δοξάζηταί σου τὸ πανάγιον ὄνομα, τοῦ Πατρὸς καὶ τοῦ Υἱοῦ καὶ τοῦ ἁγίου Πνεύματος, τῆς μιᾶς θεότητός τε καὶ βασιλείας, ᾗ πρέπει πᾶσα δόξα, τιμὴ καὶ προσκύνησις νῦν καὶ ἀεὶ καὶ εἰς τοὺς αἰῶνας.

Εὐχὴ ἑτέρα τῆς αὐτῆς ὥρας

Πάτερ ἅγιε, ὁ τὸν ἥλιον τῆς δικαιοσύνης, τὸν Κύριον ἡμῶν Ἰησοῦν Χριστὸν εὐδοκήσας ἀνατεῖλαι ἡμῖν κατὰ τὴν νύκτα τοῦ νόμου καὶ τὴν ταύτης συμπλήρωσιν, ὁ τῷ προφήτῃ Δαυῒδ ἐμπνεύσας εἰπεῖν, Τὸ πρωῒ εἰσ|²⁴²-άκουσον τῆς φωνῆς μου, τὸ πρωῒ παραστήσομαί σοι καὶ ἐπόψει με, αὐτὸς καὶ ἐφ᾽ ἡμᾶς τοὺς ἀναξίους παραστῆναι τολμῶντας τῷ προσώπῳ τῆς ἁγίας δόξης σου, διὰ τὴν σὴν φιλανθρωπίαν ἐπίβλεψον ἐν οἰκτιρμοῖς καὶ χρηστότητι· καὶ παράσχου ἡμῖν τὴν παροῦσαν ἡμέραν καὶ πάντα τὸν χρόνον τῆς ζωῆς ἡμῶν διελθεῖν εὐλαβῶς καὶ εὐσχημόνως, συντηρῶν ἡμᾶς ἐξ ἀοράτων καὶ ὁρωμένων ἐχθρῶν καὶ πᾶσαν ἐνθύμησιν καὶ πρᾶξιν ἀπταίστως ἐν ἡμῖν ἐνεργεῖσθαι ποιῶν, καὶ πάντοτε ὡς ὑπὸ τοὺς σοὺς ὀφθαλμοὺς ὄντας καὶ ὁρωμένους, ἐν εὐθύτητι καθοδηγῶν, πρεσβείαις τῆς ἀχράντου δεσποίνης ἡμῶν, Θεοτόκου καὶ ἀειπαρθένου Μαρίας, τῶν ἁγίων καὶ ἐπουρανίων δυνάμεων, τοῦ ἁγίου καὶ ἐνδόξου προφήτου, προδρόμου καὶ βαπτιστοῦ Ἰωάννου, τῶν ἁγίων ἀποστόλων, προφητῶν, μαρτύρων, ἱεραρχῶν, ὁσίων, ὁμολογητῶν καὶ πάντων καὶ πασῶν τῶν ἁγίων σου, ὅτι εὐλογητὸς εἶ εἰς τοὺς αἰῶνας· ἀμήν.

of Christ, more holy than the angels, she whom we confess to be the mother of God, who truly gave birth to the incarnate God, and she who never stops interceding for our souls.

Lord, have mercy forty times, then the

prayer: *You, God, are worshiped at every moment and in every hour* (166), and after the completion of this prayer fifteen bows, and the

prayer of the first hour: *O eternal God* (cf. Is 40:28), *you who are everlasting light without beginning, the maker of every creature, the wellspring of mercy, sea of goodness and the unsearchable well of infinite love for mankind, shine on us the **light of your countenance** (Ps 4:7). **Shine in our hearts** (cf. 2 Cor 4:6), O spiritual **sun of righteousness** (Mal 4:2), and fill our souls with your joy (cf. Ps 15:11). Teach us always to meditate on and proclaim your judgments (cf. Ps 118:108) and to confess continually to you, our master and benefactor. **Guide the works of our hands** (Ps 89:17) in the direction of your will, and lead us along the path to do what is acceptable and pleasing to you, so that even through us, the unworthy, your all-holy name be glorified: that of the Father and the Son and the Holy Spirit, the one Deity and kingdom, to whom is due all glory, honor, and worship, now and always and for ever <and ever. Amen>.*

Another prayer of the same hour: *O holy Father, you consented to make rise for us the **sun of righteousness** (Mal 4:2), our Lord Jesus Christ, during the night of the Law and its completion. You inspired the prophet David to say, "**In the morning hear my voice; in the morning I will wait upon you and you will watch over me**" (Ps 5:4). In your benevolence, look with compassion and kindness on even us, the unworthy who dare to stand in the presence of your holy glory. Grant that we may pass the coming day and the entire span of our lives piously and decently, you who preserve us safe from invisible and visible enemies, making every thought and action to be at work in us without stumbling, who always watch over us, and who guide us along the straight and narrow, through the intercessions of our undefiled sovereign lady, mother of God, and ever-virgin Mary, of the holy and heavenly powers, of the holy and glorious prophet, forerunner, and baptist, John, of the holy apostles, prophets, martyrs, hierarchs, saints, confessors, and of all your holy men and women, for you are blessed forever. Amen.*

Εὐχὴ ἑτέρα[98]

Ὁ ἀποστέλλων τὸ φῶς καὶ πορεύεται, ὁ ἀ|²⁴²ᵛ-νατέλλων τὸν ἥλιον ἐπὶ δικαίους καὶ ἀδίκους, πονηρούς τε καὶ ἀγαθούς, ὁ ποιῶν ὄρθρον καὶ φωτίζων πᾶσαν τὴν οἰκουμένην, φώτισον ἡμῶν τὰς καρδίας, Δέσποτα τῶν ἁπάντων. Χάρισαι ἡμῖν ἐν τῇ παρούσῃ ἡμέρᾳ εὐαρεστῆσαί σοι, διαφυλάττων ἡμᾶς ἀπὸ πάσης ἁμαρτίας καὶ πάσης πονηρᾶς πράξεως, ῥυόμενος ἡμᾶς ἀπὸ παντὸς βέλους πετομένου ἡμέρας καὶ πάσης ἀντικει{κει}μένης δυνάμεως, πρεσβείαις τῆς Θεοτόκου, τῶν ἀΰλων σου λειτουργῶν, καὶ πάντων τῶν ἁγίων τῶν ἀπ᾽ αἰῶνός σοι εὐαρεστησάντων. Σὸν γάρ ἐστι τὸ ἐλεεῖν καὶ σῴζειν, ὁ Θεὸς ἡμῶν, καὶ σοὶ τὴν δόξαν ἀναπέμπομεν, τῷ Πατρὶ καὶ τῷ Υἱῷ καὶ τῷ ἁγίῳ Πνεύματι νῦν.

98. εὐχὴ ἑτέρα written in the margin.

Another prayer: *You send the light and it goes. You make **the sun rise on the just and the unjust, both the wicked and the good*** (Mt 5:45). *O master of all, you who bring the dawn and illuminate the entire world, enlighten our hearts. Favor us in this coming day to please you, preserving us from all sin and every wrongful act. Keep us safe from **every arrow that flies by day*** (Ps 90:5) *and every hostile power, through the intercessions of the Theotokos, of your incorporeal ministers, and of all the saints who through the ages have been pleasing to you. For yours, O our God, is to show mercy and to save, and to you we give the glory: to the Father and the Son and the Holy Spirit, now <and always and for ever and ever. Amen>.*

Ὥρα γ΄ μεγάλη

Βασιλεῦ οὐράνιε, παράκλητε, τὸ πνεῦμα τῆς ἀληθείας· τὸ τρισάγιον, τὸ Πάτερ ἡμῶν. Ὡς ἐν μέσῳ τῶν μαθητῶν σου παρεγένου, Σωτὴρ ἡμῶν, τὴν εἰρήνην διδοὺς αὐτοῖς, ἐλθὲ καὶ μεθ᾽ ἡμῶν καὶ σῶσον ἡμᾶς. Δόξα καὶ νῦν. Θεοτόκιν, Θεοτόκε, πύλη ἐπουράνιε, ἄνοιξον ἡμῖν τὴν θύραν τοῦ ἐλέους σου. Κύριε, ἐλέησον, ιβ΄· καὶ οὕτως, |²⁴³ *τὸ Δεῦτε, προσκυνήσωμεν καὶ προσπέσωμεν Χριστῷ τῷ βασιλεῖ, ἐκ γ΄· Εἰσάκουσον, Κύριε, δικαιοσύνης· ψαλμὸς*⁹⁹ *κδ΄, Πρὸς σέ, Κύριε, ἦρα τὴν ψυχήν μου· ψαλμὸς ν΄, Ἐλέησόν με, ὁ Θεός, κατά. Δόξα καὶ νῦν. Ἀλληλούϊα, ἀλληλούϊα, δόξα σοι, ὁ Θεός, ἐκ γ΄. Κύριε, ἐλέησον, γ΄. Δόξα καὶ νῦν.*

Καὶ εἶθ᾽ οὕτως· εἰ μὲν ἑορτὴν ἦγεν ἡ ἐκκλη<σία>, ἐπάσεις τὸ τῆς ἑορτῆς τροπάριον· εἰ δ᾽ οὖν, λέγε προκείμενον, *Κύριε, ὁ τὸ πανάγιόν σου Πνεῦμα·* στίχος, *Καρδίαν καθαρὰν κτίσον ἐν ἐμοί, ὁ Θεός, καὶ πνεῦμα εὐθὲς ἐγκαίνισον ἐν τοῖς ἐγκάτοις μου·* στίχος, *Μὴ ἀπορρίψῃς με ἀπὸ τοῦ προσώπου σου καὶ τὸ Πνεῦμά σου τὸ ἅγιον μὴ ἀντανέλῃς ἀπ᾽ ἐμοῦ·* στίχος,¹⁰⁰ *Ἀπόδος μοι τὴν ἀγαλλίασιν τοῦ σωτηρίου σου· καὶ πνεύματι ἡγεμονικῷ στήριξόν με. Δόξα καὶ νῦν. Θεοτόκε,*¹⁰¹ *σὺ εἶ ἄμπελος ἡ ἀληθινή. Κύριος ὁ Θεὸς εὐλογητός, εὐλογητὸς Κύριος ἡμέραν καθημέραν· κατευοδώσαι ἡμῖν ὁ Θεὸς τῶν σωτηρίων ἡμῶν· ὁ Θεὸς ἡμῶν, ὁ Θεὸς τοῦ σῴζειν· τὸ τρισάγιον· τὸ Πάτερ ἡμῶν· Κύριε, ἐλέησον, μ΄· μετάνοιαι καὶ εὐχή,*¹⁰²

---

99. ψαλμός indicated in the margin.
100. στίχος indicated in the margin.
101. ὁ Κύριε: C.
102. καὶ εὐχή written in the margin.

(II.2)

Great Third Hour[94]

Heavenly king, comforter, spirit of truth, the

Trisagion, the

Our Father (HR 8) (and troparia:)

As when you, our savior, came into the midst of your disciples, giving them peace, come among us, too, and save us.

Glory, both now.

theotokion: *O Theotokos, heavenly gate, open for us the door of your mercy.*

Lord, have mercy twelve times, and in the following way:

Come let us worship and fall down before Christ the king three times.

Psalm 16: *Hear, O Lord, of my righteousness.*

Psalm 24: *To you, O Lord, have I lifted up my soul.*

Psalm 50: *Have mercy on me, O Lord, according.*

Glory, both now.

Alleluia, alleluia, glory to you, O God three times.

Lord, have mercy three times.

Glory, both now.

And then in the following manner: if the church is to celebrate a feast, you will sing the troparion of the feast; otherwise, say the prokeimenon: *Lord, you who sent down your all-holy Spirit* (TR 121); verse: *Create in me a clean heart, O God, and renew a right spirit within me* (Ps 50:12); verse: *Do not cast me out of your presence, and do not take your Holy Spirit from me* (Ps 50:13); verse: *Restore to me the joy of your salvation* (Ps 50:14). *And establish me with your guiding spirit* (Ps 50:12).

Glory, both now.

(theotokion) *O Theotokos, you are **the true vine*** (Jn 15:1) (TR 98).

Blessed be the Lord God; blessed be the Lord daily, and the God of our salvation shall prosper us. Our God is the God of salvation (Ps 67:20–21).

Trisagion, the

Our Father,

---

94. For the use of "great" see Parenti § III.8; the office is said privately.

Ὁ ἐν τῇ τρίτῃ ὥρᾳ τοῖς ἁγίοις σου μαθηταῖς καὶ ἀποστόλοις καταπέμψας τὸ πανάγιόν σου Πνεῦμα, τοῦτο, Ἰησοῦ, μὴ ἀντανέλῃς ἀπ᾽ ἐμοῦ, Υἱὲ τοῦ Θεοῦ καὶ Λόγε, |²⁴³ᵛ ἀλλ᾽ ἐγκαίνισον ἐν τοῖς ἐγκάτοις μου πνεῦμα εὐθὲς καὶ ζωοποιοῦν, πνεῦμα θείου φόβου καὶ κατανύξεως· καὶ εὔθυνον τὴν προσευχήν μου ἐν τῷ φωτοποιῷ καὶ ἁγιαστικῷ καὶ παντοδυνάμῳ καὶ ζωοποιῷ σου Πνεύματι. Σὺ γὰρ εἶ ὁ φωτισμὸς τῶν ψυχῶν ἡμῶν, ὁ φωτίζων πάντα ἄνθρωπον ἐρχόμενον εἰς τὸν κόσμον· καὶ σοὶ τὴν δόξαν καὶ εὐχαριστίαν καὶ προσκύνησιν ἀναπέμπομεν, τῷ Πατρὶ καὶ τῷ Υἱῷ καὶ τῷ ἁγίῳ Πνεύματι νῦν.

Εὐχὴ ἑτέρα[103]

Κύριε ὁ Θεὸς ἡμῶν, ὁ τὴν σὴν εἰρήνην δεδωκὼς τοῖς ἀνθρώποις καὶ τὴν τοῦ παναγίου Πνεύματος δωρεὰν τοῖς σοῖς μαθηταῖς καταπέμψας, καὶ τὰ τούτων χείλη ἐκ πυρίνων γλωσσῶν ἀνοίξας δυνάμει σου, διάνοιξον καὶ ἡμῶν τῶν ἁμαρτωλῶν τὰ χείλη, καὶ δίδαξον ἡμᾶς πῶς δεῖ καὶ ὑπὲρ ὧν χρὴ προσεύχεσθαι. Κυβέρνησον ἡμῶν τὴν ζωὴν ὁ εὔδιος τῶν σῳζομένων λιμήν, καὶ γνώρισον ἡμῖν ὁδὸν ἐν ᾗ πορευσόμεθα. Πνεῦμα εὐθὲς ἐγκαίνισον ἐν τοῖς ἐγκάτοις ἡμῶν, καὶ πνεύματι ἡγεμονικῷ τὸ τῆς διανοίας ἡμῶν στήριξον ὀλισθηρόν· ἵνα, |²⁴⁴ καθ᾽ ἑκάστην ἡμέραν τῷ Πνεύματί σου τῷ ἀγαθῷ πρὸς τὸ συμφέρον ὁδηγούμενοι, καταξιωθῶμεν ποιεῖν τὰς ἐντολάς σου, καὶ τῆς σῆς ἀεὶ μνημονεύειν ἐνδόξου καὶ ἐρευνητικῆς τῶν πεπραγμένων ἀνθρώποις παρουσίας, καὶ μὴ τοῖς φθειρομένοις τοῦ κόσμου τούτου ἐναπατᾶσθαι τερπνοῖς, ἀλλὰ τῶν μελλόντων ὀρέγεσθαι τῆς ἀπολαύσεως θησαυρῶν· ὅτι εὐλογητὸς εἶ καὶ αἰνετὸς ὑπάρχεις ἐν πᾶσι τοῖς ἁγίοις σου εἰς τοὺς αἰῶνας τῶν αἰώνων· ἀμήν.

---

103. εὐχὴ ἑτέρα written in the margin.

Lord, have mercy forty times,

bows,[95] and

prayer: *You who in the third hour sent down to your disciples and Apostles your all-holy Spirit, O Jesus, son of God and Word, do not take this Spirit from me, but **renew within me a right spirit** (Ps 50:12) that gives life, a **spirit of divine fear** (Is 11:3) and of contrition. Direct my prayer in accordance with your illuminating, sanctifying, almighty, and life-giving Spirit. For you are the light of our souls, **you who enlighten every man coming into the world** (Jn 1:9), and to you we give the glory, thanks and worship: to the Father and the Son and the Holy Spirit, now <and always and for ever and ever. Amen>.*

Another prayer: *O Lord our God, you who have given your peace to mankind (cf. Jn 14:27), and sent down **the gift of your all-holy Spirit** (Acts 2:38) to your disciples, and by your power opened their lips with tongues of flame, also open the lips (cf. Ps 50:17) of us sinners and teach us how we should pray (cf. Lk 11:1) and the things for which we must pray. You who are the calm harbor of those who are being saved, steer our lives and make known to us the way in which we will travel. **Renew a right spirit within us** (Ps 50:12), and by the **guiding Spirit** (Ps 50:14) stiffen our wavering resolve, so that led each day to advantage by your good Spirit (cf. Ps 142:10) we might be considered worthy to carry out your commandments and always to remember your glorious presence—which searches out men's deeds—and not to be deceived by the transitory delights of this world, but to crave the enjoyment of the rewards that are to come. For blessed are you and praised are you in all your holy places (cf. Ps 150:1) for ever and ever. Amen.*

95. At this point in the office, following the recitation of *Lord, have mercy* forty times and before the prayers, the number is likely to be fifteen; cf. first hour, 112, and ninth hour, 126.

Ὥρα ϛ' μεγάλη

Τὸ *Βασιλεῦ οὐράνιε·* τὸ τρισάγιον· τὸ *Πάτερ ἡμῶν·* τροπάρια, ἦχος β', *Τὴν ἄχραντον εἰκόνα σου. Σωτηρίαν εἰργάσω. Ὁ φωτίσας τὰ ἐπίγεια.* Καὶ θεοτόκιν, *Ὑπερευλογημένη.* Τὸ *Κύριε, ἐλέησον,* ιβ', τὸ *Δεῦτε, προσκυνήσωμεν·* καὶ τοὺς τρεῖς ψαλμοὺς τῆς ϛ', ἤγουν τὸν νγ', *Ὁ Θεός, ἐν τῷ ὀνόματι·* τὸν νδ', *Ἐνώτισαι, ὁ Θεός, τὴν προσευχήν μου·* τὸν ϙ', *Ὁ κατοικῶν ἐν βοηθείᾳ τοῦ ὑψίστου. Δόξα καὶ νῦν. Ἀλληλούϊα, ἀλληλούϊα, δόξα σοι, ὁ Θεός,* γ'· *Κύριε, ἐλέησον,* γ'.

Καὶ εἰ μὲν ἑορτὴν ἦγεν ἡ ἐκκλη<σία>, ἐπάσεις τὸ τῆς ἑορτῆς τροπάριον· εἰ δ' οὖν, λέγε προκείμενον, |²⁴⁴ᵛ *Ὁ ἐν ἕκτη ἡμέρᾳ τε καὶ ὥρᾳ τῷ σταυρῷ·* στίχος,[104] *Ἐνώτισαι, ὁ Θεός, τὴν προσευχήν μου·* ἕτερος στίχος, *Ἐγὼ πρὸς τὸν Θεὸν ἐκέκραξα·* ἕτερος στίχος, *Ἑσπέρας καὶ πρωῒ καὶ μεσημβρίας. Δόξα καὶ νῦν.* Θεοτοκίον,[105] *Ὅτι οὐκ ἔχομεν παρρησίαν διὰ τὰ πολλὰ ἡμῶν ἁμαρτήματα. Ταχὺ προκαταλαβέτωσαν ἡμᾶς οἱ οἰκτιρμοί σου, Κύριε, ὅτι ἐπτωχεύσαμεν σφόδρα. Βοήθησον ἡμῖν, ὁ Θεὸς ὁ Σωτὴρ ἡμῶν· ἕνεκεν τῆς δόξης τοῦ ὀνόματός σου, Κύριε, ῥῦσαι ἡμᾶς καὶ ἱλάσθητι ταῖς ἁμαρτίαις ἡμῶν ἕνεκεν τοῦ ὀνόματός σου.* Εἶτα τὸ τρισάγιον, τὸ *Πάτερ ἡμῶν,* τὸ *Κύριε, ἐλέησον,* μ', μετάνοιαι καὶ εὐχαί,

---

104. στίχος indicated in the margin.
105. θεοτοκίον indicated in the margin.

(II.3)

Great Sixth Hour[96]

The *Heavenly king*, the

Trisagion, the

Our Father (*HR* 8),

troparia, mode II:

> *We worship your immaculate image* (*TR* 125).

You wrought salvation (*TR* 125).

You who illuminated earthly things (*PaR* 141), and

theotokion: *You are blessed above all others* (*HR* 125).

Lord, have mercy twelve times.

Come, let us worship, the three psalms of the sixth (hour), that is:

Psalm 53: *Save me, O God, by your name.*

Psalm 54: *Hearken, O God, to my prayer.*

Psalm 90: *He that dwells in the help of the highest.*

Glory, both now.

Alleluia, alleluia, glory to you, O God three times.

Lord, have mercy three times.

And if the church is to celebrate a feast, you will sing the troparion of the feast; otherwise, say the prokeimenon: *You who on the sixth day and at the sixth hour, when nailed to the cross* (*TR* 123); verse: *Hearken, O God, to my prayer* (Ps 54:2); another verse: *I cried to God* (Ps 54:17); another verse: *Evening and morning and noon* (Ps 54:18).

Glory, both now.

theotokion: *We have no license to speak because of our many sins* (*TR* 123).

Let your mercy quickly reach us, O Lord, for we are utterly bereft. Help us, O God our savior. For the glory of your name, O Lord, deliver us and for your name's sake be merciful to our sins (Ps 78:8–9); then the

Trisagion, the

Our Father, the

Lord, have mercy forty times,

bows,[97] and prayers:

---

96. The office is said privately.

97. Likely fifteen; cf. 119n95.

Ὁ ἐν ἕκτῃ ὥρᾳ τῷ σταυρῷ προσηλωθείς, Ἰησοῦ ὁ Θεὸς ἡμῶν, καὶ τὴν μὲν ἁμαρτίαν νεκρώσας ἐν τῷ ξύλῳ· τὸν δὲ νεκρωθέντα ζωώσας, τὸ πλάσμα τῶν χειρῶν σου, τὸν ἄνθρωπον ὃν ἀπέκτεινεν ἡ ἁμαρτία. Νέκρωσόν μου τὰ πάθη τοῖς ζωοποιοῖς σου παθήμασι· καὶ τοῖς ἥλοις,[106] οἷς προσεπάρης, ἐκ τῆς τῶν |[245] ὑλικῶν προσπαθείας ἐξήλωσόν μου τὸν νοῦν καὶ προσήλωσον τῇ ἀγάπῃ σου, Χριστὲ ὁ Θεός, καὶ σῶσόν με.

Εὐχὴ ἑτέρα[107]

Θεὲ καὶ Κύριε τῶν δυνάμεων καὶ πάσης κτίσεως δημιουργέ, ὁ διὰ σπλάγχνα ἀνεικάστου ἐλέους σου τὸν μονογενῆ σου Υἱόν, τὸν Κύριον ἡμῶν Ἰησοῦν Χριστόν, καταπέμψας ἐπὶ σωτηρίᾳ τοῦ γένους ἡμῶν, καὶ διὰ τοῦ τιμίου αὐτοῦ σταυροῦ τὸ χειρόγραφον τῶν ἁμαρτιῶν ἡμῶν διαρρήξας, καὶ θριαμβεύσας ἐν αὐτῷ τὰς ἀρχὰς καὶ ἐξουσίας τοῦ σκότους, αὐτός, Δέσποτα φιλάνθρωπε, πρόσδεξαι καὶ ἡμῶν τῶν ἁμαρτωλῶν τὰς εὐχαρίστους ταύτας καὶ ἱκετηρίους ἐντεύξεις. Ῥῦσαι ἡμᾶς ἀπὸ παντὸς ὀλεθρίου καὶ σκοτεινοῦ παραπτώματος καὶ πάντων τῶν κακῶσαι ἡμᾶς ζητούντων ἀοράτων ἐχθρῶν. Καθήλωσον ἐκ τοῦ φόβου σου τὰς σάρκας ἡμῶν, καὶ μὴ ἐκκλίνῃς τὰς καρδίας ἡμῶν εἰς λόγους ἢ εἰς λογισμοὺς πονηρίας, ἀλλὰ τῷ πόθῳ σου τρῶσον ἡμῶν τὰς ψυχάς, ἵνα πρὸς σὲ διὰ παντὸς ἀτενίζοντες, καὶ τῷ παρὰ σοῦ φωτί, σὲ τὸ ἀπρόσιτον κατοπτεύοντες φῶς, ἀκατάπαυστόν |[245v] σοι τὴν ἐξομολόγησιν καὶ εὐχαριστίαν ἀναπέμπωμεν, τῷ ἀνάρχῳ Πατρὶ σὺν τῷ μονογενεῖ Υἱῷ καὶ τῷ παναγίῳ καὶ ἀγαθῷ καὶ ζωοποιῷ σου Πνεύματι νῦν καὶ ἀεὶ καὶ εἰς τούς.

Εἶτα τὰ τυπικὰ ἑορτῆς οὔσης, εἰ δ᾽ οὖν μετὰ τὴν θ᾽ ἔνθα καὶ ἐγράφησαν.

---

106. ἥλοις: C.
107. εὐχὴ ἑτέρα written in the margin.

When in the sixth hour you were nailed to the cross, O Jesus our God, you put sin to death on the tree. You brought to life the man who was dead, the creation of your hands, man whom sin had killed. Mortify my passions through your life-giving sufferings; and using the nails with which you were pierced, detach my mind from its attachment to material things and fix it to your love, O Christ our God, and save me.

Another prayer: *O God, **Lord of hosts** (Ps 45:8) and maker of all creation, through your tender, incomparable mercy (cf. Lk 1:78) you yourself sent your only-begotten Son, our Lord Jesus Christ, for the salvation of our race. Through his precious cross you ripped apart the record of our sins and **in him triumphed over the principalities and powers of darkness** (Col 2:15, Eph 6:12). O benevolent master, accept from us sinners these grateful and suppliant entreaties. Rescue us from every destructive and dark transgression and from all invisible enemies who seek to do us harm. **Pierce our flesh with the fear of you** (Ps 118:120), and **let our hearts not turn to evil words** (Ps 140:4) or thoughts. Wound our souls with longing for you, so that we may continually gaze upon you and <be led>[98] by your light—observing you, **the unapproachable light** (1 Tm 6:16)—and without ceasing offer up to you praise and thanks, to the Father without beginning and the only-begotten Son and the all-holy, good, and life-giving Spirit, now and always and <forever. Amen>.*

Then when it is a feast day, (perform) the typika; otherwise (do so) after the ninth hour, where they were written.

---

98. ὁδηγούμενοι supplied from P.

Ὥρα θ᾽

Βασιλεῦ οὐράνιε, παράκλητε, εἶτα τὸ τρισάγιον, τὸ Πάτερ ἡμῶν, τροπάρια, Βλέπων ὁ λῃστὴς τὸν ἀρχηγὸν τῆς ζωῆς ἐπί.

Θεοτοκίον,[108] *Τὸν ἀμνὸν καὶ ποιμένα καὶ σωτῆρα τοῦ κόσμου ἐπὶ σταυροῦ θεωροῦσα ἡ τεκοῦσα, ἔλεγε δακρύουσα· Ὁ μὲν κόσμος ἀγάλλεται, δεχόμενος τὴν λύτρωσιν· τὰ δὲ σπλάγχνα μου φλέγονται, ὁρώσης σου τὴν σταύρωσιν, ἣν ὑπὲρ πάντων ὑπομένεις, ὁ υἱὸς καὶ Θεός μου.*

Κύριε, ἐλέησον, ιε᾽· εἶτα τὸ Δεῦτε, προσκυνήσωμεν καί· <ψαλμὸς> πγ᾽,[109] Ὡς ἀγαπητὰ τὰ σκηνώματά σου, Κύριε· πδ᾽, Εὐδόκησας, Κύριε, τὴν γῆν σοῦ, ἀπέστρεψας τήν· πε᾽, Κλῖνον, Κύριε, τὸ οὖς σου καὶ ἐπάκουσόν μου. Δόξα καὶ νῦν. Ἀλληλούϊα, ἀλληλούϊα, δόξα σοι, ὁ Θεός, ἐκ γ᾽· Κύριε, ἐλέησον, γ᾽. Δόξα καὶ νῦν.

Καὶ εἰ μὲν ἦγεν ἑορτὴν ἡ ἐκκλη<σία>, ἐπάσεις τὸ τῆς ἑορτῆς τροπάριον· εἰ δ᾽ οὖν, λέγε |[246] *Ὁ ἐν τῇ ἐνάτῃ[110] ὥρᾳ δι᾽ ἡμᾶς σαρκὶ θανάτου· στίχος, Ἐγγισάτω ἡ δέησίς μου ἐνώπιόν σου, Κύριε. Εἰσέλθοι τὸ ἀξίωμά μου. Δόξα καὶ νῦν.*

Ὁ δι᾽ ἡμᾶς γεννηθεὶς ἐκ παρθένου καὶ σταύρωσιν ὑπομείνας. Μὴ δὴ παραδώῃς ἡμᾶς εἰς τέλος διὰ τὸ ὄνομά σου καὶ μὴ διασκεδάσῃς τὴν διαθήκην σου καὶ μὴ ἀποστήσῃς τὸ ἔλεός σου ἀφ᾽ ἡμῶν, διὰ Ἀβραὰμ[111] τὸν ἠγαπημένον ὑπὸ σοῦ καὶ διὰ Ἰσαὰκ τὸν δοῦλόν σου καὶ Ἰσραὴλ τὸν ἅγιόν σου.

---

108. θεοτοκίον indicated in the margin.
109. πγ᾽ and two subsequent psalm numbers written in the margin.
110. θ᾽: C.
111. ἀβραὰμ: C.

(II.4)

Ninth Hour[99]

Heavenly king, comforter, then the

Trisagion, the

Our Father (HR 8),

troparia: *As the thief looked at the originator of life hanging on (HR 210).*

theotokion: *As his mother beheld the lamb, shepherd and* **savior of the world** *(Jn 4:42) on the cross , she said, weeping, "Though the world rejoices at receiving its redemption, my insides burn as I witness your crucifixion, which you, O my son and God, endure on behalf of everyone."*

Lord, have mercy fifteen times, then

Come, let us worship and.

Psalm 83: *How lovely are your tabernacles, O Lord.*

Psalm 84: *O Lord, you have taken pleasure in your land; you have turned back.*

Psalm 85: *Incline, O Lord, your ear and hearken to me.*

Glory, both now.

Alleluia, alleluia, glory to you, O God three times.

Lord, have mercy three times.

Glory, both now.

And if the church is to celebrate a feast, you will sing the troparion of the feast; otherwise, say (the prokeimenon): *You who in the ninth hour* **tasted death** *(Heb 2:9) in your flesh on our behalf (HR 209);* verse: *Let my supplication come near, O Lord (Ps 118:169). Let my petition come in*[100] *(Ps 118:170).*

Glory, both now.

You who for our sake were born of a virgin and suffered crucifixion (HR 209).

For your name's sake, deliver us not into oblivion and do not break your covenant or take your mercy from us, for the sake of Abraham your beloved, Isaac your servant, and your holy Israel (Ode 7:34–35); then, the

---

99. The office is said privately.
100. Noted as the second verse to the troparion in P.

Εἶτα τὸ τρισάγιον· τὸ *Πάτερ ἡμῶν*· *Κύριε, ἐλέησον*, μ'· μετάνοιαι, ιε', ἢ κἂν προσκυνήματα, καὶ εὐχή,

Ὁ τὴν ψυχὴν ἐπὶ ξύλου κρεμάμενος ἐνάτῃ ὥρᾳ παραδοὺς τῷ Πατρί, καὶ τῷ συσταυρωθέντι σοι λῃστῇ ὁδοποιήσας τὴν εἰς τὸν παράδεισον εἴσοδον, μή με παρίδῃς, μηδὲ ἀποδοκιμάσῃς, ἀγαθέ, ἀλλὰ ἁγίασόν μου τὴν ψυχὴν καὶ φώτισον τὴν διάνοιαν· καὶ τῆς ἀθανάτου σου τρυφῆς κοινωνόν με ἀνάδειξον τῶν θείων σου μυστηρίων, ἵνα γευσάμενός σου τῆς χρηστότητος, ὕμνον ἀσιγήτως προσφέρω σοι, ὁ ὑπὲρ πάντας |²⁴⁶ᵛ *ποθήσας σου τὴν ὡραιότητα, Χριστὲ ὁ Θεός· δόξα.*

Καὶ πάλιν, εἰ βούλ<ει>, καὶ τρισάγιον καὶ τροπάριον τὸ

*Σταυρωθέντος σου, Χριστέ, ἀνῃρέθη ἡ τυραννίς, ἐπατήθη ἡ δύναμις τοῦ ἐχθροῦ· οὔτε γὰρ ἄγγελος οὐκ ἄνθρωπος, ἀλλ᾿ αὐτὸς ὁ Κύριος ἔσωσας ἡμᾶς· δόξα σοι. Δόξα.*¹¹²

Τοῦ σταυροῦ σου τὸ ξύλον προσκυνοῦμεν, φιλάνθρωπε, ὅτι ἐν αὐτῷ προσηλώθης ἡ ζωὴ τῶν ἁπάντων. Παράδεισον ἠνέῳξας, Σωτήρ, τῷ πίστει προσελθόντι σοι λῃστῇ, καὶ τρυφῆς κατηξιώθη ὁμολογῶν σοι· Μνήσθητί μου, Κύριε. Δέξαι, ὥσπερ ἐκεῖνον, καὶ ἡμᾶς κραυγάζοντας· Ἡμάρτομεν πάντες· τῇ εὐσπλαγχνίᾳ σου μὴ ὑπερίδῃς ἡμᾶς. Καὶ νῦν.

*Θεοτοκίον,*¹¹³ *Οἱ τὴν σὴν προστασίαν κεκτημένοι, ἄχραντε, καὶ ταῖς σαῖς ἱκεσίαις τῶν δεινῶν λυτρούμενοι, τῷ σταυρῷ τοῦ υἱοῦ σου ἐν παντὶ φρουρούμενοι, καταχρέως σε πάντες εὐσεβῶς μεγαλύνομεν.*

Κύριε, ἐλέησον· καὶ τὴν εὐχὴν ταύτην,

Δέσποτα, Κύριε Ἰησοῦ Χριστὲ ὁ Θεὸς ἡμῶν, ὁ μακροθυμήσας ἐπὶ τοῖς ἡμῶν παραπτώμασι καὶ πολλοῖς καὶ μεγάλοις πλημμελήμασι, καὶ ἄχρι τῆς παρούσης ὥρας ἡμᾶς |²⁴⁷ *ἀγαγών, ἐν ᾗ ἐπὶ τοῦ ζωοποιοῦ ξύλου κρεμ{μ}άμενος, τῷ εὐγνώμονι λῃστῇ τὴν εἰς τὸν παράδεισον ὡδοποίησας εἴσοδον, καὶ θανάτῳ τὸν θάνατον ἔλυσας, ἱλάσθητι ἡμῖν τοῖς ἁμαρτωλοῖς καὶ ἀναξίοις δούλοις σου, ἡμάρτομεν γὰρ καὶ ἠνομήσαμεν· καὶ οὐκ ἐσμὲν ἄξιοι ἆραι*¹¹⁴ *τὰ ὄμματα καὶ*

---

112. δόξα indicated in the margin.
113. καὶ νῦν. θεοτοκίον indicated in the margin.
114. ἆραι: C.

Trisagion, the

Our Father,

Lord, have mercy forty times,

fifteen bows or prostrations, and

prayer: *You who in the ninth hour delivered your soul to the Father while hanging on the cross, and showed the thief crucified with you the way into paradise, O you who are good, do not neglect me, neither reject (me), but sanctify my soul, illuminate my thought; and declare me to be a sharer in the deathless delight of your sacred mysteries, so that tasting of your kindness* (cf. 1 Pt 2:3), *I, who more than all long for your beauty, may unceasingly offer you praise: O Christ our God, glory <to you>.*

And again, if you wish, also a Trisagion and the troparion: *When you were crucified, O Christ, tyranny was destroyed; the power of the enemy was trampled. For neither angel nor man, but you, the Lord himself, saved us; glory to you.*

Glory.

O you who love mankind, we worship the wood of your cross, since you the life of all were nailed to it. You opened paradise, savior, to the thief who approached you in faith, and he was deemed worthy of its delights by confessing to you, "**Remember me, O Lord**" (Lk 23:42). *As you did him, receive us, too, as we cry out,* "*We are all sinners; in your compassion, do not neglect us.*"

Both now.

theotokion: *We who possess your protection, O undefiled one, and are delivered from terror by your supplications, being guarded throughout everything by the cross of your son, we all reverently extol you in our indebtedness.*

Lord, have mercy, and this

prayer: *Master, Lord Jesus Christ our God, you who were patient in the face of our transgressions and our many grievous sins and have led us up to the present hour, when hanging on the life-giving cross you showed the way into paradise for the prudent thief and annulled death by death. Be merciful to us sinners, your unworthy servants, for we have sinned and transgressed; we are not worthy to raise (our) eyes and look toward the* **height of heaven** (cf. Ode 12:9; Ps 102:11) *because we abandoned the way of your righteousness and we have conducted our lives by the wishes of our hearts. But we entreat your*

βλέψαι εἰς τὸ ὕψος τοῦ οὐρανοῦ, διότι κατελίπομεν τὴν ὁδὸν τῆς δικαιοσύνης σου καὶ ἐπορεύθημεν ἐν τοῖς θελήμασι τῶν καρδιῶν ἡμῶν· ἀλλ᾿ ἱκετεύομεν τὴν σὴν ἀγαθότητα. Φεῖσαι ἡμῶν, Κύριε, διὰ τὸ πλῆθος τοῦ ἐλέους σου καὶ σῶσον ἡμᾶς διὰ τὸ ὄνομά σου, ὅτι ἐξέλιπον ἐν ματαιότητι αἱ ἡμέραι ἡμῶν. Ἐξελοῦ ἡμᾶς τῆς τοῦ ἀντικειμένου χειρὸς καὶ ἄφες ἡμῖν τὰ ἁμαρτήματα, καὶ νέκρωσον τὸ σαρκικὸν ἡμῶν φρόνημα ἵνα, τὸν παλαιὸν ἀποθέμενοι ἄνθρωπον, τὸν νέον ἐνδυσώμεθα· καὶ σοὶ ζήσωμεν τῷ ἡμετέρῳ Δεσπότῃ καὶ κηδεμόνι· |²⁴⁷ᵛ καὶ οὕτω τοῖς σοῖς ἀκολουθοῦντες προστάγμασιν εἰς τὴν αἰωνίαν ἀνάπαυσιν καταντήσωμεν, ἔνθα πάντων τῶν ἐν σοὶ εὐφραινομένων ἐστὶν ἡ κατοικία. Σὺ γὰρ εἶ ἡ ἀληθὴς εὐφροσύνη καὶ ἀγαλλίασις τῶν ἀγαπώντων σε, Χριστὲ ὁ Θεὸς ἡμῶν, καὶ σοὶ τὴν δόξαν ἀναπέμπομεν, τῷ Πατρὶ καὶ τῷ Υἱῷ καὶ τῷ ἁγίῳ Πνεύματι εἰς τοὺς αἰῶνας τῶν αἰώνων.

goodness: spare us, O Lord, through the fullness of your mercy (Ps 5:8, 68:14), and save us for your name's sake, for our days were consumed in vanity (Ps 77:33). Rescue us from the hand of the adversary, forgive us our sins, and mortify our carnal thoughts (cf. Rom 8:6), so that, putting aside the old self (Rom 6:6), we may put on the new and live for you who are our master and guardian, and thus by following your commands, we will attain everlasting repose in the place that is the dwelling of all who rejoice in you (cf. Ps 86:7); for you are the true joy and exaltation of those who love you, O Christ our God, and to you we offer up glory: to the Father and the Son and the Holy Spirit, for ever and ever. <Amen.>

Τὰ τυπικά

Εἰ μὴ ἀπὸ τῆς ϛ' ὥρας ψαλθήτω οὕτως· τὸ τρισάγιον, τὸ *Πάτερ ἡμῶν,* τὸ *Κύριε, ἐλέησον·* εἶτα τὸ *Εὐλόγει, ἡ ψυχή <μου> τὸν Κύριον·* εὐλογητὸς εἶ, Κύριε· ρβ',[115] *Εὐλόγει, ἡ ψυχή μου, τὸν Κύριον καὶ πάντα τὰ ἐντός. Κύριε ἐλέησον, γ'· Δόξα τῷ Πατρί, καὶ τῷ Υἱῷ, καὶ τῷ ἁγίῳ Πνεύματι·* ρμε', *Αἴνει, ἡ ψυχή μου, τὸν Κύριον. Αἰνέσω Κύριον ἐν ζωῇ. Καὶ νῦν. Ὁ μονογενὴς Υἱὸς καὶ Λόγος.* Τὸ *Κύριε, ἐλέησον,* γ'· εἶτα τὸ

Μνήσθητί μου, Κύριε, ὅταν ἔλθῃς ἐν τῇ βασιλείᾳ σου.

Μακάριοι οἱ πτωχοὶ τῷ πνεύματι, ὅτι αὐτῶν ἐστιν ἡ βασιλεία τῶν οὐρανῶν.

Μακάριοι οἱ πενθοῦντες, ὅτι αὐτοὶ παρακληθήσονται. |[248]

Μακάριοι οἱ πραεῖς, ὅτι αὐτοὶ κληρονομήσουσι τὴν γῆν.

Μακάριοι οἱ πεινῶντες καὶ διψῶντες τὴν δικαιοσύνην, ὅτι αὐτοὶ χορτασθήσονται.

Μακάριοι οἱ ἐλεήμονες, ὅτι αὐτοὶ ἐλεηθήσονται.

Μακάριοι οἱ καθαροὶ τῇ καρδίᾳ, ὅτι αὐτοὶ τὸν Θεὸν ὄψονται.

---

115. ρβ' written in the margin, as is the subsequent psalm number.

(II.5)

The Typika[101]

Unless (said) after the sixth hour, they should be chanted in this way:

Trisagion,

Our Father (HR 8),

Lord, have mercy, then

Bless the Lord, O <my> soul (Ps 102:1); **blessed are you, O Lord** (Ps 118:12).[102]

Psalm 102: *Bless the Lord, O my Soul, and all that is within me*

Lord, have mercy three times.

Glory to the Father, and to the Son, and to the Holy Spirit.[103]

Psalm 145: *My soul, praise the Lord. While I live will I praise the Lord.*

Both now.

Only-begotten son and Word (Monogenes: HR 84).

Lord, have mercy three times, then:

(Beatitudes; Mt 5:3–12)

Remember me, O Lord, when you come into your kingdom (Lk 23:42).[104]

Blessed are the poor in spirit, for theirs is the kingdom of heaven.

Blessed are those who mourn, for they shall be comforted.

Blessed are the meek, for they shall inherit the earth.

Blessed are those who hunger and thirst for righteousness, for they shall be satisfied.

Blessed are the merciful, for they shall obtain mercy.

Blessed are the pure in heart, for they shall see God.

---

101. Said after the sixth hour on days when the Divine Liturgy is celebrated, but after the ninth on days when there is no liturgy. See Parenti § III.10.

102. P specifies that this be said after each verse of Ps 102.

103. P specifies that this be said after each verse of Ps 145.

104. This line is said as a refrain after each of the Beatitudes (Arranz, *Typicon de Messine*, 203.25–26; HR 185).

εἰς τὸν ἦχον

Μακάριοι οἱ εἰρηνοποιοί, ὅτι αὐτοὶ υἱοὶ Θεοῦ κληθήσονται.

καὶ μακαρισμοὶ τοῦ ἤχου

Μακάριοι οἱ δεδιωγμένοι ἕνεκεν δικαιοσύνης, ὅτι αὐτῶν ἐστιν ἡ
βασιλεία τῶν οὐρανῶν.
Μακάριοι ἐστὲ ὅταν ὀνειδίσωσιν ὑμᾶς καὶ διώξωσι καὶ εἴπωσι πᾶν
πονηρὸν ῥῆμα καθ᾽ ὑμῶν[116] ψευδόμενοι ἕνεκεν ἐμοῦ.
Χαίρετε καὶ ἀγαλλιᾶσθε, ὅτι ὁ μισθὸς ὑμῶν πολὺς ἐν τοῖς οὐρανοῖς.

Μνήσθητι ἡμῶν, Κύριε. Μνήσθητι ἡμῶν, Δέσποτα. Μνήσθητι ἡμῶν, Ἅγιε,
ὅταν ἔλθῃς ἐν τῇ βασιλείᾳ σου. Χορὸς ὁ ἐπουράνιος ὑμνεῖ σε καὶ λέγει· Ἅγιος,
ἅγιος, ἅγιος Κύριος Σαβαώθ, πλήρης ὁ οὐρανὸς καὶ ἡ γῆ τῆς δόξης σου.
Προσέλθετε πρὸς αὐτὸν καὶ φωτίσθητε, καὶ τὰ πρόσωπα ὑμῶν |[248v] οὐ μὴ
καταισχυνθῇ. Χορὸς ἁγίων ἀγγέλων καὶ ἀρχαγγέλων ὑμνεῖ σε καὶ λέγει·
Ἅγιος, ἅγιος, ἅγιος. Δόξα καὶ νῦν. Πιστεύω εἰς ἕνα Θεόν· Πάτερ ἡμῶν· τὸ
Κύριε, ἐλέησον, ιε᾽· εἶτα τὸ Εἴη τὸ ὄνομα Κυρίου εὐλογημένον, ἐκ τρίτου· καὶ
τὸ Εὐλογήσω{μεν} τὸν Κύριον ἐν παντὶ καιρῷ.

Πρὸ τῆς τῶν θείων καὶ ἁγίων μυστηρίων μεταλήψεως
Τρισάγιον, τὸν ν᾽ ψαλμόν, τὸ Ἐλέησον ἡμᾶς, Κύριε, ἐλέησον ἡμᾶς, πάσης

---

116. ἡμῶν: C.

In the mode (of the week)

Blessed are the peacemakers, for they shall be called the sons of God.

And Beatitudes of the mode (of the week)

Blessed are those who are persecuted for righteousness' sake, for theirs is the kingdom of heaven.

Blessed are you when men revile you and persecute you and utter all kinds of evil things against you falsely on my account.

Rejoice and be glad, for your reward is great in heaven.

Remember us, O Lord. Remember us, O master. Remember us, O holy One, when you come into your kingdom.

The heavenly choir praises you and says, **"Holy, holy, holy is the Lord of hosts; heaven and earth are full of your glory"** *(Is 6:3).*

Draw near to him and be enlightened, and your faces shall not be ashamed (Ps 33:6).

The choir of holy angels and archangels praises you and says, **"Holy, holy, holy** *<***is the Lord of hosts; heaven and earth are full of your glory***>."*

Glory, both now.[105]

I believe in one God (Creed: HR 30–31).

Our Father.

Lord, have mercy fifteen times, then

Let the name of the Lord be blessed (Ps 112:2) three times, and

I will bless the Lord at all times (Ps 33).[106]

Before partaking of the divine and holy mysteries[107]

Trisagion.

Psalm 50, the (troparia):

> **Have mercy on us, O Lord, have mercy on us.** (Ps 122:3, Mt 20:30)
> *We who* (82).
> *Glory.*

---

105. The performance of these lines is described in Arranz, *Typicon de Messine*, 203.26–28.

106. Entire psalm according to Arranz, *Typicon de Messine*, xli, but only Ps 33:2 according to J. Mateos, "Un Horologion inédit de Saint-Sabas. Le codex sinaïtique grec 863 (IXe siècle)," in *Mélanges Eugène Tisserant*, 1:55 (Vatican City: Biblioteca Apostolica Vaticana, 1964).

107. See Parenti § III.11.

γάρ. *Δόξα. Κύριε, ἐλέησον ἡμᾶς, ἐπὶ σοὶ γάρ. Καὶ νῦν. Τῆς εὐσπλαγχνίας τὴν πύλην.* Μετάνοιαι ἢ προσκυνήματα, καὶ εὐχὴ ἡ τῷ πεντηκοστῷ συνάδουσα ἥτις καὶ προγέγραπται.

O Lord, have mercy on us, for we have put (82).

Both now.

Open to us the gate of compassion (82).

Bows or prostrations, and the

Prayer said together with the fiftieth psalm, which has also been written out above (82–84).

Ἀκολουθία τῆς μεγάλης ε´

ὥρα α´

Δεῦτε, προσκυνήσωμεν, καὶ ψαλμὸς λε´, *Φησὶν ὁ παράνομος·* καὶ ψαλμὸς μ´, *Μακάριος ὁ συνιῶν·* τρισάγιον καὶ τροπάριον, ἦχος πλάγιος δ´,

Ὅτε οἱ ἔνδοξοι μαθηταὶ ἐν τῷ νιπτῆρι τοῦ δείπνου ἐφωτίζοντο, τότε Ἰούδας ὁ δυσσεβὴς φιλαργυρίαν νοσήσας ἐσκοτίζετο· καὶ ἀνόμοις κριταῖς σὲ τὸν δίκαιον κριτὴν παραδίδωσι. Βλέπε, χρημάτων ἐραστά, τὸν διὰ ταῦτα ἀγχόνῃ χρησάμενον· φεῦγε ἀκόρεστον ψυ|²⁴⁹-χὴν τὴν διδασκάλῳ τοιαῦτα τολμήσασαν· ὁ περὶ πάντας ἀγαθός, Κύριε, δόξα.

ὥρα γ´

Ψαλμὸς να´, *Τί ἐγκαυχᾷ ἐν κακίᾳ·* καὶ ψαλμὸς νβ´, *Εἶπεν ἄφρων ἐν καρδίᾳ αὐτοῦ·* τρισάγιον, τροπάριον, ἦχος πλάγιος δ´,

Ὦ πῶς Ἰούδας, ὁ ποτέ σου μαθητής, τὴν προδοσίαν ἐμελέτα κατὰ σοῦ; Συνεδείπνησε δολίως ὁ ἐπίβουλος καὶ ἄδικος. Πορευθεὶς εἶπε τοῖς ἱερεῦσι· Τί μοι παρέχετε, καὶ παραδώσω ὑμῖν ἐκεῖνον τὸν νόμον λύσαντα καὶ βεβηλοῦντα τὸ σάββατον; Μακρόθυμε, δόξα.

(II.6)

Offices of Maundy Thursday[108]

First hour

Come, let us worship.

> Psalm 35: *The transgressor says* and
> Psalm 40: *Blessed is the man who considers.*

Trisagion and

troparion, plagal mode IV,

When the glorious disciples were being enlightened at the supper's washing of the feet, at that moment the impious Judas was being driven into darkness, his mind sick with avarice. He surrendered you, the just judge, to the lawless judges. O lover of money, look at him who resorted to a noose on account of that. Flee the insatiable spirit that dared commit such things against the teacher. Glory <to you>, O Lord, who are good to all around you.

Third hour

<Come, let us worship.>[109]

> Psalm 51: *Why do you boast of iniquity in your* and
> Psalm 52: *The fool has said in his heart.*

Trisagion.

Troparion, plagal mode IV,

Oh how did Judas, who was once your disciple, (come to) practice betrayal against you? Treacherous and unrighteous, he deceitfully ate supper with you. He went and said to the priests, "What do you offer me and I will deliver to you (cf. Mt 26:15) that man who broke the Law and profanes the Sabbath?" Glory <to you>, O patient <Lord>.

---

108. This is an interhour (μεσώριον), like II.7. The passages are added to the canonical hours; see Parenti § III.12.

109. Presumably an omission by oversight here and in the following hours.

ὥρα ς’

Ψαλμὸς νς᾽, Ἐλέησον, ὁ Θεός, ἐλέησόν με, ὅτι ἐπὶ σοὶ πέποιθεν· καὶ ψαλμὸς νη᾽, Ἐξελοῦ με ἐκ τῶν ἐχθρῶν μου, ὁ Θεός· τρισάγιον καὶ τροπάριον, ἦχος βαρύς,

Ποῖός σε τρόπος, Ἰούδα, προδότην τοῦ Σωτῆρος εἰργάσατο; Μὴν τοῦ χοροῦ σε τῶν ἀποστόλων ἐχώρισε; Μὴν τοῦ χαρίσματος τῶν ἰαμάτων ἐστέρησε; Μὴν συνδειπνήσας ἐκείνοις σὲ τῆς τραπέζης ἀπώσατο; Μὴν τῶν ἄλλων νίψας τοὺς πόδας, τοὺς σοὺς ὑπερεῖδε;

ὥρας θ’

Ψαλμὸς ρη᾽, Ὁ Θεός, τὴν αἴνεσίν μου μὴ παρασιωπήσῃς· καὶ ψαλμὸς ρλθ᾽, Ἐξελοῦ με, Κύριε, ἐξ ἀνθρώπου πονηροῦ· τρισάγιον καὶ τροπάριον, ἦχος βαρύς,

Ἐν τῷ δείπνῳ τοὺς μαθητὰς διατρέφων καὶ τὴν σκῆψιν |²⁴⁹ᵛ τῆς προδοσίας γινώσκων, ἐν αὐτῷ τὸν Ἰούδαν διήλεγξας, ἀδιόρθωτον μὲν τοῦτον ἐπιστάμενος, γνωρίσαι δὲ πᾶσι[117] βουλόμενος ὅτι θέλων παρεδόθης, ἵνα κόσμον ἁρπάσῃς τοῦ ἀλλοτρίου· μακρόθυμε Κύριε, δόξα.

---

117. πάλιν: C; corrected after TR 667.

Sixth hour

<Come, let us worship.>

Psalm 56: *Have mercy, O God, have mercy on me; for my soul has trusted in you* and

Psalm 58: *Deliver me from my enemies, O God.*

Trisagion and

troparion, barys mode,

*What manner of circumstance turned you, O Judas, into a betrayer of the savior? He did not separate you from the band of apostles, did he? Did he deprive you of the **gifts of healing** (1 Cor 12:9)? Did he banish you from the table after eating with them? Did he perhaps overlook your feet when he washed the others'?*

Ninth hour

<Come, let us worship.>

Psalm 108: *O God, pass not over my praise in silence* and

Psalm 139: *Deliver me, O Lord, from the evil man.*

Trisagion and

troparion, barys mode,

You fed the disciples at the supper even knowing the pretext for betrayal. There you exposed Judas, the one that you knew full well to be beyond redemption. You wished, though, to make known to all mankind that you were willingly surrendered, so that you might seize the world from the grasp of the enemy.[110] *Glory <to you>, O patient Lord.*

---

110. Literally "alien," meaning Satan; see Lampe, *Lexicon, s.v.*

Εὐχὴ πρὸ τῆς ἁγίας μεταλήψεως
τοῦ ἁγίου Ἰωάννου τοῦ Χρυσοστόμου

Κύριε, οἶδα ὅτι οὐκ εἰμὶ ἄξιος, οὐδὲ ἱκανός, ἵνα μου ὑπὸ τὴν στέγην εἰσέλθῃς τοῦ οἴκου τῆς ψυχῆς, διότι ὅλη ἔρημος ἐστὶ καὶ καταπεσοῦσα· καὶ οὐκ ἔχεις ἐν ἐμοὶ τόπον ἄξιον ποῦ τὴν κεφαλὴν κλῖναι. Ἀλλ' ὡς ἐξ ἔθους δι' ἡμᾶς ἐταπείνωσας ἑαυτόν, συμμετρίασον καὶ ἐν ἐμοὶ τῷ ταπεινῷ· καὶ ὡς κατεδέξω ἐν σπηλαίῳ καὶ φάτνῃ ἀλόγων ἀνακλιθῆναι, οὕτως κατάδεξαι καὶ ἐν τῇ φάτνῃ τῆς ἀλόγου μου ψυχῆς καὶ τῷ ἐσπιλωμένῳ στόματι εἰσελθεῖν. Ὁ καταξιώσας εἰσελθεῖν καὶ δειπνῆσαι εἰς τὴν οἰκίαν Σίμωνος τοῦ λεπροῦ· αὐτός, φιλάνθρωπε, καταξίωσον εἰσελθεῖν καὶ εἰς τὴν οἰκίαν τῆς |²⁵⁰ ψυχῆς μου τοῦ νεκροῦ καὶ λεπροῦ. Ὁ καταδεξάμενος τὴν ὁμοίαν μου πόρνην τὴν ἁμαρτωλὸν ἁπτομένην σου, σπλαγχνίσθητι καὶ ἐν ἐμοὶ τῷ ἁμαρτωλῷ προσερχομένῳ καὶ ἁπτομένῳ σου· καὶ ὡς οὐκ ἐβδελύξω αὐτῆς τὸ ῥυπαρὸν στόμα καταφιλοῦν τοὺς ἀχράντους σου πόδας, μὴ βδελύξῃ μου τὸ ῥυπαρὸν στόμα καὶ ἐναγές, μὴ δὲ τὰ ἔμμυσα καὶ ἀκάθαρτα χείλη μου. Ἀλλὰ γενέσθω μοι ὁ ἄνθραξ τοῦ παναγίου σου σώματος εἰς φωτισμὸν τῆς ταπεινῆς μου ψυχῆς καὶ τοῦ σώματος, εἰς κουφισμὸν τοῦ βάρους τῶν ἐμῶν πλημμελημάτων, εἰς ἀποτροπὴν καὶ ἐμπόδιον τῆς φαύλης καὶ πονηρᾶς μου συνηθείας. Οὐ γὰρ ὡς καταφρονῶν προσέρχομαί σοι, Χριστέ, ἀλλὰ θαρρῶν τῇ σῇ ἀγαθότητι, καὶ ἵνα μὴ |²⁵⁰ᵛ ἀφιστάμενος τῶν ζωοποιῶν μυστηρίων τοῦ ἀχράντου σου σώματος καὶ τοῦ τιμίου αἵματος θηριάλωτος ὑπὸ τοῦ πονηροῦ θηρὸς γένωμαι. Ὡς οὖν μόνος ὢν ἅγιος, ἁγίασόν μου τὸν νοῦν καὶ τὴν καρδίαν, τοὺς νεφροὺς καὶ τὰ σπλάγχνα, καὶ ὅλον με ἀνακαίνισον· καὶ ἐρίζωσον τὸν φόβον σου ἐν τοῖς μέλεσί μου καὶ ἐν τῷ ἁγιασμῷ σου διατήρησόν με· καὶ γενοῦ μοι βοηθὸς καὶ ἀντιλήπτωρ, καταξιῶν με τῆς ἐκ δεξιῶν σου παραστάσεως, πρεσβείαις τῆς ἀχράντου σου μητρὸς καὶ πάντων τῶν ἁγίων τῶν ἀπ' αἰῶνος σοι εὐαρεστησάντων.

(II.7)

(Prayers before and after holy communion)[111]

Prayer before the holy partaking, by St. John Chrysostom:

O Lord, I know that I am not worthy, nor am I adequate, to have you enter under the roof (Mt 8:8) *of the house of (my) soul, for it is a total wasteland and has collapsed. You do not have in me a worthy place on which to rest your head* (Mt 8:20). *As you customarily humbled yourself for our sake, do the same, too, in my case, the humble one. As you consented to lie in a cave and in a manger of unreasoning animals, so consent also to enter the manger of my unreasoning soul and defiled mouth. You who deigned to enter and eat at the house of Simon the leper, you, O lover of mankind, deign also to enter into the soul's house of me, a corpse and a leper. You who received the harlot who is like me, she the sinner who touches you, show your compassion also in my case, the sinner who approaches and touches you. Just as you were not disgusted when her filthy mouth kissed your undefiled feet, do not be disgusted by my filthy, foul mouth, neither by my polluted and unclean lips. But be for me the burning coal*[112] *of your most holy body, to illuminate my humble soul and my body, to relieve the burden of my sins, to avert and thwart my evil and worthless habits. I approach you, O Christ, not as one who is presumptuous, but as one confident in you goodness; lest—keeping myself away from the life-giving mysteries of your undefiled body and precious blood*[113]*—I be devoured by the evil beast of prey. As, then, the only one who is holy, sanctify my mind and heart, my kidneys and bowels: renew all of me. Root the fear of you in my limbs and preserve me by your sanctification. Be for me a helper* (Ps 26:9) *and a supporter* (Ps 58:17), *one who esteems me worthy of a place at your right hand through the intercessions of your undefiled mother and of all the saints who have been pleasing to you through the ages.*

---

111. See Parenti § III.11.

112. Cf. Is 6:5–7.

113. "Your immaculate body and precious blood" is a phrase used in the liturgy: P. Trempelas, *Αἱ τρεῖς λειτουργίαι κατὰ τοὺς ἐν Ἀθήναις κώδικας* (Athens: Hypo tes M. Patriarchikes Epistemonikes Epitropes pros Anatheoresin kai Ekdosin ton Leitourgikon Vivlion, 1935), 76, 129, 212.

Εὐχὴ[118] ἑτέρα ὁμοίως

Ὁ Θεός, ἄνες, ἄφες, συγχώρησόν μοι τὰ πλημμελήματά μου ὅσα σοι ἥμαρτον, εἴτε ἐν γνώσει, εἴτε ἐν ἀγνοίᾳ, εἴτε ἐν λόγῳ, εἴτε ἐν ἔργῳ ἥμαρτον, ἥμαρτον γάρ· πάντα μοὶ συγχώρησον ὡς ἀγαθὸς καὶ φιλάνθρωπος· καί, τῇ πρεσβείᾳ τῆς ἀχράντου καὶ ἀειπαρθένου σου μητρὸς |[251] καὶ πάντων τῶν ἁγίων σου, ἀκατάκριτόν με διατήρησον δέξασθαι τὸ τίμιον καὶ ἅγιον καὶ ἄχραντον σῶμα καὶ αἷμά σου εἰς ἴασιν τῆς ψυχῆς, καὶ ἐξάλειψιν τῶν πονηρῶν μου λογισμῶν· ὅτι σοῦ ἐστιν ἡ βασιλεία καὶ ἡ δύναμις καὶ ἡ δόξα εἰς τοὺς αἰῶνας.

Εὐχὴ μετὰ τὴν θείαν μετάληψιν

Εὐχαριστῶ σοι, φιλάνθρωπε, ὅτι διὰ πολλὴν ἀγαθότητα ἠνέσχου κοινωνόν με γενέσθαι τοῦ ἀχράντου σου σώματος καὶ τοῦ τιμίου αἵματος· καὶ οὐκ ἐβδελύξω, οὐδέ, ὡς μεμολυσμένον καὶ τῆς ὑποδοχῆς τοῦ ἁγιασμοῦ σου ἀνάξιον, ἀοράτῳ σου καῖ θείᾳ δυνάμει ἀπώσω, ἀλλ' εὐδόκησας κἀμὲ τὸν ἁμαρτωλὸν τῇ ἀθανάτῳ σου καὶ θείᾳ διαθρέψαι τραπέζῃ· ἧς τὴν ζωοποιὸν χάριν ἀμείωτον ἐν τῇ ταπεινῇ μου ψυχῇ διατήρησον καὶ τὸν φωτισμὸν ἀκατάσβεστον, φωτίζων ἡμῶν πᾶσαν νόησιν, πᾶσαν αἴσθησιν, ἀ|[251v]–προσκόπους φυλάττων καὶ ἀπεριτρέπτους ἡμᾶς τοῦ σκότους τῆς ἁμαρτίας τοῦ δοξάζειν καὶ εὐχαριστεῖν σοι κατὰ τὸ σὸν θέλημα πάσας τὰς ἡμέρας τῆς ζωῆς μου, πρεσβείαις τῆς παναχράντου δεσποίνης ἡμῶν Θεοτόκου καὶ πάντων τῶν ἁγίων· ἀμήν.

Εὐχὴ ἑτέρα ὁμοίως[119]

Τὸ σῶμά σου τὸ ἅγιον, Κύριε Ἰησοῦ Χριστέ, γένοιτό μοι εἰς ζωὴν καὶ τὸ αἷμά σου τὸ τίμιον εἰς ἄφεσιν ἁμαρτιῶν, καὶ ἐν τῇ ἁγίᾳ σου κρίσει στῶ κατέναντι τοῦ προσώπου σου. Γένοιτο δέ μοι αὕτη ἡ εὐχαριστία εἰς εὐσπλαγχνίαν καὶ εἰς χαρὰν καὶ εἰς ὑγίειαν καὶ εἰς ἴασιν τῆς ταπεινῆς μου ψυχῆς· ὅτι ηὐλόγηται καὶ δεδόξασται τὸ πάντιμον καὶ μεγαλοπρεπὲς ὄνομά σου, τοῦ Πατρὸς καὶ τοῦ Υἱοῦ καὶ τοῦ ἁγίου Πνεύματος νῦν.

---

118. εὐχή is written in the margin.
119. εὐχὴ ἑτέρα ὁμοίως is written in the marrgin.

Another prayer of the same

O God, spare, remit, forgive me my sins, as many as I have sinned against you; whether I have sinned intentionally or in ignorance, in word or deed, for I have sinned. As the one who is good and loves mankind, forgive me all (my sins), and, through the intercession of your undefiled, ever-virgin mother and all your saints, preserve me free of condemnation to receive your precious, holy, and undefiled body and blood for healing the soul[114] and blotting out my wicked thoughts; **for yours is the kingdom and the power and the glory forever** (cf. Mt 6:13).

Prayer after the divine partaking

I thank you, O lover of mankind, that through (your) great goodness, you were content that I became a partaker of your undefiled body and precious blood and were not repelled; nor did you drive me away by your unseen and divine power as one defiled and unworthy of receiving your sacrament. But you consented to nourish even a sinner like me at your everlasting and divine table. Keep its life-giving grace undiminished in my poor soul and its light always burning. For it is you who illuminate every thought, every perception we have, keeping us free from stumbling and secure from the shadow of sin to glorify and thank you according to your will all the days of my life, through the intercessions of our most undefiled lady, the Theotokos, and all the saints. Amen.

Another prayer of the same

Let your holy body, O Lord Jesus Christ, bring me life, and your precious blood the remission of sins; and may I stand before you face to face at your holy Judgment. **Let the sacrament itself bring me mercy, grace and health, as well as healing for** *my poor soul* (LB: Trempelas 192.12), *for your most precious and exalted name has been blessed and glorified: (that) of the Father and the Son and the Holy Spirit, now <and always and for ever and ever. Amen>.*[115]

---

114. "For healing the soul" is a phrase used in the liturgy, e.g., Trempelas, Τρεῖς λειτουργίαι, 192.12.

115. LB = Liturgy of St. Basil: ed. Trempelas, Αἱ τρεῖς λειτουργίαι, 161–98.

Ἀκολουθία τῶν τῆς ἡμέρας μεσώρων
τῆς μεγάλης παρασκευῆς

ὥρα α´

Τὸ Δεῦτε, προσκυνήσωμεν· ψαλμὸς β´, Ἰνατί ἐφρύαξαν ἔθνη· καὶ ψαλμὸς ζ´, Κύριε ὁ Θεός μου, |²⁵² ἐπὶ σοὶ ἤλπισα· τρισάγιον καὶ τροπάριον <ἦχος α´>,¹²⁰ τὸ Σταυρωθέντος σου, Χριστέ, ἀνῃρέθη ἡ τυραννίς. Δόξα καὶ νῦν. Οἱ τὴν σὴν προστασίαν κεκτημένοι.

ὥρα γ´

Δεῦτε, προσκυνήσωμεν· ψαλμὸς λδ´, Δίκασον, Κύριε· καὶ οε´, Γνωστὸς ἐν τῇ Ἰουδαίᾳ ὁ Θεός· τρισάγιον καὶ τροπάριον, ἦχος πλάγιος β´, Σήμερον τὸ προφητικὸν πεπλήρωται λόγιον. Δόξα καὶ νῦν. Θεοτοκίον, Θεοτόκε παρθένε, ἱκέτευε τὸν υἱόν σου καὶ Θεὸν ἡμῶν τὸν [ἑ]κουσ[ίως] προσπαγέντα ἐν σταυρῷ [καὶ ἀνα]στάντα ἐκ νεκρῶν σ[ωθῆναι τὰς ψυχὰς ἡμῶν].¹²¹

ὥρα ς´

Δεῦτε, προσκυνήσωμεν· ψαλμὸς κα´, Ὁ Θεὸς ὁ Θεός μου, πρόσχες μοι· καὶ ψαλμὸς ξη´, Σῶσόν με, ὁ Θεός, ὅτι εἰσήλθοσαν· τρισάγιον· τροπάριον, ἦχος β´, Σωτηρίαν εἰργάσω ἐν μέσῳ. Δόξα καὶ νῦν. Θεοτοκίον, Εὐσπλαγχνίας ὑπάρχουσα.¹²²

---

120. Supplied from Arranz, *Typicon de Messine*, 240.20.

121. ἐκουσίως … ψυχὰς ἡμῶν was written in the margin and later erased or worn away; restitutions following *TR* 355.

122. εὐσπλαγχνίας ὑπάρχουσα is written, compressed, in the margin.

(II.8)

Offices of the interhours of the day for Good Friday[116]

First Hour

Come, let us worship.

  Psalm 2: *Why did the heathen rage* and
  Psalm 7: *O Lord my God, in you have I trusted.*

Trisagion and

troparion, mode I, *When you were crucified, O Christ, tyranny was destroyed* (126).

Glory, both now.

(theotokion) *We who possess your protection* (126).

Third Hour

Come, let us worship.

  Psalm 34: *Judge, O Lord* and
  Psalm 75: *God is known in Judea.*

Trisagion and

troparion, plagal mode II, *Today the prophesy has been fulfilled* (TR 355).

Glory, both now.

theotokion, *O virgin Theotokos, entreat your son and our God, who was willingly crucified on the cross and who rose from the dead, that our souls be saved.*

Sixth Hour

Come, let us worship.

  Psalm 21: *O God, my God, attend to me* and
  Psalm 68: *Save me, O God, for the waters have come in.*

Trisagion.

Troparion, mode II, *You wrought salvation in the midst* (TR 125).

Glory, both now.

theotokion, *You who are a spring of compassion* (TR 125).

---

116. The passages are added to the canonical hours; see Parenti § III.12.

ὥρα θʹ

Δεῦτε, προσκυνήσωμεν· καὶ ψαλμὸς πζʹ, Κύριε ὁ Θεὸς τῆς σωτηρίας μου· καὶ ρμβʹ, Κύριε, εἰσάκουσον τῆς προσευχῆς μου, ἐνώτισαι τὴν δέησίν μου· τρισάγιον καὶ τροπάριον, ἦχος πλάγιος δʹ, Βλέπων ὁ λῃστὴς τόν. Δόξα καὶ νῦν. Τὸν ἀμνὸν καὶ ποιμένα καί.

Ninth Hour

Come, let us worship.

    Psalm 87: *O Lord God of my salvation* and

    Psalm 142: *O Lord, attend to my prayer; hearken to my supplication.*

Trisagion and

troparion, plagal mode IV, *As the thief looked at* (*TR* 127).

Glory, both now.

(theotokion) *As his mother beheld the lamb, shepherd* (124).

Τῷ ἁγίῳ καὶ μεγάλῳ σαββάτῳ

ὥρα α΄

Δεῦτε, προσκυνήσωμεν· ψαλμὸς ια΄, Σῶσόν με, Κύριε, ὅτι ἐκλέλοιπεν ὅσιος· καὶ ψαλμὸς ιε΄, Φύλαξόν με, Κύριε, ὅτι ἐπὶ σοὶ ἤλπισα· τρισάγιον καὶ τροπάριον, ἦχος β΄, Ὁ εὐσχήμων Ἰωσήφ, ἀπό. Δόξα καὶ νῦν. Θεοτοκίον. |[252v]

ὥρα γ΄

Δεῦτε, προσκυνήσωμεν· ψαλμὸς κγ΄,[123] Τοῦ Κυρίου ἡ γῆ καὶ τὸ πλήρωμα αὐτῆς· καὶ ψαλμὸς κθ΄, Ὑψώσω σε, Κύριε, ὅτι ὑπέλαβες· τρισάγιον καὶ τὸ αὐτὸ τροπάριον καὶ θεοτοκίον.

ὥρα ς΄

Δεῦτε, προσκυνήσωμεν· ψαλμὸς λ΄, Ἐπὶ σοί, Κύριε, ἤλπισα, μὴ καταισχυνθείην· καὶ ψαλμὸς πα΄, Ὁ Θεὸς ἔστη ἐν συναγωγῇ θεῶν· τρισάγιον καὶ τροπάριον καὶ θεοτοκίον.

---

123. ψαλμὸς κγ΄· δεῦτε, προσκυνήσωμεν: C.

(II.9)

On the Holy and Great Saturday[117]

First Hour

Come, let us worship.

Psalm 11: *Save me, O Lord, for the godly man has failed* and
Psalm 15: *Keep me, O Lord, for I have hoped in you.*
Trisagion and
troparion, mode II, *The noble Joseph, taking from the cross the* (TR 708).
Glory, both now.
theotokion.[118]

Third Hour

Come, let us worship.

Psalm 23: *The earth is the Lord's and the fullness thereof* and
Psalm 29: *I will exalt you, O Lord, for you have lifted me up.*
Trisagion and
the same troparion and
theotokion.

Sixth Hour

Come, let us worship.

Psalm 30: *O Lord, I have hope in you; let me not be ashamed* and
Psalm 81: *God stands in the assembly of gods.*
Trisagion and
<the same> troparion and
theotokion.

117. This is an interhour (μεσώριον), like II.7. The passages are added to the canonical hours; see Parenti § III.12.

118. The theotokion, Ὑπερδεδοξασμένη ὑπάρχεις θεοτόκε (*PaR* 106), is given for this day in the Synaxaerion-Menologion (part III); a pairing of the same troparion and theotokion is observed on Holy Saturday at the Evergetis monastery: *Synaxarion of Evergetis*, ed. Jordan, 2:496–97 [O.4].

ὥρα θ'

Δεῦτε, προσκυνήσωμεν· ψαλμὸς ϙα', *Ἀγαθὸν τὸ ἐξομολογεῖσθαι·* καὶ ψαλμὸς ϙβ', *Ὁ Κύριος ἐβασίλευσεν, εὐπρέπειαν·* τρισάγιον καὶ τροπάριον ὁμοίως καὶ θεοτόκιν.

Ninth Hour

Come, let us worship.

Psalm 91: *It is a good thing to give thanks* and

Psalm 92: *The Lord reigns; he has clothed himself with majesty.*

Trisagion and

the same troparion and

theotokion.

Ἀκολουθία τοῦ λυχνικοῦ

Βασιλεῦ οὐράνιε, παράκλητε, τὸ τρισάγιον, τὸ Πάτερ ἡμῶν, τὸ Κύριε, ἐλέησον· εἶτα τὸ Δεῦτε, προσκυνήσωμεν καὶ προσπέσωμεν, ἐκ γ'· καὶ ψαλμὸς ργ',[124] *Εὐλόγει, ἡ ψυχή μου, τὸν Κύριον. Κύριε, ὁ Θεός μου, ἐμεγαλύνθης σφόδρα· καὶ μετὰ τὸ πληρῶσαι τὸν ψαλμὸν λέγε Δόξα καὶ νῦν. Ἀλληλούϊα, ἀλληλούϊα, ἐκ γ'· Κύριε, ἐλέησον, γ'· Δόξα καὶ νῦν. καὶ εὐθὺς λέγε τὸν ρμ'*[125] *ψαλμόν,*

Κύριε, ἐκέκραξα πρός
κατευθυνθήτω ἡ προσευχή
θοῦ, Κύριε, φυλακὴν τῷ
μὴ ἐκκλίνῃς τὴν καρδίαν μου
σὺν ἀνθρώποις ἐργαζομένοις
παιδεύσει με δίκαιος
ὅτι ἔτι καὶ ἡ προσευχή
ἀκούσονται τὰ ῥήματα
ὅτι πρὸς σέ, Κύριε Κύριε, οἱ ὀφθαλμοί
φύλαξόν με ἀπὸ παγίδος |[253]
πεσοῦνται ἐν ἀμφιβλήστρῳ
ρμα',[126] *Φωνῇ μου πρὸς Κύριον ἐκέκραξα*
ἐκχεῶ ἐνώπιον αὐτοῦ
ἐν τῷ ἐκλείπειν ἐξ ἐμοῦ
ἐν ὁδῷ ταύτῃ, ᾗ ἐπορευόμην
κατενόουν εἰς τά

124. ργ' written in the margin.
125. ρμ' written a second time in the margin.
126. ρμα' written in the margin.

(II.10)

Office of Vespers[119]

Heavenly king, comforter.
Trisagion, the
Our Father (HR 8),
Lord, have mercy, then
Come, let us worship and fall down three times, and
Psalm 103: *Bless the Lord, O my soul. O Lord my God, you are very great,*
and after the completion of the psalm say
Glory, both now.
Alleluia, alleluia <glory to you, O God> three times,
Lord, have mercy three times.
Glory, both now, and immediately say
Psalm 140:[120] *O Lord, I have cried to*
Let my prayer be set forth
Set a watch, O Lord
Incline not my heart
With men who work iniquity
The righteous shall chasten me
For yet shall my prayer
They shall hear my words
For my eyes are to you, O Lord, O Lord
Keep me from the snare
Sinners shall fall by their own net.
Psalm 141: *I cried to the Lord with my voice*
I will pour out before him
When my spirit was fainting within me
In the very way wherein I was walking
I looked on

119. Lychnikon: lamp-lighting; the office is communal.
120. Here, alone in the manuscript, the scribe copied the beginning words of each verse in neat double columns (final words tacitly completed in the Greek); careful and prominent versification of the same psalms also occurs in P.

ἀπώλετο φυγὴ ἀπ᾽ ἐμοῦ
ἐκέκραξα πρὸς σέ, Κύριε
πρόσχες πρὸς τὴν δέησιν
ῥῦσαί με ἐκ τῶν καταδιωκόντων
ἐξάγαγε ἐκ φυλακῆς
ἐμὲ ὑπομενοῦσι δίκαιοι
Ἐκ βαθέων ἐκέκραξα
γενηθήτω τὰ ὦτα
ἐὰν ἀνομίας παρατηρήσῃ
ἕνεκεν τοῦ ὀνόματος
ἀπὸ φυλακῆς πρωΐας
ὅτι παρὰ τῷ Κυρίῳ τὸ ἔλεος.
Στιχηρά,[127] Αἰνεῖτε τὸν Κύριον, πάντα. Ὅτι ἐκραταιώθη τὸ ἔλεος. Δόξα καὶ νῦν. Θεοτοκίον, εἶτα τὸ Φῶς ἱλαρὸν ἁγίας δόξης, καὶ εὐθὺς τὸ προκείμενον τῆς ἡμέρας.

Τὰ προκείμενα τῆς ἑβδομάδος

τῷ σαββάτῳ, ἑσπέρας, Ὁ Κύριος ἐβασίλευσεν. Ἐνεδύσατο Κύριος δύναμιν.

τῇ κυριακῇ, ἑσπέρας, Ἰδοὺ δὴ εὐλογεῖτε. Οἱ ἑστῶτες ἐν οἴκῳ.

---

127. στιχηρά indicated in the margin.

Refuge failed me
I cried unto you, O Lord
Attend to my supplication
Deliver me from them that persecute me.
Bring out of prison
The righteous shall wait for me.

Out of the depths have I cried
Let your ears be attentive (Ps 129:1, 2)

If you should mark iniquities
For your name's sake (Ps 129:3–5)

From the morning watch
For with the Lord is mercy. (Ps 129:6, 7)
stichera, *Praise the Lord, all.*
For his mercy has been abundant (Ps 116:1, 2).
Glory, both now.
theotokion, then
Joyous light of the holy glory (Phos Hilaron: *HR* 225–26),[121] then immediately the prokeimenon of the day.

The Prokeimena of the week

At Saturday vespers

The Lord reigns <he has clothed himself with majesty>[122] (Ps 92:1). (Verse)
<The> Lord has clothed <and girded> himself with strength (Ps 92:1).

At Sunday vespers

Behold now, bless <the Lord all you servants of the Lord> (Ps 133:1).
(Verse) *Who stand in the house <of the Lord, in the courts of the house of our God>* (Ps 133:1).

121. Edited with comments: Mateos, "Horologion de Saint-Sabas," 70–71. Contemporary sources indicate that the monks enter the church, presumably after gathering in the narthex, during or directly after the chanting of the Phos Hilaron (e.g., the Black Mountain Typikon, *BMFD*, 1:385 [4]; *Synaxarion of Evergetis*, ed. Jordan, 1:6 [V.3]; Arranz, *Typicon de Messine*, 12.14).

122. The same prokeimena were used in the cathedral vespers (Mateos, *Typicon*, 2:178–81); the endings here from *HR* 227 with some support from Mateos, *Typicon*.

τῇ β’, ἐσπέρας, *Κύριος εἰσακούσεταί. Ἐν τῷ ἐπικαλεῖσθαί.*

τῇ γ’, ἐσπέρας, *Τὸ ἔλεός σου, Κύριε. Κύριος ποιμαίνει με.*

τῇ δ’, ἐσπέρας, *Ὁ Θεός, ἐν τῷ ὀνόματι. Ὁ Θεός, εἰσάκουσον τῆς.*

τῇ ε’, ἐσπέρας, *Ἡ βοήθειά μου. Ἦρα τοὺς ὀφθαλμούς.*

τῇ παρασκευῇ, ἐσπέρας, *Ὁ Θεὸς ἀντιλήπτωρ. Ἐξελοῦ με ἐκ τῶν ἐχθρῶν.*

Καὶ ἀπὸ τοῦ προκειμένου λέγε *Καταξίωσον, Κύριε, ἐν τῇ·* εἶτα πάλιν ψάλλονται στιχηρὰ ὧν μεσόστιχοι τάδε, |²⁵³ᵛ *Πρὸς σὲ ἦρα τοὺς ὀφθαλμούς· Ἐλέησον ἡμᾶς, Κύριε, ἐλέησον. Δόξα καὶ νῦν.* Θεοτόκιν, εἶτα τὸ *Νῦν ἀπολύεις,*

At Monday vespers

The Lord will hear <me when I cry to him> (Ps 4:4). (Verse) *When I called upon him <the God of my righteousness heard me>* (Ps 4:2).

At Tuesday vespers

Your mercy, O Lord <shall follow me all the days of my life> (Ps 22:6). (Verse) *The Lord is my shepherd <I shall not want. In a place of green grass, there he has made me dwell>* (Ps 22:1).

At Wednesday vespers

<Save me,> O God, by your name <and judge me by your might> (Ps 53:3). (Verse) *O God, hear <my prayer; listen to the words of my mouth>* (Ps 53:4).

At Thursday vespers

My help <shall come from the Lord who made the heaven and the earth> (Ps 120:2). (Verse) *I lifted up my eyes <to the mountains from which my help shall come>* (Ps 120:1).

At Friday vespers

O God <, you are my> supporter. <As for my God, his mercy shall go before me> (Ps 58:10). (Verse) *Deliver me from my enemies <O God, and ransom me from those that rise up against me>* (Ps 58:2).

(¹²³)

After the prokeimenon, say[124] *Deign, O Lord, on <this night>* (HR 229); then the stichera are chanted again, the verses in between for them are these: *To you have I lifted up <my> eyes* (HR 229–30: Ps 122:1-2). *Have mercy upon us, O Lord, have mercy* (HR 230: Ps 122:3-4).

Glory, both now.

theotokion, then

---

123. A reading from scripture can follow the prokeimenon (e.g., *Synaxarion of Evergetis*, ed. Jordan, 1:6 [V.4–5]; Arranz, *Typicon de Messine*, xliv) and this reading generally came from the Old Testament.

124 See Parenti § III.13.4.

τὸ τρισάγιον, τὸ *Πάτερ ἡμῶν,* καὶ τὸ ἀπολυτίκιον ἐάν ἐστιν ἑορτή·[128] εἰ δ᾽ οὖν, λέγε *Θεοτόκε παρθένε, χαῖρε κεχαριτωμένη. Βαπτιστὰ τοῦ Χριστοῦ, πάντων ἡμῶν. Ἱκέτευε ὑπὲρ ἡμῶν, ἅγιοι. Ὑπὸ τὴν σὴν εὐσπλαγχνίαν. Τὸ Κύριε, ἐλέησον,* ιε᾽, καὶ ἀπολεύει.

---

128. ἐὰν ἔστι ἑορτῇ: C.

Lord, now let your servant depart (Ode 13: Symeon, Lk 2:29–32), the
Trisagion, the
Our Father, and the
apolytikion,[125] if it is a feast day; otherwise say (the troparia):

> *Hail virgin mother of God, Mary full of grace* (HR 231).
> *You who baptized Christ, remember us all* (HR 231).
> *Intercede for us holy apostles* (HR 232).
> *In your compassion we take refuge* (HR 232).

Lord, have mercy fifteen times, and dismissal.[126]

---

125. Troparion of the feast or saint of the day, if there is one, from the synaxarion-menologion (section III).

126. The dismissal can involve a brief ritual.

Ἀκολουθία τῶν ἀποδείπνων

Τὸ τρισάγιον, τὸ Πάτερ ἡμῶν, τὸ Κύριε, ἐλέησον, ιβ'· εἶτα τὸ Δεῦτε, προσκυνήσωμεν καὶ προσπέσωμεν, ἐκ γ'· καὶ ψαλμὸς δ',[129] Ἐν τῷ ἐπικαλεῖσθαί με εἰσήκουσέ μου ὁ· ς', Κύριε, μὴ τῷ θυμῷ σου ἐλέγξῃς με μὴ δὲ τῇ ὀργῇ σου παιδεύσῃς με. Ἐλέησόν με, Κύριε, ὅτι· ιβ', Ἕως πότε, Κύριε, ἐπιλήσῃ μου εἰς τέλος; Δόξα καὶ νῦν. Ἀλληλούϊα, ἀλληλούϊα· δόξα σοι, ὁ Θεός, ἐκ γ'· εἶτα κδ', Πρὸς σέ, Κύριε, ἦρα τὴν ψυχήν μου, ὁ Θεός μου· λ', Ἐπὶ σοί, Κύριε, ἤλπισα, μὴ καταισχυνθείην· ρ', Ὁ κατοικῶν ἐν βοηθείᾳ τοῦ ὑψίστου. Δόξα καὶ νῦν. Ἀλληλούϊα, ἀλληλούϊα· δόξα <σοι>, ὁ Θεός, ἐκ γ'· Κύριε, ἐλέησον, γ'. Εἶτα τὸ

Μεθ' ἡμῶν ὁ Θεός.
Γνῶτε ἔθνη καὶ ἡττᾶσθε· ὅτι μεθ' ἡμῶν ὁ Θεός. |[254]
Ἐπακούσατε ἕως ἐσχάτου τῆς γῆς· ὅτι.
Ἰσχυκότες ἡττᾶσθε· ὅτι μεθ' ἡμῶν ὁ Θεός.
Ἐὰν γὰρ πάλιν ἰσχύσητε, καὶ πάλιν ἡττηθήσεσθε· ὅτι μεθ' ἡμῶν ὁ Θεός.
Καὶ ἣν ἂν βουλὴν βουλεύσησθε, διασκεδάσει Κύριος· ὅτι μεθ' ἡμῶν ὁ Θεός.
Καὶ λόγον, ὃν ἐὰν λαλήσητε, οὐ μὴ ἐμμείνῃ ἐν ὑμῖν· ὅτι μεθ' ἡμῶν ὁ Θεός.

---

129. δ' and subsequent five psalm numbers written in the margin.

(II.11)

Office of Compline[127]

The Trisagion, the

Our Father (HR 8).

Lord, have mercy twelve times, then the

Come, let us worship and fall down three times, and

Psalm 4: *When I called upon him, the God of my righteousness heard me.*

(Psalm) 6: *O Lord, rebuke me not in your wrath, neither chasten me in your anger. Pity me, O Lord, for.*

(Psalm) 12: *How long, O Lord, will you forget me? for ever?*

Glory, both now.

Alleluia, alleluia, glory to you, O God three times, then

(Psalm) 24: *To you, O Lord, have I lifted up my soul. O my God.*

(Psalm) 30: *O Lord, I have hoped in you; let me never be ashamed.*

(Psalm) 90: *He that dwells in the shelter of the most high.*

Glory, both now.

Alleluia, alleluia, glory <to you>, O God three times.

Lord, have mercy three times, then

God Is with Us[128]

Know, O Nations, and be conquered, for God is with us.

Listen to the farthest limits of the earth, for <God is with us>.

Be conquered, you who are strong, for God is with us.

For even if you should again strengthen yourselves, you shall again be conquered, for God is with us.

And whatever counsel you shall take, the Lord shall bring it to naught, for God is with us.

Any whatever word you will speak, it shall not stand among you, for God is with us.

---

127. Apodeipnon: after supper; the office is communal. See Parenti § III.14.

128. Isaiah Canticle: a cento created from Is 8:9–10, 12–14, 17–18; 9:1, 5 (with departures from LXX, some recognized as variants in *Septuaginta*, ed. Rahlfs, and others arising from use in corporate devotions).

Τὸν δὲ φόβον ὑμῶν οὐ μὴ φοβηθῶμεν, οὐδὲ μὴ ταραχθῶμεν· ὅτι μεθ'.

Κύριον δὲ τὸν Θεὸν ἡμῶν αὐτὸν ἁγιάσωμεν, καὶ αὐτὸς ἔσται ἡμῖν φόβος· ὅτι μεθ' ἡμῶν.

Καὶ ἐὰν ἐπ' αὐτῷ πεποιθὼς ᾦ, ἔσται μοι εἰς ἁγιασμόν· ὅτι μεθ' ἡμῶν ὁ Θεός.

Καὶ πεποιθὼς ἔσομαι ἐπ' αὐτῷ, καὶ σωθήσομαι δι' αὐτοῦ· ὅτι μεθ' ἡμῶν.

Ἰδοὺ ἐγὼ καὶ τὰ παιδία ἅ μοι ἔδωκεν ὁ Θεός· ὅτι μεθ' ἡμῶν ὁ Θεός.

Ὁ λαὸς ὁ πορευόμενος ἐν σκότει εἶδε φῶς μέγα· ὅτι μεθ' ἡμῶν ὁ Θεός.

Οἱ κατοικοῦντες ἐν χώρᾳ καὶ σκιᾷ |²⁵⁴ᵛ θανάτου, φῶς λάμψει ἐφ' ὑμᾶς· ὅτι.

Ὅτι παιδίον ἐγεννήθη ἡμῖν, υἱὸς καὶ ἐδόθη ἡμῖν· ὅτι μεθ' ἡμῶν ὁ Θεός.

Οὗ ἡ ἀρχὴ ἐγενήθη ἐπὶ τοῦ ὤμου αὐτοῦ· ὅτι μεθ' ἡμῶν ὁ Θεός.

Καὶ τῆς εἰρήνης αὐτοῦ οὐκ ἔστιν ὅριον.¹³⁰ ὅτι.

Καὶ καλεῖται τὸ ὄνομα αὐτοῦ μεγάλης βουλῆς ἄγγελος· ὅτι μεθ' ἡμῶν ὁ Θεός.

Θαυμαστὸς σύμβουλος· ὅτι μεθ' ἡμῶν ὁ Θεός.

Θεὸς ἰσχυρός, ἐξουσιαστής, ἄρχων εἰρήνης· ὅτι.

Πατὴρ τοῦ μέλλοντος αἰῶνος· ὅτι μεθ' ἡμῶν.

Δόξα καὶ νῦν, ἐκ τρίτου τὸ Μεθ' ἡμῶν ὁ Θεός.

Τὴν ἡμέραν διελθὼν εὐχαριστῶ σοι, Κύριε· τὴν ἑσπέραν αἰτοῦμαι σὺν τῇ νυκτὶ ἀναμάρτητον. Παράσχου μοι, Σῶτερ, καὶ σῶσον. Δόξα.¹³¹ ἀσκανδάλιστον. Καὶ νῦν.¹³² ἀνεπίβουλόν. Πα<ράσχου>. Ἡ ἀσώματος φύσις, τὰ χερουβίμ, ἀσιγήτοις. Πιστεύω εἰς ἕνα Θεόν, Πατέρα παντοκράτορα.

---

130. ὅριον: C.
131. δόξα indicated in the margin.
132. καὶ νῦν added above the line.

Your fear we do not fear, nor are we dismayed, for <God is with us>.

We will glorify the Lord our God himself, and he will be our fear, for <God> is with us.

And if I have put trust in him, he will be for me a sanctuary, for God is with us.

And having trusted, I will be near him and I will be saved through him, for <God> is with us.

Behold, I and the children whom the Lord has given me, for God is with us.

The people who walk in darkness have seen a great light, for God is with us.

A people who dwell in the land and shadow of death, a light shall shine on you, for <God is with us>.

For a child is born to us, a son is given to us, for God is with us.

Whose government is upon his shoulder, for God is with us.

And of his peace there is no end, for <God is with us>.

And his name is called the messenger of great counsel, for God is with us.

Wonderful counselor, for God is with us.

Mighty God, highest power, prince of peace, for <God is with us>.

Father of the coming age, for <God> is with us.

Glory both now three times (after) God is with us.[129]

Coming to the end of the day, I thank you, O Lord. I beg you for an evening and night free of sin. Grant me this, O savior, and save <me>.

Glory.

<Completing the day, I glorify you, master. I beg you for an evening and night> free of dangerous traps. <Grant me this, savior, and save me>.[130]

Both now.

---

129. In the textus receptus (*HR* 249): *God is with us. / Glory to the Father and the Son and Holy Spirit. / God is with us. / Both now and always and forever and ever. / God is with us.*

130. Τὴν ἡμέραν παρελθὼν δοξολογῶ σε, Δέσποτα· τὴν ἑσπέραν αἰτοῦμαι σὺν τῇ νυκτί and repeated ending supplied from the textus receptus: *HR* 249. It is possible that the two brief phrases given by the scribe merely replace the words "free of sin" in the first complete line. In writing this triplet, the scribe gave the briefest cues for the second and third prayers, but his instruction parallels that of the San Salvatore Typikon (Arranz, *Typicon de Messine,* 206.4–9).

Παναγία δέσποινα, Θεοτόκε, πρέσβευε ὑπὲρ ἡμῶν. Πᾶσαι αἱ οὐράνιαι δυνάμεις τῶν ἁγίων ἀγγέλων καὶ ἀρχαγγέλων, πρεσβεύσατε ὑπὲρ ἡμῶν τῶν ἁμαρτωλῶν. |²⁵⁵ Ἅγιε Ἰωάννη προφῆτα, πρόδρομε καὶ βαπτιστὰ τοῦ Χριστοῦ, πρέσβευε ὑπὲρ ἡμῶν τῶν ἁμαρτωλῶν. Ἅγιοι ἀπόστολοι, προφῆται, μάρτυρες καὶ πάντες οἱ ἅγιοι, πρεσβεύσατε ὑπέρ. Ἡ ἀήττητος δύναμις τοῦ τιμίου καὶ ζωοποιοῦ σταυροῦ, μὴ ἐγκαταλίποις ἡμᾶς τοὺς ἁμαρτωλούς. Ὁ Θεός, ἱλάσθητι ἡμῖν τοῖς ἁμαρτωλοῖς καὶ ἐλέησον ἡμᾶς· ἐκ γ′.

Εἶτα τὸ τρισάγιον, τὸ Πάτερ ἡμῶν· καὶ εἰ¹³³ μὲν ἔστιν ἑορτή, λέγε τὸ τῆς ἑορτῆς ἀπολυτίκιον· εἰ δ' οὖν,

Τῶν ἀοράτων ἐχθρῶν μου τὸ ἄϋπνον ἐπίστασαι, Κύριε, καὶ τῆς ἀθλίας σαρκός μου τὸ ἄτονον ἔγνως, ὁ πλάσας με· διὸ εἰς χεῖράς σου παρατίθημι τὸ πνεῦμά μου. Σκέπασόν με πτέρυξι τῆς σῆς ἀγαθότητος, ἵνα μὴ ὑπνώσω εἰς θάνατον· καὶ τοὺς νοεροὺς ὀφθαλμούς μου φώτισον ἐν τῇ τρυφῇ τῶν θείων λόγων σου, καὶ διέγειρόν με ἐν καιρῷ εὐθέτῳ πρὸς σὴν δοξολογίαν, ὡς μόνος ἀγαθὸς καὶ φιλάνθρωπος. |²⁵⁵ᵛ Δόξα.¹³⁴

Ὡς φοβερὰ ἡ κρίσις σου, Κύριε, τῶν ἀγγέλων παρισταμένων, τῶν ἀνθρώπων εἰσαγομένων, τῶν βίβλων ἀνεῳγμένων, τῶν ἔργων ἐρευνωμένων, τῶν λογισμῶν ἀπολογουμένων. Ποία κρίσις ἔσται μοι τῷ συλληφθέντι ἐν

---

133. ἡ: C.
134. δόξα indicated in the margin.

<Finishing the day, I sing praise to you, O holy One. I beg you for an evening and night> in security. Grant *<me this, savior, and save me>*.[131]

The incorporeal order, the cherubim, by unceasing (HR 250).
I believe in one God, the Father almighty (Creed: HR 30–31).

O most holy one, sovereign lady, mother of God, intercede for us <sinners>.[132]

All heavenly powers of the holy angels and archangels, intercede for us sinners.

St. John the prophet, forerunner, and baptizer of Christ, intercede for us sinners.

Holy apostles, prophets, martyrs and all the saints, intercede for <us sinners>.

Invincible power of the precious and life-giving cross, may you not forsake us sinners.

O God, forgive us sinners and have mercy on us three times, then the

Trisagion, the
Our Father.
If it is a feast day, say the festal apolytikion; otherwise (say the troparia),
*You know that my invisible enemies go without sleep, O Lord, and you who fashioned me know the weakness of my miserable flesh; therefore **I commend my spirit into your hands*** (Ps 30:6). *Shelter me with the wings* (cf. Ps 16:8) *of your goodness, **so that I might not go sleeping into death*** (Ps 12:4). *Illuminate my mind's eye with the joy of your holy word, and awaken me at the proper time for your praise, since you alone are good and benevolent.*
Glory.
How frightening will be your judgment (cf. Heb 10:27), *O Lord, when the angels stand near, men are led in, books laid open* (cf. Dan 7:10), *deeds examined, thoughts defended! What judgment will there be for me, conceived in sin*

---

131. Τὴν ἡμέραν διαβὰς ὑμνολογῶ σε, Ἅγιε· τὴν ἑσπέραν αἰτοῦμαι σὺν τῇ νυκτί supplied from HR 250.

132. Supplied from Arranz, *Typicon de Messine*, 206.13.

ἁμαρτίαις; Τίς μοι τὴν φλόγα κατασβέσει; Τίς μοι τὸ σκότος καταλάμψει, εἰ μὴ σύ, Κύριε, ἐλεήσεις με ὡς φιλάνθρωπος; Καὶ νῦν.

Θεοτοκίον,[135] Τὴν ἀκαταίσχυντον, Θεοτόκε, ἐλπίδα σὲ ἔχων σωθήσομαι· τὴν προστασίαν σου κεκτημένος, πανάχραντε, οὐ φοβηθήσομαι. Καταδιώξω τοὺς ἐχθρούς μου καὶ τροπώσομαι, μόνην ἀμπεχόμενος ὡς θώρακα τὴν σκέπην σου· καὶ τὴν παντοδύναμον βοήθειάν <σου>[136] καθικετεύων, βοῶ σοι· Δέσποινα, σῶσόν με ταῖς πρεσβείαις σου, καὶ ἀνάστησόν με ἐκ ζοφώδους ὕπνου πρὸς σὴν δο|²⁵⁶-ξολογίαν δυνάμει τοῦ ἐκ σοῦ σαρκωθέντος Θεοῦ.

Τὸ Κύριε, ἐλέησον, μ'· καὶ εὐχήν,

Ὁ ἐν παντὶ καιρῷ καὶ πάσῃ ὥρᾳ, ἐν οὐρανῷ καὶ ἐπὶ γῆς προσκυνούμενος καὶ δοξαζόμενος Θεός, ὁ χρηστός, ὁ μακρόθυμος, ὁ τοὺς δικαίους ἀγαπῶν καὶ τοὺς ἁμαρτωλοὺς ἐλεῶν, ὁ πάντας καλῶν εἰς σωτηρίαν διὰ τῆς ἐπαγγελίας τῶν μελλόντων ἀγαθῶν, αὐτός, Κύριε, πρόσδεξαι ἡμῶν τῇ ὥρᾳ ταύτῃ τὰς ἐντεύξεις, καὶ εὔθυνον ἡμῶν τὴν ζωὴν πρὸς τὰς ἐντολάς σου. Τὰς ψυχὰς ἡμῶν ἁγίασον, τὰ σώματα ἅγνισον, τοὺς λογισμοὺς διόρθωσον, τὰς ἐννοίας κάθαρον, καὶ ῥῦσαι ἡμᾶς ἀπὸ θλίψεως, κακῶν καὶ ὀδύνης. Τείχισον ἡμᾶς ἁγίοις ἀγγέλοις σου, ἵνα τῇ παρεμβολῇ[137] τούτων φρουρούμενοι, καὶ ὁδηγούμενοι, καταντήσωμεν εἰς τὴν ἑνότητα τῆς πίστεως καὶ τῆς ἐπιγνώσεως τῆς ἁγίας Τριάδος· ὅτι εὐλογητὸς εἶ εἰς τοὺς αἰῶνας· ἀμήν. |²⁵⁶ᵛ

Δεῦτε, προσκυνήσωμεν· ψαλμὸς ν', Ἐλέησόν με, ὁ Θεός, κατὰ τὸ μέγα ἔλεος· εἶτα κανόνα τῆς παννυχίδος ἀπὸ ἕκτης ᾠδῆς· τὸ Προστασία ἄμαχε τῶν· εἶτα τρισάγιον καὶ τροπάρια, τὸ Ἐλέησον ἡμᾶς, Κύριε, ἐλέησον ἡμᾶς, πάσης γάρ. Δόξα. Κύριε, ἐλέησον ἡμᾶς· ἐπὶ σοὶ γὰρ πεποίθαμεν. Καὶ νῦν. Τῆς εὐσπλαγχνίας τὴν πύλην. Κύριε, ἐλέησον, ιε'· καὶ εὐχὴ ἡ τῷ Ν' συνάδουσα· εἶτα τὸ Δεῦτε,

---

135. θεοτοκίον indicated in the margin.   136. Supplied from *HR* 255.
137. παρεμβολή: C.

(cf. Ps 50:7)? *Who will quench the flame for me? Who will light the darkness for me, if not you, O Lord? As lover of mankind, will you show me mercy?*
Both now.

theotokion: *O Theotokos, having you as my unshakable hope, I will be saved. Having acquired your protection, most immaculate one, I will have no fear. Girt only with your protection as a breastplate, I will pursue my enemies and put them to flight. Entreating your all-powerful help, I call to you, "Sovereign lady, save me by your intercessions, and raise me out of the gloom of sleep for your praise, by the power of God, who took his flesh from you."*

Lord, have mercy forty times' and the

prayer: *You, God, are worshiped and glorified at every moment and in every hour, in heaven and on earth, as the good, the patient, he who loves the righteous and has mercy on the sinners, he who summons all to salvation through the promise of good things to come. O Lord, accept our petitions at this hour, and direct our life **according to your commandments** (Ps 118:128). Sanctify our souls, purify our bodies, correct our thoughts, cleanse our minds, and deliver us from affliction (cf. Ps 53:7), evils, and pain. Fortify us with your holy angels so that we will be guarded in their company; and, guided by them, we will **arrive at the unity of the faith and of the knowledge** (Eph 4:13) of the holy Trinity: for blessed are you forever. Amen.*

Come, let us worship.
Psalm 50: *Have mercy upon me, O God, according to your great mercy*, then
Canon of the pannychis after the sixth ode,[133] the (troparion)
Unvanquished protection of those (MR 2:393),[134] then the
Trisagion, and
troparia:
   Have mercy on us, O Lord, have mercy on us. (Ps 122:3, Mt 20:30
We who (82).
   Glory.
   O Lord, have mercy on us, for we have put our trust in you (82).
   Both now.
   (theotokion) *Open to us the gate of compassion* (82).

133. For "canon of the pannychis" see Parenti § III.14.2.
134. MR = Μηναῖα τοῦ ὅλου ἐνιαυτοῦ, 4 vols. (Rome, 1885–1901).

προσκυνήσωμεν· τὸ Δόξα ἐν ὑψίστοις Θεῷ· τὸ τρισάγιον καὶ τροπάρια,
Σῶσον, Κύριε, τὸν λαόν σου. Ὁ ὑψωθεὶς ἐν τῷ σταυρῷ. Τῶν οὐρανίων στρατ{ε}
ιῶν. Μνήμη δικαίου μετ᾽ ἐγκωμίων. Οἱ τῶν ἀποστόλων πρωτόθρονοι. Ἅγιοι
ἀνάργυροι καὶ θαυματουργοί. Ἀθλοφόροι ἅγιοι πρεσβεύσατε. Οἱ μάρτυρές σου,
Κύριε, ἐν τῇ. Δόξα καὶ νῦν. Τῇ Θεοτόκῳ ἐκτενῶς νῦν προσδράμωμεν. Κύριε,
ἐλέησον, ιε᾽, καὶ τὴν εὐχὴν τοῦ Μεγάλου Βασιλείου,[138]

Κύριε, Κύριε, ὁ ρυσάμενος ἡμᾶς ἀπὸ παντὸς βέλους πετομένου ἡμέρας,
ρῦσαι ἡμᾶς[139] *καὶ ἀπὸ παντὸς πράγματος ἐν σκότει διαπορευομένου.*
Πρόσδεξαι θυσίαν ἑσπερινὴν τὰς τῶν χειρῶν ἡμῶν ἐπάρσεις. Καταξίωσον
δὲ ἡμᾶς καὶ τὸ νυκτερινὸν στά|[257]*–διον ἀμέμπτως διελθεῖν ἀπειράστους*
κακῶν. Λύτρωσαι ἡμᾶς πάσης ταραχῆς καὶ δειλίας τῆς ἐκ τοῦ διαβόλου ἡμῖν
προσγινομένης. Χάρισαι δὲ ταῖς ψυχαῖς ἡμῶν κατάνυξιν, καὶ τοῖς λογισμοῖς
ἡμῶν μέριμναν τῆς ἐν τῇ φοβερᾷ καὶ δικαίᾳ σου κρίσει ἐξετάσεως. Καθήλωσον
ἐκ τοῦ φόβου σου τὰς σάρκας ἡμῶν καὶ νέκρωσον τὰ μέλη ἡμῶν τὰ ἐπὶ
τῆς γῆς, ἵνα καὶ ἐν τῇ καθ᾽ ὕπνον ἡσυχίᾳ ἐμφαιδρυνώμεθα τῇ θεωρίᾳ τῶν
κριμάτων σου. Ἀπόστησον ἀφ᾽ ἡμῶν πᾶσαν φαντασίαν ἀπρεπῆ καὶ ἐπιθυμίαν
βλαβεράν. Διανάστησον δὲ ἡμᾶς ἐν τῷ καιρῷ τῆς προσευχῆς ἐστηριγμένους
ἐν τῇ πίστει, καὶ προκόπτοντας ἐν τοῖς παραγγέλμασί σου, εὐδοκίᾳ καὶ
ἀγαθότητι τοῦ μονογενοῦς σου Υἱοῦ, μεθ᾽ οὗ εὐλογητὸς εἶ σὺν τῷ παναγίῳ
καὶ ἀγαθῷ καὶ ζωοποιῷ σου Πνεύματι νῦν καὶ ἀεὶ καὶ εἰς τοὺς αἰῶνας τῶν
αἰώνων· ἀμήν. |[257v]

138. εὐχή written in the margin.
139. ρῦσαι ἡμᾶς added in the margin; an insertion sign follows ἡμέρας.

Lord, have mercy fifteen times.

Prayer said in unison with the fiftieth psalm (82–84), then

Come, let us worship.[135]

Glory to God in the highest (doxology: 98), the

Trisagion, and

troparia:

> *Save, O Lord, your people* (MR 1:158).
>
> *You who were raised on the cross* (MHS 142).[136]
>
> *Commanders of the heavenly armies* (MHS 703).
>
> **The memory of the just is praised** (Prv 10:7) (MR 3:161).
>
> *The first enthroned of the apostles* (MR 5:390).
>
> *Holy anargyroi and miracle workers* (MHS 449).
>
> *Victorious saints intercede*[137]
>
> *Your martyrs, O Lord, in the trial* (TR 791).
>
> *Glory, both now.*
>
> *To the Theotokos let us hasten now in earnest* (MHS 21).

Lord, have mercy fifteen times, and the

prayer of Basil the Great: *Lord, O Lord, you who delivered us **from every arrow that flies by day** (Ps 90:5), now deliver us from every trouble that passes in the darkness. Accept the lifting-up of our hands as an evening sacrifice (cf. Ps 140:2). Consider us worthy also to finish the night's course blamelessly, free from evil's temptations. Keep us free from all unrest and fear coming upon us from the devil. Grace our souls with contrition and our thoughts with a grave concern for the examination in your fearful and righteous judgment. **From fear of you drive a nail into our flesh** (Ps 118:120) and mortify our **limbs that are (bound) to the earth** (Col 3:5), so that even in the stillness during sleep we may rejoice in the contemplation of your judgments. Keep from us every impure fantasy and **hurtful desire** (1 Tm 6:9). At the time for prayer awaken us firmly established in faith and advancing in your precepts, by the*

---

135. The use of the *Come, let us worship* at this point is likely a mistake; see Parenti § III.14.2.

136. MHS = Μέγας ἱερὸς συνέκδημος (Athens, n.d.).

137. This is likely a version of the troparion said on Oct. 16 (pt. III), but with the address plural rather than singular and no saint specified; cf. *MHS* 449 and below part III, Oct. 16, with a relevant parallel in *Synaxarion of Evergetis*, ed. Jordan, 1:132. The troparion falls within an ordered sequence beginning with two troparia addressed to Christ followed by ones celebrating the archangels, John the Baptist, Peter and Paul, Kosmas and Damian, martyrs, and the Theotokos.

Καὶ πάλιν, Δεῦτε, προσκυνήσωμεν καὶ προσπέσωμεν αὐτῷ· Κύριε
παντοκράτορ· τρισάγιον καὶ τροπάρια, Τὴν ἄχραντον εἰκόνα. Ὁ Θεὸς τῶν
πατέρων ἡμῶν. Ὅταν ἔλθῃς, ὁ Θεός. Τῆς σοφίας ὁδηγέ. Δόξα καὶ νῦν. Σὲ καὶ
τεῖχος καὶ λιμένα. Κύριε, ἐλέησον, ιε΄· καὶ εὐχὴ τοῦ ἁγίου Εὐστρατίου,

Μεγαλύνων μεγαλύνω σε, Κύριε, ὅτι ἐπεῖδες ἐπὶ τὴν ταπείνωσίν μου, καὶ οὐ
συνέκλεισάς με εἰς χεῖρας ἐχθρῶν, καὶ ἔσωσας ἐκ τῶν ἀναγκῶν τὴν ψυχήν μου·
καὶ νῦν, Δέσποτα, σκεπασάτω με ἡ χείρ σου καὶ ἔλθοι ἐπ᾽ ἐμὲ τὸ ἔλεός σου, ὅτι
τετάρακται ἡ ψυχή μου καὶ κατώδυνός ἐστιν ἐν τῷ ἐκπορεύεσθαι αὐτὴν ἐκ
τοῦ σώματος τούτου· μήποτε ἡ πονηρὰ τοῦ ἀντικειμένου βουλὴ συναντήσῃ
αὐτῇ καὶ παρεμποδίσῃ ἐν σκότει διὰ τὰς ἐν ἀγνοίᾳ καὶ γνώσει ἐν τῷ βίῳ τούτῳ
γενομένας μοι ἁμαρτίας. Ἵλεώς μοι γενοῦ, Δέσποτα, καὶ μὴ ἰδέτω ἡ ψυχή μου
τὴν ζεζοφωμένην |²⁵⁸ ὄψιν τῶν πονηρῶν δαιμόνων, ἀλλὰ παραλαβέτωσαν
αὐτὴν ἄγγελοί σου φαιδροὶ καὶ φωτεινοί. Δὸς δόξαν τῷ ὀνόματί σου τῷ ἁγίῳ
καὶ τῇ σῇ δυνάμει ἀνάγαγέ με εἰς τὸ θεῖόν σου βῆμα. Ἐν τῷ κρίνεσθαί με, μὴ
καταλάβῃ με ἡ χεὶρ τοῦ ἄρχοντος τοῦ κόσμου τούτου εἰς τὸ κατασπᾶσαί με
τὸν ἁμαρτωλὸν εἰς βυθὸν ᾅδου, ἀλλὰ παράστηθί μοι, καὶ γενοῦ μοι σωτὴρ
καὶ ἀντιλήπτωρ. Ἐλέησον, Κύριε, τὴν ῥυπωθεῖσαν τοῖς πάθεσι τοῦ βίου τούτου
ψυχήν μου· καὶ εἴ τι ὡς ἄνθρωπος κατὰ τὴν ἀσθένειαν τῆς φύσεως ἐν λόγῳ
ἢ ἔργῳ, ἢ κατὰ διάνοιαν ἐπλημμέλησα, ὁ ἔχων ἐξουσίαν ἀφιέναι ἁμαρτίας
συγχώρησόν μοι καὶ ἄνες μοι, ἵνα ἀναψύξω καὶ εὑρεθῶ ἐνώπιόν σου, μὴ ἔχων
σπίλον ἢ ῥυτίδα, ἀλλὰ ἄμωμος καὶ ἀκηλίδωτος προσδεχθείην ἐν χερσί σου,
Δέσποτα, ὅτι εὐλογητὸς εἶ εἰς τοὺς αἰῶνας· ἀμήν. |²⁵⁸ᵛ

grace and goodness of your only-begotten Son, with whom you are blessed, along with your all-holy, good, and life-giving Spirit, now and always and for ever and ever. Amen.

Then again, *Come, let us worship and fall down before him.*

Lord almighty (Ode 12: Manasses).

Trisagion, and

troparia:

> *We worship your immaculate image* (*PaR* 141).
>
> *O God of our fathers* (*MHS* 210).
>
> *Whenever you come, O God* (*TR* 38).
>
> *Guide of wisdom* (*TR* 105).
>
> *Glory, both now.*
>
> *We have you as both fortress and haven* (*PaR* 696).

Lord, have mercy fifteen times, and

prayer of St. Eustratios: *In magnifying, I magnify you, O Lord, **because you have looked upon my affliction** (Ps 30:8), and **you have not shut me up in the hands of the enemy** (Ps 30:8). **You saved my soul from suffering** (Ps 30:8). Now, master, let your hand shelter me (cf. Is 51:16) **and may your mercy come upon me** (Ps 118:41), because my soul is disturbed and is in pain at the prospect of leaving this body, for fear that the wicked plan of the adversary ever overtake it and detain it in darkness on account of the sins I committed in this life, in ignorance and in full knowledge. Be gracious to me, master; and do not let my soul see the darkening sight of wicked demons, but have your radiant and shining angels receive it. **Give glory to your holy name** (Ps 113:9), and by your power raise me up to your holy tribunal. While I am being judged may the hand of **the ruler of this world** (Jn 12:31) not seize me, the sinner, to drag me down to the depths of hell, but stand by me and be my savior and helper. Have mercy, O Lord, on my soul, defiled by the passions of this life. And if, through the weakness of my nature as a man, I offended you in word or deed or thought, forgive me, you who have the power to remit sins, and **spare me that I may be refreshed** (Ps 38:14) and may find myself in your presence **without spot or wrinkle** (Eph 5:27), but blameless and spotless may I be accepted into your hand, O master, for blessed are you forever. Amen.*

Εἶτα τὸ Δεῦτε, προσκυνήσωμεν· ψαλμὸς ριη', Μακάριοι οἱ ἄμωμοι ἐν ὁδῷ·
τρισάγιον· τροπάρια νεκρώσιμα, Μνήσθητι, Κύριε, ὡς ἀγαθός. Ἀληθῶς
ματαιότης. Μετὰ τῶν ἁγίων ἀνάπαυσον. Ὁ εἰδώς μου τὸ ἀνέτοιμον τοῦ βίου.
Κύριε, ἐλέησον, κ'· καὶ εὐχὴ εἰς κοιμηθέντας,

Μνήσθητι, Κύριε, τῶν ἐπ' ἐλπίδι ἀναστάσεως καὶ ζωῆς αἰωνίου
κεκοιμημένων πατέρων καὶ ἀδελφῶν ἡμῶν καὶ πάντων τῶν ἐν εὐσεβείᾳ
τελειωθέντων· καὶ συγχώρησον αὐτοῖς πᾶν πλημμέλημα ἑκούσιόν τε καὶ
ἀκούσιον, ἐν ἔργῳ ἢ λόγῳ ἢ κατὰ διάνοιαν πλημμεληθὲν ὑπ' αὐτῶν· καὶ
κατασκήνωσον αὐτοὺς ἐν τόποις φωτεινοῖς, ἐν τόποις χλοεροῖς ὅθεν ἀπέδρα
πᾶσα ὀδύνη καὶ λύπη καὶ στεναγμός, ὅπου ἡ ἐπισκοπὴ τοῦ προσώπου
σου εὐφραίνει πάντας τοὺς ἀπ' αἰῶνος ἁγίους σου· καὶ χάρισαι αὐτοῖς τὴν
βασιλείαν σου, καὶ τὴν μέθεξιν τῶν ἀφράστων καὶ αἰωνίων ἀγαθῶν |²⁵⁹ καὶ
τῆς σῆς ἀπεράντου καὶ μακαρίας ζωῆς. Σὺ γὰρ εἶ ἡ ζωὴ καὶ ἀνάπαυσις τῶν
κεκοιμημένων, καὶ σοὶ τὴν δόξαν ἀναπέμπομεν, τῷ Πατρὶ καὶ τῷ Υἱῷ καὶ τῷ
ἁγίῳ Πνεύματι νῦν καὶ ἀεὶ καὶ εἰς τοὺς αἰῶνας τῶν αἰώνων· ἀμήν.

Εὐχὴ ἑτέρα

Βασιλεῦ οὐράνιε, παράκλητε, τὸ πνεῦμα τῆς ἀληθείας, παρακλήθητι καὶ
συγχώρησόν μοι, τῷ ἀχρείῳ καὶ ἀναξίῳ δούλῳ σου· εἴ τι ἥμαρτον σήμερον
ὡς ἄνθρωπος μᾶλλον δὲ ὡς ἀπάνθρωπος, τὰ ἑκούσιά μου πταίσματα καὶ τὰ
ἀκούσια, τὰ ἐν γνώσει καὶ τὰ ἐν ἀγνοίᾳ, τὰ ἐκ συναρπαγῆς καὶ ἀπροσεξίας
καὶ πολλῆς μου ῥαθυμίας καὶ ἀμελείας, εἴτε τὸ ὄνομά σου τὸ ἅγιον
ὤμοσα, εἴτε αὐτὸ ἐπιώρκησα κατὰ διάνοιαν, εἰ ἐβλασφήμησα, εἴτε τινα¹⁴⁰
ἐλοιδόρησα ἢ ἐσυκοφάντησα ἢ ἐλύπησα ἢ ἔν τινι παρώργισα, εἰ ἐψευσάμην,
εἰ φίλος κατέλαβε πρός με καὶ αὐτὸν παρεῖδον, εἰ ἀδελφὸν ἔ|²⁵⁹ᵛ-θλιψα καὶ
παρεπίκρανα ἢ ἱσταμένου μου εἰς προσευχὴν καὶ ψαλμῳδίαν ὁ νοῦς μου
ὁ πονηρὸς εἰς τὰ πονηρὰ καὶ βιωτικὰ περιεπόλευσεν, ἢ παρὰ τὸ πρέπον

---

140. εἴτέ τινα: C.

Then, *Come, let us worship.*

Psalm 118: *Blessed are the blameless in the way.*

Trisagion.

troparia in remembrance of the dead:

> *Remember, O Lord, as the one who is good* (*TR* 289).
>
> *Truly, all is vanity* (*TR* 809).
>
> *Give rest with the saints* (*MHS* 323).
>
> *You who know my unpreparedness in life* (oo).

Lord, have mercy twenty times, and

prayer for the dead:[138] ***Remember, O Lord, (all) who have passed away in the hope of the resurrection and life eternal:*** *our fathers, brothers and all who have died in a state of orthodox devotion.* ***Forgive them every sin they committed, both voluntary and involuntary*** (LCh: Trempelas 119.3–120.2),[139] *in deed or word or thought. Settle them* ***in bright places, in green fields*** (cf. Ps 22:2) ***from which all pain, grief and moaning have fled*** (LB: Trempelas 185.4: cod. Δ), *and where looking upon your face gladdens all your saints of ages past* (cf. LB: Trempelas 186.6–7). *Grant them your kingdom and a share of its ineffable and eternal good things, and your boundless and blessed life. For you are the life and repose of those who have passed away, and to you we offer glory: to the Father and the Son and the Holy Spirit, now and always and forever and ever. Amen.*

Another prayer

Heavenly king, comforter, spirit of truth, hear my plea and forgive me, your useless and unworthy servant, if I committed any sin today, as a human being more than as someone inhuman. Forgive me my voluntary transgressions and my involuntary ones, those committed in full knowledge and the ones committed in ignorance, from recklessness, inattention, and my great apathy and negligence. Forgive me if I took in vain your holy name or swore it in thought,

---

138. This prayer is known from the twelfth-century typikon of the Pantokrator Monastery (P. Gautier, "Le typikon du Christ Sauveur Pantocrator," *REB* 32 [1974], 35.97–105), for which the first sentence was rewritten to convert it to one said for the emperor and founder after his death: Μνήσθητι, Κύριε, τῶν κεκοιμημένων ὀρθοδόξων ἡμῶν βασιλέων καὶ κτητόρων. The remainder of the wording is identical to that of the Harvard Psalter (C).

139. LCh = Liturgy of St. John Chrysostom, ed. Trempelas, *Αἱ τρεῖς λειτουργίαι*, 2–160. Prayer said by the priest at the reading of the diptychs; "all" supplied from it.

ἐτρύφησα, ἢ εὐτράπελα ἐλάλησα, ἢ ἀφρόνως ἐγέλασα, ἢ ἐγαστριμάργησα, ἢ ἐκενοδόξησα, ἢ ὑπερηφανευσάμην, ἢ κάλλος μάταιον ἐθεασάμην καὶ ὑπ᾽ αὐτοῦ ἐθέλχθην, ἢ τὰ μὴ δέοντα ἐφλυάρησα, ἢ τὰ ἐλαττώματα τοῦ ἀδελφοῦ μου ἔβλεψα, τὰ δὲ ἐμὰ ἀναρίθμητα καὶ ἀσυγχώρητα ἐλαττώματα παρέβλεψα, ἢ τῆς εὐχῆς μου ἠμέλησα, ἢ ἄλλο τι[141] πονηρὸν ἐποίησα, ταῦτα πάντα καὶ εἴ τινα[142] ἄλλα ἔπραξα καὶ οὐ μέμνημαι, συγχώρησόν μοι τῷ ἀχρείῳ καὶ ἀναξίῳ δούλῳ σου, ἵνα ἐν εἰρήνῃ κοιμηθήσομαι καὶ ὑπνώσω, ὁ ἄσωτος ἐγώ, καὶ ἀναστάς, ὑμνήσω καὶ προσκυνήσω καὶ δοξάσω σε, τὸ ἀγαθὸν καὶ ζωοποιὸν καὶ πα|[260]-νάγιον Πνεῦμα, ἅμα τῷ ἀνάρχῳ Πατρὶ καὶ τῷ μονογενεῖ Υἱῷ νῦν καὶ ἀεὶ καὶ εἰς τοὺς αἰῶνας τῶν αἰώνων· ἀμήν.

Εἶτα πάλιν Δεῦτε, προσκυνήσωμεν καί· ψαλμὸς ς', Κύριε, μὴ τῷ θυμῷ σου ἐλέγξῃς με μὴ δὲ τῇ ὀργῇ σου παιδεύσῃς με· ἐλέησον. Τρισάγιον. Φώτισον τοὺς ὀφθαλμούς. Δόξα. Ἀντιλήπτωρ τῆς ψυχῆς μου. Καὶ νῦν. Ἔνδοξε, ἀειπαρθένε. Κύριε, ἐλέησον, ιε'· εἶτα τὴν εὐχήν,

Δὸς ἡμῖν, Δέσποτα, εἰς ὕπνον ἀπιοῦσιν ἀνάπαυσιν σώματος, καὶ διαφύλαξον ἡμᾶς ἀπὸ τοῦ ζοφεροῦ σκότους τῆς ἁμαρτίας· ῥῦσαι ἡμᾶς ἀπὸ παντὸς μολυσμοῦ σαρκὸς καὶ πνεύματος. Δὸς ἡμῖν ἁγιωσύνην ἐπιτελεῖν τῷ φόβῳ σου, καὶ ῥῦσαι ἡμᾶς ἀπὸ πάσης σκοτεινῆς καὶ νυκτερινῆς ἡδυπαθείας. Παῦσον τὰς ὁρμὰς τῶν παθῶν, σβέσον τὴν τοῦ σώματος πύρωσιν, τὰς τῆς σαρκὸς ἐπαναστάσεις κατάργησον, τὰ σωματικὰ ἡμῶν πάθη καὶ τὰ φρονήματα τῆς

---

141. ἄλλό τι: C.
142. εἴ τινα: C.

if I blasphemed, or railed in anger against anyone, or committed slander or caused distress, or provoked anyone to anger; if I lied, if a friend came to me and I ignored him, if I distressed or embittered a brother, or if my wicked mind wandered off toward the wicked things of daily life while I stood at prayer and psalmody, or I enjoyed earthly pleasures beyond (what is) proper, or said frivolous things, or laughed foolishly, or ate like a glutton, or was conceited, or behaved arrogantly, or gazed on vain beauty and was beguiled by it, or joked about things that I ought not to have; if I looked for my brother's faults and overlooked my own innumerable and inexcusable defects, or neglected my prayer, or any other wickedness I did, for all these (transgressions) and any others that I committed but have not remembered, forgive me, your useless and unworthy servant, so that I, who am not worthy to be saved, might go to bed in peace, sleep, and arise to sing, worship, and glorify you, the good and life-giving and all-holy Spirit, together with the Father without beginning and the only-begotten Son, now and always and for ever and ever. Amen.

Then again, *Come, let us worship and,*

Psalm 6: *O Lord, rebuke me not in your wrath, and do not chasten me in your anger. Pity.*

Trisagion.

(troparia:)

> *Illuminate my eyes (MHS 87).*
> *Glory.*
> *Be a helper to my soul (MHS 88).*
> *Both now.*

(theotokion) *Glorious, ever-virgin (PG 98:481).*

Lord, have mercy fifteen times, then the

prayer: *Master, give us who depart into sleep rest for the body, and guard us from the gloomy darkness of sin. Deliver us **from every defilement of the body and spirit** (2 Cor 7:1). Allow us to achieve sanctity through a fear of you (cf. 2 Cor 7:1), and deliver us from all dark, nocturnal pleasures. Stop the attacks of passions, quench the burning of the body, quell the rebellions of the flesh. Abolish our carnal passions and calm the **thoughts of the flesh** (Rom 8:6); and give us restful sleep with a watchful mind and sober thought. Let us not fall into deep sleep, but awaken us for your nightly and morning offices.*

σαρκὸς πράϋνον· καὶ |²⁶⁰ᵛ δὸς ἡμῖν κοίτην ἀναπαύσεως ἐγρηγορότι λογισμῷ καὶ νηφούσῃ τῇ διανοίᾳ· μὴ παραλειφθῶμεν ὑπὸ βαρέος ὕπνου, ἀλλ' ἐξέγειρον ἡμᾶς πρὸς τὰς νυκτερινὰς καὶ ἑωθινὰς λειτουργίας σου· παννύχιον ἡμῖν τὴν σὴν δοξολογίαν χάρισαι τοῦ ὑμνεῖν τὸ μεγαλοπρεπὲς ὄνομά σου, τοῦ Πατρὸς καὶ τοῦ Υἱοῦ καὶ τοῦ ἁγίου Πνεύματος νῦν καὶ ἀεὶ καὶ εἰς τοὺς αἰῶνας τῶν αἰώνων· ἀμήν.

Εὐχὴ λεγομένη εἰς τὰ ἀπόδειπνα τοῦ Μεγάλου Βασιλείου

Κύριε Ἰησοῦ Χριστὲ ὁ Θεὸς ἡμῶν, ὁ τὰς κοινὰς ταύτας καὶ συμφώνους προσευχὰς ἡμῖν χαρισάμενος, ὁ καὶ δύο καὶ τρισὶ συμφωνοῦσιν ἐπὶ τῷ ὀνόματί σου τὰς αἰτήσεις παρέχειν ἐπαγγειλάμενος, καὶ διὰ τοῦτο νομοθετῶν ἡμῖν τὴν ἀγάπην, καὶ ὑπὲρ ἀλλήλων εὔχεσθαι παιδεύων ἡμᾶς, ἐπάκουσον καὶ ἡμῶν τῶν ἀναξίων δούλων σου, καὶ πρὸς τὸ συμφέρον πλήρωσον ἡμῶν τὰ αἰτήματα. Μνήσθητι, Κύριε, πάσης ἧς ἐκτήσω κληρονομίας σου καὶ παντὸς τοῦ λαοῦ σου ὃς τὸ σὸν ἐπικέκληται ἅγιον ὄνομα· εἰρήνευ|²⁶¹-σον αὐτῶν τὴν ζωήν, καὶ γενηθήτω ὡς ἐν οὐρανῷ οὕτω καὶ ἐν τῇ γῇ τὸ σὸν ἅγιον θέλημα. Μνήσθητι, Κύριε, τῶν εὐσεβεστάτων καὶ πιστοτάτων ἡμῶν βασιλέων, οὓς ἐδικαίωσας βασιλεύειν ἐπὶ τῆς γῆς. Ὅπλῳ ἀληθείας, ὅπλῳ εὐδοκίας στεφάνωσον αὐτούς, καὶ ὑπόταξον αὐτοῖς πάντα τὰ βάρβαρα ἔθνη τὰ τοὺς πολέμους θέλοντα· καὶ χάρισαι αὐτοῖς βαθεῖαν καὶ ἀναφαίρετον εἰρήνην, ἵνα ἐν τῇ γαλήνῃ αὐτῶν ἤρεμον καὶ ἡσύχιον βίον διάγωμεν. Μνήσθητι, Κύριε, πάσης ἀρχῆς καὶ ἐξουσίας καὶ παντὸς τοῦ στρατοπέδου. Τοὺς ἀγαθοὺς ἐν τῇ ἀγαθότητί σου διατήρησον· τοὺς πονηροὺς ἀγαθοὺς ποίησον ἐν τῇ χρηστότητί σου. Μνήσθητι, Κύριε, πάντων τῶν ἐν πάσῃ θλίψει καὶ ἀνάγκῃ καὶ περιστάσει ὄντων χριστιανῶν ἀδελφῶν ἡμῶν, καὶ ἐπὶ πάντας ἔκχεον τὸ σὸν πλούσιον ἔλεος. Σὺ γὰρ εἶ, Κύριε, ἡ βοήθεια τῶν ἀβοηθήτων, ἡ ἐλπὶς τῶν ἀπελπισμένων, ἡ τῶν θλιβομένων παραμυθία, ὁ τῶν πλεόντων λιμήν, ὁ τῶν χειμαζομένων σωτήρ, ὁ τῶν αἰχμαλώτων ῥύστης, ὁ τῶν χηρῶν προστάτης, ὁ τῶν ὀρφανῶν ὑπερασπιστής, ὁ τῶν νοσούντων ἰατρός, ἡ τῶν ὀλιγοψύχων παράκλησις καὶ τῶν πεπλανημένων ἐπιστροφή. Αὐτός, πολυέλεε Κύριε, τοῖς πᾶσι τὰ πάντα γενοῦ, ὁ εἰδὼς ἕκαστον |²⁶¹ᵛ καὶ τὸ αἴτημα αὐτοῦ. Μνήσθητι, Κύριε, καὶ πάντων τῶν δεομένων δι' ἡμῶν τῆς σῆς ἀγαθότητος καὶ τῶν διακονούντων ἡμῖν τὰ πρὸς τὴν χρείαν τοῦ σώματος, καὶ τῶν ἀγαπώντων ἡμᾶς καὶ μισούντων, καὶ πᾶσι τὰ πρὸς σωτηρίαν αἰτήματα παράσχου. Ῥῦσαι, Κύριε, τὴν πόλιν ταύτην

Grant us praise of you all night long to sing of your magnificent name: (that)
of the Father and the Son and the Holy Spirit, now and always and for ever
and ever. Amen.

Prayer of Basil the Great said at compline: *Lord Jesus Christ our God, you*
favor these our common prayers offered with one voice, you who promised
to grant the requests made when two and three call on your holy name (cf.
Mt 18:19) (LCh: Trempelas 36.1–3). *In this way you ordain for us brotherly*
love, and teach us to pray on behalf of one another. Hear us, your unworthy
servants, and for our benefit satisfy our request.

Remember, O Lord, your entire inheritance which you received (cf. Heb
9:15–17) *and all your people who call upon your holy name; bring peace to*
their lives, and let your holy will be done on earth as it is in heaven (cf. Mt
6:10). *Remember, O Lord, our most pious and faithful emperors, whom you*
ordained to rule on earth. Encompass them with a shield of truth, a shield
of favor, and make subject to them all foreign nations that wish for war
(Ps 67:30), *and grant them profound and irrevocable peace, so that in their*
tranquility we might lead a quiet and peaceable life (1 Tm 2:2). *Remember,*
O Lord, every magistrate and authority and the entire army. In your good-
ness watch over the virtuous; in your kindness make the wicked good (LB:
Trempelas 185.22–186.16).[140]

Remember, O Lord, all those in every affliction, suffering and stress who
are our Christian brothers; pour out your great mercy over all of them (ibid.
187.5). *For you, O Lord, are the help of the helpless, the hope of the despair-*
ing (ibid. 187.10–11), *the encouragement of the oppressed, a haven for sailors,*
savior of the storm-tossed, deliverer of captives, guardian of widows, protector
of orphans, physician to those who are sick (ibid. 187.9–11), *comfort to the*
faint of heart, the one who redirects those who have gone astray. You, Lord,
who are rich in mercy, be all things to all people, you who know each and
his plea (ibid. 187.12–13).

---

140. Here and following: prayer for the dead at the reading of the diptychs.

καὶ πᾶσαν πόλιν καὶ χώραν ἀπὸ λιμοῦ, λοιμοῦ, σεισμοῦ, καταποντισμοῦ, πυρός, μαχαίρας, ἐπιδρομῆς ἀλλοφύλων καὶ ἐμφυλίου πολέμου. Μνήσθητι, Κύριε, καὶ πάντων τῶν συνδούλων καὶ ἀδελφῶν ἡμῶν τῶν δι᾽ εὐλόγους αἰτίας ἀπολειφθέντων. Μνήσθητι, Κύριε, κατὰ τὸ πλῆθος τοῦ ἐλέους σου καὶ τῆς ἡμετέρας ἀναξιότητος καὶ συγχώρησον ἡμῖν πᾶν πλημμέλημα ἑκούσιόν τε καὶ ἀκούσιον· ἁγίασον ἡμῶν τὰς ψυχὰς καὶ τὰ σώματα, καὶ δὸς ἡμῖν ἁγιωσύνην ἐπιτελεῖν ἐν φόβῳ σου πάσας τὰς ἡμέρας τῆς ζωῆς ἡμῶν· καὶ καταξίωσον ἡμᾶς ἐν ἑνὶ στόματι καὶ μιᾷ καρδίᾳ ἀνυμνεῖν καὶ δοξάζειν τὸ πάντιμον καὶ μεγαλοπρεπὲς ὄνομά σου, καὶ εὐχαριστεῖν σοι ἀξίως τῶν εὐεργεσιῶν ὧν ἐποίησας καὶ ποιεῖς μεθ᾽ ἡμῶν τῶν ἀναξίων. Σὺ γὰρ εἶ ὁ εὐεργέτης ἡμῶν καὶ Κύριος, καὶ σοὶ τὴν δόξαν ἀναπέμπομεν σὺν τῷ ἀνάρχῳ Πατρὶ καὶ τῷ παναγίῳ καὶ ἀγαθῷ καὶ ζωοποιῷ Πνεύματι νῦν καὶ ἀεὶ καὶ εἰς τούς.

Remember too, O Lord, all who ask through us for your great goodness and who serve us in the needs of the body, **the ones who love us and the ones who hate us** (ibid. 187.2): *grant all of them their requests for salvation.* **Deliver this city and every city and land from famine, plague, earthquake, flood, fire, the sword, foreign raid, and internal strife** (ibid. 187.13–16).

Remember too, O Lord, all our fellow servants and brothers who for good reasons have departed. Also remember, O Lord, **according to the fullness of your mercy** (Neh 13:22), *the most unworthy members of our house and for-* **give their every transgression, voluntary and involuntary** (LCh: Trempelas 44.8–9). **Sanctify our souls and bodies, and give us** *the sanctity to finish* **all the days of our lives** (Ps 22:6, 26:4) *in fear of you* (LCh: Trempelas 44.9–11);[141] *consider us worthy* **to sing with one voice** (cf. Rom 15:6) *and with one heart and to glorify your all-holy and magnificent name* (cf. Ps 85:9) (LCh: Trempelas 124.10–12) *and to thank you rightfully for the benefits which you have given and are giving us, the unworthy. For you are our benefactor and Lord, and to you we give glory, along with the Father without beginning and the all-holy and good and life-giving Spirit, now and always and <forever and ever. Amen>.*

---

141. Prayer at the Trisagion.

III

SYNAXARION-MENOLOGION

Συναξάριον ἤτοι μηνολόγιον τοῦ ὅλου χρόνου,
μετὰ τῶν ἀπολυτικίων ἤγουν τῶν τροπαρίων τῶν ἑορτασίμων ἡμερῶν
καὶ τῶν ἐπισήμων ἁγίων τῶν ταῦτα ἐχόντων· ἐν αἷς δὲ ἡμέραις
οὐκ εἰσίν, τὸ Ἀλληλούϊα λέγεσθαι ὀφείλει.

Μὴν σεπτέμβριος
ἔχει ἡμέρας λ'· ἡ ἡμέρα ἔχει ὥρας ιβ' καὶ ἡ νὺξ ὥρας ιβ'.

α' Ἡ ἀρχὴ τῆς ἰνδίκτου, καὶ τοῦ ὁσίου πατρὸς ἡμῶν Συμεὼν τοῦ στυλίτου,
τροπάριον τῆς ἰνδίκτου,
Ὁ πάσης δημιουργὸς τῆς κτίσεως, ὁ καιροὺς καὶ χρόνους ἐν τῇ ἰδίᾳ ἐξουσίᾳ
θέμενος, εὐλόγησον τὸν στέφανον τοῦ ἐνιαυτοῦ τῆς χρηστότητός σου, Κύριε,
φυλάττων ἐν εἰρήνῃ τοὺς βασιλεῖς[143] *καὶ τὴν πόλιν σου, ἱκετεύοντας διὰ τῆς*
Θεοτόκου, μόνε φιλάνθρωπε.
Ἕτερον τοῦ ὁσίου, ἦχος α'·[144]
Ὑπομονῆς στύλος γέγονας, ζηλώσας τοὺς προπάτορας, ὅσιε· τὸν Ἰὼβ ἐν τοῖς
πάθεσιν, τὸν Ἰωσὴφ ἐν πειρασμοῖς καὶ τὴν τῶν ἀσωμάτων πολιτείαν ὑπάρχων
ἐν σώματι· διὸ[145] *πρέσβευε Χριστῷ τῷ Θεῷ ὑπὲρ τῶν ψυχῶν*[146] *ἡμῶν.*

β' Τοῦ ἁγίου μάρτυρος Μάμαντος, καὶ τοῦ ὁσίου πατρὸς ἡμῶν Ἰωάννου
πατριάρχου Κωνσταντινουπόλεως τοῦ νηστευτοῦ.

γ' Τοῦ ἁγίου ἱερομάρτυρος Ἀνθίμου ἐπισκόπου Νικομηδείας, καὶ τοῦ ὁσίου
πατρὸς |[262v] ἡμῶν Θεοκτίστου συνασκητοῦ τοῦ μεγάλου Εὐθυμίου.

---

143. τ(ὸν) βα(σιλεα) before erasure and correction.
144. The mode is written in the margin.
145. διὸ changed to Συμεὼν πατὴρ ἡμῶν by a later hand.
146. ὑπὲρ τῶν ψυχῶν is a correction after an erasure.

(III.1

Synaxarion-Menologion)

Synaxarion, or Menologion, of the entire year,
with the apolytikia, that is the troparia, of the feast days and the
distinguished saints that have them. On those days when there are no
troparia, the Alleluia[142] should be recited.

September

has thirty days; the day has twelve hours and the night twelve hours.

1 The beginning of the indiction; and (commemoration[143]) of our blessed
father Symeon the Stylite; troparion of the indiction <mode II[144]>:
*Creator of all things, you who made the **seasons and time by your own
authority** (Acts 1:7), **bless the crown of the year because of your goodness**
(Ps 64:12). O Lord, protect in peace the rulers and your city, who beseech you
through the Theotokos, O you who alone love mankind.*
The other (troparion) of the saint, mode I:
*O blessed one, when you became a pillar of perseverance, you emulated
the forefathers: Job in suffering, Joseph in trials, and the society of angels represented in the flesh;[145] for this intercede with Christ our God for our souls.*

2 The holy martyr Mamas; and our blessed father John the Faster, patriarch of Constantinople.

3 The holy hieromartyr St. Anthimos, bishop of Nicomedia; and our
blessed father Theoktistos, fellow-ascetic of Euthymios the Great.

---

142. Those formulas for which no reference is given appear in Common, Repeated Formulas,
27–28.
143. "Commemoration" is assumed by the possessive; see the entry for Sep. 6. Both the
understood noun and the possessive are omitted in the translation of the remaining entries.
144. *Synaxarion of Evergetis*, ed. Jordan, 1:6; Arranz, *Typicon de Messine*, 13.
145. I.e., monks.

δ Τοῦ ἁγίου ἱερομάρτυρος Βαβύλα πατριάρχου Ἀντιοχείας καὶ τῶν σὺν αὐτῷ νηπίων, τροπάριον ἦχος δʹ, *Καὶ τρόπων μέτοχος καὶ θρόνων διάδοχος.*

εʹ Τοῦ ἁγίου προφήτου Ζαχαρίου τοῦ πατρὸς τοῦ Προδρόμου, τροπάριον ἦχος δʹ,

Ἱερωσύνης στολισμὸν περιβαλλόμενος σαφῶς, κατὰ τὸν νόμον τοῦ Θεοῦ ὁλοκαυτώματα δεκτὰ ἱεροπρεπῶς προσενήνοχας, Ζαχαρία, καὶ γέγονας φωστὴρ καὶ θεατὴς μυστικῶν· τὰ σύμβολα ἐν σοὶ τὰ τῆς χάριτος φέρων ἐδείχθης, πάνσοφε, καὶ ξίφει ἀναιρεθεὶς ἐν τῷ ναῷ τοῦ Θεοῦ· Χριστοῦ προφῆτα, σὺν τῷ Προδρόμῳ πρέσβευε τοῦ σωθῆναι ἡμᾶς.

Τῇ αὐτῇ ἡμέρᾳ, τοῦ ἁγίου ἱερομάρτυρος Κυρίλλου ἐπισκόπου Γορτύνης.

ϛʹ Μνήμη τοῦ γεγονότος θαύματος ἐν Χώναις παρὰ τοῦ ἀρχιστρατήγου Μιχαήλ, τροπάριον ἦχος δʹ, *Τῶν οὐρανίων στρατιῶν·* καὶ τῇ αὐτῇ ἡμέρᾳ, τῶν ἁγίων μαρτύρων Εὐδοξίου, Ῥωμύλου, Ζήνωνος καὶ Μακαρίου.

ζʹ Προεόρτια τοῦ γενεθλίου τῆς ὑπεραγίας Θεοτόκου, τροπάριον ἦχος αʹ, Τοῦ λίθου.

Τεχθεῖσα παραδόξως στειρωτικῶν ἐκ λαγόνων παρθενικῶν, ἐξ ὠδίνων ἐκύησας ὑπὲρ φύσιν· ὡραῖος φανεῖσα γὰρ βλαστὸς ἐξήνθησας τῷ κόσμῳ τὴν ζωήν· διὰ τοῦτο αἱ δυνάμεις τῶν οὐρανῶν βοῶσί σοι, Θεοτόκε· Δόξα τῇ προόδῳ σου, ἀγνή, δόξα τῇ κυήσει σου· δόξα τῇ παρθενίᾳ σου, μῆτερ ἀνύμφευτε. |[263]

Τῇ αὐτῇ ἡμέρᾳ, τοῦ ἁγίου μάρτυρος Σώζοντος.

ηʹ Τὸ γενέθλιον τῆς παναγίας δεσποίνης ἡμῶν Θεοτόκου, τροπάριον εἰς τὸ Θεὸς Κύριος, ἦχος αʹ,

Ἡ γέννησίς σου, Θεοτόκε, χαρὰν ἐμήνυσε πάσῃ τῇ οἰκουμένῃ· ἐκ σοῦ γὰρ ἀνέτειλεν ὁ ἥλιος τῆς δικαιοσύνης, Χριστὸς ὁ Θεὸς ἡμῶν, καὶ λύσας τὴν κατάραν ἔδωκε τὴν εὐλογίαν, καὶ καταργήσας τὸν θάνατον ἐδωρήσατο ἡμῖν ζωὴν τὴν αἰώνιον.

θʹ Τῶν ἁγίων Ἰωακεὶμ καὶ Ἄννης, καὶ τοῦ ἁγίου μάρτυρος Σευηριανοῦ, τροπάριον τῆς ἑορτῆς.

4 The holy hieromartyr St. Babylas, patriarch of Antioch, and the children with him; troparion, mode IV: *You who followed in the footsteps and succeeded to the thrones* (MR 1:37).

5 The holy prophet Zechariah, father of the Forerunner; troparion, mode IV:

Once openly dressed in the robe of the priesthood, you reverently sacrificed burnt offerings acceptable according to God's law. Zechariah, you became a beacon and a seer of hidden things. You were revealed as bearing within yourself the sign of grace, and, O wisest one, you were slain by the sword in God's temple. O prophet of Christ, intercede with the Forerunner to save us.

On the same day, the holy martyr St. Cyril, bishop of Gortyna.

6 Commemoration of the miracle performed at Chonai by the Archangel Michael; troparion, mode IV: *Commander of the heavenly armies* (MR 1:65); and on the same day, the martyrs Sts. Eudoxius, Romulus, Zeno, and Macarius.

7 Forefeast of the birth of the most holy Theotokos; troparion, mode I (to the melody of the troparion) "When the stone had been sealed":

Miraculously born from barren loins, you (yourself), contrary to natural law, conceived in a virgin womb. Appearing like a beautiful bud, you made life bloom in the world. For this the powers in heaven cry out to you, O Theotokos, "Glory to your birth. O pure one, Glory to your conception. Glory to your virginity, O virgin mother."

On the same day, the martyr St. Sozon.

8 The birth of our all-holy sovereign lady, the Theotokos; troparion to God is the Lord, mode I:

*Your birth, O Theotokos, brought joy to the entire world, because from you dawned the **sun of righteousness** (Mal 4:2), Christ our God. Lifting the curse, he bestowed his blessing, and annulling death he gave us life everlasting.*

9 Saints Joachim and Anna; and the holy martyr Severianus; troparion of the feast.

ι′ Τῶν ἁγίων μαρτύρων γυναικῶν Μηνοδώρας, Μητροδώρας καὶ
Νυμφοδώρας, τροπάριον τῆς ἑορτῆς.

ια′ Τῆς ὁσίας μητρὸς ἡμῶν Θεοδώρας τῆς ἐν Ἀλεξανδρείᾳ, τροπάριον τῆς
ἑορτῆς.

ιβ′ Τοῦ ἁγίου ἱερομάρτυρος Αὐτονόμου, τροπάριον τῆς ἑορτῆς καὶ ἀποδίδει
ἡ ἑορτή.

ιγ′ Προεόρτια τῆς ὑψώσεως τοῦ τιμίου σταυροῦ, καὶ τοῦ ἁγίου Κορνηλίου
τοῦ ἑκατοντάρχου, τροπάριον εἰς τὸ Θεὸς Κύριος, ἦχος β′,
Τὸν ζωοποιὸν σταυρὸν τῆς σῆς ἀγαθότητος, ὅν ἐδωρήσω ἡμῖν τοῖς ἀναξίοις,
Κύριε, σοὶ προσάγομεν εἰς πρεσβείαν· σῷζε τοὺς βασιλεῖς καὶ τὴν πόλιν σου,
ἱκετεύοντας διὰ τῆς Θεοτόκου, μόνε πολυέλεε.
Τῇ αὐτῇ ἡμέρᾳ, τὰ ἐγκαίνια τῆς ἁγίας Ἀναστάσεως.

ιδ′ Ἡ ὕψωσις τοῦ τιμίου σταυροῦ, τροπάριον εἰς τὸ Θεὸς Κύριος, ἦχος α′,
Σῶσον, Κύριε, τὸν λαόν σου· καὶ τῇ αὐτῇ ἡμέρᾳ, ἡ κοίμησις τοῦ ἐν ἁγίοις
πατρὸς ἡμῶν Ἰωάννου τοῦ Χρυσοστόμου, ἥτις ψάλλεται εἰς τὴν ιγ′ τοῦ
νοεμβρίου μηνός. |²⁶³ᵛ

ιε′ Μεθέορτον τοῦ σταυροῦ, καὶ τοῦ ἁγίου μάρτυρος Νικήτα, τροπάριον
τῆς ἑορτῆς.

ις′ Τῆς ἁγίας καὶ πανευφήμου μάρτυρος Εὐφημίας, τροπάριον ἦχος δ′,
Τὸν νυμφίον σου Χριστὸν ἀγαπήσασα, τὴν λαμπάδα σου φαιδρῶς
εὐτρεπίσασα, ταῖς ἀρεταῖς διέλαμψας, πανεύφημε· ὅθεν εἰσελήλυθας σὺν
αὐτῷ εἰς τὸν γάμον, τὸ στέφος τῆς ἀθλήσεως παρ᾽ αὐτοῦ δεξαμένη· ἀλλ᾽ ἐκ
κινδύνων λύτρωσαι ἡμᾶς τοὺς ἐκτελοῦντας ἐν πίστει τὴν μνήμην σου.

ιζ′ Τῆς ἁγίας μάρτυρος Σοφίας καὶ τῶν τριῶν θυγατέρων αὐτῆς, Πίστεως,
Ἐλπίδος καὶ Ἀγάπης, καὶ τοῦ ὁσίου πατρὸς ἡμῶν καὶ θαυματουργοῦ
Εὐμενίου ἐπισκόπου Γορτύνης.

ιη′ Τοῦ ἁγίου ἱερομάρτυρος Συμεὼν ἀρχιεπισκόπου Ἱεροσολύμων.

ιθ′ Τῶν ἁγίων ἱερομαρτύρων Τροφίμου, Σαββατίου καὶ Δορυμέδοντος, καὶ
τῆς ἁγίας ὁσιομάρτυρος Σωσάννης τῆς παρθένου.

10 The holy martyred women Menodora, Metrodora, and Nymphodora; troparion of the feast.

11 Our blessed mother Theodora of Alexandria; troparion of the feast.

12 The holy hieromartyr Autonomos; troparion of the feast, and the feast concludes.

13 Forefeast of the elevation of the precious cross; and holy Cornelius the centurion; troparion to God is the Lord, mode II:

For its advocacy, we bring before you, O Lord, the life-giving cross, which of your goodness you gave to us, the unworthy. Save your city and the emperors who beseech (you) through the Theotokos, O you who alone are full of mercy
On the same day, the dedication of the Holy Anastasis.[146]

14 The elevation of the precious cross; troparion to God is the Lord, mode I: *Save, O Lord, your people (MR 1:158)*; and on the same day, the dormition of our father among the saints John Chrysostom; (the same troparion) or any one chanted on November 13.

15 Afterfeast of the cross; and the holy martyr Niketas; troparion of the feast.

16 The holy and all-blessed martyr Euphemia; troparion, mode IV:

You, O all-blessed one, loved Christ your bridegroom, joyously prepared your lamp, (and) shone forth in virtue. When you had gone with him to the wedding, you received the crown of martyrdom from him. But (now) rescue us from danger, the ones who celebrate your feast in faith.

17 The holy martyr Sophia and her three daughters, Pistis, Elpis and Agape; and our blessed father and miracle worker Eumenios, bishop of Gortyna.

18 The holy hieromartyr Symeon, archbishop of Jerusalem.

19 The holy hieromartyrs Trophimos, Sabbatios, and Dorymedon; and the holy hosiomartyr Sosanna the Virgin.

---

146. Jerusalem: H. Delehaye, *Synaxarium Ecclesiae Constantinopolitanae e codice Sirmondiano nunc Berolinensi adiectis synaxariis selectis opera et studio*, Propylaeum ad Acta sanctorum Novembris (Brussels: Socios Bollandianos, 1902), 42.

κ᾽ Τοῦ ἁγίου μεγαλομάρτυρος Εὐσταθίου καὶ τῆς συνοδίας αὐτοῦ, τροπάριον ἦχος δ᾽, *Οἱ μάρτυρες*.

κα᾽ Τοῦ ἁγίου προφήτου Ἰωνᾶ, καὶ ἑτέρου Ἰωνᾶ πρεσβυτέρου τοῦ πατρὸς τοῦ ἁγίου Θεοφάνους τοῦ ποιητοῦ.

κβ᾽ Τοῦ ἁγίου ἀποστόλου Κοδράτου τοῦ ἐν Μαγνησίᾳ, τροπάριον ἦχος γ᾽, *Ἀπόστολε ἅγιε, πρέσβευε·* καὶ τῇ αὐτῇ ἡμέρᾳ, τοῦ ἁγίου ἱερομάρτυρος Φωκᾶ τοῦ ἐν Σινώπῃ.

κγ᾽ Ἡ σύλληψις τοῦ ἁγίου Ἰωάννου τοῦ προδρόμου,[147] τροπάριον ἦχος δ᾽,
Ἡ πρώην οὐ τίκτουσα στεῖρα εὐφράνθητι· ἰδοὺ γὰρ συνέλαβες ἡλίου |[264] *λύχνον σαφῶς φωτίζειν τὸν μέλλοντα πᾶσαν τὴν οἰκουμένην ἀβλεψίαν νοσοῦσαν· χόρευσον, Ζαχαρία, ἐκβοῶν παρρησίᾳ· προφήτης τοῦ ὑψίστου ἐστὶν ὁ μέλλων τίκτεσθαι.*

κδ᾽ Τῆς ἁγίας πρωτομάρτυρος καὶ ἰσαποστόλου Θέκλας, τροπάριον ἦχος δ᾽,
Ἡ ἀμνάς σου, Ἰησοῦ, κράζει μεγάλῃ τῇ φωνῇ· σὲ νυμφίε μου, ποθῶ, σὲ καὶ ζητοῦσα ἀθλῶ, καὶ συσταυροῦμαι καὶ συνθάπτομαι τῷ βαπτισμῷ σου· καὶ πάσχω διὰ σὲ καὶ βασιλεύω ἐν σοὶ καὶ θνῇσκω ὑπὲρ σοῦ, ἵνα καὶ ζήσω σὺν σοί· ἀλλ᾽ ὡς θυσίαν ἄμωμον προσδέχου τὴν μετὰ πόθου τυθεῖσάν σοι· αὐτῆς πρεσβείαις, ὡς ἐλεήμων, σῶσον τὰς ψυχὰς ἡμῶν.

κε᾽ Τῶν ἁγίων μαρτύρων Σαβινιανοῦ, Παύλου καὶ Τάττης, καὶ τῆς ὁσίας Εὐφροσύνης.

κς Ἡ μετάστασις τοῦ ἁγίου ἀποστόλου καὶ εὐαγγελιστοῦ Ἰωάννου τοῦ θεολόγου, τροπάριον ἦχος β᾽,
Ἀπόστολε Χριστοῦ τοῦ Θεοῦ ἠγαπημένε, ἐπιτάχυνον ῥῦσαι λαὸν ἀναπολόγητον· δέχεταί σε προσπίπτοντα ὁ ἐπιπεσόντα τῷ στήθει καταδεξάμενος, ὃν ἱκέτευε, θεολόγε, καὶ ἐπίμονον νέφος ἐθνῶν διασκεδάσαι, αἰτούμενος ἡμῖν εἰρήνην καὶ τὸ μέγα ἔλεος.

κζ᾽ Τοῦ ἁγίου μάρτυρος Καλλιστράτου καὶ τῆς συνοδίας αὐτοῦ.

κη᾽ Τοῦ ὁσίου πατρὸς ἡμῶν καὶ ὁμολογητοῦ Χαρίτωνος, τροπάριον ἦχος πλάγιος δ᾽, |[264v]

---

147. ἡ σύλληψις ... τοῦ προδρόμου is written in red ink.

20 The holy great martyr Eustathios and his companions; troparion, mode IV: *Your martyrs* (*MR* 1:212)

21 The holy prophet Jonah; and the other Jonah, priest (and) father of the holy Theophanes the Poet.

22 The holy apostle Kodratos of Magnesia; troparion, mode III: *Holy apostle intercede* (*MR* 1:221); and on the same day, the holy hieromartyr Phokas of Sinope.

23 The conception of the holy John the Forerunner; troparion, mode IV:
*Rejoice barren woman who has not given birth until now, for behold: you conceived a lamp of the sun destined to illuminate clearly the entire world, which suffered in blindness. Join in the chorus Zecariah, calling out with confidence, "The **prophet of the highest** (Lk 1:76) is the one about to be born."*

24 The holy protomartyr Thekla, equal to the apostles; troparion, mode IV:
Your lamb, O Jesus, cries out with a strong voice, "I long for you, O my bridegroom, I struggle seeking after you; I am crucified alongside you and am buried with you in your baptism (cf. Col 2:14). I suffer through you, I reign in you, I die for you, so that I might live with you." Accept as an immaculate sacrifice what has been offered to you with love. As one who is merciful, save our souls through her intercession.

25 The holy martyrs Savinian, Paul, and Tatte; and the blessed Euphrosyne.

26 The translation of the holy apostle and evangelist John the Theologian; troparion, mode II:
Beloved apostle of Christ our God, rush to save a defenseless people. He who allowed (you to) rest on his breast accepts your supplication. Beseech him, theologian, to disperse the constant throng of nations, you who beg for us (his) peace and great mercy.

27 The holy martyr Kallistratos and his companions.

28 Our blessed father and confessor Chariton; troparion, plagal mode IV:
In you, father, "according to the image"[147] was accurately preserved, for

---

147. Cf. Col 3:10 (conceptualizing Gn 1:26); patristic use: Lampe, *Lexicon*, s.v. at III.B.

Ἐν σοί, πάτερ, ἀκριβῶς διεσώθη τὸ κατ᾽ εἰκόνα· λαβὼν γὰρ τὸν σταυρὸν ἠκολούθησας τῷ Χριστῷ, καὶ πράττων ἐδίδασκες τὸ ὑπερορᾶν σαρκός, παρέρχεται γάρ, ἐπιμελεῖσθαι δὲ ψυχῆς, πράγματος ἀθανάτου· διὸ καὶ μετὰ ἀγγέλων συναγάλλεται τὸ πνεῦμά σου.

κθ᾽ Τοῦ ὁσίου Κυριακοῦ τοῦ ἀναχωρητοῦ.

λ᾽ Τοῦ ἁγίου ἱερομάρτυρος Γρηγορίου ἐπισκόπου τῆς Μεγάλης Ἀρμενίας, τροπάριον ἦχος δ᾽, Καὶ τρόπων μέτοχος καὶ θρόνων.

Μὴν ὀκτώβριος
ἔχει ἡμέρας λα᾽· ἡ ἡμέρα ἔχει ὥρας ια᾽ καὶ ἡ νὺξ ὥρας ιγ᾽.

α᾽ Τοῦ ἁγίου ἀποστόλου καὶ μάρτυρος Ἀνανίου, τροπάριον ἦχος γ᾽, Ἀπόστολε ἅγιε, πρέσβευε· καὶ τῇ αὐτῇ ἡμέρᾳ, τοῦ ὁσίου Ῥωμανοῦ τοῦ μελῳδοῦ.

β᾽ Τοῦ ἁγίου ἱερομάρτυρος Κυπριανοῦ, καὶ Ἰουστίνας, τροπάριον ἦχος δ᾽, Καὶ τρόπων μέτοχος καὶ θρόνων διάδοχος.

γ᾽ Τοῦ ἁγίου ἱερομάρτυρος Διονυσίου τοῦ Ἀρεοπαγίτου, τροπάριον ἦχος δ᾽,

Χρηστότητα ἐκδιδαχθεὶς καὶ νήφων ἐν πᾶσι, ἀγαθὴν συνείδησιν ἱεροπρεπῶς ἐνδυσάμενος, ἤντλησας ἐκ τοῦ σκεύους τῆς ἐκλογῆς τὰ ἀπόρρητα· καὶ τὴν πίστιν τηρήσας, τὸν ἴσον δρόμον ἐτέλεσας· ἱερόμαρτυς Διονύσιε, πρέσβευε Χριστῷ τῷ.

δ᾽ Τοῦ ἁγίου ἀποστόλου Ἱεροθέου τοῦ πρεσβυτέρου.

ε᾽ Τῆς ἁγίας μάρτυρος Χαριτίνης, καὶ τῆς ἁγίας Μαμέλχθας |²⁶⁵

ϛ᾽ Τοῦ ἁγίου ἀποστόλου Θωμᾶ, τροπάριον ἦχος γ᾽, Ἀπόστολε ἅγιε, πρέσβευε.

taking up the cross you followed Christ, and by actions you taught, on the one hand, the disregard of flesh, for it passes away, and, on the other, cultivation of the soul, which is an immortal being. For this your spirit rejoices with the angels.

29 The blessed Kyriakos the Anchorite.

30 The holy hieromartyr Gregory, bishop of Greater Armenia; troparion, mode IV: *You who followed in the footsteps and succeeded to the thrones* (cf. Sep. 4).

October

has thirty-one days; the day has eleven hours and the night thirteen hours.

1 The holy apostle and martyr Ananias; troparion, mode IV: *Holy apostle, intercede* (cf. Sep. 22); and on the same day the blessed Romanos the Melode.

2 The holy hieromartyr Cyprian, and Justina; troparion, mode IV: *You who followed in the footsteps and succeeded to the thrones* (cf. Sep. 4).

3 The holy hieromartyr Dionysios the Areopagite; troparion, mode IV: *You were well educated in goodness and sober-minded in all things. Having been clothed in a good conscience, as befits a holy man, you drew the hidden meanings from the **chosen instrument** (Acts 9:15);[148] and having kept the faith, you finished the race fairly (cf. 2 Tm 4:7). O holy martyr Dionysios, intercede with Christ our <God that our souls be saved >.[149]*

4 The holy apostle Hierotheos the priest.

5 The holy martyr Charitine, and St. Mamelchtha.

6 The holy apostle Thomas; troparion, mode III: *Holy apostle, intercede* (cf. Sep. 22).

148. I.e., an interpreter of Paul, his teacher in Athens, for whom this term is an epithet (cf. Basil the Great, *Against Eunomius*, PG 29:540B; and John Chrysostom, *In terrae montum*, PG 48:1041). The author plays on the verb "draw from" and the sense of σκεῦος as "vessel."

149. Supplied from Arranz, *Typicon de Messine*, 36.

ζ´ Τῶν ἁγίων μαρτύρων Σεργίου καὶ Βάκχου, τροπάριον ἦχος δ´, *Οἱ μάρτυρές σου, Κύριε.*

η´ Τῆς ὁσίας Πελαγίας τῆς πόρνης, Ἀλληλούϊα.

θ´ Τοῦ ἁγίου ἀποστόλου Ἰακώβου τοῦ Ἀλφαίου, τροπάριον ἦχος γ´, *Ἀπόστολε ἅγιε, πρέσβευε.*

ι´ Τῶν ἁγίων μαρτύρων Εὐλαμπίου καὶ Εὐλαμπίας τῆς ἀδελφῆς αὐτοῦ, Ἀλληλούϊα.

ια´ Τοῦ ἁγίου ἀποστόλου Φιλίππου, ἑνὸς τῶν ἑπτὰ διακόνων, τροπάριον ἦχος γ´, *Ἀπόστολε ἅγιε·* καὶ τοῦ ὁσίου πατρὸς ἡμῶν Θεοφάνους τοῦ ποιητοῦ, καὶ τῆς ἁγίας μάρτυρος Ζηναΐδος,

ιβ´ Τῶν ἁγίων μαρτύρων Ταράχου, Πρόβου καὶ Ἀνδρονίκου, τροπάριον ἦχος δ´, *Οἱ μάρτυρές σου.*

ιγ´ Τῶν ἁγίων μαρτύρων Κάρπου καὶ Παπύλου, Ἀλληλούϊα.

ιδ´ Τῶν ἁγίων μαρτύρων Ναζαρίου, Γερβασίου, Προτασίου καὶ Κελσίου.

ιε´ Τοῦ ἁγίου μάρτυρος Λουκιανοῦ, καὶ τοῦ ὁσίου Κοσμᾶ τοῦ ποιητοῦ, Ἀλληλούϊα.

ις´ Τοῦ ἁγίου μάρτυρος Λογγίνου τοῦ ἑκατοντάρχου, τροπάριον ἦχος γ´, *Ἀθλοφόρε.*

ιζ´ Τοῦ ἁγίου προφήτου Ὡσηέ, Ἀλληλούϊα.

ιη´ Τοῦ ἁγίου ἀποστόλου καὶ εὐαγγελιστοῦ Λουκᾶ, τροπάριον ἦχος γ´, *Ἀπόστολε ἅγιε, πρέσβευε.*

ιθ´ Τοῦ ἁγίου προφήτου Ἰωήλ, καὶ τοῦ ἁγίου μάρτυρος Οὐάρου καὶ τῆς συνοδίας αὐτοῦ.

κ´ Τοῦ ἁγίου μεγαλομάρυρος Ἀρτεμίου, τροπάριον ἦχος δ´, *Ὁ μάρτυς σου, Κύριε, ἐν τῇ.*

κα´ Τοῦ ὁσίου πατρὸς ἡμῶν Ἱλαρίωνος,[148] τροπάριον ἦχος πλάγιος δ´, *Ταῖς τῶν δακρύων σου ῥοαῖς τῆς ἐρήμου τὸ ἄγονον ἐγεώργησας, καὶ τοῖς*

---

148. Ἱλαρίωνος: C; the troparion carries the customary breathing.

7 The holy martyrs Sergios and Bakchos; troparion, mode IV: *Your martyrs, O Lord (MR* 1:212).

8 The blessed Pelagia the Harlot: Alleluia.

9 The holy apostle James, son of Alphaeus; troparion, mode III: *Holy apostle, intercede* (cf. Sep. 22).

10 The holy martyrs Eulampios and Eulampia, his sister: Alleluia.

11 The holy apostle Philip, one of the seven deacons; troparion, mode III: *Holy apostle* (cf. Sep. 22); and our blessed father Theophanes the Poet, and the holy martyr Zenaïs.

12 The holy martyrs Tarachos, Probos, and Andronikos; troparion, mode IV: *Your martyrs* (cf. Oct. 7).

13 The holy martyrs Karpos and Papylos: Alleluia.

14 The holy martyrs Nazarios, Gerbasios, Protasios, and Kelsios.

15 The holy martyr Loukianos, and the blessed Kosmas the Poet: Alleluia.

16 The holy martyr Longinus the centurion; troparion, mode III: *Victorious.*

17 The holy prophet Hosea: Alleluia.

18 The holy apostle and evangelist Luke; troparion, mode III: *Holy apostle, intercede* (cf. Sep. 22).

19 The holy prophet Joel, and the holy martyr Varus and his companions.

20 The holy great martyr Artemios; troparion, mode IV: *Your martyr, O Lord, in the (MR* 1:27).

21 Our blessed father Hilarion; troparion, plagal mode mode IV:
With the rivers of your tears you cultivated the barren desert, and by your deep groans you brought forth a hundredfold the fruit of labor (cf. Mt 13:23) *and became a beacon illuminating the entire world by your wonders. Hilarion our father, intercede with Christ our <God that our souls be saved>.*[150]

---

150. Supplied from *MR* 1:38.

ἐκ βάθους στεναγμοῖς εἰς ἑκατὸν τοὺς πόνους ἐκαρποφόρησας· καὶ γέγονας
φωστήρ, τῇ οἰκουμένῃ λάμπων τοῖς θαύμασιν· Ἱλαρίων πατὴρ ἡμῶν, πρέσβευε
Χριστῷ τῷ.

κβ′ Τοῦ ἐν ἁγίοις πατρὸς ἡμῶν Ἀβερκίου, τροπάριον ἦχος δ′, Κανόνα
πίστεως.|²⁶⁵ᵛ

κγ′ Τοῦ ἁγίου ἀποστόλου Ἰακώβου τοῦ ἀδελφοθέου, τροπάριον ἦχος β′,
Ὡς τοῦ Κυρίου μαθητὴς ἀνεδέξω, δίκαιε, τὸ εὐαγγέλιον, ὡς μάρτυς ἔχεις τὸ
ἀπαράγραπτον, τὴν παρρησίαν ὡς ἀδελφόθεος, τὸ πρεσβεύειν ὡς ἱεράρχης·
ἱκέτευε Χριστὸν τὸν Θεὸν¹⁴⁹ σωθῆναι τὰς ψυχὰς ἡμῶν.

κδ′ Τοῦ ἁγίου μάρτυρος Ἀρέθα καὶ τῆς συνοδίας αὐτοῦ, τροπάριον ἦχος
δ′, Οἱ μάρτυρές σου, Κύριε.

κε′ Τῶν ἁγίων μαρτύρων Μαρκιανοῦ καὶ Μαρτυρίου τῶν νοταρίων.

κϛ′ Τοῦ ἁγίου μεγαλομάρτυρος Δημητρίου, τροπάριον ἦχος γ′, Μέγαν
εὕρατο ἐν τοῖς.

κζ′ Τοῦ ἁγίου μάρτυρος Νέστορος, Ἀλληλούϊα.

κη′ Τοῦ ἁγίου μάρτυρος Τερεντίου καὶ τῆς συνοδίας αὐτοῦ.

κθ′ Τοῦ ὁσίου πατρὸς ἡμῶν Ἀβραμίου,¹⁵⁰ καὶ τῆς ἁγίας ὁσιομάρτυρος
Ἀναστασίας τῆς Ῥωμαίας.

λ′ Τοῦ ἁγίου ἱερομάρτυρος Ζηνοβίου καὶ τῆς ἀδελφῆς αὐτοῦ Ζηνοβίας,
καὶ τῶν ἁγίων ἀποστόλων ἐκ τῶν ο′, Στάχυος καὶ τῶν λοιπῶν.

λα′ Τοῦ ἁγίου ἱερομάρτυρος Μαρκιανοῦ ἐπισκόπου Συρακούσης, καὶ τοῦ
ἁγίου μάρτυρος Ἐπιμάχου, Ἀλληλούϊα.

Μὴν νοέμβριος

ἔχει ἡμέρας λ′· ἡ ἡμέρα ἔχει ὥρας ι′ καὶ ἡ νὺξ ὥρας ιδ′.

α′ Τῶν ἁγίων καὶ θαυματουργῶν ἀναργύρων Κοσμᾶ καὶ Δαμιανοῦ,
τροπάριον ἦχος πλάγιος δ′, Ἅγιοι ἀνάργυροι καὶ θαυματουργοί.

---

149. Emended by the scribe from Χριστῷ τῷ Θεῷ (cf. Arranz, *Typicon de Messine*, 43).
150. Ἀβραμίου: C.

22 Our father among the saints Aberkios; troparion, mode IV: *Rule of faith* (*MR* 1:27).

23 The holy apostle James, brother of the Lord; troparion, mode II:

As a disciple of the Lord, O just one, you received the Gospel, as a martyr you are unassailable, as brother of God you have the confidence to speak (with him), and as bishop the (power of) intercession. Beseech Christ our God that our souls be saved.

24 The holy martyr Arethas and his companions; troparion, mode IV: *Your martyrs, O Lord* (cf. Oct. 7).

25 The holy martyrs Markianos and Martyrios, the notaries.

26 The holy great martyr Demetrios; troparion, mode III: *When in peril, the world found in you a powerful figure* (*MR* 1:522).

27 The holy martyr Nestor: Alleluia.

28 The holy martyr Terence and his companions.

29 Our blessed father Abramios, and the holy hosiomartyr Anastasia the Roman.

30 The holy hieromartyr Zenobius and his sister Zenobia, and the holy apostles numbered among the Seventy, Stachys and the others.[151]

31 The holy hieromartyr Markianos, bishop of Syracuse, and the holy martyr Epimachos: Alleluia.

November

has thirty days; the day has ten hours and the night fourteen hours.

1 The holy anargyroi and miracle workers Kosmas and Damian; troparion, plagal mode mode IV: *Holy anargyroi and miracle workers* (*MR* 2:5).

---

151. The seventy apostles (Lk 10:1): Delehaye, *Synaxarium Constantinopolitanae*, 779–90.

β′ Τῶν ἁγίων μαρτύρων Ἀκινδύνου καὶ τῆς συνοδίας αὐτοῦ, τροπάριον,
Οἱ μάρτυρές σου, Κύριε.

γ′ Τῶν ἁγίων ἱερομαρτύρων Ἀκεψιμᾶ, Ἰωσὴφ καὶ Ἀειθαλᾶ, τροπάριον ἦχος
α′, Τὰς ἀλγηδόνας τῶν ἁγίων, ἃς ὑπὲρ σοῦ. |²⁶⁶

δ′ Τοῦ ὁσίου πατρὸς ἡμῶν Ἰωαννικίου τοῦ ἐν τῷ Ὀλύμπῳ, τροπάριον ἦχος
πλάγιος δ′, Ἐν σοί, πάτερ, ἀκριβῶς διεσώθη· ζήτει σεπτέμβριον κη′.
Τῇ αὐτῇ ἡμέρᾳ, τῶν ἁγίων ἱερομαρτύρων Ἑρμαίου καὶ Νικάνδρου.

ε′ Τῶν ἁγίων ὁσιομαρτύρων Γαλακτίωνος καὶ Ἐπιστήμης, Ἀλληλούϊα.

ϛ′ Τοῦ ὁσίου πατρὸς ἡμῶν Παύλου τοῦ ὁμολογητοῦ, τροπάριον ἦχος γ′,
Θείας πίστεως ὁμολογίᾳ ἄλλον Παῦλόν σε ἡ ἐκκλησία ζηλωτὴν ἐν ἱερεῦσιν
ἀνέδειξε· συνεκβοᾷ σοι καὶ Ἄβελ πρὸς Κύριον, καὶ Ζαχαρίου τὸ αἷμα τὸ δίκαιον·
πάτερ ὅσιε, Χριστὸν τὸν Θεὸν ἱκέτευε δωρήσασθαι ἡμῖν τὸ μέγα ἔλεος.

ζ′ Τοῦ ἁγίου μάρτυρος Ἱέρωνος καὶ τῶν σὺν αὐτῷ ἀθλησάντων λγ′
μαρτύρων.

η′ Τῶν ἀσωμάτων ἡ σύναξις, τροπάριον ἦχος δ′, Τῶν οὐρανίων στρατιῶν.

θ′ Τῶν ἁγίων μαρτύρων Ὀνησιφόρου καὶ Πορφυρίου, Ἀλληλούϊα.

ι′ Τοῦ ἁγίου μάρτυρος Ὀρέστου, καὶ τῶν ἁγίων ἀποστόλων ἐκ τῶν ο′,
Ὀλυμπᾶ, Ῥοδίωνος καὶ τῶν σὺν αὐτῷ, Ἀλληλούϊα.

ια′ Τῶν ἁγίων μαρτύρων Μηνᾶ τοῦ Αἰγυπτίου, Βίκτορος καὶ Βικεντίου,
τροπάριον ἦχος δ′, Οἱ μάρτυρές σου, Κύριε, ἐν τῇ ἀθλήσει· καὶ τῇ αὐτῇ
ἡμέρᾳ, τοῦ ὁσίου πατρὸς ἡμῶν καὶ ὁμολογητοῦ Θεοδώρου ἡγουμένου
τῶν Στουδίου, τροπάριον ἦχος πλάγιος δ′,
Ὀρθοδοξίας ὁδηγέ,¹⁵¹ εὐσεβείας διδάσκαλε καὶ σεμνότητος, τῆς οἰκουμένης
ὁ φωστήρ, τῶν ἱερέων θεόπνευστον ἐγκα<λ>λώπισμα, λύρα τοῦ Πνεύματος,
ταῖς διδαχαῖς σου |²⁶⁶ᵛ πάντας ἐφώτισας· πατὴρ ἡμῶν Θεόδωρε, πρέσβευε
Χριστῷ τῷ.

---

151. ὁδηγέ: C.

2 The holy martyrs Akindynos and his companions; troparion <mode IV[152]>: *Your martyrs, O Lord* (cf. Oct. 7).

3 The holy hieromartyrs Akepsimas, Joseph, and Aeithalas; troparion, mode I: *Be moved by the suffering of the saints, which they endured for your sake* (MR 2:718).

4 Our blessed father Ioannikios of (Mt.) Olympos; troparion, plagal mode mode IV: *In you, father, "according to the image" was accurately preserved;* see Sep. 28.
On the same day, the holy hieromartyrs Hermaios and Nikandros.

5 The holy hosiomartyrs Galaktion and Episteme: Alleluia.

6 Our blessed father Paul the Confessor; troparion, mode III:
For (your) profession of divine faith, the church declared you to be another Paul, zealot among priests. The righteous blood of Abel and Zechariah cries out with you to the Lord. Blessed father, beseech Christ our God to bestow upon us (his) great mercy.

7 The holy martyr Hieron and the thirty-three martyrs who struggled with him.

8 The service for the incorporeal beings; troparion, mode IV: *Commanders of the heavenly armies* (MR 2:79).

9 The holy martyrs Onesiphoros and Porphyrios: Alleluia.

10 The holy martyr Orestes and of the Seventy Holy Apostles, Olympas, Rodion, and the ones with him: Alleluia.

11 The holy martyrs Menas the Egyptian, Victor, and Vincent; troparion, mode IV: *Your martyrs, O Lord, in the trial* (cf. Oct. 7); and on the same day, our blessed father and confessor Theodore, abbot of the Stoudios; troparion, plagal mode IV:
Guide of orthodoxy, teacher of piety and solemnity, beacon to the world, divinely-inspired adornment of priests (and) lyre of the Holy Spirit, you il-

---

152. As Sep. 20, Oct. 7 and 12, etc.

ιβ′ Τοῦ ἐν ἁγίοις πατρὸς ἡμῶν Ἰωάννου τοῦ ἐλεήμονος πατριάρχου Ἀλεξανδρείας, καὶ τοῦ ὁσίου πατρὸς ἡμῶν Νείλου τοῦ ἀσκητοῦ, τροπάριον ἦχος δ′, *Ὁ Θεὸς τῶν πατέρων ἡμῶν, ὁ ποιῶν ἀεί.*

ιγ′ Τοῦ ἐν ἁγίοις πατρὸς ἡμῶν Ἰωάννου ἀρχιεπισκόπου Κωνσταντινουπόλεως τοῦ Χρυσοστόμου, τροπάριον ἦχος πλάγιος δ′, *Ἡ τοῦ στόματός σου καθάπερ.*

ιδ′ Τοῦ ἁγίου ἀποστόλου Φιλίππου, τροπάριον ἦχος γ′, *Ἀπόστολε ἅγιε, πρέσβευε.*

ιε′ Τῶν ἁγίων ὁμολογητῶν Γουρία, Σαμωνᾶ καὶ Ἀβίβου, τροπάριον ἦχος πλάγιος α′, *Τὰ θαύματα τῶν ἁγίων σου μαρτύρων.*

ις′ Τοῦ ἁγίου ἀποστόλου καὶ εὐαγγελιστοῦ Ματθαίου, τροπάριον ἦχος γ′, *Ἀπόστολε ἅγιε.*

ιζ′ Τοῦ ἁγίου Γρηγορίου τοῦ θαυματουργοῦ, τροπάριον ἦχος πλάγιος δ′, *Ἐν προσευχαῖς γρηγορῶν, ταῖς τῶν θαυμάτων ἐργασίαις ἐγκαρτερῶν, ἐπωνυμίαν ἐκτήσω τὰ κατορθώματα· ἀλλὰ πρέσβευε Χριστῷ τῷ Θεῷ, πάτερ Γρηγόριε, φωτίσαι τὰς ψυχὰς ἡμῶν, μήποτε ὑπνώσωμεν εἰς θάνατον.*

ιη′ Τοῦ ἁγίου μάρτυρος Πλάτωνος, καὶ ῾Ρωμανοῦ, Ἀλληλούϊα.

ιθ′ Τοῦ ἁγίου προφήτου Ἀβδιοῦ, καὶ τοῦ ἁγίου μάρτυρος Βαρλαάμ.

κ′ Προεόρτια τῆς Θεοτόκου, τροπάριον εἰς τὸ Θεὸς Κύριος, ἦχος α′, *Δικαίων ὁ καρπὸς Ἰωακεὶμ καὶ τῆς Ἄννης προσφέρεται Θεῷ ἱερῷ ἐν ἁγίῳ· σαρκὶ νηπιάζουσα ἡ τροφὸς τῆς ζωῆς ἡμῶν, ἣν εὐλόγησεν ὁ ἱερὸς* |²⁶⁷ *Ζαχαρίας· ταύτην ἅπαντες, ὡς τοῦ Κυρίου μητέρα, πιστῶς μακαρίσωμεν.*

Τῇ αὐτῇ ἡμέρᾳ, τῶν ὁσίων πατέρων ἡμῶν Πρόκλου πατριάρχου Κωνσταντινουπόλεως καὶ Γρηγορίου τοῦ Δεκαπολίτου.

luminated all men with your teaching. Theodore, our father, intercede with Christ our <God that our souls be saved>.[153]

12 Our father among the saints John the Merciful, patriarch of Alexandria, and our blessed father Nilus the Ascetic; troparion, mode IV: *God of our fathers, who always treats (MR 2:202).*

13 Our father among the saints John Chrysostom, archbishop of Constantinople; troparion, plagal mode mode IV: *Inasmuch as the grace of your mouth (MR 3:387).*

14 The holy apostle Philip; troparion, mode III: *Holy apostle, intercede* (cf. Sep. 22).

15 The holy confessors Gourias, Samonas, and Abibos; troparion, plagal mode I: *The miracles of your holy martyrs (MR 2:163).*

16 The holy apostle and evangelist Matthew; troparion, mode III: *Holy apostle* (cf. Sep. 22).

17 St. Gregory the Wonder-worker; troparion, plagal mode IV:
*Being vigilant in prayer (and) persevering in the work of miracles, you gained as a surname your accomplishments; but now, father Gregory, intercede with Christ our God to illuminate our souls, **lest we go sleeping into death** (Ps 12:4).*

18 The holy martyr Platon, and Romanos: Alleluia.

19 The holy prophet Abdias,[154] and the holy martyr Barlaam.

20 Forefeast of the (presentation in the temple of the) Theotokos; troparion to God is the Lord, mode I:
The fruit of righteous Joachim and Anna is offered to God in the holy sanctuary (, where) being a child in the flesh, she who is the nursemaid to our life was blessed by the holy Zechariah. Let every one of us faithfully declare this woman blessed as the mother of the Lord.

On the same day, our blessed fathers Proklos, patriarch of Constantinople, and Gregory of Dekapolis.

---

153. Supplied from *Synaxarion of Evergetis*, ed. Jordan, 1:188.
154. I.e., Obadiah.

κα' Τὰ ἅγια τῶν ἁγίων,[152] τροπάριον εἰς τὸ Θεὸς Κύριος, ἦχος δ',

Σήμερον τῆς εὐδοκίας Θεοῦ τὸ προοίμιον καὶ τῆς τῶν ἀνθρώπων σωτηρίας ἡ προκήρυξις· ἐν ναῷ τοῦ Θεοῦ τρανῶς ἡ παρθένος δείκνυται καὶ τὸν Χριστὸν τοῖς πᾶσιν εὐαγγελίζεται· αὐτῇ καὶ ἡμεῖς μεγαλοφώνως βοήσωμεν· Χαῖρε, τῆς οἰκονομίας τοῦ κτίστου ἡ ἐκπλήρωσις.

κβ' Μεθέορτον, καὶ τῆς ἁγίας μάρτυρος Κικιλίας καὶ τῶν σὺν αὐτῇ, τροπάριον τῆς ἑορτῆς.

κγ' Μεθέορτον, καὶ τοῦ ἀποστόλου Φιλήμωνος[153] καὶ τῶν σὺν αὐτῷ, τροπάριον τῆς ἑορτῆς, καὶ ἀποδίδει ἡ ἑορτή.

Τῇ αὐτῇ ἡμέρᾳ, τοῦ ὁσίου πατρὸς ἡμῶν Ἀμφιλοχίου ἐπισκόπου Ἰκονίου.

κδ' Τῆς ἁγίας μάρτυρος Αἰκατερίνης,[154] τροπάριον ἦχος δ', *Ἡ ἀμνάς σου, Ἰησοῦ.*

Τῇ αὐτῇ ἡμέρᾳ, τοῦ ὁσίου πατρὸς ἡμῶν Γρηγορίου τοῦ Ἀκραγαντίου.

κε' Τῶν ἁγίων ἱερομαρτύρων Κλήμεντος πάπα Ῥώμης καὶ Πέτρου Ἀλεξανδρείας, τροπάριον ἦχος δ', *Καὶ τρόπων μέτοχοι, καί.*

Τῇ αὐτῇ ἡμέρᾳ, τοῦ ἁγίου μάρτυρος Μερκουρίου.

κϛ' Τοῦ ὁσίου πατρὸς ἡμῶν Ἀλυπίου τοῦ στυλίτου, Ἀλληλούϊα.

κζ' Τοῦ ἁγίου μάρτυρος Ἰακώβου τοῦ Πέρσου, Ἀλληλούϊα.

κη' Τοῦ ὁσίου πατρὸς ἡμῶν καὶ ὁμολογητοῦ Στεφάνου τοῦ νέου, τροπάριον ἦχος δ',

Ἀσκητικῶς προγυμνασθεὶς ἐν τῷ |267v *ὄρει, τὰς νοητὰς τῶν δυσμενῶν παρατάξεις τῇ πανοπλίᾳ ὤλεσας, παμμάκαρ, τοῦ σταυροῦ· αὖθις δὲ πρὸς ἄθλησιν ἀνδρικῶς ἀπεδύσω, κτείνας τὸν Κοπρώνυμον τῷ τῆς πίστεως ξίφει, καὶ δι' ἀμφοῖν[155] ἐστέφθης πρὸς Χριστοῦ· ὁσιόμαρτυς ἀοίδιμε Στέφανε.*

κθ' Τοῦ ἁγίου Παραμόνου, καὶ τοῦ ὁσίου Ἀκακίου τοῦ ἐν τῇ κλίμακι.

λ' Τοῦ ἁγίου ἀποστόλου Ἀνδρέου τοῦ πρωτοκλήτου, τροπάριον ἦχος δ',

Ὡς τῶν ἀποστόλων πρωτόκλητος καὶ τοῦ κορυφαίου αὐτάδελφος, τὸν Δεσπότην τῶν ὅλων, Ἀνδρέα, ἱκέτευε εἰρήνην τῇ οἰκουμένῃ δωρήσασθαι καὶ ταῖς ψυχαῖς ἡμῶν τὸ μέγα ἔλεος.

---

152. τὰ ἅγια τῶν ἁγίων is written in red ink.
153. Φιλίμωνος: C.   154. Αἰκατερίνης: C.
155. διαμφοῖν: C.

21 The (ascent of the Theotokos to the) Holy of Holies; troparion to God is the Lord, mode IV:

Today is the preamble to God's gracious will and the herald of mankind's salvation. The virgin is openly presented in God's temple, and she proclaims the news of Christ to all. With a strong voice let us, too, cry to her: "Hail, fulfillment of the Creator's plan."

22 Afterfeast, and the holy martyr Cecilia and the ones with her; troparion of the feast.

23 Afterfeast, and the apostle Philemon and the ones with him; troparion of the feast, and the feast concludes.

On the same day, our blessed father Amphilochios, bishop of Iconium.

24 The holy martyr Catherine; troparion, mode IV: *Your lamb, O Jesus* (cf. Sep. 24).

On the same day, our blessed father Gregory of Agrigentum.

25 The holy hieromartyrs Clement, head of the church of Rome, and Peter of Alexandria; troparion, mode IV: *You who followed in the footsteps and* (cf. Sep. 4).

On the same day, the holy martyr Mercurius.

26 Our blessed father Alypios the Stylite: Alleluia.

27 The holy martyr James the Persian: Alleluia.

28 Our blessed father and confessor Stephen the Younger; troparion, mode IV:

You received your ascetic education on the mountain, (and) by the armor of the cross you destroyed the unearthly ranks of the enemies, O most blessed one. Moreover, after you courageously stripped for the fight, you slew the copronymos with the sword of faith, and for both of these (victories) you were crowned for Christ, O blessed martyr, Stephen of renown.

29 The holy Paramonos, and the blessed Akakios of the Ladder.[155]

30 The holy apostle Andrew, the first-called; troparion, mode IV:

155. Delehaye, *Synaxarium Constantinopolitanae*, 261: "who is memorialized in the *(Heavenly) Ladder*" (see chap. 4: PG 88:719B–722A).

Μὴν δεκέμβριος

ἔχει ἡμέρας λα'· ἡ ἡμέρα ἔχει ὥρας θ' καὶ ἡ νὺξ ὥρας ιε'.

α' Τοῦ ἁγίου προφήτου Ναούμ.

β' Τοῦ ἁγίου προφήτου Ἀββακούμ.

γ' Τοῦ ἁγίου προφήτου Σοφονίου, καὶ τῶν ἁγίων μαρτύρων Ἴνδη, Πέτρου, Δωροθέου καὶ τῶν λοιπῶν.

δ' Τῆς ἁγίας μάρτυρος Βαρβάρας, τροπάριον ἦχος δ', Ἡ ἀμνάς σου, Ἰησοῦ. Τῇ αὐτῇ ἡμέρᾳ, τοῦ ὁσίου πατρὸς ἡμῶν Ἰωάννου τοῦ Δαμασκηνοῦ.

ε' Τοῦ ὁσίου πατρὸς ἡμῶν Σάβα, τροπάριον ἦχος πλάγιος δ', Ταῖς τῶν δακρύων σου ῥοαῖς, τῆς ἐρήμου τὸ ἄγονον· ζήτει σεπτεμβρίου κα'.

ς' Τοῦ ὁσίου πατρὸς ἡμῶν Νικολάου, τροπάριον ἦχος δ', Κανόνα πίστεως.

|268

ζ' Τοῦ ὁσίου πατρὸς ἡμῶν Ἀμβροσίου ἐπισκόπου Μεδιολάνων, Ἀλληλούϊα.

η' Τοῦ ὁσίου πατρὸς ἡμῶν Παταπίου, Ἀλληλούϊα.

θ' Ἡ σύλληψις τῆς ἁγίας Ἄννης τῆς μητρὸς τῆς Θεοτόκου, τροπάριον ἦχος δ',

Σήμερον ἡ ἀπαρχὴ τῆς σωτηρίας ἡμῶν φύεται καὶ καρπογονεῖ ἐν τῇ μήτρᾳ τῆς ἀκάρπου γαστρός, καὶ ἀγάλλεται λοιπὸν ἡ Ἄννα σὺν τῷ Ἰωακείμ, καὶ ὁ Ἀδὰμ συγχαίρει ἐλευθερούμενος· διὸ καὶ ἡμεῖς τῇ συλληφθείσῃ βοήσωμεν· Χαῖρε, κεχαριτωμένη, ὁ Κύριος μετὰ σοῦ.

ι' Τῶν ἁγίων μαρτύρων Μηνᾶ, Ἑρμογένους καὶ Εὐγράφου, τροπάριον ἦχος δ', Οἱ μάρτυρές σου, Κύριε, ἐν τῇ.

ια' Τοῦ ὁσίου πατρὸς ἡμῶν Δανιὴλ τοῦ στυλίτου, τροπάριον ἦχος α', Ὑπομονῆς στύλος γέγονας, ζηλώσας· ζήτει σεπτεμβρίου α'.

As the first apostle called and brother of the chief apostle,[156] *O Andrew, beseech the Master of all to give peace to the world and to our souls (his) great mercy.*

December

has thirty-one days; the day has nine hours and the night fifteen hours.

1 The holy prophet Nahum.

2 The holy prophet Habakkuk.

3 The holy prophet Sophonias;[157] and the holy martyrs Indes, Peter, Doro-theos and the rest.

4 The holy martyr Barbara; troparion, mode IV: *Your lamb, O Jesus* (cf. Sep. 24).
On the same day, our blessed father John of Damascus.

5 Our blessed father Sabas; troparion, plagal mode IV: *With the rivers of your tears you cultivated the barren desert*; see Sep. 21.

6 Our blessed father Nicholas; troparion, mode IV: *Rule of faith* (cf. Oct. 22).

7 Our blessed father Ambrose, bishop of Milan: Alleluia.

8 Our blessed father Patapios: Alleluia.

9 The conception of St. Anna, mother of the Theotokos; troparion, mode IV:
Today the beginning of our salvation is planted and flourishes in the womb of a barren belly. Finally, Anna rejoices with Joachim, and Adam, who is set free, joins in. For this let us, too, cry out to her who has been conceived, "Hail, full of grace, the Lord is with you" (Lk 1:28).

10 The holy martyrs Menas, Hermogenes, and Eugraphos; troparion, mode IV: *Your martyrs, O Lord, in the* (cf. Oct. 7).

11 Our blessed father Daniel the Stylite; troparion, mode I: *O blessed one, when you became a pillar of perseverance, you emulated*; see Sep. 1.

---

156. I.e., Peter.   157. I.e., Zephaniah.

ιβʹ Τοῦ ὁσίου πατρὸς ἡμῶν Σπυρίδωνος, Ἀλληλούϊα.

ιγʹ Τοῦ ἁγίου μεγαλομάρτυρος Εὐστρατίου καὶ τῆς συνοδίας αὐτοῦ, τροπάριον ἦχος αʹ, *Οἱ μάρτυρές σου, Κύριε, ἐν τῇ ἀθλήσει αὐτῶν.*

ιδʹ Τοῦ ἁγίου μάρτυρος Θύρσου καὶ τῶν σὺν αὐτῷ, Ἀλληλούϊα.

ιεʹ Τοῦ ἁγίου μάρτυρος Ἐλευθερίου, Ἀλληλούϊα.

ιςʹ Τοῦ ἁγίου προφήτου Ἀγγαίου, καὶ τοῦ ἁγίου μάρτυρος Μαρίνου, Ἀλληλούϊα.

ιζʹ Τῶν ἁγίων τριῶν παίδων καὶ Δανιὴλ τοῦ προφήτου, τροπάριον εἰς τὸ Θεὸς Κύριος, ἦχος βʹ,

Μεγάλα τὰ τῆς πίστεως κατορθώματα· ἐν τῇ πηγῇ τῆς φλογὸς ὡς ἐπὶ ὕδατος ἀναπαύσεως οἱ ἅγιοι παῖδες |²⁶⁸ᵛ *ἠγάλλοντο, καὶ ὁ προφήτης Δανιὴλ λεόντων ποιμὴν ὡς προβάτων ἐδείκνυτο· ταῖς αὐτῶν ἱκεσίαις, Χριστὲ ὁ Θεός, ἐλέησον ἡμᾶς.*

ιηʹ Τοῦ ἁγίου μάρτυρος Σεβαστιανοῦ καὶ τῆς συνοδίας αὐτοῦ.

ιθʹ Τοῦ ἁγίου μάρτυρος Βονιφατίου, καὶ τοῦ ἁγίου ὁσιομάρτυρος Ἀθηνοδώρου.

Κυριακὴ πρὸ τῶν ἁγίων πατέρων, ἤγουν τῶν προπατόρων, τροπάριον ἦχος βʹ,

*Ἐν πίστει τοὺς προπάτορας ἐδικαίωσας, τὴν ἐξ ἐθνῶν*¹⁵⁶ *δι' αὐτῶν προμνηστευσάμενος ἐκκλησίαν σου. Καυχῶνται ἐν δόξῃ οἱ ἅγιοι, ὅτι ἐκ σπέρματος αὐτῶν ὑπάρχει καρπός, ἡ ἀσπόρως τεκοῦσά σε· ταῖς αὐτῶν ἱκεσίαις, Χριστὲ ὁ Θεός, ἐλέησον ἡμᾶς.*

Κυριακὴ βʹ πρὸ τῆς Χριστοῦ γεννήσεως, τῶν ἁγίων πατέρων, τροπάριον ἦχος βʹ, *Μεγάλα τὰ τῆς πίστεως·* ζήτει εἰς τὴν ιζʹ τοῦ αὐτοῦ μήνος.

κʹ Προεόρτια τῆς Χριστοῦ γεννήσεως, καὶ τοῦ ἁγίου ἱερομάρτυρος Ἰγνατίου τοῦ θεοφόρου, τροπάριον προεόρτιον ἦχος δʹ,

Ἑτοιμάζου Βηθλεέμ· ἤνοικται πᾶσιν ἡ Ἐδέμ. Εὐτρεπίζου Ἐφραθά, νῦν γὰρ τὸ ξύλον τῆς ζωῆς ἐν τῷ σπηλαίῳ ἐξήνθησεν ἐκ τῆς παρθένου· παράδεισος καὶ γὰρ ἡ ἐκείνης γαστὴρ ἐδείχθη νοητῶς, ἐν ᾧ τὸ θεῖον φυτόν, ἐξ οὗ φαγόντες

---

156. ἐξεθνῶν: C.

12 Our blessed father Spyridon: Alleluia.

13 The holy great martyr Eustratios and his companions; troparion, mode
   I: *Your martyrs, O Lord, in the trial* (cf. Oct. 7).

14 The holy martyr Thyrsos and the ones with him: Alleluia.

15 The holy martyr Eleutherios: Alleluia.

16 The holy prophet Haggai, and the holy martyr Marinos: Alleluia.

17 The Three Holy Children[158] and Daniel the prophet; troparion to God
   is the Lord, mode II:

   Great are the successes of the faith. The Holy Youths rejoiced in the wellspring of fire as if **in peaceful waters** (Ps 22:2), and the prophet Daniel proved
   to be a shepherd to lions that were like sheep; through their supplications,
   Christ our God, have mercy on us.

18 The holy martyr Sebastian and his companions.

19 The holy martyr Boniface, and the holy hosiomartyr Athenodoros.

Sunday before (that) of the holy fathers,[159] that is, of the Forefathers;
troparion, mode II:

   *Through faith you vindicated the forefathers, having courted your church
   of the gentiles through them. The saints exult in glory, because from their seed
   issues fruit, she*[160] *who bore you without seed. Through their supplications,
   Christ our God, have mercy on us.*

Second Sunday before Christ's birth, and (that) of the holy fathers; troparion, mode II: *Great are the successes of the faith*; see the seventeenth of this
month.

20 Forefeast of Christ's birth, and of the holy hieromartyr Ignatios Theophoros; forefeast troparion, mode IV:

   Get ready, O Bethlehem: Eden is opened to all. Be prepared, O Ephrath,[161]
   for now **the tree of life** (Gn 2:9) *blooms forth from the Virgin in a cave. For
   that woman's womb is revealed in spirit to be paradise, in which is (found) the*

---

158. Shadrach, Meshach, Abednego (Dn 3).
159. Abraham, Isaac, and Jacob. This is the third Sunday before Christmas.
160. I.e., the church.   161. Cf. Gn 48:7, as Bethlehem.

ζήσομεν·[157] οὐχὶ δὲ ὡς ὁ Ἀδὰμ τεθνηξόμεθα· Χριστὸς γεννᾶται τὴν πρὶν πεσοῦσαν ἀναστήσων εἰκόνα. |[269]

Ἕτερον τροπάριον τοῦ ἁγίου, ἦχος δ᾽, Καὶ τρόπων μέτοχος, καὶ θρόνων.

κα᾽ Προεόρτια, καὶ τῆς ἁγίας μάρτυρος Ἰουλιανῆς, τροπάριον προεόρτιον.

κβ᾽ Προεόρτια, καὶ τῆς ἁγίας μάρτυρος Ἀναστασίας, τροπάριον προεόρτιον.

κγ᾽ Προεόρτια, καὶ τῶν ἁγίων ι᾽ μαρτύρων τῶν ἐν Κρήτῃ, τροπάριον προεόρτιον.

κδ᾽ Προεόρτια, καὶ τῆς ἁγίας ὁσιομάρτυρος Εὐγενίας καὶ τῶν σὺν αὐτῇ, τροπάριον προεόρτιον τῆς ἀπογραφῆς, ἦχος δ᾽,

Ἀπεγράφετο ποτὲ σὺν τῷ πρεσβύτῃ Ἰωσήφ, ὡς ἐκ σπέρματος Δαυῒδ ἐν Βηθλεέμ, ἡ Μαριὰμ κυοφοροῦσα τὴν ἄσπορον κυοφορίαν. Ἐπέστη δὲ καιρὸς ὁ τῆς γεννήσεως καὶ τόπος ἦν οὐδεὶς τῷ καταλύματι· ἀλλ᾽ ὡς τερπνὸν παλάτιον τὸ σπήλαιον τῇ βασιλίδι ἐδείκνυτο· Χριστὸς γεννᾶται τὴν πρὶν πεσοῦσαν ἀναστήσων εἰκόνα.

κε᾽ Τὰ ἅγια χριστούγεννα,[158] τροπάριον ἦχος δ᾽,

Ἡ γέννησίς σου, Χριστὲ ὁ Θεὸς ἡμῶν, ἀνέτειλε τῷ κόσμῳ τὸ φῶς τὸ τῆς γνώσεως· ἐν αὐτῇ γὰρ οἱ τοῖς ἄστροις λατρεύοντες, ὑπὸ ἀστέρος ἐδιδάσκοντο σὲ προσκυνεῖν τὸν ἥλιον τῆς δικαιοσύνης, καὶ σὲ γινώσκειν ἐξ ὕψους ἀνατολήν· Κύριε, δόξα σοι.

κϛ᾽ Ἡ σύναξις τῆς ὑπεραγίας Θεοτόκου καὶ τοῦ δικαίου Ἰωσὴφ τοῦ μνηστῆρος, καὶ τοῦ ἁγίου Εὐθυμίου ἐπισκόπου Σάρδης, τροπάριον τῆς ἑορτῆς |[269v]

Κυριακὴ μετὰ τὴν Χριστοῦ γέννησιν, τελεῖται ἡ μνήμη τῶν ἁγίων καὶ δικαίων Ἰωσὴφ τοῦ μνηστῆρος, Δαυῒδ τοῦ θεοπάτορος καὶ Ἰακώβου τοῦ ἀδελφοθέου, τροπάριον εἰς τὸ Θεὸς Κύριος, ἦχος β᾽,

Εὐαγγελίζου, Ἰωσήφ, τῷ Δαυῒδ <τὰ θαύματα>[159] τῷ θεοπάτορι· παρθένον εἶδες κυοφορήσασαν, μετὰ ποιμένων ἐδοξολόγησας, διὰ ἀγγέλου χρηματισθείς· ἱκέτευε Χριστὸν τὸν Θεὸν σωθῆναι τὰς ψυχὰς ἡμῶν.

---

157. ζήσωμεν: C.
158. τὰ ἅγια χριστούγεννα is written in red ink.
159. Supplied from Mateos, *Typicon* 1:160; *MR* 2.685.

divine tree, eating of which we shall live; we will not die like Adam. Christ is born who will raise the image[162] *that had once fallen.*

The other troparion, of the saint; mode IV: *You who followed in the footsteps and succeeded to the thrones* (cf. Sep. 4).

21 Forefeast, and the holy martyr Juliana; forefeast troparion.

22 Forefeast, and the holy martyr Anastasia; forefeast troparion.

23 Forefeast, and the holy Ten Martyrs of Crete; forefeast troparion.

24 Forefeast, and the holy hosiomartyr Eugenia and the ones with her; forefeast troparion (to the melody of) "Of the registration," mode IV:

At the time when Mary was registered with the aged Joseph, from the line of David in Bethlehem, she was pregnant, having conceived without seed. When the moment of birth was close at hand, there was no room in the inn (Lk 2:7), but the cave was shown to be like a fine palace for the queen. Christ is born who will raise the image that had once fallen.

25 Holy nativity of Christ; troparion, mode IV:

O Christ our God, your birth brought forth into the world the light of knowledge; through it the men who worshipped the stars were instructed by the (one) star to worship you, the sun of righteousness (Mal 4:2), and to know you, the dawning from on high. Glory to you, O Lord.

26 Service for the most-holy Theotokos and the righteous Joseph the Betrothed, and St. Euthymios, bishop of Sardis: troparion of the feast.

Sunday after Christ's birth; the commemoration of the holy and righteous Joseph the Betrothed, David, the ancestor of the Lord, and James, the brother of the Lord, concludes; troparion to God is the Lord, mode II:

Joseph, announce <the wonders> to God's ancestor David. You have seen a virgin who conceived; you have praised God with the shepherds, you who were delivered a message by an angel. Beseech Christ our God that our souls be saved.

162. Of God in humankind, as Gn 1:26.

κζ´ Τοῦ ἁγίου πρωτομάρτυρος καὶ ἀποστόλου Στεφάνου, τροπάριον τῆς ἑορτῆς καὶ ἕτερον τοῦ ἁγίου, ἦχος δ´,

Βασίλειον διάδημα ἐστέφθη σῇ κορυφῇ ἐξ ἄθλων ὧν ὑπέμεινας ὑπὲρ Χριστοῦ τοῦ Θεοῦ, μαρτύρων πρωτόαθλε· σὺ γὰρ τῶν Ἰουδαίων ἀπελέγξας μανίαν, εἶδές σου τὸν Σωτῆρα τοῦ Πατρὸς δεξιόθεν· αὐτὸν οὖν ἐκδυσώπει ἀεὶ ὑπὲρ τῶν ὑμνούντων σε.

κη´ Τῶν ἁγίων δισμυρίων, καὶ τοῦ ὁσίου καὶ ὁμολογητοῦ Θεοδώρου τοῦ γραπτοῦ, τροπάριον τῆς ἑορτῆς.

κθ´ Τῶν ἁγίων νηπίων, καὶ τοῦ ὁσίου πατρὸς ἡμῶν Μαρκέλλου, τροπάριον τῆς ἑορτῆς.

λ´ Τῆς ἁγίας μάρτυρος Ἀνυσίας, τροπάριον τῆς ἑορτῆς.

λα´ Τῆς ὁσίας Μελάνης τῆς Ῥωμαίας, τροπάριον τῆς ἑορτῆς καὶ ἀποδίδει.

Μὴν ἰαννουάριος
ἔχει ἡμέρας λα´· ἡ ἡμέρα ἔχει ὥρας ι´ καὶ ἡ νὺξ ὥρας ιδ´.

α´ Ἡ περιτομὴ τοῦ Κυρίου ἡμῶν Ἰησοῦ Χριστοῦ, καὶ τοῦ ἐν ἁγίοις πατρὸς ἡμῶν Βασιλείου τοῦ μεγάλου, τροπάριον ἦχος α´, |²⁷⁰

Εἰς πᾶσαν τὴν γῆν ἐξῆλθεν ὁ φθόγγος σου ὡς δεξαμένην τὸν λόγον σου, δι᾽ οὗ θεοπρεπῶς ἐδογμάτισας, τὴν φύσιν τῶν ὄντων ἐτράνωσας, τὰ τῶν ἀνθρώπων ἤθη κατεκόσμησας· βασίλειον ἱεράτευμα, πάτερ ὅσιε, πρέσβευε Χριστῷ τῷ Θεῷ σωθῆναι τὰς ψυχὰς ἡμῶν.

β´ Προεόρτια τῶν φώτων, καὶ τοῦ ὁσίου πατρὸς ἡμῶν Σιλβέστρου πάπα Ῥώμης, τροπάριον προεόρτιον ἦχος δ´,

Ἑτοιμάζου Ζαβουλών, καὶ εὐτρεπίζου Νεφθαλείμ· Ἰορδάνη ποταμέ, στῆθι, ὑπόδεξαι σκιρτῶν τοῦ βαπτισθῆναι ἐρχόμενον τὸν Δεσπότην· ἀγάλλου ὁ Ἀδὰμ σὺν τῇ προμήτορι, μὴ κρύπτεσθε αὐτὸν ὡς ἐν παραδείσῳ ποτέ· καὶ γὰρ γυμνοὺς ἰδὼν ἡμᾶς ἐπέφανεν, ἵνα ἐνδύσῃ τὴν πρώτην στολήν· Χριστὸς ἐφάνη, τὴν πᾶσαν κτίσιν θέλων ἀνακαινίσαι.

27 The holy protomartyr and apostle Stephen; troparion of the feast and the other of the saint, mode IV:

The imperial crown sits about your head for the hardships which you, O protomartyr, endured for Christ our God. Exposing the madness of the Jews, you saw your savior seated at the right hand of the Father. Eternally importune him, therefore, on behalf of the ones who sing your praises.

28 The holy Twenty Thousand (martyred in Nicomedia[163]), and the blessed confessor Theodore Graptos: troparion of the feast.

29 The Holy Innocents,[164] and our blessed father Marcellus; troparion of the feast.

30 The holy martyr Anysia; troparion of the feast.

31 The blessed Melane the Roman; troparion of the feast, and it concludes.

January

has thirty-one days; the day has ten hours and the night fourteen hours.

1 The circumcision of our Lord Jesus Christ, and our father among the saints Basil the Great; troparion, mode I:

Your voice reached throughout all the earth, which accepted your word. Through it you taught a theology worthy of God; you explained the nature of beings; you beautified men's character, O you of the imperial priesthood. Blessed father, intercede with Christ our God that our souls be saved.

2 Forefeast of Lights,[165] and our blessed father Silvester, head of the church of Rome; forefeast troparion, mode IV:

Get ready, O Zebulun, and prepare yourself, O Naphtali.[166] O River Jordan, stop to receive, leaping, the master who is coming to be baptized. Adam, exalt with the first mother; do not hide yourself from him as you once (did) in paradise. For seeing us naked he has appeared so that he might clothe us in the best robe (Lk 15:22). Christ has come: he who wishes to renew all of creation.

---

163. Delehaye, *Synaxarium Constantinopolitanae*, 349.
164. Victims of Herod's decree (Mt 2:16).
165. The celebration of Christ's baptism; see the following note.
166. Cf. Mt 4:15–16 (from Is 9:1–2): The land of Zebulum and the land of Naphtali, / toward the

γ′ Προεόρτια, καὶ τοῦ ἁγίου προφήτου Μαλαχίου, καὶ τοῦ ἁγίου μάρτυρος Γορδίου, τροπάριον τῆς ἑορτῆς.

δ′ Προεόρτια, καὶ τοῦ ὁσίου Θεοκτίστου ἡγουμένου, τροπάριον τῆς ἑορτῆς.

ε′ Προεόρτια, τροπάριον τῆς ἑορτῆς.

ϛ′ Τὰ ἅγια φῶτα,[160] τροπάριον ἦχος α′, *Ἐν Ἰορδάνῃ βαπτιζομένου σου, Κύριε, ἡ τῆς Τριάδος ἐφανερώθη προσκύνησις.*

ζ′ Ἡ σύναξις τοῦ ἁγίου Ἰωάννου τοῦ προδρόμου καὶ βαπτιστοῦ, τροπάριον τῆς ἑορτῆς καὶ ἕτερον τοῦ ἁγίου, ἦχος β′, *Μνήμη δικαίου μετ᾽ ἐγκωμίων.*

η′ Μεθέορτα, καὶ τῆς ὁσίας Δομνίκας, καὶ τῶν ἁγίων μαρτύρων Ἰουλιανοῦ καὶ Βασιλίσσης, τροπάριον τῆς ἑορτῆς. |[270v]

θ′ Μεθέορτα, καὶ τοῦ ἁγίου μάρτυρος Πολυεύκτου, καὶ τοῦ ὁσίου Μαρκιανοῦ.

ι′ Μεθέορτα, καὶ τοῦ ἐν ἁγίοις πατρὸς ἡμῶν Γρηγορίου τοῦ Νύσης, τροπάριον τῆς ἑορτῆς καὶ ἕτερον τοῦ ἁγίου, ἦχος πλάγιος δ′, *Ὀρθοδοξίας ὁδηγέ.*

ια′ Μεθέορτα, καὶ τοῦ ὁσίου πατρὸς ἡμῶν Θεοδοσίου τοῦ κοινοβιάρχου, τροπάριον τῆς ἑορτῆς καὶ ἕτερον τοῦ ἁγίου, ἦχος πλάγιος δ′, *Ταῖς τῶν δακρύων σου.*

ιβ′ Μεθέορτα, καὶ τῆς ἁγίας μάρτυρος Τατιανῆς, τροπάριον τῆς ἑορτῆς.

ιγ′ Μεθέορτα, καὶ τῶν ἁγίων μαρτύρων Ἑρμύλου καὶ Στρατονίκου, τροπάριον τῆς ἑορτῆς καὶ ἀποδίδει.

ιδ′ Τῶν ἁγίων ἀββάδων, τροπάριον ἦχος δ′, *Ὁ Θεὸς τῶν πατέρων ἡμῶν.*

ιε′ Τοῦ ὁσίου πατρὸς ἡμῶν Ἰωάννου τοῦ καλυβίτου, τροπάριον ἦχος πλάγιος δ′, *Ἐν σοί, πάτερ, ἀκριβῶς διεσώθη τὸ κατ᾽ εἰκόνα.*

---

160. τὰ ἅγια φῶτα is written in red ink.

3 Forefeast, and the holy prophet Malachi, and the holy martyr Gordios; troparion of the feast.

4 Forefeast, and the blessed Theoktistos, abbot; troparion of the feast.

5 Forefeast; troparion of the feast.

6 The Holy Lights; troparion, mode I: *When you were baptized in the Jordan, O Lord, worship of the Trinity was made manifest* (MR 3:144).

7 Service for the holy John the Forerunner and Baptist; troparion of the feast and the other for the saint, mode II: *The memory of the just is praised* (Prv 10:7) (MR 3:161).

8 Afterfeast, and the blessed Domnika, and the holy martyrs Julian and Basilissa; troparion of the feast.

9 Afterfeast, and the holy martyr Polyeuktos, and the blessed Marcian.

10 Afterfeast, and our holy father among the saints Gregory of Nyssa; troparion of the feast, and the other for the saint, plagal mode IV: *Guide of orthodoxy* (cf. Nov. 11).

11 Afterfeast, and our blessed father Theodosios the Cenobiarch; troparion of the feast and the other for the saint, plagal mode IV: *With the rivers of your tears* (cf. Oct. 21).

12 Afterfeast, and the holy martyr Tatiane; troparion of the feast.

13 Afterfeast, and the holy martyrs Hermylos and Stratonikos; troparion of the feast, and it concludes.

14 The holy fathers (of Sinai[167]); troparion, mode IV: *God of our fathers* (cf. Nov. 12).

15 Our blessed father John the Calybite; troparion, plagal mode IV: *In you, father, "according to the image" was accurately preserved* (cf. Sep. 28).

---

sea, across the Jordan, / Galilee of the Gentiles— / the people who sat in darkness have seen a great light, / and for those who sat in the region and shadow of death / light has dawned.

167. Delehaye, *Synaxarium Constantinopolitanae*, 389.

ις᾽ Ἡ προσκύνησις τῆς τιμίας ἁλύσεως τοῦ ἁγίου ἀποστόλου Πέτρου, τροπάριον ἦχος δ᾽,

Τὴν Ῥώμην μὴ λιπὼν πρὸς ἡμᾶς ἐπεδήμησας, δι᾽ ὧν ἐφόρεσας τιμίων ἁλύσεων, τῶν ἀποστόλων πρωτόθρονε· ἃς ἐν πίστει προσκυνοῦντες, δεόμεθα ταῖς πρὸς Θεὸν πρεσβείαις σου δώρησαι ἡμῖν τὸ μέγα ἔλεος.

ιζ᾽ Τοῦ ὁσίου πατρὸς ἡμῶν Ἀντωνίου τοῦ μεγάλου, τροπάριον ἦχος δ᾽,

Τὸν ζηλωτὴν Ἠλίαν τοῖς τρόποις μιμούμενος, τῷ βαπτιστῇ εὐθείαις ταῖς τρίβοις ἑπόμενος, πάτερ ὅσιε, τῆς ἐρήμου γέγονας οἰκιστὴς καὶ τὴν οἰκουμένην ἐστήριξας εὐχαῖς· διὸ πρέσβευε Χριστῷ τῷ Θεῷ, πάτερ |²⁷¹ Ἀντώνιε, σωθῆναι τὰς ψυχὰς ἡμῶν.

ιη᾽ Τῶν ὁσίων πατέρων ἡμῶν Ἀθανασίου καὶ Κυρίλλου πατριαρχῶν Ἀλεξανδρείας, τροπάριον ἦχος δ᾽, Ὁ Θεὸς τῶν πατέρων ἡμῶν, ὁ.

ιθ᾽ Τοῦ ὁσίου Μακαρίου τοῦ Αἰγυπτίου, Ἀλληλούϊα.

κ᾽ Τοῦ ὁσίου πατρὸς ἡμῶν Εὐθυμίου τοῦ μεγάλου, τροπάριον ἦχος δ᾽,

Εὐφραίνου ἔρημος ἡ οὐ τίκτουσα, εὐθύμησον ἡ οὐκ ὠδίνουσα· ὅτι ἐπλήθυνέ σοι τέκνα ἀνὴρ ἐπιθυμιῶν τῶν τοῦ Πνεύματος, εὐσεβείᾳ φυτεύσας, ἐγκρατείᾳ ἐκθρέψας εἰς ἀρετῶν τελειότητα· ταῖς αὐτοῦ ἱκεσίαις, Χριστὲ ὁ Θεός, ἐλέησον ἡμᾶς.

κα᾽ Τοῦ ὁσίου μάρτυρος Νεοφύτου, καὶ τοῦ ὁσίου πατρὸς ἡμῶν καὶ ὁμολογητοῦ Μαξίμου, τροπάριον ἦχος πλάγιος δ᾽, Ὀρθοδοξίας ὁδηγέ, εὐσεβείας.

κβ᾽ Τοῦ ἁγίου ἀποστόλου Τιμοθέου, τροπάριον ἦχος δ᾽, Χρηστότητα ἐκδιδαχθεὶς καὶ νήφων ἐν πᾶσιν· ζήτει ὀκτωβρίου γ᾽.

κγ᾽ Τοῦ ἁγίου ἱερομάρτυρος Κλήμεντος Ἀγκύρας, καὶ Ἀγαθαγγέλου, τροπάτιον ἦχος πλάγιος δ᾽,

Κλῆμα ὁσιότητος καὶ στέλεχος ἀθλήσεως, ἄνθος ἱερώτατον καὶ κάρπωσις θεόσδοτος, τοῖς πιστοῖς, πανάγιε ἀειθαλές, δεδώρησαι· ἀλλ᾽ ὡς μαρτύρων σύναθλος καὶ ἱεραρχῶν σύνθρονος, πρέσβευε Χριστῷ τῷ Θεῷ σωθῆναι τὰς ψυχὰς ἡμῶν.

16 Veneration of the precious chains of the holy apostle Peter; troparion, mode IV:

Not deserting Rome, O chief of the apostles, you came to stay among us because of the precious chains that you bore. Worshiping them in faith, we ask for your intercession with God to grant us (his) great mercy.

17 Our blessed father Anthony the Great; troparion, mode IV:

In your way of life you imitated the zealous Elijah. O blessed father, you followed the straight paths of the Baptist. After you made a city of the wilderness, you steadied the world through prayer. Therefore, O father Anthony, intercede with Christ the God that our souls be saved.

18 Our blessed fathers Athanasios and Cyril, patriarchs of Alexandria; troparion, mode IV: *God of our fathers* (cf. Jan. 14).

19 The blessed Makarios of Egypt: Alleluia.

20 Our blessed father Euthymios the Great; troparion, mode IV:

Rejoice, wilderness that has not born fruit. Be of good cheer, you who do not experience the pain of childbirth, for a man of desire for things of the spirit has filled you with children. You conceive through piety (and) you are reared by self-control to a perfection of virtue. Through his supplications, O Christ our God, have mercy on us.

21 The blessed martyr Neophytos, and our blessed father and confessor Maximos; troparion, plagal mode IV: *Guide of orthodoxy, teacher of piety* (cf. Nov. 11).

22 The holy apostle Timothy; troparion, mode IV: *You were well educated in goodness and sober-minded in all things*; see Oct. 3.

23 The holy hieromartyr Clement of Ankyra, and Agathangelos; troparion, plagal mode IV:

O all-holy one ever-flourishing, you have been given to the faithful as a shoot of holiness and a trunk of struggle, a most sacred flower and a God-given fruit. As a contender alongside the martyrs and one sharing a throne with holy fathers, intercede with Christ our God that our souls be saved.

κδ΄ Τῆς ὁσίας μητρὸς ἡμῶν Ξένης, Ἀλληλούϊα. |²⁷¹ᵛ

κε΄ Τοῦ ἐν ἁγίοις πατρὸς ἡμῶν Γρηγορίου τοῦ θεολόγου, τροπάριον ἦχος α΄,
   Ὁ ποιμενικὸς αὐλὸς τῆς θεολογίας σου τὰς τῶν ῥητόρων ἐνίκησε
   σάλπιγγας· ὡς γὰρ τὰ βάθη τοῦ Πνεύματος ἐκζητήσαντι καὶ τὰ κάλλη τοῦ
   φθέγματος προσετέθη σοι· διὸ πρέσβευε Χριστῷ τῷ Θεῷ σωθῆναι τὰς ψυχὰς
   ἡμῶν.

κϛ΄ Τοῦ ὁσίου Ξενοφῶντος καὶ τῶν τέκνων αὐτοῦ.

κζ΄ Ἡ ἀνακομιδὴ τοῦ λειψάνου τοῦ ἁγίου Ἰωάννου τοῦ Χρυσοστόμου,
   τροπάριον ἦχος πλάγιος δ΄, *Ἡ τοῦ στόματός σου καθάπερ.*

κη΄ Τοῦ ὁσίου πατρὸς ἡνῶν Ἐφραὶμ τοῦ Σύρου, τροπάριον ἦχος πλάγιος δ΄,
   Ταῖς τῶν δακρύων σου ῥοαῖς· ζήτει ὀκτωβρίου κα΄.

κθ΄ Ἡ ἀνακομιδὴ τοῦ λειψάνου τοῦ ἁγίου Ἰγνατίου τοῦ θεοφόρου, τροπάριον
   ἦχος δ΄, *Καὶ τρόπων μέτοχος, καί.*

λ΄ Τοῦ ἁγίου ἱερομάρτυρος Ἱππολύτου πάπα Ῥώμης.

λα΄ Τῶν ἁγίων καὶ θαυματουργῶν ἀναργύρων Κύρου καὶ Ἰωάννου,
   τροπάριον ἦχος πλάγιος α΄, *Τὰ θαύματα τῶν ἁγίων σου μαρτύρων.*

Μὴν φεβρουάριος
ἔχει ἡμέρας κη΄· <ἡ> ἡμέρα ἔχει ὥρας ια΄ καὶ ἡ νὺξ ὥρας ἔχει ιγ΄.

α΄ Προεόρτια τῆς ὑπαπαντῆς τοῦ Σωτῆρος, καὶ τοῦ ἁγίου μάρτυρος
   Τρύφωνος, τροπάριον τῆς ἑορτῆς, ἦχος α΄,
   Χορὸς ἀγγελικὸς ἐκπληττέσθω τὸ θαῦμα· βροτοὶ δὲ ταῖς φωναῖς
   ἀνακράξομεν αἶνον, ὁρῶντες τὴν ἄφατον |²⁷² τοῦ Θεοῦ συγκατάβασιν, ὃν
   γὰρ τρέμουσι τῶν οὐρανῶν αἱ δυνάμεις· νῦν γηραλέαι[161] *ἐναγκαλίζονται*
   χεῖρες τὸν μόνον φιλάνθρωπον.

β΄ Ἡ ὑπαπαντὴ τοῦ Κυρίου ἡμῶν Ἰησοῦ Χριστοῦ, τροπάριον εἰς τὸ Θεὸς
   Κύριος, ἦχος α΄,
   Χαῖρε, κεχαριτωμένη Θεοτόκε παρθένε· ἐκ σοῦ γὰρ ἀνέτειλε Χριστὸς ὁ

---

161. γηράλεοι: C.

24 Our blessed mother Xene: Alleluia.

25 Our father among the saints Gregory (of Nazianzen) the Theologian; troparion, mode I:

The shepherd's flute of your teaching vanquished the rhetoricians' trumpets. For on you who sought the depths of the Spirit, the beauty of the language was bestowed. For this intercede with Christ our God that our souls be saved.

26 The blessed Xenophon and his children.

27 The translation of the relics of St. John Chrysostom; troparion, plagal mode IV: *Inasmuch as the grace of your mouth* (cf. Nov. 13).

28 Our blessed father Ephrem the Syrian; troparion, plagal mode IV: *With the rivers of your tears*; see Oct. 21.

29 The translation of the relics of St. Ignatios Theophoros; troparion, mode IV: *You who followed in the footsteps and* (cf. Sep. 4).

30 The holy hieromartyr Hippolytus, head of the church of Rome.

31 The holy anargyroi and miracle workers Cyrus and John; troparion, plagal mode I: *The miracles of your holy martyrs* (cf. Nov. 15).

February

has twenty-eight days; the day has eleven hours and the night has thirteen hours.

1 Forefeast of the meeting (in the Temple) of the savior (and Symeon),[168] and the holy martyr Tryphon; troparion of the feast, mode I:

Angelic choir be astonished at the wonder. Mortals, in a strong voice we will sing out praise at seeing the unutterable condescension of God, before whom the powers of heaven tremble. Now the aged hands take up and hold the one who alone loves mankind.

2 The meeting of our Lord Jesus Christ (and Symeon in the temple); troparion to God is the Lord, mode I:

*Hail, **full of grace** (Lk 1:28), virgin mother of God; for from you arose*

---

168. Presentation of Christ in the Temple.

Θεὸς ἡμῶν φωτίζων τοὺς ἐν σκότει. Εὐφραίνου καὶ σύ, πρεσβῦτα δίκαιε, δεξάμενος ἐν ἀγκάλαις τὸν ἐλευθερωτὴν τῶν ψυχῶν ἡμῶν χαριζόμενον ἡμῖν καὶ τὴν ἀνάστασιν.

γ´ Μεθέορτα, καὶ τοῦ ἁγίου Συμεὼν τοῦ θεοδόχου, τροπάριον τῆς ἑορτῆς.

δ´ Μεθέορτα, καὶ τοῦ ὁσίου Ἰσιδώρου τοῦ Πηλουσιώτου, τροπάριον τῆς ἑορτῆς.

ε´ Μεθέορτα, καὶ τῆς μάρτυρος Ἀγάθης, τροπάριον τῆς ἑορτῆς.

ς´ Μεθέορτα, καὶ τοῦ ὁσίου Βουκόλου α´ ἐπισκόπου Σμύρνης, τροπάριον τῆς ἑορτῆς καὶ ἀποδίδει ἡ ἑορτή.

ζ´ Τοῦ ὁσίου πατρὸς ἡμῶν καὶ θαυματουργοῦ Λουκᾶ τοῦ ἐν τῷ Στειρίῳ, τροπάριον ἦχος πλάγιος δ´, Ἐν σοί, πάτερ, ἀκριβῶς.

Τῇ αὐτῇ ἡμέρᾳ, τοῦ ὁσίου πατρὸς ἡμῶν Παρθενίου ἐπισκόπου Λαμψάκου, καὶ τοῦ ἁγίου μεγαλομάρτυρος Θεοδώρου τοῦ στρατηλάτου· ζήτει ἰουνίου η´.

η´ Τοῦ ἁγίου προφήτου Ζαχαρίου, Ἀλληλούϊα.

θ´ Τοῦ ἁγίου μάρτυρος Νικηφόρου, τροπάριον ἦχος δ´, Ὁ μάρτυς σου, Κύριε.

ι´ Τοῦ ἁγίου ἱερομάρτυρος Χαραλάμπους καὶ τῶν σὺν αὐτῷ, Ἀλληλούϊα.

ια´ Τοῦ ἁγίου ἱερομάρτυρος Βλασίου, τροπάριον ἦχος δ´, Καὶ τρόπων μέτοχος.|272v

ιβ´ Τοῦ ὁσίου πατρὸς ἡμῶν Μελετίου πατριάρχου Ἀντιοχείας, καὶ τῶν ἁγίων ͵αγ´ μαρτύρων τῶν ἐν Νικομηδείᾳ, Ἀλληλούϊα.

ιγ´ Τοῦ ὁσίου Μαρτινιανοῦ, Ἀλληλούϊα.

ιδ´ Τοῦ ὁσίου πατρὸς ἡμῶν Αὐξεντίου, Ἀλληλούϊα.

ιε´ Τοῦ ἁγίου ἀποστόλου Ὀνησίμου, τροπάριον ἦχος γ´, Ἀπόστολε ἅγιε, πρέσβευε.

ις´ Τοῦ ἁγίου ἱερομάρτυρος Παμφίλου καὶ τῶν σὺν αὐτῷ.

Christ our God, illuminating those in darkness. You, O righteous old man, rejoice as well; you have taken in embrace the deliverer of our souls, he who willingly offers us even resurrection.

3 Afterfeast, and the holy Symeon the Theodochos;[169] troparion of the feast.

4 Afterfeast, and the blessed Isidore of Pelousion; troparion of the feast.

5 Afterfeast, and the martyr Agatha; troparion of the feast.

6 Afterfeast, and the blessed Boukolos, first bishop of Smyrna; troparion of the feast, and the feast concludes.

7 Our blessed father and miracle worker Luke of Stiris; troparion, plagal mode IV: *In you, father, "according to the image" was accurately* (cf. Sep. 28).

On the same day, our blessed father Parthenios, bishop of Lampsakos, and the holy great martyr Theodore Stratelates: see June 8.

8 The holy prophet Zachariah: Alleluia.

9 The holy martyr Nikephoros; troparion, mode IV: *Your martyr, O Lord* (cf. Oct. 20).

10 The holy hieromartyr Charalampos and the ones with him: Alleluia.

11 The holy hieromartyr Blasios; troparion, mode IV: *You who followed in the footsteps* (cf. Sep. 4).

12 Our blessed father Meletios, patriarch of Antioch, and the holy 1,003 martyrs of Nicomedia: Alleluia.

13 The blessed Martinianos: Alleluia.

14 Our blessed father Auxentios: Alleluia.

15 The holy apostle Onesimos; troparion, mode III: *Holy apostle, intercede* (cf. Sep. 22).

16 The holy hieromartyr Pamphilos and the ones with him.

---

169. "Who received God," the Symeon of the previous two days.

ιζ’ Τοῦ ἁγίου μεγαλομάρτυρος Θεοδώρου τοῦ τήρωνος, ζήτει τὸ α’ σάββατον· καὶ τῇ αὐτῇ ἡμέρᾳ, τῆς ἁγίας ἀποστόλου Μαριάμνης ἀδελφῆς τοῦ ἁγίου ἀποστόλου Φιλίππου.

ιη’ Τοῦ ἐν ἁγίοις πατρὸς ἡμῶν Λέοντος πάπα Ῥώμης, τροπάριον ἦχος πλάγιος δ’, Ὀρθοδοξίας ὁδηγέ, εὐσεβείας διδάσκαλε καί.

ιθ’ Τῶν ἁγίων μαρτύρων Μαξίμου, Θεοδότου καὶ Ἀσκληπιοδότης.

κ’ Τοῦ ἁγίου ἀποστόλου Ἀρχίππου, Ἀλληλούϊα.

κα’ Τοῦ ὁσίου πατρὸς ἡμῶν Λέοντος ἐπισκόπου Κατάνης.

κβ’ Ἡ εὕρεσις τῶν λειψάνων τῶν ἁγίων μαρτύρων τῶν ἐν τοῖς Εὐγενίου.

κγ’ Τοῦ ἁγίου ἱερομάρτυρος Πολυκάρπου ἐπισκόπου Σμύρνης.

κδ’ Ἡ α’ καὶ β’ εὕρεσις τῆς τιμίας κεφαλῆς τοῦ Προδρόμου, τροπάριον ἦχος β’, Μνήμη δικαίου μετ’ ἐγκωμίων.

κε’ Τοῦ ὁσίου πατρὸς ἡμῶν Ταρασίου πατριάρχου Κωνσταντινουπόλεως.

κϛ’ Τοῦ ὁσίου Πορφυρίου ἐπισκόπου Γάζης, Ἀλληλούϊα.

κζ’ Τοῦ ὁσίου πατρὸς ἡμῶν Προκοπίου τοῦ Δεκαπολίτου.

κη’ Τοῦ ὁσίου πατρὸς ἡμῶν καὶ ὁμολογητοῦ Βασιλείου· καὶ τῇ αὐτῇ ἡμέρᾳ, τοῦ ἁγίου ἱερομάρτυρος Προτερίου πατριάρχου Ἀλεξανδρείας. |²⁷³

Μὴν μάρτιος
ἔχει ἡμέρας λα’· ἡ ἡμέρα ἔχει ὥρας ιβ’ καὶ ἡ νὺξ ὥρας ιβ’.

α’ Τῆς ἁγίας ὁσιομάρτυρος Εὐδοκίας, Ἀλληλούϊα.

β’ Τοῦ ἁγίου μάρτυρος Κοΐντου, Ἀλληλούϊα.

γ’ Τῶν ἁγίων μαρτύρων Εὐτροπίου, Κλεονίκου καὶ Βασιλίσκου.

δ’ Τοῦ ἁγίου Ἡσυχίου, Ἀλληλούϊα.

ε’ Τοῦ ἁγίου μάρτυρος Κόνωνος, Ἀλληλούϊα.

ϛ’ Τῶν ἁγίων μβ’ μαρτύρων τῶν ἐν τῷ Ἀμορίῳ ἀθλησάντων.

17 The holy great martyr Theodore Tiron; see the first Saturday (of Lent, below 246); and on the same day, the holy apostle Miriam, sister of the holy apostle Philip.

18 Our father among the saints Leo, head of the church of Rome; troparion, plagal mode IV: *Guide of orthodoxy, teacher of piety and* (cf. Nov. 11).

19 The holy martyrs Maximos, Theodotos, and Asklepiodote.

20 The holy apostle Archippos: Alleluia.

21 Our blessed father Leo, bishop of Catania.

22 Discovery of the relics of the holy martyrs of the Eugenios.[170]

23 The holy hieromartyr Polycarp, bishop of Smyrna.

24 The first and second discovery of the precious head of the Forerunner; troparion, mode II: **The memory of the just is praised** (Prv 10:7) (cf. Jan. 7).

25 Our blessed father Tarasios, patriarch of Constantinople.

26 The blessed Porphyrios, bishop of Gaza: Alleluia.

27 Our blessed father Prokopios of Dekapolis.

28 Our blessed father and confessor Basil; and on the same day the holy hieromartyr Proterios, patriarch of Alexandria.

March

has thirty-one days, the day has twelve hours and the night twelve hours.

1 The holy hosiomartyr Eudokia: Alleluia.

2 The holy martyr Kointos: Alleluia.

3 The holy martyrs Eutropios, Kleonikos, and Basiliskos.

4 St. Hesychios: Alleluia.

5 The holy martyr Konon: Alleluia.

---

170. A quarter of Constantinople: R. Janin, *Constantinople byzantine: développement urbain et répertoire topographique*, 2nd ed. (Paris: Institut Français d'Études Byzantines, 1964), 349.

ζ´ Τῶν ἁγίων ἱερομαρτύρων τῶν ἐν Χερσῶνι ἐπισκοπησάντων, Βασιλέως, Ἐφραὶμ καὶ τῶν λοιπῶν.

η´ Τοῦ ὁσίου πατρὸς ἡμῶν καὶ ὁμολογητοῦ Θεοφυλάκτου ἐπισκόπου Νικομηδείας.

θ´ Τῶν ἁγίων μ´ μαρτύρων τῶν ἐν Σεβαστείᾳ ἀθλησάντων, τροπάριον ἦχος α´, Τὰς ἀλγηδόνας τῶν ἁγίων, ἃς ὑπὲρ σοῦ.

ι´ Τοῦ ἁγίου μάρτυρος Κοδράτου τοῦ ἐν Κορίνθῳ καὶ τῶν σὺν αὐτῷ.

ια´ Τοῦ ὁσίου πατρὸς ἡμῶν Σωφρονίου ἀρχιεπισκόπου Ἱεροσολύμων.

ιβ´ Τοῦ ὁσίου Θεοφάνους τοῦ τῆς Σιγριανῆς.

ιγ´ Ἡ ἀνακομιδὴ τοῦ λειψάνου τοῦ ἁγίου Νικηφόρου πατριάρχου Κωνσταντινουπόλεως.

ιδ´ Τοῦ ἁγίου μάρτυρος Ἀλεξάνδρου τοῦ ἐν Πύδνῃ.

ιε´ Τοῦ ἁγίου μάρτυρος Ἀγαπίου καὶ τῶν σὺν αὐτῷ.

ις´ Τοῦ ἁγίου μάρτυρος Πάπα.

ιζ´ Τοῦ ὁσίου πατρὸς ἡμῶν Ἀλεξίου τοῦ ἀνθρώπου τοῦ Θεοῦ.

ιη´ Τοῦ ὁσίου πατρὸς ἡμῶν Κυρίλλου ἀρχιεπισκόπου Ἱεροσολύμων. |273v

ιθ´ Τῶν ἁγίων μαρτύρων Χρυσάνθου καὶ Δαρείας, Ἀλληλούϊα.

κ´ Τοῦ ὁσίου πατρὸς ἡμῶν Γερασίμου, Ἀλληλούϊα.

κα´ Τοῦ ἁγίου ἀποστόλου Βηρύλλου[162] ἐπισκόπου Κατάνης.

κβ´ Τοῦ ἁγίου ἱερομάρτυρος Βασιλείου, Ἀλληλούϊα.

κγ´ Τοῦ ἁγίου ἱερομάρτυρος Νίκωνος καὶ τῶν σ´ αὐτοῦ μαθητῶν.

κδ´ Προεόρτια εἰς τὸν εὐαγγελισμὸν τῆς ὑπεραγίας Θεοτόκου, τροπάριον ἦχος δ´, Τὸ ἀπ᾽ αἰῶνος ἀπόκρυφον καὶ ἀγγέλοις· καὶ τῇ αὐτῇ ἡμέρᾳ, τοῦ ὁσίου Ἰακώβου ὁμολογητοῦ καὶ ἐπισκόπου.

---

162. Βυρίλλου: C.

6 The holy forty-two martyrs who died at Amorion.

7 The holy hieromartyrs who were bishops of Cherson: Basileus, Ephrem, and the rest.

8 Our blessed father and confessor Theophylact, bishop of Nicomedia.

9 The holy forty martyrs who died at Sebaste; troparion, mode I: *Be moved by the suffering of the saints, which they endured for your sake* (cf. Nov. 3).

10 The holy martyr Kodratos of Corinth and the ones with him.

11 Our blessed father Sophronios, archbishop of Jerusalem.

12 The blessed Theophanes of Sigriane.

13 The translation of the relics of the holy Nikephoros, patriarch of Constantinople.

14 The holy martyr Alexander of Pydna.

15 The holy martyr Agapios and the ones with him.

16 The holy martyr Papas.

17 Our blessed father Alexios, Man of God.

18 Our blessed father Cyril, archbishop of Jerusalem.

19 The holy martyrs Chrysanthos and Dareia: Alleluia.

20 Our blessed father Gerasimos: Alleluia.

21 The holy apostle Byrillos,[171] bishop of Katane.

22 The holy hieromartyr Basil: Alleluia.

23 The holy hieromartyr Nikon and his two hundred disciples.

24 Forefeast of the Annunciation to the most-holy Theotokos; troparion, mode IV: *The secret of the ages and mystery unknown to the angels* (MR 2:392); and on the same day, the blessed James, confessor and bishop.

---

171. The reading here conforms to that of the Evergetis Synaxarion (*Synaxarion of Evergetis*, ed. Jordan, 2:26), whereas the Messina Typikon and that of the Great Church read Βηρύλλου, bishop of Katane (Arranz, *Typicon de Messine*, 129; Mateos, *Typicon*, 1:252).

κεʹ Ὁ εὐαγγελισμὸς τῆς ὑπεραγίας δεσποίνης ἡμῶν Θεοτόκου,[163] τροπάριον
ἦχος δ᾽,
Σήμερον τῆς σωτηρίας ἡμῶν τὸ κεφάλαιον καὶ τοῦ ἀπ᾽ αἰῶνος μυστηρίου ἡ
φανέρωσις· ὁ Υἱὸς τοῦ Θεοῦ, υἱὸς τῆς παρθένου γίνεται, καὶ Γαβριὴλ τὴν χάριν
εὐαγγελίζεται· διὸ σὺν αὐτῷ τῇ Θεοτόκῳ βοήσωμεν· Χαῖρε, κεχαριτωμένη,
ὁ Κύριος μετὰ σοῦ.

κϛʹ Ἡ σύναξις τοῦ ἀρχιστρατήγου Γαβριήλ, τροπάριον ἦχος α᾽, *Τοῦ Γαβριὴλ*
φθεγξαμένου σοι, παρθένε, τό.

κζʹ Τῆς ἁγίας Ματρώνης τῆς ἐν Θεσσαλονίκῃ, Ἀλληλούϊα.

κηʹ Τοῦ ἁγίου ἱερομάρτυρος [Μάρκου][164] ἐπισκόπου Ἀρεθουσίων καὶ
Κυρίλλου διακόνου.

κθʹ Τῶν ἁγίων μαρτύρων Ἰωνᾶ καὶ Βαραχησίου[165] καὶ τῶν σὺν αὐτοῖς.

λʹ Τοῦ ὁσίου πατρὸς ἡμῶν Ἰωάννου τοῦ τῆς κλίμακος, Ἀλληλούϊα.

λαʹ Τοῦ ἁγίου μάρτυρος Θεοφίλου, Ἀλληλούϊα. |[274]

Μὴν ἀπρίλιος
ἔχει ἡμέρας λ᾽· ἡ ἡμέρα ἔχει ὥρας ιγ᾽ καὶ ἡ νὺξ ὥρας ια᾽.

αʹ Τῆς ὁσίας Μαρίας τῆς Αἰγυπτίας.

βʹ Τοῦ ὁσίου πατρὸς ἡμῶν Τίτου τοῦ θαυματουργοῦ.

γʹ Τοῦ ὁσίου Νικήτα τοῦ {τοῦ} Μηδικίου.[166]

δʹ Τῶν ἁγίων μαρτύρων Θεοδούλου καὶ Ἀγαθόποδος τῶν ἐν Θεσσαλονίκῃ.

εʹ Τῆς ὁσίας Θεοδώρας τῆς ἐν Θεσσαλονίκῃ.

ϛʹ Τοῦ ὁσίου πατρὸς ἡμῶν Εὐτυχίου πατριάρχου Κωνσταντινουπόλεως.

ζʹ Τοῦ ὁσίου Γεωργίου μητροπολίτου Μιτυλήνης.[167]

ηʹ Τῶν ἁγίων ἀποστόλων ἐκ τῶν ο᾽, Ἡροδίωνος,[168] Ἀγάβου καὶ τῶν σὺν
αὐτοῖς.

---

163. ὁ εὐαγγελισμὸς … Θεοτόκου is written in red ink.
164. The scribe left a space, which can be restored with certainty.
165. Βαραχίου: C.   166. Μηδεικείου: C.
167. Μιτυλίνης: C.   168. Ἡροδίωνος: C.

25 Annunciation to our most-holy sovereign lady, the Theotokos; troparion, mode IV:

*Today is the beginning of our salvation and the unveiling of the mystery of the ages. The Son of God becomes the son of the Virgin, and Gabriel announces the grace. For this let us call out with him to the mother of God: "**Hail, full of grace, the Lord is with you**"* (Lk 1:28).

26 Service for the archangel Gabriel; troparion, mode I: *After Gabriel had clearly spoken the greeting to you, O Virgin (PaR 4).*

27 St. Matrona of Thessaloniki: Alleluia.

28 The holy martyr [Mark], bishop of Arethousa, and Cyril the deacon.

29 The holy martyrs Jonah and Barachesios and the ones with them.

30 Our blessed father John Klimakos: Alleluia.

31 The holy martyr Theophilos: Alleluia.

April

has thirty days, the day thirteen has hours and the night eleven hours.

1 The blessed Mary of Egypt.

2 Our blessed father Titus the miracle worker.

3 The blessed Niketas of Medikion.

4 The holy martyrs Theodoulos and Agathopous of Thessaloniki.

5 The blessed Theodora of Thessaloniki.

6 Our blessed father Eutychios, patriarch of Constantinople.

7 The blessed George, metropolitan of Mitylene.

8 The holy apostles from among the Seventy, Herodion, Agabos and the ones with them.

θ' Τοῦ ἁγίου μάρτυρος Εὐψυχίου τοῦ ἐν Καισαρείᾳ.

ι' Τῶν ἁγίων μ' μαρτύρων, Τερεντίου, Ἀφρικανοῦ καὶ τῶν σὺν αὐτοῖς.

ια' Τοῦ ἁγίου ἱερομάρτυρος Ἀντίπα ἐπισκόπου Περγάμου.

ιβ' Τοῦ ὁσίου πατρὸς ἡνῶν Βασιλείου ἐπισκόπου Παρείου.[169]

ιγ' Τοῦ ὁσίου πατρὸς ἡμῶν Μαρτίνου πάπα Ῥώμης.

ιδ' Τῶν ἁγίων ἀποστόλων ἐκ τῶν ο', Ἀριστάρχου, Πούδη καὶ Τροφίμου.

ιε' Τοῦ ἁγίου μάρτυρος Κρίσκεντος τοῦ ἐν Λυκίᾳ.

ις' Τῶν ἁγίων τριῶν παρθένων καὶ αὐταδέλφων, Εἰρήνης, Ἀγάπης καὶ Χιονίας.

ιζ' Τοῦ ἁγίου ἱερομάρτυρος Συμεὼν ἐπισκόπου Περσίδος καὶ τῶν σὺν αὐτῷ.

ιη' Τοῦ ὁσίου Ἀκακίου ἐπισκόπου Μελιτηνῆς.[170]

ιθ' Τοῦ ἁγίου μάρτυρος Θεοδώρου τοῦ ἐν Πέργῃ τῆς Παμφυλίας καὶ τῶν σὺν αὐτῷ.

κ' Τοῦ ὁσίου Θεοδώρου τοῦ Τριχινᾶ.

κα' Τοῦ ἁγίου ἱερομάρτυρος Ἰαννουαρίου καὶ τῶν σὺν αὐτῷ. |274v

κβ' Τοῦ ὁσίου καὶ θαυματουργοῦ Θεοδώρου τοῦ Συκεώτου.[171]

κγ' Τοῦ ἁγίου μεγαλομάρτυρος Γεωργίου, τροπάριον ἦχος δ', *Ὁ μάρτυς σου, Κύριε, ἐν τῇ.*

κδ' Τῆς ὁσίας Ἐλισάβετ τῆς θαυματουργοῦ.

κε' Τοῦ ἁγίου ἀποστόλου καὶ εὐαγγελιστοῦ Μάρκου, τροπάριον ἦχος γ', *Ἀπόστολε ἅγιε.*

κς' Τοῦ ἁγίου ἱερομάρτυρος Βασιλέως ἐπισκόπου Ἀμασείας,[172] τροπάριον ἦχος δ', *Καὶ τρόπων μέτοχος, καὶ θρόνων διάδοχος.*

---

169. Παρίου: C.
171. Σικεώτου: C.
170. Μελιτινῆς: C.
172. Ἀμασίας: C.

9 The holy martyr Eupsychios of Caesarea.

10 The forty holy martyrs, Terence, Africanus and the ones with them.

11 The holy hieromartyr Antipas, bishop of Pergamon.

12 Our blessed father Basil, bishop of Pareion.

13 Our blessed father Martin, head of the church of Rome.

14 The holy apostles from among the Seventy, Aristarchos, Poudes, and Trophimos.

15 The holy martyr Kriskes of Lycia.

16 The holy three virgins and sisters, Eirene, Agape, and Chionia.

17 The holy hieromartyr Symeon, bishop of Persia, and the ones with him.

18 The blessed Akakios, bishop of Melitene.

19 The holy martyr Theodore of Perge in Pamphylia and the ones with him.

20 The blessed Theodore of Trichina.

21 The holy hieromartyr Iannouarius and the ones with him.

22 The blessed miracle worker Theodore of Sykeon.

23 The holy great martyr George; troparion, mode IV: *Your martyr, O Lord, in the* (cf. Oct. 20).

24 The blessed Elizabeth the miracle worker.

25 The holy apostle and evangelist Mark; troparion, mode III: *Holy apostle* (cf. Sep. 22).

26 The holy hieromartyr Basileus, bishop of Amaseia; troparion, mode IV: *You who followed in the footsteps and succeeded to the thrones* (cf. Sep. 4).

27 The holy hieromartyr Symeon, kinsman of the Lord, brother of James the Greater: Alleluia.

κζ′ Τοῦ ἁγίου ἱερομάρτυρος Συμεὼν τοῦ συγγενοῦς τοῦ Κυρίου, ἀδελφοῦ δὲ Ἰακώβου τοῦ μεγάλου, Ἀλληλούϊα.

κη′ Τοῦ ἁγίου ἀποστόλου Ἰάσωνος, ἑνὸς τῶν ο′.

κθ′ Τοῦ ὁσίου πατρὸς ἡμῶν καὶ θαυματουργοῦ Μέμνονος τοῦ ἐν Λυκίᾳ.

λ′ Τοῦ ἁγίου ἀποστόλου Ἰακώβου ἀδελφοῦ Ἰωάννου τοῦ θεολόγου, τροπάριον ἦχος γ′, Ἀπόστολε ἄγιε.

Μὴν μάϊος

ἔχει ἡμέρας λα′· ἡ ἡμέρα ἔχει ὥρας ιδ′ καὶ ἡ νὺξ ὥρας ι′.

α′ Τοῦ ἁγίου προφήτου Ἱερεμίου· καὶ τῇ αὐτῇ ἡμέρᾳ, τοῦ ἁγίου μάρτυρος Σάβα τοῦ στρατηλάτου καὶ τῶν σὺν αὐτῷ.

β′ Τοῦ ἐν ἁγίοις πατρὸς ἡμῶν Ἀθανασίου πατριάρχου Ἀλεξανδρείας, τροπάριον ἦχος πλάγιος δ′, Ὀρθοδοξίας ὁδηγέ, εὐσεβείας.

γ′ Τῶν ἁγίων μαρτύρων Τιμοθέου καὶ Μαύρας, Ἀλληλούϊα.

δ′ Τῆς ἁγίας μάρτυρος Εἰρήνης, Ἀλληλούϊα.

ε′ Τῆς ἁγίας ὁσιομάρτυρος Πελαγίας, Ἀλληλούϊα.

ϛ′ Τοῦ δικαίου Ἰώβ, Ἀλληλούϊα.

ζ′ Τοῦ ὁσίου πατρὸς ἡμῶν Μαξίμου τοῦ ὁμολογητοῦ, καὶ τοῦ ἁγίου μάρτυρος Ἀκακίου. |²⁷⁵

η′ Τοῦ ἁγίου ἀποστόλου καὶ εὐαγγελιστοῦ Ἰωάννου τοῦ θεολόγου, τροπάριον ἦχος β′, Ἀπόστολε Χριστοῦ τοῦ Θεοῦ ἠγαπημένε· ζήτει σεπτεμβρίου κϛ′.

Τῇ αὐτῇ ἡμέρᾳ, τοῦ ὁσίου πατρὸς ἡμῶν Ἀρσενίου τοῦ μεγάλου.

θ′ Τοῦ ἁγίου προφήτου Ἡσαΐου, καὶ τοῦ ἁγίου μάρτυρος Χριστοφόρου.

ι′ Τοῦ ἁγίου ἀποστόλου Σίμωνος τοῦ ζηλωτοῦ, τροπάριον ἦχος γ′, Ἀπόστολε ἄγιε, πρέσβευε τῷ ἐλεήμονι.

ια′ Τὰ ἐγκαίνια τῆς πόλεως, καὶ τοῦ ἁγίου ἱερομάρτυρος Μωκίου.

28 The holy apostle Jason, one of the Seventy.

29 Our blessed father and miracle worker Memnon of Lycia.

30 The holy apostle James, brother of John the Theologian; troparion, mode III: *Holy apostle* (cf. Sep. 22).

May

has thirty-one days, the day has fourteen hours and the night ten hours.

1 The holy prophet Jeremiah; and on the same day, the holy martyr Sabas Stratelates and the ones with him.

2 Our father among the saints Athanasios, patriarch of Alexandria; troparion, plagal mode IV: *Guide of orthodoxy, teacher of piety* (cf. Nov. 11).

3 The holy martyrs Timothy and Maura: Alleluia.

4 The holy martyr Eirene: Alleluia.

5 The holy hosiomartyr Pelagia: Alleluia.

6 The righteous Job: Alleluia.

7 Our blessed father Maximos the Confessor, and the holy martyr Akakios.

8 The holy apostle and evangelist John the Theologian; troparion, mode II: *Beloved Apostle of Christ our God;* see Sep. 26.
On the same day, our blessed father Arsenios the Great.

9 The holy prophet Isaiah; and the holy martyr Christopher.

10 The holy apostle Simon Zelotes; troparion, mode III: *Holy apostle, intercede with God the merciful* (cf. Sep. 22).

11 The dedication of the city,[172] and the holy hieromartyr Mokios.

---

172. Constantinople: Delehaye, *Synaxarium Constantinopolitanae*, 673.

ιβ´ Τῶν ἁγίων πατέρων ἡμῶν Γερμανοῦ πατριάρχου Κωνσταντινουπόλεως καὶ Ἐπιφανίου ἀρχιεπισκόπου Κύπρου, τροπάριον ἦχος δ´, Ὁ Θεὸς τῶν πατέρων ἡμῶν, ὁ ποιῶν ἀεὶ μεθ᾽ ἡμῶν.

ιγ´ Τῆς ὁσίας μάρτυρος Γλυκερίας, καὶ τοῦ ὁσίου Γεωργίου τοῦ ἐν τῷ Μαλέῳ.[173]

ιδ´ Τοῦ ἁγίου μάρτυρος Ἰσιδώρου τοῦ Χιώτου.

ιε´ Τοῦ ὁσίου πατρὸς ἡμῶν Παγχωμίου[174] καὶ Θεοδώρου μαθητοῦ αὐτοῦ τοῦ ἡγιασμένου, τροπάριον ἦχος πλάγιος δ´, Ταῖς τῶν δακρύων σου.

ις´ Τοῦ ὁσίου Νεαδίου τοῦ θαυματουργοῦ.

ιζ´ Τοῦ ἀποστόλου Ἀνδρονίκου ἐκ τῶν ο´.

ιη´ Τοῦ ἁγίου μάρτυρος Πέτρου τοῦ ἐν τῇ Λαμψάκῳ καὶ τῶν σὺν αὐτῷ.

ιθ´ Τοῦ ἁγίου ἱερομάρτυρος Πατρικίου καὶ τῶν σὺν αὐτῷ.

κ´ Τοῦ ἁγίου μάρτυρος Θαλελαίου καὶ τῶν σὺν αὐτῷ.

κα´ Τῶν ἁγίων καὶ ἐνδόξων μεγάλων βασιλέων Κωνσταντίνου καὶ Ἑλένης τῆς μητρὸς αὐτοῦ, τροπάριον ἦχος πλάγιος δ´,
Τοῦ σταυροῦ σου τὸν τύπον ἐν οὐρανῷ θεασάμενος |[275v] καὶ ὡς ὁ Παῦλος τὴν κλῆσιν οὐκ ἐξ ἀνθρώπων δεξάμενος, ὁ ἐν βασιλεῦσι ἀπόστολός σου, Κύριε, βασιλεύουσαν πόλιν τῇ χειρί σου παρέθετο· ἣν περίσῳζε διαπαντὸς ἐν εἰρήνῃ, πρεσβείαις τῆς Θεοτόκου, μόνε φιλάνθρωπε.

κβ´ Τοῦ ἁγίου μάρτυρος Βασιλίσκου.

κγ´ Τοῦ ὁσίου πατρὸς ἡμῶν καὶ ὁμολογητοῦ Μιχαὴλ ἐπισκόπου Συνάδων.

κδ´ Τοῦ ὁσίου πατρὸς ἡμῶν καὶ θαυματουργοῦ Συμεὼν τοῦ ἐν τῷ Θαυμαστῷ Ὄρει, τροπάριον ἦχος α´, Ὑπομονῆς στύλος γέγονας.

κε´ Ἡ τρίτη εὕρεσις τῆς τιμίας κεφαλῆς τοῦ Προδρόμου, τροπάριον ἦχος β´, Μνήμη δικαίου μετ᾽ ἐγκωμίων.

κς´ Τοῦ ἁγίου ἀποστόλου Κάρπου ἐκ τῶν ο´.

173. Μαλέα: C.
174. Παγχομίου: C.

12 Our holy fathers Germanos, patriarch of Constantinople, and Epiphanios, archbishop of (Konstantia on[173]) Cyprus; troparion, mode IV: *God of our fathers, who always treats* (cf. Nov. 12).

13 The blessed martyr Glykeria, and the blessed George of (Mt.) Maleon.

14 The holy martyr Isidore of Chios.

15 Our blessed father Pachomios and his disciple Theodore the Sanctified; troparion, plagal mode IV: *With the rivers of your tears* (cf. Oct. 21).

16 The blessed Neadios the miracle worker.

17 The apostle Andronikos of the Seventy.

18 The holy martyr Peter of Lampsakos and the ones with him.

19 The holy hieromartyr Patrikios and the ones with him.

20 The holy martyr Thalelaios and the ones with him.

21 The holy and glorious, great rulers Constantine and Helen, his mother; troparion, plagal mode IV:

He beheld the sign of your cross in the heavens and, like Paul, accepted the call that was not from men. Your apostle among emperors, he placed in your hands, O Lord, the imperial city. Through the intercession of the Theotokos, save it always in peace, O you who alone love mankind.

22 The holy martyr Basiliskos.

23 Our blessed father and confessor Michael, bishop of Synada.

24 Our blessed father and miracle worker Symeon of the Wondrous Mountain; troparion, mode I: *O blessed one, when you became a pillar of perseverance* (cf. Sep. 1).

25 The third discovery of the precious head of the Forerunner; troparion, mode II: ***The memory of the just is praised*** (Prv 10:7) (cf. Jan. 7).

26 The holy apostle Karpos of the Seventy.

27 The holy hieromartyr Helladios.

---

173. Delehaye, *Synaxarium Constantinopolitanae*, 675.

κζ' Τοῦ ἁγίου ἱερομάρτυρος Ἑλλαδίου.[175]

κη' Τοῦ ἁγίου μάρτυρος Εὐτυχίου τοῦ ἐν Μελιτηνῷ.[176]

κθ' Τῆς ἁγίας μάρτυρος Θεοδοσίας.

λ' Τοῦ ἁγίου ἀποστόλου καὶ μάρτυρος Εὐτυχοῦς[177] μαθητοῦ τοῦ ἁγίου Ἰωάννου τοῦ θεολόγου.

λα' Τοῦ ἁγίου μάρτυρος Ἑρμείου καὶ τῶν σὺν αὐτῷ.

Μὴν ἰούνιος
ἔχει ἡμέρας λ'· ἡ ἡμέρα ἔχει ὥρας ιε' καὶ ἡ νὺξ ἔχει ὥρας θ'.

α' Τοῦ ἁγίου μάρτυρος Ἰουστίνου καὶ τῶν σὺν αὐτῷ.

β' Τοῦ ὁσίου πατρὸς ἡμῶν καὶ ὁμολογητοῦ Νικηφόρου πατριάρχου.

γ' Τῶν ἁγίων μαρτύρων Λουκιλλιανοῦ καὶ Παύλης[178] καὶ τῶν σὺν αὐτοῖς.
|276

δ' Τοῦ ὁσίου πατρὸς ἡμῶν Μητροφάνης πατριάρχου.

ε' Τοῦ ὁσίου Ἱλαρίωνος τοῦ νέου ἡγουμένου τῶν Δαλμάτων.

ϛ' Τοῦ ἁγίου ἱερομάρτυρος Δωροθέου ἐπισκόπου Τύρου.

ζ' Τοῦ ἁγίου μάρτυρος Θεοδότου τοῦ ἐν Ἀγκύρᾳ.

η' Ἡ ἀνακομιδὴ τοῦ λειψάνου τοῦ ἁγίου μεγαλομάρτυρος Θεοδώρου τοῦ στρατηλάτου, τροπάριον ἦχος δ', Ὁ μάρτυς σου, Κύριε, ἐν τῇ ἀθλήσει· καὶ τῇ αὐτῇ ἡμέρᾳ, τοῦ ἁγίου μάρτυρος Παύλου τοῦ ἐν τοῖς Καϊουμᾶ.

θ' Τοῦ ἁγίου μάρτυρος Ὀρέστου καὶ τῶν σὺν αὐτῷ.

ι' Τοῦ ἁγίου μάρτυρος Βενιαμὶν τοῦ Λευΐτου.

ια' Τοῦ ἁγίου ἀποστόλου Βαρθολομαίου καὶ Βαρνάβα, τροπάριον ἦχος γ', Ἀπόστολοι ἅγιοι, πρεσβεύσατε τῷ ἐλεήμονι.

ιβ' Τοῦ ὁσίου πατρὸς ἡμῶν Ὀνουφρίου, τροπάριον ἦχος α', Τῆς ἐρήμου πολίτης.

---

175. Ἑλλαδίου: C.   176. Μελιτῷ: C.
177. Εὐτυχίου: C.   178. Λουκιανοῦ καὶ Παύλου: C.

28 The holy martyr Eutychios of Meletine.[174]

29 The holy martyr Theodosia.

30 The apostle and martyr Eutyches, disciple of St. John the Theologian.

31 The holy martyr Hermeias and the ones with him.

June
has thirty days, the day has fifteen hours and the night has nine hours.

1   The holy martyr Justin and the ones with him.

2   Our blessed father and confessor Nikephoros, patriarch (of Constantinople).

3   The holy martyrs Loukillianos and Paula and the ones with them.

4   Our blessed father Metrophanes, patriarch (of Constantinople).

5   The blessed Hilarion the Younger, abbot of the (monastery of) Dalmatos.

6   The holy hieromartyr Dorotheos, bishop of Tyre.

7   The holy martyr Theodotos of Ankyra.

8   The translation of the relics of the holy great martyr Theodore Stratelates; troparion, mode IV: *Your martyr, O Lord, in the trial* (cf. Oct. 20); and on the same day, the holy martyr Paul of the (monastery of) Kaïouma.

9   The holy martyr Orestes and the ones with him.

10 The holy martyr Benjamin the Levite.[175]

11 The holy apostle Bartholomew, and Barnabas: *Holy apostles intercede with God the merciful* (MHS 915).

12 Our blessed father Onouphrios; troparion, mode I: *A citizen of the wilderness* (MR 1:290).

---

174. Ibid., 713, gives Eutychios τοῦ ἐν Μελίτῳ and Eutyches bishop of Μελιτηνῆς, both for this day.
175. The epithet is unknown to the other sources cited here.

ιγ᾽ Τῆς ἁγίας μάρτυρος Ἀκυλίνης.

ιδ᾽ Τοῦ ἁγίου προφήτου Ἐλισσαίου.

ιε᾽ Τοῦ ἁγίου προφήτου Ἀμώς.

ις᾽ Τοῦ ὁσίου καὶ θαυματουργοῦ Τύχωνος ἐπισκόπου Κύπρου.

ιζ᾽ Τῶν ἁγίων μαρτύρων Μανουήλ, Σαβὲλ καὶ Ἰσμαήλ, τροπάριον ἦχος δ᾽,
    Οἱ μάρτυρές σου, Κύριε, ἐν τῇ ἀθλήσει.

ιη᾽ Τοῦ ἁγίου μάρτυρος Λεοντίου.

ιθ᾽ Τοῦ ἁγίου ἀποστόλου Ἰούδα τοῦ ἀδελφοθέου, τροπάριον ἦχος γ᾽,
    Ἀπόστολε ἅγιε, πρέσβευε.

κ᾽ Τοῦ ἁγίου μάρτυρος Ζωσίμου.

κα᾽ Τοῦ ἁγίου μάρτυρος Ἰουλιανοῦ.

κβ᾽ Τοῦ ἁγίου ἱερομάρτυρος Εὐσεβίου ἐπισκόπου Σαμοσάτων. |²⁷⁶ᵛ

κγ᾽ Τῆς ἁγίας μάρτυρος Ἀγριππίνης.

κδ᾽ Τὸ γενέθλιον τοῦ ἁγίου Ἰωάννου τοῦ προδρόμου, τροπάριον ἦχος δ᾽,
    Προφῆτα καὶ πρόδρομε τῆς παρουσίας Χριστοῦ, ἀξίως εὐφημῆσαί σε οὐκ
εὐποροῦμεν ἡμεῖς οἱ πόθῳ τιμῶντές σε· στείρωσις γὰρ τεκούσης καὶ πατρὸς
ἀφωνία λέλυνται τῇ ἐνδόξῳ καὶ σεπτῇ σου γεννήσει, καὶ σάρκωσις Υἱοῦ τοῦ
Θεοῦ κόσμῳ κηρύττεται.

κε᾽ Τῆς ἁγίας ὁσιομάρτυρος Φευρωνίας.

κς᾽ Τοῦ ὁσίου Δαυῒδ τοῦ ἐν Θεσσαλονίκῃ.

κζ᾽ Τοῦ ὁσίου Σαμψὼν τοῦ ξενοδόχου.

κη᾽ Ἡ ἀνακομιδὴ τῶν λειψάνων τῶν ἁγίων καὶ θαυματουργῶν ἀναργύρων
    Κύρου καὶ Ἰωάννου, τροπάριον ἦχος πλάγιος α᾽, *Τὰ θαύματα τῶν ἁγίων*
σου μαρτύρων.

13 The holy martyr Aquilina.

14 The holy prophet Elisha.

15 The holy prophet Amos.

16 The blessed miracle worker Tychon, bishop of (Amathountos on[176]) Cyprus.

17 The holy martyrs Manuel, Sabel, and Ishmael; troparion, mode IV: *Your martyrs, O Lord, in the trial* (cf. Oct. 7).

18 The holy martyr Leontios.

19 The holy apostle Jude, brother of the Lord; troparion, mode III: *Holy apostle, intercede* (cf. Sep. 22).

20 The holy martyr Zosimos.

21 The holy martyr Julian.

22 The holy hieromartyr Eusebios, bishop of Samosata.

23 The holy martyr Agrippina.

24 The birth of St. John the Forerunner; troparion, mode IV:

O prophet and forerunner of the coming of Christ, we who revere you longingly are unable to praise you justly. With your glorious and august birth, your mother's barrenness and father's speechlessness were undone, and the incarnation of the Son of God was announced to the world.

25 The holy hosiomartyr Febronia.

26 The blessed David of Thessaloniki.

27 The blessed Sampson the Xenodochos.

28 The translation[177] of the relics of the holy miracle workers and anargyroi Cyrus and John; troparion, plagal mode I: *The miracles of your holy martyrs* (cf. Nov. 15).

---

176. Delehaye, *Synaxarium Constantinopolitanae*, 751.
177. Ibid., 775: discovery of the relics.

κθ' Τῶν ἁγίων καὶ κορυφαίων ἀποστόλων Πέτρου καὶ Παύλου, τροπάριον ἦχος δ', *Οἱ τῶν ἀποστόλων πρωτόθρονοι.*

λ' Τῶν ἁγίων ιβ' ἀποστόλων ἡ σύναξις, τροπάριον ἦχος γ', *Ἀπόστολοι ἅγιοι, πρεσβεύσατε.*

Μὴν ἰούλιος
ἔχει ἡμέρας λα'· ἡ ἡμέρα ἔχει ὥρας ιδ' καὶ ἡ νὺξ ὥρας ι'.

α' Τῶν ἁγίων καὶ θαυματουργῶν ἀναργύρων Κοσμᾶ καὶ Δαμιανοῦ τῶν Ῥωμαίων, τροπάριον ἦχος πλάγιος δ', *Ἅγιοι ἀνάργυροι καὶ θαυματουργοί.*

β' Τὰ καταθέσια τῆς τιμίας ἐσθῆτος τῆς ὑπεραγίας Θεοτόκου ἐν Βλαχέρναις, τροπάριον ἦχος πλάγιος δ',
Θεοτόκε ἀειπάρθενε, |²⁷⁷ τῶν ἀνθρώπων ἡ σκέπη, ἐσθῆτα καὶ ζώνην τοῦ ἀχράντου σου σώματος κραταιὰν τῇ πόλει σου περιβολὴν ἐδωρήσω, τῷ ἀσπόρῳ τόκῳ σου ἄφθαρτα διαμείναντα·¹⁷⁹ ἐπὶ σοὶ γὰρ καὶ φύσις καινοτομεῖται καὶ χρόνος· διὸ δυσωποῦμέν σε εἰρήνην τῇ πολιτείᾳ σου δώρησαι καὶ ταῖς ψυχαῖς ἡμῶν τὸ μέγα.

γ' Τοῦ ἁγίου μάρτυρος Ὑακίνθου τοῦ κουβικουλαρίου.

δ' Τοῦ ὁσίου πατρὸς ἡμῶν Ἀνδρέου ἐπισκόπου Κρήτης.

ε' Τοῦ ἁγίου ἱερομάρτυρος Ἀστείου ἐπισκόπου Δυρραχίου.

ϛ' Τοῦ ὁσίου πατρὸς ἡμῶν Σισόη τοῦ μεγάλου.

ζ' Τοῦ ὁσίου πατρὸς ἡμῶν Θωμᾶ τοῦ ἐν τῷ Μαλέῳ.

η' Τοῦ ἁγίου μεγαλομάρτυρος Προκοπίου, τροπάριον ἦχος δ', *Ὁ μάρτυς σου, Κύριε, ἐν τῇ.*

θ' Τοῦ ἁγίου ἱερομάρτυρος Παγκρατίου ἐπισκόπου Ταυρομενίου.

ι' Τῶν ἁγίων με' μαρτύρων τῶν ἐν Νικοπόλει.

ια' Τῆς ἁγίας μάρτυρος Εὐφημίας· τοῦ ὅρου¹⁸⁰ τῶν χλ' ἁγίων πατέρων τῆς δ' συνόδου, τροπάριον ἦχος δ', *Τὸν νυμφίον σου Χριστὸν ἀγαπήσασα·* ζήτει σεπτεμβρίου ις'.

---

179. διὰ μείνατα: C.   180. ὅρου: C.

29 The holy chief apostles Peter and Paul; troparion, mode IV: *First en-thronened of the apostles* (*MR* 5:390).

30 Service for the holy twelve apostles; troparion, mode III: *Holy apostles intercede* (cf. June 11).

July

has thirty-one days, the day has fourteen hours and the night ten hours.

1 The holy miracle workers and anargyroi Kosmas and Damian the Ro-mans; troparion, plagal mode IV: *Holy anargyroi and miracle workers* (cf. Nov. 1).

2 The installation of the precious robe of the most-holy Theotokos in the Blachernae (church of Constantinople); troparion, plagal mode IV:

O Theotokos ever-virgin, shelter of mankind, you gave the robe and belt from your undefiled body to be a mighty wall around your city, a wall that endured, indestructible because of your bearing the child begotten without seed. In you both nature and time are made new. For this we importune you to give peace to your state and great mercy to our souls.

3 The holy martyr Hyakinthos the Koubikoularios.

4 Our blessed father Andrew, bishop of Crete.

5 The holy hieromartyr Asteios, bishop of Dyrrachium.

6 Our blessed father Sisoes the Great.

7 Our blessed father Thomas of (Mt.) Maleon.

8 The holy great martyr Prokopios; troparion, mode IV: *Your martyr, O Lord, in the* (cf. Oct. 20).

9 The holy hieromartyr Pancratius, bishop of Taormina.

10 The forty-five holy martyrs of Nikopolis.

11 The holy martyr Euphemia; the Definition of the 630 holy fathers of the Fourth Council (of Chalcedon); troparion, mode IV: *You, O all-blessed one, loved Christ your bridegroom*; see Sep. 16.

ιβ' Τῶν ἁγίων μαρτύρων Πρόκλου καὶ Ἱλαρίου,[181] Ἀλληλούϊα.

ιγ' Τοῦ ἁγίου μάρτυρος Σεραπίωνος, Ἀλληλούϊα.

ιδ' Τοῦ ἁγίου ἀποστόλου Ἀκύλα, Ἀλληλούϊα.

ιε' Τῶν ἁγίων μαρτύρων Κηρύκου καὶ Ἰουλίττης, τροπάριον ἦχος δ', *Οἱ μάρτυρές σου, Κύριε, ἐν τῇ ἀθλήσει.*

ις' Τοῦ ἁγίου μάρτυρος Πέτρου Κρήτης τοῦ νέου, Ἀλληλούϊα. |[277v]

ιζ' Τῆς ἁγίας μάρτυρος Μαρίνας, τροπάριον ἦχος δ', *Ἡ ἀμνάς σου, Ἰησοῦ, κράζει.*

ιη' Τοῦ ἁγίου μάρτυρος Αἰμιλιανοῦ.[182]

ιθ' Τοῦ ὁσίου πατρὸς ἡμῶν [...],[183] καὶ τῆς ὁσίας Μακρίνας ἀδελφῆς τοῦ μεγάλου Βασιλείου.

κ' Τοῦ ἁγίου προφήτου Ἠλιοῦ, τροπάριον ἦχος δ',

   Ὁ ἔνσαρκος ἄγγελος, τῶν προφητῶν ἡ κρηπίς, ὁ δεύτερος πρόδρομος τῆς παρουσίας Χριστοῦ, Ἠλίας ὁ ἔνδοξος ἄνωθεν καταπέμπει. Ἐλισσαίῳ τὴν χάριν νόσους ἀποδιώκειν καὶ λεπροὺς καθαρίζειν· διὸ καὶ τοῖς τιμῶσιν αὐτὸν βρύει ἰάματα.

κα' Τοῦ ἁγίου προφήτου Ἰεζεκιήλ,[184] καὶ τῶν ὁσίων πατέρων ἡμῶν Συμεὼν τοῦ διὰ Χριστὸν σαλοῦ καὶ Ἰωάννου.

κβ' Τῆς ἁγίας Μαρίας τῆς Μαγδαληνῆς, τροπάριον ἦχος α',

   Χριστῷ τῷ δι' ἡμᾶς ἐκ παρθένου τεχθέντι, σοφὴ Μαγδαληνή, ἠκολούθεις, Μαρία, αὐτοῦ τὰ δικαιώματα καὶ τοὺς νόμους φυλάττουσα· ὅθεν χαίροντες τὴν παναγίαν σου μνήμην ἑορτάζομεν ἀνευφημοῦντές σε πίστει καὶ πόθῳ γεραίροντες.

κγ' Τοῦ ἁγίου μάρτυρος Ἀπολλωνίου ἀθλήσαντος ἐν Σάρδῃ.

κδ' Τῆς ἁγίας μάρτυρος Χριστίνης,[185] τροπάριον ἦχος δ', *Ἡ ἀμνάς σου, Ἰησοῦ.*

---

181. Ἱλαρίου: C.
183. The scribe left a space for the name.
185. Χριστίνας: C.

182. Αἰμιλιανοῦ: C.
184. Ἰεζεκιήλ: C.

12 The holy martyrs Proklos and Hilarios: Alleluia.

13 The holy martyr Serapion: Alleluia.

14 The holy apostle Akylas: Alleluia.

15 The holy martyrs Kyrikos and Ioulitta; troparion, mode IV: *Your martyrs, O Lord, in the trial* (cf. Oct. 7).

16 The holy martyr Peter the Younger (bishop) of Crete: Alleluia.

17 The holy martyr Marina; troparion, mode IV: *Your lamb, O Jesus, cries out* (cf. Sep. 24).

18 The holy martyr Aemilianos.

19 Our blessed father [...];[178] and the blessed Makrina, sister of Basil the Great.

20 The holy prophet Elijah; troparion, mode IV:
An angel made flesh, the foundation stone of prophets, (and) a second forerunner of Christ's coming, Elijah the glorious sends down grace from heaven on Elisha to chase away disease and to purify the lepers; thus to them who honor him he gives abundant healing.

21 The holy prophet Ezekiel, and our blessed fathers Symeon the Fool for Christ and John.

22 St. Mary Magdalene; troparion, mode I:
O wise Mary Magdalene, preserving his laws and ordinances, you followed Christ, born for us from a virgin, for which we acclaim your most holy memory (and) celebrate your feast, faithfully proclaiming and ardently honoring you.

23 The holy martyr Apollonios who struggled (for the faith) in Sardis.[179]

24 The holy martyr Christina; troparion, mode IV: *Your lamb, O Jesus* (cf. Sep. 24).

---

178. Possibly St. Dios: Arranz, *Typicon de Messine*, 168; Mateos, *Typicon*, 1:346.

179. Delehaye, *Synaxarium Constantinopolitanae*, 812, lists Apollonios of Sardis on July 10. On July 23 (ibid., 835) is celebrated Apollonios the bishop of Rome.

κε’ Ἡ κοίμησις τῆς ἁγίας Ἄννης τῆς μητρὸς τῆς Θεοτόκου, τροπάριον ἦχος
δ’,

Ζωὴν τὴν κυήσασαν ἐκυοφόρησας, |[278] *ἀγνὴν θεομήτορα, θεόφρον Ἄννα·
διὸ πρὸς λῆξιν ἀθάνατον, ἔνθα εὐφραινομένων κατοικία ἐν δόξῃ χαίρουσα νῦν
μετέστης, τοῖς τιμῶσί σε πόθῳ πταισμάτων αἰτουμένη ἱλασμόν, ἀειμακάριστε.*
Καὶ τῇ αὐτῇ ἡμέρᾳ, τῶν ὁσίων γυναικῶν Εὐπραξίας καὶ Ὀλυμπιάδος.

κϛ’ Τοῦ ἁγίου ἱερομάρτυρος Ἑρμολάου καὶ τῶν σὺν αὐτῷ, καὶ τοῦ ὁσίου
Ἰωάννου τοῦ Παλαιολαυρίτου, Ἀλληλούϊα.

κζ’ Τοῦ ἁγίου μεγαλομάρτυρος Παντελεήμονος, τροπάριον ἦχος δ’, *Ὁ
μάρτυς σου, Κύριε.*

κη’ Τῶν ἁγίων ἀποστόλων καὶ διακόνων Προχόρου, Νικάνωρος,[186] Τίμωνος
καὶ Παρμενᾶ, τροπάριον ἦχος γ’, *Ἀπόστολοι ἅγιοι, πρεσβεύσατε.*

κθ’ Τοῦ ἁγίου μάρτυρος Καλλινίκου, Ἀλληλούϊα.

λ’ Τῶν ἁγίων ἀποστόλων ἐκ τῶν ο’, Σίλα, Σιλουανοῦ καὶ τῶν λοιπῶν.

λα’ Τοῦ ὁσίου καὶ δικαίου Εὐδοκίμου.

Μὴν αὔγουστος
ἔχει ἡμέρας λα’· ἡ ἡμέρα ἔχει ὥρας ιγ’ καὶ ἡ νὺξ ὥρας ια’.

α’ Τῶν ἁγίων Μακκαβαίων, τροπάριον ἦχος α’, *Τὰς ἀλγηδόνας τῶν.*

β’ Ἡ ἀνακομιδὴ τοῦ λειψάνου τοῦ ἁγίου πρωτομάρτυρος καὶ ἀποστόλου
Στεφάνου, τροπάριον ἦχος γ’, *Ἀπόστολε ἅγιε, πρέσβευε τῷ.*

γ’ Τῶν ὁσίων πατέρων ἡμῶν Ἰσαακίου, Δαλμάτου καὶ Φαύστου, τροπάτιον
ἦχος δ’, *Ὁ Θεὸς τῶν πατέρων ἡμῶν, ὁ ποιῶν.*

δ’ Τῶν ἁγίων ἑπτὰ παίδων τῶν ἐν Ἐφέσῳ, καὶ τοῦ ὁσίου Ἰωάννου τῆς
Πατελαραίας.

ε’ Προεόρτια τῆς μεταμορφώσεως τοῦ Σωτῆρος, καὶ τοῦ ἁγίου μάρτυρος
Εὐσιγνίου, |[278v] τροπάριον ἦχος δ’,[187]

---

186. Νικάνορος: C.
187. τροπάριον ἦχος δ’ is written in the upper margin.

25 The dormition of St. Anna, the mother of the Theotokos; troparion, mode IV:

You, O godly-minded Anna, bore her who conceived life, the pure mother of God; because now you have gone rejoicing in glory to eternal life that is the dwelling place of those who live in gladness (cf. Ps 86:7), you beseech forgiveness of sins for those who yearningly honor you, O forever blessed.

And on the same day, the blessed women Eupraxia and Olympias.

26 The holy hieromartyr Hermolaos and the ones with him, and the blessed John Palaiolaurites: Alleluia.

27 The holy great martyr Panteleimon; troparion, mode IV: *Your martyr, O Lord* (cf. Oct. 20).

28 The holy apostles and deacons Prochoros, Nikanor, Timon, and Parmenas; troparion, mode III: *Holy apostles, intercede* (cf. June 30).

29 The holy martyr Kallinikos: Alleluia.

30 The holy apostles from among the Seventy: Silas, Silvanus, and the others.

31 The blessed and righteous Eudokimos.

August

has thirty-one days, the day has thirteen hours and the night eleven hours.

1 The holy Maccabees; troparion, mode I: *Be moved by the suffering of* (cf. Nov. 3).

2 The translation of the relic of the holy protomartyr and apostle Stephen; troparion, mode III: *Holy apostle, intercede* (MHS 680).

3 Our blessed fathers Isaac, Dalmatos, and Faustos; troparion, mode IV: *God of our fathers who always treats* (cf. Nov. 12).

4 The seven holy children of Ephesus, and the blessed John (abbot) of Patalarea.

5 Forefeast of the savior's transfiguration; and the holy martyr Eusignios; troparion, mode IV:

Χριστοῦ τὴν μεταμόρφωσιν[188] *προϋπαντήσωμεν, φαιδρῶς πανηγυρίζοντες τὰ προεόρτια πιστοί, καὶ βοήσωμεν·Ἔφθασεν ἡ ἡμέρα τῆς ἐνθέου εὐφροσύνης· ἄινεσιν εἰς τὸ ὄρος τὸ Θαβὼρ ὁ Δεσπότης, τῆς θεότητος ἀπαστράψαι τὴν ὡραιότητα.*

ς' Ἡ μεταμόρφωσις τοῦ μεγάλου Θεοῦ καὶ Σωτῆρος ἡμῶν Ἰησοῦ Χριστοῦ,[189] τροπάριον ἦχος βαρύς,

Μετεμορφώθης ἐν τῷ ὄρει, Χριστὲ ὁ Θεός, δείξας τοῖς μαθηταῖς τὴν δόξαν σου, καθὼς ἠδύναντο· λάμψῃ[190] *καὶ ἡμῖν τοῖς ἁμαρτωλοῖς τὸ φῶς σου τὸ ἀΐδιον, πρεσβείαις τῆς Θεοτόκου, μόνε φιλάνθρωπε.*

ζ' Μεθέορτα, καὶ τοῦ ἁγίου ὁσιομάρτυρος Δομετίου τοῦ Πέρσου καὶ τῶν σὺν αὐτῷ, τροπάριον τῆς ἑορτῆς.

η' Μεθέορτα, καὶ τοῦ ὁσίου Αἰμιλιανοῦ[191] ἐπισκόπου Κυζίκου, τροπάριον τῆς ἑορτῆς.

θ' Μεθέορτα, καὶ τοῦ ἁγίου ἀποστόλου Ματθίου τοῦ ἀντὶ τοῦ Ἰούδα, τροπάριον τῆς ἑορτῆς καὶ ἕτερον τοῦ ἁγίου, ἦχος γ', *Ἀπόστολε ἅγιε, πρέσβευε.*

ι' Μεθέορτα, καὶ τοῦ ἁγίου μάρτυρος Λαυρεντίου καὶ τῶν σὺν αὐτῷ, τροπάριον τῆς ἑορτῆς.

ια' Μεθέορτα, καὶ τοῦ ἁγίου μάρτυρος Εὔπλου, τροπάριον τῆς ἑορτῆς.

ιβ' Μεθέορτα, καὶ τῶν ἁγίων μαρτύρων Φωτίου καὶ Ἀνικήτου, τροπάριον τῆς ἑορτῆς.

ιγ' Μεθέορτα, καὶ τοῦ ὁσίου πατρὸς ἡνῶν Μαξίμου τοῦ ὁμολογητοῦ, τροπάριον τῆς ἑορτῆς καὶ ἀποδίδει, καὶ ἕτερον τοῦ ὁσίου, *Ὀρθοδοξίας ὁδηγέ.*

ιδ' Προεόρτια τῆς κοιμήσεως τῆς ὑπεραγίας Θεοτόκου, καὶ τοῦ ἁγίου προφήτου Μιχαίου, τροπάριον ἦχος δ',

Λαοὶ προσκιρτήσατε |[279] *χεῖρας κροτοῦντες πιστῶς καὶ πόθῳ ἀθροίσθητε σήμερον χαίροντες, καὶ φαιδρῶς ἀλαλάζοντες πάντες ἐν εὐφροσύνῃ· τοῦ*

---

188. μεταμορφώσει: C, corrected by another hand.
189. ἡ μεταμόρφωσις … Χριστοῦ is written in red ink.
190. λάμψοι: C.   191. Αἰμιλιανοῦ: C.

Let us, the faithful who joyously celebrate the forefeast, go in advance to meet the transfiguration of Christ, and let us joyously cry out, "The day of enthusiastic celebration comes. The Master approaches near Mount Tabor and will shine forth the beauty of divinity."

6 The transfiguration of our great God and savior Jesus Christ; troparion, barys mode:

When you were transfigured on the mountain, O Christ our God, you revealed your glory to the disciples in accordance with (their ability to) bear it. May your everlasting light shine on us sinners, too, (we pray) through the intercession of the Theotokos, O you who alone love mankind.

7 Afterfeast, and the holy hosiomartyr Dometios the Persian and the ones with him; troparion of the feast.

8 Afterfeast, and the blessed Aemilianos, bishop of Kyzikos; troparion of the feast.

9 Afterfeast, and the holy apostle Matthias, who took the place of Judas; troparion of the feast and the other of the saint, mode III: *Holy apostle, intercede* (cf. Sep. 22).

10 Afterfeast, and the holy martyr Lawrence and the ones with him; troparion of the feast.

11 Afterfeast, and the holy martyr Euplos; troparion of the feast.

12 Afterfeast, and the holy martyrs Photios and Aniketos; troparion of the feast.

13 Afterfeast, and our blessed father Maximos the Confessor; troparion of the feast and it concludes; and the other (troparion) for the blessed one <plagal mode IV[180]>: *Guide of orthodoxy* (cf. Nov. 11).

14 Prefeast of the dormition of the most-holy Theotokos, and the holy Prophet Micah; troparion, mode IV:

People: jump clapping your hands with confidence, and fervently gather, rejoicing today, everyone blissfully shouting out in celebration because the

---

180. As Jan. 10 and 21, Feb. 18, etc.

Θεοῦ γὰρ ἡ μήτηρ μέλλει τῶν ἐπιγείων πρὸς τὰ ἄνω ἀπαίρειν ἐνδόξως, ἣν ὕμνοις ἀεὶ ὡς Θεοτόκον δοξάζομεν.

ιε΄ Ἡ κοίμησις τῆς ὑπεραγίας Θεοτόκου, τροπάριον ἦχος α΄, Ἐν τῇ γεννήσει τὴν παρθενίαν ἐφύλαξας· ἐν τῇ κοιμήσει.

ις΄ Ἡ μετακομιδὴ τοῦ ἁγίου μανδηλίου τοῦ Χριστοῦ ἀπὸ Ἐδέσης, καὶ τοῦ ἁγίου μάρτυρος Διομήδους, τροπάριον τῆς ἑορτῆς τῆς κοιμήσεως, καὶ ἕτερον τοῦ ἁγίου μανδηλίου, ἦχος β΄, Τὴν ἄχραντον εἰκόνα σου προσκυνοῦμεν.

ιζ΄ Μεθέορτα τῆς κοιμήσεως, καὶ τοῦ ἁγίου μάρτυρος Μύρωνος, τροπάριον τῆς ἑορτῆς, Ἐν τῇ γεννήσει τὴν παρθενίαν.

ιη΄ Μεθέορτα, καὶ τῶν ἁγίων μαρτύρων Φλώρου καὶ Λαύρου, τροπάριον τῆς ἑορτῆς.

ιθ΄ Μεθέορτα, καὶ τοῦ ἁγίου μάρτυρος Ἀνδρέου τοῦ στρατηλάτου, τροπάριον τῆς ἑορτῆς.

κ΄ Τοῦ ἁγίου προφήτου Σαμουήλ, τροπάριον τῆς ἑορτῆς.

κα΄ Τοῦ ἁγίου ἀποστόλου Θαδδαίου, τροπάριον τῆς ἑορτῆς.

κβ΄ Τοῦ ἁγίου μάρτυρος Ἀγαθονίκου καὶ τῶν σὺν αὐτῷ, τροπάριον τῆς ἑορτῆς.

κγ΄ Μεθέορτα, καὶ τοῦ ἁγίου μάρτυρος Λούππου, τροπάριον τῆς ἑορτῆς καὶ ἀπόδιδει.

κδ΄ Ἡ κατάθεσις τοῦ λειψάνου τοῦ ἁγίου ἀποστόλου Βαρθολομαίου ἐν Σικελίᾳ, τροπάριον ἦχος γ΄, Ἀπόστολε ἅγιε, πρέσβευε τῷ.

κε΄ Τοῦ ἁγίου <ἀ>ποστόλου Τίτου, τροπάριον ἦχος δ΄, Χρηστότητα ἐκδιδαχθείς.

κς΄ Τῶν ἁγίων μαρτύρων Ἀδριανοῦ καὶ Ναταλίας καὶ τῶν σὺν αὐτοῖς, τροπάριον ἦχος δ΄, Οἱ μάρτυρές σου, Κύριε. |279v

κζ΄ Τοῦ ὁσίου πατρὸς ἡμῶν Ποιμένος τοῦ ἀναχωρητοῦ.

mother of God is gloriously about to depart earthly things for those above, she whom we ever glorify through hymns as the bearer of God.

15 The dormition of the most-holy Theotokos; troparion, mode I: *In birth you preserved your virginity, in death* (*MR* 6:406).

16 The translation of the holy mandylion of Christ from Edessa, and the holy martyr Diomedes; troparion of the feast of the dormition and the other of the holy mandylion, mode II: *We worship your immaculate image* (*MR* 6:422).

17 Afterfeast of the dormition, and the holy martyr Myron; troparion of the feast <mode I[181]>: *In birth you preserved your virginity* (cf. Aug. 15).

18 Afterfeast, and the holy martyrs Phloros and Lauros; troparion of the feast.

19 Afterfeast, and the holy martyr Andrew Stratelates; troparion of the feast.

20 The holy prophet Samuel; troparion of the feast.

21 The holy apostle Thaddeus; troparion of the feast.

22 The holy martyr Agathonikos and the ones with him; troparion of the feast.

23 Afterfeast, and the holy martyr Louppos; troparion of the feast and it concludes.

24 The discovery of the relics of the holy apostle Bartholomew in Sicily; troparion, mode III: *Holy apostle, intercede* (cf. Sep. 22).

25 The holy apostle Titus; troparion, mode IV: *You were well educated in goodness* (cf. Oct. 3).

26 The holy martyrs Adrianos and Natalia and the ones with them; troparion, mode IV: *Your martyrs, O Lord* (cf. Oct. 7).

27 Our blessed father Poimen the Anchorite.

---

181. As above, Aug. 15.

κηʹ Τοῦ ὁσίου Μωυσέως τοῦ Αἰθίοπος.

κθ Ἡ ἀποτομὴ τοῦ τιμίου προδρόμου καὶ βαπτιστοῦ Ἰωάννου, τροπάριον ἦχος βʹ, *Μνήμη δικαίου μετ᾽ ἐγκωμίων.*

λʹ Τοῦ ἁγίου ἱερομάρτυρος Φίλικος καὶ τῶν σὺν αὐτῷ.

λαʹ Τὰ καταθέσια τῆς τιμίας ζώνης τῆς ὑπεραγίας Θεοτόκου ἐν τοῖς Χαλκοπρατίοις, τροπάριον ἦχος πλάγιος δʹ, *Θεοτόκε ἀειπάρθενε, τῶν ἀνθρώπων ἡ σκέπη, ἐσθῆτα καὶ ζώνην τοῦ ἀχράντου σου σώματος·* ζήτει ἰουλίου βʹ.

28 The blessed Moses the Ethiopian.

29 The decapitation of the honored Forerunner and Baptist John; troparion, mode II: *The memory of the just is praised* (Prv 10:7) (cf. Jan. 7).

30 The holy hieromartyr Felix and the ones with him.

31 The installation of the precious belt of the most-holy Theotokos in the Chalkoprateia (church of Constantinople); troparion, plagal mode IV: *O Theotokos ever-virgin, shelter of mankind, you gave the robe and belt from your undefiled body;* see July 2.

Ἕτερα τροπάρια τῆς μεγάλης ἁγίας τεσσαρακοστῆς[192]

Τῷ σαββάτῳ τῆς ἀπόκρεω, τροπάριον ἦχος πλάγιος δ', *Ὁ βυθοῖς σοφίας πάντα οἰκονομῶν.*

Τῇ β' τῆς τυροφάγου, τῇ γ' καὶ τῇ ε', *Θεὸς Κύριος καὶ ἐπέφανεν.*

Τῷ σαββάτῳ τῆς τυροφάγου, εἰς τοὺς ὁσίους πατέρας ἡμῶν καὶ ἀσκητάς, τροπάριον εἰς τὸ Θεὸς Κύριος, ἦχος δ', *Ὁ Θεὸς τῶν πατέρων ἡμῶν.*

Σάββατον α' τῶν ἁγίων νηστειῶν, τοῦ ἁγίου μεγαλομάρτυρος Θεοδώρου τοῦ τήρωνος, τροπάριον ἦχος β',
    Μεγάλα τὰ τῆς πίστεως κατορθώματα· ἐν τῇ πηγῇ τῆς φλογός, ὡς ἐπὶ ὕδατος ἀναπαύσεως, ὁ ἅγιος μάρτυς ἠγάλλετο, πυρὶ γὰρ ὁλοκαυτωθείς, ὡς ἄρτος ἡδὺς τῇ Τριάδι προσήνεγκται· ταῖς αὐτοῦ ἱκεσίαις, Χριστὲ ὁ Θεός, ἐλέησον ἡμᾶς. |[280]

Κυριακῇ α' τῶν νηστειῶν ἤτοι τῆς ὀρθοδοξίας, τροπάριον ἦχος β', *Τὴν ἄχραντον εἰκόνα σου προσκυνοῦμεν.*

Κυριακῇ γ' τῶν νηστειῶν, ἡ προσκύνησις τοῦ τιμίου σταυροῦ, τροπάριον ἦχος α', *Σῶσον, Κύριε, τὸν λαόν σου καὶ εὐλόγησον τὴν κληρονομίαν.*

Τῇ τετράδι τῆς μεσονηστείμου, τροπάριον πάλιν τὸ αὐτὸ καὶ ἕτερον, ἦχος ὁ αὐτός,
    Τοῦ σταυροῦ σου τὸ ξύλον προσκυνοῦμεν, Χριστέ, ὅτι ἐν αὐτῷ προσηλώθης, ἡ ζωὴ τῶν ἁπάντων. Παράδεισον ἠνέῳξας Σωτὴρ τῷ πίστει προσελθόντι σοι ληστῇ, καὶ τρυφῆς κατηξιώθη ὁμολογῶν σοι· Μνήσθητί μου Κύριε. Δέξαι ὥσπερ ἐκεῖνον καὶ ἡμᾶς, κραυγάζομεν· Ἡμάρτομεν πάντες τῇ εὐσπλαγχνίᾳ σου μὴ ὑπερίδῃς ἡμᾶς.

Τῷ σαββάτῳ τοῦ δικαίου Λαζάρου, τροπάριον εἰς τὸ Θεὸς Κύριος, ἦχος α', *Τὴν κοινὴν ἀνάστασιν πρὸ τοῦ σοῦ πάθους πιστούμενος, ἐκ νεκρῶν ἤγειρας.*

192. μ': C.

(III.2)

Other Troparia of Great Holy Lent[182]

On Saturday of Apokreos; troparion, plagal mode IV: *You who ordain all things from the depths of your wisdom* (*TR* 20).

On Monday of Cheesefare, Tuesday, and Thursday: *God is the Lord, and he has shined* (28).

On Saturday of Cheesefare, of our blessed fathers and ascetics; troparion to God is the Lord: *God our fathers* (cf. Nov. 12).

On the first Saturday of holy Lent, (that) of the holy great martyr Theodore Tiron; troparion, mode II:

> *Great are the successes of the faith. The holy martyr rejoiced in the well-spring of fire as if in peaceful waters* (Ps 22:2); *for consumed by fire like an offering, he was brought before the Trinity as sweet-tasting bread; by his supplications, Christ our God, have mercy on us.*

On the first Sunday of Lent, that is, of Orthodoxy; troparion, mode II: *We worship your immaculate image* (cf. Aug. 16).

On the third Sunday of Lent: the adoration of the precious cross; troparion, mode I: *Save, O Lord, your people and bless your inheritance* (Ps 27:2) (*TR* 352).

On Wednesday of mid-Lent, the same troparion again, and the other, the same mode:

> *We worship the wood of your cross, O Christ, since you the life of all were nailed to it. You opened paradise, savior, to the thief who approached you in faith, and he was deemed worthy of its delights by confessing to you, "Remember me, O Lord"* (Lk 23:42). *As you did him, receive us, too, as we cry out, "We are all sinners; in your compassion, do not neglect us."*

On Saturday of the righteous Lazarus; troparion to God is the Lord, mode I: *Making known before your passion the resurrection common to all, you raised Lazarus from among the dead* (*TR* 590).

---

182. Troparia for select movable feasts, followed by miscellaneous entries.

Τῇ κυριακῇ τῶν βαΐων, εἰς τὸ Θεὸς Κύριος τὸ αὐτὸ τροπάριον καὶ ἕτερον, ἦχος δ᾽,

Συνταφέντες σοι διὰ τοῦ βαπτίσματος, Χριστὲ ὁ Θεὸς ἡμῶν, τῆς ἀθανάτου ζωῆς ἠξιώθημεν τῇ ἀναστάσει σου, καὶ ἀνυμνοῦντες κράζομεν· Ὡσαννά,[193] *εὐλογημένος ὁ ἐρχόμενος ἐν ὀνόματι Κυρίου.*

Τῇ ἁγίᾳ καὶ μεγάλῃ β᾽ καὶ γ᾽ καὶ τετράδι, τροπάριον εἰς τὸ Ἀλληλούϊα, ἦχος πλάγιος δ᾽, |[280v] ἀντὶ τοῦ Τριαδικοῦ, *Ἰδού, ὁ νυμφίος ἔρχεται ἐν τῷ μέσῳ τῆς.*

Τῇ ἁγίᾳ καὶ μεγάλῃ ε᾽, καὶ τῇ μεγάλῃ παρασκευῇ, τροπάριον εἰς τὸ Ἀλληλούϊα, ἦχος πλάγιος δ᾽, *Ὅτε οἱ ἔνδοξοι μαθηταὶ ἐν τῷ νιπτῆρι·* καὶ ἀπολυτίκιον τοῦ ὄρθρου τῆς μεγάλης παρασκευῆς, ἦχος α᾽, *Σταυρωθέντος σου, Χριστέ, ἀνῃρέθη ἡ τυραννίς, ἐπατήθη ἡ δύναμις.*

Τῷ ἁγίῳ καὶ μεγάλῳ σαββάτῳ, τροπάριον εἰς τὸ Θεὸς Κύριος, ἦχος β᾽, *Ὁ εὐσχήμων Ἰωσήφ·* καὶ θεοτοκίν, *Ὑπερδεδοξασμένη ὑπάρχεις.*

Τῇ ἁγίᾳ καὶ μεγάλῃ κυριακῇ τοῦ πάσχα[194] ἀντὶ τοῦ Θεὸς Κύριος, *Χριστὸς ἀνέστη.*

Κυριακῇ τοῦ ἀντίπασχα ἤτοι τοῦ ἁγίου Θωμᾶ, τροπάριον ἦχος βαρύς, *Ἐσφραγισμένου τοῦ μνήματος, ἡ ζωὴ ἐκ τάφου ἀνέτειλας.*

Κυριακῇ γ᾽ τῶν μυροφόρων ἁγίων γυναικῶν, καὶ Ἰωσὴφ τοῦ εὐσχήμωνος, τροπάριον, *Ὁ εὐσχήμων Ἰωσήφ·*[195] ἕτερον, *Ταῖς μυροφόροις γυναιξὶ παρὰ τὸ μνῆμα ἐπιστάσαις ἐβόα.*

Κυριακῇ δ᾽ τοῦ παραλύτου, τροπάριον ἦχος γ᾽, *Εὐφραινέσθω τὰ οὐράνια, ἀγαλλιάσθω τὰ ἐπίγεια.*

Τῇ δ᾽ τῆς μεσοπεντηκοστῆς, τροπάριον ἦχος πλάγιος δ᾽, *Μεσούσης τῆς ἑορτῆς διψῶσάν μου τὴν ψυχὴν εὐσεβαίας.*

Κυριακῇ ε᾽ τῆς Σαμαρίτιδος, τροπάριον τοῦ δ᾽ ἤχου, *Τὸ φαιδρὸν τῆς ἀναστάσεως κήρυγμα ἐκ τοῦ ἀγγέλλου.*

---

193. ὡς ἀννά: C.
194. τῇ ἁγίᾳ ... πάσχα is written in red ink.
195. τροπάριον, Ὁ εὐσχήμων Ἰχσὴφ is written in the margin with an insertion sign.

On Palm Sunday, to God is the Lord, the same troparion and the other, mode IV:

Having been buried with you in baptism (cf. Col 2:14), *O Christ our God, we have been made worthy of everlasting life by your resurrection; singing in praise, we cry out, "Hosanna: blessed is he who comes in the name of the Lord"* (Mt 21:9).

On Monday, Tuesday, and Wednesday (of Holy Week) instead of the Trinitarian Hymns (the) troparion to the Alleluia, plagal mode IV: *Behold, the bridegroom comes in the middle of the* (cf. matins, 86).

On Maundy Thursday and on Good Friday; troparion to Alleluia, plagal mode IV: *When the glorious disciples were being enlightened* (136); and apolytikion of matins on Good Friday, mode I: *When you were crucified, O Christ, tyranny was destroyed; the power of the enemy was trampled* (126).

On Holy Great Saturday; troparion to God is the Lord, mode II: *The noble Joseph* (PaR 106); and the theotokion: *You are supremely glorified* (PaR 106).

On Easter Sunday, instead of God is the Lord <plagal mode I[183]>: *Christ is risen.*

On the Sunday of Antipascha, that is, of St. Thomas; troparion, barys mode: *When the tomb was sealed, you who are the life arose from the grave* (PaR 540).

On the third Sunday, that of the holy myrrh-bearing women and of the noble Joseph; troparion <mode II[184]>: *The noble Joseph* (PaR 106); the other: *The angel standing by the tomb proclaimed to the women bringing myrrh* (PaR 106).

On the fourth Sunday, that of the Paralytic; troparion, mode III: *Let the heavens rejoice; let the earthly exalt* (PaR 187).

On Wednesday of mid-Pentecost; troparion, plagal mode IV: *At the middle of the feast, you watered my thirsty soul with a stream of celebration* (MHS 623).

On the fifth Sunday, that of the woman of Samaria; troparion, mode IV: *Having understood the joyful proclamation of the resurrection from the angel* (PaR 274).

---

183. See Arranz, *Typicon de Messine*, 247–48; Mateos, *Typicon*, 1:258.17.
184. Arranz, *Typicon de Messine*, 243; Mateos, *Typicon*, 2.114.

Κυριακῇ ς᾽ τοῦ τυφλοῦ, τοῦ πλαγίου α᾽ ἤχου, *Τὸν συνάναρχον Λόγον, Πατρὶ, καὶ Πνεύματι, τὸν ἐκ παρθένου τεχθέντα.*

Τῇ ε᾽ τῆς ἀναληψίμου, τροπάριον εἰς τὸ Θεὸς Κύριος, ἦχος δ᾽,[196] *Ἀνελήφθης ἐν δόξῃ.* |[281]

Κυριακῇ ζ᾽ τῶν {ἁγίων} τιη᾽ ἁγίων θεοφόρων πατέρων τῶν ἐν Νικαίᾳ τῆς α᾽ συνόδου, τροπάριον ἦχος πλάγιος δ᾽,

Ὑπερδεδοξασμένος εἶ, Χριστὲ ὁ Θεὸς ἡμῶν, ὁ φωστῆρας ἐπὶ γῆς τοὺς πατέρας ἡμῶν θεμελιώσας καὶ δι᾽ αὐτῶν πρὸς τὴν ἀληθινὴν πίστιν πάντας ἡμᾶς ὁδηγήσας· πολυεύσπλαγχνε, δόξα.

Τῷ σαββάτῳ τῆς ἁγίας πεντηκοστῆς, τροπάριον νεκρώσιμον εἰς τὸ Θεὸς Κύριος, ἦχος πλάγιος δ᾽, *Ὁ βυθοῖς σοφίας·* καὶ τὴν λοιπὴν πᾶσαν ἀκολουθίαν καθώς ἐστι τῷ σαββάτῳ τῆς ἀπόκρεω.

Κυριακῇ τῆς ἁγίας πεντηκοστῆς, τροπάριον ἦχος πλάγιος δ᾽,

Εὐλογητὸς εἶ, Χριστὲ ὁ Θεὸς ἡμῶν, ὁ πανσόφους τοὺς ἁλιεῖς ἀναδείξας, καταπέμψας αὐτοῖς τὸ Πνεῦμα τὸ ἅγιον καὶ δι᾽ αὐτῶν τὴν οἰκουμένην σαγηνεύσας· φιλάνθρωπε, δόξα σοι.

Κυριακῇ τῶν ἁγίων πάντων, τροπάριον ἦχος δ᾽, *Τῶν ἐν ὅλῳ τῷ κόσμῳ μαρτύρων σου, ὡς πορφύραν καὶ βύσσον τά.*

Τῶν ἐγκαινίων, τροπάριον ἦχος δ᾽,

Τὰ πέρατα ἐφώτισε τῇ παρουσίᾳ Χριστός, τὸν κόσμον ἀνεκαίνισε Πνεύματι θείῳ αὐτοῦ· ψυχαὶ ἐγκαινίζονται· οἶκος γὰρ ἀνετέθη νῦν εἰς δόξαν Κυρίου, ἔνθα καὶ ἐγκαινίζει τῶν πιστῶν τὰς καρδίας Χριστὸς ὁ Θεὸς ἡμῶν εἰς σωτηρίαν βροτῶν.

Κοντάκιον ἦχος δ᾽,

Ὡς[197] τοῦ ἄνω στερεώματος τὴν εὐπρέπειαν καὶ τὴν κάτω συναπέδειξας ὡραιότητα τοῦ ἁγίου σκηνώματος τῆς δόξης σου, Κύριε· κραταίωσον |[281v] *αὐτὸ[198] εἰς αἰῶνα αἰῶνος, καὶ πρόσδεξαι ἡμῶν τὰς ἐν αὐτῷ ἀπαύστως προσαγομένας σοι δεήσεις διὰ τῆς Θεοτόκου· ἡ πάντων ζωὴ καὶ ἀνάστασις.*

---

196. ἦχος δ᾽ added later in the lower margin.
197. Ὅς: C.   198. αὐτὴν: C.

On the sixth Sunday, that of the blind man; plagal mode I: *Let us praise in song the Word that is of the same source as the Father and the Holy Spirit* (*PaR* 364).

On Ascension Thursday; troparion to God is the Lord, mode IV: *You were taken up in glory* (*MHS* 636).

On the seventh Sunday, that of the holy 318 God-bearing Fathers of the First Council of Nicaea; troparion, plagal mode IV:

You are the one who has been glorified above all, O Christ our God: you who established our fathers to be stars on the earth, and through them you showed us all the way to the true faith. O most merciful one, glory to you.

On the Saturday of (the week of) holy Pentecost; troparion in honor of the dead to God is the Lord: plagal mode IV: *You who ordain all things from the depths of your wisdom* (cf. Saturday of Apokreos). The rest of the office is just like that of the Saturday of Apokreos.

On Pentecost Sunday; troparion, plagal mode IV:

Blessed are you, O Christ our God, who made fishermen to be all wise; you sent down to them the Holy Spirit, and through them you pulled the world into your net. O you who love mankind, glory to you.

On the Sunday of All Saints; troparion, mode IV: *The rivers of blood from your martyrs throughout the whole world are, as purple and fine linen* (*PaR* 316).

(The celebration of) consecrations;[185] troparion, mode IV:

By the advent Christ illuminated the ends of the earth. By his divine Spirit he made the world new; souls are renewed. A church is dedicated to the glory of the Lord; for the salvation of mortals, Christ our God renews within it the hearts of the faithful.

Kontakion,[186] fourth mode:

Together, O Lord, you established the majesty of the firmament above and

---

185. The last four entries stand outside the calendar. They are miscellaneous additions of a sort found in other kinds of liturgical manuscripts, for example, calendar appendices in the Gospel lectionary; cf. Gregory, *Textkritik des Neuen Testaments*, 1:384–86. This troparion was used at the monastery of the Theotokos Evergetis, on Dec. 29, for the commemoration of the dedication of its church; cf. *Synaxarion of Evergetis*, ed. Jordan, 1:362.

186. Found among the supplements to the Typikon of the Great Church, where it is used for

Ὁ οἶκος,

Τὴν ἐν σώματι θείαν τοῦ λόγου ἑορτάζοντες ἐπιδημίαν, τῆς αὐτοῦ ἐκκλησίας τὰ τέκνα πυκασμῷ ἀρετῶν λαμπρυνθῶμεν ἀξίως τῆς χάριτος, καὶ Θεοῦ ἄξιον ἀναδειχθῶμεν φωτισμῷ γνώσεως οἰκητήριον, ἐν σοφίᾳ τῆς πίστεως τὰς αἰνέσεις ἐξαγγέλλοντες· ἡ σοφία γὰρ ἀληθῶς τοῦ Πατρὸς ἀνῳκοδόμησεν ἑαυτῇ οἶκον σαρκός, καὶ ἐσκήνωσεν ἐν ἡμῖν ὑπὲρ νοῦν, ἡ πάντων ζωὴ καὶ ἀνάστασις.

Χερουβικὸν τῆς μεγάλης ἐκκλησίας, ἦχος β',

Σιγησάτω πᾶσα σὰρξ βροτεία, καὶ στήτω μετὰ φόβου καὶ τρόμου, καὶ μηδὲν γήϊνον ἐν ἑαυτῇ λογιζέσθω· ὁ γὰρ βασιλεὺς τῶν βασιλευόντων, Χριστὸς ὁ Θεὸς ἡμῶν, προέρχεται σφαγιασθῆναι, καὶ δοθῆναι εἰς βρῶσιν τοῖς πιστοῖς· προηγοῦνται δὲ τούτου οἱ χοροὶ τῶν ἀγγέλων μετὰ πάσης ἀρχῆς καὶ ἐξουσίας, τὰ πολυόμματα χερουβίμ, τὰ ἑξαπτέρυγα σεραφίμ, τὰς ὄψεις καλύπτοντα καὶ βοῶντα τὸν ὕμνον· Ἀλληλούϊα.

the beauty of the holy tabernacle of your glory below; strengthen it for ever and ever, and accept our prayers offered in it and without ceasing to you, through the Theotokos, the life and resurrection of all.

The oikos,

Celebrating the holy arrival of the Logos in the flesh, let us, the children of his church, be brightly adorned with a covering of virtues as befits (our) gratitude; let us be shown forth by the illumination of knowledge as a dwelling place worthy of God as we proclaim praises in the wisdom of the faith; for it was in truth the wisdom of the Father (that) raised up for itself a dwelling of flesh, and **he dwelt among us** *(Jn 1:14) beyond understanding: the life and resurrection of all.*

The Cherubikon of the Great Church,[187] mode II:

Let all mortal flesh be silent, and stand in fear and trembling; and let its thinking be in no way earthly, for the king of kings, Christ our God, enters to be sanctified and to be given as food to the faithful. He is conducted by the choirs of angels with every principality and power, the many-eyed cherubim, the six-winged seraphim, covering their faces and crying out the hymn, "Alleluia, <alleluia, alleluia>."

anniversaries of church dedications: Mateos, *Typicon*, 2:186–87. Cited by incipit for use in the dedication of the church of the monastery of the Theotokos Evergetis (*Synaxarion of Evergetis*, ed. Jordan, 1:364, 370), where it is found in the Kontakarion under Sep. 13, which is the day of the dedication of the Anastasis church in Jerusalem. This entry and the next are extracts from a hymn said to have been composed to celebrate the consecration of St. Sophia, Constantinople: Anonymous, "Un antichissimo 'kontakion' inedito," *Roma e l'Oriente* 1 (1910): 182.

187. Not the hymn traditionally known as the "Cherubikon," but its replacement on Holy Saturday: R. Taft, *The Great Entrance. A History of the Transfer of Gifts and Other Preanaphoral Rites of the Liturgy of St. John Chrysostom*, OCA 200 (Rome: Pontificio Instituto Orientale, 1975), 53, 76–77. In light of the absence from the *Horologion* of material directly pertinent to the celebration of the liturgy, as well as the nature of the two preceding entries, it is relevant to note that this hymn has been identified as one used on the anniversaries of church dedications: O. Strunk, "Chants of the Byzantine-Greek Liturgy," in Strunk, *Essays on Music in the Byzantine World* (New York: W. W. Norton, 1977), 325.

PART 2

THE HARVARD MANUSCRIPT AND THE HISTORY OF THE HOROLOGION OF THE GREEK LITURGICAL PSALTER

Stefano Parenti

Translated from the Italian
by Isella O'Rourke with the collaboration of
J. Anderson and Gabriel I. Radle

To the memory of Juan Mateos, SJ (1917–2003),
magister magistrum

Introduction

When, in 1932, Anton Baumstark formulated the first of his laws, which states that liturgical rites evolve from diversity toward unity, he wished to emphasize how the study of the Christian liturgy is above all a study of local rites.[1] Today, despite the movement in favor of cultural integration and creativity, there are fewer liturgical rites than in the Christian world of late antiquity, the Middle Ages, or even after the advent of the printing press at the end of the fifteenth century. These early rites were regional recensions from the same liturgical family, strongly marked by their own unique features. As a concrete illustration, one need only cite the Byzantine rite at the beginning of the twelfth century, when the Harvard Liturgical Psalter was written. The city of Constantinople had a cathedral rite and several monastic rites. At the same time, other recensions were in use in Greece and the Middle East. In southern Italy regional differences are so pronounced that it is possible to distinguish a Calabrian recension from a Salentine one, and the same can be said of the Slavic world, where the traditions of Kiev and Novgorod differed significantly from those of the Balkans.[2] The variety of local recensions of the Byzantine rite is known to us through the handwritten liturgical texts, which deserve special attention for their diversity alone.

In the last half century, the study of the Eastern Christian liturgies has taken many significant steps forward,[3] but, as far as the sources of worship

---

1. A. Baumstark, *Liturgie comparée. Principes et méthodes pour l'étude historique des liturgies chrétiennes*, ed. B. Botte, 3rd rev. ed. (Chevetogne-Paris, 1953), 18–22. However, still foremost is Baumstark, *Vom geschichtlichen Werden der Liturgie* (Freiburg i.B., 1923), 33; for a critical evaluation see R. F. Taft, "Anton Baumstark's Comparative Liturgy Revisited," in *Comparative Liturgy Fifty Years after Anton Baumstark (1872–1948)*, ed. R. F. Taft, SJ, and G. Winkler, OCA 265 (Rome: Pontificio Instituto Orientale, 2001). On the circumstances leading to the publication of the *Liturgie comparée* see E. Lanne, "Les dix leçons de liturgie comparée d'Anton Baumstark au monastère d'Amay-sur-Meuse en 1932: leur contexte et leur publication," in *Comparative Liturgy Fifty Years after Anton Baumstark*, ed. Taft and Winkler, 145–61.

2. See E. Velkovska, "La liturgia presso gli Slavi ortodossi," in *Lo spazio letterario del Medievo*, vol. 3, *Le culture circostanti*, part 3, *Le culture slave*, ed. M. Capaldo (Rome: Salerno, 2006), 405–37.

3. R. F. Taft, "Über die Liturgiewissenschaft heute," *Theologische Quartalschrift* 177 (1997): 243–

go, we still lack a serious and reliable *typologie des sources*, following the example of what has been done for Latin texts.[4] Valuable studies taking up the problem have been published, and they offer new research opportunities.[5] For the psalter we have Georgi R. Parpulov's recent monograph covering the principal Byzantine manuscripts from the ninth to the fifteenth century; Parpulov carefully examines the material and artistic aspects of the books in relation to their patrons' needs and the social and religious contexts of their production.[6] The study includes appendices containing texts of primary importance in the history of Constantinopolitan monasticism, ones such as the *Hypotyposis* of Niketas of Stoudios (d. ca. 1090).[7] Works of a more strictly liturgical nature remain to be investigated.[8] As for the study of the horologion, a number of editions with commentary are available: that of the earliest known copy, which is attributed to the ninth century, Mt. Sinai, MSC, gr. 863 (+ Chest I, no. 58),[9] the contemporary

---

55; Taft, "The Liturgical Enterprise Twenty-Five Years After Alexander Schmemann (1921–1983); the Man and His Heritage," *St. Vladimir's Theological Quarterly* [hereafter "SVThQ"] 53 (2009): 141–56.

4. See especially M. Huglo, *Les livres de chant liturgique* (Turnhout: Brepols, 1988); J. Szövérffy, *Latin Hymns*, Typologie des sources du moyen âge occidental 55 [hereafter "TSMO"] (Turnhout: Brepols, 1989); A. G. Martimort, *Les "ordines," les ordinaires et les cérémoniaux* (Turnhout: Brepols, 1991); Martimort, *Les lectures liturgiques et leurs livres* (Turnhout: Brepols, 1992); M. Metzger, *Les sacramentaires* (Turnhout: Brepols, 1994).

5. An initial division of liturgical books by function was proposed by E. Velkovska, "Byzantine Liturgical Books," in *Handbook for Liturgical Studies*, vol. 1, *Introduction to the Liturgy*, ed. A. J. Chupungco (Collegeville, Minn: Liturgical Press, 1997), 225–40, and expanded in Velkovksa, "Система на византийските и славянските богослужебни книги в периода на възникването им," in *Medieval Christian Europe: East and West. Tradition, Values, Communications* (Sofia: Gutenberg, 2002), 220–36. More recently this division was taken up by R. F. Taft, "I libri liturgici," in *Lo spazio letterario del Medioevo*, vol. 3, *Le culture circostanti*, part 1, *La cultura bizantina*, ed. G. Cavallo (Rome: Salerno, 2004), 229–56.

6. Parpulov, *Byzantine Psalters*. I wish to thank Georgi R. Parpulov, Francesco D'Aiuto, and the staff of the library of the Pontificio Ateneo S. Anselmo, Rome, for help in obtaining the entire work.

7. Paruplov, *Byzantine Psalters*, 1:444–92. See also G. R. Parpulov, "Psalters and Personal Piety in Byzantium," in *The Old Testament in Byzantium*, ed. Paul Magdalino and Robert Nelson (Washington, D.C.: Dumbarton Oaks Research Library and Collection, 2010), 77–105.

8. E.g., G. M. Hanke, "Der Odenkanon des Tagzeitenritus Konstantinopels im Licht der Beiträge H. Schneiders und O. Strunk—eine Relecture," in *Crossroad of Cultures. Studies in Liturgy and Patristics in Honor of Gabriele Winkler*, ed. H.-J. Feulner et al., OCA 260 (Rome: Pontificio Instituto Orientale, 2000), 345–67.

9. Mateos, "Horologion de Saint-Sabas," 47–76; the fragments of Mt. Sinai, Μονὴ Ἁγίας Αἰκατερίνης [hereafter "MSC"], chest I, no. 58, discovered and partially published by Parpulov (*Byzantine Psalters*, 1:61–62n36), were subsequently published in full in S. Parenti, "Un fascicolo ritrovato dell'horologion Sinai gr. 863 (IX secolo)," *OCP* 75 (2009): 346–49.

Mt. Sinai, MSC, gr. 864,[10] and, since 1954, the edition of the so-called Melkite Horologion (1187/88 A.D.).[11] Stig R. Frøyshov's research on the tenth-century manuscript Mt. Sinai, MSC, georg. 34, opens up new research prospects for the history of the horologion.[12] Scholarly interest has understandably focused on the earliest Greek, Syriac, and Georgian examples surviving from the eastern parts of the Empire, where the horologion originated. For southern Italy we have a partial edition of the psalter-horologion Turin, BNU, cod. B.VII.30 of the ninth century,[13] but, with respect to the other regions of the Byzantine world, we know little or nothing: there is no repertorium, checklist, or even simple survey of the currently available horologia in manuscript form. Under these circumstances, the publication of a psalter horologion like Cambridge, Harvard University, Houghton Library, gr. 3, assumes an altogether special meaning and significance.

Altered political conditions and the enormous opportunities offered by computers, along with easier access to the manuscript collections of the Russian Federation, have resulted in the circulation of works by scholars of the liturgical schools flourishing in Moscow and Kiev during the pre-Soviet period.[14] Today, many of their contributions are available online at *www. mzh.mrezha.ru*. The studies published by Diakovskij in 1909 and 1913[15] are

10. M. Ajjoub and J. Paramelle, ed. and trans., *Livre d'Heures du Sinaï (Sinaiticus graecus 864)*, SC 486 (Paris: Éditions du Cerf, 2004). The liturgical and philological commentary prompts numerous reservations, however; see my review in *OCP* 72 (2006): 266–69, that of G. Papagiannis in *Byzantinische Zeitschrift* [hereafter "*BZ*"] 100 (2007): 189–96, and the detailed account of S. S. Frøyshov, "Часослов без последований Больших Часов (вечерни и утрени): Исследование недавно изданного Часослова Sin. gr. 864 (IX в.)," *Богословские Труды* 43–44 (1912): 381–400.

11. M. Black, *A Christian Palestinian Syriac Horologion (Berlin MS. Or. Oct. 1019)* (Cambridge: Cambridge University Press, 1954).

12. S. S. Frøyshov, "The Georgian Witness to the Jerusalem Liturgy: New Sources and Studies," in *Inquiries into Eastern Christian Worship: Selected Papers of the Second International Congress of the Society of Oriental Liturgy, Rome, 17–21 September 2008*, ed. B. Groen, S. Hawkes-Teeples, and S. Alexopoulos, Eastern Christian Studies 12 (Leuven: Brill, 2012), 227–67, here 249–59.

13. BNU = Biblioteca Nazionale Universitaria. S. Parenti, "Nota sul Salterio-Horologion del IX secolo Torino, Biblioteca Universitaria B. VII. 30," *Bollettino della Badia Greca di Grottaferrata* [hereafter "*BollGrott*"] 4 (2007): 275–87.

14. In this regard see the recent studies of P. Galadza, "Baumstark's Kievan Contemporary, Mikhail N. Skaballanovich (1871–1931[?]): A Sketch of His Life and Heortology," in *Comparative Liturgy Fifty Years after Anton Baumstark*, ed. Taft and Winkler, 761–75, and J. Getcha, "Les études liturgiques russes au XIXe–XXe siècles et leur impact sur la pratique," in *Les mouvements liturgiques. Corrélations entre pratiques et recherches*, ed. C. Braga and A. Pistoia (Rome: Edizioni Liturgiche, 2004), 279–90.

15. E. Diakovskij, "Последование ночных часов (чин 12-ти псалмов)," *Труды Киевской Ду-*

still important for the history of the horologion: this author uses manuscript sources such as Mt. Sinai, MSC, gr. 863 and 864, only accessible to Western scholars after the microfilming was carried out, in 1950, by the Library of Congress in Washington, D.C. Nevertheless, the research, mainly concerning Slavic manuscripts, currently underway in Russia should not be overlooked, since it provides important comparative material for the study of Greek horologia[16] for which there is as yet no reliable study. Unfortunately the recent monograph of Carolina Lutzka dedicated to the "Lesser Hours" does not advance our understanding.[17]

I

The Greek Liturgical Psalter and Its Typology

I.1. Preface

The liturgical psalter of the Septuagint was designed for recitation or chanting.[18] It contains the 150 psalms "of David," the supernumerary Psalm 151 (ἔξωθεν τοῦ ἀριθμοῦ), the biblical odes of the Old and New Testaments, and various supplements or liturgical appendices. Some examples contain marginal catenae comprising comments on the Psalms by the Fathers.[19]

The oldest Greek psalters, whether destined for liturgical use or not, fall into two categories established by Alfred Rahlfs at the beginning of the twentieth century: "hagiopolite," or Jerusalem psalters, and "ecclesiastical," or Constantinoplitan psalters.[20] The terminology derives from the manu-

---

ховной Академии 2 (1909): 547–95, and *Последование часов и изобразительных. Историческое исследоване* (Kiev: Mejnander, 1913).

16. E. E. Sliva, "Часословы студийской традиции в славянских списках XIII–XIV веков," *Труды Отдела древнерусской литературы* 51 (1999): 91–106.

17. C. Lutzka, *Die Kleinen Horen des byzantinischen Stundengebetes und ihre geschichtliche Entwicklung* (Berlin: Berlin-Münster LIT, 2007).

18. The melodies for the sung execution of the psalms are not found in the psalter, which is devoid of musical notation, but in codices of the Hasmatikòn and the Psaltikòn, cf. C. Thodberg, *Der byzantinische Alleluiarionzyklus. Studien im kurzen Psaltikonstil*, Monumenta Musicae Byzantinae, Subsidia VIII (Kopenhagen: E. Munksgaard, 1966).

19. *Clavis Patrum Graecorum*, 5 vols., ed. M. Geerard (Turnhout: Brepols, 1974–87) [hereafter "CPG"], 4:C10–C50; G. Dorival, *Les Chaînes exégétiques grecques sur les Psaumes: Contribution à l'étude d'une forme littéraire*, Spicilegium Sacrum Lovaniense, Études et documents 43–46 (Leuven: Peeters, 1986–95), 1:1–4.

20. A. Rahlfs, *Verzeichnis der griechischen Handschriften des Alten Testaments* (Berlin: Weidmann, 1914), 18–19n1, and 225n1.

scripts themselves. "Hagiopolitis" (ἁγιοπολίτης) is a technical (in addition to geographical) term that denotes the liturgical tradition of the cathedral of Jerusalem, whereas "ecclesiastical" (ἐκκλησιαστής) refers to the tradition of the cathedral of Hagia Sophia in Constantinople, the "Great Church" par excellence.[21] The principal difference between the two systems concerns the stichometry, or verse division: 4,782 in Jerusalem, 2,542 in Constantinople.[22] On average, therefore, a verse in the Constantinopolitan psalter is double the length of one in the Jerusalem psalter. The different stichometry thus corresponds to two different cathedral liturgies, but it has important implications for the composition and compilation of the exegetic chains; these are divided into Palestinian and Constantinopolitan, as are the psalters that employ them.[23] The stichometry is a microdivision of the psalter that underlies the macrodivisions of the psalms carried out according to the methods of the two traditions.

I.2. *Hagiopolite, or Jerusalem psalter*

In the hagiopolite system, the 150 psalms were divided into 20 sections (καθίσματα); each section—κάθισμα, which, as we shall see below (§ II.3), simply means "structure"—is in turn divided into three subsections, called "antiphons" (ἀντίφωνα), for a total of 60 units. By way of an example, kathisma I is illustrated in table 1:

Table 1: Kathisma I

Kathisma	Antiphon	Psalms
	1a	1, 2, 3
I	2a	4, 5, 6
	3a	7, 8

21. G. Mercati, *Osservazioni a proemi del Salterio di Origene, Ippolito, Eusebio, Cirillo Alessandrino e altri, con frammenti inediti* (Vatican City: Biblioteca Apostolica Vaticana, 1948), 23.

22. Schneider, "Oden," 442–45. There is some variance in the manuscript numeration.

23. Dorival, *Chaînes exégétiques*, 1:1–4.

The macrodivision by kathismata is attested in the middle of the sixth century in the Purple Psalter of Zurich.[24] Following it are the oldest specimens of the Jerusalem psalter, such as Mt. Sinai, MSC, gr. 30, made in the first half of the ninth century,[25] where, at the end of the third antiphon (ἀντίφωνον) of each section, the scribe wrote the number of verses that make up both the antiphon as well as the entire κάθισμα. [26] Following Psalm 150, he added a table that gives in summary form the psalms and the verses of each κάθισμα, followed in turn by the indication denoting its use in the cathedral of Jerusalem: "ὡς πρόκειται στίχοι, δψπ᾽ καθῶς ψάλλομεν ἐν τῇ ἁγίᾳ Χριστοῦ τοῦ Θεοῦ ἡμῶν Ἀναστάσει. [As has been said, 4,780 verses in the manner in which we sing them in the Holy Anastasis of Christ our God.]"[27]

In the hagiopolite liturgical tradition, the psalter text itself is introduced by the Nicene-Constantinoplitan Creed, the Our Father, with the distinctive clause "ἐν Χριστῷ Ἰησοῦ τοῦ Κυρίου ἡμῶν," and patristic and/or poetic texts.[28] There are nine biblical odes, followed by an appendix usually consisting of the lucernarium hymn of vespers (Φῶς ἱλαρόν), the matins hymn (ὕμνος ἑωθινός) *Gloria in excelsis*, the Beatitudes (Μακαρισμοί) of Matthew (Mt 5:3–13), the Canticle (literally προφητεία) of Isaiah (Is 8:9, 13, 17–18; 9:1–2, 6), and the deuterocanonical Prayer (Προσευχή) of Manasses.

---

24. Zentralbibliothek, RP 1 (C 84, App. 19). C. von Tischendorf, ed., *Psalterium Turicense purpureum, septimi fere saeculis, addito Danihelis libro ex codice prophetarum Marchaliano, nunc Vaticano, sexti vel septimi saeculi* (Leipzig, 1869), xix, 63, 168, 175, 179, 195, 200, 207; bibliography in A. Rahlfs, *Verzeichnis der griechischen Handschriften des Alten Testaments*, vol. 1, part 1, *Die Überlieferung bis zum VIII. Jahrhundert*, ed. D. Fraenkel (Göttingen: Vandenhoeck and Ruprecht, 2004), 445. For the date I follow E. Crisci, "Studio codicologico e paleografico," in E. Crisci et al., "Il Salterio purpureo Zentralbibliothek Zürich, RP 1," *Segno e Testo* 5 (2007): 31–67 (the volume includes a compact disc with a complete reproduction of the codex). However, the subdivisions were added later: according to Parpulov, "Psalters and Personal Piety," 89n51, they were added before the year 780.

25. K. Weitzmann and G. Galavaris, *The Monastery of Saint Catherine at Mount Sinai: The Illuminated Manuscripts*, vol. 1, *From the Ninth to the Twelfth Century* (Princeton, N.J.: Princeton University Press, 1990), 15–16; L. Perria, "Scritture e codici di origine orientale (Palestina e Sinai) dal IX al XII secolo. Rapporto preliminare," *RSBN* 36 (1999): 24. A description of the codex is found in Parpulov, "Psalters and Personal Piety," 101–2.

26. E.g., on fol. 66r: Τὸ γ᾽ ἀντίφωνον στίχους νγ᾽, ὡς τὸ εἶναι τὸ α᾽ κάθισμα στίχους ροδ᾽.

27. Sinai. gr. 30, fols. 367v–368r; transcription in Weitzmann-Galavaris, *Illuminated Manuscripts*, 15, fig. 2.

28. An inventory of prefatory texts, independent of provenance, is given in Parpulov, *Byzantine Psalters*, 1:256–99.

The best known hagiopolite psalter is the so-called Uspenskij Psalter (St. Petersburg, RNB, gr. 216 + Mt. Sinai, MSC, NE МГ 33), previously in St. Catherine's monastery.[29] It was copied, in 862–63, by Theodore, deacon of the Anastasis in Jerusalem, on the commission of Noah, bishop of Tiberias.[30] Both the Sinai. gr. 30 and the Uspenskij Psalter direct the recitation of psalmody in the manner of the Anastasis. From the contemporary Mt. Sinai, MSC, gr. 32, we learn that the same system was also in use on Sinai itself, where the codex was probably copied.[31] It follows that the hagiopolite psalter was common to the cathedral and monastic churches of the entire patriarchate of Jerusalem; what might possibly differ was the *pensum*, that is, the quantity of psalmody, usually greater in the liturgical use and in the private prayer of the monk.

Despite possible gaps, the ninth-century manuscripts Mt. Sinai, MSC, gr. 28 (800 A.D.), 29, 31, 33 (+ St. Petersburg, RNB, gr. 262), and Mt. Sinai, MSC, NE МГ 51, the Greek-Arabic psalters Mt. Sinai, MSC, gr. 34 and 35, and the four palimpsest folios with the so-called Greek-Arabic biblical odes in Milan, BA, cod. L 120 sup.,[32] all belong to the same editorial and liturgical types.[33] They are generally codices of small format and modest appearance,

29. RNB = Российская Национальная Библиотека, St. Petersburg. Rahlfs, *Verzeichnis*, 224–25n1. See the brief description in E. E. Granstrem, "Каталог греческих рукописей ленинградских хранилищ, I, Рукописи IV–IX веков," *Византийский Временник* [hereafter "*VizVrem*"] 16 (1959): 234–35. For the fragments at Sinai, see Holy Monastery and Archdiocese of Sinai, *The New Finds of Sinai* (Athens: Mount Sinai Foundation, Ministry of Culture, 1999), 147, pl. 9.

30. The precise date of 862 was established by E. Follieri, "Tommaso di Damasco e l'antica minuscola libraria greca," *Rendiconti dell'Accademia Nazionale dei Lincei*, Classe di scienze morali, storiche e filologiche 29 (1974): 145–63, reprinted in *Byzantina e Italograeca: Studi di filologia e di paleografia*, ed. A. Longo et al. (Rome: Edizioni di Storia e Letteratura, 1997), 163–84.

31. G. Galavaris, "'Sinaitic' Manuscripts in the Time of the Arabs," Δελτίον τῆς Χριστιανικῆς Ἀρχαιολογίας Ἑταιρείας [hereafter "Δελτίον"] 2 (1984): 118–20; Weitzmann-Galavaris, *Illuminated Manuscripts*, 16–17, with the colophon and reproduction (fig. 5); Perria, "Scritture e codici di origine orientale," 24. For the Uspenski Psalter, cf. Parpulov, "Psalters and Personal Piety," 100.

32. BA = Biblioteca Ambrosiana, Milano. C. Pasini, "Un frammento greco-arabo delle Odi bibliche nel palinsesto Ambrosiano L 120 sup.," *Rivista di studi bizantini e neoellenici* [hereafter "*RSBN*"] 39 (2002): 33–53. The dimensions and order of texts (Odes IV and VII) make it likely that the biblical fragments are ones lost from a psalter of the type Sinai gr. 34 or 35 and not from a "libro delle Odi" (ibid., 42), which, as such, never existed. On the problems posed by the grouping of the Odes in the edition of Rahlfs, see Taft, "Mount Athos," 181n19.

33. For a concise description see the outdated work of V. Gardthausen, *Catalogus codicum graecorum Sinaiticorum* (Oxford: Oxford University Press, 1886), 8–10; Holy Monastery and Archdiocese of Sinai, *New Finds of Sinai*, 150 and pl. 73; see also Perria, "Scritture e codici di origine orientale," 25; and also the ninth-century fragments of the trilingual (Greek-Syriac-Arabic) psalter

devoid of ornament or illustration, and for these reasons they are overlooked by the scholarly community.[34]

I.3. *The ecclesiastical, or Constantinopolitan, psalter*

The liturgical psalter of the capital collected the 150 psalms in 68 liturgical units called "antiphons" (ἀντίφωνα). As in Jerusalem, each included a variable number of psalms; the Alleluia was intercalated between the verses of the odd antiphons and a brief invocation between the even antiphons.[35] As an example, the first five antiphons are displayed in table 2.

In the psalter Rome, Biblioteca Apostolica Vaticana [hereafter "BAV"], gr. 342 (1087/88 A.D.), which belonged to Michael Attaliates (ca. 1020 to at least 1085),[36] the "Canon of the antiphons of the Psalms of the Great Church of God" is attributed to the Patriarch Anthimos I (535–36).[37] The fixed psalms of matins (Pss 3, 50, 148–50) were excluded from the system, as were those of vespers (Pss 85 and 140), called, respectively, κατόρθρον and κατὰ λυχνικόν.[38]

There are fifteen odes, which followed the psalms. The appendix could

ex. coll. Norov, Moscow, Российская Государственная Библиотека, Moscow [hereafter "RGB"], F. 201. No. 18.1, on which see N. V. Pigulevskaja, "Греко-сиро-арабская рукопись IX в.," *Палестинский сборник* 1 (1954): 59–90; B. L. Fonkič and F. B. Poljakov, "Paläographische Grundlagen der Datierung des Kölner Mani-Kodex," *BZ* 83 (1990): 24.

34. But see the cataloguing project illustrated by L. Perria and A. Luzzi, "Manoscritti greci delle province orientali dell'impero bizantino," in *Atti del VI Congresso Nazionale dell'Associazione Italiana di Studi Bizantini*, ed. T. Creazzo and G. Strano (Catania: Facoltà di Lettere e Filosofia, Università di Catania, 2004) (= *Siculorum Gymnasium* 57), 667–90, and, most recently, D. Harlfinger, "Beispiele der Maiuscula Ogivalis Inclinata von Sinai und aus Damaskus," in *Alethes Philia: Studi in onore di Giancarlo Prato*, ed. M. D'Agostino and P. Degni (Spoleto: Centro Italiano di studi sull'alto Medioevo, 2010), 2:461–77.

35. For a table with the distribution of the psalms see O. Strunk, "The Byzantine Office at Hagia Sophia," *DOP* 9–10 (1955–56): 200–201, reprinted in Strunk, *Essays on Music*, 140–41. M. Arranz, "L'office de l'Asmatikos Hesperinos ('vêpres chantées') de l'ancien Euchologe byzantin. IIe Partie: la psalmodie," *OCP* 44 (1978): 393–99; Arranz, "L'office de l'Asmatikos Orthros ('matines chantées') de l'ancien Euchologe byzantin. Ie Partie: Les prières des euchologes," *OCP* 47 (1981): 137–44.

36. On whom see the notice by A. Kazhdan in *ODB*, 1:229. On the codex see Parpulov, *Byzantine Psalters*, 98–104.

37. R. Devreesse, *Bibliothecae Apostolicae Vaticanae codices manu scripti recensiti. Codices Vaticani graeci*, vol. 2, *Codices 330–603* (Vatican City: Biblioteca Vaticana, 1937), 2:16; J. B. Pitra, *Iuris ecclesiastici graecorum historia et monumenta*, 2 vols. (Rome, 1864–68), 2:209.

38. And not κατόρθωσον and κατὰ λύχνης as transcribed by Pitra (*Iuris ecclesiastici graecorum*, 2:209). For the Constantinopolitan antiphons in the Slavic psalters see C. M. MacRobert, "The Classificatory Importance of Headings and Liturgical Directions in Church Slavonic Psalters of the 11th–15th Centuries," *Byzantinoslavica* [hereafter "*BSl*"] 57 (1996): 167–68, 174–75.

Table 2: The First Five Antiphons

Antiphon	Psalms	Refrain
I	1, 2	Ἀλληλούϊα
II	4, 5, 6	Οἰκτείρησόν με, Κύριε
III	9	Ἀλληλούϊα
IV	7–8	Σῶσον ἡμᾶς, Κύριε
V	10, 11, 12, 13	Ἀλληλούϊα

include the matins hymn (ὕμνος ἑωθινός), but in a different recension from that of the hagiopolite psalters, the Nicene-Constantinoplitan Creed, the Beatitudes of Matthew (Mt 5:3–13), and hymns from the Divine Liturgy. A particularly significant example of a Constantinopolitan psalter is the uncial codex Moscow, GIM, gr. 129D, better known as the Chludov Psalter; dated in the second half of the ninth century and famous for its marginal illumination, it was partially rewritten in minuscule at a later date.[39] The psalters Paris, BNF, gr. 20, and Mt. Athos, MP, cod. 61, belong to the same artistic and liturgical family as the Chludov.[40] A valuable table is found in the Chludov at the end of the psalms; it shows the hagiopolite subdivisions of the psalter in twenty καθίσματα and sixty Glorias (δόξαι),[41] a term which

39. GIM = Государственный Исторический Музей, Moscow. M. V. Ščepkina, *Миниатюры Хлудовской Псалтыри. Греческий иллюстрированный кодекс IX века* (Moscow: Iskusstvo, 1977). Published in this work are facsimiles of only the illuminated leaves; for the cathedral antiphons and other materials in the liturgical appendix see S. Amfilochij, *Археологическия заметки греческой псалтири, писанной в конце IX века и переписанной почти всей в XII веке с миниатюрами X–XII века, принадлежащей действительному члену Общества Древнерусского Искусства при Румянцевском Московском Музее и других Обществ А. Н. Лобков* (Moscow, 1866), 10–14. I was unable to consult the facsimile edition published by the Historical Museum of Moscow and accompanied by *Salterio griego Jlúdov (ms. gr. 129, Museo Histórico del Estado, Moscú). Libro de estudios* (Madrid: Archivo Histórico de la Ciudad de Moscú, 2007).

40. MP = Μονὴ Παντοκράτορος, Mount Athos; BNF = Bibliothèque Nationale, Paris. S. Dufrenne, *L'Illustration des psautiers grecs du Moyen âge*, vol. 1, *Pantocrator 61, Paris grec 20, British Museum 40731* (Paris: C. Klincksieck, 1966), but for the relationship of the psalters with the cathedral rite see J. Anderson, "The Palimpsest Psalter, Pantokrator Cod. 61: Its Content and Relationship to the Bristol Psalter," *DOP* 48 (1994): 199–220, esp. 207; Anderson, "The Content of the Marginal Psalter Paris. gr. 20," *RSBN* 35 (1998): 25–35, esp. 29n9.

41. Moscow, GIM, gr. 129Д, fol. 137v, Ψαλμοὶ ρν' καὶ ἰδιόγραφος α', καθίσματα κ', δόξαι ξ', reproduced in Ščepkina, *Миниатюры Хлудовской Псалтыри*, reprinted in K. Corrigan, "Salterio, arte bizantina," *Enciclopedia dell'Arte Medievale* (Rome: Istituto della Enciclopedia Italiana, 1999), 10:289.

here, perhaps for the first time, replaces ἀντίφωνον, presumably in order to avoid confusion with the Constantinopolitan system, which shares the same name but is completely different.[42]

The second half of the ninth century thus registers the first signs of interaction between the cathedral traditions of Jerusalem and Constantinople, a process that will subsequently become ever more apparent. Scribes annotate both stichometries, but with some hesitation over which system has precedence.[43] For example, we find the following notice in the psalter with exegetical catenae Oxford, BodL, Auct. D.4.1:[44]

Ὁμοῦ πάντες ψαλμοὶ ΡΝ᾽, ἀντίφωνα Ξ᾽, καθίσματα Κ᾽, στίχοι ,ΔΩΠΒ᾽ καθὼς ψάλλει ἡ ἁγία Χριστοῦ τοῦ Θεοῦ ἡμῶν πόλις· ἐν δὲ τῇ μεγάλῃ ἐκκλησίᾳ καθὼς ψάλλουσιν ἤτοι ὁ ἐκκλησιαστής, εἰσίν οἱ πάντες στίχοι ,ΒΦΜΒ᾽ δόξαις ΟΒ᾽. [All together, 150 psalms, 60 antiphons, 20 kathismata, 4,882 verses as sung in the Holy City of Christ our God; instead, in the Great Church in the manner in which they sing, that is, the ecclesiastical, they are in total 2,542 verses and 72 doxai.]

The Oxford codex was copied, in 950–51, by one Anthimos, on the commission of someone identified only as George.[45] As in Palestine, the Creed and Our Father precede the psalms, but in accordance with the Constantinopolitan tradition the vespers hymn (Φῶς ἱλαρόν) and the Canticle of Isaiah of the hagiopolite rite (fol. 314) follow the odes.[46] In Rome, BAV, Barb.

42. To the contrary, J. Mateos, *La célébration de la Parole dans la Liturgie byzantine. Étude historique*, OCA 191 (Rome: Pontificium Institutum Studiorum Orientalium, 1971), 13n21, believes that the use of ἀντίφωνον is the result of Constantinopolitan influence on the Palestinian psalter.

43. See Dorival, *Chaînes exégétiques*, 2:79–80, 123–25, 226; 3:7; 4:105.

44. Ibid., 2:123–24. BodL = Bodleian Library, Oxford.

45. The palaeographers attribute the manuscript, with reservations, to south Italy: I. Hutter, *Corpus der byzantinischen Miniaturenhandschriften*, vol. 1, *Oxford Bodleian Library*, part 1 (Stuttgart: A. Hiersemann, 1977), 27–28n18 and pls. 105–8; E. Gamillscheg et al., *Repertorium der griechischen Kopisten 800–1600*, vol. 1, *Handschriften aus Bibliotheken Grossbritanniens*, part A, *Verzeichnis der Kopisten* (Vienna: Verlag der Österreichischen Akademie der Wissenschaften, 1981), 37, no. 21; M. L. Agati, *La minuscola "bouletée,"* 2 vols. (Vatican City: Scuola Vaticana di Paleografia, Diplomatica e Archivistica, 1992), 1:32–33, 311, 329, and pl. 15 in vol. 2. On the iconographic program see I. Ševčenko, "Caption to a David Cycle in the Tenth-Century Oxford Auct. D.4.1," in *Πολύπλευρος νοῦς. Miscellanea für Peter Schreiner zum 60. Geburtstag*, ed. C. Sholtz and G. Makris (Leipzig: Saur, 2000), 324–41. See also Parpulov, *Byzantine Psalters*, 65–70.

46. Designated ὕμνος νυκτερινὸς ἐκ τῆς προφητείας Ἡσαίου. S. Korakides, Ἀρχαῖοι ὕμνοι, vol. 1, Ἡ ἐπιλύχνιος εὐχαριστία: Φῶς ἱλαρὸν ἁγίας δόξης … (PhD diss., Ethnikon kai Kapodistriakon Panepistemion Athenon, 1979), pl. 19 reproduces fol. 314.

gr. 285, an Italo-Greek manuscript of the eleventh century (?), we have a provincial and by now perfected example of a "bi-ritual" psalter, one resulting from the fusion of the hagiopolite and Constantinopolitan systems. The scribe does not limit himself to supplying the two stichometries with the division into καθίσματα–δόξαι and ἀντίφωνα; he also highlights the Constantinopolitan stichometry using initial letters that are both superscript and larger than those of the Jerusalem stichometry. Here, for example, is Psalm 132:

'Ιδοὺ δὴ τί καλὸν ἢ τί τερπνὸν
ἀλλ' ἢ τὸ κατοικεῖν ἀδελφοὺς ἐπὶ τὸ αὐτό;
ὡς μύρον ἐπὶ κεφαλῆς τὸ καταβαῖνον ἐπὶ πώγωνα,
τὸν πώγωνα τὸν Ἀαρών,
Τὸ καταβαῖνον ἐπὶ τὴν ᾤαν τοῦ ἐνδύματος αὐτοῦ·
ὡς δρόσος Ἀερμὼν ἡ καταβαίνουσα ἐπὶ τὰ ὄρη Σιών·
ὅτι ἐκεῖ ἐνετείλατο κύριος τὴν εὐλογίαν
καὶ ζωὴν ἕως τοῦ αἰῶνος.

The system of biblical canticles is also doubled, including the Hymn of the Three Youths (Dn 3:57–90), given according to both the Septuagint (Constantinople) and Theodotion (Jerusalem) editions,[47] and the matins hymn *Gloria in excelsis*, duplicated in recension, while from the hagiopolite psalters the vespers hymn and the Canticle of Isaiah are inserted expressly for the (monastic) prayer of the evening (εἰς τὰ ἀποδείπνια).[48] Gregor Hanke is therefore correct when he speaks of "hybride liturgische Psalters," but it is precisely in the second half of the eleventh century that we see the change. Rather than having the two traditions exist side by side, they begin to flow into one another. Two Constantinopolitan psalters of exceptional historic and artistic value, Rome, BAV, Barb. gr. 372, from the beginning of the sixth decade of the eleventh century,[49] and the BAV, gr. 342, of 1087–88 (the one that contains the canon of the psalm antiphons of the Great Church), attest

47. Schneider, "Oden," 433–41.

48. Hanke, "Odenkanon," 360–62.

49. See J. Anderson, "The Date and Purpose of the Barberini Psalter," *Cahiers archéologiques* 31 (1983): 35–67, and the facsimile J. Anderson et al., *The Barberini Psalter Codex Vaticanus Barberinianus Graecus 372* (Zurich: Belser, 1989); I. Hutter, "Theodoros βιβλιογράφος und die Buchmalerei in Studiu," *BollGrott* 51 (1997): 177–208.

to the dissemination of the hagiopolite stichometry in the Byzantine capital.[50] The eleventh- or twelfth-century psalter Florence, BML, plut. 5.5, has cathedral antiphons, but the stichometry is hagiopolite, as is the macrodivision into καθίσματα;[51] this same division, but without cathedral antiphons, is found in the Constantinopolitan psalter Venice, BM, gr. I.32, dated 1083.[52] Naturally, the opposite combination is also attested; it is, in fact, seen in the Harvard Psalter, which has the hagiopolite macrodivision into καθίσματα but stichometry of the Constantinopolitan type. The model destined to establish itself will be precisely this type, in which the nine canticles and several hymns for the Divine Liturgy follow the psalms.

I.4. *The augmented psalter*

Although the practice of adding liturgical appendices of various lengths at the end of the psalter is ancient, its evolution is difficult to trace. In fact, the psalter was and remains a liturgical text used on a daily basis, so it was more subject to wear and tear than other kinds of books. For this reason many handwritten copies, including ones of considerable importance, lack their initial or final gatherings, sometimes both.

Among contemporary editions for the Russian Orthodox Church, there is still an "augmented psalter" (Ψалтирь следованнаѧ), in the sense that the book of psalms continues with a supplement and the supplement may be the horologion, which remains the most natural complement.[53] The oldest specimen of the psalter horologion is the above-mentioned Turin, BNU, cod. B.VII.30, seriously damaged in the 1904 fire that devastated what was then the Biblioteca Reale.[54] The codex was copied in an upright ogival hand and

---

50. For Vat. gr. 342 see Devreesse, *Codices Vaticani graeci*, 2:16.

51. BML = Biblioteca Medicea Laurenziana, Florence. A. M. Bandini, *Catalogus codicum manuscriptorum Bibliothecae Mediceae Laurentianae*, ed. E. Rostagno et al. (Leipzig: Zentral-Antiquariat der Deutschen Demokratischen Republik, 1961), 1:13–14.

52. BM = Biblioteca Marciana, Venice. E. Mioni, *Bibliothecae Divi Marci Venetiarum Codices Graeci Manuscripti*, 3 vols. in 6 parts (Rome: Instituto Poligrafico dello Stato, 1981–85), 1.1:40–41.

53. N. Egender, introduction to *La Prière des Heures (Horologion)* (Chevetogne: Éditions de Chevetogne, 1975), 51–52.

54. *Codices manuscripti Bibliothecae Regii Taurinensis athenei, per linguas digesti, & binas in partes distribuiti, in quarum prima hebraei & graeci, in altera latini, italici, & gallici*, ed. J. Pasinus et al. (Turin, 1749), 470–71: "Sequuntur nonnulla ad *Officium* Ecclesiasticum spectantia, *troparia* nimirum, hymni, aliaque variis horis diei, & media nocte canenda cum propriis tonis." Parenti, "Nota sul Salterio-Horologion," 275–87.

is likely to be of ninth-century Italo-Greek origin,[55] and the scribe included catenae for both psalms and odes (Catena Typus XXVI).[56]

For the eleventh century, there is the Italo-Greek psalter of the Constantinopolitan type Rome, BAV, gr. 1966, where the appendix includes the ἀπόδειπνον, unfortunately mutilated.[57] In the recently discovered final part of the Glagolitic psalter at Mt. Sinai, MSC, sl. 1/N, the vespers of the Stoudite tradition are described.[58] With the twelfth century, the horologion reappears as an appendix to the Harvard Psalter of 1105, and Athens, EBE, 15 (ca. 1180).[59] For the subsequent eras, I note, without claim to comprehensiveness: Mt. Sinai, MSC, gr. 125 (1248 A.D.);[60] Mt. Athos, MI, cod. 65 (997 A.D.);[61] Mt. Athos, MDoch, cod. 50; Rome, BAV, gr. 1866,[62] and Madrid,

---

55. According to Parpulov, *Byzantine Psalters*, 55–56, the leaves with the prologues to the psalms by Hesychios of Jerusalem and Cyril of Alexandria—and now Verona, Biblioteca Capitolare, CXIX/109—would be *membrum disiectum* of the Turin manuscript. On the leaf in Verona, attributed to south Italy on the basis of script, see the note by M. D'Agostino, "Esichio di Gerusalemme ... Verona, Biblioteca Capitolare, cod. 119," in *Splendori di Bisanzio. Testimonianze e riflessi d'arte e cultura bizantina nelle Chiese d'Italia* (Milan: Fabbri, 1990), 216–17; further bibliography in Rahlfs-Fraenkel, *Verzeichnis*, 370.

56. See M. Geerard, ed., *Clavis patrum graecorum* (Turnhout: Brepols, 1974–87) 4:C1027, C39; Dorival, *Chaînes exégétiques*, 2:126–41.

57. Vat. gr. 1966, fol. 183r, Ἀκολουθία τῶν ἀποδειπνίων· Συναγώμεθα καὶ λέγωμεν· Δόξα Πατρί ... des. Παναγία Τριὰς ὁμοούσιε μὴ χωρί [...]. The manuscript belongs to the so-called scuola niliana; see M. Ceresa-S. Lucà, "Frammenti greci di Dioscoride Pedanio e Aezio Amideno in una edizione a stampa di Francesco Zanetti (Roma 1576)," in *Miscellanea Bibliothecae Apostolicae Vaticanae XV* (Vatican City: Biblioteca Apostolica Vaticana, 2007), 200, 200n23, 226, pl. XII.

58. P. Fetková et al., *Psalterii Sinaitici pars nova (monasterii s. Catharinae codex slav. 2/N)* (Vienna: Österreichische Akademie der Wissenschaften, 1977), 128–31. E. Velkovska, "Денонощното богослужение в Синайския евхологий," *Palaeobulgarica* 24, no. 4 (2000): 32–34.

59. E. C. Constantinides, "The Tetraevangelion Manuscript 93 of the Athens National Library," Δελτίον 9 (1977–79): 208–14; A. Cutler, *The Aristocratic Psalters in Byzantium* (Paris: Picard, 1984), 17–18.

60. Gardthausen, *Catalogus Sinaiticorum*, 25.

61. MI = Μονὴ Ἰβήρων, Mount Athos. P. Soteroudes, *Κατάλογος ἑλληνικῶν χιερογράφων* (Mt. Athos, 1998), 1:124–26.

62. MDoch = Μονὴ Δοχειαρίου, Mount Athos. P. Canart, *Bibliothecae Apostolicae Vaticanae Codices manu scripti ... Codices Vaticani graeci: Codices 1745–1962*, vol. 1, *Codicum enarrationes* (Vatican City: Biblioteca Apostolica Vaticana, 1970), 395–403, with textual additions, after 1480, of hieromonachos Gioacchino di Casole, on whom see M. Re, "Copisti salentini in Calabria e in Sicilia," *RSBN* 41 (2004): 109, 111–12. According to Re (112), the additions to the codex by the copyist Gioacchino—those regarding the determination of solar and lunar cycles, of the indiction, leap years, the date of Easter, together with predictions (*sortes*) from the Psalms—show a certain interest in chronological calculations ("sembra fosse interessato ai calcoli cronologici"). In reality such psalter complements are normal and have nothing to do with copyists' mathematical interests. On this subject see Parpulov, *Byzantine Psalters*, 20, 508–15; "Psalters and Personal Piety," 86 and 88.

BNE, Vitr. 26–5[63] (fourteenth century); the later Mt. Athos, MK, cod. 88, and MDoch, cod. 57;[64] Paris, BNF, gr. 12 (1419 A.D.);[65] Rome, BC, cod. 240 (*olim* G.VI.5) (late fifteenth to early sixteenth century);[66] and, in a certain sense, Mt. Sinai, MSC, gr. 49 (1120 A.D.).[67] In these cases, only the incipit is given for the psalms, since the complete text is to be found in the attached psalter. With the passage of time, the appendix to the psalter expands to include private prayers or the Akathistos Hymn.[68]

In the Russian church, the augmented psalter also includes a series of hymns and prayers to be recited at the end of each kathisma; designed for private devotion, they constitute what is called the "Office of the Psalter,"[69] but there are also editions in which these supplements are inserted directly after each kathisma.[70] A connection between the augmented Russian psalter and the Greek manuscript tradition was first established in 1885 by Nikolaj Krasnosel'cev in the description of the fourteenth-century psalter, Rome, BAV, gr. 778,[71] but the practice of adding supplements is earlier and begins

63. I. Pérez Martín, "El 'estilo Hodegos' y su proyección en las escrituras constantinopolitanas," *Segno e testo* 6 (2008), 389–458. BNE = Biblioteca Nacional de España, Madrid.

64. Dated to the thirteenth century by S. Lambros, *Catalogue of the Greek Manuscripts on Mount Athos* (Cambridge, 1895), 1:282, it contains a horologion similar to the *textus receptus*, therefore datable to at least the fifteenth century in Mt. Athos, MDoch, cod. 57 (twelfth century), fol. 131r, there is another horologion like the *textus receptus*. MK = Μονὴ Κουτλουμουσίου, Mount Athos.

65. H. Omont, *Inventaire sommaire des manuscrits grecs de la Bibliothèque Nationale* (Paris, 1886), 1:3. E. Gamillscheg et al., *Repertorium der griechischen Kopisten 800–1600*, vol. 2, *Handschriften aus Bibliotheken Frankreichs* (Vienna: Österreichische Akademie der Wissenschaften, 1989), part A, 141, no. 371; 137–38, no. 371; part C, pl. 205.

66. BC = Biblioteca Casanatense, Rome. S. Moretti, "Vulgo 'miniatura' appellatur: i manoscritti greci miniati e decorati delle biblioteche pubbliche statali di Roma," *Nuovi Annali della Scuola Speciale per Archivisti e Bibliotecari* 18 (2004): 72–73, with bibliography.

67. Described in D. Harlfinger et al., *Specimina Sinaitica. Die datierten griechischen Handschriften des Katharinen-Klosters auf dem Berge Sinai: 9. bis 12. Jahrhundert* (Berlin: Dietrich Reimer, 1983), 42–43, pls. 99–103; following the various appendices is the ordinary for the hours of the day.

68. In Mt. Athos, Μονὴ Βατοπεδίου [hereafter "MV"], cod. 761 (1088 A.D.), fol. 235r+v, a prayer to the guardian angel; in Mt. Athos, MDoch, cod. 53 (thirteenth century), fol. 207r, the Akathistos, as in the Tomič Psalter (Moscow, Государственный Исторический Музей [hereafter "GIM"], 2752), a Bulgarian manuscript datable to around 1360–62; facsimile edition: A. Džurova, *Tomič Psalter*, vol. 2 (Sofia: Tsentăr za Slavjano-Vizantijski Prouchvanija "Ivan Duichev," 1990), ff. 273r–302v; cf. Parpulov, *Byzantine Psalters*, 23; "Psalters and Personal Piety," 93–94.

69. Egender, "Introduction," 52; also the solution adopted among the Copts: U. Zanetti, "La distribution des psaumes dans l'horologion copte," *OCP* 56 (1990): 323–69.

70. E.g., Ѱалтирь (Moscow: Sinodal'naja Tipografija, 1913).

71. N. F. Krasnosel'cev, *Сведения о некоторых литургических рукописях Ватиканской Би-*

precisly with our Harvard Psalter. In the twelfth and following centuries we have, for example, Mt. Sinai, MSC, gr. 44 (ca. 1121),[72] the previously cited Athens, EBE, 15 (ca. 1180) and Venice, BM, gr. II.113 (coll. 565),[73] Vienna, ÖNb, theol. gr. 177 (ca. 1150),[74] Venice, BM, gr. I. 49 (coll. 1213),[75] Mt. Athos, MI, cod. 22 (187) (twelfth century), 65 (997), and 74 (1194) (thirteenth century),[76] Rome, BAV, gr. 341 (1021 A.D.),[77] Venice, BM, gr. I.27 (coll. 1398) (late fourteenth century),[78] and others, including the late examples[79] and the printed editions.[80] The Greek model then spread to the Balkans, introduced by St. Sava, Archbishop of Serbia (d. 1235) and attested by the Norov Psalter (fourteenth century),[81] and in Russia by the Simonovs- kaja Psalter of 1280.[82] The Russian tradition thus continues an editorial type

блиотеки, Kazan 1885, 37–39; cf. Devreesse, *Codices Vaticani graeci*, 3:293–96, and C. Giannelli, *Bibliothecae Apostolicae Vaticanae codices manu scripti … Codices Vaticani Graeci. Codices 1485– 1683* (Vatican City: Bibliotheca Vaticana, 1950), 111 (Rome, BAV, gr. 1541).

72. Harlfinger et al., *Specimina Sinaitica*, 43–44.

73. Mioni, *Codices Venetiarum*, 1.1:335–36; in addition, see the entry by P. Eleuteri, "Salterio [Venice, Biblioteca Marciana gr. Z 540]" [hereafter "BM"], in *Oriente cristiano e santità. Figure e storie di santi tra Bisanzio e l'Occidente*, ed. S. Gentile (Rome: Centro Tibaldi, 1998), 199–200, with bibliography.

74. ÖNb = Österreichische Nationalbibliothek, Vienna. H. Hunger et al., *Katalog der griechischen Handschriften der Österreichischen Nationalbibliothek*, 4 vols. in 6 parts (Vienna: Ös- terreichische Nationalbibliothek, 1961–64), 3.2:316–27.

75. Mioni, *Codices Venetiarum*, 1.1:65–66, dates the codex to the eleventh century, but cf. Mar- gherita Losacco, "Venezia, Biblioteca Nazionale Marciana, gr. I 49 (coll 1213), c. 252v," www.bml. firenze.sbn.it/rinascimentovirtuale/pannello22.shtm.

76. Soteroudes, *Κατάλογος*, 141–42.

77. Devreesse, *Codices Vaticani graeci*, 2:13–15. The supplement is from the thirteenth century.

78. Mioni, *Codices Venetiarum*, 1.1:32–33.

79. P. Canart, *Catalogue des manuscrits grecs de l'Archivio di San Pietro* (Vatican City: Biblioteca Apostolica Vaticana, 1966), 53–57; Athens, Byzantine Museum, cod. 171 (nineteenth century), for which see D. I. Pallas, *Κατάλογος τῶν χειρογραφῶν τοῦ Βυζαντινοῦ Μουσείου Ἀθηνῶν* (Athens: Typographeion Katastematon S. Kousoulinou, 1955), 3:57–58.

80. For the editions of the Greek psalter in the fifteenth and sixteenth centuries see E. Layton, *The Sixteenth Century Greek Book in Italy: Printers and Publishers for the Greek World* (Venice: In- stituto Ellenico di Studi bizantini e Postbizantini di Venezia, 1994), 131–32; and Parpulov, "Psalters and Personal Piety," 92n1. There also exists a contemporary French translation: P. D. Guillaume, *Psaumes et Cantiques avec les cathismes et les prières de la tradition byzantine* (Rome: Diaconie Apostolique, 1990).

81. *Норовская Псалтырь. Среднеболгарская рукопись XIV века* (Sofia: Bălgarska akademija na naukite, 1989), 1:52–56. On the role of St. Sava, cf. Parpulov, "Psalters and Personal Piety," 91–92.

82. S. Amfilochij, *Древле-славянская Псалтирь Симоновская до 1280 года*, 3 vols. (Mos- cow, 1880–82); see also M. Momina, "Песнопения древних славяно-русских рукописей," in *Методическе рекомендации по описанию славяно-русских рукописей для Сводного каталога рукописей, хранящихся в СССР, вып. 2* (Moscow: Institut istorii CCCP, 1976), 462–66.

that is well-documented in the Greek sphere and is far from being "singulière" or "unusual."[83] No studies exist with respect to the augmented psalter,
and the presentation of the Harvard Psalter may represent an opportunity
to offer an initial investigation.

I.5. Conclusion

The manuscript tradition of the oldest Greek psalters, those of the ninth
and tenth centuries, reveals the existence of two cathedral systems that can
be traced to the Anastasis of Jerusalem (*hagiopolitis*) and the Great Church
of Constantinople (*ekklesiastis*). The Jerusalem system was divided into
kathismata and antiphons, whereas the Constantinopolitan relied solely on
antiphons; and in both systems the psalms were grouped in numerical succession. The widespread view that the division of the psalter by kathismata
is peculiar to Palestinian monasticism must therefore be abandoned.

Antiphons and/or kathismata are only grouping systems, and they have
parallels in other liturgical traditions. All that really distinguished the *hagiopolitis* from the *ekklesiastis* was the stichometry—double in number in
Jerusalem over that of Constantinople, where the verses were twice as long—
which gave rise to differences in the performance of antiphonated psalmody.
When, in the ninth century, Constantinopolitan monasteries adopt the hagiopolite division of the psalter into kathismata—but not necessarily the
simple stichometry—the antiphon begins to take the name of "Doxa" and
then "stasis." By the tenth century bi-ritual psalters appear which take into
account both stichometries.

The augmented type of psalter with horologion is confirmed in southern
Italy from the end of the ninth century, and in Constantinople at the beginning of the twelfth century. Byzantine examples of augmented psalters with
hymns and prayers at the conclusion of each kathisma are known at the
beginning of the twelfth century, precisely the time of the Harvard Psalter.

---

83. See R. Devreesse, *Introduction à l'étude des manuscrits grecs* (Paris: C. Klincksieck, 1954),
193: "une présentation singulière, où les vingt καθίσματα sont accompagnés de prières, d'hymnes
et de tropaires: c'est le 'psautier continué.'" According to MacRobert, *The Classificatory Importance*, 167n47: "Some ... manuscripts also share unusual devotional texts for recitation between
the *kathismata*."

II

The Harvard Psalter

II.1. *Definition and structure*

The discussion of the manuscript tradition of the Greek psalter now allows us to define the Cambridge manuscript as an augmented psalter using cathedral stichometry, divided into kathismata followed by hymns and prayers (fols. 9r–215r) and completed by a horologion (fols. 233r–261r), with menologion (fols. 262r–279v), appendices (fols. 279v–281r), and Paschal tables for the years from 1105–24 (fols. 282r–289r).

According to the augmented psalter type, each of the twenty kathismata presents the following structure:[84]

1) Trisagion-Pater
2) Kyrie eleison (forty times)
3) hymnography
4) prayer

II.2. *Trisagion-Pater and Kyrie eleison*

This is the well-known set of prayers that opens and closes the offices in various Eastern traditions. As Juan Mateos has shown and Gabriele Winkler[85] confirmed, they were originally final prayers, later duplicated at the beginning of the celebration according to a process that is completed by the ninth-century horologion Mt. Sinai, MSC, gr. 863.[86] Evident here is the editorial tendency to standardize the beginnings and endings of rites.[87]

---

84. On the hymns and prayers that eventually conclude the kathismata of the augmented psalter one should note S. Amfilochij, "О покаянных тропарях и молитвах или стихирах, в древне-Греческих и древне-Славянских Псалтирях после каждой кафисмы," *Чтения в Обществе любителей духовного просвящения* 17 suppl. (1880): 132–49. I wish to thank to Fr. Michael Zheltov for providing me with a copy of this (hard to find) work.

85. J. Mateos, "Prières initiales fixes des offices syrien, maronite et byzantin," *L'Orient Syrien* 11 (1966): 488–98; Mateos, "La synaxe monastique des vêpres byzantines," *OCP* 36 (1970): 251–55; G. Winkler, "The Armenian Night Office I: The Historical Background of the Introductory Part of Gišerayin Žam," *Journal of the Society for Armenian Studies* 1 (1984): 95–100.

86. Mateos, "Horologion de Saint-Sabas," 48, 76.

87. R. F. Taft, "How Liturgies Grow: The Evolution of the Byzantine 'Divine Liturgy,'" *OCP* 43 (1977): 378, reprinted in Taft, *Beyond East and West: Problems in Liturgical Understanding*, 2nd ed. (Rome: Pontificio Instituto Orientale, 1997), 231–32.

II.3. *Hymnography: the problem of the kathisma*

The hymnographic section includes three elements intercalated in the doxology:

1) Penitential troparion

    Glory to the Father, the Son and the Holy Spirit.

2) Penitential troparion

    Now and forever and ever. Amen.

3) Theotokion (Marian troparion)

"Troparion" (literally *refrain*) is the generic term specific to the Constantinopolitan rite, and it refers to each liturgical hymn of ecclesiastical (that is, non-biblical) composition.[88] Originally conceived in terms of a psalm, the troparion later became an element that was independent.[89] In terms of structure and liturgical function, it corresponds to the Roman *antiphona*,[90] the Palestinian *hypakoe*, and the Eastern-Syrian *hepakta* / *ōnītā*.[91] In the Harvard Psalter the first troparion that follows the second kathisma of the psalter (Pss 9–16) is defined as penitential because of its content (κατανυκτικόν), but looking more closely it becomes apparent that all forty troparia are penitential, since they invoke divine mercy using the first person. It should also be noted that the forty troparia and the twenty theotokia are arranged in descending order according to the eight modes; the "authentic" modes cover the first ten kathismata and the plagal cover the second set of ten, as shown in table 3.[92]

88. Mateos, *Typicon*, 2:323–25.

89. R. F. Taft, "Christian Liturgical Psalmody: Origins, Development, Decomposition, Collapse," in *Psalms in Community: Jewish and Christian Textual, Liturgical, and Artistic Traditions*, ed. H. W. Attridge and M. E. Fassler (Atlanta: Society of Biblical Literature, 2003), 20.

90. In translating the Greek version of the *Dialogues* of Gregory the Great (IV, 35), Pope Zaccaria (741–52) rendered *antiphona* as τροπάριον. See *Patrologiae cursus completus, Series latina*, ed. J.-P. Migne, 220 vols. (Paris, 1844–64), 77:375 [hereafter "PL"]; C. Hannick, "Hymnen: II. Orthodoxe Kirche," in *Theologische Realenzyklopädie*, ed. H. Balz (Berlin: De Gruyter, 1976–86), 15:763.

91. Mateos, *Célébration de la Parole*, 15–21; cf. J. Mateos, *Lelya-Sapra. Essai d'interprétation des matines chaldéennes* (Rome: Pontificium Institutum Studiorum Orientalium, 1959), 488, 492–93.

92. On the Byzantine tonal system see P. Jeffery, "The Earliest Oktôêchoi: The Role of Jerusalem and Palestine in the Beginning of Modal Ordering," in *The Study of Medieval Chant: Paths and Bridges, East and West: In Honor of Kenneth Levy*, ed. P. Jeffery (Woodbridge: Boydell, 2001), 147–209, and, in particular, the study of S. S. R. Frøyshov, "The Early Development of the Liturgical Eight-mode System in Jerusalem," *SVThQ* 51 (2007): 193–203.

Table 3: Arrangement of
Kathisma and Modes

Kathisma	Mode
I–III	I
IV–V	II
VI–VII	III
VIII–X	IV
XI–XIII	I plagal
XIV–XV	II plagal
XVI–XVII	grave
XIX–XX	IV plagal

The tonal system and penitential content direct our inquiry to the manuscript tradition of hymnographic collections, such as the contemporary manuscripts of the "parakletike," where, unlike modern editions, the texts are ordered one after another according to the hymnographic genre and with no attempt to distribute them by the days of the week. From such generic collections it is almost impossible to know how many of the hymns were actually used in the services.[93] If, for example, we compare the penitential troparia and theotokia of kathismata IV and V (mode II) of the Harvard Psalter with the eleventh-century "parakletike" Mt. Sinai, MSC, gr. 778,[94] we have the arrangement displayed in table 4.

According to the definition established by Christian Hannick, and as indicated in the title of the manuscript, the Sinai. gr. 778 is a stichero-kathismatarion,[95] that is, a collection of stichera (troparia to be inserted into the fixed psalms of vespers and the lauds) and of kathismata. Our texts are found precisely among the latter, which are arranged as follows in the Sinai manuscript:

93. C. Hannick, "Le texte de l'Oktoechos," in *La Prière des Églises de rite byzantine* (Chevetogne: Éditions de Chevetogne, 1972–75), 3:42.

94. On the manuscript see H. Husmann, "Hymnus und Troparion. Studie zur Geschichte der musikalischen Gattungen von Horologion und Tropologion," *Jahrbuch der Staatlichen Instituts für Musikforschung Preussischer Kulturbesitz* (1971): 41.

95. Sinai. gr. 778, fol. 1r: ἀρχὴ σὺν Θεῷ τῶν στιχηρῶν καθισμάτων τῶν ὀκτὼ ἤχων. Hannick, "Oktoechos," 42–43; for the corresponding Slavic tradition see M. Jovčeva, *Солунският Октоих в контекста на южнославянските октоиси до XIV в.* (Sofia: Kirilo-Metodievski Naučen Centăr, 2004).

Table 4: Comparison of Harvard Psalter and Mt. Sinai, gr. 778

Sinai MSC gr. 778	Harvard Psalter
Ἐγὼ ὑπάρχω τὸ δένδρον…	Ὡς κύματα θαλάσσης…
Ὡς κύματα θαλάσσης…	Ἐγὼ ὑπάρχω τὸ δένδρον…
Ἐλέησόν με, εἶπεν ὁ Δαβίδ…	Ἐλέησόν με ὁ Θεός, ἐλέησόν με, ἐπὶ δυσὶν…
Ἐλέησόν με ὁ Θεός, ἐλέησόν με, ἐπὶ δυσὶν…	Ἐλέησόν με, εἶπεν ὁ Δαβίδ…
Φοβερός σου ὁ θρόνος…	
…	
	Θεοτόκε μὴ παρίδης με…
Σὲ μεγαλύνομεν, Θεοτόκε, βοῶντες· χαῖρε τὸ ὄρος…	Σὲ μεγαλύνομεν, Θεοτόκε, βοῶντες…
Σὲ μεγαλύνομεν, Θεοτόκε, βοῶντες· χαῖρε ἁγίων ἁγιωτέρα…	

1) Καθίσματα ἀναστάσιμα εἰς τὸ Θεὸς Κύριος

2) Ὕμνοι τριαδικοί

3) Καθίσματα κατανυκτικά

4) Καθίσματα θεοτοκία

Here is a perfect example of the ambiguity and superimposition of meanings that is so common in Greek liturgical terminology. According to lexicons, dictionaries, and glossaries,[96] a κάθισμα is (1) one of the twenty sections of the hagiopolite psalter and (2) the matins hymn that follows the reading of the psalm kathisma; and (3) in the Muscovite recension, the hymn placed after the sixth ode in the Marian canon of apodeipnon.[97]

In order to avoid possible confusion, a few contemporary translators have thought to distinguish between (a) the *kathisma* that is simply recited,

---

96. E.g., L. Clugnet, *Dictionnaire grec-français des noms liturgiques en usage dans l'Église grecque* (Paris, 1895, reprinted in London: Valorium, 1971), 71; Arranz, *Typicon de Messine*, 407; G. Vergoti, *Λεξικὸ λειτουργικῶν καὶ τελετουργικῶν ὅρων* (Thessaloniki: Ektyposis Bibliodesia, 1988), 62–63.

97. E.g., *Октоихъ, сирѣчь осмогласникъ*, 2 vols. (Moscow: Izdatel'skij Sovet Russkoj Pravoslavnoj Cerkvi, 2004), 1:62.

and (b) the *poetic kathisma*.[98] As regards its literal meaning, "kathisma" appears to indicate a hymn to be sung while sitting following the psalms (from καθίζω, sit); they, in turn, are collected in a kathisma of three στάσεις, thus called because read and heard while standing. The Slavs resolved the problem by reserving the loan word Каθисма for the section of the psalter and indicating the "poetic kathisma" with Сѣдаленъ (literally, "session").[99]

The proposed etymology is not altogether convincing. As we have already seen, in the oldest dated and datable examples of the hagiopolite psalter—all from the ninth century, in which the Byzantinization of the Jerusalem rite was at its initial stage[100]—the subsections of the psalter were not called "staseis." They were instead called "antiphonon,"[101] thus removing from the stasis-kathisma (standing/sitting) equation one of the necessary elements. We have also seen that the eleventh-century stichero-kathismatarion Mt. Sinai, MSC, gr. 778, denotes the hymn to be intercalated in the Θεὸς Κύριος (Ps 117:27) as a kathisma, a choice that also occurs in the earlier Mt. Sinai, MSC, gr. 1593 (ninth or tenth century), which has survived without the first four modes.[102] The kathisma at Θεὸς Κύριος is one of the most solemn elements of the matins. In Byzantine terminology it would be called the principal "troparion of the day" (τροπάριον τῆς ἡμέρας), and it would

---

98. *Prière des Heures*, 505; *Dimanche*, 595.

99. See Ѱалтирь, 13; Октωихъ, 1:30–31.

100. J. Nasrallah, "La liturgie des patriarchats melchites de 969 à 1300," *Oriens Christianus* 71 (1987): 156–81; C. Hannick, "Annexions et reconquêtes byzantines. Peut-on parler d''uniatisme' byzantin?," *Irénikon* 66 (1993): 151–74; K. Leeming, "The Adoption of Arabic as a Liturgical Language by the Palestinian Melkites," *Aram* 15 (2003): 239–46; K.-P. Todt, "Region und griechisch-orthodoxes Patriarchat von Antiocheia in mittelbyzantinischer Zeit (969-1084)," *BZ* 94 (2001): 239–67; D. Galadza, "Liturgical Byzantinization in Jerusalem: al-Bīrunī's Melkite Calendar in Context," *BollGrott* 7 (2010): 69–85, and especially D. Galadza, *Worship in the Holy City in Captivity: The Liturgical Byzantinization of the Orthodox Patriarchate of Jerusalem After the Arab Conquest (8th–13th c.)* (Excerpta ex Dissertatione ad Doctoratum, PIO, Roma, 2013).

101. See above § I.2; nonetheless, M. Arranz erroneously supposed that the division into staseis is also found in the hagiopolite RNB, gr. 216 (+ Sinai, MSC, NE ΜΓ 33), of 862 A.D.; cf. M. Arranz, "Les grandes étapes de la Liturgie byzantine: Palestine-Byzance-Russie. Essai d'aperçu historique," in *Liturgie de l'Église particulière et liturgie de l'Église universelle* (Rome: Edizioni Liturgiche, 1976), 57–58.

102. The surviving sections of the manuscript are poorly preserved and difficult to read in the microfilm; at fol. 13v is found Καθίσματα ἀναστάσιμα εἰς τὸ Θεὸς Κύριος· Τὸ φαιδρὸν τῆς ἀναστάσεως κήρυγμα …; for further analysis, see the recent study of O. A. Krašeninnikova, *Древне-неславянский Октоих св. Климента архиепископа Охридского по древнерусским спискам XIII–XV веков* (Moscow: Jazyki Slavjanskih Kul'tur, 2006), 302–15.

be repeated at the end of the celebration, where and for which reason it is called the troparion "of dismissal" (ἀπολυτίκιον).[103] Thus, it is difficult to imagine the recitation while sitting of at least this one type of kathisma. In reality, the distinction between kathisma/stasis is subsequent to kathisma/antiphonon, and it is documented in the eleventh-century Byzantine—not hagiopolite—psalters.[104]

Juan Mateos, who held this then-current opinion, gets credit for at least having clarified kathisma as the Palestinian term for the Byzantine troparion.[105] As an example of the rudimentary manner of performing, he offered the then unpublished example taken from the horologion Mt. Sinai, MSC, gr. 864:

> [1] *Kathisma, mode II:* Lift me up, Lord, to adore you, open my lips to sing you hymns, cancel the multitudes of my sins, give me a spirit of authentic compunction for salvation: welcome, Christ God, my prayer,
> * you who can do anything, O only friend of man.
>
> [2] *Verse:* [Ps 56:2] Have mercy on me, O God, mercy on me,
> in you I entrust my soul
> and I hope, in the shadow of your wings, as long as iniquity will pass
> * you who can do anything, O only friend of man.
>
> [3] *Doxology:* [Glory to the Father ... for ever and ever. Amen]
>
> [4] *Theotokion:* Mother of God do not reject me when I beg for your assistance ...[106]

The structural similarity with the Constantinople troparion is evident: we have [1] a non-biblical refrain (kathisma) intercalated into [2] psalmody, which in our case appears already in contracted form, [3] the Gloria, a distinguishing element of antiphonal psalmody, and [4] a concluding refrain

---

103. Mateos, *Typicon*, 2:285; Arranz, *Typicon de Messine*, 387.

104. Mateos, "Horologion de Saint-Sabas," 59–60; Mateos, *Célébration de la Parole*, 21n59. Vat. gr. 341, cited by Mateos as thirteenth century, is dated 1021, and the indication of κά(θισμα) at the end of each kathisma is by a hand other than the principal scribe's.

105. Mateos, *Célébration de la Parole*, 21.

106. Ibid., now available in the edition Ajjoub and Paramelle, ed., *Livre d'Heures du Sinaï*, 240–41, but see in this regard my review in *OCP* 72 (2006): 268.

which is different from the initial one (the perisse of Constantinople).[107] This manner of chanting the kathisma, despite some secondary modifications (final disappearance of the psalm), is still preserved in the Muscovite and Italo-Byzantine recensions.[108] The kathisma is quite a different thing from a troparion to be sung while sitting, as has long been thought. What, then, is its etymology?

The problem was posed by Heinrich Husmann, who advanced the lexicographical and etymological aspects of the question. In classical Greek, κάθισμα can mean "place," "location," "support," or "foundation"[109]; in short, I would be tempted to translate "kathisma" as "supporting unit." A kathisma is the supporting unit of the hagiopolite psalter, as it is of the antiphonal psalmody in the same tradition. Resorting to architectural terminology is not new and should not be surprising; it is enough to remember that the verses of a kontakion are still called οἶκοι, that is, "homes," a term which finds a valid parallel in the "stanzas" of Italian renaissance poetry.[110] In late Greek, a kathisma is a "residence,"[111] and in the monastic terminology of Mt. Athos the annex to a monastery.[112]

Finally, it is significant that in the Harvard Psalter, divided into kathismata and no longer into antiphona, the hymnographic kathismata which follow the psalmody are called "troparia," almost as if to avoid any possible confusion. From this standpoint, we can clearly see that in the mind of an early twelfth-century Constantinopolitan, kathisma and troparion are perfectly identical in function and musical performance, so much so that both can be sung using the same melodic pattern. In confirmation, it can be added that a certain number of hymnographic manuscripts of the eleventh

107. The Perisse (Περισσή) or "appendix" is a concluding refrain of antiphonal psalmody, which is located after the doxology "Glory to the Father ..." and which is at times diverse from the intercalated refrain between the Psalm verses, cf. Mateos, *Typicon*, II, 313–14, *s.v.* Περισσή.

108. Οκτωιχъ, 1:39–40, and Ὡρολόγιον σὺν Θεῷ ἁγίῳ περιέχον τὴν ἡμερονύκτιον τῆς Ἐκκλησίας ἀκολουθίαν τῆς ἱερᾶς καὶ περιβλέπτου μονῆς τῆς Κρυπτοφέρρης (Grottaferrata, 1950), 453–56 (also weekdays).

109. Husmann, "Hymnus und Troparion," 71–77, esp. 74.

110. Cf. C. Aslanov, "*Bayt* ('House') as 'Strophe' in Hebrew, Byzantine and Near Eastern Poetry," *Le Muséon* 121 (2008): 297–310.

111. G. Caracausi, *Lessico greco della Sicilia e dell'Italia Meridionale (secoli X–XIV)* (Palermo: Centro di Studi Filologici e Linguistici Siciliani, 1990), 250 s.v.

112. P. D. Day, *The Liturgical Dictionary of Eastern Christianity* (Collegeville, Minn.: Liturgical Press, 1993), 141–42.

century, ones copied in the Middle East or in southern Italy, transfer the term kathisma to the troparion that in the Constantinopolitan tradition is the apolytikion.[113] In the final analysis, neither the exercise of a free choice nor instability in the liturgical vocabulary underlies the apparent linguistic range. It is the consequence of the introduction of hagiopolite hymnography via the Constantinopolitan monastery of St. John Stoudios.

II.4. *Prayers*

The last element of the liturgical unit comprises prayers, which I present in the same order as the manuscript and for which I provide the incipit:

1. Εὐλογῶ σε Κύριε τὸν μόνον μακρόθυμον καὶ ἀνεξίκακον …
2. Κύριε Ἰησοῦ Χριστέ, υἱὲ τοῦ Θεοῦ, λόγε ἀθάνατε …
3. Ὁ Θεὸς ὁ δίκαιος καὶ αἰνετός, ὁ Θεὸς ὁ μέγας …
4. Ὁ Θεὸς ὁ παντοκράτορ, ὁ πατὴρ τοῦ Χριστοῦ σου …
5. Κύριε σωτήρ μου, ἵνα τί μὲ ἐγκατέλιπες …
6. Κύριε ὁ τὰ ὕψη τῶν οὐρανῶν σπιθαμῇ καὶ τὴν γῆν …
7. Κύριε ὑπὲρ πάντων καὶ διὰ πάντων καὶ ἐν πᾶσιν ὑμνῶ …
8. Κύριε ὡς ἀγαθὸς καὶ φιλάνθρωπος Θεὸς πολλὰ ἐλέη …
9. Ὁ Θεὸς ὁ ἐπὶ τῶν χερουβὶμ καθεζόμενος …
10. Πτωχὸς καὶ πένης αἰνέσουσί σε, Κύριε …
11. Κύριε ὁ Θεὸς ἡμῶν ὁ θέλων πάντας ἀνθρώπους σωθῆναι …
12. Κύριε οἰκτίρμον καὶ ἐλεῆμον …
13. Κύριε Ἰησοῦ Χριστέ, υἱὲ τοῦ Θεοῦ τοῦ ζῶντος ἄφελε …
14. Δεόμεθά σου Κύριε ὁ Θεὸς ἡμῶν, μακροθύμησον ἐφ᾽ ἡμᾶς …
15. Παναγία δέσποινα Θεοτόκε ἀποδίωξον τοὺς πονηροὺς …
16. Προσευχὴ τοῦ Μανασσῆ· Κύριε παντοκράτωρ ὁ Θεός …
17. Ἐγὼ εἶπα ἐν τῷ ὕψει τῶν ἡμερῶν μου …
18. Πολλῶν καὶ μεγάλων ἀπολαύσας τῶν δωρημάτων …
19. Πάλιν ὑπεσκελίσθην ὁ τάλας τὸν νοῦν …
20. Σὲ καὶ νῦν εὐλογοῦμεν, Χριστέ μου, λόγε Θεοῦ …

As is true for the troparia-kathismata, the prayers are texts primarily written in the first person. Two of them, the prayers of Manasses (16) and

---

113. Husmann, "Hymnus und Troparion," 71–77.

Hezekiah (17), are biblical odes, and they are used in the cathedral psalter of Constantinople as well as in the monastic horologion.[114] Some prayers are attributed to specific saints: Basil (1), Nikon (3), Auxentios (10), and Gregory the Theologian (20); others are presidential prayers of the asmatike akolouthia (9, 12, 14).[115] The patristic-hagiographic attributions are verifiably accurate. Basil's authorship of prayer (1) is confirmed by the *Constitutiones Basilianae*;[116] the text attributed to Nikon (3) comes from the *Vita* of Symeon of Emesa by Leontios of Neapolis (seventh century), where the prayer is recited by the hermit Nikon.[117] The prayer of Auxentios (10) is taken from his Metaphrastic *Vita* (BHG 199),[118] and the last text is the vespertine hymn (*Carmina dogmatica* 32) by Gregory of Nazianzus (CPG and CPGs 3034).[119]

Several prayers that are anonymous in the Harvard Psalter carry specific attributions in other manuscripts. In Vienna, ÖNb, theol. gr. 177 (ca. 1150), prayer (2) is attributed to Symeon of the Wondrous Mountain (d. 592)[120] and is, in fact, found in his *Vita* (BHG 1689).[121] Prayer (19)—which the modern euchologion attributes to Martinian (fourth century?) and employs in the rite of purification of nocturnal emission—is also likely to be of hagiographic origin.[122] The Marian prayer (15) is taken from a homily on the Theotokos's

114. See below, 293, for further details.

115. The asmatike akolouthia (literally "Sung Office") is the Liturgy of the Hours according to the cathedral rite of Constantinople, see S. Parenti, "The Cathedral Rite of Constantinople: Evolution of a Local Tradition," OCP 77 (2011), 449–69 (with earlier bibliography).

116. *Constitutiones Basilianae* 1.2 (PG 31:1329A5–14); P. J. Fedwick, *Bibliotheca Basiliana Universalis: A Study of the Manuscript Tradition of the Works of Basil of Caesarea* (Turnhout: Brepols, 1993–2004), 3:736–45, 4.3:1523 [hereafter "*BiblBasil*"].

117. CPG 4068, Bibliotheca Hagiographica Graeca [hereafter "BHG"] 1677 (PG 93:1692–93); L. Rydén, *Das Leben des Heiligen Narren Symeon von Leontios von Neapolis* (Stockholm: Almqvist and Wiksell, 1963), 134–35.

118. PG 94:1416B–C.

119. I. M. Phountoulis, "Τοῦ ἁγίου Γρηγορίου τοῦ Θεολόγου Ὕμνος ἑσπερινός' -Ἡ λειτουργικὴ χρήση τοῦ," *Κληρονομία* 22 (1990): 32–34; see also B. Phragkeskos, "Ὁ ὕμνος ἑσπερινὸς σὲ λειτουργικὰ καὶ γρηγοριάνα χειρόγραφα," *Κληρονομία* 24 (1992): 259–62.

120. Hunger et al., *KatalogÖNb*, 3.2:318.

121. P. Van den Ven, *La vie ancienne de S. Syméon Stylite le Jeune (521–592)*, 2 vols. (Brussels: Société des Bollandistes, 1962, 1970), 1:25.

122. J. Goar, *Εὐχολόγιον, sive rituale Græcorum* ..., 2nd ed. (Venice, 1730; reprinted in Graz: Akademische Druck und Verlagsanstalt, 1960), 703; at times the prayer is attributed to Basil the Great: see Fedwick, *BiblBasil*, 4.3:1526. S. Alexopoulos and A. van den Hoek, "The Endicott Scroll and Its Place in the History of Private Communion Prayers," *DOP* 60 (2006): 146–88, here 176–77.

entrance into the temple by Germanos of Constantinople (d. 730) (CPG 4079).[123] Prayer (5) originates in the *Sermo asceticus* by Ephrem the Syrian (CPG and CPGs 3909),[124] which, like the second Marian prayer (18), is at times attributed to the monk Mark (fourth or fifth century); this text has been considered unpublished by more than one author,[125] even though it was included in the *Ephraem graecus* (CPG 4079)[126] and published, in 1746, by Joseph Assemani from the late manuscript Rome, BAV, gr. 1190 (sixteenth century). In the Assemani edition, the prayer is preceded by another Marian prayer that Jacques Noret has shown to have originated in the *Life* of Mary of Egypt.[127] The manuscript Noret used, the Sinai. gr. 80, is an augmented psalter copied in the second half of the fifteenth century. Unlike the Assemani codex, it distinguishes the two sources of the prayer through the rubric: "ἡ μὲν ἀρχὴ τῆς ὁσίας Μαρίας τὴν Αἰγυπτίας, ἡ δὲ λοιπὴ (which would be ours) Λέοντος τοῦ Σοφοῦ" (but the text seems not to occur in the published work of Leo the Wise [886–912]).[128] The origins of the remaining prayers (6–8, 11, 13) remain unclear, though their styles suggest that they, too, may come from patristic or hagiographical sources. In any case, an investigation of TLG did not provide positive results.

---

123. A date for the unpublished piece in A. Jacob, "Un euchologe du Saint-Sauveur 'in Lingua Phari' de Messine. Le Bodleianus Auct. E.5.13," *Bulletin de l'Institut Historique Belge de Rome* 50 (1980): 65.4, with reference to Devreesse, *Codices Vaticani graeci*, 2:295, where one finds no indication of its existence, and N. F. Krasnosel'cev, *Сведения о некоторых литургических рукописях Ватиканской Библиотеки* (Kazan, 1885), 34; see instead S. G. Mercati, *De nonnullis versibus dodecasyllabis S. Germani I CP. Patriarchae homiliae Εἰς τὰ εἰσόδια τῆς Θεοτόκου insertis*, 2nd ed. (Grottaferrata, 1915), 15, reprinted in *Collectanea Byzantina*, ed. A. Longo (Bari: Dedalo Libri, 1970), 1:35; the first edition appeared in *Roma e l'Oriente* 8 (1915): 147–65.

124. J. S. Assemani, *Sancti Patris Nostri, Ephraem Syri opera omnia quae exstant …*, vol. 3, *Graece et latine* (Rome, 1746), 158.3.

125. Canart, *Codices Vaticani graeci*, 398; Jacob, *Saint-Sauveur*, 65.1.

126. Assemani, *Ephraem Syri Opera Omnia*, 548–50. For Vat. gr. 1190, see P. Canart, "A propos du *Sermo de Sanctissimae Dei Genitricis Virginis Mariae Laudibus* d'Ephrem le Syrien," *Byzantion* 75 (2005): 499–500, a study that completes W. Bakker, "The Origin of the *S. Patris Ephraem Syri Sermo de Sanctissimae Dei Genitricis Mariae laudibus* (Assemani, III: 575–577)," *Byzantion* 74 (2004): 147–97.

127. J. Noret, "La vie de Marie l'Égyptienne (BHG 1042) source partielle d'une prière pseudo-éphrémienne," *Analecta Bollandiana* [hereafter "*AB*"] 96 (1978): 386–87.

128. Ibid., 286. On 286n2 Noret recognizes that the only similarity between the prayer and the work of Leo the Wise lies in their common citation of Ps 86:7. The attribution to Leo is affirmed in the psalter Vienna, ÖNb, theol. gr. 177 (ca. 1150); see Hunger et al., *KatalogÖNb*, 3.2:324.

II.5. *The ἀκολουθία for the forgiveness of sins*

Between the first and second sets of kathismata the author inserted penitential verses attributed to someone identified merely as the monk Gregory.[129] The same verses are present in the Constantinopolitan psalter Mt. Athos, MDion, cod. 86 (1037 A.D.),[130] where they likewise serve to ask forgiveness of sins committed during the day. The ἀκολουθία is organized in the following manner:

a) Trisagion-Pater

b) Kyrie eleison (three times)

c) *Venite adoremus* + Psalm 50

d) Trisagion-Pater

e) Penitential troparia in mode pl. II

f) Kyrie eleison (twenty times)

g) Prayer: Κύριε ὁ Θεὸς ἡμῶν ὁ τὴν διὰ μετανοίας ἄφεσιν ...

The ensemble is structured as an independent liturgical unit modeled on the hours of the day, but with only one psalm instead of three. The most interesting element is represented by the prayer (g) of the cathedral and Stoudite matins, where it accompanied Psalm 50—which it paraphrases—and was recited by the celebrant.[131] As will be shown below (§ V.1), the ἀκολουθία for the forgiveness of sins is useful in understanding the overall order and use of the augmented psalter in relation to the horologion, and thus to the ascetic-liturgical program of the Harvard Psalter.

II.6. Excursus: *Hymns and prayers of the monk Thikara:*
       some clarifications

In describing the psalter Athens, EBE, 15 (ca. 1180), the compilers of the catalogue wrote that "it contains the psalms with the hymns and the

---

129. Τοῦ μακαριωτάτου μοναχοῦ κυροῦ Γρηγορίου στίχοι κατανυκτικοί· Ὦ τῆς δριμείας πικρίας τοῦ θανάτου ...; see I. Vassis, *Initia carminum byzantinorum* (Berlin: De Gruyter, 2005), 910.

130. MDion = Μονὴ Διονυσίου, Mount Athos. S. N. Kadas, ed., *Τὰ σημειώματα τῶν χειρογράφων τῆς Μονῆς Διονυσίου Ἁγίου Ὄρους* (Mt. Athos: Ekdose Hieras Mones Dionysiou, 1996), 19–20. However, the verses are of a later hand. I wish to thank Christo Kanavas for having obtained this work for me.

131. S. Parenti and E. Velkovska, ed. and trans., *L'Eucologio Barberini gr. 336*, 2nd ed. (Rome: C.L.V.-Edizioni Liturgiche, 2000), 102 (§ 78); Arranz, "Les prières presbytérales," 426–28.

prayers of John Θηκαρᾶ,"[132] even though the name never appears in the codex. As has been discussed, the Athens Psalter belongs to the same type as the Harvard Psalter (§ I.4); it would therefore not be out of place to clarify the possible dependency of the psalter with appendix on the Θηκαρᾶ, the *editio princeps* of which appeared in Venice, in 1643, edited by the Cretan monk Agapios Landos.[133]

The Θηκαρᾶ is a collection of "hymns and prayers to the glory of the Indivisible Trinity, worthy of every praise, Father, Son, and Holy Spirit." It is arranged according to the synaxes of hourly prayer, almost a *cursus*, but one that is alternative and supplemental to that established by the horologion. The manuscript tradition of the Θηκαρᾶ is both extensive and heterogeneous,[134] and the collection of prayers, in the strict sense of the word, may be preceded by an *Explanation* (Διήγησις) of the hymns. The Landos edition, like the others that would follow, does not, however, reproduce the work in its entirety. Various parts were omitted; among them were "the prayers and hymns for the psalter" that correspond to many of the troparia and some of the prayers present in the Harvard and Athens Psalters, and to the augmented psalter in general.

The identity of the monk Θηκαρᾶ, the presumed author of the euchological collection, is obscure, as is the period in which he lived. The available evidence was collected and analyzed by Stephanos Skalistes in his dissertation on the life and works of Thomas Magistros (d. after 1347).[135] In fact, Karl Krumbacher[136] and Hans-Georg Beck[137]—to cite only the most eminent scholars—have associated Θηκαρᾶ with Magistros, the erudite Byzantine who took the name

132. J. and A. Sakkelion, *Κατάλογος τῶν χειρογράφων τῆς Ἐθνικῆς Βιβλιοθήκης τῆς Ἑλλάδος* (Athens, 1892), 4, also in the later Codd. Athen. gr. 16, 27, 55.

133. *Βιβλίον καλούμενον Θηκαρᾶς, ἐν ᾧ εἰσί γεγραμμένοι ὕμνοι τε καὶ εὐχαί* ... (Venice, 1643). For the various editions see S. K. Skalistes, *Θωμᾶς Μάγιστρος· Ὁ βίος καὶ τὸ ἔργο του· Διατριβὴ ἐπὶ Διδακτορίᾳ ὑποβληθεῖσα εἰς τὸ Τμῆμα Θεολογίας τοῦ Ἀριστοτελείου Πανεπιστημίου Θεσσαλονίκης* (Thessaloniki: Aristoteleio Panepistemio Thessalonikes, 1984), 223–24. I wish to thank Dr. Dorotei Getov for having provided me with a photocopy of the *Θηκαρᾶ* (Venice, 1783) and the work of Skalistes.

134. Skalistes, *Θωμάς Μάγιστρος*, 224–40.

135. Ibid., 248–62.

136. K. Krumbacher, *Geschichte der byzantinischen Litteratur von Justinian bis zum Ende des oströmischen Reiches (527–1453)* (Munich, 1891, reprinted in New York: Burt Franklin, 1958), 548–50.

137. H.-G. Beck, *Kirche und theologische Literatur im byzantinischen Reich* (Munich: C. H. Beck, 1959), 704–5, with the earlier bibliography.

Theodoulos when he became a monk, thus assuming the name of the man to whom the hymns are attributed in the *Explanation* (Διήγησις).[138] Skalistes, however, challenges the identification of Θηκαρᾶ as Thomas (Theodoulos) Magistros and maintains that an eleventh-century Constantinopolitan monk stands behind the eponymous Θηκαρᾶ.[139] If that were indeed the case, we would have resolved the problem of the origin of the augmented psalter type, identifying the compiler as well. The fact that the most recent catalogues of the Greek manuscripts in Vienna do not accept the identification of Θηκαρᾶ as Magistros[140] prompts a closer examination of of Skalistes's conclusions.

Skalistes bases his argument on a number of paper codices containing the Θηκαρᾶ; they are preserved in Jerusalem (PB, codd. Sabas 44, 90, 279, 305, 340) and dated to the eleventh century by Papadopoulos-Kerameus.[141] Although some Greek manuscripts written on paper are known from the period,[142] the Papadopoulos-Kerameus attribution arouses more than a little suspicion. Confirmation of his error comes from the *Checklist* of the Greek manuscripts in Jerusalem that were microfilmed, in 1949–50, for the Library of Congress in Washington, D.C. In the introduction to the *Checklist*, mission director Kenneth W. Clark gives the year 1600 as the upper limit and lists the criteria that guided the choice of manuscripts to be reproduced.[143] The dating criterion accounts for the reason why, of the five codices noted by Skalistes, only Sabas 44 (itself dated to the sixteenth century[144]) appears in the *Checklist*. The four remaining copies were deemed to be later than the sixteenth century and were therefore not microfilmed.

138. See also the information collected in E. Follieri, *Initia hymnorum Ecclesiae Graecae* (Vatican City: Biblioteca Apostolica Vaticana, 1960–66), 5.1:267 (Θεόδουλος Θηκαρᾶ) and 275–76 (Ἰωάννης Θηκαρᾶ).

139. Skalistes, *Θωμᾶς Μάγιστρος*, 259–60.

140. See Hunger et al., *KatalogÖNb*, 3.3:311–12 (cod. theol. gr. 289, sixteenth century); ibid, 4:159 (cod. suppl. gr. 91, fourteenth century).

141. PB = Πατριαρχικὴ Βιβλιοθήκη, Jerusalem. A. Papadopoulos-Kerameus, Ἱεροσολυμιτικὴ Βιβλιοθήκη ... (St. Petersburg, 1899, reprinted in Brussels: Culture et Civilisation, 1963), 4:90–91, 166, 399–400, 428–29, 463.

142. M. L. Agati, *Il libro manoscritto. Introduzione alla codicologia* (Rome: Bretschneider, 2003), 80, cites MI, cod. 258, of 1042/43 A.D., and MML, cod. Θ 70, of 1070 A.D.

143. K. W. Clark, ed., *Checklist of Manuscripts in the Libraries of the Greek and Armenian Patriarchates in Jerusalem, Microfilmed for the Library of Congress, 1949–50* (Washington, D.C.: Library of Congress, 1953), viii.

144. Ibid., 9.

In fact, the handwritten tradition of Θηκαρᾶ, an eponym documented with certainty at Philadelphia in 1348,[145] does not reach back earlier than the fourteenth century. The oldest known example of the work appear to be the Athens, EBE, 2045, copied ca. 1328, Moscow, GIM, gr. 305 (269/CCLVI), copied in 1341,[146] and Sofija, Sofia University, Dujčev Center, MS gr. 1, made in the second half of the fourteenth century.[147] The Slavic versions are even later, known only from the sixteenth century, although they derive from a version produced during the course of the fourteenth century in one of the great translation centers, such as Tărnovo in Bulgaria, the Serbian Monastery of Dečani, or, in the context of the Neo-Hesychast revival, Mount Athos itself.[148] In conclusion, it is the collection by Θηκαρᾶ that depends on the augmented psalters with appendix and not vice versa.

II.7. *Conclusions*

In the augmented psalter type we have the Trisagion-Our Father, three hymnographic kathismata, and a prayer following each kathisma. Our study has provided the opportunity finally to clarify the significance of the term "kathisma," which, like "oikos," was borrowed from architecture. In the hagiopolite sphere it designated the "supporting structure" of antiphonated psalmody or the division of the psalter. Altogether unfounded is the etymology of stasis-kathisma as denoting, on the one hand, the psalms recited while

145. See E. Trapp et al., *Prosopographisches Lexikon der Palaiologenzeit. Addenda et Corrigenda zu Faszikel 1–8* (Vienna: Österreichische Akademie der Wissenschaften, Veröffentlichungen der Kommission für Byzantinistik, 1988), 107, no. 92041: Θηκαρᾶς Μιχαήλ.

146. L. Politis, *Κατάλογος των χειρογράφων τῆς Ἐθνικῆς Βιβλιοθήκης τῆς Ἑλλάδος: αρ. 1857–2500*. Πραγματεῖαι τῆς Ἀκαδημίας Ἀθηνῶν 54 (Athens: Academy of Athens, 1991), 93–94; Archimandrite Vladimir, *Систематическое описание рукописей Московской Синодальной (Патриаршей) Библиотеки*, vol. 1, Рукописи греческия (Moscow, 1894), 418–19; B. L. Fonkič and F. B. Poljakov, *Греческие рукописи Московской Синодальной Библиотеки. Палеографические, кодикологические и библиографические дополнения к каталогу архимандрита Владимира (Филантропова)* (Moscow: Синодальная библиотека, 1993), 104–5.

147. D. Getov, *A Catalogue of Greek Liturgical Manuscripts in the "Ivan Dujčev Centre for Slavo-Byzantine Studies"* (Rome: Pontificio Instituto Orientale, 2007), 27–38; see also M. Stavrou, "Une prière inédite de Nicephore Blemmydès transmise dans le 'Thékaras,'" in *La Prière liturgique* (Rome: C.L.V.-Edizioni Liturgiche, 2001), 119–28.

148. T. D. Ivanova-Sullivan, *Lexical Variation in the Slavonic Thekara Texts: Semantic and Pragmatic Factors in Medieval Translations* (PhD diss., Ohio State University, 2005). Thikaras's dating of the fourteenth century is also shared by P. Skaltis, ed., *Θηκαρᾶς. Στίχοι εἰς τοὺς θείους Ὕμνους Διονυσίου καὶ Μητροφάνους Περὶ τῶν Ὕμνων, Θηκαρᾶ μοναχοῦ Λόγοι περὶ πίστεως ..., Εἰσαγωγή* (Mt. Athos: Ekdosis Hieras Mones Pantokratoros, 2008), 39.

standing, followed, on the other, by the hymnographic kathisma performed while sitting.

In manuscripts of the Byzantine periphery, the apparent confusion between troparion (Constantinopolitan) and kathisma (hagiopolite) stems from the fact that both have the same metrical-melodic pattern and were interchangeable with respect to liturgical function, in relation, for example, to the "God is the Lord" (Θεὸς Κύριος) of the matins. It would be interesting to verify whether this is an isolated case or if the lexicographical ambiguities all derive from the flow of the monastic rite of Palestine (with its hagiopolite *tréfonds*) into the Byzantine rite.[149]

The hymnographic kathismata of the psalter originate in a parakletike of an ancient type, and they are distributed in order of succession according to the musical modes. They undoubtedly represent an improvised solution based on the use of penitential and Marian texts. The prayers, almost all of which were in the first person, mainly originate in hagiographic and patristic texts, but presidential prayers from the Constantinopolitan cathedral office also appear. Finally, the edifying collection known as "Thikara," which dates from the fourteenth century, is not the source of the prayers of the augmented psalter.

III

The Horologion

III.1. *The context*

Despite the strong tendency toward conservation, the liturgical book always interacts most immediately with its user; yet precisely because it is liturgical, it also interacts with a society at the moment when it assembles for prayer. The book, or better, the rite that the book describes, exercises an influence on whoever uses it, but it is also the case that the liturgical book absorbs and reflects contemporary spiritual movements, which give rise to new editions. This is particularly true of the horologion, the most personal, and in a certain sense the most private, of liturgical books, one whose

---

149. Still valid is P. Peeters, *Orient et Byzance. Le tréfonds oriental de l'hagiographie byzantine* (Louvain: Société des Bollandistes, 1950).

synaxes were not necessarily all carried out in a public, communal setting.

Thanks to the Paschal tables,[150] the Harvard Psalter can be dated to 1105, during the reign of Alexios Komnenos (ca. 1057–1118). It was precisely in the years 1105–7 that John the Hesychast, a monk from Mt. Athos, submitted to the Patriarch Nicholas III Grammatikos (1084–1111) a series of liturgical and canonical questions that began on the subject of the typika of Theodore the Stoudite and Athanasios of Athos.[151] Half a century earlier, in a typikon composed around 1055–60, Nikon of the Black Mountain (1025 to at least 1088)—a virtual predecessor to Baumstark—compared the liturgical typikon of Stoudios with that of Mar Saba in Jerusalem; significantly, although a native of Constantinople, Nikon granted greater credit and preference to the Neo-Sabaite rule.[152] In 1049, the monk Paul founded the monastery of the Theotokos Evergetis in Constantinople, and around 1055 his successor, Timothy, provided it with the liturgical and foundation typikon (1098–1118).[153] Both are preserved in the codex Athens, EBE, cod. 788, variously dated from the first quarter of the twelfth century to the first decade of the fourteenth.[154] It is generally recognized that the Evergetis Typikon is the first member of the Stoudite family in which the effects of the incipient Neo-Sabaite reform can be clearly seen.[155] The path of the reform may lead back through the tradition of Mount Galesios, which is north of Ephesus; the Mount Galesios tradition was codified in the lost typikon[156] drafted by Lazaros (d. 1053), who entered the monastic life at Mar Saba.

In the course of the twelfth century, the founding typikon of Evergetis experienced a great success and was adopted in other important Constantinopolitan monasteries, such as those of *Kosmosoteira, Phoberos, Kechari-*

150. F. Piper, *Karls des Grossen Kalendarium und Ostertafel, ... nebst einer Abhandlung über die lateinischen und griechischen Ostercyklen des Mittelalters* (Berlin, 1858), 110–62.

151. I. Oudot, ed., *Patriarchatus Constantinopolitani acta selecta* (Vatican City: Typis Polyglottis Vaticanis, 1941), 1:12–27. On the document and its various redactions see V. Grumel, *Les regestes des actes du Patriarcat de Constantinople*, vol. 1, *Les actes des patriarches*, parts 2–3, *Les regestes de 715 à 1206*, ed. J. Darrouzès, 2nd ed. (Paris: Institut Français d'Études Byzantines, 1989), 434–40.

152. *BMFD*, 1:379.

153. *BMFD*, 2:465–68.

154. B. Crostini Lappin, "Structure and Dating of Codex *Atheniensis Graecus 788, Typikon* of the Monastery of the Theotokos Evergetis (Founded in 1049)," *Scriptorium* 52 (1998): 330–49.

155. R. F. Taft, *The Byzantine Rite: A Short History* (Collegeville, Minn.: Liturgical Press, 1992), 81.

156. See the review by E. Velkovska of *Synaxarion of Evergetis*, ed. Jordan, in *BZ* 97 (2004): 213.

tomene, and *Pantokrator*.[157] Could one say the same thing for the liturgical tradition of this monastery? Two recent studies have allowed us to discover the liturgical typikon of Philanthropos, conserved in the codex Panaghia Kamariotissa 26 of the Patriarchal Library in Istanbul, datable between the second half of the twelfth century and the beginning of the thirteenth.[158] Besides some local rites of this monastery, like the feast of the dedication of the church on March 25, the liturgical practice is identical to that of Evergetis. This happy discovery, while confirming the wide diffussion of the liturgical and canonical tradition of Evergetis, renders the dating of the codex Athens, EBE, cod. 788, a much more secondary problem.

A second movement, which is evident from the end of the eleventh century, relates to private versus communal monastic offices. Dirk Krausmüller has emphasized the tendency to make offices, such as compline, communal and public when in earlier times they were left to private recitation.[159] This, in brief, is the historical framework in which the analysis of the horologion of the Harvard Psalter must be conducted.

III.2. *The daily* cursus

The horologion does not carry a main title, but the individual celebrations follow one another in this order:

1. Prayers upon rising
2. The ἀκολουθία for the forgiveness of sins
3. Trisagion for the deceased
4. Midnight hour
5. Matins
6. First hour

---

157. *BMFD*, 2:455–56. By examining dietary regulations, D. Krausmüller has relativized the influence of the Typikon of Evergetis, notwithstanding our observations regarding exclusively the liturgical practice: D. Krausmüller, "The Abbots of Evergetis as Opponents of "Monastic Reform": A Re-Appraisal of the Monastic Discourse in 11th and 12th-Century Constantinople," *REB* 61 (2011): 111–34.

158. A. M. Pentkovskij, "Евергетидский монастырь и императорские монастыри в Константинополе в конце XI – начале XII века," *VizVrem* 63, no. 88 (2004): 76–88; M. Kouroupou and J.-F. Vannier, "Commémoraisons des Comnènes dans le typikon liturgique du monastère du Christ Philanthrope (ms. Panaghia Kamariotissa 29)," in *REB* 63 (2005): 41–69.

159. Krausmüller, "Private vs communal," 312.

7. Third "great" hour

8. Sixth "great" hour

9. Ninth hour

10. Typika

11. Prayer before and after communion

12. Intermediate hour of the Paschal Triduum

13. Vespers

14. Apodeipnon

III.3. *Prayers upon rising*

The horologion of the Harvard Psalter begins with a "prayer to be said upon awakening from sleep," and in this it is not unlike current practice.[160] Stoudite custom directed the prayer to be said before going to sleep, but here, located prior to mesonyktikon, it becomes de facto the first office of the day.[161] The prayer, which is not of widespread use, is directed to the Trinity.[162]

The second formula (εὐχὴ ἑτέρα) is equally rare but particularly important because of its relationship with the Constantinopolitan euchologion Paris, BNF, Coislin 213, dated 1027. The index of the euchologion makes it clear that in the cathedral rite a group of prayers attributed to Basil follows the fifth presidential prayer of the ninth hour;[163] those attributed to Basil are to be said on awakening, at matins, the hours, "and others."

The euchologion has lost the leaf following fol. 73, and with it the last two prayers of the ninth hour and a large part of the first of the "Basilian" prayers. The text resumes on fol. 74 with the final doxology: "[. . . . . ἀει]παρθένου Μαρίας, καὶ τῶν θείων καὶ νοερῶν λειτουργῶν σου σεραφίμ, τῆς πρώτης ἱεραρχίας καὶ διακοσμήσεως, καὶ δοξάζειν σὺν τῷ πατρὶ καὶ τῷ παναγίῳ καὶ ἀγαθῷ καὶ παντοδυνάμῳ καὶ ζωοποιῷ σου πνεύματι, νῦν καὶ ἀεὶ καὶ εἰς τοὺς αἰῶνας τῶν αἰώνων. Ἀμήν."

---

160. See *HR* 7–10; Ὡρολόγιον τὸ μέγα περιέχον ἄπασαν τὴν ἀνήκουσαν αὐτῷ ἀκολουθίαν, 5th ed. (Athens, 2005) [hereafter "*HA*"], 13–15.

161. See below and also note III.6.

162. Among the rare witnesses I note the horologion Sinai. gr. 865, fol. 46r+v (twelfth century).

163. Paris. Coislin. 213, fol. 4r:Ἕτεραι τοῦ ἁγίου Βασιλείου μετὰ τὴν τῆς κλίνης ἐξανάστασιν καὶ ἑωθιναί, τῶν ὡρῶν καὶ λοιπαί, ἀμφότεραι θ᾽; cf. Dmitrievskij, *Opisanie*, 2:1004. The prayers are not listed in Fedwick, *BiblBasil*, 4.3.

The characteristic designation of the seraphim (τῆς πρώτης ἱεραρχίας καὶ διακοσμήσεως) associates the prayer with the second of the horologion, which in turn lets us complete the lacuna in the Paris euchologion. As far as the attribution to Basil, made in the euchologion but not the psalter horologion, it is only necessary to note the inspiration the author took from a passage in the saint's *Regulae fusius tractatae* (37):[164]

Regulae basilianae ... τὸν μὲν ὄρθρον, ὥστε τὰ πρῶτα κινήματα τῆς ψυχῆς, καὶ τοῦ νοῦ, ἀναθήματα εἶναι Θεοῦ ...

Harvard Psalter ... καὶ ἀκαταγνώστως προσφέρειν σοι ὥσπερ ἀπαρχὰς τὰς πρώτας κινήσεις τῆς καρδίας ἡμῶν τὰς μετὰ τὴν ἐξ ὕπνου ἐξέγερσιν ...

III.4. *The ἀκολουθία for the forgiveness of sins*

Following the prayers for rising, the psalter horologion presents a brief office that is easily recognized as the ἀκολουθία for the forgiveness of sins, the office previously noted between the first and second sets of psalm kathismata:

a) *Venite adoremus* + Psalm 50

b) Trisagion [-Pater]

c) Penitential troparia of mode pl. II

d) Kyrie eleison (twenty times)

e) Prayer: Κύριε ὁ Θεὸς ἡμῶν ὁ τὴν διὰ μετανοίας ...

The repetition of the unit at the beginning of the liturgical day should be understood as an invocation for the forgiveness of sins committed during the night; these sins are specifically dreams, whether or not followed by an emission, which according to the view prevailing at the time were considered to be a psychosomatic disorder (as menstruation was for women) requiring purification and forgiveness.[165]

---

164. PG 31:1013.

165. See *Responsa Canonica* 7 and 12, attributed to Patriarch Timothy I of Alexandria (380–85), ed. P.-P. Joannou, *Discipline générale antique (IVe – IXe s.)*, vol. 2, *Les canons des pères grecs (IVe – IXe s.)* (Grottaferrata: Tipografia Italo-Orientale "S. Nilo," 1963), 244, 247–48; see also Goar, Εὐχολόγιον, 704–5; R. F. Taft, "Women at Church in Byzantium: Where, When—and Why?" *DOP* 52 (1998): 74–79; V. Larin, "What Is Ritual Im/Purity and Why?" *SVThQ* 52 (2008): 275–92.

III.5. *Trisagion for the deceased*

A brief remembrance of the dead—which follows at the beginning of the day and consists of a Trisagion, two troparia, a theotokion, and fifteen Kyries, but no specific prayer—is likely the result of devotional practice. In the *textus receptus,* a prayer for the deceased follows the midnight hour[166] and the remembrance is more structured; it includes Psalms 120 and 133, several troparia, and a prayer that we find at compline in the psalter horologion. What is found in the *textus receptus,* though, is the structure of a late office, absent from the oldest codices of Sinai and Athos; it never became part of the horologia of southern Italy and to my knowledge is found only at the end of the fourteenth century, in Mt. Sinai, MSC, gr. 866, fols. 1r–4v. [167]

III.6. *Mesonyktikon*

The midnight hour appears without title and is given in the double feast day and weekday type (table 5).

It is precisely the weekday type with the distinctive troparion "Of the groom" (Ἰδοὺ ὁ νυμφίος ἔρχεται . . .), common to the nocturnal offices of several traditions,[168] that permits the association of the brief rite of the psalter horologion with the office of mesonyktikon.

Psalm 26, which celebrates the Lord, light, defense, and safety from all terror, is particularly appropriate to nocturnal prayer. The psalm also inaugurates mesonyktikon in the horologia Mt. Sinai, MSC, gr. 904, fol. 216r (1211 A.D.), and gr. 903, fols. 48r–5or (thirteenth or fourteenth century), and it is prescribed with other psalms in the *Hypotyposis* of Niketas of Stoudios (before 1090) in a synaxis that immediately follows the prayers for awakening.[169] Psalm 26 is part of the hexapsalmos of compline in the ninth-century horologion Sinai, MSC, gr. 863, published by Mateos and this author,[170] and it is interpolated in the Italo-Greek Erlangen, Ubibl, cod. A2,

---

166. HR 38–40; HA 34–36 (Monday–Friday), HR 58; HA 52–53 (Saturday).

167. The thirteenth-century date proposed by Gardthausen, *Catalogus Sinaiticorum*, 187, and followed in K. W. Clark, ed., *Checklist of Manuscripts in St. Catherine's Monastery, Mount Sinai, Microfilmed for the Library of Congress, 1950* (Washington, D.C.: Library of Congress, 1952), 10, is hardly tenable.

168. *La Prière des Heures*, 95.

169. Parpulov, *Byzantine Psalters*, 480.

170. Mateos, "Horologion de Saint-Sabas," 58; Parenti, "Un fascicolo ritrovato," 346.

Table 5

Feast day mesonyktikon	Weekday mesonyktikon
Venite adoremus	=
Psalm 26	=
Prayer of Manasses	=
Gloria in excelsis	=
Trisagion	=
Sunday kathisma or troparion of the saint/feast	Penitential kathismata Troparion "Of the groom"
Theotokion	

Table 6: Comparison of Chludov Psalter, Sinai gr. 864, and Harvard Psalter

Chludov Psalter[1]	Sinai. gr. 864[2]	Harvard Psalter
Prayer of Hezekiah	Prayer of Hezekiah	
Prayer of Manasses	Prayer of Manasses	Prayer of Manasses
Gloria in excelsis		Gloria in excelsis

1. Ščepkina, Миниатюры Хлудовской Псалтыри, 157v–164r.
2. Ajjoub and Paramelle, ed., Livre d'Heures du Sinaï, 232–37.

fols. 50v–51r, of 1025;[171] finally, it reappears in the last part of the Lenten apodeipnon in the Typikon of Grottaferrata (1299–1300 A.D.).[172]

The presence of the deuterocanonical Manasses prayer in mesonyktikon has a precedent in the ninth-century horologion Mt. Sinai, MSC, gr. 864, where it is preceded by the Prayer of Hezekiah, whereas in the Harvard Psalter it is followed by the *Gloria in excelsis*. The Prayer of Manasses and *Gloria in excelsis* are two fixed elements of the Sabaite compline; above all, though, the Manasses prayer and the Gloria constitute the conclusion of the Constantinopolitan canon of fourteen biblical odes, preserved, for example, in the ninth-century Chludov Psalter (see table 6).

171. Ubibl = Universitätsbibliothek, Erlangen. For the Italo-Greek provenance of the manuscript see E. Velkovska, "A Liturgical Fragment in Majuscule in the Codex A2 in Erlangen," in *Στέφανος. Studia byzantina ac slavica Vladimiro Vavřinek ad annum sexagesimum quintum dedicata* (= *BSl* 56 [1995]), 483–92; Velkovska, "La liturgia italo-bizantina negli eucologi e lezionari del Nuovo Testamento della 'scuola niliana,'" in *Il monachesimo d'Oriente e d'Occidente nel passaggio dal primo al secondo Millennio* (Grottaferrata: Monastero Esarchico, 2009), 197, 211.

172. Grottaferrata, BB, Γ.α.I, fol. 114r.

It is possible that the Sinai. gr. 864 and the Harvard Psalter Horologion reflect an original sequence that has been excerpted in two different ways.

However, the tradition of our codex is not completely isolated. In the psalter Paris gr. 22, written in southern Italy around 1126, we find in the appendices a singular Akolouthia attributed to Ephrem the Syrian with instruction on how a monk should get out of bed, go to church, and participate in the common celebration of the mesonyktikòn.[173] The outline follows:

INITIAL PRAYERS

Psalm 138

Psalm 139

Gloria ... Alleluia three times.

Psalm 31

Prayer of Hezekiah

Prayer of Manasses

Gloria ... Alleluia three times.

Alleluia + troparion "Of the groom"

This structure must be compared with Sinai gr. 864 where we have:

Prayer of Hezekiah

Prayer of Manasses

Psalm 90

Troparion "Of the groom"

Psalm 118

It is clear that these various regional recensions are part of a very ancient common tradition that later decomposed, providing us another proof of the pluralism that prevailed in the twelfth century in the various regions that practiced the Byzantine rite.

More noteworthy in the Harvard manuscript is the absence of Psalm 118, which, as we will see, the Harvard Psalter reserves for the last part of apodeipnon. In the *ritus receptus*, Psalm 118 is recited in mesonyktikon from Monday to Friday, but on Saturday its place is taken by kathisma IX

173. Paris gr. 20, ff. 239 ss. The manuscript is available at http://gallica.bnf.fr/ark:/12148/btv1b8478956z/.

Table 7: Comparison of Horologia

Psalter Horologion	Sinai. gr. 904 and 903
Venite adoremus	=
Psalm 26	=
Prayer of Manasses	Psalm 118

(Pss 64–69) and on Sunday by a canon in honor of the Trinity composed by Metrophanes, metropolitan of Smyrna (857–80).[174] This, though, is a late solution reached within a system of weekly commemorations that considers Sunday to be the day of the Trinity[175] and that was devised to avoid duplicating Psalm 118, recited at the Saturday and Sunday orthros.[176] The psalter horologion shows a similar approach; here it is the Prayer of Manasses that takes the place of Psalm 118, as we can see from a comparison (table 7) with the horologia Mt. Sinai, MSC, gr. 904 and gr. 903.

In our horologion, Psalm 118 is prescribed for the end of apodeipnon—that is, before awakening—following a Stoudite tradition that will be taken up below, in paragraph III.14.4.

III.7. Matins

Juan Mateos addressed and resolved the most important questions posed by the Byzantine office of matins (ὄρθρος) in a fundamental study he accurately, if euphemistically, entitled "Quelques problèmes de l'orthros byzantin." Because of the multiple structures that comprise matins, the office is inherently a problem in all of the liturgical traditions.[177] Adding to the difficulty is the loss, if not removal, of the relevant leaves from the oldest or most important Greek horologia: the ninth-century Sinai. gr. 863 and gr. 864, Erlangen, Ubibl, cod. A2 (1025 A.D.), and Mt. Athos, MV, cod. 1248 (1077 A.D.).

174. See *HR* 59; *HA* 54.

175. Hannick, "Oktoechos," 54.

176. J. Mateos, "La psalmodie variable dans l'office byzantin," *Acta Philosophica et Theologica* (Societas Academica Dacoromana) 2 (1964): 327–31. For the manuscript tradition see Sinai. gr. 877 (1467 A.D.); at an earlier date the same psalms were recited on Sunday as on Saturday: see, e.g., Sinai. gr. 865 (twelfth century) and Sinai. gr. 904 (1211 A.D.).

177. J. Mateos, "Quelques problèmes de l'orthros byzantin," *Proche-Orient Chrétien* 11 (1961): 17–35, 201–20; Taft, *Liturgy of the Hours*.

III.7.1. *Initial section and celebratory forms*

Like mesonyktikon, matins has no separate title in the psalter horologion; the absence is a sign that the two synaxes were celebrated one after another. Conforming to a book of the ordinary, the horologion takes no account of the roles of the priest and deacon in the celebration or the prayers and litanies associated with their participation, ones normally found in the euchologion.[178]

The celebration begins with the Trinitarian doxology (Δόξα τῇ ἁγίᾳ ... Τριάδι ...), likely of hagiopolite origin, that is common to the *Taktikon* of Nikon of the Black Mountain (1055–60),[179] the typika of Alexios the Stoudite and Evergetis,[180] and the second edition of the *Hypotyposis* of Stoudios.[181] The doxology is followed by the usual group of six psalms, or ἑξάψαλμος (Pss 3, 37, 62, 87, 102, 142), introduced by Luke 2:14 and Psalm 50:17. Note that the conclusion of each group of psalms ("Alleluia, alleluia, glory to you O God") has two Alleluias—and not three as in the *textus receptus*—in accordance with the tradition retained in Russia until Patriarch Nikon's reform of 1657.[182]

After the hexapsalmos, three celebratory options are outlined: (1) Sunday and feast days, (2) Saturday, and (3) simple weekday commemorations (λιτή), also called "of the Alleluia." In this context, the adjective "feast day"

178. For the distinction between the books of the proper and the ordinary see Taft, "Mount Athos," 180–82.

179. B. N. Beneševič, *Тактикон Никона Черногорца. Греческий текст по рукописи № 441 Синайскаго монастыря св. Екатерины*, vol. 1 (St. Petersburg: St. Petersburg University, 1917), § 17 (26.17–18); *BMFD*, 1:387–88.

180. A. M. Pentkovskij, *Типикон Патриарха Алексия Студита в Византии и на Руси* (Moscow: Izd-vo Moskovskoĭ Patriarkhii, 2001), 256; Klentos, *Evergetis*, 133–34; J. E. Klentos, *Byzantine Liturgy in Twelfth-Century Constantinople. An Analysis of the Synaxarion of the Monastery of the Theotokos of Evergetis (Codex Athens Ethnike Bibliotheke 788)* (PhD diss., University of Notre Dame, 1995). For the Palestinian origin see J. Mateos, "'Sedre' et prières connexes dans quelques anciennes collections," *OCP* 28 (1962): 239–87; Mateos, "Trois recueils anciens de Proemia syriens," *OCP* 33 (1967): 457–82; Mateos, "Synaxe monastique," 257–58.

181. Dmitrievskij, *Opisanie*, 1:226.3–4; *BMFD*, 1:98, left col.

182. *Деяния Московских сборов 1666–1667 годов, II, Книга соборных деяний 1667 года* (Moscow, 1893), fols. 29r–31r (chap. 56). On the reforms of Nikon see P. Meyendorff, *Russia, Ritual and Reform: The Liturgical Reforms of Nikon in the 17th Century* (Crestwood, N.Y.: St. Vladimir's Seminary Press, 1991); T. Pott, *La réforme liturgique byzantine. Étude du phénomène de l'évolution non-spontanée de la liturgie byzantine* (Rome: C.L.V.-Edizioni Liturgiche, 2000), 214–22; see also B. Uspenskij, *Il segno della croce e lo spazio sacro* (Naples: Napoli D'Auria, 2005), 105–46.

refers to the great feasts of the Lord and the Theotokos, and to the memories of the saints.[183]

III.7.2. *Sunday and feast day matins*

The Sunday and feast day celebrations are characterized by the responsorial singing of several verses from Psalm 117, using the refrain "God is the Lord ..." (Θεὸς Κύριος ...). There follows antiphonal responsorial psalmody with a concluding doxology ("Glory to the Father ..."), the troparion, and the hymnographic refrain of the day.[184] Psalm 117 opens the Paschal matins in the Armenian Lectionary of Jerusalem (fifth century) and in the Stoudite tradition of Constantinople and southern Italy. It is natural to find it again in the Sunday celebrations, but its use in the feast day celebrations of any degree is less obvious. For Nicolas Egender, the choice "indique toujours le caractère pascal de l'heure du matin,"[185] but I believe that it is necessary to consider a more prosaic phenomenon common to various liturgical traditions: the progressive solemnization of feasts and memorials modeled on the Sunday office or eucharist.[186]

For the continuous psalmody, the horologion only gives instructions for Sunday, ordering two kathismata followed by the ὑπακοή;[187] nothing further is indicated, thus aligning the practice with the distribution of the *pensum* recorded later in the Evergetis Typikon.[188] The compiler kept to the fixed elements of the Sunday and feast day matins without addressing Psalms 134–35, called the "polyeleos" owing to the refrain "because his mercy (ἔλεος) is eternal." To be noted instead is the presence of the gradual hymns (ἀναβαθμοί).

---

183. For a detailed discussion see below § IV, devoted to the calendar.

184. On the antiphonalization of responsorial psalmody see Taft, "Psalmody," 28.

185. *La Prière des Heures*, 126.

186. Mateos, "Quelques problèmes," 203; on the phenomenon see also S. Parenti, "Lo studio e la storia della messa romana nella prospettiva della liturgia comparata," *Ecclesia Orans* 25 (2008): 193–226.

187. Mateos, *Célébration de la Parole*, 20; L. Calì, "Le ipacoè dell'Octoichos bizantino," *BollGrott* 19 (1965): 161–74, who is concerned with the musical aspect.

188. Mateos, "Psalmodie variable," 331–36; Klentos, *Evergetis*, 140–42.

Table 8: Comparison of Schema

schema I	schema II
[Fixed prokeimenon: Psalm 9:33]	Prokeimena of the eight modes
Psalm 150:6	Psalm 150:6
Gospel	Gospel
Ἀνάστασιν Χριστοῦ θεασάμενοι...	Ἀνάστασιν Χριστοῦ θεασάμενοι...

III.7.2.1. *Fixed and variable prokeimena and Psalm 150:6*

The horologion continues with a double description (shown in table 8).

In schema II, which closely follows schema I, the copyist transcribed the Sunday prokeimena according to the cycle of the eight modes. The rubric of schema I—ἔπειτα ἀντὶ τοῦ Ἀνάσθητι (Ps 9:33) τὸ Πᾶσα πνοή (Ps 150:6)—is unclear; in fact, it appears to direct the singing of Psalm 150:6 in place of the fixed Sunday prokeimenon (Ps 9:33).

The Barberini Euchologion (Rome, BAV, Barb. gr. 336), copied at the close of the eighth century, shows that matins in the cathedral rite of Constantinople contained a prokeimenon well before the introduction of the Gospel pericopes of Sunday or feast days, which occurred at the end of the ninth century:[189] "Εὐχὴ κατηχουμένων γινομένης εἰσόδου μετὰ τὸ τρισάγιον, λεγομένου προκειμένου. [Prayer of the catechumens, once the entrance with the Trisagion is completed and the prokeimenon has been sung.]"[190] The Barberini Euchologion does not specify the precise text. It is nevertheless highly probable, if not absolutely certain, that it is a fixed prokeimenon identifiable as Psalm 9:33, as is found in various manuscripts from every corner of the Byzantine world from the tenth century to the commentary of Symeon of Thessaloniki (d. 1429).[191]

But in the second half of the tenth century, the Jerusalem manuscript of the Typikon of the Great Church (PB, cod. Staurou 40) contains an appendix that includes a list of ten matins prokeimena organized according

189. E. Velkovska, "Lo studio dei lezionari bizantini," *Ecclesia Orans* 13 (1996): 265–66.

190. Parenti-Velkovska, *Eucologio Barberini*, 103 (§ 80.1).

191. Cf. E. Velkovska, "I 'dodici prokeimena' del mattutino cattedrale bizantino," in *Crossroad of Cultures*, ed. Feulner, 714.

to the cycle of the eight modes.[192] Juan Mateos, who devoted a note to the list, thinks that it is a compilation based on an earlier series of only seven prokeimena.[193] Each prokeimenon is followed by Psalm 150:6, which, in turn, we can consider to be a second fixed feast day prokeimenon that is of the hagiopolite tradition, not the Constantinopolitan.[194] Supporting this view is the reading of the so-called Typikon of the Anastasis, copied at Jerusalem in 1122[195] and preserved in Jerusalem, PB, cod. Staurou 43 (+ St. Petersburg, RNB, gr. 359). Here, in the matins of Palm Sunday, the prokeimenon of the day (Ps 117:27) supplants Ps 150:6: "Καὶ ἀντὶ τοῦ Πᾶσα πνοή, λέγεται Θεὸς Κύριος καὶ ἐπέφανεν. Στίχος·Ἐξομολογεῖσθε, εἶθ᾽ οὕτως ἀναγινώσκεται εὐαγγέλιον ἀναστάσιμον. [Instead of the 'Let every thing that hath breath,' the Lord is God is sung. Verse: Confess. Then the Gospel of the resurrection is read.]"[196]

It is thus possible to consider Psalm 150:6 as a fixed element of the ordinary Sunday matins; this supposition is confirmed by the fact that in the same Jerusalem manuscript the Gospel of the day for matins of Holy Monday is preceded only by the prokeimenon.[197] There are, however, also examples of the overlapping of prokeimena, both fixed and specific to the day, as in the pannychis of Tuesday, Wednesday, and Good Friday.[198] These

192. Mateos, *Typicon*, 2:170–72.

193. Ibid., 171n1, to be preferred over Mateos, "Quelques problèmes," 211–12.

194. To the contrary, Egender, "Introduction," 132, considers Ps 150:6 a "fixed prokeimenon" of the Constantinopolitan pannychis.

195. A. Papadopoulos-Kerameus, Ἀνάλεκτα Ἱεροσολυμιτικῆς σταχυολογίας, 5 vols. (St. Petersburg, 1891–98, reprinted in Brussels: Culture et Civilisation, 1963), to be read in light of the observations of A. Dmitrievskij, Древнейшие патриаршие типиконы: Святогорский Иерусалимский и Великой Константинопольской Церкви (Kiev: I. I. Gorbunova, 1907), 41–59. The Leningrad folios were briefly described in E. E. Granstrem, "Каталог греческих рукописей ленинградских хранилищ, 4, Рукописи XII века," VizVrem 23 (1963): 171. The best introduction to the typikon remains that of G. Bertonière, *The Historical Development of the Easter Vigil and Related Services in the Greek Church* (Rome: Pontificium Institutum Orientalium Studiorum, 1972), 12–18. The term "typikon" has been criticized by G. Shurgaia, "Formazione della struttura dell'ufficio del Sabato di Lazzaro nella tradizione di Gerusalemme," *Annali di Ca' Foscari* 36, no. 3 (1997): 147–48n4, who suggests defining the manuscript as a hymnal or tropologion, but one should remember that, first, the beginning is defective (lacking a title) and, second, the scribe himself calls it a δέλτος or τεῦχος, that is, a codex, according to the ordo (κατὰ τὴν τάξιν) of the Anastasis of Jerusalem (cf. Papadopoulos-Kerameus, Ἀνάλεκτα, 252–53).

196. Papadopoulos-Kerameus, Ἀνάλεκτα, 11.

197. Ibid., 41.

198. Ibid., 66, 83, 137.

are elements that likewise confirm the ongoing process of fusion between different traditions. The matins Gospel of the Resurrection,[199] followed by the hymn Ἀνάστασιν Χριστοῦ θεασάμενοι, closes the Sunday vigil.

III.7.2.2. *Exaposteilarion and Psalm 98:9*

The presentation of matins in two forms continues, detailing the different aspects and providing complementary information, as shown in table 9.

The two patterns have Psalm 50 and the hymnographic canons in common. In schema I the exaposteilarion of the resurrection (ἀναστάσιμον), which concludes the canons, is given as an alternative to "Holy is the Lord our God" (Ps 98:9). Schema II directs the performance of the kathismata of the day and the exaposteilaria or "Holy is the Lord our God" in the mode of the day, then the exaposteilarion heothinon (relative to the Gospel of the resurrection read Sunday) and that of the feast of the Lord if it falls on a Sunday. "Holy is the Lord our God" is then also to be sung if it is a feast of the Theotokos. The complexity at this point requires several explanations.

As in contemporary practice, several hymns are intercalated into the poetic canon: a kathisma or a hypakoe after the third ode, a kontakion or a kathisma after the sixth, and the exapostilarion after the ninth. Obviously, it is an improvised construction that tends to provide a triple three-part structure to the canon, when in fact:

1) in the oldest hagiopolite books the canon is always given consecutively without interruptions; [200]
2) the kontakion had its own, original position at the end of the Constantinopolitan cathedral vigil (παννυχίς);[201]

199. S. Janeras, "I vangeli domenicali della Resurrezione nelle tradizioni liturgica agiopolita e bizantina," in *Paschale Mysterium. Studi in memoria dell'Abate Prof. Salvatore Marsili*, ed. G. Farnedi (Rome: Pontificio Ateneo S. Anselmo, 1986), 64–69.

200. On the configuration of the hymnographical canon in the ancient hagiopolite books, see the studies of R. Krivko, "A Typology of Byzantine Office Menaia of the Ninth–Fourteenth Centuries," *Scrinium 7–8, Ars Christiana. In memoriam Michail F. Murianov (21.XI.1928–6.VI.1995)*, ed. R. Krivko, B. Lourié, A. Orlov, part 2 (2011–12), available at www.academia.edu/1145451/A_Typology_of_Byzantine_Office_Menaia_of_the_9th_-_14th_cc; A. Nikiforova, "The Tropologion Sin. gr. NE/ΜΓ 56–5 of the Ninth Century: A New Source for Byzantine Hymnography," *Scripta & e-Scripta* 12 (1913): 157–85.

201. A. Lingas, "The Liturgical Place of the Kontakion in Constantinople," in *Liturgy, Architecture and Art of the Byzantine World: Papers of the XVIII International Byzantine Congress (Moscow,*

Table 9: Presentation of Matins

schema I	schema II
Psalm 50	Psalm 50
Hymnographic canons	Hymnographic canons
Exapostilarion of the mode	Hagios Kyrios
or Hagios Kyrios	Heothinon exaposteilarion or of the feast

3) the kathismata are multipurpose canticles, and they may conclude the singing of "God is the Lord" (Ps 117:27) or the session of common psalmody.[202]

The sole original element appears to be the exaposteilarion (ἐξαπο-στειλάριον), which is the troparion followed by the hymnographic canon and the psalms of the lauds. According to an etymology proposed by Symeon of Thessaloniki (d. 1429), the selection appears to derive from the plea addressed to Christ, present in the texts of modes II, III, and plagal I, to send his light (ἐξαπόστειλον τὸ φῶς σου) to those who pray.[203]

The Sunday exaposteilarion is replaced by the responsorial singing of Psalm 98:9 ("Holy is the Lord our God"), which Juan Mateos appropriately terms a prokeimenon.[204] During the first half of the tenth century, Emperor Constantine VII Porphyrogennetos (913–59) composed eleven Sunday exaposteilaria to complement the cycle of eleven pericopes of the resurrection of the Lord.[205] Since Psalm 98 acclaims the regality of the Κύριος "great in

---

8–15 August 1991) and Other Essays Dedicated to the Memory of Fr. John Meyendorff, ed. C. C. Akentiev (St. Petersburg: Vizantinorossika, 1995), 50–57.

202. See the discussion above § II.3.

203. PG 155:572; cf. Mateos, "Quelques problèmes," 219n78, referring to Clugnet, Dictionnaire, 48.

204. Mateos, "Quelques problèmes," 219.

205. Bibliography in A. Luzzi, "L'ideologia costantiniana' nella liturgia dell'età di Costantino VII Porfirogenito," RSBN 28 (1991): 115–68; G. Wolfram, "Das Zeremonienbuch Konstantins VII. und das liturgische Typikon der Hagia Sophia als Quellen der Hymnographie," in Wiener Byzantinistik und Neogräzistik. Beiträge zum Symposion vierzig Jahre Institut für Byzantinistik und Neogräzistik der Universität Wien im Gedenken an Herbert Hunger (Wien, 4.–7. Dezember 2002), ed. W. Hörandner, J. Koder, M. A. Stassinopoulou, Byzantina et Neograeca Vindobonensia 24 (Wien: Verlag der Österreichischen Akademie der Wissenschaften, 2004), 487–96; G. Wolfram,

Zion" (98:3), it is well adapted to the risen Christ and therefore to Sunday. In terms of structure, we again witness the phenomenon of partial antiphonalization of what was originally responsorial psalmody (Ps 98:9) through the addition of a concluding troparion.[206]

For the saints' feast days the psalter horologion prescribes the singing of the exaposteilarion Ὁ οὐρανὸν τοῖς ἄστροις κατακοσμήσας, although without giving the text, which it is necessary to know in order to understand the reasons behind the choice. As Juan Mateos has noted,[207] in the horologion of the eleventh century (Paris, BNF, gr. 331, fols. 21v–22r), the exaposteilarion presents an interesting reading with respect to the *textus receptus* (*tr*): "Ὁ οὐρανὸν τοῖς ἄστροις κατακοσμήσας ὡς Θεός, καὶ διὰ τῶν σῶν ἁγίων (*tr*: τῶν σῶν ἀγγέλων) πᾶσαν τὴν γῆν φωταγωγῶν, δημιουργὲ τῶν ἀπάντων τοὺς ἀνυμνοῦντάς σε σῶσον (*tr*: σῶζε)." The τῶν σῶν ἁγίων reading must be considered original, and only at a later date was it replaced by τῶν σῶν ἀγγέλων; the substitution transformed an exaposteilarion common to all the feasts of the saints into the exaposteilarion for Monday, a day devoted to the angels. The change gave rise to an improvised series of weekly exaposteilaria, which were still unknown to the liturgical typikon of Evergetis.[208]

III.7.2.3. *Doxology and conclusion*

The description of the feast day matins continues in schema I with the group of the Psalms known as the lauds (Pss 148–50); the resurrection stichera (ἀναστάσιμα στιχηρά) are intercalated into the last verses, followed by the doxology and ending with the Trisagion. Schema II presents a lengthier sequence and includes other elements that are found in the Lenten matins in the *textus receptus* (table 10).

The doxology (δοξολογία) is the celebrated hymn "Glory to God in the

---

"Ein neumiertes Exaposteilarion anastasimon Konstantins VII.," in *Byzantios. Festschrift für Herbert Hunger zum 70. Geburtstag*, ed. W. Hörandner, J. Koder, O. Kresten, E. Trapp (Wien: Becvar, 1984), 333–38.

206. On antiphonalization see above, n184.

207. Mateos, "Quelques problèmes," 219.

208. Cf. Jordan, ed., *Synaxarion of Evergetis*, 1:19, 21, 23, 73, 81, 87, 89, 93, 103, etc., as in the typikon of the monastery of Christ Philanthropos (Panaghia Kamariotissa 26), for which it is not possible to cite folio numbers, as these are not visible on microfilm of the Dumbarton Oaks Research Library. Here I would like to extend my gratitude to Dumbarton Oaks for placing this microfilm at my disposal.

Table 10

schema I	schema II
Psalms 148–50	Psalms 148–50
+ stichera of the resurrection	+ stichera
Doxology	Doxology
+ Trisagion	+ Kataxioson
	Psalm 89:14–17 + stichera
	Psalm 91:2–3
	Trisagion-Pater
	Kyrie eleison
First hour	First hour

highest," attested as early as the *Apostolic Constitutions* (ca. 380) and the Codex Alexandrinus (early fifth century),[209] and used in matins in many Eastern traditions, as well as in the Ambrosian rite.[210] The contemporary horologion presents two recensions: the "great" for Sundays and feast days and the "small" for weekdays.[211] But this is just another example of imprecise and banal terminology, even if widely applied (for example, great and small apodeipnon, great and small omophorion, etc).[212] The "great doxology" is nothing other than the Constantinopolitan recension, and the "small" one is the hagiopolite; the former ends with the Trisagion, the latter with a type of psalm litany known from the incipit Καταξίωσον. Even before the time of the Harvard Horologion, the versions of the doxology are confirmed in the psalter; the hagiopolite psalters present a recension different from that of the

209. C. Renoux, "Le *Gloria in excelsis Deo* de l'Église arménienne," in *Crossroad of Cultures*, ed. Feulner, 603–18.

210. Taft, *Liturgy of the Hours*, 393: Index of Liturgical Pieces, s.v. *Gloria in excelsis*; for the Ambrosian rite: "Principi e norme per la Liturgia ambrosiana delle Ore," in *Liturgia delle Ore secondo il rito della Santa Chiesa Ambrosiana, Riformata a norma dei decreti del Concilio Vaticano II e promulgata dal Cardinale Carlo Maria Martini Arcivescovo di Milano* (Milan: Centro Ambrosiano di Documentazione e Studi Religiosi, 1983), 36 (§ IV.69).

211. *HR* 126–30; *HA* 108–11.

212. For the omophorion, see R. F. Taft, "The Case of the Missing Vestment: The Byzantine Omophorion Great and Small," *BollGrott* 1 (2004): 273–304.

Constantinopolitan. The distinction between the two is clearly marked in the Italo-Greek psalter Rome, BAV, Barb. gr. 285, the eleventh-century work that, as noted above at § I.3, combines the two traditions. The Constantinopolitan recension of the "Glory to God in the highest" appears under the title ὕμνος ἑωθινὸς τοῦ κορυφαίου Πέτρου (fol. 155v), whereas the Jerusalem recension has the explicit rubric κατὰ τὸν ἁγιοπολίτην (fol. 156v).[213]

The information in the psalters allows us to assign schema I to the Constantinopolitan tradition and schema II to the hagiopolite. Nevertheless, if schema I models the conclusion of matins on the cathedral of Constantinople, this does not mean that schema II follows the pattern set by the cathedral of Jerusalem. In fact, schema II is also related to practice in the Byzantine capital, specifically to that of the monastery of St. John Stoudios. We learn this from the *Taktikon* of Nikon (1055–60), the monk of the Black Mountain monastery north of Antioch in Syria.[214] In listing the differences between the liturgical typika of Stoudios and Mar Saba, he explains:

> It is necessary to understand that in the Stoudite typikon there is no great doxology whatsoever, either on Sundays or on the major feast days, but on these days the stichera are recited at the lauds, as at the aposticha; on the lesser feast days instead, the stichera are recited only at the aposticha, as on other days.
>
> In the Jerusalem typikon, however, it is not so; but every Sunday has the great doxology, as during all of Pentecost, from the birth of Christ to St. Basil's and also from the Theophany to its apodosis. The other great feast-days have only a single day, while Saturday and the other middle feast-days the stichera are recited at lauds, as at the aposticha; on the other little feast-days and on the other days the stichera are not at all recited at the lauds, but only at the aposticha.
>
> Thus it must be done here as well, according to the Jerusalem model, and in all the akolouthia and for the entire year, while the other ordo is not written in the current typikon.[215]

The long conclusion of schema II is therefore easily attributed to the Stoudite tradition. The century after the *Taktikon* of Nikon sees the situation evolving. The monastic typikon of Mar Saba, in Palestine, saves the long conclusion for the Lenten weekdays,[216] and in this it is followed by

---

213. See Parenti, "Nota sul Salterio-Horologion," 278, with bibliography.
214. On the complex Greek and/or Slavic textual tradition see *BMFD*, 1:377–78 and notes.
215. Slavonic text in Beneševič, *Тактикон*, 30; cf. *BMFD*, 2:390–91.
216. As precisely in Sinai. gr. 1094, ed. Dmitrievskij, *Описание*, 3:9.

the typika of southern Italy (though strongly influenced by the Stoudite tradition) and by the Sinaitic recension of the Palestinian typikon.[217] But the horologion of the Harvard Psalter also maintains the original practice common to Stoudios on feast days (schema II), though in competition with the new usage (schema I). We again have confirmation of the survival in Lent of ritual structures and elements that in previous eras were common and daily elements of the office.[218]

III.7.3. Saturday matins

In the cycle of weekly commemorations, Saturday is the day devoted to all the saints and the deceased.[219] Following the singing of "God is our Lord ..." (Θεὸς Κύριος ...) is a troparion in honor of the saints (Ἀπόστολοι, μάρτυρες καὶ προφῆται ...), one for the deceased (Μνήσθητι, Κύριε, ὡς ἀγαθός ...), and a theotokion (Μῆτερ ἁγία ἡ τοῦ ἀφράστου ...) inserted at the Glory to the Father. In the same manner, the exaposteilarion is the one already examined for the commemoration of the saints (Ὁ οὐρανὸν τοῖς ἄστροις ...), followed by a second exaposteilarion for the deceased (Ὁ καὶ νεκρῶν ...) and a theotokion (Ὁ γλυκασμός ...).

III.7.4. Weekday matins
III.7.4.1. Alleluia and triadic hymns

Following the hexapsalmos on weekdays and days of simple commemoration (ἡμέρα λιτή), the Canticle of Isaiah (Is 26:9, 11, 15, 17) is sung in a responsorial manner with the Alleluia as the refrain. For this reason the weekdays are called "of the Alleluia." In the horologion Mt. Sinai, MSC, gr 864 (ninth century) the Canticle of Isaiah still belongs to the ἀκολουθία τῶν μεσονυκτινῶν, where it is followed by the Trinitarian troparion (τριαδικόν) "Behold, the bridegroom comes in the middle of the night ..."[220] The same

217. For Sinai. gr. 1097, copied at St. Catherine's in 1214, see N. P. Ševčenko, "The liturgical typikon of Symeon of Sinai," in Metaphrastes, or, Gained in translation. Essays and translations in honour of Robert H. Jordan, ed. M. Mullett (Belfast: Belfast Byzantine Enterprises, 2004), 274–86; the author expresses the hope that "someone will undertake an edition of the entire text" (ibid., 274).

218. Taft, "Comparative Liturgy Revisited," 200, 206–8.

219. O. A. Krašeninnikova, "К истории формирования седмичных памятей октоиха," Богословские Труды 32 (1996): 260–68; Parenti, "Un fascicolo ritrovato," 355–56.

220. Ajjoub and Paramelle, ed., Livre d'Heures du Sinaï, 236–38. Dr. Nina Glibetić has recently published a Glagolitic fragment from the eleventh century, which appears to be connected to the same textual tradition as the Sinai Horologion: N. Gilbetić, "A New Eleventh-Century Glagolitic

troparion is sung at matins during the first three days of Holy Week in the Stoudite and Sabaite Byzantine traditions, and it is directed in the calendar of our horologion as well. This is further confirmation of a hypothesis of Mateos, who had detected remnants of an ancient nighttime office in the first part of orthros.[221]

In the horologion of the Harvard Psalter the Isaiah Canticle is followed, as it is today, by Trinitarian Hymns (τριαδικά), three for each of the eight modes. All have the same conclusion: the angelic hymn or the biblical Trisagion of Isaiah 6:3 ("Holy, Holy, Holy Lord"). Juan Mateos sees a more ancient layer to the Trinitarian Hymns; it is identifiable in hymns I.3 and III.3, for example, through the simpler and more thematically centered structure (awakening from sleep and arrival of the divine judge at midnight).[222] At a later time, other hymns were apparently added for the purpose of creating a weekly cycle in accordance with the eight modes. Mateos based his observations on the *textus receptus*. A glance at the manuscript tradition, as yet uninvestigated, reveals a situation already underway and in flux in the oldest manuscripts. In the stichero-kathismatarion Mt. Sinai, MSC, gr. 1593, of the ninth and tenth centuries, there are four triadika for modes III, IV, plagal I and II, five for the grave mode, and a good seven for plagal IV (the manuscript is defective at the point of the first two modes).[223]

In the tenth-century stichiro-kathismatarion Mt. Sinai, MSC, gr. 824 there are two Trinitarian Hymns for each mode.[224] In the eleventh-century "parakletike" Mt. Sinai, MSC, gr. 776 there are three for modes II–IV, plagal II, grave, and plagal IV, four in mode I and plagal I.[225] All of this points to a process of development that corroborates Mateos's theory. In the Harvard Psalter, the Trinitarian Hymns are already the same as in contemporary editions, although in a different order.

Fragment from St. Catherine's Monastery: The Midnight Prayer of Early Slavic Monks in the Sinai," *Archeografski prilozi/Archeographical Papers* 37 (2015): 11–48.

221. Mateos, "Quelques problèmes," 30, writes: "Si cette place du tropaire est ancienne, comme forcément elle doit l'être, nous avons ici un autre argument solide pour interpréter le début de l'orthros comme un office de minuit."

222. Ibid., 28.

223. Krašeninnikova, *Древнеславянский Октоих*, 304 (plagal tone I).

224. D. Bucca, "Un antico manoscritto innografico di origine orientale: il Sin. gr. 824," *RSBN* 43 (2006): 87–136, esp. 117–25.

225. Krašeninnikova, *Древнеславянский Октоих*, 304 (plagal tone I).

III.7.4.2. *The exaposteilarion*[226]

The weekday psalmody is denoted by the technical term στιχολογία, which literally means reading the psalms one verse (στίχος) after another, but the number of kathismata, which could vary according to the liturgical schedule, is not indicated.[227]

After Psalm 50 and the rest of the celebration (ἡ λοιπὴ ἀκολουθία), the description of the weekday orthros resumes with the exaposteilaria according to the eight modes following the lauds of the feast day orthros. In contrast to the Sunday exaposteilarion, which is psalmic (Ps 98:9), the weekday exaposteilaria are hymnographic texts. Thus, one asks whether the latter were at one time short troparia standing in relation to a fixed psalm that has now disappeared. The phrase ἐξαπόστειλον τὸ φῶς σου—which, as we have seen, characterizes the hymns of modes II, III, and plagal I—corresponds to Psalm 43:3 and suggests the hypothesis, surely to be verified, that the exaposteilarion was originally a short troparion. Its name, ἐξαποστειλάριον, derives from a structural function relating to the performance of Psalm 43:3. Therefore, ἐξαποστειλάριον from ἐξαπόστειλον τὸ φῶς σου (Ps 43:3), as κεκραγάριον from Κύριε ἐκέκραξα (Ps 140:1) or στιχηρόν from στίχος, refers not to the text of the hymn but to its structural function with respect to the psalm. It is also likely that the exaposteilarion came to antiphonalize a previously responsorial structure, later removed from the troparion. The Sunday psalmic structure (Ps 98:9) was saved because it was used less frequently with respect to the presumed weekday structure (Ps 43:3). If things were actually so, the responsorial structure would correspond to those mesodia, which in the *Narrations* by Nilos of Sinai (seventh and eighth century) came to intercalate the canons of the scriptural odes.[228]

The original role of the exaposteilarion is difficult to establish; it may, however, be noted that both the psalms refer to Zion (Ps 98:3) and the "sacred mountain" (Ps 43:3), and they do so in a pronounced processional context that may relate them to the stational liturgy of Jerusalem. However things

---

226. In this paragraph, I summarize what I wrote in the study "Върху историята на ексапостилария," in *Пение мало Георгию. Сборник в чест на 65-годишнината на проф. Георги Попов* (Sofia: Издателски център Боян Пенев, 2010), 285–96.

227. Mateos, "Psalmodie variable."

228. S. Parenti, "Mesedi–Mesodion," in *Crossroad of Cultures*, ed. Feulner, 543–55.

stand, the modern distinction between the exaposteilaria and photagogika is arbitrary: they are only two ways of denoting the same liturgical structure.[229]

The last part of weekday matins shows analogies with the modern rite: the lauds (Pss 148–50) without the intercalated hymnography, the hagiopolite doxology concluding with the Καταξίωσον, and stichera of the day, perhaps with Psalm 91:2–3.[230]

III.8. *The great hours*

In the contemporary observance of the Byzantine rite, the term "great hours" (Αἱ Μεγάλαι Ὧραι) refers to the particularly solemn form of psalms, hymns, and readings that the first, third, sixth, and ninth monastic hours assume three times a year: Holy Friday, Christmas vigil, and the vigil of the Theophany.[231] The terminology, used to distinguish the great hours from the ordinary and daily observances, considered in some manner "small," is not universally employed. To the present day, the typika of Moscow and Constantinople call the "great hours" simply "the hours" (Αἱ Ὧραι - Часы).[232] In our manuscript the opposite occurs. The normal hours of third and sixth are called "great," but not the first and ninth. This is another problem of ambiguous terminology that needs to be resolved.

In his 1963 doctoral thesis on the uninterrupted prayer "of the twenty-four hours," the Greek liturgist Ioannis Phountoulis studied two horologia that present a nearly unique daily *cursus*.[233] One is Paris, BNF, gr. 331 (cf. § III.7.2.2), dated by Omont to the eleventh century[234] and assigned by Bordier

229. The commentary of Mark of Ephesus (d. 1444) puts the photagogika and exaposteilaria on the same level, with no distinction between them; see *Expositio Officii ecclesiastici* (PG 160:1180C–D). For an appreciation of Mark as a theologian see N. Constas, "Mark Eugenikos," in *La théologie byzantine et sa tradition*, vol. 2, *XIIIe – XIXe s.*, ed. C. G. Conticello and V. Conticello (Turnhout: Brepols, 2002), 411–75.

230. HR 122–25, 128–32; HA 106–11.

231. K. Papagianne, Ἡ ἁγία καὶ μεγάλη Ἑβδομὰς, περιέχουσα πᾶσαν τὰς ἱερᾶς ἀκουλουθίας ἀπὸ τῆς Κυριακῆς τῶν βαΐων μέχρι τῆς Κυριακῆς τοῦ Πάσχα (Athens: Apostolike Diakonia, 1990), 225; Μηναῖον τοῦ Δεκεμβρίου μηνός (Athens, 2002), 468; Μηναῖον τοῦ Ἰαννουαρίου μηνός (Athens, 2002), 127.

232. G. Biolake, Τυπικὸν τῆς τοῦ Χριστοῦ Μεγάλης Ἐκκλησίας (Constantinople, 1888), 360; Типиконъ сиесть Уставъ (Moscow, 2002), 362–65, 405–6, 939–43.

233. Phountoulis, Ἀκοίμητος δοξολογία. Two manuscripts found by Parpulov ("Psalters and Personal Piety," 84n39) should be added to those cited by Phountoulis: Sinai gr. 869 (formerly part of Sinai gr. 51) and Atene, EBE 15, of the twelfth century.

234. Omont, *Inventaire sommaire*, 34. Parpulov, "Psalters and Personal Piety," 84n38.

Table 11

Hours of the day	Hours of the night
Orthros	
<First hour>[1]	
First little hour (Ὥρα Α᾽ μικρά)	First hour
Second hour	Second hour
Third little hour (Ὥρα Γ᾽ μικρά)	Third hour
Third great hour (Ὥρα Γ᾽ μεγάλη)	
Fourth hour	Fourth hour
Fifth hour	Fifth hour
Sixth little hour (Ὥρα ς᾽ μικρά)	Sixth hour
Sixth great hour (Ὥρα ς᾽ μεγάλη)	<Mesonyktikon>[4]
Seventh hour	Seventh hour
Eighth hour	Eighth hour
Ninth little hour (Ὥρα θ᾽ μικρά)	Ninth hour
Ninth great hour (Ὥρα θ᾽ μεγάλη)	
Typika[2]	
Tenth hour	Tenth hour
Eleventh hour	Eleventh hour
Twelfth hour	Twelfth hour
Vespers[3]	

1. Owing to the loss of a folio, the first hour begins without title on fol. 29r at Ps 5:8b: "προσκυνήσω πρὸς ναὸν ἅγιόν σου ἐν φόβῳ σου..."

2. Lacunae between fols. 103 and 104, and between fols. 104 and 105.

3. Lacuna between fols. 120 and 121.

4. Although the name "mesonyktikon" does not appear in the manuscript, the office is certain.

to Constantinople.[235] The other is Lesbos, ML, cod. 295, a richly illustrated manuscript that has been dated to the twelfth or thirteenth century and attributed to the Palestinian-Cypriot region.[236]

The unique characteristic of the Paris and Lesbos manuscripts is the daily *cursus* for each hour of the day and night. The framework of the Paris. gr. 331, can serve here as an example (table 11).

235. H.-L. Bordier, *Description des peintures et autres ornements contenus dans les manuscrits grecs de la Bibliothèque Nationale* (Paris, 1883), 184; see also Parpulov, *Byzantine Psalters*, 118–19.

236. ML = Μονὴ τῶν Λειμῶνος, Lesbos. P. Vokotopoulos, "Ἡ εἰκονογράφηση τοῦ κανόνος εἰς ψυχορραγοῦντα στὸ Ὡρολόγιον 295 τῆς Μονῆς Λειμῶνος," *Symmeikta* 9 (1994): 97; a reproduction appears in Phountoulis, "῾Ύμνος ἑσπερινός," 36. In the fourteenth century the codex arrived

The compiler of this particular horologion has joined two distinct traditions: (1) the hours of the Byzantine horologion (orthros, first, third, sixth, ninth, typika, vespers [apodeipnon], mesonyktikon), and (2) an akolouthia for the twenty-four hours of the day and night. Phountoulis believed that he could connect the latter with the Constantinopolitan monastery of the Akoimetoi and the *laus perennis* that was celebrated there.[237] The hours of the Byzantine horologion come to be called "great" to distinguish them from the "small" of the *cursus* of the twenty-four hours; the terminology and distinction were very clear to the copyist of the psalter horologion, who was aware of this unique tradition, which will be examined below (§ V).

III.9. *The first, third, sixth, and ninth hours*

The four hours of the day in the horologion of the Harvard Psalter are one of the many local recensions attested by horologia and typika from every corner of the Byzantine Empire. In the final analysis they all descend from the ordo represented by the ninth-century Sinai. gr. 863. One could more precisely speak of regional developments within a common rite of Palestinian origin, as illustrated in table 12.

The comparison presented here is exclusively concerned with fundamental structures and the linking of the individual elements; for the psalmody, it is enough to note that the psalms in the Harvard Psalter, as in the *textus receptus*, correspond to the first three psalms in the Sinai. gr. 863.[238] With respect to the remainder, I would only draw attention to a few other specific aspects, such as the initial prayers, the prokeimenon, the "verses," and the final prayers.

---

in Constantinople, as revealed by eleven marginal notes written between 1328 and 1393, for which see P. Schreiner, *Die byzantinischen Kleinchroniken*, vol. 1, *Einleitung und Text* (Vienna: Österreichische Akademie der Wissenschaften, 1975), 101–4. See also E. Follieri, *I calendari in metro innografico di Cristoforo Mitileneo*, vol. 1, *Introduzione, testo e traduzione* (Brussels: Société des Bollandistes, 1980), 20, 35–40; http://84.205.233.134/pdfs/2008730114435.pdf.

237. Phountoulis, Ἀκοίμητος δοξολογία; Phontoulis, Εἰκοσιτετράωρον ὡρολόγιον, Κείμενα Λειτουργικῆς 16 (Thessaloniki, 1978), translated by P. D. Guillaume, *Horologe des veilleurs. Les 24 heures des Acémètes* (Rome: Diaconie Apostolique, 1990). The Constantinopolitan monastery of the Akoimetoi (sleepless ones) was founded by the monk Alexander in 405. He organized the community into three groups in order to ensure a continual liturgical service in church (cf. the notice by A.-M. Talbot and R. F. Taft in *ODB*, 1:46).

238. Mateos, "Horologion de Saint-Sabas," 62; Diakovskij, *Posledovanie časov*, 94–96.

Table 12

Sinai. gr. 863	Harvard Psalter Horologion
Initial prayers	=
Hymn	=
Psalms [from 8 to 4]	[3]
Antiphonated Psalmody	=
"Verses"	=
Trisagion	=
Creed	=
Our Father	=
	Prayer or prayers

III.9.1. *Initial prayers*

In the third, sixth, and ninth hours the initial prayers are supplemented by other elements. The original group of the Trisagion-Pater is prefaced by the troparion to the Holy Spirit (Βασιλεῦ οὐράνιε ...), and following the Our Father are others that are inspired by the themes of the individual hours. The first hour—which is an exception since it was recited following matins—begins directly after the invitatory (Δεῦτε προσκυνήσωμεν ...). The hymn "Heavenly King," originally of the hagiopolite liturgy for the feast of Pentecost,[239] appears at the beginning of the initial prayers in the *Hypotyposis* of Niketas of Stoudios (before 1090), but becomes a fixed element only in the fifteenth century.[240]

III.9.2. *The prokeimenon*

On feast days, after the fixed psalmody for each hour, the psalter horologion prescribes the singing of the feast day troparion, and a prokeimenon in its place on the other days. According to the definition of Juan Mateos,

239. A. Ju. Nikiforova, *Из истории Минеи в Византии. Гимнографические памятники VIII–XII вв. из собрания монастыря святой Екатерины на Синае* (Moscow: Изд-во ПСТГУ, 2012), 233.

240. S. Parenti and E. Velkovska, "'Re celeste, paraclito, Spirito di verità.' Il *Veni creator Spiritus* della liturgia bizantina," in *Spiritus spiritalia nobis dona potenter infundit. A proposito di tematiche liturgico-pneumatologiche. Studi in onore di Achille M. Triacca, sdb*, ed. E. Carr (Rome: Centro Studi S. Anselmo, 2005), 387–404.

"le terme προκείμενον ... désigne un verset psalmique placé avant le début du psalme ... le prokeimenon, par opposition à l'antiphone, n'est jamais terminé par le *Gloria Patri*."[241] Prokeimenon is thus synonymous with responsorial psalmody.[242] In our case, the situation is more complex. At the first hour, the prokeimenon follows a fundamentally responsorial structure, concluded, however, by the *Gloria Patri* with a troparion. For the third, sixth, and ninth hours, the structure, although still called prokeimenon, is entirely antiphonal, with a troparion not only with the *Gloria Patri*, but also with the psalm verses.

As Heinrich Husmann notes,[243] the same phenomenon is in part reflected in the horologia Mt. Sinai, MSC, gr. 904 (1211 A.D.)[244] and gr. 883 (1392 A.D.);[245] it is also found in other manuscripts of the horologion unknown to him.[246] Husmann infers that troparion and prokeimenon are at times used as synonyms, and his assumption finds support in Mt. Sinai, MSC, gr. 904 (1211 A.D.), where, at the sixth hour, the liturgical unit under discussion is designated "troparion-prokeimenon." Ultimately, though, Husmann's inference is unsupportable, for despite the abundance of synonyms found in the Byzantine liturgical rubrics the remaining impression is one of a certain propriety and correctness in the language. The responsorial psalmody of the first hour can easily be called prokeimenon, because that is what it is—up to the *Gloria Patri*. The insertion of the Gloria reveals yet another example of the process of antiphonalization, which Husmann has called "tropiert,"[247] and which in the other hours appears to be fully realized. Beginning by the sixth century, antiphonalization appears in the rites of the Great Church.[248] The scribes do not, therefore, use "troparion" and "prokeimenon" as synonyms. The words are chosen by analogy and with respect to the position that the liturgical unit occupies in the ordinary of each individual hour. The term "prokeimenon," in part correct for the first hour, is automatically repeated

---

241. Mateos, *Célébration de la Parole*, 12–13.

242. Taft, "Psalmody," 17–18; see also Parenti, "Mesedi-Mesodion" (above, n228), 554–55.

243. Husmann, "Hymnus und Troparion," 69–70.

244. Sinai. gr. 904, fols. 81r–82v (first), 100v–102r (third), 117v–119v (sixth).

245. Sinai. gr. 883, fol. 5r+v (ninth).

246. Sinai. gr. 903 (thirteenth or fourteenth century), fol. 5r+v; Sinai. gr. 870 (thirteenth century), fols. 49r–50r.

247. Husmann, "Hymnus und Troparion," 69.

248. Taft and Parenti, *Il Grande Ingresso* (below n382), 206–28.

in the other hours, not with regard to the internal structure but in respect to the position that it occupies.

III.9.3. *Verses of the hours*

In the ninth-century Mt. Sinai, MSC, gr. 863, several scriptural verses of an undefined role follow the antiphonal canticle:

First: Psalms 118:133–35, 70:8
Third: Psalm 67:19–21
Sixth: Psalm 78:8–9
Ninth: Daniel 3:34–35

The manuscripts and printed horologia do not provide a title for them, and some scholarly translations call them "versets"[249] because of their content, not their function. The only hypothesis that I am aware of is that of Juan Mateos, for whom the verses "semblent être une finale fixe de l'heure, après les pièces variables."[250]

The problem of the verses is open to a solution when viewed in the light of comparative liturgy. The scriptural verses are, in fact, invocations placed toward the end of every hour, precisely where the insistant supplication pronounced by the deacon occurs in the cathedral system. A parallel from monastic ritual can be found in the *Dignare Domine* ... (Καταξίωσον Κύριε ...), which concludes the vespers in the Sinai. gr. 863. Furthermore, a psalm litany, the *capitellum* or *capitella*, occurs at the end of the hours of the monastic offices celebrated in Gaul at the time of Caesarius of Arles (ca. 470–542). Ours is a case of a use explicitly mentioned in Canon 30 of the Council of Adge, presided over by Caesarius in 506.[251] Thus, the "verses," including the Καταξίωσον of vespers and matins, are the final petitions of the monastic rite.[252]

---

249. *La prière des heures*, 261, 279, 299, 315. The same solution ("versetti") has been adopted in S. Parenti, *Liturgia delle Ore Italo-bizantina (Rito di Grottaferrata)* (Vatican City: Libreria Editrice Vaticana, 2001), 107, 118, 126, 138.

250. Mateos, "Horologion de Saint-Sabas," 64.

251. O. Heiming, "Zum monastischen Offizium von Kassianus bis Kolumbanus," *Archiv für Liturgiewissenschaft* 7 (1961): 121; Taft, *Liturgy of the Hours*, 147–48.

252. More extensively in Parenti, "Nota sul Salterio-Horologion," 284.

III.9.4. *Concluding prayers*

All of the hours end with two prayers, all, that is, except the first hour, which has four:

(1) Ὁ ἐν παντὶ καιρῷ καὶ πάσῃ ὥρᾳ ...

(2) Ὁ Θεὸς ὁ αἰώνιος, τὸ ἄναρχον ...

(3) Πάτερ ἅγιε, ὁ τὸν ἥλιον τῆς δικαιοσύνης ...

(4) Ὁ ἀποστέλλων τὸ φῶς καὶ πορεύεται ...

Only the incipit is given of prayer (1), since the text is found in its entirety later, at apodeipnon (§ III.14.6). It appears, in fact, that the prayer was originally meant for evening or nighttime offices, as demonstrated for instance by the Italo-Greek tradition, which reserves its use for mesonyktikon.[253] In prescribing it not only at apodeipnon but also at the first hour, our manuscript is the first horologion to attest to a trend, which is the promotion of prayer at every hourly synaxis with the exception of orthros and vespers. Although ours is the first horologion to do so, prayer is prescribed for first, third, and ninth hours, and apodeipnon in the Evergetis Typikon, attributed to the first quarter of the twelfth century.[254] Over the course of the twelfth century, prayer can be found in the first hour and its mesorion (the "interhours" are discussed below, § III.12);[255] by the thirteenth, prayers are also found in the third, sixth, and ninth hours,[256] or in the mesoria of the first, sixth, and ninth hours, and in mesonyktikon (weekdays and Saturday–Sunday).[257] Thus, before the end of the fourteenth century, the use of prayer had been broadened and generalized, as in the *textus receptus*.[258] According to N. Egender, the prayer "fait partie de la couche ancienne de l'Horologion

253. Egender, "Introduction," 252. I. Phontoulis, "Αἱ ἀκολουθίαι τῶν ὡρῶν τοῦ νυχθημέρου κατὰ τὸ Ὡρολόγιον τῆς Κρυπτοφέρρης ἐν συγκρίσει πρὸς τὸ Κωνσταντινουπολιτικὸν Ὡρολόγιον," in *La Chiesa greca in Italia dall'VIII al XVI secolo* (Padua: Antenore, 1972–73), 2:581, maintaining that in the oldest manuscripts the prayer was recited only at mesonyktikon. This is also the case with the "Melkite Horologion" (1187/88 A.D.); see Black, *Syriac Horologion*, 92.

254. Jordan, ed., *Synaxarion of Evergetis*, 1:201–2, 328; 2:359, 361, 367; for the first hour see also the foundation typikon in P. Gautier, "Le Typikon de la Théotokos Évergétis," *REB* 40 (1982): 19; *BMFD*, 2:473. The regulation of the liturgical typikon of Evergetis is taken verbatim from that of Christ Philanthropos.

255. Sinai. gr. 865 (twelfth century), fols. 98v–99r, 105r.

256. Sinai. gr. 870 (thirteenth century), fols. 8r, 33v, 50r, 90v.

257. Sinai. gr. 904 (1211 A.D.), fols. 92v, 127r, 161v, 239v, 268r.

258. E.g., Sinai. gr. 898 (1335 A.D.), fols. 24r, 93v, 106r, 116r, 140r, 174v.

qui l'attribue à S. Basile,"[259] but since the assignment to Basil is a rather late phenomenon[260] it would be beneficial to return to the manuscript tradition for clarification or confirmation.

Prayer (2), which in current practice is assigned to the mesorion of the first hour and attributed to Basil,[261] was known to the practice of the Constantinopolitan monastery of Evergetis, as shown by its foundation typikon.[262] Its use at the Evergetis notwithstanding, the prayer seems not, at least in the distant past, to have enjoyed much popularity.[263] The text exhibits surprising affinities—if not literally, then at least conceptually—with the prayer of the Gospel in the Liturgy of St. James, adopted for orthros in Constantinopolitan monasteries during the course of the tenth century.[264] In table 13, I compare the text of the psalter horologion with the prayer of the Gospel in the euchologion Paris, BNF, Coislin 213, written in Constantinople in 1027.

Prayer (3) belongs to the series for the various times in the day credited to St. Basil in the Constantinopolitan euchologion Paris. Coislin. 213.[265] The text also appears in Oxford, Bodleian Lib., Auct. E.5.13 (1121/22–1132 A.D.), the euchologion of the monastery of San Salvatore of Messina,[266] and in the mesorion of the first hour in the horologion Mt. Sinai, MSC, gr. 904, fols. 83v–85r (1211 A.D.). The last prayer of the first hour (4) is also attributed to Basil in the *textus receptus*, but this finds no support in the limited manuscript tradition. The *textus receptus* has prayer (4) in the mesorion of the first hour, immediately after our prayer (2).[267] In fact, we always find prayer (4) after prayer (2): in the thirteenth-century Mt. Sinai, MSC, gr.

259. Egender, "Introduction," 77, with reference to *HR* 122, comparing the prayer "of all the hours" with the eucharistic prayer of inclination in the *Apostolic Constitutions* 8:7–9, 15: M. Metzger, *Les Constitutions Apostoliques* (Paris: Éditions du Cerf, 1987), 3:214–15.

260. Among the Sinai manuscripts of the horologion accessible to me I found the attribution to Basil for the first time in Sinai. gr. 877 (1467 A.D.), fols. 10v–11r.

261. *HR* 147–48; see also Fedwick, *BiblBasil*, 4.3:1524.

262. *BMFD*, 2:473.

263. Cf. Sinai. gr. 870 (thirteenth century), fols. 8v–9v, and Vat. Pal. gr. 288, fol 190r+v.

264. Arranz, "Prières des matines," 425–26.

265. Dmitrievskij, *Описание*, 2:1004–5; M. Arranz, "Les prières presbytérales des Petites Heures dans l'ancien Euchologe byzantin," *OCP* 39 (1973): 63.

266. Arranz, "Petites Heures," 65; Jacob, "Saint-Sauveur," 55.1.

267. *HR* 148–49, with the incipit "Ὁ ἐξαποστέλλων τὸ φῶς ..."; see also Fedwick, *BiblBasil*, 4.3:1524.

Table 13: Comparison of Psalter Horologion
and Prayer of the Gospel

Paris, BNF, Coislin 213	Psalter Horologion
	Ὁ Θεὸς ὁ αἰώνιος…
	τὸ φῶς τοῦ προσώπου σου·
Ἔλλαμψον ἐν ταῖς καρδίαις ἡμῶν,	λάμψον ἐν ταῖς καρδίαις ἡμῶν,
Δέσποτα,	νοητὲ ἥλιε τῆς δικαιοσύνης,
τὸ τῆς θεογνωσίας σου	καὶ τῆς σῆς εὐφροσύνης
ἀπρόσιτον φῶς,	τὰς ψυχὰς ἡμῶν πλήρωσον.
καὶ τοὺς τῆς διανοίας ἡμῶν	Δίδαξον ἡμᾶς τὰ σὰ μελετᾶν ἀεὶ
ὀφθαλμοὺς ἄνοιξον	καὶ φθέγγεσθαι κρίματα
εἰς τὴν τῶν εὐαγγελικῶν	καὶ ἐξομολογεῖσθαί σοι διηνεκῶς
κηρυγμάτων κατανόησιν·	τῷ ἡμετέρῳ Δεσπότῃ καὶ εὐεργέτῃ.
ἔνθες ἡμῖν καὶ τὸν φόβον	Τὰ τῶν χειρῶν ἡμῶν ἔργα
τῶν μακαρίων σου ἐντολῶν,	
ἵνα τὰς σαρκικὰς ἐπιθυμίας	
καταπατήσαντες,	
πνευματικὴν πολιτείαν	πρὸς τὸ σὸν κατεύθυνον θέλημα,
μετέλθωμεν,	καὶ πράττειν ἡμᾶς τὰ σοὶ εὐάρεστα
πάντοτε τὰ πρὸς εὐαρέστησιν σὴν	καὶ φίλα εὐόδωσον…
καὶ φρονοῦντες καὶ πράττοντες.	

Table 14: Comparison of Typikon
and Horologion

Evergetis Typikon	Psalter Horologion
Prayer 1	Prayer 1
Prayer 2	Prayer 2
Communal meditation	Prayer 3
Prayer 4	Prayer 4

870, fols. 9v–10v, and in the mesorion of the first hour in Rome, BAV, Pal. gr. 288, fol. 190v, also from the thirteenth century. Perhaps more important than a possible attribution to St. Basil, at least in terms of the issue here, is the constant association of prayers (2) and (4) in the foundation Typikon of the Evergetis.[268] If we compare the prescriptions of the typikon and the ordo of our horologion, an interesting picture emerges (see table 14).

268. Gautier, "Typikon Évergétis," 19–21; BMFD, 2:473.

The private use of the Harvard Psalter Horologion is indicated by its substitution of prayer (3) for what was communal meditation at the Evergetis. Given that the liturgical rule of Evergetis at this time was followed also in other Constantinopolitan foundations, this detail could indicate that our manuscript was not destined for a monastic environment.

The third, sixth, and ninth hours each have two concluding prayers, although the first of each series is not a prayer in the strict sense, but is rather a revised troparion. The first prayer of the third hour is dependent on a troparion that I publish in table 15 from the horologion Mt. Sinai, MSC, gr. 904, fol. 101r+v (1211 A.D.).[269]

The first person plural of the troparion has been changed to the first person singular, an adaptation that underscores the private nature of the book.

The first prayers of the sixth and ninth hours are a light recasting of troparia already in use in the ninth-century horologion Mt. Sinai, MSC, gr. 863.[270] The process by which troparia were converted into prayers continued for a long time and left its traces in the *textus receptus*, where the beautiful prayer of the first hour (Χριστέ, τὸ φῶς τὸ ἀληθινόν ...) is a later reworking of the troparion "Τὸ φῶς τὸ ἀληθινόν ..." known from the Sinai gr. 863.[271]

The three alternative prayers that follow are true concluding prayers, taken into the *textus receptus*, where they are attributed to Basil,[272] although here, too, the observations made above are valid: they are late attributions not supported by the manuscript tradition.[273] The prayer of the third hour is a different recension of the second prayer of the Pentecost vespers of genuflection.[274]

---

269. Also in Sinai. gr. 870 (thirteenth century), f. 32v. The presumption that it is unpublished is based on its absence in Follieri, *Initia*, and P. Plank et al., *Das byzantinische Eigengut der neuzeitlichen slavischen Menäen und seine griechischen Originale*, vol. 3, *Incipitarium und Edition Theotokia, Index hymnorum graecorum, Index hymnorum slavicorum, Epimetra tria* (Paderborn: Schöningh, 2006).

270. Mateos, "Horologion de Saint-Sabas," 52, 54.

271. Ibid., 52.

272. As precisely in the mesorion of the third, sixth, and ninth hours: *HR* 164, 174–75, 211–12.

273. See Fedwick, *BiblBasil*, 4.3:1524–25.

274. M. Arranz, "Les prières de la gonyklisia ou de la génuflexion du jour de la Pentecôte dans l'ancien Euchologe byzantin," *OCP* 48 (1982): 92–123, does not take into consideration the manuscript tradition of all the prayers, which still remains unstudied.

Table 15: Troparion

Sinai. gr. 904	Psalter Horologion
Ὁ ἐν τῇ τρίτῃ ὥρᾳ	Ὁ ἐν τῇ τρίτῃ ὥρᾳ
τοῖς ἁγίοις σου	τοῖς ἁγίοις σου
καταπέμψας μαθηταῖς	μαθηταῖς καὶ ἀποστόλοις
	καταπέμψας
τὸ πανάγιόν σου πνεῦμα,	τὸ πανάγιόν σου πνεῦμα,
τοῦτο, Ἰησοῦ,	τοῦτο, Ἰησοῦ,
μὴ ἀντανέλῃς ἀφ᾽ ἡμῶν,	μὴ ἀντανέλῃς ἀπ᾽ ἐμοῦ,
υἱὲ Θεοῦ καὶ λόγε,	υἱὲ Θεοῦ καὶ λόγε,
ἀλλ᾽ ἐγκαίνισον	ἀλλ᾽ ἐγκαίνισον
ἐν τοῖς ἐγκάτοις ἡμῶν	ἐν τοῖς ἐγκάτοις μου
πνεῦμα τὸ εὐθὲς καὶ ζωοποιοῦν,	πνεῦμα εὐθὲς καὶ ζωοποιοῦν,
πνεῦμα συνέσεως,	πνεῦμα θείου φόβου
πνεῦμα υἱοθεσίας καὶ ἁγιασμοῦ·	καὶ κατανύξεως·
καὶ κατεύθυνον	καὶ εὔθυνον
τὰς προσευχὰς ἡμῶν	τὴν προσευχὴν μου
τῷ φωτοποιῷ καὶ ἁγιαστικῷ	τῷ φωτοποιῷ καὶ ἁγιαστικῷ
καὶ παντοδυνάμῳ	καὶ παντοδυνάμῳ καὶ ζωοποιῷ
σου πνεύματι·	σου πνεύματι·
σὺ γὰρ εἶ ὁ φωτισμὸς	σὺ γὰρ εἶ ὁ φωτισμὸς
τῶν ψυχῶν ἡμῶν,	τῶν ψυχῶν ἡμῶν,
ὁ φωτίζων πάντα ἄνθρωπον	ὁ φωτίζων πάντα ἄνθρωπον
εἰς τὸν κόσμον ἐρχόμενον.	ἐρχόμενον εἰς τὸν κόσμον,
	καὶ σοὶ τὴν δόξαν καὶ

III.10. *Typika*

The so-called typika (τυπικά) are what remains of an ancient monastic office of communion. The first and thus far only written evidence comes to us from the ninth-century book of hours, Sinai. gr. 863.[275] In the Sinai manuscript the office is entitled εἰς τὴν μετάληψιν and comes immediately after the ninth hour, where a troparion alludes to communion as imminent. In fact, among the monastic *consuetudines* was the rule that during certain

275. Mateos, "Horologion de Saint-Sabas," 54–55.

times of the year the only meal of the day was the one taken after the ninth hour.[276] The origins and significance of the rite of communion in relation to the later office of typika were already uncovered by Dmitrievskij and Diakovskij.[277] When Juan Mateos wrote on the same topic nearly forty years later it was an unconscious repetition since he did not have the works of the two Russian liturgists at his disposal. The analysis of the rite proposed by Diakovskij, Dmitrievskij, and Mateos remains substantially valid, though in some respects it may require more precise definitions and some corrections.

As I have previously observed,[278] the celebrative model of the typika is to be sought in the hagiopolite formulary of the Liturgy of the Presanctified, known as the Liturgy of St. James, and this connection should constitute the basis for all future investigation regarding the typika.[279] While the monastic rite of communion was still honored at Sinai during the ninth century, the Stoudios monastery of Constantinople had already abandoned the practice in favor of the cathedral formulary of the Presanctified.[280] The *Hypotyposis* of Stoudios [§ 27], compiled a few years after Theodore's death, in 826, presents the typika as the former office of communion and does so in relation to the distribution of the blessed bread, the antidoron, which took place following the eucharistic liturgy, by then a daily celebration.[281] In its further evolution, the typika became a moveable office destined to precede the celebration of the eucharistic rite, whether the complete liturgy or the Liturgy of the

276. See E. Trapp et al., *Lexikon zur byzantinischen Gräzität: besonders des 9.–12. Jahrhunderts* (Vienna: Österreichische Akademie der Wissenschaften, Veröffentlichungen der Kommission für Byzantinistik, 1999), 515, s.v. ἡ ἐννάτη ("fasten bis zur neunten Stunde").

277. See A. Dmitrievskij, "Что такое κανὼν τῆς ψαλμῳδίας, так нередко упоминаемый в жизнеописании препод. Саввы Освященного?" *Руководство для сельских пастырей* 38 (1889): 69–73; Diakovskij, *Posledovanie časov*, 283–84.

278. See A.-A. Thiermeyer, "Das Typikon-Ktetorikon und sein literarhistorischer Kontext," *OCP* 58 (1992): 482n18.

279. On the hagiopolite Liturgy of the Presanctified see S. Verhelst, "Les Présanctifiés de saint Jacques," *OCP* 61 (1995): 381–405; S. Alexopoulos, *The Presanctified Liturgy in the Byzantine Rite. A Comparative Analysis of its Origins, Evolution, and Structural Components* (Leuven: Peeters, 2009), 107–12.

280. R. F. Taft, "Changing Rhythms of Eucharistic Frequency in Byzantine Monasticism," in *Il monachesimo tra eredità e aperture*, ed. M. Bielawski and D. Hombergen (Rome: Pontificio Ateneo S. Anselmo, 2004), 419–58.

281. PG 99:1713; Dmitrievskij, *Описание*, 1:233; *BMFD*, 1:108–9; commentary in Pott, *La réforme liturgique byzantine*, 116. On antidoron see R. F. Taft, *A History of the Liturgy of St. John Chrysostom*, vol. 6, *The Communion, Thanksgiving, and Concluding Rites* (Rome: Pontificio Istituto Orientale, 2008), 699–719.

Presanctified; at this stage of development, the typika took the form of an appendix to the sixth hour on the days of liturgical celebration (when it did not take the place of the antiphons of the liturgy[282]) and to the ninth hour on the days when the liturgy was not celebrated. It is in this latter variation, of non-eucharistic moveable office, that the typika appears in the psalter horologion, although the memory of communion is retained in the ninth-hour troparion "Ὁ τὴν ψυχὴν ἐπὶ ξύλου κρεμάμενος ..."

III.11. *Prayers before and after communion*

Following the τυπικά is a brief office in preparation and thanksgiving for communion. It appears in a rather disorganized fashion owing to the insertion of special hours of Holy Thursday among the introductory prayers. Preceding everything is the liturgical unit previously examined between the two sets of psalter kathismata (§ II.5) and after prayers for rising (§ III.4). The prayers have nothing to do with the rite of the typika; they are meant for the communion in the liturgy (complete or of the Presanctified), which follows or incorporates the typika.

Of the two prayers in preparation for communion, the first can also be found in Paris, BNF, Coislin 213—but without the attribution to Chrysostom, found in the Harvard Psalter Horologion—and in the *textus receptus* of the ἀκολουθία τῆς μεταλήψεως.[283] The second prayer is a well-known and studied text, the renowned Syro-Palestinian formula for forgiveness: ἄνες, ἄφες, συγχώρησον. Of possible Jewish origin, it was in use from the tenth century, primarily in southern Italy, as a prayer in preparation for communion within the liturgical formulary.[284] There are also two thanksgiving prayers. The first is not widespread: I have found two other examples, one

---

282. The substitution is first attested in the Italo-Greek Liturgy of St. Peter, found in the euchologion Grottaferrata, BB, Γ.β.VII, from the end of the tenth century: H. W. Codrington, *The Liturgy of Saint Peter* (Munster: Aschendorff, 1936), 130.10–15; G. Passarelli, *L'Eucologio cryptense Γ.β.VII (sec. X)* (Thessaloniki: Patriarchikon Hidryma Paterikon Meleton, 1982), 167, (§§ 308–10); see also G. Andreou, "Alcune osservazioni sul menologion del lezionario Paris gr. 382 (X sec. ex.)," *BollGrott* 2 (2005): 6.

283. Canart, *Codices Vaticani graeci*, 343–44.

284. I mention only the recent work of Taft, *A History of the Liturgy of St. John Chrysostom*, vol. 6, 151–52, 168–72, and S. Verhelst, *Les traditions Judéo-chrétiennes dans la liturgie de Jérusalem, spécialement la Liturgie de saint Jacques frère de Dieu* (Leuven: Peeters, 2003), 91–104, with the earlier bibliography.

in the Italo-Greek paraklitike Rome, BAV, gr. 1853, copied in 1173,[285] and the other in the Middle-Eastern Euchologion "of Archimedes," from the beginning of the thirteenth century.[286] The second prayer appears for the first time around the end of the eleventh century in a euchologion from southern Italy, Grottaferrata, BB, Γ.β.XVA.[287] In the *textus receptus* it appears in the thanksgiving ἀκολουθία after communion.[288]

In sum, like the prayers for rising and rest, the prayers before and after communion belong to the sphere of private devotion. They can be found in the most varied manuscripts, whether of date or place of origin, and can be selected to suit the taste and judgment of the patron or the copyist. The prayers are found in euchologia, horologia, hymnographic, and patristic texts, as well as in rolls, especially ones of the thirteenth and fourteenth centuries,[289] that in the Middle East are already known by the ninth century.[290] If the prayers in preparation for communion came into existence earlier in southern Italy than elsewhere in the same eucharistic formulary, it is attributable to the tendency, attested as early as the second half of the tenth century, to produce plenary formularies that included both diakonika and more detailed rubrics.[291] An identical phenomenon, limited to the prayers

---

285. Canart, *Codices Vaticani graeci*, 244, no. 9.

286. S. Parenti, "The Liturgical Tradition of the Euchologion 'of Archimedes,'" *BollGrott* 2 (2005): 85–86, § 73.

287. BB = Biblioteca della Badia, Grottaferrata. V. Polidori, "L'eucologio criptense Γ. β. XV," *BollGrott* 6 (2009): 233.

288. Taft, *A History of the Liturgy of St. John Chrysostom*, 154–55, including "Γένοιτό μοι, Κύριε Ἰησοῦ Χριστέ, ὁ Θεὸς ἡμῶν τὸ σῶμά σου ..."

289. Taft, *A History of the Liturgy of St. John Chrysostom*, 162–68; S. Alexopoulos and A. van den Hoek, "The Endicott Scroll and Its Place in the History of Private Communion Prayers," *DOP* 60 (2006): 146–88.

290. The rolls Sinai, MSC, NE ΜΓ 81 and ΜΓ 86, summarily described in Holy Monastery and Archdiocese of Sinai, *The New Finds of Sinai*, 154–55, pls. 93–94, 98, and on which see the corrections in P. Géhin and S. Frøyshov, "Nouvelles découvertes sinaïtiques: à propos de la parution de l'inventaire des manuscrits grecs," *REB* 58 (2000): 177–78.

291. A. Jacob, "L'evoluzione dei libri liturgici bizantini in Calabria e in Sicilia dall'VIII al XVI secolo con particolare riguardo ai riti eucaristici," in *Calabria bizantina: vita religiosa e strutture amministrative* (Reggio: Parallelo, 1938), 49. Thanks to the research of Gabriel Radle, the insertion of diakonikà and rubrics into eucharistic formularies should no longer be considered a phenomenon born in Byzantine Italy in the course of the tenth century, since this practice is found already at the end of the ninth century in the Middle East: G. Radle, "Sinai Greek NE / ΜΓ 22: Late 9th / Early 10th Century Euchology Testimony of the Liturgy of St John Chrysostom and the Liturgy of Presanctified Gifts in the Byzantine Tradition," *BollGrott* III s. 8 (2011): 169–211.

prior to communion, can be observed once again in the Middle East in the Liturgy of St. James.[292]

III.12. *Hours and "interhours" of the Paschal triduum*

In the hagiopolite tradition, the death of the Lord on Good Friday was commemorated from noon to three in the afternoon with hymns and twenty biblical readings.[293] According to current understanding, the Byzantine rite of southern Italy began to absorb Jerusalem usage at the end of the tenth century; the hymns and readings were distributed in the horologion among the the first, third, sixth, and ninth hours.[294] The manuscripts (particularly Gospel lectionaries and typika) of the various local recensions of the Byzantine rite naturally attest to a wide variety of combinations and lead to the current synthesis, which has seen a reduction of the readings from twenty to fifteen.

The hours for Good Friday are analogous in origin to the hours of the Christmas vigil and those of Theophany,[295] although toward the end of the tenth century there are already signs of an enlargement of the system of special hours from Good Friday to other days of the Paschal triduum, such as Maundy Thursday. This we learn from the index (the text unfortunately has been lost) of Moscow, RGB, f. 270–Ia, No. 15 (Sevast'janov 474, gr. 27), a luxurious "pocket" euchologion, copied at the end of the tenth century and textually related to the Middle East:[296] "Αἱ ὧραι τῆς μεγάλης ε' καὶ τῆς μεγάλης παρασκευῆς· ὅπως χρὴ ψά[λλειν.........]."[297]

Hours for the Paschal triduum also appear in the psalter St. Petersburg,

292. B.-C. Mercier, *La Liturgie de saint Jacques. Édition critique du texte grec avec traduction latine*, Patrologia Orientalis 26.2 (Paris: Firmin-Didot, 1946), 234; A. K. Kazamias, Ἡ θεία Λειτουργία τοῦ ἁγίου Ἰακώβου τοῦ Ἀδελφοθέου καὶ τὰ νέα Σιναϊτικὰ χειρόγραφα (Thessaloniki: Hiera Mone Theovadistou Orous Sina, 2006), 216–17.

293. S. Janeras, *Le vendredi-saint dans la tradition liturgique byzantine. Structure et histoire des ses offices* (Rome: Pontificio Ateneo S. Anselmo, 1988), 189–277, 325–30.

294. S. Parenti, "La celebrazione delle Ore del Venerdì Santo nell'Eucologio Γ.β.X di Grottaferrata (X–XI sec.)," *BollGrott* 44 (1990): 81–125.

295. Janeras, *Le vendredi-saint* (see above, n293), 252–59.

296. I wish to express my deepest gratitude to Dr. Tat'jana Ivanova of the Department of Manuscripts of the National Library (Российская Национальная Библиотека) of Moscow for her help in facilitating my research.

297. S. I. Koster, *Das Euchologion Sevastianov 474 (X. Jhdt.) der Staatsbibliothek in Moskau. Edition* (PhD diss., PIO Roma, 1996), 43 (text), 36–38 (commentary). Recently the manuscript has been attributed to Constantinople on the basis of the script and decoration: I. Mokretsova et al., *Materials and Techniques on Byzantine Manuscripts* (Moscow: Indrik, 2003), 107–9, 262–63.

RNB, gr. 64, fol. 222v (994 A.D.),[298] and those for Maundy Thursday are listed in the tables of the praxapostolos Grottaferrata, BB, A.β.III, fols. 175r–176v, which is the work of the eleventh-century scribe Leon.[299] But it is the twelfth-century psalter Athens, EBE, 7, that gives us—despite the inevitable differences—the complete series of the hours for Maundy Thursday, Good Friday, and Holy Saturday analogous to those provided in the horologion of the Harvard Psalter.[300] The Athens series calls the first, third, sixth, and ninth hours simply "the hours" (αἱ ὧραι).[301] In our codex, those of Maundy Thursday appear under the name of Ἀκολουθία, the ones for Friday are designated Ἀκολουθία ... τῶν μεσώρων, and no specific designation accompanies the ones for Saturday. Thus, in addition to the "great" and "small" hours, this important manuscript also attests to the existence of the "interhours."

The term "interhours" (μεσώρια) refers to supplementary hours that nowadays follow the four daily hours only during the penitential periods; thus, after the first hour there is an intermediate first hour, after the third an intermediate third hour, and so forth. The origin of the interhours must be moved back from the twelfth century[302] to the second half of the eleventh, as demonstrated by both the horologion Mt. Athos, MV, cod. 1248, copied in 1077,[303] and the *Hypotyposis* by Niketas Stethatos, composed before 1090.[304]

---

298. Noted in Parpulov, *Byzantine Psalters*, 16n16.

299. See A. A. Aletta, "Grottaferrata, Biblioteca del Monumento Nazionale, Crypt. A.β.III," in *Codici greci dell'Italia meridionale*, ed. P. Canart and S. Lucà (Rome: Ufficio Centrale per i Beni Librari, le Instituzioni Culturali e l'Editoria, 2000), 69–70.

300. I. Phountoulis, "Αἱ μεγάλαι ὧραι τῆς μεγάλης πέμπτης, μεγάλης παρασκευῆς καὶ τοῦ μεγάλου σαββάτου (κατὰ τὸν ὑπ' ἀριθ. 7 κώδικα τῆς ἐν Ἀθήναις Ἐθνικῆς Βιβλιοθήκης)," Ἐπιστημονικὴ Ἐπετηρὶς τῆς Θεολογικῆς Σχολῆς τοῦ Πανεπιστημίου Θεσσαλονίκης 7 (1962): 217–43. On the manuscript see Cutler, *Aristocratic Psalters*, 15–17, dated second half of the twelfth century, and P. Buberl, *Die Miniaturenhandschriften der Nationalbibliothek in Athen* (Vienna: A. Hölder, 1917); a reproduction with script in Phountoulis, "Ὕμνος ἑσπερινός," 30.

301. The title "great" (μεγάλαι) attributed to the hours by the editor (see preceding note) actually belongs by analogy to the "great hours" of Good Friday.

302. Thus Egender, "Introduction," 253.

303. S. Eustratiades and Arcadius Vatopedinos, *Catalogue of the Greek Manuscripts in the Library of the Monastery of Vatopedi on Mt. Athos* (Cambridge, Mass.: Harvard University Press, 1924; reprinted in New York: H. P. Kraus, 1969), 208, omit reference to the Paschal tables on fol. 77v, which give the date 1077; cf. S. N. Kadas, Τὰ σημειώματα τῶν χειρογράφων τῆς ἱερᾶς Μεγίστης Μονῆς Βατοπεδίου (Mt. Athos: Hiera Megiste Mone Vatopaidiou, 2000), 226.

304. Krausmüller, "Private vs communal," 318–20, and more in detail in D. Krausmüller, "Liturgica Innovation in 11th- and 12th Century Constantinople. Hours and Inter-Hours in Evergetis Typikon, its 'Daughters' and its 'Grand-Daughters,'" *REB* 71 (2013): 149–72.

The usage then passes into the typikon of the monastery of the Theotokos Kecharitomene, founded at the beginning of the twelfth century[305] and in the liturgical typika of the monasteries of Evergetis and Christ Philanthropos.[306]

It appears reasonable to assume that despite the different titles (ἀκολουθία or μεσώρια) for the structure, which fails to provide the characteristic psalm for each hour (Pss 5, 50, 90, 85), the function of the special intermediate hours for the Paschal triduum was not as a substitute for the normal hours of the day.

III.13. *Vespers*

Vespers, more properly called the lucernarium (ἀκολουθία τοῦ λυχνικοῦ), does not present significant peculiarities; the celebration retains as essential the framework of the monastic Sabaite vespers as we know them from the ninth-century Mt. Sinai, MSC, gr. 863.[307] It is instructive to compare the two rites (see table 16).

III.13.1. *The absence of the variable psalmody*

The akolouthia of lucernarium (τοῦ λυχνικοῦ) is introduced by the group of initial prayers. The absence of the eighteenth kathisma (the gradual psalms, Pss 119–33) from the psalter horologion confirms that it belongs to the Stoudite, and later Evergetis tradition, as was argued in the examination of matins. As Juan Mateos showed in his historic study on the distribution of the psalmic *pensum* in the Byzantine rite, at the Evergetis the eighteenth kathisma of the weekday vespers (Monday–Friday) was omitted in the summer period, which ran from the Sunday after Easter to September 14, and in the remaining half of the year was subject to significant restrictions.[308]

That the eighteenth kathisma appears as a fixed unit of the ordinary in the old horologion Sinai. gr. 863 possibly speaks to the *cursus* of its user. It may, alternatively, reflect a system of psalm distribution not otherwise known, one in which the eighteenth kathisma was a fixed element of vespers

---

305. Gautier, "Le typikon," 81, 85; *BMFD*, 2:687–88.

306. For example, Jordan, ed., *Synaxarion of Evergetis*, 1:200 (ferial days of the Nativity Fast) and 2:692 (Apostles' Fast).

307. Mateos, "Horologion de Saint-Sabas," 56–58.

308. Mateos, "Psalmodie variable," 331–32.

Table 16: Comparison of Two Rites

Sinai. gr. 863 (ninth century)	Psalter Horologion (1105 A.D.)
	Initial Prayers
Psalm 103	Psalm 103
Psalms 119–33	
Psalm 140	Psalm 140
Psalm 141	Psalm 141
Psalm 129	Psalm 129 + hymnography
Psalm 116	Psalm 116
Gloria…	Gloria… + theotokion
Φῶς ἱλαρόν…	Φῶς ἱλαρόν…
Alleluia + verses	Prokeimena of the week
Καταξίωσον Κύριε…	Καταξίωσον Κύριε …
	Psalm 122 + hymnography
	Gloria … + theotokion
Canticle of Simeon (Lk 2:29–32)	Canticle of Simeon (Lk 2:29–32)
Trisagion	Trisagion + Pater
	Apolytikion of the day
	Or weekday troparia
	Kyrie eleison (15x) and closing

well beyond the days of penitence.[309] As support, one could point to the use of the eighteenth kathisma in the "tempi forti" vespers up to the present day; here the operation of Baumstark's Second Law[310] is evident, as it is to an even greater extent in the fixed assignment of kathisma seventeen (Ps 118) to the Saturday matins. Juan Mateos pointed out that the distribution of psalmody among the possible cycles of the liturgical year was always governed by the fixed assignment of Psalm 118 to Saturday because of the weekly commemoration of the saints and the dead.[311] Nothing, therefore, prevents the vespertine use of the eighteenth kathisma in the Sinai. gr. 863 from obeying the same rule.

309. Ibid., 339.
310. Taft, "Comparative Liturgy Revisited," 200, 206–8.
311. Mateos, "Psalmodie variable," 330–31. For Ps 118 in the context of funeral rites see E. Velkovska, "Funeral Rites according to the Byzantine Liturgical Sources," DOP 55 (2001): 38.

III.13.2. *Stichera of lucernarium*

In the last psalms of lucernarium (Pss 129, 116) only three stichera are intercalated, not the six or eight of Stoudite practice. Although the difference deserves investigation, the number of hymnographic manuscripts that need to be surveyed would take the study beyond what is envisioned here.

III.13.3. *Prokeimenon*

The weekday prokeimena, absent in the Sinai. gr. 863, come from the cathedral tradition of Constantinople. A prokeimenon after the entrance of the celebrants is attested as early as the end of the eighth century in the non-monastic vespers recorded in Rome, BAV, Barb. gr. 336,[312] and texts identical to those currently in use are given in the appendix of the tenth-century kanonarion-synaxarion Jerusalem, PB, cod. Staurou 40, also known as the "Typikon" of the Great Church.[313] The fact that the prokeimena were not at that time organized to follow the system of eight modes is a certain sign of antiquity. The semi-responsorial chanting of the Alleluia, present in the Sinai. gr. 863,[314] has been reserved in the contemporary horologion for the penitential days,[315] but its performance remains somewhat hypothetical.

III.13.4. *Aposticha*

The verse stichera (στίχοι) of the psalms, called εἰς τὸν στίχον or ἀπόστιχα,[316] are another feature of the Harvard Psalter Horologion that is absent from the Sinai. gr. 863. As in the *textus receptus*, the psalm is Psalm 122; for Sundays the liturgical typika prescribe Psalm 92 and for feast days the verses themselves.[317] Juan Mateos—who recognized the possible absence of the stichera in the ninth century—established the relationship between Psalm 92 and its dependent liturgical poetry and the stational procession to the cross that concluded the hagiopolite vespers as early as the time of Egeria (§§ 24, 7);[318] Mateos therefore considers the adoption of Psalm 122 for week-

312. Parenti-Velkovska, *Eucologio Barberini*, 90 (§ 57.1); Mateos, *Typicon*, 2:316–17. For the often ignored musical aspect see S. Harris, "The Byzantine prokeimena," *Plainsong and Medieval Music* 3 (1994): 133–47.

313. Mateos, *Typicon*, 2:179–80.   314. Mateos, "Horologion de Saint-Sabas," 75.
315. *HR* 227–28; *HA* 192–94.   316. *HR* 229–30; *HA* 194–95.
317. E.g., *Synaxarion of Evergetis*, ed. Jordan, 1:27–28, 54–55, etc.
318. P. Maraval, ed., *Égérie, Journal de voyage (Itinéraire)* (Paris: Éditions du Cerf, 1997), 240–41.

Table 17

Vespers	Lauds
Καταξίωσον	Doxology
	Καταξίωσον
	[Litany of the petitions
	Kephaloklisia]
Aposticha	Aposticha
Canticle of Simeon	
Trisagion-Pater	Trisagion-Pater
[Troparion]	[Troparion]
Dismissal	Dismissal

N.B.: The elements in brackets belong to the Constantinopolitan cathedral tradition

days to be in emulation of the use of Psalm 92 on Sundays.[319] N. Egender shares Mateos's view of the role of the stational procession and considers the hymnographic element a monastic doublet of the final apolytikion troparion of cathedral use. Egender introduces a new element into the argument;[320] he compares the final parts of lauds and the weekday vespers in the *textus receptus* and highlights the symmetry common to their structures (table 17).

In his study of the *Commentary on the Liturgy of the Hours* written by Bishop Step'anos Siwnec'i (d. 735), Michael Findykian notes that the "structural symmetry" between the final parts of vespers and lauds is also found in the Armenian tradition. More precisely, at lauds we have Psalm 112, "of the down," and at vespers Psalm 120 or "of rest." The latter has in common with Psalm 122 some aposticha belonging to the gradual psalms, as well as a nearly identical *incipit*: "Ἦρα τοὺς ὀφθαλμούς μου εἰς τὰ ὄρη …" (Ps 120) and "Πρὸς σὲ ἦρα τοὺς ὀφθαλμούς μου …" (Ps 122). According to Findykian's reconstruction, Psalm 120 was possibly added at the end of vespers in the second half of the seventh century, at the time of Catholicos Ezr (630–41), in order to counterbalance structurally the insertion of Psalm 112 at the end of lauds.[321]

319. Mateos, "Horologion de Saint-Sabas," 75–76.
320. *La Prière des heures*, 370–71.
321. M. D. Findikyan, ed. and trans., *The Commentary of the Armenian Daily Office by Bishop Step'anos Siwnec'i († 735)* (Rome: Pontificio Instituto Orientale, 2004), 431–35, 494–95.

It is not implausible that something similar had taken place in the Palestine horologion after the ninth century. Unfortunately, the lacuna in the Sinai. gr. 863 (ninth century) prevents us from verifying whether or not Psalm 89:14–17 was then present after lauds, as the matins *pendent* to Psalm 122 at vespers. In the final analysis, the Mateos-Egender theory, which considers the aposticha to be processional chants connected to the matins and vespertine hagiopolite processions to the cross, finds little support.[322] Alone, the fact that the aposticha precede the Trisagion-Pater, the ancient conclusion of vespers and other hours, shows that they are an internal development and not a stational appendix.[323]

III.13.5. *Concluding troparia*

After the Trisagion and the Our Father, the apolytikion troparion of the day is prescribed, or, in its absence, a series of four troparia that are the same ones sung today at the Lenten vespers:

1. Θεοτόκε παρθένε …
2. Βαπτιστὰ τοῦ Χριστοῦ …
3. Ἱκετεύσατε ὑπὲρ ἡμῶν …
4. Ὑπὸ τὴν σὴν εὐσπλαγχνίαν …

The chanting of the apolytikion or dismissal troparion at the end of the celebrations is a characteristic of the Constantinopolitan rite,[324] and it is in that setting that it is possible to find text (1), specifically at the vespers of September 1.[325] The other texts, known in the same order in the Italo-Greek horologion Erlangen, Ubibl, cod. A2 (1025 A.D.),[326] may reflect a monastic development. The presence of the following troparion, in honor of the Baptist, would point toward—and this is only a theory—the Stoudios monastery of Constantinople; the third troparion generically appeals for the intercession of the apostles and all the saints, and the last is the celebrated Marian troparion *Sub tuum praesidium*.[327]

---

322. Egender, "Introduction," 139–40.

323. Cf. also what is written in G. Woolfenden, "The Processional Appendix to Vespers: Some Problems and Questions," in *Inquires into Eastern Christian Worship*, ed. B. Groen et al., 121–34, esp. 123–27.

324. Mateos, *Typicon*, 2:285, s.v. ἀπολυτίκιον.   325. Mateos, *Typicon*, 1:2.

326. Husmann, "Hymnus und Troparion," 10.   327. Ibid., 9–13.

III.14. *Apodeipnon*

In the monastic tradition the last office of the day, analogous to the Roman compline, is the ἀπόδειπνον, so called because it comes after dinner (δεῖπνον).[328] It is an extremely complex office and one still little studied.[329] It is known through manuscripts in various regional traditions, all traceable to two recensions: (1) the Stoudite and (2) the Sabaite. The Stoudite recension is, in turn, divided into two families: (1a) the Constantinopolitan and (1b) the Italo-Greek. The current distinction of "great" and "small" apodeipnon[330]—the "small" being none other than the final section of the "great"—appears in the horologia of the Sabaite recension toward the end of the fourteenth century.[331] In thirteenth-century Constantinople, following the Latin occupation of the city (1204–61), it took the place of the Stoudite recension within the context of the "Neo-Sabaite" reform.[332]

The apodeipnon (ἀκολουθία τῶν ἀποδείπνων) of the psalter horologion is consistent with the Stoudite-Constantinopolitan recension and rather closely parallels the prescriptions of the contempory Evergetis Typikon, which gives the concrete details of the ordinary.[333] These are generally absent from the typika since the compilers considered it to be known by the users of the book. A comparison between the psalter horologion and the typikon will be useful to clarify several apparent anomalies. The rite of the horologion includes five liturgical units.

III.14.1. *First liturgical unit*

This first unit holds no surprises and is almost identical in all the recensions; it constitutes in common with the Coptic tradition[334] what is doubtless

---

328. For the Patristic testimony in the various traditions see Taft, *Liturgy of the Hours*, 407, General Index, s.v. compline.

329. A. Raes, "Les Complies dans les Rites orientaux," *OCP* 17 (1951): 133–45; Egender, "Complies," in *La Prière des Heures*, 423–26.

330. Cf. *HR* 237, 280.

331. The small apodeipnon in the horologion Sinai. gr. 883 (1392 A.D.), fol. 40r, is introduced by the rubric: τὸ μικρὸν ἀπόδειπνον τὸ ψαλλόμενον ἐν ταῖς κελλίοις.

332. Taft, *Short History*, 78–84.

333. Klentos, *Evergetis*, 180–86. The same pattern is also in the typikon of the monastery of Christ Philanthropos.

334. O. H. Burmester, "The Canonical Hours of the Coptic Church," *OCP* 2 (1936): 95–96; to which should be added H. Quecke, "Neue griechische Parallelen zum koptischen Horologion," *Le Muséon* 77 (1964): 285–94.

Table 18: First Liturgical Unit

Psalter Horologion	Evergetis Typikon
Trisagion-Pater	=
Kyrie eleison	
Psalms 4, 6, 12, 24, 30, 90	=
Canticle, Isaiah 8	= "and the rest"
Τὴν ἡμέραν διελθών ...	
Ἡ ἀσώματος φύσις ...	
Creed	
Litanies of the saints	
Trisagion-Pater	
Apolytikion of the feast	
or weekday apolytikia:	=
Τῶν ἀοράτων ἐχθρῶν...	=
Ὡς φοβερὰ ἡ κρίσις σου...	=
Τὴν ἀκαταίσχυντον...	=
Kyrie eleison	
Prayer: You, God, are	Prayer: You, God, are
worshipped at every ...	worshipped at every...
	Prayer: Lord, O Lord, you
	who delivered us...
	(during penitential days
	outside Great Lent)

the oldest stratum of the apodeipnon. The first three psalms (Pss 4, 6, 12) and the Canticle of Isaiah are found in the Armenian tradition as well, and from at least the beginning of the eighth century.[335] Psalms 4, 12, 30, 90, and the Canticle of Isaiah appear in the ninth-century horologion published by Mateos and myself (Mt. Sinai, MSC, gr. 863 + Chest I, no. 58).[336] With respect to our horologion we can note that the Evergetis Typikon reserves the prayer "Lord, O Lord, you who delivered us ..." to penitential days. This means that our horologion conserves a more ancient practice with respect to the liturgical typos of Evergetis, before the diffusion of the prayer "You, God, are worshipped at every ..." to all the hours.

335. Findikyan, Commentary, 503, 505–6.
336. Mateos, "Horologion de Saint-Sabas," 58; Parenti, "Un fascicolo ritrovato," 346–48, 351–54.

Table 19: Second Liturgical Unit

Psalter Horologion	Evergetis Typikon
Psalm 50	=
Canon of the panychis	=
Trisagion	
Penitential troparia	
Kyrie eleison	
Prayer of Psalm 50	
Gloria	
Trisagion	
Troparia	=
Kyrie eleison	=
	Supplication
Lord, O Lord, you who delivered us...	=

III.14.2. *Second liturgical unit*

The second unit consists of the pannychis, a daily vigil structured around a hymnographic canon; from a chronological, but not structural, standpoint it is related as a daily *cursus* to the partial vigil of the cathedral.[337] In the rite that is in effect today there remain a few examples in the mesonyktikon of Sunday, the Easter Vigil, and the first Saturday in lent (the commemoration of Theodore Tiron).[338] In the Evergetis Typikon, the pannychis is usually expected to follow vespers, except in Great Lent, when it is inserted as the second section of apodeipnon,[339] where it is also found in the Italo-Byzantine tradition.[340]

For the Harvard Psalter Horologion, the Evergetis-type pannychis was adapted to meet the editorial criteria of a horologion: the supplication (ἐκτενής), which was an element of public worship, was omitted and a long

---

337. M. Arranz, "Les prières presbytérales de la 'Pannychis' de l'ancien Euchologe byzantin et la 'Panikhida' des défunts," *OCP* 40 (1974): 314–43; *OCP* 41 (1975): 119–39. The information of Arranz should be supplemented with the study of Tinatin Chronz, *Die Feier des Heiligen Öles nach Jerusalemer Ordnung*, Jerusalemer Theologisches Forum 18 (Münster: Aschendorff, 2012), 298–302.

338. *HR* 59–61; Bertonière, *Easter Vigil*, 158, 191–93, 238–39, 266, 277, 287–88; cf. *TR* 206–9; Трїωдь Постнаѧ, vol. 1 (Moscow, 2002), fols. 131v–134r.

339. Jordan, ed., *Synaxarion of Evergetis*, 2:692; cf. Klentos, *Evergetis*, 179–80.

340. See Arranz, *Typicon de Messine*, xlvii.

Table 20: Third Liturgical Unit

Psalter Horologion	Evergetis Typikon
Prayer of Manasses	=
	Prayer for family members
Trisagion	Trisagion
Troparia	
Kyrie eleison	
Prayer of St. Eustratios	

series of troparia added (from the choice we cannot learn anything useful in attributing the manuscript to a specific monastery).[341] In the process of making the adaptation, the scribe mistakenly added the invitatory (Δεῦτε προσκυνήσωμεν ...), which normally precedes a psalmic unit, before the doxology (*Gloria in excelsis*).[342] In its "great" and "little" forms—a late terminology meant to distinguish the Constantinopolitan ("great") from the hagiopolite recension ("small")—the doxology is traditionally found at the end of offices or liturgical units.[343] Linking it with the invitatory of psalmody, which is found at the beginning of an office or of one of its sections, is surprising and constitutes an aberration.[344]

III.14.3. *Third liturgical unit*

The third unit of the horologion has only the apocryphal Prayer of Manasses and the Trisagion in common with the Evergetis Typikon, and

341. "Σῶσον Κύριε τὸν λαόν σου ..., Ὁ ὑψωθεὶς ἐν τῷ σταυρῷ ..., Τῶν οὐρανίων στρατιῶν ..., Μνήμη δικαίου ..., Οἱ τῶν ἀποστόλων πρωτόθρωνοι ..., Ἅγιοι ἀνάργυροι ..., Ἀθλοφόροι ἅγιοι ..., Οἱ μάρτυρές σου ..., Τῇ Θεοτόκῳ ἐκτενῶς ..." The order of troparia reflects that of the weekly commemorations preceded by two texts in honor of the cross and finds a parallel in the final intercession of the litany supplications before the Gospel in the Liturgy of St. James. See Mercier, *La Liturgie de saint Jacques*, 172; Kazamias, Ἡ θεία Λειτουργία τοῦ ἁγίου Ἰακώβου (above, n292), 164.

342. Mateos, "Synaxe monastique," 255–58.

343. Cf. above, 278–79.

344. The testimony of our horologion is nevertheless not isolated; it is comparable to that of a twelfth- or thirteenth-century horologion in the British Library, London (fols. 224r–226v, 225r), which I know through old photographs in the library of the monastery of Grottaferrata; unfortunately, the photographs do not give the manuscript shelfmark.

Table 21: Fourth Liturgical Unit

Psalter Horologion	Evergetis Typikon
Psalm 118	
Funeral troparia	Funeral troparia
Μνήσθητι, Κύριε, ὡς ἀγαθός	Μνήσθητι, Κύριε, ὡς ἀγαθός
Ἀληθῶς ματαιότης	Ὁ βυθοῖς σοφίας
Μετὰ τῶν ἁγίων ἀνάπαυσον	Μετὰ τῶν ἁγίων ἀνάπαυσον
Ὁ εἰδώς μου τὸ ἀνέτοιμον	Σὲ καὶ τεῖχος
Kyrie eleison	Kyrie eleison
Prayer for the deceased	Prayer for the deceased
Private prayer of forgiveness	Rite of forgiveness

here, too, the series of troparia is generic.[345] The "prayer for family members" of Evergetis tradition is absent from the psalter horologion.

III.14.4. Fourth liturgical unit

The fourth section is an authentic funeral office of intercession, and it finds in the Evergetis Typikon an almost perfect correspondence in text and structure; the exception is Psalm 118. As noted in § III.6, the use of the psalm within the daily *cursus* can follow one of two different traditions attested in the sources.

The recitation of Psalm 118 precedes the awakening from sleep in the Stoudite sources: the *Diatyposis* by Athanasios of Athos (984–93),[346] the *Ascetic Discourse* by Symeon the Pious,[347] the *Catechesis* by Symeon the New Theologian (d. 1022?),[348] the horologion Mt. Athos, MV, cod. 1248, of 1077 (fol. 25r), and the *Hypotyposis* of Niketas Stethatos (before 1090). As usual, the sources associate the psalm with ὁ ἄμωμος, and it is not always clear if the term is synonymous with mesonyktikon as an hour of the daily *cursus*,

---

345. "Τὴν ἄχραντον εἰκόνα σου ..., Ὁ Θεὸς τῶν πατέρων ἡμῶν ...,Ὅταν ἔλθῃς ..., Τῆς σοφίας ὁδηγέ ..., Σὲ καὶ τεῖχος καὶ λιμένα ..."

346. Dmitrievskij, *Описание*, 1:247. For the date of the document, composed in 963 and probably revised in 1020, see *BMFD*, 1:216n1.

347. L. Neyrand, ed. and trans., *Syméon le Studite, Discours Ascétique* (Paris: Éditions du Cerf, 2003), 103.

348. Catechesis 26: B. Krivochéine and I. Paramelle, ed. and trans., *Syméon le Nouveau Théologien*, vol. 3, *Catéchèses 23–34. Action de grâces 1–2* (Paris: Éditions du Cerf, 1965), 95.

Table 22: Fifth Liturgical Unit

Horologion	Evergetis Typikon
Venite adoremus	
Psalm 6	
Trisagion	
Troparia	
Φώτισον τοὺς ὀφθαλμούς...	
Ἀντιλήπτωρ τῆς ψυχῆς μου...	
Ἔνδοξε ἀειπαρθένε...	
Kyrie eleison	
Prayer	
Other prayer of St. Basil	
The rest is done in the cell	

or if it indicates a private prayer, which in the Harvard Psalter Horologion assumes the function of intercession for the deceased.

Dirk Krausmüller noted that at the end of the eleventh century a significant change occurred, the first signs of which can already be observed in the Athanasian *Diatyposis*; once a private prayer said before sleeping, Psalm 118 becomes one recited as a communal prayer after awakening in the hour permanently called mesonyktikon.[349] The shift is noticeable in the foundation typika of the Pantokrator monastery[350] and the Phoberou,[351] in the liturgical and foundation typika of the monastery of Evergetis,[352] as well as in the *Taktikon* of Nikon of the Black Mountain;[353] theirs is a tradition shared with the Stoudite typika of southern Italy, but not by the Sabaite typika, in which the mesonyktikon follows the awakening and remains a private office.[354]

III.14.5. *Fifth liturgical unit*

The final unit presents a structure symmetrical to the akolouthia for the forgiveness of sins (cf. § II.5 and III.4) and to the prayers appended to the psalter kathismata (§ II.1), that is, to a type of prayer that was strictly per-

349. Krausmüller, "Private vs communal," 313–16.

350. P. Gautier, "Le Typikon du Christ Sauveur Pantocrator," *REB* 32 (1974): 31, 33.

351. A. Papadopoulos-Kerameus, *Noctes Petropolitanae. Сборник византийских текстов XII–XIII веков* (St. Petersburg: V. F. Kirshbaum, 1913), 24; BMFD, 3:898.

352. Gautier, "Typikon Évergétis," 27; Dmitrievskij, *Описание*, 1:604.

353. Beneševič, *Тактикон*, 25.20. 354. Dmitrievskij, *Описание*, 3:17, 60.

sonal. It is not by accident that the Evergetis Typikon mentions a "remnant" of the apodeipnon to be performed in the cell. We do not have the evidence needed to compare the Evergetis office with that of the Harvard Psalter Horologion, but there is surely an affinity between them that was, at the very least, spiritual in nature. What is surprising is that the series of three troparia found in the first unit of apodeipnon in the Vatopedi Horologion and in the Sabaite tradition were moved to this location.[355]

III.14.6. Prayers of apodeipnon

Every section of apodeipnon concludes with a prayer. The first section concludes on the prayer "You, God, are worshipped at every hour," already noted in the first hour. The second ("Κύριε, Κύριε, ὁ ῥυσάμενος ἡμᾶς ἀπὸ παντὸς βέλους…") was taken into the Constantinopolitan cathedral vespers, where as early as the eighth century it served as a prayer of the second "little antiphon."[356] The third prayer, attributed to Eustratios (d. 303),[357] and supported by his Passio (BHGna 646e), is one that the textus receptus assigns to the Saturday mesonyktikon.[358] The prayer for the deceased is the same as that found in the typikon ktitorikon of the Constantinopolitan monastery of the Pantokrator, where it was adapted to commemorate the death of the emperors who founded the monastery.[359]

As we have seen in § III.14.4, the private prayer for forgiveness of sins committed during the day corresponds to the rite of mutual forgiveness of the Evergetis Typikon. The references to the distractions during prayer and psalmody and to the trespasses against the other brothers reveal the strictly monastic origin of a text occasionally attributed to Ephrem the Syrian, the reason for its inclusion in the eighteenth-century Assemani edition.[360]

At the end of the last section we find two interesting prayers. The first is attributed in the textus receptus to the monk Antiochos of the Pandektes,[361] an attribution supported by the Homilia XIX de fornicatione (περὶ πορνείας)

---

355. Dmitrievskij, Описание, 1:17, and as such has passed into horologia.

356. Parenti-Velkovska, Eucologio Barberini, 91 (§ 58).

357. PG 116:505; see also Assemani, Ephraem Syri Opera Omnia, 485.

358. HR 57–58 and, e.g., in the manuscripts of the horologion Sinai. gr. 865, fols. 44r–46r, Sinai. gr. 904 (1211 A.D.), fols. 245v–247r: Saturday, Sinai. gr. 903, fols. 79v–80v.

359. Gautier, "Typikon Pantocrator," 35; BMFD, 2:739.

360. Assemani, Ephraem Syri Opera Omnia, 484–85 (CPG 4070), from Vat. gr. 341.

361. HR 274–75.

(CPG 7843),[362] also attributed to Antiochos; the author is sometimes identified, although without conclusive evidence, as Antiochos Strategos, responsible for the account of the capture of Jerusalem by the Persians in 614.[363] The prayer enjoyed wide circulation. Toward the end of the tenth century it appears in the euchologion Grottaferrata, BB, Γ.β.IV (fol. 122r), where it is attributed to Epiphanios (of Salamis?), and it appears in a difference recension in the euchologion Paris, BNF, Coislin 213 (Cple, 1027 A.D.).[364] From the second half of the eleventh century, the prayer is found in the *Hypotyposis* of Niketas Stethatos (fol. 202r), in the Slavic Euchologion of Sinai,[365] and in the celebrated Euchologion "of Archimedes," of the thirteenth century.[366] It appears in the apodeipnon of the horologia, beginning with Mt. Athos, MV, cod. 1248, fol. 23r+v (1077 A.D.), Mt. Sinai, MSC, gr. 865, fols. 154v–155r (twelfth century), and gr. 903, fols. 36v–37v (thirteenth or fourteenth century),[367] and the paper codices Mt. Sinai, MSC, gr. 883, fols. 47r–48r (1392 A.D.), and gr. 877, fols. 116v–117r (1467 A.D.).

The last and lengthy prayer with which apodeipnon closes, and with it the horologion, is attributed to Basil the Great; the attribution is justified by the content, largely repeated in the intercessions of the anaphora that goes under Basil's name.[368]

III.15. *Conclusions*

As we have seen above, the daily *cursus* of the horologion that forms part of the Harvard Psalter begins with mesonyktikon, which is preceded by several devotional offices; the absence of Psalm 118 connects it to the

---

362. PG 89:1428–1894.

363. A. Kazhdan, "Antiochos Strategos," in *ODB*, 1:119–20.

364. M. Arranz, ed., *L'Eucologio costantinopolitano agli inizi del secolo XI. Hagiasmatarion & Archieratikon (Rituale & Pontificale) con l'aggiunta del Leitourgikon (Messale)* (Rome: Pontificia Università Gregoriana, 1996), 389.

365. S. Parenti and E. Velkovska, "Една молитва 'за болни' в Синайския евхологий (One Prayer 'for the Sick' in the Slavic Euchology of Sinai)," in *Филологически изследвания в чест на Климентина Иванова в чест на нейната 65-годишнина* (= *Старобългарска литература* 33–34 [2005]), 154–66.

366. Parenti, "The Liturgical Tradition," 85, § 69.

367. Repeated by another hand on fol. 47r+v.

368. Cf. the English translation where the parallels with the Liturgy of St. Basil are cited. The prayer also occurs in Vat. gr. 341, fols. 295r–296v, and probably also in the thirteenth-century Marc. gr. I. 16 (coll. 1415); see Mioni, *Codices Venetiarum*, 1.1:22–23.

early Stoudite tradition. Matins presents three celebrative structures: for Sundays and feast days, for Saturday, and for weekdays. One should not, for the purpose of study, consider them as three modes of celebration but rather as three moments in their history. Each of the practices has retained elements useful for a reconstruction of the oldest common structures. This is particularly evident in the case of the exaposteilarion at the end of the hymnographic canon. Hypothetically, what was originally responsorial psalmody—preserved in the psalter horologion, as today, only in Sunday matins (Ps 89:9)—had been antiphonalized in the first half of the tenth century with the introduction of the hymnographic exaposteilaria of Constantine VII Porphyrogennetos (913–59). Then for weekdays there are only short troparia and no longer a psalm. The *incipit* of some hymns ("ἐξαπόστειλον τὸ φῶς σου . . .") would point to Psalm 42:3 ("ἐξαπόστειλον τὸ φῶς σου καὶ τὴν ἀλήθειάν σου· αὐτά με ὡδήγησαν . . ."). Psalms 89 and 43 would lead one to think of a processional use.

The Sunday and feast day matins present two celebratory possibilities: the first is closer to the Stoudite tradition and the second reveals the influence of what would establish itself as the Neo-Sabaite tradition, apparent in the adoption of the series of prokeimena in accordance with the series of eight modes. Thus—and while keeping in mind the relationship with the Stoudite tradition—the Harvard Psalter Horologion reveals evidence of transition. The study of the first, third, sixth, and ninth hours has allowed us to explore the process of antiphonalization of the prokeimenon and to identify in the "verses" of each hour a psalmic litany of the monastic type. The choice and number of prayers of the first hour bring the horologion closer to what would become the Evergetis tradition; the two prayers of the remaining hours are lightly revised troparia.

In accordance with the liturgical schedule, the typika precedes the liturgy or the vespers and does not entail an office of communion. The absence from the horologion of the eighteenth kathisma as a fixed element of vespers yet again points to the Stoudite tradition. A further element demonstrating how the horologion belongs within the Stoudite liturgical *milieu* is the use of Psalm 118 within apodeipnon.

IV

The Synaxarion-Menologion

The third major section of the Harvard Psalter is the "Synaxarion or Menologion" (συναξάριον ἤτοι μηνολόγιον); the title phrase uses two multi-purpose terms as synonyms to indicate little other than a simple calendar.[369] It lists the saint of the day arranged according to the Byzantine calendar that runs from September 1 to August 31.[370]

The oldest liturgical calendars preserved begin in the ninth century and are found in the initial or final pages of Gospel books, lectionaries, and the praxapostoloi. Despite their importance, calendars have attracted little or no interest from a heortological perspective[371] simply because of the large number of examples that survive. (The exceptions are the calendars of southern Italian manuscripts, which are used for the purpose of identifying the places where books were copied.[372]) We do not, for instance, have a study that examines the relationships among calendars in regard to liturgical types or the selections of saints as they relate to the various families of the Constantinopolitan Synaxarion.[373] In the case of the Harvard Psalter, the observances of the second half of the year (March–August) generally agree with those of the Family D* manuscripts, which reflect an edition made prior to 1095,[374] and with the "Little Synaxarion" of the Evergetis Typikon.

369. For the multiple meanings of the term *synaxarion* see J. Noret, "Ménologes, Synaxaires, Ménées. Essai de clarification d'une terminologie," *AB* 86 (1968): 21–24.

370. R. F. Taft, "Calendar, Church," in *ODB*, 1:366; and N. Oikonomides, "Indiction," in *ODB*, 2:993.

371. See, for example, A. Ehrhard, *Überlieferung und Bestand der hagiographischen und homiletischen Literatur der griechischen Kirche von den Anfängen bis zum Ende des 16. Jahrhunderts* (Leipzig: J. C. Hinrichs, 1937), 1:25–35; see also S. Salaville, "La formation du calendrier liturgique byzantin d'après les recherches critiques de mgr. Ehrhard," *Ephemerides Liturgicae* 50 (1936): 312–23.

372. H. Delehaye, "Un synaxaire italo-grec," *AB* 21 (1902): 23–28, reprinted in *Synaxaires byzantins, ménologes, typica* (London: Variorum, 1977), II.

373. J. M. Birdsall, "A Byzantine Calendar from the Menology of Two Biblical Mss.," *AB* 84 (1966): 29–57.

374. J. Noret, "Le Synaxaire Leningrad gr. 240. Sa place dans l'évolution du Synaxaire byzantin," Античная древность и Средние века 10 (1973): 124–30, to be preferred over H. Delehaye, *Synaxarium Ecclesiae Constantinopolitanae e codice Sirmondiano nunc Berolinensi adiectis synaxariis selectis opera et studio* (Brussels: Socios Bollandianos, 1902), xvi–xx; see also A. Luzzi, *Studi sul Sinassario di Costantinopoli* (Rome: Dipartimento di filologia greca e latina, Sezione bizantino-neoellenica, Università di Roma, 1995), 223, s.v., in index.

We cannot, however, assign the manuscript to a particular church on the basis of a distinctive selection of saints. The celebration of the anniversary of the dedication of Constantinople, on May 11, passes without a troparion specific to the occasion,[375] but as a clue this is too slight to be of value. Although elegantly copied and richly decorated, the manuscript has a calendar that is strikingly anonymous and impersonal, a familiar characteristic that hampers the study of Byzantine (and non-Byzantine) liturgical manuscripts. Unfortunately, the Gospel book Baltimore, WAM, cod. W 522, which Georgi R. Parpulov attributed to the copyist of the Harvard Psalter,[376] is mutilated and lacks its calendar; it is thus of no help in reaching a more precise location where the scribe carried out his work.

We should therefore turn to some strictly liturgical observations. For feast days and the days on which the most important saints are commemorated the text (or incipit) of the apolytikion troparion is given. For weekdays of simple commemoration the Alleluia is prescribed. At the end of the calendar come several troparia for pre-Lent, Lent, and the Paschal period up to the Sunday after Pentecost, the Feast of All Saints. In the manuscript, feasts and commemorations are classified in summary fashion, but a general correspondence exists with the *Taktikon* of Nikon of the Black Mountain (1025 to at least 1088), which distinguishes among great (μεγάλαι), middle (μεσαῖαι), and small (μικραί) feasts.[377] In concrete terms, we have: (1) days with the indication of the troparion, (2) days without the indication of troparia, and (3) days of the Alleluia.

Among the days for which a troparion is given, it is possible to identify the most important feasts, which have one or more forefeast days (προεόρτια), some after-feast days (μεθέορτα), and a conclusion (ἀπόδοσις).

Taking into account the days with a double commemoration, the calendar

---

375. Mateos, *Typicon*, 1:286.

376. Parpulov, "Catalogue," 89.

377. Benešević, *Тактикон*, 61; see also J. B. Pitra, *Spicilegium Solesmense* (Paris, 1858), 4:445–55. For other designations and classifications see E. Velkovska, "The Liturgical Year in the East," in *Handbook for Liturgical Studies*, vol. 5, *Liturgical Time and Space*, ed. A. J. Chupungco (Collegeville, Minn.: Liturgical Press, 2000), 164; for contemporary practice: R. F. Taft, "The Veneration of Saints in the Byzantine Liturgical Tradition," in Θυσία αἰνέσεως. *Mélanges liturgiques offerts à la mémoire de l'archevêque Georges Wagner (1930–1993)*, ed. J. Getcha and A. Lossky (Paris: Saint Serge, 2005), 353–60.

Table 23: The Most Important Feasts

Date	Feast	Forefeast	After-feast
Sep. 8	Nativity of the Theotokos	1	4
Sep. 14	Exaltation of the Cross	1	–
Nov. 21	Entry of Theotokos	1	2
Dec. 25	Birth of the Lord	5	6
Jan. 6	Theophany	4	7
Feb. 2	Presentation	1	4
Mar. 25	Annunciation	1	–
Aug. 6	Transfiguration	1	7
Aug. 15	Dormition of the Theotokos	1	8

lists 52 dates with their own troparia, 89 with a shared troparion, 46 with a pre- or post-feast day troparion, 133 without troparia, and 49 days of Alleluia. There are no unpublished texts. One should note a choice in common with the Evergetis Typikon; the Typikon assignment of a theotokion in the series of the eight modes[378] to March 24 is repeated in our calendar on March 26.[379] The affinity with the Evergetis Typikon is additionally apparent in the troparia of the pre-Lenten and Lenten periods; in particular, the troparion for the third Sunday of Lent and the very distinctive one for the Wednesday of Mid-Lent[380] are both absent from the typikon of Alexios the Stoudite.[381] One notes at Eastertide the use in the third to fifth Sundays of troparia in the cycle of eight modes.

The calendar concludes with troparia, a kontakion (the only example in the entire manuscript), and the Cherubikon hymn for the feast of the consecration of a church, where the Constantinopolitan tradition of the Great

378. *Synaxarion of Evergetis*, ed. Jordan, 2:29; "Tὸ ἀπ' αἰῶνος ἀπόκρυφον ...," which Jordan (2:28n76) calls Troparion of the Forefeast of the Annunciation. The same troparion is also in the typikon of the monastery of Philanthropos.

379. A matter of the Sunday troparion of mode I, "Τοῦ Γαβριὴλ φθεγξαμένου σοι, παρθένε, τὸ χαῖρε ...," particularly adapted to the feast of the Archangel Gabriel, celebrated the day after the Annunciation; see *PaR* 4–5. This troparion is also prescribed for the same day in the Typikon of Philanthropos.

380. A. Luzzi, "Il *dies festus* di Costantino il Grande e di sua madre Elena nei libri liturgici della Chiesa Greca," in *Costantino il Grande dall'Antichità all'Umanesimo*, ed. G. Bonamente and F. Fusco (Macerata: Università degli Studi di Macerata, 1992), 2:597–98.

381. Cf. Pentkovskij, *Типикон*, 242–43.

Church (Hagia Sophia) is followed, in particular in the choice of the hymn *Sileat omnis caro*.[382]

V

The Twenty-Four-Hour *Cursus* and Monastic Prayer in Constantinople

Above, at § III.8, we examined the typical twenty-four hour *cursus* in the manuscripts Paris, BNF, gr. 331 (late eleventh century) and Lesbos, ML, cod. 295 (late twelfth century), erroneously considered by Phountoulis to be examples of the hourly prayer of the Akoimetoi. In a review of the Greek colleague's work,[383] Juan Mateos pointed out the very close relationship that exists between the psalms of the Paris. gr. 331 and the *Canones diurni et nocturni psalmorum*, attributed to Eusebius of Caesarea (d. ca. 340) and published by Migne in the *Patrologia Graeca*.[384] In all probability, the series in the *Patrologia* corresponds to that of the fifth-century Codex Alexandrinus (London, BL, MS Royal I.D.vii),[385] published by H. B. Swete.[386]

Mateos then highlighted three psalters that cite the *Canones*—all discussed above—Oxford, BodL, Auct. D. 4. 1, as of the ninth century (but in fact, 950–51),[387] Athens, EBE, cod. 7 (twelfth century), and a twelfth-century psalter known to him through a pamphlet published at the end of the nineteenth century by Archimandrite Amfilochij. The last can be identified as the famous Chludov Psalter (Moscow, GIM, gr. 129D), a Stoudite work of the ninth century.[388] We should also note that in the second half of the nineteenth century, Jean-Baptiste Pitra published the *Canones* from the no less celebrated Rome, BAV, Reg. gr. 1, the first volume of a Bible written during

---

382. R. Taft and S. Parenti, *Storia della Liturgia di S. Giovanni Crisostomo, II: Il Grande Ingresso. Edizione italiana rivista, ampliata e aggiornata*, Ἀνάλεκτα Κρυπτοφέρρης 10 (Grottaferrata, 2014), 191–97.

383. In *OCP* 32 (1966): 287.

384. PG 23:1395–96.

385. BL = British Library, London. Rahlfs-Fraenkel, *Verzeichnis*, 221–26.

386. H. B. Swete, *An Introduction to the Old Testament in Greek* (Cambridge, 1902; reprinted in New York: KTAV, 1968), 359.

387. See above, n383.

388. Amfilochij, *Заметки*, 25; color reproductions of only the morning psalms in Ščepkina, *Миниатюры Хлудовской Псалтыри*, fol. 169r.

the "Macedonian Renaissance" (the first half of the tenth century) for Leo, patrician, praepositos, and sakellarios.[389]

In the middle of the 1970s, Heinrich Husmann brought together the psalms of the "little" Hours of the Paris. gr. 331 and a group of twelve psalms which immediately follow the psalmody of the ninth hour in the horologion Sinai. gr. 864 (ninth century).[390] Even if Husmann's assignment of the *cursus* to a Melkite milieu is unconvincing, his choice and comparison of the two sources are of value.[391] The whole subject has recently been taken up and organized by Stig S. R. Frøyshov,[392] who has, first and foremost, revived the studies of the *cursus* of twenty-four hours, not only those of Phountoulis, but also the ones carried out in the early years of the twentieth century by the Russians Diakovskij and Skaballanovič.[393]

According to Frøyshov, the origin of the *cursus* is to be found in the common prayer of Egypt, as attested by the Codex Alexandrinus of the fifth century and a papyrus fragment, also Egyptian, from the sixth century. This system, which assigned a psalm to each of the hours of the day and night, probably corresponds to the practice of the so-called Rule of the Angel— known in the fourth century by John Cassian at the time of his visit to Skete in Egypt, from 380 to 399,[394] and Palladius of Helenopolis. In it every hour included one psalm and one prayer. The study of the witnesses has shown the existence of two distinct series of nocturnal psalms, ancient and new, and within the ancient series, two dominant recensions, a) and b). Recension

---

389. Pitra, *Iuris ecclesiastici graecorum*, 2:209; cf. S. Dufrenne and P. Canart, ed., *Die Bibel des Patricius Leo: Codex Reginensis graecus I B*, vol. 2 (Zurich: Belser, 1988), 55, and P. Canart, *La Bible du Patrice Lèon - Codex Reginensis Graecus 1* - Commentaire codicologique, Paléographique, Philologique et Artistique, Studi e Testi [hereafter "ST"] 463 (Vatican City: Biblioteca Apostolica Vaticana, 2011).

390. H. Husmann, "Eine alte orientalische christliche Liturgie: altsyrisch-melkitish," *OCP* 42 (1976): 175–77. The text of the Sinai. gr. 864 is now published in Ajjoub and Paramelle, ed., *Livre d'Heures du Sinaï*, 175–79, but the editor has not taken into account the work of Husmann.

391. Husmann, "Alte orientalische Liturgie," 177: "Sinai gr. 864 und Paris gr. 331 sind damit Vertreter einer echten altgriechish-melkitischen Stundenordnung."

392. S. S. R. Frøyshov, "Двенадцати псалмов чин," in *Православная энциклопедия* 14 (Moscow: Tserkovno-nauchnyj tsentr "Pravoslavnaia Entsiklopediia," 2006): 232–34.

393. S. S. R. Frøyshov, "The Cathedral-Monastic Distinction Revisited. Part I: Was Egyptian Desert Liturgy a Pure Monastic Office?," *Studia Liturgica* 37 (2007): 208–13.

394. A. Veilleux, *La liturgie dans le cénobitisme pachômien au quatrième siècle* (Rome: "I.B.C." Libreria Herder, 1968), 324–39; Taft, *Liturgy of the Hours*, 418 (Rule of the Angel and rule of twelve psalms per office).

a) is that of the Codex Alexandrinus and of the Egyptian papyrus taken up in the horologia Sinai gr. 864 and georg. 34, and, in Constantinople, in the Chludov Psalter and Athens, EBE, 7, also a psalter.[395] Recension b) is found in horologia Paris, BNF, gr. 331, Lesbos, ML, cod. 295, and in the later Sinai. gr. 868 (twelfth or fourteenth century) studied by Diakovskij.[396] The series of the Leo Bible, however, reveals particular characteristics.

A certain continuity in metropolitan practice from the first half of the tenth century to the second half of the twelfth is demonstrated by the presence of the *Canones* of the Psalters in Milan, BA, cod. +24 sup., by the scribe Γρηγορᾶς,[397] in Rome, BAV, gr. 342, of 1087–88 (belonging to Michael Attaliates), and in examples of the aristocratic psalters, ones such as Athens, EBE, codd. 7 and 15.[398]

In 1909, E. Diakovskij drew attention to the horologion Mt. Athos, MV, cod. 1248 (1077 A.D.),[399] as yet unpublished horologion of great interest for the history of hourly monastic prayer in Byzantium.[400] After apodeipnon the *cursus* provides for a series of "supplementary" hours that are identical in structure and analogous in content to the appendices of the Harvard Psalter kathismata and to the "little" hours of the Paris and Lesbos horologia (see table 24).

Diakovskij[401] noted another example that should be examined alongside the three illustrated immediately above; it is the twelfth-century horologion Sinai. gr. 865. Diakovskij points to a special "interhour" of the night, after apodeipnon, meant for the third nocturnal hour.[402] It is useful to compare it with the same hour of the Paris. gr. 331 (see table 25).

395. Frøyshov, "Двенадцати псалмов чин" (above, n392), 233.

396. E. Diakovskij, "Последование ночных часов (чин 12-ти псалмов)," *Труды Киевской Духовной Академии* (Kiev, 1909), 2:557–78; Diakovskij, *Posledovanie časov*, 163–64. Gardthausen, *Catalogus Sinaiticorum*, 188, dates the horologion to the fourteenth or fifteenth century. The manuscript was not microfilmed by the mission led by Kenneth W. Clark and is therefore inaccessible to me.

397. Cf. A. Martini and D. Bassi, *Catalogus codicum graecorum Bibliothecae Ambrosianae* (Milan: Hoepli, 1906), 2:783; Agati, *Minuscola "bouletée*," 1:36–37; Parpulov, "Psalters and Personal Piety," fig. 1–2.

398. Other testimony is cited in Parpulov, *Byzantine Psalters*, C5.

399. Diakovskij, "Чин 12-ти псалмов," 547; Diakovskij, *Последование часов*, 159. The Vatopedi manuscript has been cited by the older number 350/984, and dated in the twelfth century; for the Slavic horologia with the same *cursus* now see Sliva, "Часословы студийской традиции," 91–106.

400. See above, n303.

401. Diakovskij, "Чин 12-ти псалмов," 556; Diakovskij, *Последование часов*, 174.

402. Sinai. gr. 865 (twelfth century), fols. 165r–171v: Μεσώριον τῆς νυκτὸς ψαλλόμενον τῇ γ' ὥρᾳ τῆς νυκτός.

Table 24: Supplementary Hours

Harvard Psalter	Paris. gr. 331[1]	Vatopedi 1248[2]
Kathisma XIX	Third hour of the night	
		Trisagion-Pater
Psalms 134–42	Psalm 55	Psalms 6, 31, 76
Trisagion-Pater		Trisagion-Pater
Hymnography	Hymnography	Hymnography
Kyrie eleison		
Prayer: Πάλιν…	Prayer: Πάλιν…	Prayer: Πάλιν…

1. Paris. gr. 331, fols. 128r–133v.
2. Mt. Athos, MV, cod. 1248, fols. 25v–26r.

Table 25: Comparison of Hours

Sinai. gr. 865	Paris. gr. 331
Mesorion of the night: third hour	Third hour of the night
Psalm 74	
Psalm 26	
Psalm 55	Psalm 55
Hymnography	Hymnography
Prayer: Πάλιν…	Prayer: Πάλιν…

Psalm 74 belongs to the first nocturnal hour in the Chludov Psalter and the Codex Alexandrinus; Psalm 26 is assigned to the second hour in Paris. gr. 331. Also in the twelfth century, the liturgical typikon of Evergetis informs us that these intermediate hours of the night were also practiced in that monastery. In the directives for ferial days during the Apostles' Fast, it expressly states that before beginning mesonyktikon, the monks must celebrate "the last mesorion, of None." It is clear that we are dealing with the ninth hour of the night here,[403] so the Apodeipnon is found at first hour, followed by three mesoria at third, sixth, and ninth hours of the night, followed by mesonyktikon, which is found at the twelfth.

403. Jordan, ed., Synaxarion of Evergetis, 2:694.

The thirteenth-century manuscript Oxford, BodL, MS Clarke 2, preserves (fols. 193v–204r) an interesting text credited to Niketas Stethatos of Stoudios (d. 1090); it is entitled "Ὑποτύπωσις εὐσύνοπτος τοῦ ἡμερονυκτίου τῆς ἀκολουθίας τῶν ὡρῶν γινομένη παρὰ τοῦ ὁσίου πατρὸς ἡμῶν Νικήτα τοῦ Στηθάτου μονῆς τῶν Στουδίου."[404] This is an ascetic rule meant to regulate the personal prayer that a Stoudite monk recited in his cell between one communal synaxis and another.[405] The document, defined by Dirk Krausmüller as "a combination of a disciplinary typikon for the individual and a purely technical Book of Hours,"[406] illustrates some little-noted aspects of the daily life of the Stoudites in Constantinople during the last quarter of the eleventh century, and documents the evolution of the ascetic discipline in the context of the corpus of legislative writings attributed to the founder, Theodore (d. 826), or those slightly later than him.[407]

According to the *Hypotyposis* of Niketas, a monk was required to participate daily in four public synaxes, orthros, the Divine Liturgy, vespers, and apodeipnon, but he recited in private the first, third, sixth, and ninth hours, the respective "interhours" (μεσώρια), and the mesonykytikon, or midnight hour. Added to these is a series of occasions for private prayer, which we can also define as "intermediate," even if not specifically named in the *Hypotyposis*. Meant to fill the times between the principal hours, these supplementary hours have a structure and elements in common with the hymnographic-euchological *cursus* of the "Akoimetoi" horologia and the augmented psalters. We may compare, for example, the first of the supplementary hours of the *Hypotyposis* of Niketas with kathisma III of the Harvard Psalter (see table 26).

---

404. Parpulov, *Byzantine Psalters*, 444–92. The text was first noted by J. Darrouzès, *Nicétas Stéthatos, Opuscules et Lettres* (Paris, 1961), 13, 40–41, and again taken up by D. Krausmüller, "The monastic communities of Stoudios and St Mamas in the second half of the tenth century," in *The Theotokos Evergetis and eleventh-century monasticism*, ed. M. Mullet and A. Kirby (Belfast: Belfast Byzantine Enterprises, 1994), 67–85, especially 69n5. Thanks to the kindness of Prof. Krausmüller I was able to examine Niketas's text in his transcription, which he kindly put at my disposal. For the latest see also E. Morini, "Il monachesimo italo-greco e l'influenza di Stoudios," in *L'Ellenismo Italiota dal VII al XII secolo. Alla memoria di Nikos Panagiotakis* (Athens: National Hellenic Research Foundation, Institute for Byzantine Research, 2001), 140n57.

405. Analysis in Krausmüller, "Private vs communal," 309–28.

406. Ibid., 312.

407. *BMFD*, 1:4–119, with English translation and bibliography. The liturgical problems have been studied by J. Leroy, "La vie quotidienne du Moine studite," *Irénikon* 27 (1954): 21–50.

Table 26: Comparison of Supplementary Hours

Harvard Psalter	Hypotyposis of Niketas
Psalmody [kathisma III: Pss 17–23]	Psalms 91, 112, 69
Glory to the Father..	Glory to the Father...
Trisagion-Pater	Trisagion-Pater
Hymnography	Hymnography
Kyrie eleison	Kyrie eleison
Prayer: Ὁ Θεὸς ὁ δίκαιος…	Prayer: Ὁ Θεὸς ὁ δίκαιος…

Beyond the identical structure, we can note that: (1) the hymnography belongs to the same type; the psalter orders two penitential kathismata and a theotokion of mode I and the *Hypotyposis* two penitential kathismata of mode I and two of mode II; and (2) the concluding prayer is the same in both examples.

All the evidence points to the existence of a direct link between the Harvard Psalter—and in general the twelfth-century psalters with an appendix—and the horologion Mt. Athos, MV, cod. 1248 (1077 A.D.), the *Hypotyposis* of Niketas of Stoudios (before 1090), and, secondarily, the "Akoimetoi" horologia of the eleventh and twelfth centuries. Furthermore, the lexical parallels that the Vatopedi Horologion and the *Hypotyposis* of Niketas share with the writings of Symeon the New Theologian (d. 1022) mean that it is necessary to look to the monastic circles of Constantinople as the place where the augmented psalter originated. The use of three presidential prayers from the cathedral Liturgy of the Hours (9, 12, 14; cf. § II.4) supports the theory. It is possible to object, arguing that the hymnographic component is drawn entirely from Palestinian kathismata, but in this regard it is necessary to emphasize: (1) the Palestinian hymnography was in daily use by the Stoudites, and (2) the oldest parakletike known—Mt. Sinai, MSC, gr. 1593 and gr. 824, copied in Palestine—have fewer penitential kathismata than the examples from the tenth and eleventh centuries; their number is insufficient to complete the twenty sections of the psalter.[408]

408. Krašeninnikova, *Древнеславянский Октоих*, 305 (plagal tone I); D. Bucca, "Un antico manoscritto innografico," 117–25.

V.1. *From psalter to horologion and vice versa*

The sources cited in the preceeding paragraph share with the augmented psalter some of the hymns and prayers and their specific use; in fact, the supplemental hours of the horologion Mt. Athos, MI, cod. 1248, the *Hypotyposis* of Niketas of Stoudios, and augmented psalter are somehow destined for use in private prayer.

As we have seen, between the two sets of kathismata (I–X and XI–XX) the Harvard Psalter contains a rite for the forgiveness of sins committed during the day. The same rite is also present in the "Akoimetoi" horologion Paris. gr. 331 (late eleventh century).[409] It also appears in the earlier Vatopedi Horologion (1077 A.D.), though in a different configuration and with the direction that the monk recite it immediately before going to sleep.[410] Considering that in the Paris Horologion the ἀκολουθία divides the daytime hours from the nighttime, and in the Vatopedi it concludes the monk's day, the location of the rite between the tenth and eleventh kathismata of the Harvard Psalter suggests that the first set of kathismata was meant for the daytime hours and the second for the nighttime hours. Confirmation comes from the choice in some codices of assigning one of the final prayers of the cathedral matins[411] to the twentieth kathisma, the last in the psalter and the nighttime set. Is it possible then to hypothesize that our psalter was used for private reading of the kathismata distributed throughout the day? In addition, what is the relationship between this reading and the *cursus* of the horologion?

In the horologion—as previously noted—the psalms are indicated only by incipit, since their text is found in the psalter. In the description of the lauds the scribe writes: "Praise the Lord from the heavens. Praise becomes you, O Lord, according to the mode, [the psalm] is in the psalter." But a deeper and more organic relationship exists between the two sections of the book. The *cursus* of the twenty-four hours was meant to ensure a moment of prayer at each hour of the day and night. Private reading of the psalter also met the

---

409. At the end of the twelfth hour of the day (fol. 112v) is the notice: "ποιεῖ δὲ μετὰ τὰς ιβ᾽ ὥρας τρισάγιον ὑπὲρ τῶν συμβαινόντων σφαλμάτων δι᾽ ὅλης τῆς ἡμέρας."

410. MV, cod. 1248, fols. 26v–27r: "Εἶθ᾽ οὕτως ποιῇ τρισάγιον ὑπὲρ τῶν δι᾽ ὅλης τῆς ἡμέρας συμπιπτόντων σφαλμάτων ἐν ἔργοις ἢ ῥήμα ἢ διὰ νοήμα, ἑκουσίως ἢ ἀκουσίως, ἐν γνώμη καὶ ἀγνοία ... αὖθις δὲ κοίτας θεὶς ἀναπαύθη μέχρι ἂν ὁ τοῦ ὄρθρου κρουσθεὶς σημαντήρ ..."

411. And the prayer: "Κύριε, Κύριε, σή ἐστιν ἡ ἡμέρα καὶ σή ἐστιν ἡ νύξ ..." (Parenti-Velkovska, *Eucologio Barberini*, 103, § 81).

need for continuous prayer, although at first sight there appears to be an inconsistency. It arises from the numerical difference between the ἀκολουθία of the twenty-four hours and the twenty kathisma of the psalter; they are four units apart. The inconsistency is only superficial, and the resolution of the difference is provided by the horologion itself. Upon examination, it is apparent that a good number of prayers and synaxes are grouped together:

1. Prayers for rising
    The ἀκολουθία for the forgiveness of sins
    Trisagion for the deceased
    Hour of midnight
    Matins
    First hour
2. "Great" third hour
    "Great" sixth hour
3. Ninth hour
    Typika
    Vespers
4. Apodeipnon

The result is four grand synaxes that when added to the twenty psalter kathismata lead, at least nominally, to twenty-four moments of daily prayer. The reconstruction proposed here finds support in other sources. An appendix to the psalter Rome, BAV, gr. 341 (1021 A.D.),[412] bearing the title Ἀρχὴ σὺν Θεῷ τῶν νυκτερινῶν εὐχῶν, organizes a *cursus* in which the twenty psalter kathismata are distributed throughout the nighttime hours between apodeipnon and mesonyktikon. The tenth kathisma is followed by the prayers before going to sleep and a formula for remission of sins, while the eleventh kathisma is prescribed after awakening and mesonyktikon.

The augmented psalter Vienna, ÖNb, theol. gr. 177 (1150 A.D.), almost half a century after the Harvard Psalter, presents for each psalm kathisma a double series of hymnographic kathismata and prayers for the day and night (κατανυκτικὰ ἡμερινά/νυκτερινά followed by εὐχὴ ἡμερινή/νυκτερινή).[413]

412. Devreesse, *Codices Vaticani graeci*, 2:13–15.
413. Hunger et al., *KatalogÖNb*, 3.2:316–27.

The choice presented cannot but refer to a twice daily recitation of the psalter distributed among the daytime and nighttime hours. The selection of prayers is also significant; out of a total of sixty-two pieces, fourteen belong to the cathedral Liturgy of the Hours and two are common to the Constantinopolitan euchologion Paris, BNF, Coislin 213, of 1027.[414] It is without doubt a private cursus that the fourteenth-century psalter, Rome, BAV, gr. 778, calls Ἀκολουθία ψαλλομένη ἐν τοῖς κελλίοις ἐν ἑκάστῃ ἡμέρᾳ.[415]

VI

Conclusion

Like every handwritten liturgical text, the Harvard Psalter, copied in 1105, probably in Constantinople, represents a moment in the slow evolution of a local rite, in our case that of a monk's communal and private prayers. Nothing in the manuscript permits attribution to a specific monastery, but the absence of the "royal office" prior to matins may be a clue that points to a cenobitic institution, neither aristocratic nor patriarchal, of recent foundation.[416]

The editorial type—of which it is the oldest dated specimen—is that of a psalter with hymns and prayers, one that is "augmented" with a horologion and a calendar. The psalter is the supporting structure of the manuscript because of the double use for which it was intended. In relation to liturgical prayer, the psalter contains the psalms required for the celebration of the hours of the daily *cursus*, and the relationship is emphasized by the fact that only the psalm incipits are given in the horologion. In support of personal devotion, each kathisma of the psalter is followed by several hymns and a prayer. The only element of the manuscript that lacks a direct relationship with the psalter is the calendar, which is connected only to the horologion.

With respect to the history of the Byzantine prayer of the hours, the

414. Dmitrievskij, *Описание*, 2:1004–8.

415. Devreesse, *Codices Vaticani graeci*, 3:293.

416. The "royal office" is presented in the typikon of Alexios Stoudites and that of the Evergetis, for which see Pentkovskij, *Типикон* 9, 398; Gautier, "Typikon Évergétis," 27; *BMFD*, 2:467; V. Larin, "The Origins and History of the Royal Office at the Beginning of Matins," *BollGrott* 5 (2008): 199–218.

horologion of the Harvard Psalter documents a process of evolution within the Stoudite Liturgy of the Hours. The fundamental structure of the daily *cursus* remains Stoudite, as shown by: a) the contracted form of mesonyktikon and b) the presence of Psalm 118 in apodeipnon, in any case prior to awakening. In the Evergetine sources the psalm moves into mesonyktikon, the first real liturgical hour of the new day (that is, after the nighttime rest). The feast day matins, while remaining within the Stoudite sphere, show two celebratory patterns, with the first more strictly Stoudite and the second oriented more toward what will become the Evergetis rite, with the Lenten matins remaining in a Stoudite style. With respect to the phenomenology of liturgical reforms, it is possible here as well to note that within the internal evolution of the rite the substitution of new customs for old ones is preceded by a period of coexistence.[417]

As regards the history of the individual liturgical services, our manuscript underscores several certainties, permits the clarification of terminology and, as for methodology, shows the usefulness of the unitary study of a manuscript. The weekday, Saturday, Sunday, and feast day divisions are not three methods of celebrating matins, but rather three evolutionary phases in the same celebration. More generally, the study of the horologion has permitted us to advance new hypotheses regarding the origins of ritual structures and sequences hitherto unexamined in a satisfactory manner; in particular, in the final section of vespers and that of matins, we have brought to light the developmental phenomenon that leads to standardization of the structure underlying the two celebrations.

Use of the adjective "great" (μεγάλη) in the context of the third and sixth hours reveals that the compiler of the horologion was aware of the *cursus* of twenty-four hours that is known through several twelfth-century horologia and connected in the past to the hourly system of the Constantinopolitan monastery of the Akoimetoi. The division of the twenty kathismata of the psalter into two sets of ten separated by a "Prayer for the forgiveness of the sins of the day" permits us to identify a private *cursus*. It assigned to each hour of the day and night the recitation of a psalm kathisma, with hymns and a prayer. In turn, the private *cursus* of the twenty kathismata comple-

417. Taft, "Comparative Liturgy Revisited," 200.

mented that of the horologion in order to satisfy, at least notionally, the demand for prayers at each of the twenty-four hours. In this way, a monk could live up to the apostolic call for praying without ceasing (1 Thes 5:17).

Hourly prayer is not only a question of *pensum*, of quantity. As we have seen, the *cursus* of the augmented psalter makes use of penitential hymns that underscore themes such as pain for personal sins, compunction—the *penthos*—and the final judgment according to the eschatology of the *tremendum*. All are themes touched on in the verses (στίχοι κατανυκτικοί) copied at the end of the first ten kathismata and ones largely present in Niketas Stethatos's *Life* of Symeon the New Theologian.[418] The daily repetition of hymns formed the spiritual character and the psychology of the monk and, as a consequence, of the *homo byzantinus*.[419]

The choice of prayers highlights the interaction between the liturgical book and hagiographical literature; examples of this process even survive in the contemporary horologion. But no less interesting in the context of private prayer is the use of presidential prayers from the cathedral Liturgy of the Hours.[420] The hermeneutical criterion of "cathedral versus monastery" remains fundamental when approaching the celebrative structures of the Divine Office,[421] but this does not exclude the possibility that in the documents the margins can become blurred.

At this point, the reader is entitled to ask: to whom was the Harvard Psalter Horologion destined? The manuscript is classified among the "aristocratic" psalters and certainly is the result of an important commission. Unfortunately the figure prostrate at Christ's feet in the miniature of the initial Deesis—the possible portrait of the patron—is too abraded to discern whether he is an hegumen, a monk, or a layperson. Paradoxically, the answer is not that important because in Constantinople of the early twelfth

---

418. I. Hausherr and G. Horn, ed. and trans., *Un grand mystique byzantin. Vie de Syméon le Nouveau Théologien (949–1022) par Nicétas Stéthatos* (Rome: Pontificium Institutum Orientalium Studiorum, 1928), 12.

419. On the subject the monograph of I. Hausherr,

420. Arranz, "Prières des matines," 406: "tout en étant l'apanage du prêtre célébrant, de par leur texte auraient pu être prononcées par n'importe quel membre de l'assemblée; et en disant cela nous songeons aux communautés de moines dépourvues de presbytres."

421. R. F. Taft, "Cathedral vs. Monastic Liturgy in the Christian East: Vindicating a Distinction," *BollGrott* III s. 2 (2005): 173–219.

century the monastic rite was already practiced in all the churches of the city, monastic and non-monastic. Certainly the ancient cathedral rite was still surviving at Hagia Sophia, but already at the end of the eleventh century it too was widely influenced by hagiopolite practices mediated by Stoudite monasticism.[422]

According to the incisive witness of the *Strategikòn* of Kekaumenos (d. after 1070) the hagiopolite Liturgy of the Hours mediated by the Stoudites eventually became the norm even for the laity of the capital[423] and a century later the patriarch Luke Chrysoberges (d. 1170) explains to a hermit that his prayer in his cell must be "the same as that carried out by the Christians [that is, laity]: mesonyktikon, matins, hours, vespers, and compline."[424] Under such circumstances, determining the socio-religious position of the user of our manuscript becomes a secondary concern.

To a certain extent the Harvard Psalter offers a new and as yet unseen glimpse of liturgical practice in Constantinople at the beginning of the twelfth century. For too many years, the scholarly community has been focused on evaluating liturgical practice through the euchologion and the typikon, examples of prime importance for the history of liturgy, but too "official" in origin and use. Apart from a few exceptions, the euchologion and typikon express the point of view of the hierarchy or of the founder of a monastery, that is, the perspective of authority. The psalter and the horologion remain the most personal of the liturgical books, and therefore complete the picture with a view of prayer from below, closer to the actual experience of everyday life,[425] as shown for example in the hagiographic literature.[426]

422. E. Velkovska, "Il lezionario patriarcale Ottoboni gr. 175," in *Alethes Philia. Studi in onore di Giancarlo Prato*, ed. M. D'Agostino, P. Degni, vol. I–II, Collectanea 23 (Spoleto: Centro Italiano di studi sull'alto Medioevo, 2010), 687–94.

423. *Cecaumeno, Raccomandazioni e consigli di un galantuomo (Στρατηγικόν)*, ed. and trans. M. D. Spadaro, Hellenica 2 (Alessandria, 1998), 136–39.

424. Parpulov, *Byzantine Psalters*, 494; see also Parpulov, "Psalters and Personal Piety," 85.

425. And which Kallistos Ware calls "the influence of the liturgy on the daily personal life of the people." See his "The Meaning of the Divine Liturgy for the Byzantine Worshipper," in *Church and People in Byzantium*, ed. R. Morris (Birmingham: Centre for Byzantine, Ottoman, and Modern Greek Studies at University of Birmingham, 1990), 7.

426. R. F. Taft, "Eastern Saints' Lives and Liturgy. Hagiography and New Perspectives in Liturgiology," in *In God's Hands: Essays on the Church and Ecumenism in Honour of Michael A. Fahey, S.J.*, ed. J. Z. Skira and M. S. Attridge (Leuven: Peeters, 2006), 33–53.

All of this is true, not only because of anthropological considerations, but because of the history of the Byzantine rite itself. As John E. Klentos summarized in the abstract of his doctoral thesis on the typikon of the Constantinopolitan monastery of the Evergetis: "This study indicates the need for further investigation of the development of the horologia to understand more fully the process of liturgical synthesis prior to the Neo-Sabaitic canonization of the Byzantine Office."[427] Everything written thus far seeks to be an initial response.

427. Klentos, *Evergetis*, second initial page without numeration.

SELECTED BIBLIOGRAPHY

Agati, M. L. *Il libro manoscritto. Introduzione alla codicologia.* Studia Archaeologica 124. Rome: Bretschneider, 2003.

———. *La minuscola "bouletée."* 2 vols. Littera Antiqua 9.1–2. Vatican City: Scuola Vaticana di Paleografia, Diplomatica e Archivistica, 1992.

Ajjoub, M., and J. Paramelle, ed. and trans. *Livre d'heures du Sinaï (Sinaiticus graecus 864).* SC 486. Paris: Éditions du Cerf, 2004.

Aletta, A. A. "Grottaferrata, Biblioteca del Monumento Nazionale, Crypt. A.β.III." In *Codici greci dell'Italia meridionale,* edited by P. Canart and S. Lucà, 69–70. Rome: Ufficio Centrale per i Beni Librari, le Instituzioni Culturali e l'Editoria, 2000.

Alexopoulos, S. *The Presanctified Liturgy in the Byzantine Rite: A Comparative Analysis of its Origins, Evolution, and Structural Components.* Liturgia Condenda 21. Leuven: Peeters, 2009.

Alexopoulos, S., and A. van den Hoek. "The Endicott Scroll and Its Place in the History of Private Communion Prayers." *DOP* 60 (2006): 145–88.

Amfilochij (Sergievskij). *Археологическия заметки греческой псалтири, писанной в конце IX века и переписанной почти всей в XII веке с миниатюрами X–XII века, принадлежащей действительному члену Общества Древнерусского Искусства при Румянцевском Московском Музее и других Обществ А. Н. Лобкову.* Moscow, 1866.

———. *Древле-славянская Псалтирь Симоновская до 1280 года.* 3 vols. Moscow, 1880–82.

———. "О покаянных тропарях и молитвах или стихирах, в древне-Греческих и древне-Славянских Псалтирях после каждой кафисмы." *Чтения в Обществе любителей духовного просвящения* 17 suppl. (1880): 132–49.

Anderson, J. "The Content of the Marginal Psalter Paris. gr. 20." *RSBN* 35 (1998): 25–35.

———. "The Date and Purpose of the Barberini Psalter." *Cahiers archéologiques* 31 (1983): 35–67.

———. "The Palimpsest Psalter, Pantokrator Cod. 61: Its Content and Relationship to the Bristol Psalter." *DOP* 48 (1994): 199–220.

———. "The Walters Praxapostolos and Liturgical Illustration." *DChAE* 19 (199697): 9–34.

Anderson, J., et al. *The Barberini Psalter Codex Vaticanus Barberinianus Graecus 372.* Zurich: Belser, 1989.

Andreou, G. "Alcune osservazioni sul menologion del lezionario Paris gr. 382 (X sec. ex.)." *BollGrott* 2 (2005): 5–16.

Anonymous. Βιβλίον καλούμενον Θηκαρᾶς, ἐν ᾧ εἰσί γεγραμμένοι ὕμνοι τε καὶ εὐχαί ... Venice, 1643.

————. Деяния Московских соборов 1666–1667 годов, II, Книга соборных деяний 1667 года. Moscow: Sinodal'naja Tipografija, 1893.

————. "Un antichissimo 'kontakion' inedito. Saggio di testi liturgici." Roma e l'Oriente 1 (1910): 165–87.

————. Paris: une thèse de doctorat apporte un éclairage nouveau sur les origines du cycle liturgique quotidian. Service Orthodoxe de Presse 285 (February 2004).

Arranz, M., ed. L'Eucologio costantinopolitano agli inizi del secolo XI. Hagiasmatarion & Archieratikon (Rituale & Pontificale) con l'aggiunta del Leitourgikon (Messale). Rome: Pontificia Università Gregoriana, 1996.

————. "Les grandes étapes de la Liturgie byzantine: Palestine-Byzance-Russie. Essai d'aperçu historique." In Liturgie de l'Église particulière et liturgie de l'Église universelle, 43–72. BELS 7. Rome: Edizioni Liturgiche, 1976.

————. "L'office de l'Asmatikos Hesperinos ('vêpres chantées') de l'ancien Euchologe byzantin. IIe Partie: la Psalmodie." OCP 44 (1978): 391–419.

————. "L'office de l'Asmatikos Orthros ('matines chantées') de l'ancien Euchologe byzantin. Ie Partie: Les prières des eucologes." OCP 47 (1981): 122–57.

————. "Les prières de la gonyklisia ou de la génuflexion du jour de la Pentecôte dans l'ancien Euchologe byzantin." OCP 48 (1982): 92–123.

————. "Les prières presbytérales de la 'Pannychis' de l'ancien Euchologe byzantin et la 'Panikhida' des défunts." OCP 40 (1974): 314–43; OCP 41 (1975): 119–39.

————. "Les prières presbytérales des matines byzantines." OCP 37 (1971): 406–36.

————. "Les prières presbytérales des Petites Heures dans l'ancien Euchologe byzantin." OCP 39 (1973): 29–82.

————. Le Typicon du monastère du Saint-Sauveur à Messine. Codex Messinensis gr. 115, A.D. 1131. OCA 185. Rome: Pontificium Institutum Orientalium Studiorum, 1969.

Aslanov, C. "Bayt ('House') as 'Strophe' in Hebrew, Byzantine and Near Eastern Poetry." Le Muséon 121 (2008): 297–310.

Assemani, J. S. Sancti patris nostri Ephraem Syri opera omnia quae exstant Graece, Syriace, Latine ... ad mss. codices Vaticanos, aliosque castigata, multis aucta, interpretatione, praefationibus notis ... illustrata. 3 vols. Rome, 1732–46.

Auzépy, M.-F. La Vie d'Étienne le Jeune. Birmingham Byzantine and Ottoman Monographs 3. Aldershot: Variorum, 1997.

Bakker, W. "The Origin of the S. Patris Ephraem Syri Sermo de Sanctissimae Dei Genitricis Mariae laudibus (Assemani, III: 575-577)." Byzantion 74 (2004): 147–97.

Bandini, A. M. Catalogus codicum manuscriptorum Bibliothecae Mediceae Laurentianae, varia continens opera graecorum patrum ... Supplementa. Edited by E. Rostagno et al. 3 vols. Leipzig: Zentral-Antiquariat der Deutschen Demokratischen Republik, 1961.

Baumstark, A. Liturgie comparée. Principes et méthodes pour l'étude historique des liturgies chrétiennes. Edited by B. Botte. 3rd ed. Chevetogne: Éditions de Chevetogne, 1953.

————. Vom geschichtlichen Werden der Liturgie. Ecclesia Orans 10. Freiburg i.B.: Herder, 1923.

Beck, H.-G. *Kirche und theologische Literatur im byzantinischen Reich*. Handbuch der Altertumswissenschaft Abt. 12, Byzantinisches Handbuch 2.1. Munich: C. H. Beck, 1959.

Beneševič, B. N. *Тактикон Никона Черногорца. Греческий текст по рукописи № 441 Синайскаго монастыря св. Екатерины*. St. Petersburg: St. Petersburg University, 1917.

Bertonière, G. *The Historical Development of the Easter Vigil and Related Services in the Greek Church*. OCA 193. Rome: Pontificium Institutum Orientalium Studiorum, 1972.

Biolake, G. *Τυπικὸν τῆς τοῦ Χριστοῦ Μεγάλης Ἐκκλησίας*. Constantinople, 1888.

Birdsall, J. M. "A Byzantine Calendar from the Menology of Two Biblical Mss." *AB* 84 (1966): 29–57.

Black, M. *A Christian Palestinian Syriac Horologion (Berlin MS. Or. Oct. 1019)*. Cambridge: Cambridge University Press, 1954.

Bordier, H. L. *Description des peintures et autres ornements contenus dans les manuscrits grecs de la Bibliothèque Nationale*. Paris: H. Champion, 1883.

Brakmann, H. "Der Gottesdienst der östlichen Kirchen." *Archiv für Liturgiewissenschaft* 30 (1988): 303–410.

Brenton, L. C. L., trans. *The Septuagint Version of the Old Testament, with an English Translation; and with Various Readings and Critical Notes*. London: Samuel Bagster, 1879; and New York: Harper and Brothers, 1879.

Buberl, P. *Die Miniaturenhandschriften der Nationalbibliothek in Athen*. Vienna: A. Hölder, 1917.

Burmester, O. H. "The Canonical Hours of the Coptic Church." *OCP* 2 (1936): 78–100.

Calì, L. "Le Ipacoè dell'Octoichos bizantino." *BollGrott* 19 (1965): 161–74.

Canart, P. "A propos du *Sermo de Sanctissimae Dei Genitricis Virginis Mariae Laudibus* d'Ephrem le Syrien." *Byzantion* 75 (2005): 499–500.

———. *Bibliothecae Apostolicae Vaticanae codices manu scripti recensiti. Codices Vaticani graeci: Codices 1745–1962*. Vol. 1, *Codicum enarrationes*. Vatican City: Biblioteca Apostolica Vaticana, 1970.

———. *Catalogue des manuscrits grecs de l'Archivio di San Pietro*. ST 246. Vatican City: Biblioteca Apostolica Vaticana, 1966.

Caracausi, G. *Lessico greco della Sicilia e dell'Italia Meridionale (secoli X–XIV)*. Lessici siciliani 6. Palermo: Centro di Studi Filologici e Linguistici Siciliani, 1990.

Ceresa, M., and S. Lucà. "Frammenti greci di Dioscoride Pedanio e Aezio Amideno in una edizione a stampa di Francesco Zanetti (Roma 1576)." In *Miscellanea Bibliothecae Apostolicae Vaticanae XV*, 191–229. ST 453. Vatican City: Biblioteca Apostolica Vaticana, 2007.

Clark, K. W., ed. *Checklist of Manuscripts in the Libraries of the Greek and Armenian Patriarchates in Jerusalem, Microfilmed for the Library of Congress, 1949–50*. Washington, D.C.: Library of Congress, 1953.

———. *Checklist of Manuscripts in St. Catherine's Monastery, Mount Sinai, Microfilmed for the Library of Congress, 1950*. Washington, D.C.: Library of Congress, 1952.

Clugnet, L. *Dictionnaire grec-français des noms liturgiques en usage dans l'Église grecque*. Paris, 1895; reprinted in London: Variorum, 1971.

Codrington, H. W. *The Liturgy of Saint Peter.* Liturgiegeschichtliche Quellen und Forschungen 30. Munster: Aschendorff, 1936.

Constantinides, E. C. "The Tetraevangelion Manuscript 93 of the Athens National Library." *DChAE* 9 (1977–79): 185–215.

Constas, N. "Mark Eugenikos." In *La théologie byzantine et sa tradition,* edited by C. G. Conticello and V. Conticello, 411–75. Corpus Christianorum Claves Subsidia 2. Turnhout: Brepols, 2002.

Corrigan, K. "Salterio, arte bizantina." In *Enciclopedia dell'Arte Medievale,* 10:289. 12 vols. Rome: Istituto della Enciclopedia Italiana, 1991–2002.

Crisci, E., et al. "Il Salterio purpureo Zentralbibliothek Zürich, RP 1." *Segno e Testo* 5 (2007): 31–98.

Cutler, A. *The Aristocratic Psalters in Byzantium.* BCA 13. Paris: Picard, 1984.

D'Agostino, M. "Esichio di Gerusalemme, Cirillo Alessandrino: Proemio ai Salmi." Verona, Biblioteca Capitolare, cod. 119." In *Splendori di Bisanzio. Testimonianze e riflessi d'arte e cultura bizantina nelle Chiese d'Italia,* 216–17. Milan: Fabbri, 1990.

Darrouzès, J. *Nicétas Stéthatos, Opuscules et lettres.* SC 81. Paris: Éditions du Cerf, 1961.

Day, P. D. *The Liturgical Dictionary of Eastern Christianity.* Collegeville, Minn.: Liturgical Press, 1993.

De Andrés, G. *Catálogo de los códices griegos de la Biblioteca Nacional.* Madrid: Ministerio de Cultura, Dirección General del Libro y Bibliotecas, 1987.

De Wald, E. *The Illustrations of the Manuscripts of the Septuagint.* Vol. 3, *Psalms and Odes.* Part 2, *Vaticanus Graecus 752.* Princeton, N.J.: Princeton University Press, 1942.

Delehaye, H. "Un synaxaire italo-grec." *AB* 21 (1902): 23–28. Reprinted in Delehaye, *Synaxaires byzantins, ménologes, typica.* London: Variorum, 1977.

———. *Synaxarium Ecclesiae Constantinopolitanae e codice Sirmondiano nunc Berolinensi adiectis synaxariis selectis opera et studio.* Propylaeum ad Acta sanctorum Novembris. Brussels: Socios Bollandianos, 1902.

Der Nersessian, S. "A Psalter and New Testament Manuscript at Dumbarton Oaks." *DOP* 19 (1965): 155–83.

Devreesse, R. *Bibliothecae Apostolicae Vaticanae codices manu scripti recensiti. Codices Vaticani graeci.* Vol. 2, *Codices 330–603.* Vatican City: Biblioteca Vaticana, 1937.

———. *Bibliothecae Apostolicae Vaticanae codices manu scripti recensiti. Codices Vaticani graeci.* Vol. 3, *Codices 604–866.* Vatican City: Biblioteca Vaticana, 1959.

———. *Introduction à l'étude des manuscrits grecs.* Paris: C. Klincksieck, 1954.

Diakovskij, E. "Последование ночных часов (чин 12-ти псалмов)." *Труды Киевской Духовной Академии* 2 (1909): 547–95.

———. *Последование часов и изобразительных. Историческое исследование.* Kiev: Mejnander, 1913.

Dimanche, office selon les huits tons: Ὀκτώηχος. La Prière des Églises de rite byzantin, vol 3. Chevetogne: Éditions de Chevetogne, 1972.

Dmitrievskij, A. *Древнейшие патриаршие типиконы: Святогробский Иерусалимский и Великой Константинопольской Церкви.* Kiev: I. I. Gorbunova, 1907.

———. *Описание литургических рукописей хранящихся в библиотеках православнаго Востока.* 3 vols. Kiev, 1895–1917; reprinted in Hildesheim: G. Olms, 1965.

———. "Что такое κανὼν τῆς ψαλμῳδίας, так нередко упоминаемый в жизнеописании препод. Саввы Освященного?" *Руководство для сельских пастырей* 38 (1889): 69–73.

Dorival, G. *Les Chaînes exégétiques grecques sur les Psaumes: Contribution à l'étude d'une forme littéraire.* 4 vols. Spicilegium Sacrum Lovaniense, Études et documents 43–46. Leuven: Peeters, 1986–95.

Dossetti, G. *Il Simbolo di Nicea e Costantinopoli.* Testi e ricerche di scienze religiose 2. Basel: Herder, 1967.

Dufrenne, S. *L'Illustration des psautiers grecs du Moyen âge.* Vol. 1, *Pantocrator 61, Paris grec 20, British Museum 40731.* BCA 1. Paris: C. Klincksieck, 1966.

Dufrenne, S., and P. Canart. *Die Bibel des Patricius Leo: Codex Reginensis graecus I B.* 2 Vols. Zurich: Belser, 1988.

Džurova, A. *Tomič Psalter.* 2 vols. Sofia: Tsentăr za Slavjano-Vizantijski Prouchvanija "Ivan Dujčev" 1990.

Egender, N. "Introduction." In *La Prière des Heures (Horologion),* 11–90. Chevetogne: Éditions de Chevetogne, 1975.

Ehrhard, A. *Überlieferung und Bestand der hagiographischen und homiletischen Literatur der griechischen Kirche von den Anfängen bis zum Ende des 16. Jahrhunderts.* 3 vols. Texte und Untersuchungen zur Geschichte der altchristlichen Literatur 50–52. Leipzig: J. C. Hinrichs, 1937–39.

Eleuteri, P. "Salterio [Venice, BM, gr. Z 540]." In *Oriente cristiano e santità. Figure e storie di santi tra Bisanzio e l'Occidente,* edited by S. Gentile, 199–200. Rome: Centro Tibaldi, 1998.

Eustratiades, S., and Arcadius Vatopedinos. *Catalogue of the Greek Manuscripts in the Library of the Monastery of Vatopedi on Mt. Athos.* Cambridge, Mass.: Harvard University Press, 1924; reprinted in New York: H. P. Kraus, 1969.

Everett, E. "An Account of Some Greek Manuscripts Procured at Constantinople in 1819, and now Belonging to the Library of the University at Cambridge." *Memoirs of the American Academy of Arts and Sciences* 4 (1820): 409–15.

Fedwick, P. J. *Bibliotheca Basiliana Universalis: A Study of the Manuscript Tradition of the Works of Basil of Caesarea.* 5 vols. in 8 parts. Turnhout: Brepols, 1993–2004.

Fetková, P., et al. *Psalterii Sinaitici pars nova (monasterii s. Catharinae codex slav. 2/N).* Österreichische Akademie der Wissenschaften. Philosophisch-historische Klasse. Schriften der Balkan-Kommission, Philologische Abteilung 38, Fontes 2. Vienna: Österreichische Akademie der Wissenschaften, 1977.

Feulner, H.-J., et al., eds. *Crossroad of Cultures: Studies in Liturgy and Patristics in Honor of Gabriele Winkler.* OCA 260. Rome: Pontificio Instituto Orientale, 2000.

Findikyan, M. D., ed. and trans. *The Commentary of the Armenian Daily Office by Bishop Step'anos Siwnec'i († 735).* OCA 270. Rome: Pontificio Instituto Orientale, 2004.

Follieri, E. *I calendari in metro innografico di Cristoforo Mitileneo.* 2 vols. SH 63. Brussels: Société des Bollandistes, 1980.

———. *Initia hymnorum Ecclesiae graecae.* 5 vols. in 6 parts. ST 211–15bis. Vatican City: Biblioteca Apostolica Vaticana, 1960–66.

———. "Tommaso di Damasco e l'antica minuscola libraria greca." *Rendiconti* dell'Accademia Nazionale dei Lincei, Classe di scienze morali, storiche e filologiche 29 (1974): 145–63. Reprinted in Follieri, *Byzantina e Italograeca: Studi di filologia e di paleografia*, ed. A. Longo et al., 163–84. Storia e Letteratura 195. Rome: Edizioni di Storia e Letteratura, 1997.

Fonkič, B. L., and F. B. Poljakov. *Греческия рукописи Московской Синодальной Библиотеки. Палеографические, кодикологические и библиографические дополнения к каталогу архимандрита Владимира (Филантропова).* Moscow: Sinodal'naia Biblioteka, 1993.

———. "Paläographische Grundlagen der Datierung des Kölner Mani-Kodex." *BZ* 83 (1990): 22–30.

Fragkeskou, B. "Ὁ ὕμνος ἑσπερινὸς σὲ λειτουργικὰ καὶ γρηγοριανὰ χειρόγραφα." *Κληρονομία* 24 (1992): 259–62.

Frøyshov, S. S. R. "The Cathedral-Monastic Distinction Revisited. Part I: Was Egyptian Desert Liturgy a Pure Monastic Office?" *Studia Liturgica* 37 (2007): 198–216.

———. "Двенадцати псалмов чин." In *Православная энциклопедия*, 14:232–34. 38 vols. Moscow: Tserkovno-nauchnyj tsentr "Pravoslavnaia Entsiklopedija," 2000–.

———. "The Early Development of the Liturgical Eight-mode System in Jerusalem." *SVThQ* 51 (2007): 139–78.

Galadza, D. "Liturgical Byzantinization in Jerusalem: al-Bīrunī's Melkite Calendar in Context." *BollGrott* 7 (2010): 69–85.

Galadza, P. "Baumstark's Kievan Contemporary, Mikhail N. Skaballanovich (1871–1931[?]): A Sketch of His Life and Heortology." In *Comparative Liturgy Fifty Years After Baumstark*, edited by Taft and Winkler, 761–75.

Galavaris, G. "'Sinaitic' Manuscripts in the Time of the Arabs." *DChAE* 2 (1984): 117–44.

Gamillscheg, E., et al. *Repertorium der griechischen Kopisten 800–1600.* 3 vols. in 6 parts. Vienna: Österreichische Akademie der Wissenschaften, 1981–89.

Gardthausen, V. *Catalogus codicum graecorum Sinaiticorum.* Oxford: Oxford University Press, 1886.

Gautier, P. "Le typikon du Christ Sauveur Pantocrator." *REB* 32 (1974): 1–145.

———. "Le typikon de la Théotokos Évergétis." *REB* 40 (1982): 5–101.

———. "Le typikon de la Théotokos Kécharitôménè." *REB* 43 (1985): 5–165.

Geerard, M., ed. *Clavis patrum graecorum.* 5 vols. Turnhout: Brepols, 1974–87.

Géhin, P., and S. Frøyshov. "Nouvelles découvertes sinaïtiques: à propos de la parution de l'inventaire des manuscrits grecs." *REB* 58 (2000): 164–84.

Getcha, J. "Les études liturgiques russes au XIXe–XXe siècles et leur impact sur la pratique." In *Les mouvements liturgiques. Corrélations entre pratiques et recherches*, edited by C. Braga and A. Pistoia, 279–90. BELS 129. Rome: Edizioni Liturgiche, 2004.

Getov, D. *A Catalogue of Greek Liturgical Manuscripts in the "Ivan Dujčev Centre for Slavo-Byzantine Studies."* OCA 279. Rome: Pontificio Instituto Orientale, 2007.

Giannelli, C. *Bibliothecae Apostolicae Vaticanae codices manu scripti recensiti. Codices Vaticani graeci. Codices 1485–1683.* Vatican City: Bibliotheca Vaticana, 1950.

Goar, J. *Εὐχολόγιον, sive rituale Græcorum . . .* 2nd ed. Venice, 1730; reprinted in Graz: Akademische Druck und Verlagsanstalt, 1960.

Granstrem, E. E. "Каталог греческих рукописей ленинградских хранилищ, I, Рукописи IV–IX веков." *VizVrem* 16 (1959): 216–43.

————. "Каталог греческих рукописей ленинградских хранилищ, 4, Рукописи XII века." *VizVrem* 23 (1963): 166–204.

Gregory, C. R. *Textkritik des Neuen Testamentes.* 3 vols. Leipzig: J. C. Hinrichs, 1900–1909.

Grumel, V. *Les regestes des actes du Patriarcat de Constantinople.* Edited by V. Laurent and J. Darrouzès. 7 vols. Paris: Institut Français d'Études Byzantines, 1972–89.

Guillaume, P. D., trans. *Horologe des veilleurs. Les 24 heures des Acémètes.* Rome: Diaconie Apostolique, 1990.

————. *Psaumes et Cantiques avec les cathismes et les prières de la tradition byzantine.* Rome: Diaconie Apostolique, 1990.

Hanke, G. M. "Der Odenkanon des Tagzeitenritus Konstantinopels im Licht der Beiträge H. Schneiders und O. Strunks—eine Relecture." In *Crossroad of Cultures,* edited by Feulner et al., 345–67.

Hannick, C. "Annexions et reconquêtes byzantines. Peut-on parler d'"uniatisme' byzantin?" *Irénikon* 66 (1993): 151–74.

————. "Hymnen: II. Orthodoxe Kirche." In *Theologische Realenzyklopädie,* edited by H. Balz, 15:762–70. 36 vols. Berlin and New York: De Gruyter, 1976–86.

————. "Le texte de l'Oktoechos." In *Dimanche, office selon les huit tons,* 37–60.

Harlfinger, D. "Beispiele der Maiuscula Ogivalis Inclinata von Sinai und aus Damaskus." In *Alethes Philia. Studi in onore di Giancarlo Prato,* edited by M. D'Agostino and P. Degni, 2:461–77. 2 vols. Spoleto: Centro Italiano di studi sull'alto Medioevo, 2010.

Harlfinger, D., et al. *Specimina Sinaitica. Die datierten griechischen Handschriften des Katharinen-Klosters auf dem Berge Sinai: 9. bis 12. Jahrhundert.* Berlin: Dietrich Reimer, 1983.

Harris, S. "The Byzantine prokeimena." *Plainsong and Medieval Music* 3 (1994): 133–47.

Hausherr, I. *Penthos. La doctrine de la componction dans l'Orient chrétien.* OCA 132. Rome: Pontificium Institutum Orientalium Studiorum, 1944.

Hausherr, I., ed. *Un grand mystique byzantin. Vie de Syméon le Nouveau Théologien (949–1022) par Nicétas Stéthatos.* Translated by G. Horn. Orientalia Christiana 45. Rome: Pontificium Institutum Orientalium Studiorum, 1928.

Heiming, O. "Zum monastischen Offizium von Kassianus bis Kolumbanus." *Archiv für Liturgiewissenschaft* 7 (1961): 89–156.

Holy Monastery and Archdiocese of Sinai. *The New Finds of Sinai.* Athens: Mount Sinai Foundation, Ministry of Culture, 1999.

Ὡρολόγιον περιέχον τὴν ἡμερονύκτιον ἀκολουθίαν μετὰ τῶν συνήθων προσθήκων. 2nd ed. Rome, 1937.

Ὡρολόγιον σὺν Θεῷ ἁγίῳ περιέχον τὴν ἡμερονύκτιον τῆς Ἐκκλησίας ἀκολουθίαν τῆς ἱερᾶς καὶ περιβλέπτου μονῆς τῆς Κρυπτοφέρρης. Grottaferrata, 1950.

Ὡρολόγιον τὸ μέγα περιέχον ἅπασαν τὴν ἀνήκουσαν αὐτῷ ἀκολουθίαν. 5th ed. Athens, 2005.

Huglo, M. *Les livres de chant liturgique.* TSMO 52. Turnhout: Brepols, 1988.

Hunger, H., et al. *Katalog der griechischen Handschriften der Österreichischen National-bibliothek.* 4 vols. in 6 parts. Vienna: Österreichische Nationalbibliothek, 1961–94.

Husmann, H. "Eine alte orientalische christliche Liturgie: altsyrisch-melkitish." *OCP* 42 (1976): 157–96.

———. "Hymnus und Troparion. Studie zur Geschichte der musikalischen Gattungen von Horologion und Tropologion." *Jahrbuch der Staatlichen Instituts für Musikforschung Preussischer Kulturbesitz* (1971): 7–86.

Hutter, I. *Corpus der byzantinischen Miniaturenhandschriften.* 5 vols. in 8 parts. Stuttgart: Hiersemann, 1977–97.

———. "Theodoros βιβλιογράφος und die Buchmalerei in Studiu." *BollGrott* 51 (1997): 177–208.

Ivanova-Sullivan, T. D. *Lexical Variation in the Slavonic Thekara Texts: Semantic and Pragmatic Factors in Medieval Translations.* PhD diss., Ohio State University, 2005.

Jacob, A. "Un euchologe du Saint-Sauveur 'in Lingua Phari' de Messine. Le Bodleianus Auct. E.5.13." *Bulletin de l'Institut Historique Belge de Rome* 50 (1980): 283–364.

———. "L'evoluzione dei libri liturgici bizantini in Calabria e in Sicilia dall'VIII al XVI secolo con particolare riguardo ai riti eucaristici." In *Calabria bizantina: vita religiosa e strutture amministrative,* 47–69. Reggio: Parallelo, 1938.

Janeras, S. "I vangeli domenicali della Resurrezione nelle tradizioni liturgica agiopolita e bizantina." In *Paschale Mysterium. Studi in memoria dell'Abate Prof. Salvatore Marsili,* edited by G. Farnedi, 55–69. Studia Anselmiana 91 (= Analecta liturgica 10). Rome: Pontificio Ateneo S. Anselmo, 1986.

———. *Le vendredi-saint dans la tradition liturgique byzantine. Structure et histoire des ses offices.* Studia Anselmiana 99 (= Analecta liturgica 13). Rome: Pontificio Ateneo S. Anselmo, 1988.

Janin, R. *Constantinople byzantine: développement urbain et répertoire topographique.* 2nd ed. Paris: Institut Français d'Études Byzantines, 1964.

Jeffery, P. "The Earliest Oktôêchoi: The Role of Jerusalem and Palestine in the Beginning of Modal Ordering." In *The Study of Medieval Chant. Paths and Bridges, East and West: In Honor of Kenneth Levy,* edited by P. Jeffery, 147–209. Woodbridge: Boydell, 2001.

Joannou, P.-P. *Discipline générale antique (IVe–IXe s.).* 3 vols. in 4 parts. Grottaferrata: Tipografia Italo-Orientale "S. Nilo," 1962–64.

Jordan, R. H., ed. and trans. *The Synaxarion of the Monastery of the Theotokos Evergetis.* 3 vols. BBTT 6.5–7. Belfast: Belfast Byzantine Enterprises, 2000–2007.

Jovčeva, M. *Солунският Октоих в контекста на южнославянските октоиси до XIV в. Кирило-Методиевски студии* 46. Sofia: Kirilo-Metodievski Naučen Centăr, 2004.

Kadas, S. N. *Τὰ σημειώματα τῶν χειρογράφων τῆς ἱερᾶς Μεγίστης Μονῆς Βατοπεδίου.* Mt. Athos: Hiera Megiste Mone Vatopaidiou, 2000.

———. *Τὰ σημειώματα τῶν χειρογράφων τῆς Μονῆς Διονυσίου Ἁγίου Ὄρους.* Mt. Athos: Ekdose Hieras Mones Dionysiou, 1996.

Kavrus-Hoffmann, N. "Catalogue of Greek Medieval and Renaissance Manuscripts in the Collections of the United States of America. Part V.1: Harvard University, The Houghton Library." *Manuscripta* 54 (2010): 64–151.

Kazamias, A. K. Ἡ *θεία Λειτουργία τοῦ ἁγίου Ἰακώβου τοῦ Ἀδελφοθέου καὶ τὰ νέα Σιναϊτικὰ χειρόγραφα.* Thessaloniki: Hiera Mone Theovadistou Orous Sina, 2006.

Kazhdan, A. "Antiochos Strategos." In *ODB*, 1:119–20.

———. "Michael Attaleiates." In *ODB*, 1:229.

Kazhdan, A., et al., eds. *The Oxford Dictionary of Byzantium*. 3 vols. Oxford: Oxford University Press, 1991.

Klentos, J. E. *Byzantine Liturgy in Twelfth-Century Constantinople. An Analysis of the Synaxarion of the Monastery of the Theotokos of Evergetis (Codex Athens Ethnike Bibliotheke 788)*. PhD diss., University of Notre Dame, 1995.

———. "The *Synaxarion* of Evergetis: algebra, geology and Byzantine monasticism." In *Work and Worship at the Theotokos Evergetis 1050–1200*, edited by M. Mullett and A. Kirby, 329–55. BBTT 6.2. Belfast: Belfast Byzantine Enterprises, 1997.

Korakides, A. Ἀρχαῖοι ὕμνοι. Vol. 1, Ἡ ἐπιλύχνιος εὐχαριστία: Φῶς ἱλαρὸν ἁγίας δόξης . . . 2 vols. PhD diss., Ethnikon kai Kapodistriakon Panepistemion Athenon, 1979.

Koster, S. I. *Das Euchologion Sevastianov 474 (X. Jhdt.) der Staatsbibliothek in Moskau. Edition*. PhD diss., Pontificio Instituto Orientale, Rome, 1996.

Kotter, B. *Die Schriften des Johannes von Damaskos*. 8 vols. Patristische Texte und Studien 7, 12, 17, 22, 29, 60, 61, 68. Berlin: De Gruyter, 1969–2013.

Kotzabassi, S., and N. P. Ševčenko, *Greek Manuscripts at Princeton, Sixth to Nineteenth Century. A Descriptive Catalogue*. Princeton, N.J.: Princeton University Press, 2010.

Krašeninnikova, O. A. Древнеславянский Октоих св. Климента архиепископа Охридского по древнерусским спискам XIII–XV веков. Moscow: Jazyki Slavjanskih Kul'tur, 2006.

———. "К истории формирования седмичных памятей октоиха." Богословские Труды 32 (1996): 260–68.

Krasnosel'cev, N. F. Сведения о некоторых литургических рукописях Ватиканской Библиотеки. Kazan, 1885.

Krausmüller, D. "The Monastic Communities of Stoudios and St Mamas in the Second Half of the Tenth Century." In *The Theotokos Evergetis and Eleventh-Century Monasticism*, edited by M. Mullet and A. Kirby, 67–85. BBTT 6.1. Belfast: Belfast Byzantine Enterprises, 1994.

———. "Private vs Communal: Niketas Stethatos's *Hypotyposis* for Stoudios, and Patterns of Worship in Eleventh-Century Byzantine Monasteries." In *Work and Worship at the Theotokos Evergetis 1050–1200*, edited by M. Mullett and A. Kirby, 309–28. BBTT 6.2. Belfast: Belfast Byzantine Enterprises, 1997.

Krivochéine, B., and I. Paramelle, eds. and trans. *Syméon le Nouveau Théologien*. 3 vols. SC 96, 104, 113. Paris: Éditions du Cerf, 1963–65.

Krumbacher, K. *Geschichte der byzantinischen Litteratur von Justinian bis zum Ende des oströmischen Reiches (527–1453)*. Handbuch der klassischen Altertums-Wissenschaft 9.1. Munich, 1891; reprinted in New York: Burt Franklin, 1958.

Lambros, S. *Catalogue of the Greek Manuscripts on Mount Athos*. 2 vols. Cambridge: Cambridge University Press, 1895–1900.

Lampe, G. *A Patristic Greek Lexicon*. Oxford: Oxford University Press, 1968.

Lanne, E. "Les dix leçons de liturgie comparée d'Anton Baumstark au monastère d'Amay-sur-Meuse en 1932: leur contexte et leur publication." In *Comparative Liturgy Fifty Years after Baumstark*, edited by Taft and Winkler, 145–61.

Lappin, B. Crostini. "Structure and Dating of Codex *Atheniensis Graecus 788*, Typikon of the Monastery of the Theotokos Evergetis (Founded in 1049)." *Scriptorium* 52 (1998): 330–49.

Larin, V. "The Origins and History of the Royal Office at the Beginning of Matins." *BollGrott* 5 (2008): 199–218.

———. "What Is Ritual Im/Purity and Why?" *SVThQ* 52 (2008): 275–92.

Layton, E. *The Sixteenth Century Greek Book in Italy: Printers and Publishers for the Greek World*. Venice: Instituto Ellenico di Studi bizantini e Postbizantini di Venezia, 1994.

Leeming, K. "The Adoption of Arabic as a Liturgical Language by the Palestinian Melkites." *ARAM* 15 (2003): 239–46.

Leroy, J. "La vie quotidienne du Moine studite." *Irénikon* 27 (1954): 21–50.

Lingas, A. "The Liturgical Place of the Kontakion in Constantinople." In *Liturgy, Architecture and Art of the Byzantine World: Papers of the XVIII International Byzantine Congress (Moscow, 8–15 August 1991) and Other Essays Dedicated to the Memory of Fr. John Meyendorff*, edited by C. C. Akentiev, 50–57 (= Byzantinorossica 1). St. Petersburg: Vizantinorossika, 1995.

Lossky, A. *Le typicon bizantin: édition d'une version grecque (partiellement inédite): analyse de la partie liturgique*. PhD diss., Université de Strasbourg, 1987.

Lutzka, C. *Die Kleinen Horen des byzantinischen Stundengebetes und ihre geschichtliche Entwicklung*. Berlin: Berlin-Münster LIT, 2007.

Luzzi, A. "Il *dies festus* di Costantino il Grande e di sua madre Elena nei libri liturgici della Chiesa Greca." In *Costantino il Grande dall'Antichità all'Umanesimo*, edited by G. Bonamente and F. Fusco, 2:585–643. 2 vols. Macerata: Università degli Studi di Macerata, 1992.

———. "L'ideologia costantiniana' nella liturgia dell'età di Costantino VII Porfirogenito." *RSBN* 28 (1991): 113–24.

———. *Studi sul Sinassario di Costantinopoli*. Testi e studi bizantino-neoellenici 8. Rome: Dipartimento di filologia greca e latina, Sezione bizantino-neoellenica, Università di Roma, 1995.

Maas, P., and C. Trypanis. *Sancti Romani Melodi cantica*. Oxford: Oxford University Press, 1963.

MacRobert, C. M. "The Classificatory Importance of Headings and Liturgical Directions in Church Slavonic Psalters of the 11th–15th Centuries." *BSl* 57 (1996): 156–81.

Maraval, P., ed. Égérie, *Journal de voyage (Itinéraire)*. SC 296. Paris: Éditions du Cerf, 1997.

Martimort, A. G. *Les lectures liturgiques et leurs livres*. TSMO 64. Turnhout: Brepols, 1992.

———. *Les "ordines," les ordinaires et les cérémoniaux*. TSMO 56. Turnhout: Brepols, 1991.

Martini, A., and D. Bassi. *Catalogus codicum graecorum Bibliothecae Ambrosianae*. 2 vols. Milan: Hoepli, 1906.

[Mother] Mary and K. Ware. *The Festal Menaion*. London: Faber, 1969.

———. *The Lenten Triodion*. London: Faber and Faber, 1978.

Mateos, J. *La célébration de la Parole dans la Liturgie byzantine. Étude historique.* OCA 191. Rome: Pontificium Institutum Studiorum Orientalium, 1971.

———. "Un Horologion inédit de Saint-Sabas. Le codex sinaïtique grec 863 (IXe siècle)." In *Mélanges Eugène Tisserant,* 3:47–76. 7 vols. ST 231–37. Vatican City: Biblioteca Apostolica Vaticana, 1964.

———. *Lelya-Sapra. Essai d'interprétation des matines chaldéennes.* OCA 156. Rome: Pontificium Institutum Studiorum Orientalium, 1959.

———. "Prières initiales fixes des offices syrien, maronite et byzantin." *L'Orient Syrien* 11 (1966): 488–98.

———. "La psalmodie variable dans l'office byzantin." *Acta Philosophica et Theologica* 2 (1964): 327–39.

———. "Quelques problèmes de l'orthros byzantin." *Proche-Orient Chrétien* 11 (1961): 17–35, 201–20.

———. "'Sedre' et prières connexes dans quelques anciennes collections." *OCP* 28 (1962): 239–87.

———. "La synaxe monastique des vêpres byzantines." *OCP* 36 (1970): 248–72.

———. "Trois recueils anciens de Procemia syriens." *OCP* 33 (1967): 457–82.

———. *Le Typicon de la Grande Église. Ms. Sainte-Croix no 40.* 2 vols. OCA 165–66. Rome: Pont. Institutum Studiorum Orientalium, 1962–63.

Μέγας ἱερὸς συνέκδημος. Athens, n.d.

Μηναῖα τοῦ ὅλου ἐνιαυτοῦ. 4 vols. Rome, 1885–1901.

Μηναῖον τοῦ Δεκεμβρίου μηνός. Athens, 2002.

Μηναῖον τοῦ Ἰαννουαρίου μηνός. Athens, 2002.

Mentz, A. *Beiträge zur Osterfestberechnung bei den Byzantinern.* PhD diss., Albertus-Universität, Königsberg, 1906.

Mercati, G. *Osservazioni a proemi del Salterio di Origene, Ippolito, Eusebio, Cirillo Alessandrino e altri, con frammenti inediti.* ST 142. Vatican City: Biblioteca Apostolica Vaticana, 1948.

Mercati, S. G. *De nonnullis versibus dodecasyllabis S. Germani I CP. Patriarchae homiliae Εἰς τὰ εἰσόδια τῆς Θεοτόκου insertis.* 2nd ed. Studi Liturgici 8. Grottaferrata, 1915. Reprinted in Mercati, *Collectanea Byzantina,* ed. A. Longo, 2:25–43. Bari: Dedalo Libri, 1970. The first edition appeared in *Roma e l'Oriente* 8 (1915): 147–65.

Mercier, B.-C. *La Liturgie de saint Jacques. Édition critique du texte grec avec traduction latine.* Patrologia Orientalis 26.2. Paris: Firmin-Didot, 1946.

Metzger, M. *Les Constitutions Apostoliques.* 3 vols. SC 320, 329, 336. Paris: Éditions du Cerf, 1985–87.

———. *Les Sacramentaires.* TSMO 70. Turnhout: Brepols, 1994.

Meyendorff, P. *Russia, Ritual and Reform: The Liturgical Reforms of Nikon in the 17th Century.* Crestwood, N.Y.: St. Vladimir's Seminary Press, 1991.

Migne, J.-P., ed. *Patrologiae cursus completus. Series graeca.* 161 vols. Paris, 1857–66.

———. *Patrologiae cursus completus. Series latina.* 220 vols. Paris, 1844–64.

Mioni, E. *Bibliothecae Divi Marci Venetiarum Codices Graeci Manuscripti.* 3 vols. in 6 parts. Rome: Instituto Poligrafico dello Stato, 1981–85.

Mitsakis, K. *The Language of Romanos the Melodist.* Byzantinisches Archiv 11. Munich: C. H. Beck, 1967.

Mokretsova, I., et al. *Materials and Techniques on Byzantine Manuscripts.* Moscow: Indrik, 2003.

Momina, M. "Песнопения древних славяно-русских рукописей." In *Методическе рекомендации по описанию славяно-русских рукописей для Сводного каталога рукописей, хранящихся в СССР,* вып. 2, ser. 2, 462–66. Moscow: Institut istorii CCCP, 1976.

Moran, N. *Singers in Late Byzantine and Slavonic Painting.* Byzantina Neerlandica 9. Leiden: E. J. Brill, 1986.

Moravcsik, G., and R. Jenkins, eds. and trans. *Constantine Porphyrogenitus De Administrando Imperio.* CFHB 1. Washington, D.C.: Dumbarton Oaks Center for Byzantine Studies, 1967.

Moretti, S. "Vulgo 'miniatura' appellatur: i manoscritti greci miniati e decorati delle biblioteche pubbliche statali di Roma." *Nuovi Annali della Scuola Speciale per Archivisti e Bibliotecari* 18 (2004): 72–73.

Morini, E. "Il monachesimo italo-greco e l'influenza di Stoudios." In *L'Ellenismo italiota dal VII al XII secolo. Alla memoria di Nikos Panagiotakis,* edited by N. Oikonomides, 125–51. Athens: National Hellenic Research Foundation, Institute for Byzantine Research, 2001.

Nasrallah, J. "La liturgie des patriarcats melchites de 969 à 1300." *Oriens Christianus* 71 (1987): 156–81.

Nees, L. "An Illuminated Byzantine Psalter at Harvard University." *DOP* 29 (1975): 205–24.

————. "Psalter [Cambridge, Harvard College Lib., cod. Gr. 3]." In *Illuminated Greek Manuscripts from American Collections: An Exhibition in Honor of Kurt Weitzmann,* edited by G. Vikan, 128–29. Princeton, N.J.: Art Museum, Princeton University, 1973.

Neyrand, L., and H. Alfeyev, eds. and trans. *Syméon le Studite, Discours ascétique.* SC 460. Paris: Éditions du Cerf, 2001.

Nicol, D. *The Byzantine Family of Kantakouzenos (Cantacuzenus), ca. 1100–1460. A Genealogical and Prosopographical Study.* Dumbarton Oaks Studies 11. Washington, D.C.: Dumbarton Oaks Center for Byzantine Studies, 1968.

Noret, J. "Ménologes, Synaxaires, Ménées. Essai de clarification d'une terminologie." *AB* 86 (1968): 21–24.

————. "Le Synaxaire Leningrad gr. 240. Sa place dans l'évolution du Synaxaire byzantin." *Античная древность и Средние века* 10 (1973): 124–30.

————. "La vie de Marie l'Égyptienne (BHG 1042) source partielle d'une prière pseudo-éphrémienne." *AB* 96 (1978): 385–87.

Норовская Псалтырь. Среднеболгарская рукопись XIV века. Vol. 1. Sofia: Bălgarska akademija na naukite, 1989.

Oikonomides, N. "Indiction." In *ODB,* 2:993.

Октоихъ, сирѣчь осмогласникъ. 2 vols. Moscow: Izdatel'skij Sovet Russkoj Pravoslavnoj Cerkvi, 2004.

Omont, H. *Inventaire sommaire des manuscrits grecs de la Bibliothèque Nationale.* Vol. 1, *Ancien fonds grec: théologie.* Paris: Alphonse Picard, 1886.

Oudot, I., ed. *Patriarchatus Constantinopolitani acta selecta.* Vol. 1. *Codificazione*

Canonica Orientale Fonti. Ser. 2, fasc. 3. Vatican City: Typis Polyglottis Vaticanis, 1941.

Pallas, D. I. *Κατάλογος τῶν χειρογραφῶν τοῦ Βυζαντινοῦ Μουσείου Ἀθηνῶν.* Vol. 3. Athens: Typographeion Katastematon S. Kousoulinou, 1955.

Papadopoulos-Kerameus, A. *Ἀνάλεκτα Ἱεροσολυμιτικῆς σταχυολογίας . . .* Vol. 2. St. Petersburg, 1884; reprinted in Brussels: Culture et Civilisation, 1963.

————. *Ἱεροσολυμιτικὴ Βιβλιοθήκη . . .* Vol. 4. St. Petersburg, 1899; reprinted in Brussels: Culture et Civilisation, 1963.

————. *Noctes Petropolitanae.* Сборник византийских текстов *XII–XIII* веков. St. Petersburg: V. F. Kirshbaum, 1913.

Papagianne, K., ed. *Ἡ ἁγία καὶ μεγάλη Ἑβδομᾶς, περιέχουσα πᾶσας τὰς ἱερὰς ἀκουλουθίας ἀπὸ τῆς Κυριακῆς τῶν βαΐων μέχρι τῆς Κυριακῆς τοῦ Πάσχα.* 2nd ed. Athens: Apostolike Diakonia, 1990.

Papagiannis, G. Book review of M. Ajjoub and J. Paramelle, *Livre d'Heures du Sinaï. BZ* 100 (2007): 189–96.

Papazoglou, G. Βιβλιοθήκες στήν Κωνσταντινούπολη τοῦ ις᾽ αἰώνα (κώδ. *Vind. hist. gr. 98*). Thessaloniki, 1983.

————. "Le Michel Cantacuzène du codex Mavrocordatianus et le possesseur homonyme du Psautier de Harvard." *REB* 46 (1988): 161–65.

————. "Un manuscrit de la collection des Cantacuzènes à la Pierpont Morgan Library de New York." *Byzantion* 67 (1997): 517–23.

————. "Un manuscrit inconnu provenant de la bibliothèque de l'archonte phanariote Nikolaos Karatzas," *REB* 49 (1991): 255–61.

Παρακλητικὴ ἤτοι ὀκτώηχος ἡ μεγάλη. Rome, 1885.

S. Parenti, "Върху историята на ексапостилария." In *Пение мало Георгию Сборник в чест на 65–годишнината на проф. Георги Попов*, 285–96. Sofia: Издателски център Боян Пенев, 2010.

————. Book review of M. Ajjoub and J. Paramelle, *Livre d'Heures du Sinaï. OCP* 72 (2006): 266–69.

————. "La celebrazione delle Ore del Venerdì Santo nell'Eucologio Γ.β.X di Grottaferrata (X–XI sec.)." *BollGrott* 44 (1990): 81–125.

————. "Un fascicolo ritrovato dell'*horologion Sinai gr. 863* (IX secolo)." *OCP* 75 (2009): 343–58.

————. *Liturgia delle Ore Italo-bizantina (Rito di Grottaferrata).* Monumenta Studia Instrumenta Liturgica 12. Vatican City: Libreria Editrice Vaticana, 2001.

————. "The Liturgical Tradition of the Euchologion 'of Archimedes.'" *BollGrott* 2 (2005): 68–88.

————. "Nota sull'impiego e l'origine dell'inno Σιγησάτω πᾶσα σάρξ βροτεία." In *Κυπριολογία. Ἀφιέρωμα εἰς Θεόδωρον Παπαδοπούλλον*, 191–99 (= Κυπριακαὶ Σπουδαί 64–65 [2000–2001]).

————. "Nota sul Salterio-Horologion del IX secolo Torino, Biblioteca Universitaria B. VII. 30." *BollGrott* 4 (2007): 275–87.

————. "Lo studio e la storia della messa romana nella prospettiva della liturgia comparata." *Ecclesia Orans* 25 (2008): 193–226.

Parenti, S., and E. Velkovska. "Една молитва 'за болни' в Синайския евхологий

(One Prayer 'for the Sick' in the Slavic Euchology of Sinai)." In *Филологически изследвания в чест на Климентина Иванова в чест на нейната 65-годишнина* (= *Старобългарска литература* 33–34 [2005]), 154–66.

———, eds. and trans. *L'Eucologio Barberini gr. 336*. 2nd ed. BELS 80. Rome: C.L.V.-Edizioni Liturgiche, 2000.

———. "'Re celeste, paraclito, Spirito di verità.' Il *Veni creator Spiritus* della liturgia bizantina." In *Spiritus spiritalia nobis dona potenter infundit. A proposito di tematiche liturgico-pneumatologiche. Studi in onore di Achille M. Triacca, sdb*, edited by E. Carr, 387–404. Studia Anselmiana 139 (= Analecta Liturgica 35). Rome: Centro Studi S. Anselmo, 2005.

Parpulov, G. R. "A Catalogue of the Greek Manuscripts at the Walters Art Museum." *Journal of the Walters Art Museum* 62 (2004): 70–187.

———. *Toward a History of Byzantine Psalters*. 2 vols. PhD diss., University of Chicago, 2004.

———. "Psalters and Personal Piety in Byzantium." In *The Old Testament in Byzantium*, edited by Paul Magdalino and Robert Nelson, 77–105. Washington: Dumbarton Oaks Research Library and Collection, 2010.

Pasini, G. "Un frammento greco-arabo delle Odi bibliche nel palinsesto Ambrosiano L 120 sup." *RSBN* 39 (2002): 33–53.

Pasinus, J., et al. *Codices manuscripti Bibliothecae Regii Taurinensis Athenaei* ... Turin, 1749.

Passarelli, G. *L'Eucologio cryptense Γ.β.VII (sec. X)*. Analekta Blatadon 36. Thessaloniki: Patriarchikon Hidryma Paterikon Meleton, 1982.

Peeters, P. *Orient et Byzance. Le tréfonds oriental de l'hagiographie byzantine*. SH 26. Brussels: Société des Bollandistes, 1950.

Pentkovskij, A. M. *Типикон Патриарха Алексия Студита в Византии и на Руси*. Moscow: Izd-vo Moskovskoj Patriarkhii, 2001.

Perria, L. "Scritture e codici di origine orientale (Palestina e Sinai) dal IX al XII secolo. Rapporto preliminare." *RSBN* 36 (1999): 19–33.

Perria, L., and A. Luzzi. "Manoscritti greci delle province orientali dell'impero bizantino." In *Atti del VI Congresso Nazionale dell'Associazione Italiana di Studi Bizantini*, 667–90 (= Siculorum gymnasium 57). Catania: Facoltà di Lettere e Filosofia, Università di Catania, 2004.

Phountoulis, I. M. "Τοῦ ἁγίου Γρηγορίου τοῦ Θεολόγου 'Ὕμνος ἑσπερινός' - Ἡ λειτουργικὴ χρήση τοῦ." *Κληρονομία* 22 (1990): 29–37.

———. "Αἱ ἀκολουθίαι τῶν ὡρῶν τοῦ νυχθημέρου κατὰ τὸ Ὡρολόγιον τῆς Κρυπτοφέρρης ἐν συγκρίσει πρὸς τὸ Κωνσταντινουπολιτικὸν Ὡρολόγιον." In *La Chiesa greca in Italia dall'VIII al XVI secolo, Atti del Convegno storico interecclesiale*, 2:579–88. 3 vols. Italia Sacra 20–22. Padua: Antenore, 1972–73.

———. *Εἰκοσιτετράωρον ὡρολόγιον*. Κείμενα Λειτουργικῆς 16. Thessaloniki, 1977.

———. *Ἡ εἰκοσιτετράωρος ἀκοίμητος δοξολογία*. Athens: Aster, 1963.

———. "Αἱ μεγάλαι ὧραι τῆς μεγάλης πέμπτης, μεγάλης παρασκευῆς καὶ τοῦ μεγάλου σαββάτου (κατὰ τὸν ὑπ' ἀριθ. 7 κῶδικα τῆς ἐν Ἀθήναις Ἐθνικῆς Βιβλιοθήκης)." *Ἐπιστημονικὴ Ἐπετηρὶς τῆς Θεολογικῆς Σχολῆς τοῦ Πανεπιστημίου Θεσσαλονίκης* 7 (1962): 217–43.

Pigulevskaja, N. V. "Греко-сиро-арабская рукопись IX в." *Палестинский сборник* 1 (1954): 59–90.

Piper, F. *Karls des Grossen Kalendarium und Ostertafel ... , nebst einer Abhandlung über die lateinischen und griechischen Ostercyklen des Mittelalters.* Berlin, 1858.

Pitra, J. B. *Iuris ecclesiastici graecorum historia et monumenta.* 2 vols. Rome, 1864–68.

———. *Spicilegium Solesmense.* 4 vols. Paris, 1852–58.

Plank, P., et al. *Das byzantinische Eigengut der neuzeitlichen slavischen Menäen und seine griechischen Originale.* Vol. 3, *Incipitarium und Edition Theotokia, Index hymnorum graecorum, Index hymnorum slavicorum, Epimetra tria.* Patristica slavica 12. 3 vols. Paderborn: Schöningh, 2006.

Polidori, V. "L'eucologio criptense Γ. β, XV." *BollGrott* 6 (2009): 215–39.

Pott, T. *La réforme liturgique byzantine. Étude du phénomène de l'évolution non-spontanée de la liturgie byzantine.* BELS 104. Rome: C.L.V.-Edizioni Liturgiche, 2000.

La Prière des Heures: Ὡρολόγιον (Horologion). La Prière des Églises de rite byzantine, vol. 1. Chevetogne: Éditions de Chevetogne, 1975.

"Principi e norme per la Liturgia ambrosiana delle Ore." In *Liturgia delle Ore secondo il rito della Santa Chiesa Ambrosiana, Riformata a norma dei decreti del Concilio Vaticano II e promulgata dal Cardinale Carlo Maria Martini Arcivescovo di Milano.* Milan: Centro Ambrosiano di Documentazione e Studi Religiosi, 1983.

Ѱалтирь. Moscow: Sinodal'naja Tipografija, 1913.

Quecke, H. "Neue griechische Parallelen zum koptischen Horologion." *Le Muséon* 77 (1964): 285–94.

Raes, A. "Les Complies dans les Rites orientaux." *OCP* 17 (1951): 133–45.

Rahlfs, A. ed. *Septuaginta: Id est Vetus Testamentum graece iuxta LXX interpretes.* 3rd ed. Stuttgart: Privilegierte württembergische Bibelanstalt, 1949.

———. *Verzeichnis der griechischen Handschriften des Alten Testaments.* Berlin: Weidmann, 1914.

———. *Verzeichnis der griechischen Handschriften des Alten Testaments.* Vol. 1.1, *Die Überlieferung bis zum VIII. Jahrhundert,* ed. D. Fraenkel. 2nd ed. Göttingen: Vandenhoeck and Ruprecht, 2004.

Re, M. "Copisti salentini in Calabria e in Sicilia." *RSBN* 41 (2004): 95–112.

Renoux, C. "Le *Gloria in excelsis Deo* de l'Église arménienne." In *Crossroad of Cultures,* edited by Feulner et al., 603–18.

Ricci, S. de, and W. Wilson, *Census of Medieval and Renaissance Manuscripts in the United States and Canada.* 3 vols. New York: H. W. Wilson, 1935–40.

Rydén, L. *Das Leben des Heiligen Narren Symeon von Leontios von Neapolis.* Stockholm: Almqvist and Wiksell, 1963.

Sakkelion, J., and A. Sakkelion. *Κατάλογος τῶν χειρογράφων τῆς Ἐθνικῆς Βιβλιοθήκης τῆς Ἑλλάδος.* Athens, 1892.

Salaville, S. "La formation du calendrier liturgique byzantin d'après les recherches critiques de mgr. Ehrhard." *Ephemerides Liturgicae* 50 (1936): 312–23.

Sautel, J.-H. *Répertoire de réglures dans les manuscrits grecs sur parchemin: base de données établie par Jacques-Hubert Sautel à l'aide du fichier Leroy et des catalogues récents à l'Institut de recherche et d'histoire des textes (CNRS).* Bibliologia 13. Turnhout: Brepols, 1995.

Ščepkina, M. V. *Миниатюры Хлудовской Псалтыри. Греческий иллюстрированный кодекс IX века.* Moscow: Iskusstvo, 1977.

Schneider, H. "Die Biblischen Oden in Jerusalem und Konstantinopel." *Biblica* 30 (1949): 28–65, 239–72, 433–52, 479–500.

Schreiner, P. *Die byzantinischen Kleinchroniken.* Vol. 1, *Einleitung und Text.* CFHB 12.1. Vienna: Österreichische Akademie der Wissenschaften, 1975.

Ševčenko, I. "Caption to a David Cycle in the Tenth-Century Oxford Auct. D.4.1." In *Πολύπλευρος νοῦς. Miscellanea für Peter Schreiner zum 60. Geburtstag,* edited by C. Sholtz and G. Makris, 324–41. Byzantinisches Archiv 19. Leipzig: Saur, 2000.

Ševčenko, N. P. "The liturgical *typikon* of Symeon of Sinai." In *Metaphrastes, or, Gained in translation: Essays and translations in honour of Robert H. Jordan,* edited by M. Mullett, 274–86. BBTT 9. Belfast: Belfast Byzantine Enterprises, 2004.

Shurgaia, G. "Formazione della struttura dell'ufficio del Sabato di Lazzaro nella tradizione di Gerusalemme." *Annali di Ca' Foscari* 36, no. 3 (1997): 147–67.

Skalistes, S. K. *Θωμάς Μάγιστρος. Ο βίος και το έργο του.* Διατριβὴ ἐπὶ Διδακτορίᾳ ὑποβληθεῖσα εἰς τὸ Τμῆμα Θεολογίας τοῦ Ἀριστοτελείου Πανεπιστημίου Θεσσαλονίκης. Thessaloniki: Aristoteleio Panepistemio Thessalonikes, 1984.

Skaltsis, P., ed. *Θηκαρᾶς. Στίχοι εἰς τοὺς θείους Ὕμνους Διονυσίου καὶ Μητροφάνους Περὶ τῶν Ὕμνων, Θηκαρᾶ μοναχοῦ Λόγοι περὶ πίστεως ..., Εἰσαγωγή.* Mt. Athos: Ekdosis Hieras Mones Pantokratoros, 2008.

Sliva, E. E. "Часословы студийской традиции в славянских списках XIII–XIV веков." *Труды Отдела древнерусской литературы* 51 (1999): 91–106.

Soteroudes, P. *Κατάλογος ἑλληνικῶν χειρογράφων.* Vol. 1. Mt. Athos: Hiera Mone Iveron, 1998.

Spatharakis, I. *The Portrait in Byzantine Illuminated Manuscripts.* Byzantina Neerlandica 6. Leiden: E. J. Brill, 1976.

Stavrou, M. "Une prière inédite de Nicephore Blemmydès transmise dans le 'Thékaras.'" In *La Prière liturgique,* 119–28. BELS 115. Rome: C.L.V.-Edizioni Liturgiche, 2001.

Strunk, O. "The Byzantine Office at Hagia Sophia." *DOP* 9–10 (1955–56): 175–202. Reprinted in Strunk, *Essays on Music in the Byzantine World,* 112–42. New York: W. W. Norton, 1977.

———. "Chants of the Byzantine-Greek Liturgy." In Strunk, *Essays on Music in the Byzantine World,* 297–335. New York: W. W. Norton, 1977. Originally published as "Die Gesänge der byzantinisch-griechischen Liturgie," in *Geschichte der katholischen Kirchenmusik,* edited by K. Fellerer, 1:128–47. 2 vols. Kassel: Bärenreiter, 1972–76.

Stuhlfauth, G. "A Greek Psalter with Byzantine Miniatures." *Art Bulletin* 15 (1933): 311–26.

Swete, H. B. *An Introduction to the Old Testament in Greek.* Cambridge, 1902; reprinted in New York: KTAV, 1968.

Szövérffy, J. *Latin Hymns.* TSMO 55. Turnhout: Brepols, 1989.

Taft, R. F., SJ. "Anton Baumstark's Comparative Liturgy Revisited." In *Comparative Liturgy Fifty Years after Baumstark,* edited by Taft and Winkler, 191–232.

————. "The Armenian 'Holy Sacrifice (Surb Patarag)' as a Mirror of Armenian Liturgical History." In *The Armenian Christian Tradition. Scholarly Symposium in Honor of the Visit to the Pontifical Oriental Institute, Rome, of His Holiness Karekin I, Supreme Patriarch and Catholikos of All Armenians, December 12, 1966*, edited by Taft, 175–97. OCA 254. Rome: Pontificio Instituto Orientale, 1997.

————. "The Byzantine Office in the *Prayerbook* of New Skete: Evaluation of a Proposed Reform." *OCP* 48 (1982): 336–70.

————. *The Byzantine Rite: A Short History*. Collegeville, Minn.: Liturgical Press, 1992.

————. "Calendar, Church." In *ODB* 1:366.

————. "The Case of the Missing Vestment: The Byzantine Omophorion Great and Small." *BollGrott* 1 (2004): 273–304.

————. "Changing Rhythms of Eucharistic Frequency in Byzantine Monasticism." In *Il monachesimo tra eredità e aperture: Atti del Simposio "Testi e temi nella tradizione del monachesimo cristiano" per il 500 Anniversario dell'Istituto Monastico di Sant'Anselmo, Roma, 28 maggio–1 giugno 2002*, edited by M. Bielawski and D. Hombergen, 419–58. Studia Anselmiana 140. Rome: Pontificio Ateneo S. Anselmo, 2004.

————. "Christian Liturgical Psalmody: Origins, Development, Decomposition, Collapse." In *Psalms in Community. Jewish and Christian Textual, Liturgical, and Artistic Traditions*, edited by H. W. Attridge, 7–32. Atlanta: Society of Biblical Literature, 2003.

————. "Eastern Saints' Lives & Liturgy. Hagiography and New Perspectives in Liturgiology." In *In God's Hands. Essays on the Church and Ecumenism in Honour of Michael A. Fahey, S.J.*, edited by J. Z. Skira and M. S. Attridge, 33–53. Bibliotheca Ephemeridum Theologicarum Lovaniensium 199. Leuven: Peeters, 2006.

————. *The Great Entrance. A History of the Transfer of Gifts and Other Preanaphoral Rites of the Liturgy of St. John Chrysostom*. OCA 200. Rome: Pontificio Instituto Orientale, 1975.

————. *A History of the Liturgy of St. John Chrysostom*. Vol. 6, *The Communion, Thanksgiving, and Concluding Rites*. OCA 281. Rome: Pontificio Instituto Orientale, 2008.

————. "How Liturgies Grow: The Evolution of the Byzantine 'Divine Liturgy.'" *OCP* 43 (1977): 355–78. Reprinted in Taft, *Beyond East and West: Problems in Liturgical Understanding*, 203–32. 2nd ed. Rome: Pontificio Instituto Orientale, 1997.

————. "I libri liturgici." In *Lo spazio letterario del Medioevo*. Vol. 3, *Le culture circostanti*. Part 1, *La cultura bizantina*, edited by G. Cavallo, 229–56. Rome: Salerno, 2004.

————. "The Liturgical Enterprise Twenty-Five Years after Alexander Schmemann (1921–1983); the Man and His Heritage." *SVThQ* 53 (2009): 139–77.

————. *The Liturgy of the Hours in East and West. The Origins of the Divine Office and its Meaning for Today*. 2nd ed. Collegeville, Minn.: Liturgical Press, 1993.

————. "Mount Athos: A Late Chapter in the History of the Byzantine Rite." *DOP* 42 (1988): 179–94.

————. "Über die Liturgiewissenschaft heute." *Theologische Quartalschrift* 177 (1997): 243–55.

―――. "The Veneration of Saints in the Byzantine Liturgical Tradition." In Θυσία αἰνέσεως. Mélanges liturgiques offerts à la mémoire de l'archevêque Georges Wagner (1930–1993), edited by J. Getcha and A. Lossky, 353–60. Analecta Sergiana 2. Paris: Saint Serge, 2005.

―――. "Women at Church in Byzantium: Where, When—and Why?" DOP 52 (1998): 27–87.

Taft, R. F., SJ, and G. Winkler, eds. Comparative Liturgy Fifty Years after Anton Baumstark (1872–1948). OCA 265. Rome: Pontificio Instituto Orientale, 2001.

Talbot, A.-M., and R. F. Taft, SJ. "Akoimetoi." In ODB 1:46.

Thiermeyer, A.-A. "Das Typikon-Ktetorikon und sein literarhistorischer Kontext." OCP 58 (1992): 475–513.

Thomas, J., and A. Constantinides Hero, eds. Byzantine Monastic Foundation Documents. 5 vols. Washington, D.C.: Dumbarton Oaks Center for Byzantine Studies, 2000.

Tischendorf, C. von. Psalterium Turicense Purpureum, septimi fere saeculis, addito Danihelis libro ex codice prophetarum Marchaliano, nunc Vaticano, sexti vel septimi saeculi. Monumenta Sacra Inedita, Nova Collectio 4. Leipzig, 1869.

Todt, K.-P. "Region und griechisch-orthodoxes Patriarchat von Antiocheia in mittelbyzantinischer Zeit (969–1084)." BZ 94 (2001): 239–67.

Trapp, E., W. Hörandner, and J. Diethart. Lexikon zur byzantinischen Gräzität: besonders des 9.–12. Jahrhunderts. 7 vols. Vienna: Österreichische Akademie der Wissenschaften, Veröffentlichungen der Kommission für Byzantinistik, 1994–2011.

Trapp, E., and H.-V. Beyer. Prosopographisches Lexikon der Palaiologenzeit. 12 vols. Vienna: Österreichische Akademie der Wissenschaften, Veröffentlichungen der Kommission für Byzantinistik, 1976–96.

Trempelas, P. Μικρὸν Εὐχολόγιον. 2 vols. Athens, 1955.

―――. Αἱ τρεῖς λειτουργίαι κατὰ τοὺς ἐν ᾿Αθήναις κώδικας. Athens: Hypo tes M. Patriarchikes Epistemonikes Epitropes pros Anatheoresin kai Ekdosin ton Leitourgikon Vivlion, 1935.

Τριῴδιον κατανυκτικὸν περιέχον ἅπασαν τὴν ἀνήκουσαν αὐτῷ ἀκολουθίαν τῆς ἁγίας καὶ μεγάλης τεσσαρακοστῆς. Rome, 1879.

Uspenskij, B. Il segno della croce e lo spazio sacro. Naples: Napoli D'Auria, 2005.

Van den Ven, P. La vie ancienne de S. Syméon Stylite le Jeune (521–592). 2 vols. SH 32–33. Brussels: Société des Bollandistes, 1962, 1970.

Vassis, I. Initia carminum byzantinorum. Supplementa byzantina, Texte und Untersuchungen 8. Berlin: De Gruyter, 2005.

Veilleux, A. La liturgie dans le cénobitisme pachômien au quatrième siècle. Studia Anselmiana 57. Rome: "I.B.C." Libreria Herder, 1968.

Velkovska, E. Book review of R. Jordan, Synaxarion of Evergetis. BZ 97 (2004): 213–14.

―――. "Byzantine Liturgical Books." In Handbook for Liturgical Studies., edited by A. J. Chupungco, 1:225–40. 5 vols. Collegeville, Minn.: Liturgical Press, 1997–2000.

―――. "Денонощното богослужение в Синайския евхологий." Palaeobulgarica 24, no. 4 (2000): 19–34.

―――. "I 'dodici prokeimena' del mattutino cattedrale bizantino." In Crossroad of Cultures, edited by Feulner et al., 705–16.

————. "Funeral Rites according to the Byzantine Liturgical Sources." *DOP* 55 (2001): 21–51.

————. "La liturgia italo-bizantina negli eucologi e lezionari del Nuovo Testamento della 'scuola niliana.'" In *Il monachesimo d'Oriente e d'Occidente nel passaggio dal primo al secondo Millennio*, 187–229. Ἀνάλεκτα Κρυπτοφέρρης 6. Grottaferrata: Monastero Esarchico, 2009.

————. "La liturgia presso gli Slavi ortodossi." In *Lo spazio letterario del Medievo,* vol. 3, *Le culture circostanti*, part 3, *Le culture slave*, edited by M. Capaldo, 405–37. Rome: Salerno, 2006.

————. "A Liturgical Fragment in Majuscule in the Codex A2 in Erlangen." In Στέφανος: *Studia byzantina ac slavica Vladimiro Vavřinek ad annum sexagesimum quintum dedicata*, edited by R. Dostálová and V. Konzal, 483–92 (= *BSl* 56 [1995]). Prague: Slovanský ústav, 1995.

————. "The Liturgical Year in the East." In *Handbook for Liturgical Studies*, edited by A. J. Chupungco, 5:157–76. 5 vols. Collegeville, Minn.: Liturgical Press, 1997–2000.

————. "Система на византийските и славянските богослужебни книги в периода на възникването им." In *Medieval Christian Europe: East and West. Tradition, Values, Communications*, 220–36. Sofia: Gutenberg, 2002.

————. "Lo studio dei lezionari bizantini." *Ecclesia Orans* 13 (1996): 265–66.

Vergoti, G. Λεξικὸ λειτουργικῶν καὶ τελετουργικῶν ὄρων. Thessaloniki: Ektyposis Bibliodesia, 1988.

Verhelst, S. "Les Présanctifiés de saint Jacques." *OCP* 61 (1995): 381–405.

————. *Les traditions Judéo-chrétiennes dans la liturgie de Jérusalem, spécialement la Liturgie de saint Jacques frère de Dieu*. Textes et études liturgiques 18. Leuven: Peeters, 2003.

Vladimir [Archimandrite]. *Систематическое описание рукописей Московской Синодальной (Патриаршей) Библиотеки*. Vol. 1, *Рукописи греческия*. Moscow, 1894.

Vokotopoulos, P. "Ἡ εἰκονογράφηση τοῦ κανόνος εἰς ψυχορραγοῦντα στὸ Ὡρολόγιον 295 τῆς Μονῆς Λειμῶνος." *Symmeikta* 9 (1994): 95–114.

Wagner, M., trans. *Saint Basil: Ascetical Works*. Washington, D.C.: The Catholic University of America Press, 1950.

Ware, K. "The Meaning of the Divine Liturgy for the Byzantine Worshipper." In *Church and People in Byzantium*, edited by R. Morris, 7–28. Birmingham: Centre for Byzantine, Ottoman and Modern Greek Studies at University of Birmingham, 1990.

Weitzmann, K., and G. Galavaris. *The Monastery of Saint Catherine at Mount Sinai. The Illuminated Manuscripts*. Vol. 1, *From the Ninth to the Twelfth Century*. Princeton, N.J.: Princeton University Press, 1990.

Wellesz, E. *A History of Byzantine Music and Hymnography*. Oxford: Oxford University Press, 1963.

Westerink, L., ed. *Michaelis Pselli poemata*. Stuttgart: Teubner, 1992.

Winkler, G. "The Armenian Night Office I: The Historical Background of the Introductory Part of Gišerayin Žam." *Journal of the Society for Armenian Studies* 1 (1984): 93–113.

Zanetti, U. "La distribution des psaumes dans l'horologion copte." *OCP* 56 (1990): 323–69.

LITURGICAL INDEX

Scriptural Passages
Note: Excluding the psalms of the kathismata and quotations in troparia and prayers.

Psalms

2: 144
3: 88
4: 160
4.2, 4: 156
5: 110
5.2, 3, 4: 110
6: 160, 174
7: 144
7.2, 7–8: 100
9.2, 33, 37: 102
11: 148
11.6, 7: 100
12: 160
15: 148
16: 116
21: 144
22.1, 6: 156
23: 148
24: 116, 160
26: 84
29: 148
30: 148, 160
33.6: 132, 133n106
34: 144
35: 136
37: 88
40: 136
42.3: 106, 108
43.2, 27: 102
50: 52, 82, 90, 98, 104, 116,
    132, 166
50.12, 13, 14: 116
50.17: 88
51: 136
52: 136
53: 120
53.3, 4: 156
54: 120

54.2, 17, 18: 120
56: 138
58: 138
58.2, 10: 156
62: 88
64: 108
67.20–21: 116
68: 144
70.8: 111
75: 144
78.8–9: 120
79.2, 3: 102
81: 148
83: 124
84: 124
85: 124
87: 88, 146
89: 110
89.14, 17: 108
90: 120, 160
91: 108, 150
91.2–3: 109n89
92: 150
92.1: 154
95.1, 10: 102
98.2: 104
98.9: 98, 104
100: 110
102: 88, 130
102.1: 130
103: 152
108: 138
112.2: 132
116.1, 2: 154
117.1, 10, 17, 23: 88
118: 172
118.12: 130
118.133–35: 110
118.169, 170: 124

120.1, 2: 156
122.1–2, 3–4: 156
129. 1–7: 154
133.1: 154
139: 138
140: 152
141: 152–54
141.8: 154
142: 88, 146
145: 130
145.1–2, 10: 102
148–50: 98, 104, 108
150.1–2: 100
150.6 (Pasa Pnoe): 98,
    100, 102

Odes

5.9, 11, 15, 17: 88–90
7.34, 35: 124
11: 64
12: 62, 84, 170
13: 158
14: 100

Isaiah
6.3: 132
8.9–10, 12–14, 17–18:
    160–62
9.1, 5: 160–62

Matthew
5.3–12: 130–32

Luke
2.14: 84, 88
23.42: 130

Prayers

Troparia, Chants, and Formulas

Note: With the exception of Δόξα καὶ νῦν

Θείας πίστεως ὁμολογίᾳ ἄλλον, Nov. 6

Θεὸς Κύριος, καὶ ἐπέφανεν, 88, 96, 104, 246, 248, 250; Sept. 8, 13, 14; Nov. 20, 21; Dec. 17, 26; Feb. 2

Θεοτόκε, μὴ παρίδης με δεόμενον ἀντιλήψεως, 38

Θεοτόκε, πύλη ἐπουράνιε, ἄνοιξον, 116

Θεοτόκε, σὺ εἶ ἄμπελος, 116

Θεοτόκε ἀειπαρθένε, τῶν ἀνθρώπων, July 2; Aug. 31

Θεοτόκε παρθένε, ἱκέτευε, 144

Θεοτόκε παρθένε, χαῖρε κεχαριτωμένη, 158

Θρήνησον, ψυχή μου, τὴν ἑαυτῆς ῥαθυμίαν, 58

Ἰδού, ὁ νυμφίος ἔρχεται ἐν τῷ μέσῳ, 86, 248

Ἱερωσύνης στολισμὸν περιβαλλόμενος, Sept. 5

Ἱκετεύσατε ὑπὲρ ἡμῶν, ἅγιοι, 158

Καὶ τρόπων μέτοχοι, Nov. 25

Καὶ τρόπων μέτοχος, Sept. 4, 30; Oct. 2; Dec. 20; Jan. 29; Feb. 11; April 26

Κανόνα πίστεως, Oct. 22; Dec. 6

Κατακαμπτόμενοι τῷ πλήθει τῶν πταισμάτων, 96

Καταξίωσον, Κύριε, ἐν τῇ, 156

Καταφυγὴ καὶ δύναμις ἡμῶν, Θεοτόκε, 42

Κλῆμα ὁσιότητος καὶ στέλεχος, Jan. 23

Κριτοῦ καθεζομένου καὶ ἀγγέλων ἑστώτων, 54

Κύριε, ἐλέησον, 30, 32, 34, 38, 40, 42, 44, 46, 48, 52, 54, 56, 58, 60, 62, 64, 66, 70, 74, 82, 84, 86, 108, 110, 112, 116, 120, 124, 126, 130, 132, 152, 158, 160, 166, 168, 170, 172, 174

Κύριε, ὁ τὸ πανάγιόν σου Πνεῦμα, 116

Κύριε, τὰ χείλη μου ἀνοίξεις, 88

Κύριε ἐλέησον ἡμᾶς· ἐπὶ σοὶ γάρ, 52, 82, 134, 166

Κύριος ὁ Θεὸς εὐλογητός, εὐλογητὸς Κύριος, 116

Λαοὶ προσκιρτήσατε χεῖρας, Aug. 14

Μακάριοι οἱ πτωχοὶ τῷ πνεύματι, 130

Μεγάλα τὰ τῆς πίστεως ... ὁ ἅγιος μάρτυς, 246

Μεγάλα τὰ τῆς πίστεως ... οἱ ἅγιοι παῖδες, 204; Dec. 17

Μέγαν εὕρατο ἐν τοῖς, Oct. 26

Μεθ' ἡμῶν ὁ Θεός, 160–62

Μεσούσης τῆς ἑορτῆς διψῶσάν μου, 248

Μετανοεῖν ἐπαγγέλλομαι ἐν τῇ ὥρᾳ τῆς προσευχῆς, 64

Μετὰ πασῶν τῶν οὐρανίων δυνάμεων χερουβικῶς, 90

Μετὰ τῶν ἁγίων ἀνάπαυσον, 84, 172

Μετεμορφώθης ἐν τῷ ὄρει, Χριστὲ ὁ Θεός, Aug. 6

Μὴ δὴ παραδῷς ἡμᾶς εἰς τέλος, 124

Μητέρα σε Θεοῦ ἐπιστάμεθα πάντες· παρθένον, 34

Μήτηρ ἁγία τοῦ ἀφράστου, 96

Μήτηρ Θεοῦ παναγία, τὸ τεῖχος τῶν χριστιανῶν, 56

Μνήμη δικαίου μετ' ἐγκωμίων, 168; Jan. 7; Feb. 24; May 25; Aug. 29

Μνήσθητι, Κύριε, ὡς ἀγαθός, 84, 96, 172

Μνήσθητί ἡμῶν, Κύριε, μνήσθητί ἡμῶν, Δέσποτα, 132

Νῦν ἀπολύεις, 156

Ὁ βυθοῖς σοφίας πάντα οἰκονομῶν, 246, 250

Ὁ γλυκασμός, 106

Ὁ δι' ἡμᾶς γεννηθεὶς ἐκ παρθένου καὶ σταύρωσιν, 124

Ὁ εἰδώς μου τὸ ἀνέτοιμον τοῦ βίου, 74, 172

Ὁ ἐκ παρθένου ἀνατείλας τῷ κόσμῳ, Χριστέ, 58

Ὁ ἐν ἕκτῃ ἡμέρᾳ τε καὶ ὥρᾳ, 120

Ὁ ἐν μήτρᾳ παρθενικῇ, 94

Ὁ ἔνσαρκος ἄγγελος, τῶν προφητῶν, July 20

Ὁ ἐν τῇ ἐνάτῃ ὥρᾳ δι' ἡμᾶς, 124

Ὁ εὐσχήμων Ἰωσήφ, ἀπό, 148, 150, 248

Ὁ Θεὸς τῶν πατέρων ἡμῶν, ὁ ποιῶν, 170, 246; Nov. 12; Jan. 14, 18; May 12; Aug. 3

Οἱ μάρτυρές σου, Κύριε, ἐν τῇ ἀθλήσει, 168; Sept. 20; Oct. 7, 12, 24; Nov. 2, 11; Dec. 10, 13; June 17; July 15; Aug. 26

Οἱ τὴν σὴν προστασίαν κεκτημένοι, ἄχραντε, 32, 126, 144

Οἱ τῶν ἀποστόλων πρωτόθρονοι, 168, June 29

Ὁ καὶ νεκρῶν καί, 106

Ὁ καρπὸς τῆς κοιλίας σου, ἄχραντε, τῶν προφητῶν, 64

Ὅλον μου τὸν βίον ἐρρύπωσα τῇ ἁμαρτίᾳ, 48

Ὁ μάρτυς σου, Κύριε, ἐν τῇ, Oct. 20; Feb. 9; April 23; June 8; July 8, 27

Ὄμματι εὐσπλάγχνῳ, Κύριε, ἴδε, 64

Ὁ μονογενὴς Υἱὸς καὶ Λόγος, 130

Ὁ οὐρανὸν τοῖς ἄστροις, 104, 106

Ὁ πάσης δημιουργὸς τῆς κτίσεως, Sept. 1

Ὁ ποιμενικὸς αὐλὸς τῆς θεολογίας σου, Jan. 25

Ὁρᾶν σε μὴ τολμῶντα, 96

Saints and Fixed Commemorations

Note: Identifications follow those of the MS. Additional information is abbreviated as follows: a. = apostle; ab. = archbishop; abt. = abbot; b. = bishop; cfs. = confessor; comps. = and others unspecified; evg. = evangelist; m. = martyr; p. = papa; pr. = prophet; pt. = patriarch.

INDEX OF MANUSCRIPTS CITED

GENERAL INDEX